The Oxford
Children's Dictionary

a b c d e f g h i j

Third Edition

Compiled by
John Weston and Alan Spooner

Illustrated by
Bill le Fever, Paul Thomas, Kathy Baxendale,
and Celia Hart

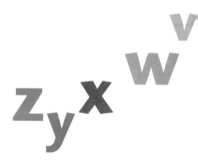

The Oxford Children's Dictionary

k l m n o p q r s t u

Oxford Toronto Melbourne

OXFORD UNIVERSITY PRESS

Oxford University Press, Walton Street, Oxford OX2 6DP

Oxford   New York
Athens   Auckland   Bangkok   Bombay
Calcutta   Cape Town   Dar es Salaam   Delhi
Florence   Hong Kong   Istanbul   Karachi
Kuala Lumpur   Madras   Madrid   Melbourne
Mexico City   Nairobi   Paris   Singapore
Taipei   Tokyo   Toronto

and associated companies in
Berlin   Ibadan

Oxford is a trade mark of Oxford University Press
© Oxford University Press 1976, 1985, 1993

First published 1976
Second edition 1985
Third edition 1993
Redesigned impression 1994
3 5 7 9 10 8 6 4 2

ISBN 0 19 910321 6 (net hardback)
ISBN 0 19 910320 8 (non-net hardback)

A CIP catalogue record for this book is available from the British Library

Printed in Hong Kong

OWLS
OXFORD ENGLISH
DICTIONARY
WORD AND
LANGUAGE
SERVICE

Do you have a query about words, their origin, meaning, use spelling
pronunciation, or any other aspect of the English language? Then write to
OWLS at Oxford University Press, Walton Street, Oxford OX2 6DP

All queries will be answered using the full resources of the
Oxford Dictionary Department

Preface to the Third Edition

In the seventeen years since the publication of the first edition of this dictionary, the English language has changed considerably. New technologies and changing social attitudes keep bringing new words into being, or giving new meanings to old ones. For this edition, we removed some words which are now out of date, and added a good number more which children are now likely to use in their day-to-day reading and writing. We have also rewritten many of the definitions. We have not included many slang words, as they tend to have a short life; nor can we claim to have included all terms belonging to more specialized hobbies or enthusiasms, since children's interests are wide-ranging and space is limited.

As in earlier editions, our object has been to provide a dictionary which is friendly and easy to use but which at the same time paves the way towards using adult dictionaries later on. One major innovation in this edition is the introduction of a part-of-speech label after each headword to indicate whether the word is defined as *noun*, *verb*, *adjective*, and so on. In other respects, the main features of earlier editions remain: definitions are kept as simple and accessible as possible; there are no abbreviations or cryptic symbols; we spell out in full all viable plurals of nouns, parts of verbs, and comparatives and superlatives of adjectives. We do not, however, attempt to give guidance on pronunciation, as we believe that in a children's dictionary this would be as likely to confuse as to help.

We would like to take this opportunity to thank Adrian Stenton for his help in preparing copy for the printers.

John Weston
Alan Spooner

What you will find in this dictionary

....

Headwords The words you look up are called *headwords*. They are arranged in alphabetical order, and are printed clearly in blue so that you can see them easily.

Entries A headword together with the printing that follows it (up to the line before the next headword) is called an *entry*.

Parts of speech Immediately after the headword, we tell you whether the word is used as a *noun*, *verb*, *adjective*, and so on. This is the headword's *part of speech*.

Other forms of the headword If the headword is a noun, you might need to spell the plural form of it. If it is a verb, you might need to spell the form ending *-ing*, or *-ed*, for example. So, when a word can have other forms, we spell the other forms for you (in brackets).

Definitions The *definition* is the part of the entry that gives you the meaning of the headword.

Numbers If a headword has more than one meaning, we separate the different definitions and give them each a number. These numbers are printed in blue, like the headwords.

Examples To help explain a word, we sometimes give you a short sentence or phrase to show how the word might be used. These examples are printed in *italic type like this*.

Phrases Sometimes a headword can be used in a phrase or expression with a special meaning. Phrases like this are printed in **bold type**, followed by a definition.

Derived words Often you can make (or *derive*) other words from the headword. For instance, from the adjective *able* you can derive the adverb *ably* and the noun *ability*. Words like this are printed in blue at the end of the entry.

Aa

a, an 1 One, any. **2** Each, every. *He earns £5 an hour.*

aback *adverb* **taken aback** surprised.

abandon *verb* (abandons, abandoning, abandoned) **1** To give up. *When night fell, they abandoned the search.* **2** To leave without intending to return. *Abandon ship!*

abbey *noun* (abbeys) **1** A group of buildings where monks or nuns live and work. **2** A church which was part of an abbey. *Westminster Abbey.*

abbot *noun* (abbots) The head of an abbey.

abbreviation *noun* (abbreviations) A short way of writing a word.

abdicate *verb* (abdicates, abdicating, abdicated) To give up the throne. **abdication** *noun*.

abdomen *noun* (abdomens) The part of the body containing the stomach.

abduct *verb* (abducts, abducting, abducted) To kidnap. **abduction** *noun*.

abhorrent *adjective* Hateful, disgusting.

abide *verb* (abides, abiding, abode) **1** (old-fashioned) To stay. *Abide with me.* **2** To bear, to put up with. *I can't abide it!* **abide by** to keep to. *Abide by the rules!*

ability *See* **able**

ablaze *adjective* On fire, burning brightly.

able *adjective* **1** Having the freedom or opportunity to do something. *Are you able to come with us?* **2** (abler, ablest) Having the intelligence, knowledge, or skill to do something well. *She's the ablest player in the school.* **ably** *adverb*, **ability** *noun*.

able seaman A fully-trained seaman.

abnormal *adjective* Not normal, unusual. **abnormally** *adverb*, **abnormality** *noun*.

aboard *adverb and preposition* On or into a ship, plane or vehicle.

abode *noun* (abodes) A place where someone lives.

abolish *verb* (abolishes, abolishing, abolished) To put an end to something. **abolition** *noun*.

abominable *adjective* Hateful, unpleasant.

Aborigines *noun* The original inhabitants of a country, especially of Australia. **aboriginal** *adjective*.

abortion *noun* (abortions) The taking away of a baby from its mother's womb before it has developed enough to stay alive.

abound *verb* (abounds, abounding, abounded) To be present in large quantity.

about[1] *preposition* **1** Nearly, almost, roughly. *It was about a metre long.* **2** On a particular subject, concerning. *I told the police about it.* **3** In various places, all round. *They ran all about the house.* **be about it** to be doing something. *While you are about it.*

about[2] *adverb* **1** Near, near by. *Is anybody about?* **2** In various directions. *Shake it about a bit.* **about to** going to.

above[1] *preposition* **1** Higher than. *Keep your head above water.* **2** More than, greater than. *I can't pay above £10.*

above[2] *adverb* To a higher place, on a higher place. *It's above me*, it's too hard for me.

above-board *adjective* Thoroughly honest.

abrasive *adjective* Scraping, rough, liable to scratch.

abreast *adverb* Side by side.

abridged *adjective* Shortened.

abroad *adverb* In or to another country.

abrupt *adjective* Sudden. **abruptly** *adverb*.

abscess *noun* (abscesses) A sore on the body full of pus.

abscond *verb* (absconds, absconding, absconded) To run away secretly.

abseil *verb* (abseils, abseiling, abseiled) To lower yourself down a rock face by a rope looped from the top.

absence *noun* (absences) **1** Being away from somewhere. *Did they notice my absence?* **2** Lack of something. *The plants died in the absence of water.*

absent *adjective* Away. *Absent from school.*

absentee *noun* (absentees) A person who is absent.

absent-minded *adjective* Forgetful, vague.

absolute *adjective* Complete, not restricted. *It was absolute madness.* **absolutely** *adverb*.

absorb *verb* (absorbs, absorbing, absorbed) To soak up. **absorbent** *adjective*. **absorbed** very interested. **absorbing** interesting.

abstain *verb* (abstains, abstaining, abstained) **1** To do without. **2** To refrain from voting. **abstainer** *noun*.

abstract *adjective* Concerned with ideas rather than things. **abstraction** *noun*.

absurd *adjective* Silly, unreasonable. **absurdly** *adverb*, **absurdity** *noun*.

abundant *adjective* Plentiful, more than enough. **abundantly** *adverb*, **abundance** *noun*.

abuse[1] *verb* (abuses, abusing, abused) **1** To treat something badly. **2** To say insulting things to someone. **abusive** *adjective*, **abusively** *adverb*.

abuse[2] *noun* (abuses) **1** Insults. **2** Wrong use. **child abuse** cruelty to children.

abysmal *adjective* (informal) Very bad.

abyss *noun* (abysses) A very deep hole.

academic *adjective* **1** Concerned with studying and learning. **2** Theoretical, not practical.

academy *noun* (academies) **1** A college. **2** A school, especially in Scotland.

accelerate *verb* (accelerates, accelerating, accelerated) To increase speed. **acceleration** *noun*.

accelerator *noun* (accelerators) The pedal in a motor vehicle which you press down to make the engine run faster.

accent *noun* (accents) **1** The way in which a language is pronounced. *Mr O'Reilly speaks English with an Irish accent.* **2** A mark written above a letter, as in *café*.

accept *verb* (accepts, accepting, accepted) **1** To take something which is offered. **2** To agree to something.

acceptable *adjective* Pleasing, worth accepting.

access[1] *noun* A way to reach something.

access[2] *verb* (accesses, accessing, accessed) To get back information stored in a computer.

accessible *adjective* Easily reached.

accession *noun* (accessions) A coming to the throne.

accessory *noun* (accessories) An extra part.

accident *noun* (accidents) An unexpected event, usually unfortunate. **by accident** accidentally.

accidental *adjective* Happening by chance, not intended. **accidentally** *adverb*.

accommodate *verb* (accommodates, accommodating, accommodated) To provide a room for someone in a hotel or house. **accommodation** *noun*.

accommodating *adjective* Helpful.

accompany *verb* (accompanies, accompanying, accompanied) **1** To go with somebody or something. **2** To happen at the same time as something else. **3** To make music to support a singer or player. **accompanist** *noun*, **accompaniment** *noun*.

accomplice *noun* (accomplices) A

helper, a companion in wrongdoing.

accomplish *verb* (accomplishes, accomplishing, accomplished) To finish something successfully.

accomplished *adjective* Skilful.

accomplishment *noun* (accomplishments) A skill.

accord *noun* Agreement. **of your own accord** without being asked.

accordingly *adverb* **1** Therefore. **2** As the circumstances suggest. *Act accordingly.*

according to **1** In the opinion of. *According to the doctor, I've got measles.* **2** In proportion to. *You're paid according to the work you do.*

accordion *noun* (accordions) A musical instrument with bellows and often with a keyboard.

account¹ *verb* (accounts, accounting, accounted) To make a record of how money was spent. **account for** to explain.

account² *noun* (accounts) **1** A statement of money received or spent or owing, a bill. **2** A description, a story. **on account of** because of. **on my account** for my sake. **on no account** for no reason. **take into account** to consider.

accountant *noun* (accountants) An expert in looking after accounts.

accumulate *verb* (accumulates, accumulating, accumulated) To pile up, to collect together. **accumulation** *noun*.

accurate *adjective* Exact, correct, precise. **accurately** *adverb*, **accuracy** *noun*.

accursed *adjective* Cursed, hateful.

accuse *verb* (accuses, accusing, accused) To blame somebody, to state that he or she has done something wrong. **accusation** *noun*.

accustomed *adjective* Usual. *in its accustomed place.* **be accustomed to** to be used to something.

ace¹ *noun* (aces) **1** The 'one' on playing-cards. **2** In tennis, a service that the other player cannot return. **3** A champion, an expert.

ace² *adjective* (informal) Excellent.

ache¹ *noun* (aches) A continuous pain.

ache² *verb* (aches, aching, ached) To have an ache.

achieve *verb* (achieves, achieving, achieved) To do something successfully, to reach a certain point. **achievement** *noun*.

acid¹ *noun* (acids) A chemical containing hydrogen which makes litmus turn red.

acid² *adjective* **1** Sour, sharp-tasting. **2** Containing too much acid. *acid rain.*

ackee *noun* (ackees) A West Indian vegetable.

acknowledge *verb* (acknowledges, acknowledging, acknowledged) **1** To admit that something is true. **2** To show thanks for something. **acknowledgement** *noun*.

acorn *noun* (acorns) The seed of an oak tree.

acoustics *noun* **1** The science of sound. **2** *a hall with good acoustics*, a hall where you can hear clearly.

acquaintance *noun* (acquaintances) a person you have met but who is not yet a friend. **make someone's**

acquaintance to get to know someone.

acquainted *adjective* **be acquainted with**, to know.

acquire *verb* (acquires, acquiring, acquired) To get, to obtain. **acquisition** *noun*.

acquit *verb* (acquits, acquitting, acquitted) To declare that somebody is not guilty.

acre *noun* (acres) A measure of area of land, 4,840 square yards or 4,047 square metres.

acrid *adjective* Sharp, bitter-smelling.

acrobat *noun* (acrobats) An entertainer who performs exciting gymnastic feats. **acrobatic** *adjective*.

across *adverb and preposition* **1** From one side to the other of. *a bridge across the Thames.* **2** On the other side of. *just across the street.*

acrylic *noun and adjective* A kind of fibre, plastic or resin.

act[1] *noun* (acts) **1** An action. **2** A law passed by parliament. **3** Part of a play. **4** A performance or a pretence. *He's only putting on an act.*

act[2] *verb* (acts, acting, acted) **1** To do something. *Act now to save our wild animals!* **2** To perform in a play or a film. **3** To pretend.

acting *adjective* Temporary. *acting Captain.*

action *noun* (actions) **1** The doing of something, something which tries to achieve some result. *a kind action.* **2** A battle. **action stations** positions taken up before a battle. **take action** to do something. **out of action** not working properly.

activate *verb* (activates, activating, activated) To start something working.

active *adjective* Energetic, doing things. **actively** *adverb*.

activity *noun* (activities) **1** Liveliness. **2** Something you do, an occupation.

actor *noun* (actors) A performer in a play or a film.

actress *noun* (actresses) A female actor.

actual *adjective* Real. **actually** *adverb*.

acupuncture *noun* A medical treatment involving pricking the body with needles. **acupuncturist** *noun*.

acute *adjective* Sharp, keen. **acutely** *adverb*. **acute angle** an angle smaller than a right angle. **acute accent** the mark (´) as used in *café*.

AD *Anno Domini*, in the year of our Lord, after the birth of Jesus Christ. *AD 1066 is the year of the Battle of Hastings.*

ad *noun* (ads) (informal) An advertisement.

adamant *adjective* Very firm, determined.

Adam's apple The lump seen in the front of a man's neck.

adapt *verb* (adapts, adapting, adapted) To make or become suitable for a new purpose or for new circumstances. **adaptable** *adjective*, **adaptation** *noun*.

adaptor *noun* (adaptors) A device used to connect pieces of electrical equipment.

add *verb* (adds, adding, added) To join one thing to another. **add to** to increase. **add up** to find the total of several numbers.

adder *noun* (adders) A poisonous snake.

addict *noun* (addicts) A person who is addicted to something.

addicted *adjective* Doing or using something because you cannot give it up. **addiction** *noun*.

addition *noun* (additions) **1** Adding up. **2** Something which has been added. **additional** *adjective*.

additive *noun* (additives) A chemical which is added in small amounts to food when it is processed in a factory.

address[1] *noun* (addresses) The details of the place where somebody lives, as written on an envelope.

address[2] *verb* (addresses, addressing,

addressed) **1** To write an address on a letter or parcel. **2** To speak to a person or to an audience.

adenoids *noun* A mass of spongy flesh growing at the back of the nose.

adequate *adjective* Just enough, just acceptable. **adequately** *adverb*.

adhere *verb* (adheres, adhering, adhered) To stick to something.

adhesive¹ *noun* (adhesives) A substance used to stick things together, such as glue or paste.

adhesive² *adjective* Sticky. *adhesive tape*.

adjacent *adjective* Lying alongside or near.

adjective *noun* (adjectives) A word that describes a noun. *Hard* and *tall* are used as adjectives in phrases like *hard work* and *a tall building*.

adjourn *verb* (adjourns, adjourning, adjourned) **1** To break off a meeting until another time. **2** To move to another place.

adjudicate *verb* (adjudicates, adjudicating, adjudicated) To judge in a competition or quarrel. **adjudicator** *noun*, **adjudication** *noun*.

adjust *verb* (adjusts, adjusting, adjusted) To alter something to make it exactly right.

administer *verb* (administers, administering, administered) **1** To look after business affairs. **2** To give. *to administer punishment*.

administrate *verb* (administrates, administrating, administrated) To manage a large business or organization. **administrator** *noun*, **administration** *noun*.

admirable *adjective* Excellent, worth admiring.

admiral *noun* (admirals) An officer of high rank in the navy.

admire *verb* (admires, admiring, admired) **1** To have a high opinion of somebody or something. **2** To look at something with pleasure. *We admired the view*. **admirable** *adjective*, **admirer**, **admiration** *nouns*.

admit *verb* (admits, admitting, admitted) **1** To let someone in. *He admitted the guests*. **2** To agree that something is true. *He admitted that he was guilty*. **admittedly** *adverb*, **admission** *noun*.

ado *noun* Fuss, excitement.

adolescence *noun* The time between being a child and being grown up. **adolescent** *noun and adjective*.

adopt *verb* (adopts, adopting, adopted) To take somebody into your family and treat him or her as your own child. **adoption** *noun*.

adore *verb* (adores, adoring, adored) To worship, to love very much. **adorable** *adjective*, **adoration** *noun*.

adorn *verb* (adorns, adorning, adorned) To decorate. **adornment** *noun*.

adrift *adjective and adverb* Drifting.

adult *noun* (adults) A fully grown person or animal.

adultery *noun* (adulteries) Unfaithfulness to your husband or wife. **adulterer** *noun*.

advance¹ *verb* (advances, advancing, advanced) To move forward.

advance² *noun* (advances) A forward movement, progress. **in advance of** before.

advanced *adjective* **1** Highly developed. *advanced technology*. **2** Difficult, at a high level. *an advanced driving test*.

advantage *noun* (advantages) Something useful or helpful. **to my advantage** helpful to me. **take advantage of something** to use it profitably. **take advantage of people** to make unfair use of them. **advantageous** *adjective*.

Advent *noun* **1** The coming of Jesus. **2** The period before Christmas.

adventure *noun* (adventures) A strange, exciting, or dangerous event or journey. **adventurous** *adjective*, **adventurously** *adverb*.

adverb *noun* (adverbs) A word which tells you how, when, or where something happens. *Loudly*, *yesterday*, and *here* are used as adverbs in sentences like: *She sang loudly. He came yesterday. Sit here.*

adversary *noun* (adversaries) An enemy.

adverse *adjective* Harmful, opposing. **adversely** *adverb*.

adversity *noun* (adversities) A trouble or misfortune.

advert *noun* (adverts) (informal) An advertisement.

advertise *verb* (advertises, advertising, advertised) To make something known to other people in order to encourage sales. **advertiser** *noun*.

advertisement *noun* (advertisements) Something which advertises.

advice *noun* A helpful suggestion.

advisable *adjective* Sensible, wise. **advisability** *noun*.

advise *verb* (advises, advising, advised) To give advice, to recommend. **adviser** *noun*.

aerial *noun* (aerials) A device, often made of rods or wire, used in transmitting and receiving radio and television signals.

aerobatics *noun* Clever flying of aircraft in an exciting display.

aerobics *noun* A kind of dancing which you do to take exercise.

aerodrome *noun* (aerodromes) An airfield.

aeroplane *noun* (aeroplanes) A flying machine with wings.

aerosol *noun* (aerosols) A device which releases its contents in a fine misty spray.

afar *adverb* Far off.

affair *noun* (affairs) A thing, an event. **affairs** business.

affect *verb* (affects, affecting, affected) To have an effect on someone or something. *Damp weather affects my health.*

affection *noun* (affections) Kindly feeling, love. **affectionate** *adjective*, **affectionately** *adverb*.

affirmative *adjective* Answering 'yes'.

afflict *verb* (afflicts, afflicting, afflicted) To cause someone pain or trouble. **affliction** *noun*.

affluent *adjective* Wealthy, rich. **affluence** *noun*.

afford *verb* (affords, affording, afforded) To provide. **able to afford something** having enough money for it, able to spare what is needed for it.

aflame *adjective* In flames.

afloat *adjective* **1** Floating. **2** At sea.

afraid *adjective* **1** Frightened. **2** *I'm afraid I'm late* I'm sorry I'm late.

afresh *adverb* Again, in a new way.

African *adjective* Of Africa, from Africa.

Africaner *noun* (Africaners) A South African of Dutch descent whose language is called Africaans.

Afro-Caribbean *adjective* Of the Caribbean people whose ancestors came from Africa.

aft *adverb* Towards the stern of a boat.

after[1] *preposition* **1** Later than, following, behind. *I'll play after tea. She ran after me. Our bus is coming after the lorry.* **2** In honour of. *We named the baby after her aunt.* **3** About, concerning. *They asked after you.* **after all** in spite of everything.

after[2] *adverb* Later. *I realized after what she meant.*

afternoon *noun* (afternoons) The time between midday and evening.

afterwards *adverb* Later.

again *adverb* **1** Once more. **again and again** often. **now and again** occasionally. **2** As before. *Put it back again!*

against *preposition* **1** In opposition to, not in favour of. *Mum was against our plan.* **2** Touching or hitting. *The ladder stood against the wall. I hit my toe against a stone.*

age[1] *noun* (ages) **1** The length of time a person has lived or a thing has existed. *Guess my age.* **2** A period of your life. *old age.* **3** A period of history. *the Stone Age.*

age[2] *verb* (ages, ageing, aged) **1** To become older. **2** To make something look older.

agency *noun* (agencies) An office where an agent works. *a travel agency.*

agent *noun* (agents) A person who arranges things for other people. **secret agent** a spy.

aggravate *verb* (aggravates, aggravating, aggravated) **1** To make worse. **2** (informal) To annoy. **aggravation** *noun.*

aggressive *adjective* **1** Liable to attack people. **2** Strong and forceful. *an aggressive player.* **aggressively** *adverb,* **aggressor, aggression** *nouns.*

aggro *noun* (informal) Deliberate trouble-making.

aghast *adjective* Shocked, horrified.

agile *adjective* Quick-moving. **agility** *noun.*

agitate *verb* (agitates, agitating, agitated) To stir up, to disturb. **agitator** *noun,* **agitation** *noun.*

agnostic *noun* (agnostics) A person who believes that you cannot be sure whether God exists or not.

ago *adverb* In the past.

agonizing *adjective* Very painful. **agonizingly** *adverb.*

agony *noun* (agonies) Severe pain.

agree *verb* (agrees, agreeing, agreed) **1** To consent, to say 'yes'. *I agree to your plan.* **2** To have the same ideas and opinions. *Jack and Jill don't quarrel, they always agree.* **agree with** to suit, to be good for the health of. *Onions don't agree with me.* **agreement** *noun.*

agreeable *adjective* Pleasant. **agreeably** *adverb.*

agriculture *noun* Farming, the cultivation of the soil. **agricultural** *adjective.*

aground *adjective and adverb* Stranded, touching the bottom in shallow water.

ahead *adverb* **1** In front. *to stay ahead.* **2** Into the future. *to think ahead.* **3** Forwards. *to go ahead.*

ahoy A cry used by seamen to attract attention.

aid[1] *verb* (aids, aiding, aided) To help.

aid[2] *noun* **1** Help. **2** (aids) Something which gives help. *a hearing aid.*

AIDS *noun* A disease that weakens your ability to resist infections.

ailment *noun* (ailments) An illness.

aim[1] *verb* (aims, aiming, aimed) **1** To point a gun or other weapon at something. **2** To throw or kick something in a certain direction. *He aimed the ball at the stumps.* **3** To have a particular plan in mind. *We aim to arrive for dinner.*

aim[2] *noun* (aims) **1** The ability to aim a gun or other weapon. **2** A purpose or plan. **aimless** *adjective,* **aimlessly** *adverb.*

air[1] *noun* **1** The mixture of gases which surrounds the earth and which people breathe. **2** (airs) A tune, a melody.

air[2] *verb* (airs, airing, aired) **1** To put something in a warm place to dry. **2** To let air into a room. **3** To make known. *to air your opinions.*

airborne *adjective* **1** In the air. **2** Carried by air.

air-conditioning *noun* Apparatus which supplies fresh air at a comfortable temperature. **air-conditioned** *adjective.*

aircraft *noun* (aircraft) A flying machine such as an aeroplane or a helicopter.

aircraft-carrier *noun* (aircraft-carriers) A ship with a flat deck on which aircraft can take off or land.

airfield *noun* (airfields) An area of land where aeroplanes may land and take off.

air force A body of people and aircraft organized for fighting.

airgun *noun* (airguns) A gun worked by compressed air.

airline *noun* (airlines) A company whose business is to carry passengers or goods by aeroplane.

airliner *noun* (airliners) A large passenger aircraft.

airmail *noun* Letters and parcels which are carried by aircraft.

airman *noun* (airmen) The pilot or a member of the crew of an aircraft.

airport *noun* (airports) An airfield from which aircraft make regular flights carrying passengers or goods.

airship *noun* (airships) A large balloon with engines, designed to carry people or goods.

airstrip *noun* (airstrips) A strip of land cleared for aircraft to take off and land.

airtight *adjective* Fitting so closely that air cannot get in or out.

airworthy *adjective* Safe to fly. **airworthiness** *noun*.

airy *adjective* 1 Breezy, with plenty of fresh air. 2 Light-hearted, careless. **airily** *adverb*.

aisle *noun* (aisles) A passage between rows of seats in a church, theatre, or aeroplane.

ajar *adjective* Partly open.

akin *adjective* Related, similar.

alarm[1] *verb* (alarms, alarming, alarmed) To frighten, to disturb, **alarmingly** *adverb*.

alarm[2] *noun* (alarms) A warning.

alas *adverb* A cry of sorrow.

albatross *noun* (albatrosses) A large seabird with long wings.

albino *noun* (albinos) A person or animal with no colouring in the skin, hair, or feathers.

album *noun* (albums) A book or record containing many items.

alcohol *noun* A colourless intoxicating liquid present in drinks like beer, wine, and whisky.

alcoholic[1] *adjective* Containing alcohol.

alcoholic[2] *noun* (alcoholics) A person addicted to alcohol.

alcove *noun* (alcoves) Part of a room set back into a wall.

ale *noun* (ales) Beer.

alert[1] *adjective* Watchful, lively. **on the alert** on guard, ready. **alertly** *adverb*, **alertness** *noun*.

alert[2] *verb* (alerts, alerting, alerted) To warn someone of danger.

algebra *noun* A kind of mathematics in which letters are used to represent numbers.

alias *noun* (aliases) A false name.

alibi *noun* (alibis) Evidence which proves that a person suspected of a crime was somewhere else when it was committed.

alien[1] *adjective* From another place, foreign, strange.

alien[2] *noun* (aliens) An alien person or creature.

alight *adjective* Burning, on fire.

alike *adjective and adverb* Like one another, in the same way. *The twins are very alike. They behave alike.*

alive *adjective* Living, lively.

alkali *noun* (alkalis) A chemical which neutralizes acids and makes litmus turn blue.

all[1] *adjective* The whole number or the whole amount of something. *All trains stop here.*

all[2] *noun* Everything, everybody. *All sang together.*

all[3] *adverb* Completely. *She was dressed all in white.*

Allah *noun* The Muslim name of God.

allege *verb* (alleges, alleging, alleged) To say something without being able to prove it. **allegation** *noun*.

allegiance *noun* Loyal duty to your king or government.

alleluia Praise God!

allergic *adjective* **allergic to** liable to become ill if you touch or eat something. **allergy** *noun*.

alley *noun* (alleys) A narrow lane or passage.

alliance *noun* (alliances) A friendly agreement between countries or groups.

alligator *noun* (alligators) A kind of crocodile found in America.

allot *verb* (allots, allotting, allotted) To distribute, to give out in proper shares.

allotment *noun* (allotments) A small area of land which you rent in order to grow vegetables, fruit, or flowers.

allow *verb* (allows, allowing, allowed) **1** To permit. *Smoking is not allowed.* **2** To give, to set aside. *The teacher allowed them an hour for painting.* **allowance** *noun*.

alloy *noun* (alloys) A mixture of two or more metals. *Brass is an alloy of copper and zinc.*

all right 1 Well, in good condition. *Are you all right?* **2** Satisfactory. *The food is all right.* **3** Yes. *All right, I'm coming.*

all-rounder *noun* (all-rounders) A person gifted in various ways.

allude *verb* (alludes, alluding, alluded) To refer to something. **allusion** *noun*.

alluring *adjective* Fascinating, charming.

ally *noun* (allies) A person or country that has agreed to support another.

almighty *adjective* Great, having all power. **The Almighty** God.

almond *noun* (almonds) A kind of nut.

almost *adverb* Nearly, very close to, not far from. *almost bedtime. almost home. almost finished.*

alms *noun* Money given to the poor.

aloft *adverb* High up.

alone *adjective and adverb* **1** Without anyone else. *I was alone in the dark.* **2** Untouched. *Leave my things alone.*

along[1] *preposition* Moving or positioned between one end of something and the other. *She ran along the road. A hedge runs along the path.*

along[2] *adverb* **1** On, onwards. *We pushed the cart along.* **2** Accompanying the person or people mentioned. *They brought the dog along.* **Come along!** Hurry up!

alongside *adverb and preposition* Beside.

aloof *adjective* Unfriendly.

aloud *adverb* In an ordinary voice, not in a whisper. *to read aloud.*

alphabet *noun* (alphabets) The letters of a language arranged in order. **alphabetical** *adjective*.

alpine *adjective* Of or like rugged mountains such as the Alps, the mountains in and around Switzerland.

already *adverb* By now, before now.

Alsatian *noun* (Alsatians) A kind of large dog.

also *adverb* As well, besides, too.

altar *noun* (altars) **1** The communion table in a church. **2** A special table for religious offerings to a god.

alter *verb* (alters, altering, altered) To change. **alteration** *noun*.

alternative¹ *noun* (alternatives) A choice between two or more things.

alternative² *adjective* **1** Available instead of the usual one. *an alternative route avoiding traffic jams.* **2** Different, not what most people think of as usual. *alternative medicine.*

although Though.

altitude *noun* (altitudes) Height, height above sea-level.

altogether *adverb* **1** Entirely, completely. **2** On the whole.

aluminium *noun* A light, silvery-white metal.

always *adverb* **1** All the time, every time. **2** Often, again and again.

am *See* **be**

a.m. The abbreviation for Latin *ante meridiem*, before midday. *Breakfast is at 8 a.m.*

amalgamate *verb* (amalgamates, amalgamating, amalgamated) To join together. **amalgamation** *noun*.

amateur¹ *adjective* **1** Doing something for the love of it, not for money. *an amateur footballer.* **2** Amateurish.

amateur² *noun* (amateurs) A person who is not paid for what he or she does, not a professional.

amateurish *adjective* Badly done, not skilful. **amateurishly** *adverb*.

amaze *verb* (amazes, amazing, amazed) To astonish, to surprise. **amazement** *noun*.

ambassador *noun* (ambassadors) An important official who is sent abroad to represent his or her government.

amber *noun* **1** A hard, clear, yellowish substance used for making ornaments and jewellery. **2** Its yellowish colour.

ambiguous *adjective* Not clear in meaning, having more than one meaning. **ambiguously** *adverb*, **ambiguity** *noun*.

ambition *noun* (ambitions) **1** A strong wish to become successful or famous. **2** The thing a person wants to do more than anything else. *John's ambition is to be a musician.* **ambitious** *adjective*, **ambitiously** *adverb*.

amble *verb* (ambles, ambling, ambled) To walk without hurrying.

ambulance *noun* (ambulances) A motor vehicle for carrying sick or injured people.

ambush *verb* (ambushes, ambushing, ambushed) To lie hidden and attack by surprise. **ambush** *noun*.

amen A word used at the end of prayers and hymns.

amend *verb* (amends, amending, amended) To change something, to improve it. **amendment** *noun*.

American *adjective* Of or from America.

amiable *adjective* Good-natured. **amiably** *adverb*.

amicable *adjective* Friendly. **amicably** *adverb*.

amid or **amidst** *preposition* In the middle of.

amidships *adverb* In the middle of a ship.

ammonia *noun* A sharp-smelling gas or liquid.

ammunition *noun* Shells and cartridges for guns.

amnesia *noun* Loss of memory.

amnesty *noun* (amnesties) A pardon, a promise to set prisoners free.

among, amongst *prepositions* **1** Surrounded by, in the middle of. *hiding among trees.* **2** One of. *among our oldest inhabitants.* **3** Between. *food shared amongst friends.*

amount¹ *verb* (amounts, amounting,

amounted) **amount to** to add up to. *The bill amounted to £47.*

amount² *noun* (amounts) **1** The total, the whole. **2** A quantity.

amphibious *adjective* Able to live or move on land and in water.

ample *adjective* Quite enough, plentiful, rather generous. **amply** *adverb*.

amplify *verb* (amplifies, amplifying, amplified). **1** To make sounds louder. **amplifier** *noun*. **2** To give more details about something. **amplification** *noun*.

amputate *verb* (amputates, amputating, amputated) To cut off a part of the body such as an arm or a leg. **amputation** *noun*.

amuse *verb* (amuses, amusing, amused) **1** To make time pass pleasantly for somebody. **2** To make somebody laugh or smile. **amusingly** *adverb*.

amusement *noun* **1** (amusements) Something that makes time pass pleasantly, entertainment. **2** Being amused.

an *See* **a**

anaemia *noun* A poor condition of the blood which makes you pale and feeble. **anaemic** *adjective*.

anaesthetic *noun* (anaesthetics) A drug or a gas used so that you do not feel pain.

analyse *verb* (analyses, analysing, analysed) To examine something closely to find out what it is made of. **analyst** *noun*, **analysis** *noun*.

anarchy *noun* Disorder, lack of good government. **anarchist**.

anatomy *noun* The scientific study of the structure of the body. **anatomical** *adjective*.

ancestor *noun* (ancestors) Anybody from whom you are descended. **ancestry** *noun*.

anchor¹ *noun* (anchors) A heavy device with hooks which can be lowered to the bottom of the sea to stop a ship from moving.

anchor² *verb* (anchors, anchoring, anchored) **1** To moor a ship by means of an anchor. **2** To fix anything firmly. **anchorage** *noun*.

ancient *adjective* **1** Very old. **2** Belonging to times long past.

and *conjunction* A joining word.

android *noun* (androids) A robot made to look like a person.

angel *noun* (angels) A messenger from God. **angelic** *adjective*, **angelically** *adverb*.

anger *noun* The strong feeling that makes people want to quarrel or fight.

angle *noun* (angles) The space between two lines or surfaces that meet.

angler *noun* (anglers) A person who fishes with a fishing-rod.

angling *noun* Fishing with a fishing-rod.

angry *adjective* (angrier, angriest) Filled with anger. **angrily** *adverb*.

anguish *noun* Severe suffering.

animal *noun* (animals) A living creature that can breathe, feel, and move about. Horses, flies, fish, birds, snakes, and humans are all animals.

animation *noun* **1** Liveliness. **2** The art of making cartoons, puppets, and models appear to move in cinema and television films. **animated** *adjective*.

ankle *noun* (ankles) The joint connecting the foot and the leg.

annexe *noun* (annexes) An extra building.

annihilate *verb* (annihilates, annihilating, annihilated) To destroy completely. **annihilation** *noun*.

anniversary *noun* (anniversaries) A day when you remember something special that happened on the same date in a previous year.

announce *verb* (announces, announcing, announced) To make something generally known. **announcer** *noun*, **announcement** *noun*.

annoy *verb* (annoys, annoying, annoyed) To make someone rather angry. **annoyance** *noun*.

annual¹ *adjective* Coming every year. **annually** *adverb*.

annual² *noun* (annuals) **1** A book that is published each year with new contents. **2** A plant which lives only one year.

anonymous *adjective* **1** Without a known name. *The author is anonymous.* **2** By an anonymous person. *The gift was anonymous.* **anonymously** *adverb*.

anorak *noun* (anoraks) A thick, warm jacket with a hood.

anorexia *noun* An illness that makes you not want to eat. **anorexic** *adjective*.

another A different one, one more of a similar kind.

answer¹ *noun* (answers) **1** Something you say, write, or do to try to satisfy someone who has asked a question, written a letter, or communicated with you in some other way. **2** A solution to a problem.

answer² *verb* (answers, answering, answered) **1** To say, write, or do something as an answer. *answer a question, answer a letter, answer the phone.* **2** To solve. **answer back** to answer rudely.

ant *noun* (ants) A kind of small insect.

antagonize *verb* (antagonizes, antagonizing, antagonized) To make an enemy of someone. **antagonism** *noun*.

Antarctic *noun* The regions round the South Pole.

antelope *noun* (antelope) An animal like a deer.

antenatal *adjective* Before the time when a baby is born.

antenna *noun* **1** (antennae) One of the two feelers on the heads of some insects. **2** (antennas) An aerial.

anthem *noun* (anthems) A song to be sung in church or on special occasions.

anthology *noun* (anthologies) A collection of poems or other kinds of writing.

anthracite *noun* A kind of hard coal.

anti-aircraft *adjective* For use against aircraft.

antibiotic *noun* (antibiotics) A drug such as penicillin which fights bacteria.

anticipate *verb* (anticipates, anticipating, anticipated) **1** To look forward to something. **2** To do something before the proper time. **3** To do something before someone else does. **anticipation** *noun*.

anticlimax *noun* (anticlimaxes) A disappointment after an exciting preparation.

anticlockwise *adjective and adverb* Moving round in the opposite direction to a clock's hands.

anticyclone *noun* (anticyclones) An area in which the pressure of the air is high, generally causing fine weather.

antidote *noun* (antidotes) A medicine which acts against the effects of a poison.

antifreeze *noun* A liquid added to water to prevent it from freezing.

antiquated *adjective* Old-fashioned.

antique[1] *adjective* Old and valuable.

antique[2] *noun* (antiques) An antique object.

antiseptic *noun* (antiseptics) Something that prevents infection.

antisocial *adjective* Unpleasant for other people.

antler *noun* (antlers) The branching horns of a deer.

anvil *noun* (anvils) A heavy block of iron on which heated metal is hammered into shape.

anxious *adjective* **1** Worried. **2** Eager. *anxious to please.* **anxiously** *adverb*, **anxiety** *noun*.

any[1] *adjective and pronoun* **1** Some amount of something. *Have you any wool? No, I haven't any.* **2** No matter which. *Come any time you like.*

any[2] *adverb* At all, to some extent. *Is Timothy any better?*

anybody Any person.

anyhow *adverb* **1** In any way. *Do it anyhow.* **2** Carelessly or untidily. *It was written all anyhow.* **3** At any rate, in any case. *It is too late, anyhow.*

anyone Any person.

anything Any thing.

anyway *adverb* Whatever happens, in any case.

anywhere *adverb* In any place, to any place.

apart *adverb* **1** Away from each other. *The two houses are far apart.* **2** To one side. *He stood apart and watched.* **3** To pieces. *The model I was making fell apart.* **apart from** except.

apartheid *noun* Keeping people of different races separate from each other.

apartment *noun* (apartments) A flat.

ape *noun* (apes) A tailless monkey, such as a chimpanzee or a gorilla.

apex *noun* (apexes) The highest point of something.

apiary *noun* (apiaries) A place where bees are kept.

apologize *verb* (apologizes, apologizing, apologized) To make an apology.

apology *noun* (apologies) A statement that you are sorry for doing something wrong. **apologetic** *adjective*, **apologetically** *adverb*.

apostle *noun* (apostles) One of the twelve men sent out by Jesus to spread his teaching.

apostrophe *noun* (apostrophes) A punctuation mark . It is used where letters have been left out (*don't*, do not) or with 's' to show ownership (*Jean's hat*, the hat owned by Jean).

appal *verb* (appals, appalling, appalled) To shock deeply, to fill with horror.

apparatus *noun* (apparatuses) Machinery, instruments, or other equipment put together for a scientific experiment or to do a particular job.

apparent *adjective* **1** Clearly seen, obvious. **2** Likely to be true. **apparently** *adverb*.

apparition *noun* (apparitions) A ghost.

appeal *verb* (appeals, appealing, appealed) **1** To ask very seriously for something. **2** To ask for a decision of a lawcourt to be reconsidered. **3** To be interesting or attractive. *This picture appeals to me.*

appear *verb* (appears, appearing, appeared) **1** To come into sight. **2** To seem. **3** To act in a play or film. **appearance** *noun.*

appease *verb* (appeases, appeasing, appeased) To make peace with someone by doing what he or she wants. **appeasement** *noun.*

appendicitis *noun* Inflammation of a person's appendix.

appendix *noun* **1** (appendixes) A part of your body attached to your intestines. **2** (appendices) A section added at the end of a book.

appetite *noun* (appetites) A desire, usually for food. **appetizing** *adjective.*

applaud *verb* (applauds, applauding, applauded) To clap, to give loud approval to something. **applause** *noun.*

apple *noun* (apples) A crisp, round fruit.

appliance *noun* (appliances) An apparatus, a machine. *electrical appliances.*

apply *verb* (applies, applying, applied) **1** To ask officially. *My sister has applied for a job.* **2** To put something onto some other thing. *He applied some ointment to the cut.* **3** *It applies to you* it concerns you. **apply yourself** to give your full attention to something. **applicable** *adjective*, **applicant** *noun*, **application** *noun.*

appoint *verb* (appoints, appointing, appointed) **1** To choose someone for a job. *Naomi was appointed librarian.* **2** *The appointed hour* the time arranged.

appointment *noun* (appointments) **1** A time agreed for a meeting or visit. *an appointment at the dentist's.* **2** A position or job.

appreciably *adverb* To a noticeable extent.

appreciate *verb* (appreciates, appreciating, appreciated) **1** To know the value of something, to enjoy it. **2** To

become higher in value. **appreciative** *adjective*, **appreciation** *noun.*

apprehensive *adjective* Anxious, rather frightened. **apprehensively** *adverb.*

apprentice *noun* (apprentices) A young person learning a trade. **apprenticeship** *noun.*

approach¹ *noun* (approaches) **1** A way towards something. **2** An advance.

approach² *verb* (approaches, approaching, approached) To come near to somebody or something.

appropriate *adjective* Suitable. **appropriately** *adverb.*

approve *verb* (approves, approving, approved) To be in favour of something. **approval** *noun.*

approximate *adjective* Roughly correct, about right. **approximately** *noun.*

apricot *noun* (apricots) An orange-coloured fruit like a small peach.

April *noun* The fourth month of the year.

apron *noun* (aprons) A garment worn in front of you to keep clothes clean.

apt *adjective* **1** Quick to learn. **2** Suitable. **apt to** likely to. **aptly** *adverb.*

aptitude *noun* A natural gift for doing something well.

aquarium *noun* (aquariums) **1** A glass tank for keeping fish in. **2** A building which contains tanks for fish.

aquatic *adjective* Of, on, or in water.

aqueduct *noun* (aqueducts) A bridge which carries water across a valley.

Arab *noun* (Arabs) One of a race of people originally from Saudi Arabia.

Arabic *adjective* Of the Arabs.

arable land Land which is ploughed for growing crops.

arbitrary *adjective* Unreasonable. **arbitrarily** *adverb*.

arbitrate *verb* (arbitrates, arbitrating, arbitrated) To help the two sides in an argument to settle their differences. **arbitrator** *noun*, **arbitration** *noun*.

arc *noun* (arcs) A curved line, part of a circle.

arcade *noun* (arcades) A covered walk or pavement. **amusement arcade** an indoor area containing electronic games and slot-machines.

arch¹ *noun* (arches) A curved shape in a bridge, or in any other piece of architecture.

arch² *verb* (arches, arching, arched) To make a curved shape like an arch. *The cat arched its back.*

archaeology *noun* The digging up and study of ancient remains. **archaeological** *adjective*, **archaeologist** *noun*.

archbishop *noun* (archbishops) A chief bishop.

archer *noun* (archers) A person who shoots with a bow and arrow. **archery** *noun*.

archipelago *noun* (archipelagos) A group of islands.

architect *noun* (architects) A person who designs buildings.

architecture *noun* The art of designing buildings. **architectural** *adjective*.

archives *noun* Historical records.

arctic *adjective* Very cold. **the Arctic** the regions round the North Pole.

arduous *adjective* Hard and difficult.

are *See* **be**. *Are you ready? Yes, we are.*

area *noun* (areas) **1** The measurement of a flat surface. *an area of six square metres.* **2** A part of the surface of something. *a sensitive area of your body.*

arena *noun* (arenas) A space for competitions or fighting.

aren't (informal) Are not.

argue *verb* (argues, arguing, argued). **1** To quarrel in words. **2** To give reasons for something. **argumentative** *adjective*, **argument** *noun*.

arid *adjective* Dry and lifeless. *arid desert.*

arise *verb* (arises, arising, arose, arisen) **1** To get up. **2** To come into being. *A problem has arisen.*

aristocrat *noun* (aristocrats) A nobleman. **aristocratic** *adjective*, **aristocratically** *adverb*, **aristocracy** *noun*.

arithmetic *noun* The science of numbers, working with numbers. **arithmetical** *adjective*, **arithmetically** *adverb*.

Ark *noun* The ship in which Noah escaped the Flood.

arm¹ *noun* (arms) **1** One of the two upper limbs of the body. **2** Anything which sticks out or moves like an arm. **arms** weapons. *to take up arms.*

arm² *verb* (arms, arming, armed) **1** To supply somebody with weapons. **2** To prepare to fight.

armada *noun* (armadas) A fleet of warships. **Spanish Armada** the Spanish fleet sent against England in 1588.

armaments *noun* Weapons and fighting equipment.

armchair *noun* (armchairs) A chair with supports for the arms.

armed *adjective* Having weapons. **armed forces** the army, navy, and air force.

armful *noun* (armfuls) As much as you can carry in your arms.

armistice *noun* (armistices) An agreement between enemies to stop fighting.

armour *noun* A covering usually of metal to protect men, ships, or vehicles in battle. **armoured** *adjective*.

armoury *noun* (armouries) A place where weapons are kept.

army *noun* (armies) A large number of people trained for fighting.

aroma *noun* (aromas) A pleasant smell.

arose *See* **arise**

around *adverb and pronoun* All round, about.

arouse *verb* (arouses, arousing, aroused) To awaken, to stir up.

arrange *verb* (arranges, arranging, arranged) **1** To put things in their proper place. **2** To make plans for something. *We arranged a party.* **3** To adapt music. *We arranged some carols for recorder band.* **arranger** *noun*, **arrangement** *noun*.

arrest[1] *verb* (arrests, arresting, arrested) **1** To take someone prisoner. **2** To stop something.

arrest[2] *noun* (arrests) The act of arresting someone. **under arrest** being held prisoner by the police.

arrive *verb* (arrives, arriving, arrived) **1** To reach the end of a journey. **2** To come in due time. *At last Christmas*

arrived. **arrive at** to reach. **arrival** *noun*.

arrogant *adjective* Proud and scornful. **arrogantly** *adverb*, **arrogance** *noun*.

arrow *noun* (arrows) **1** A thin, straight stick which is shot from a bow. **2** A sign shaped like an arrow.

arsenal *noun* (arsenals) A place where weapons or ammunition are made or stored.

arsenic *noun* A deadly poison.

arson *noun* Deliberately starting a fire to damage someone's property.

art *noun* (arts) **1** Something which needs imagination and skill, such as painting, drawing, modelling, and other ways of making beautiful things. **2** A skill. *the art of spin bowling*.

artery *noun* (arteries) A tube carrying blood from the heart to other parts of the body.

artful *adjective* Crafty. **artfully** *adverb*.

arthritis *noun* A disease causing pain in the joints.

article *noun* (articles) **1** Any particular thing. **2** A piece of writing published in a newspaper or magazine.

articulated lorry A lorry built in two parts so that it bends at the joint.

artificial *adjective* Manufactured, not found in nature. **artificially** *adverb*.

artillery *noun* **1** Big guns. **2** The soldiers who use them.

artist *noun* (artists) A person who is good at painting or some other art. **artistic** *adjective*, **artistically** *adverb*.

as This word has many uses including the following: **1** A word used in making comparisons. *I am as tall as you and can run as fast.* **2** When, while. *I saw him as I went in.* **3** Because. *As you won't come with me, I'll go alone.* **4** In the form of. *John went to the party as a pirate.* **5** In the same way that. *Do as I do.* **as long as** provided that. *I'll come as long as it doesn't rain.* **as well** as an addition, also. *The dog can come as well.*

asbestos *noun* A fire-proof material.

ascend *verb* (ascends, ascending, ascended) To go up. **ascent** *noun*.

Ascension Day The day when Christians remember the ascent of Jesus into heaven.

ash[1] *noun* (ashes) Powder which is left after a fire. **The Ashes** the trophy for which England and Australia play each other at cricket.

ash[2] *noun* (ashes) A large kind of tree.

ashamed *adjective* Feeling shame, upset by your own behaviour.

ashore *adverb* To the shore, on the shore.

ashtray *noun* (ashtrays) A small bowl for cigarette ash.

Asian *adjective* Of Asia, from Asia.

aside *adverb* To one side, on one side.

ask *verb* (asks, asking, asked) **1** To put a question, to seek information. *We asked what time the bus was due.* **2** To say you want to be allowed to do something. *He asked to leave.* **3** To invite. *I asked her to my party.*

asleep *adjective* Sleeping.

asparagus *noun* A vegetable grown for its tender edible shoots.

aspect *noun* (aspects) A way of looking at something.

asphalt *noun* A substance like tar. It is mixed with gravel to make the surface of roads and playgrounds.

aspirin *noun* (aspirins) A drug, usually in the form of a tablet, taken to reduce pain.

ass *noun* (asses) **1** A donkey. **2** (informal) A stupid person.

assail *verb* (assails, assailing, assailed) To attack.

assassinate *verb* (assassinates, assassinating, assassinated) To murder a ruler, a politician, or other well-known person. **assassin, assassination** *nouns*.

assault[1] *verb* (assaults, assaulting, assaulted) To attack suddenly and violently.

assault[2] *noun* (assaults) A sudden attack.

assemble *verb* (assembles, assembling, assembled) To gather together, to put together.

assembly *noun* **1** Assembling. **2** (assemblies) A gathering of people, especially at the beginning of the day at school.

assert *verb* (asserts, asserting, asserted) To state something firmly. **assert yourself** to stand up for yourself. **assertive** *adjective*, **assertion** *noun*.

assess *verb* (assesses, assessing, assessed) To decide the value or cost of something. **assessor, assessment** *nouns*.

asset *noun* (assets) Something useful or valuable.

assign *verb* (assigns, assigning, assigned) **1** To give somebody something to do or use. **2** To tell somebody to do a job.

assignment *noun* (assignments) A job somebody is set to do.

assist *verb* (assists, assisting, assisted) To help. **assistant, assistance** *nouns*.

association *noun* (associations) A society or organization. **association football** (also called *soccer*) the type of football played with a round ball by two teams of eleven a side.

assorted *adjective* Mixed, of various sorts. **assortment** *noun*.

assume *verb* (assumes, assuming, assumed) To accept something as true before it is known for certain.

I assumed Dad would give me a lift.
an assumed name a false name.
assumption *noun*.

assure *verb* (assures, assuring, assured)
To tell someone something definitely.
assurance *noun*.

assured *adjective* Confident.

asterisk *noun* (asterisks) The mark *.

asteroid *noun* (asteroids) A tiny planet.

asthma *noun* A disease which makes
breathing difficult. **asthmatic** *adjective*.

astonish *verb* (astonishes, astonishing,
astonished) To give someone a big
surprise. **astonishment** *noun*.

astound *verb* (astounds, astounding,
astounded) To astonish.

astray *adverb* Away from the right path.

astride *preposition* With one leg on
each side of something. *to sit astride
a horse.*

astrology *noun* The study of how the
positions of the stars and planets are
supposed to affect our lives.
astrologer *noun*.

astronaut *noun* (astronauts) A traveller
in space.

astronomy *noun* The scientific study of
the sun, moon, planets, and stars.
astronomer *noun*.

astute *adjective* Clever, crafty. **astutely**
adverb.

asylum *noun* (asylums) **1** Refuge,

shelter. **2** (old-fashioned) A mental
hospital.

asymmetrical *adjective* Not symmetrical.

at *preposition* A word which shows the
place, direction, time, or manner of
something. **1** *We live at home.* **2** *Throw
the ball at the stumps!* **3** *We have breakfast at eight.* **4** *She ran at top speed.*

ate *See* **eat**

atheist *noun* (atheists) Someone who
believes that there is no God.
atheism *noun*.

athlete *noun* (athletes) A person who is
good at athletics. **athletic** *adjective*.

athletics *noun* Competitive sports like
running, jumping, or throwing.

atlas *noun* (atlases) A book of maps.

atmosphere *noun* **1** The air which we
breathe. **2** A feeling, a vague general
impression. *Your home has a friendly
atmosphere.* **atmospheric** *adjective*.

atom *noun* (atoms) A tiny part of a substance. **atom bomb** an early kind of
nuclear weapon. **atomic** *adjective*.

atrocious *adjective* Very wicked, very
bad.

atrocity *noun* (atrocities) A violent and
cruel crime.

attach *verb* (attaches, attaching,
attached) **1** To fasten or join something to something else. **2** *To be
attached to something*, to be fond of it.
attachment *noun*.

attack¹ *noun* (attacks) **1** A violent
attempt to hurt, damage, or defeat
somebody. **2** A sudden pain or illness.

attack² *verb* (attacks, attacking,
attacked) To make an attack.

attain *verb* (attains, attaining, attained)
To succeed in doing, getting, or learning something. **attainment** *noun*.

attempt *verb* (attempts, attempting,
attempted) To do your best to succeed in something, to try. **attempt**
noun.

attend *verb* (attends, attending,

a b c d e f g h i j k l m

attended) **1** To give care and thought to something or somebody. *Attend to your work!* **2** To be present somewhere, to go somewhere regularly. *Which school do you attend?* **attendance** *noun*.

attendant *noun* (attendants) A person on duty to help people. *a car-park attendant.*

attention *noun* **1** The action of attending to something. *Pay attention to your work.* **2** A kind or polite action. **3** A position in military drill with heels together and arms by your sides.

attentive *adjective* Paying attention. **attentively** *adverb*.

attic *noun* (attics) A room in the roof of a house.

attire *noun* Dress, clothes.

attitude *noun* (attitudes) **1** A way of thinking or behaving. **2** A way of standing or holding your body.

attract *verb* (attracts, attracting, attracted) **1** To pull something with a power that cannot be actually seen. *Magnets attract steel.* **2** To get somebody's attention or interest. **attraction** *noun*.

attractive *adjective* Pleasant. **attractively** *adverb*.

auburn *adjective* Reddish brown.

auction[1] *noun* (auctions) A sale where goods are sold to the person who offers the highest price.

auction[2] *verb* (auctions, auctioning, auctioned) To sell at an auction. **auctioneer** *noun*.

audible *adjective* Loud enough to be heard. **audibly** *adverb*, **audibility** *noun*.

audience *noun* (audiences) People gathered together to see or hear something.

audio-visual *adjective* **audio-visual aids** Apparatus used by teachers, such as projectors and tape-recorders.

audition *noun* (auditions) A test taken by a performer hoping to get a job.

August *noun* The eighth month of the year.

aunt *noun* (aunts) The sister of your father or mother, or the wife of your uncle.

aunty *noun* (aunties) (informal) An aunt.

au pair (au pairs) A young person who works for a time in somebody's home in another country.

au revoir Good-bye till we meet again.

austere *adjective* **1** Strict. **2** Simple and plain. **austerely** *adverb*, **austerity** *noun*.

Australian *adjective* Of or from Australia.

authentic *adjective* Genuine, known to be true. **authentically** *adverb*, **authenticity** *noun*.

author *noun* (authors) The writer of a book, play, or poem. **authorship** *noun*.

authority *noun* (authorities) **1** A person or group of people with the power to give orders. **2** The right to give orders. **3** An expert. *an authority on stamp-collecting.*

authorize *verb* (authorizes, authorizing, authorized) To give official permission to someone to do something.

autistic *adjective* Suffering from a handicap which makes you unable to communicate with people or respond to surroundings. **autism** *noun*.

autobiography *noun* (autobiographies) The story of a person's life written by that person. **autobiographical** *adjective*.

autograph *noun* (autographs) A signature, someone's name written in his or her own handwriting.

automatic[1] *adjective* **1** Done without thinking. *an automatic reply.* **2** Working on its own and not needing continuous attention. *an automatic washing-machine.* **automatically** *adverb*.

automatic² *noun* (automatics) A kind of pistol.

automation *noun* The use of automatic equipment in factories.

automobile *noun* (automobiles) A car.

autumn *noun* (autumns) The season of the year between summer and winter. **autumnal** *adjective*.

auxiliary *adjective* Helping.

available *adjective* **1** Ready for use, within reach. **2** On sale. **availability** *noun*.

avalanche *noun* (avalanches) A sudden fall of snow and ice down a steep slope.

avenge *verb* (avenges, avenging, avenged) To take revenge on somebody for something. **avenger** *noun*.

avenue *noun* (avenues) A road or pathway with trees along both sides.

average¹ *noun* The number you get when you add several quantities together and divide by the number of quantities. The average of 11, 12, and 16 is 13 $(11 + 12 + 16 = 39 \div 3 = 13)$.

average² *adjective* **1** Worked out as an average. *the average age of a class*. **average speed**, the total distance divided by the time taken. **2** Usual, normal. *an average sort of day*.

average³ *verb* (averages, averaging, averaged) To have or get as an average.

aversion *noun* (aversions) A dislike.

aviary *noun* (aviaries) A place to keep birds in.

aviation *noun* Flying in aircraft.

avid *adjective* Eager, greedy. **avidly** *adverb*.

avoid *verb* (avoids, avoiding, avoided) To keep out of the way of something or somebody. **avoidance** *noun*.

awake¹ *adjective* Not sleeping.

awake² *verb* (awakes, awaking, awoke, awoken, awaked) To wake.

awaken *verb* (awakens, awakening, awakened) To wake.

award¹ *noun* (awards) A prize or payment.

award² *verb* (awards, awarding, awarded) To give officially. *to award prizes*.

aware *adjective* **be aware of** to know about. **awareness** *noun*.

awash *adjective* Under water, flooded.

away *adverb* **1** At a distance. *Stay away!* **2** Not at home. *They are away this weekend*. **3** Continuously. *We chatted away for over an hour*. **4** To nothing. *The snow melted away*. **right away** at once.

awe *noun* Respect combined with fear or reverence.

awful *adjective* **1** Fearful, dreadful. **2** (informal) Very bad, very great. **awfully** *adverb*.

awkward *adjective* **1** Not convenient. **2** Clumsy. **awkwardly** *adverb*, **awkwardness** *noun*.

awning *noun* (awnings) A roof or shelter made of canvas.

awoke, awoken *See* **awake**

axe *noun* (axes) A tool for chopping wood.

axle *noun* (axles) The rod which passes through the centre of a wheel.

ayatollah *noun* (ayatollahs) A Muslim religious leader.

azure *adjective* Sky-blue.

babble *verb* (babbles, babbling, babbled) To talk in a meaningless way, to make sounds like a baby. **babbler** *noun*.

babe *noun* (babes) A baby.

baboon *noun* (baboons) A large kind of monkey.

baby *noun* (babies) A new-born child, a very young child. **babyish** *adjective*.

baby-sit *verb* (baby-sits, baby-sitting, baby-sat) To look after a child while its parents are out. **baby-sitter** *noun*.

bachelor *noun* (bachelors) An unmarried man.

back¹ *noun* (backs) **1** The rear part of anything, the side opposite to the front. **2** The part of a person's body between the shoulders and the bottom, the top of an animal's body. **3** A defending player in football and other games.

back² *verb* (backs, backing, backed) **1** To move backwards. **2** To bet on something. **3** To support. *Back me up*, give me your help. **backer** *noun*.

back³ *adjective* At the back, furthest from the front. *the back row*.

back⁴ *adverb* **1** To where you have come from. *Go back!* **2** To an earlier time. *Think back to last year*. **3** Backwards. *Lean back*.

backbone *noun* (backbones) The spine.

backfire *verb* (backfires, backfiring, backfired) To make a loud explosion in a petrol engine.

background *noun* (backgrounds) **1** The back part of a scene, picture, or display. *distant hills in the background*. **2** The circumstances surrounding and influencing something. *the background to the French Revolution*.

backing *noun* (backings) **1** Support. **2** A musical accompaniment.

backside *noun* (backsides) A person's bottom.

backstroke *noun* A way of swimming on your back.

backward *adjective* **1** Towards the back, towards where you started from. **2** Having made less than normal progress. **backwardness** *noun*.

backwards *adverb* **1** Towards the back. **2** In reverse. *I can say the alphabet backwards*.

bacon *noun* Smoked or salted meat from the back or sides of a pig.

bacteria *noun* Tiny organisms, some of which cause diseases.

bad *adjective* (worse, worst) **1** Of the kind that people do not want, like, or approve of. *bad advice. bad behaviour*. **2** unfit to eat. *bad meat*. **3** Serious. *a bad mistake*. **4** (informal) Ill. *I feel bad today*. **badness** *noun*.

bade *See* **bid²**

badge *noun* (badges) A sign worn to show you belong to a school or club, a sign of your rank or position.

badger *noun* (badgers) An animal that burrows in the ground.

badly *adverb* **1** In a bad or unsatisfactory way. *I played badly*. **2** Severely, seriously. *He was badly hurt*. **3** Very much. *They badly want to win*. **badly off** having little money.

badminton *noun* A game like tennis, played with a shuttlecock instead of a ball.

bad-tempered *adjective* Having a bad temper.

baffle *verb* (baffles, baffling, baffled) To puzzle.

bag¹ *noun* (bags) A container made of something flexible such as paper or plastic. *a shopping bag. a tool bag.*

bag² *verb* (bags, bagging, bagged) **1** To put in bags. **2** To seize or capture.

baggage *noun* Luggage.

baggy *adjective* Hanging in loose folds.

bagpipes *noun* A musical instrument with pipes and a bag to supply air.

bail¹ *noun* A payment or promise of money which allows an accused person to go free until his trial. The money is forfeited if he does not come to court at the proper time.

bail² *noun* (bails) One of the pieces of wood placed on top of the stumps in cricket.

bail³ *verb* (bails, bailing, bailed) To scoop water out of a boat.

bairn *noun* (bairns) In Scotland, a child.

bait¹ *noun* Food which is put on a hook or in a trap to catch fish or animals.

bait² *verb* (baits, baiting, baited) **1** To put bait on a hook or in a trap. **2** To tease or torment somebody.

bake *verb* (bakes, baking, baked) **1** To cook in an oven. **2** To heat something, to make a thing hard by heating. **3** To become very hot.

baker *noun* (bakers) A person whose business is baking bread and cakes. **bakery** *noun*.

balance¹ *noun* **1** Steadiness. **2** An equal distribution of weight or quantity. **3** A device for weighing things. **4** The money left after you have spent some of it, the money you have in a bank account.

balance² *verb* (balances, balancing, balanced) **1** To make a thing steady. **2** To be steady, to make yourself steady. **3** To distribute weight equally on each side of something.

balcony *noun* (balconies) **1** An outside platform which can be reached from an upstairs window. **2** The upstairs part of a cinema or theatre.

bald *adjective* (balder, baldest) Without hair. **baldness** *noun*.

bale¹ *noun* (bales) A large bundle of hay, straw, or wool.

bale² *verb* (bales, baling, baled) To make into bales. **baler** *noun*. **bale out** to jump with a parachute from an aircraft.

ball *noun* (balls) **1** A round object for playing games, such as a football. **2** A round shape. *a ball of string.* **3** A big party with dancing.

ballad *noun* (ballads) A song or poem that tells a story.

ballerina *noun* (ballerinas) A woman ballet-dancer.

ballet *noun* (ballets) A stage entertainment telling a story or expressing an idea in dancing and mime.

balloon *noun* (balloons) **1** A large rounded container filled with air or gas, sometimes with a basket beneath to carry passengers. **2** A small bag filled with air or gas, used as a toy.

ballot *noun* (ballots) Secret voting on pieces of paper.

ball-point *noun* (ball-points) A kind of pen with a tiny steel ball for a nib.

balmy *adjective* Peaceful, healing.

balsa *noun* A light wood.

bamboo *noun* (bamboos) A plant with hollow stems or canes.

ban *verb* (bans, banning, banned) To forbid, to make something illegal.

banana *noun* (bananas) A finger-shaped yellow fruit.

band *noun* (bands) **1** A strip, often in the form of a loop. *a rubber band.*

a **b** c d e f g h i j k l m

2 A group of people. *a band of robbers*.
3 A group of musicians.

bandage *noun* (bandages) A strip of material used to cover a wound.

bandit *noun* (bandits) An outlaw, a robber.

bandstand *noun* (bandstands) A covered platform where a band can play in the open air.

bandy *adjective* Having legs curved outward so that the knees are wide apart.

bang¹ *noun* (bangs) **1** A heavy blow. **2** A sudden loud noise.

bang² *verb* (bangs, banging, banged) To make a bang, to do something with a bang.

banger *noun* (bangers) (informal) **1** An exploding firework. **2** A sausage. **3** An old car.

Bangladeshi *adjective* Of or from Bangladesh.

bangle *noun* (bangles) An ornament worn round the arm or leg.

banish *verb* (banishes, banishing, banished) To punish someone by sending him away from his country.

banisters *noun* A handrail with upright supports at the side of stairs.

banjo *noun* (banjos) A musical instrument with metal strings played by plucking.

bank¹ *noun* (banks) **1** Raised or sloping ground. **2** The dry ground at the edge of a pond, river, or canal.

bank² *noun* (banks) A business which looks after people's money. **banker** *noun*.

bank³ *verb* (banks, banking, banked) **1** To put money in a bank. **2** To lean over, or lift one side higher than the other, while turning a corner. *The plane banked as it turned in to land.* **bank on** to rely on. **bank up** to heap up.

bankrupt *adjective* Unable to pay all your debts. **bankruptcy** *noun*.

banner *noun* (banners) A flag carried in procession.

banns *noun* An announcement in church that two people are going to be married.

banquet *noun* (banquets) A feast.

bantam *noun* (bantams) A small kind of chicken.

banter *noun* Good-humoured teasing.

baptize *verb* (baptizes, baptizing, baptized) To sprinkle or cover someone with water in a religious ceremony. **baptism** *noun*.

bar¹ *noun* (bars) **1** A long piece of any hard substance. *a bar of chocolate. a metal bar.* **2** A place where drinks are served. **3** A term used in music. *In a waltz you count three beats to the bar.*

bar² *verb* (bars, barring, barred) **1** To fasten with a bar. **2** To keep somebody out.

barbarian *noun* (barbarians) An uncivilized, savage person. **barbaric** *adjective*, **barbarous** *adjective*.

barbecue¹ *noun* (barbecues) **1** A metal framework for cooking meat over a fire. **2** An open-air party where food is cooked on a barbecue.

barbecue² *verb* (barbecues, barbecueing, barbecued) To cook on a barbecue.

barbed *adjective* With jagged hooks or points. *barbed wire*.

barber *noun* (barbers) A men's hairdresser.

ISBN 0-19-861297-4

9 780198 612971

bar-code *noun* (bar-codes) A pattern of stripes such as is printed on goods in shops to be read by a special computer at the check-out.

bard *noun* (bards) A minstrel, a poet.

bare¹ *adjective* (barer, barest) **1** Uncovered, without protection or decoration. **2** Empty or nearly empty. *a bare room*. **3** Just enough. *a bare possibility*.

bare² *verb* (bares, baring, bared) To uncover, to reveal.

barely *adverb* Only just, scarcely.

bargain¹ *noun* (bargains) **1** An agreement to buy or sell something. **2** Something bought unusually cheaply.

bargain² *verb* (bargains, bargaining, bargained) To argue about the price of something.

barge *noun* (barges) A large flat-bottomed boat used especially on canals.

bark¹ *noun* (barks) **1** The sound made by a dog or a fox. **2** The outer covering of the trunk of a tree.

bark² *verb* (barks, barking, barked) **1** To make the sound of a dog or a fox. **2** To injure yourself by scraping your skin on something. *I barked my shin*.

barley *noun* **1** A cereal plant. **2** Its seed used for food and in making various drinks.

barley-sugar *noun* A sweet made of boiled sugar.

barmaid, barman *nouns* (barmaids, barmen) A person who serves drinks at a bar.

bar mitzvah The ceremony at which a Jewish boy aged 13 takes on adult responsibilities.

barn *noun* (barns) A storage building on a farm.

barnacle *noun* (barnacles) A shellfish that sticks to rocks and the bottoms of ships.

barometer *noun* (barometers) An instrument that measures air pressure, used in studying the weather.

baron *noun* (barons) A nobleman.

baroness *noun* (baronesses) **1** A noble woman. **2** A baron's wife.

barracks *noun* A building where soldiers live.

barrage *noun* (barrages) **1** Heavy gunfire. **2** A dam across a river, a barricade.

barrel *noun* (barrels) **1** A container with curved sides and flat ends. **2** The tube of a gun through which the shot is fired.

barren *adjective* Not producing fruit or offspring. *a barren tree*.

barricade *noun* (barricades) A barrier quickly put together to keep out an enemy.

barrier *noun* (barriers) A fence or obstacle.

barrister *noun* (barristers) A lawyer with the right to conduct a case in the higher lawcourts.

barrow *noun* (barrows) **1** A small cart. **2** A mound of earth made in prehistoric times to cover a grave.

base¹ *noun* (bases) **1** The lowest part of anything, the part on which a thing stands. **2** A headquarters, a place where stores and reinforcements are kept.

base² *verb* (bases, basing, based) To put on or in a base. *He based his story on fact*, he used something that had really happened as the basis for his story.

base³ *adjective* (baser, basest) Mean, selfish, cowardly. **basely** *adverb*, **baseness** *noun*.

baseball *noun* An American game played rather like rounders.

basement *noun* (basements) A room or rooms below the ground floor.

bash *verb* (bashes, bashing, bashed) (informal) To hit hard.

bashful *adjective* Shy. **bashfully** *adverb*.

basic *adjective* **1** Forming a basis.
2 Most important. **basically** *adverb*.

basin *noun* (basins) A deep dish, a bowl,
an open container for liquids.

basis *noun* (bases) **1** A foundation,
a starting-point. **2** The main
ingredient of something.

bask *verb* (basks, basking, basked) To
enjoy warmth and light.

basket *noun* (baskets) A kind of container, usually woven from canes,
raffia, or similar material.

basket-ball *noun* A game in which
a ball is thrown into basket-shaped
nets which are the goals.

bass *noun* (basses) **1** A male singer with
the lowest type of voice. **2** The lowest
part in a piece of music.

bassoon *noun* (bassoons) A woodwind
instrument which can produce low
notes.

bastard *noun* (bastards) An illegitimate
child.

bat[1] *noun* (bats) A small flying animal.
blind as a bat, unable to see clearly.

bat[2] *noun* (bats) A wooden implement
used to hit the ball in cricket, baseball, and other games.

bat[3] *verb* (bats, batting, batted) To use
a bat, to hit with a bat.

batch *noun* (batches) A set of things.

bated *adjective* **with bated breath**
anxiously, hardly daring to speak.

bath[1] *noun* (baths) **1** A washing of the
whole body. **to have a bath**, to sit in
water and wash yourself all over. **2** A
large container for water in which to
have a bath. **3** The water used in having a bath. *to run a bath*.

bath[2] *verb* (baths, bathing, bathed)
1 To have a bath. **2** To give someone
a bath.

bathe *verb* (bathes, bathing, bathed)
1 To go swimming. **bather** *noun*.
2 To wash something gently. *Bathe
your sore finger*.

bathroom *noun* (bathrooms) A room
where you can have a bath.

baths *noun* A swimming-pool.

baton *noun* (batons) A short stick such
as the stick used to conduct an
orchestra.

batsman *noun* (batsmen) A person batting in cricket.

battalion *noun* (battalions) A unit of
the army.

batten *noun* (battens) A strip of wood.

batter[1] *verb* (batters, battering, bat-
tered) To strike hard and often, to
beat out of shape.

batter[2] *noun* A mixture of flour, eggs,
and milk used in cooking.

battering-ram *noun* (battering-rams)
A post swung to hammer down gates
and walls.

battery *noun* (batteries) **1** A portable
device for storing and supplying electricity. **2** A number of guns organized
together. **battery hens** hens kept in
small cages.

battle *noun* (battles) A fight between
armies.

battle-axe *noun* (battle-axes) A heavy
axe formerly used as a weapon.

battlefield *noun* (battlefields) A place
where a battle is fought.

battlements *noun* The top of a castle
wall.

battleship *noun* (battleships) A large
and powerful warship.

bawl *verb* (bawls, bawling, bawled) To
shout or cry out loudly.

bay *noun* (bays) **1** A wide inlet, a curved
part of the sea-shore. **2** An alcove, or
an area between two partitions. **3** The
bark of a hound. **keep at bay** to fight

off. **bay window** a window which curves outwards from the wall of a house.

bayonet *noun* (bayonets) A dagger fixed to the end of a rifle.

bazaar *noun* (bazaars) **1** A market in Eastern countries. **2** A kind of shop. **3** A sale to raise money for charity.

BBC The British Broadcasting Corporation.

BC Before Christ. *Julius Caesar came to Britain in 55 BC.*

be *verb* (am, are, is; being; was, were; been) **1** To exist, to live. **2** To have a particular name, or quality, or condition. *This is Mr Eliot. He is famous.* **3** To become. *What are you going to be when you grow up?* **4** To happen, to take place. *When will sports day be?* **5** To remain. *I'll be here all day.* **6** To go, to visit. *Have you been to school today?*

beach *noun* (beaches) A sea-shore covered in sand or pebbles.

beacon *noun* (beacons) A light used as a warning signal.

bead *noun* (beads) **1** A small, pretty ball with a hole through it for making necklaces. **2** A small drop of liquid.

beagle *noun* (beagles) A small hound.

beak *noun* (beaks) The hard, horny part of a bird's mouth.

beaker *noun* (beakers) A large cup or mug.

beam¹ *noun* (beams) **1** A long, thick bar of wood. **2** Rays of light or radio waves.

beam² *verb* (beams, beaming, beamed) **1** To smile happily. **2** To send out a light or radio beam.

bean *noun* (beans) **1** A kind of plant with seeds growing in pods. **beans** these seeds or pods used as food.

bear¹ *verb* (bears, bearing, bore, borne) **1** To carry, to support. **2** To produce. *to bear fruit.* **3** To suffer, to put up with. *I can't bear it any longer.*

bear² *verb* (bears, bearing, bore, born) To give birth to offspring.

bear³ *noun* (bears) A large heavy animal with rough hair.

beard *noun* (beards) The hair on the lower part of a man's face.

bearings *noun* Where one place is in relation to another. **lose your bearings** to lose your sense of direction.

beast *noun* (beasts) **1** A four-footed animal. **2** (informal) A cruel, disgusting, or badly behaved person. **beastly** *adverb*, **beastliness** *noun*.

beat¹ *verb* (beats, beating, beaten) **1** To hit often, usually with a stick. **2** To stir up something briskly before cooking it. *to beat eggs.* **beater** *noun*. **3** To hammer into shape, to make metal flat. **4** To defeat. **dead beat** tired out. **beat time** to move your hand in time with music.

beat² *noun* (beats) **1** Regular rhythm. **2** A repeated stroke. *the beat of a drum.* **3** The regular route of a policeman.

beauty *noun* (beauties) The pleasant quality in something that makes you admire it and enjoy its loveliness. *the beauty of the sunset.* **beautiful** *adjective*, **beautifully** *adverb*.

beaver *noun* (beavers) A fur-covered animal living on land and water.

becalmed *adjective* Unable to sail on because the wind has dropped.

became *See* **become**

because For the reason that. **because of** for the reason of.

beckon *verb* (beckons, beckoning, beckoned) To make a sign to someone asking him to come.

become *verb* (becomes, becoming, became) **1** To come to be. *It became darker.* **2** To look attractive on someone. *That new dress becomes you.* **become of** to happen to. *What became of Dick when he went to London?*

becoming *adjective* Suitable, attractive.

bed *noun* (beds) **1** A piece of furniture for sleeping on. **2** A place to sleep or rest. *a bed of straw.* **3** A piece of ground for growing flowers, fruit, or vegetables. **4** The bottom of the sea or of a river. **5** A base or foundation.

bedclothes *noun* Sheets, blankets, pillows, and other things that go on a bed.

bedding *noun* Things for making a bed.

bedlam *noun* Noisy confusion.

bedraggled *adjective* Untidy, limp, wet.

bedridden *adjective* Unable to get out of bed because of illness.

bedroom *noun* (bedrooms) A room to sleep in.

bedspread *noun* (bedspreads) A top cover for a bed.

bedstead *noun* (bedsteads) The framework of a bed.

bedtime *noun* (bedtimes) The time for going to bed.

bee *noun* (bees) An insect which makes honey.

beech *noun* (beeches) A kind of tree.

beef *noun* The meat of an ox, bull, or cow.

beefburger *noun* (beefburgers) A round cake of minced beef.

beefeater *noun* (beefeaters) A Yeoman of the Guard, a guard at the Tower of London.

beefy *adjective* Strong, with large muscles.

beehive *noun* (beehives) A box or other container made for bees to live in.

been *See* **be**

beer *noun* An alcoholic drink made from malt and hops.

beetle *noun* (beetles) An insect with hard, shiny wing-covers.

beetroot *noun* A dark red root vegetable.

befall *verb* (befalls, befalling, befell) To happen.

before[1] *adverb* At an earlier time. *I have been here before.*

before[2] *preposition and conjunction* **1** Earlier than. *before lunch.* **2** Ahead of, in front of. *leg before wicket.*

beg *verb* (begs, begging, begged) **1** To ask strangers for money, food, and other necessities. **2** To ask earnestly and with feeling. *He begged me not to report him.*

began *See* **begin**

beggar *noun* (beggars) Somebody who lives by begging.

begin *verb* (begins, beginning, began, begun) To start, to come into existence.

beginner *noun* (beginners) A learner.

beginning *noun* (beginnings) A starting-point.

begrudge *verb* (begrudges, begrudging, begrudged) To envy someone about something.

begun *See* **begin**

behalf **on my behalf** for me.

behave *verb* (behaves, behaving, behaved) **1** To act. *My dog behaved* *badly at Granny's.* **2** To act well. *Try to behave!* **behaviour** *noun.*

behead *verb* (beheads, beheading, beheaded) To cut off somebody's head.

behind[1] *preposition* **1** To the rear of. *The driver sits behind the wheel.* **2** Causing. *Who's behind all this trouble?*

behind[2] *adverb* **1** At the rear, after others have gone. *The old man lagged behind. The bus left us behind.* **2** Not making good progress. *I'm getting behind with my work.*

behind[3] *noun* (behinds) (informal) A person's bottom.

behindhand *adverb* Late.

behold *verb* (beholds, beholding, beheld) (old-fashioned) To see.

being[1] *See* be

being[2] *noun* (beings) A creature. *human beings.*

belated *adjective* Late, too late. **belatedly** *adverb.*

belch *verb* (belches, belching, belched) **1** To send out. *The chimney belched smoke and flames.* **2** To let gases from the stomach noisily out through the mouth.

belfry *noun* (belfries) A tower in which bells are hung.

belief *noun* (beliefs) What a person believes.

believe *verb* (believes, believing, believed) **1** To feel sure that something is true. *I believe your story.* **2** To feel sure that someone is telling the truth. *I believe you.* **believe in** to trust, to have faith in.

bell *noun* (bells) **1** A hollow metal instrument that rings when struck. **2** Any instrument that makes a ringing sound, such as a door-bell or a bicycle bell.

belligerent *adjective* Warlike.

bellow *noun* (bellows, bellowing, bellowed) To roar like a bull, to shout.

bellows *noun* A device for blowing air.

belly *noun* (bellies) The stomach, the abdomen.

belong *verb* (belongs, belonging, belonged) **1** **belong to** to be owned by someone. **2** *The butter belongs in the fridge,* its proper place is in the fridge.

belongings *noun* Possessions.

beloved *adjective* Much loved.

below[1] *adverb* To a lower level, underneath.

below[2] *preposition* Lower than, under. *below zero.*

belt *noun* (belts) **1** A strip of material worn round the waist. **2** A strip, a band, a long line. *a belt of trees.*

bench *noun* (benches) **1** A long, hard seat. **2** A work table, such as a carpenter's bench. **3** The seat for a judge or a magistrate in a lawcourt.

bend[1] *verb* (bends, bending, bent) **1** To force something into a curved or crooked shape. **2** To become curved or crooked. **3** To bow or stoop.

bend[2] *noun* (bends) A curve, a turn.

beneath *preposition* Below, underneath.

benediction *noun* (benedictions) A blessing.

benefactor *noun* (benefactors) Someone who has generously given something to another person or to a charity.

benefit *noun* (benefits) Help, advantage. **beneficial** *adjective.*

benevolent *adjective* Kindly, helpful. **benevolently** *adverb,* **benevolence** *noun.*

bent[1] *See* bend[1]

bent[2] *noun* (bents) A natural liking for something.

bequest *noun* (bequests) A gift left to somebody in a will.

bereaved *adjective* Left sad because somebody has died. **bereavement** *noun.*

beret *noun* (berets) A round soft cap.

berry *noun* (berries) A small juicy fruit containing seeds.

berserk *adjective* **go berserk** to become violent and behave wildly.

berth *noun* (berths) 1 A sleeping place on a ship or train. 2 A place where ships tie up in harbour.

beside *preposition* 1 At the side of. *A spider sat down beside her.* 2 Compared with. *You don't seem tall beside your father.* **beside yourself** no longer in control of yourself.

besides 1 In addition to, as well as. *I have two more besides these.* 2 Moreover, also. *It's too late to go now. Besides, I don't want to any more.*

besiege *verb* (besieges, besieging, besieged) To surround a place and try to capture it.

best[1] *adjective* Most excellent. **best man** the friend who stands by the bridegroom at a wedding.

best[2] *adverb* 1 In the best way. 2 most usefully, most wisely. *If you aren't well, you'd best go to bed.*

bet[1] *verb* (bets, betting, betted, bet) To take a chance of losing or winning money on the result of a race or some other event.

bet[2] *noun* (bets) 1 The agreement you make with someone when you bet. 2 The money you risk losing in betting.

betray *verb* (betrays, betraying, betrayed) 1 To be false to someone, to give someone up to the enemy. 2 To let something become known which should be kept secret. *to betray your feelings.* **betrayer, betrayal** *nouns.*

betrothed *adjective* Engaged to be married.

better[1] *adjective* 1 More excellent, more satisfactory. 2 Recovered after an illness. *Are you better today?*

better[2] *adverb* 1 In a better way. 2 More usefully, more wisely. *If you aren't well, you'd better go the bed.*

better[3] *verb* (betters, bettering, bettered) 1 To improve on something. *She bettered her own fastest time.* 2 To do better than someone else.

between *preposition* 1 A word showing within which limits something is. *We live between the park and the river. I go to bed between 8 and 9 o'clock. They walked between 3 and 4 miles.* 2 In shares. *We'll divide it between us, we shall have equal shares.* 3 When comparing. *Can't you tell the difference between right and wrong?*

beverage *noun* (beverages) A drink.

beware *verb* Be careful. *Beware of the dog.*

bewilder *verb* (bewilders, bewildering, bewildered) To puzzle, to confuse. **bewilderment** *noun.*

bewitch *verb* (bewitches, bewitching, bewitched) To put a magic spell on someone.

beyond *preposition* 1 On the far side of, further than. *Don't go beyond the fence.* 2 Too difficult for. *The problem is beyond me.*

biased *adjective* Preferring one side rather than the other. *a biased referee.*

bib *noun* (bibs) A piece of cloth or plastic tied under a child's chin during meals.

Bible *noun* (Bibles) The holy book of Christians and of Jews. **biblical** *adjective.*

bicycle *noun* (bicycles) A two-wheeled vehicle driven by pedals.

bid[1] *verb* (bids, bidding, bid) To offer a price for something. **bidder** *noun.*

bid[2] *verb* (bids, bidding, bade, bidden) (old-fashioned) To order or invite someone.

bide *verb* (bides, biding, bided) To stay. **bide your time** to wait for a good opportunity.

bifocals *noun* Spectacles with divided lenses, the lower part for reading, the upper part for seeing at a distance.

big *adjective* (bigger, biggest) 1 Of great size or importance. 2 Older. *my big sister.*

bigamy *noun* The crime of having two

wives or two husbands at a time. **bigamous** *adjective*, **bigamist** *noun*.

biggish *adjective* Fairly large.

bike *noun* (bikes) (informal) A bicycle.

bikini *noun* (bikinis) A two-piece bathing costume for women.

bilge *noun* **1** (bilges) The bottom of a ship where water collects. **2** (informal) Nonsense.

bilingual *adjective* Able to speak two languages equally well.

bilious *adjective* Feeling sick. **bilious attack** an illness with headache and sickness.

bill *noun* (bills) **1** A bird's beak. **2** An account showing how much money is owing. **3** A poster. **4** A proposed law, to be discussed by Parliament.

billiards *noun* An indoor game played with balls and long sticks called cues on a cloth-covered table.

billion *noun* (billions) In Britain, a billion used to mean one million million (1,000,000,000,000). In USA and nowadays in Britain and elsewhere it means one thousand million (1,000,000,000).

billow *verb* (billows, billowing, billowed) To swell up, to rise like great waves.

billy (billies) or **billycan** *noun* (billycans) A tin used by campers to cook in and eat out of.

billy-goat *noun* (billy-goats) A male goat.

bin *noun* (bins) A large container, usually with a lid.

binary *adjective* Consisting of two parts or units. **binary system** a system of counting using only the two digits 1 and 0.

bind *verb* (binds, binding, bound) **1** To tie up. *bound in chains.* **2** To fasten material round something. *to bind up a wound, to bind the edge of a carpet.* **3** To fasten the pages of a book into a cover. **binder** *noun*.

binding *noun* (bindings) A book cover.

bingo *noun* A gambling game in which each player has a card on which numbers are printed, and covers these when they are called.

binoculars *noun* An instrument with lenses you look through with both eyes to make distant objects seem nearer.

biodegradable *adjective* Able to be destroyed by bacteria.

biography *noun* (biographies) The written story of a person's life.

biology *noun* The branch of science dealing with living things. **biological** *adjective*, **biologist** *noun*.

biplane *noun* (biplanes) An aircraft with two pairs of wings, one above the other.

birch *noun* (birches) A kind of tree.

bird *noun* (birds) An animal with feathers and wings.

birdcage *noun* (birdcages) A cage in which a bird is kept.

birdseed *noun* Seed used as food for birds.

Biro *noun* (Biros) The trade name of a kind of ball-point pen.

birth *noun* (births) The process of being born. **birth control** ways of avoiding conceiving a baby.

birthday *noun* (birthdays) The date of a person's birth.

birthmark *noun* (birthmarks) A mark which has been on a person's body since birth.

birthplace *noun* (birthplaces) The place where a person was born.

biscuit *noun* (biscuits) A flat thin crisp cake.

bishop *noun* (bishops) **1** A clergyman of high rank. **2** A piece in chess.

bison *noun* (bison) An American buffalo, a wild ox.

bit[1] *noun* (bits) **1** A small piece or quantity of anything. **2** The metal part of a horse's bridle that goes into its mouth. **3** A digit in the binary system, 1 or 0. **bit by bit** gradually.

bit[2] *See* bite

bitch *noun* (bitches) A female dog.

bite *verb* (bites, biting, bit, bitten) **1** To cut into something with the teeth. **2** To sting. **bite the dust** to be killed.

bitter *adjective* (bitterest) **1** Unpleasant-tasting, the opposite of sweet. **2** Filled with envy or hatred. **3** Very cold. *a bitter wind*. **bitterly** *adverb*, **bitterness** *noun*.

black[1] *noun* The darkest of all colours, the colour of coal, the opposite of white.

black[2] *adjective* (blacker, blackest) **1** Black in colour. **2** Very dirty. **3** Gloomy, evil, sinister. **black ice** dangerous ice on roads. **blackly** *adverb*, **blackness** *noun*.

Black[3] *noun* (Blacks) A person with dark or black skin.

black-beetle *noun* (black-beetles) A cockroach.

blackberry *noun* (blackberries) A juicy black berry that grows on brambles.

blackbird *noun* (blackbirds) A common European song-bird.

blackboard *noun* (blackboards) A dark surface for writing on with chalk.

blacken *verb* (blackens, blackening, blackened) **1** To become black, to make something black.

blackguard *noun* (blackguards) A rogue, a scoundrel.

blackhead *noun* (blackheads) A pimple with a black top.

blackmail *verb* (blackmails, blackmailing, blackmailed) To demand money from someone in return for keeping quiet about something. **blackmailer** *noun*.

black-out *noun* (black-outs) **1** An electric power failure. **2** The switching off of all lights. **3** A period of unconsciousness.

blacksmith *noun* (blacksmiths) A person who forges and repairs things made of iron, a person who makes shoes for horses.

bladder *noun* (bladders) The part of the body in which waste liquid collects before it is passed out of the body.

blade *noun* (blades) **1** The sharp part of a knife or any other cutting instrument. **2** Something shaped like a blade. *a blade of grass*.

blame *verb* (blames, blaming, blamed) To say that someone or something is the cause of what is wrong. *Jo broke the window, but Mum blamed me! He was to blame, it was his fault*. **blameless** *adjective*.

blancmange *noun* (blancmanges) A pudding made with cornflour and milk.

blank[1] *adjective* (blanker, blankest) **1** Not written or recorded on. *a blank page, a blank tape*. **2** Without interest or expression. *a blank look*. **blankly** *adverb*.

blank[2] *noun* (blanks) **1** An empty space. **2** A cartridge which makes a noise but does not fire a bullet.

blanket *noun* (blankets) A piece of thick cloth used as a warm covering on a bed.

blare *verb* (blares, blaring, blared) To make a loud, harsh noise.

blasphemous *adjective* Wicked and irreverent. **blasphemously** *adverb*, **blasphemy** *noun*.

blast¹ *noun* (blasts) **1** A sudden rush of air. **2** A loud noise, such as the sound of a trumpet.

blast² *verb* (blasts, blasting, blasted) To blow up something with explosives.

blatant *adjective* Very obvious. *a blatant foul.* **blatantly** *adverb*.

blaze *verb* (blazes, blazing, blazed) **1** To burn brightly. **2** To be full of strong feelings. **blaze away** to fire guns continually. **blaze a trail** to make cuts on trees to mark a path.

blazer *noun* (blazers) A type of jacket sometimes worn as part of school uniform.

bleach *verb* (bleaches, bleaching, bleached) To become white or make something white.

bleak *adjective* (bleaker, bleakest) Bare, cold, and miserable. **bleakly** *adverb*.

bleary *adjective* Not seeing clearly.

bleat *verb* (bleats, bleating, bleated) To make a noise like the cry of a lamb or calf.

bleed *verb* (bleeds, bleeding, bled) To lose blood.

bleep *noun* (bleeps) The short, high sound produced by an electronic device.

blemish *noun* (blemishes) A mark, a flaw.

blend *verb* (blends, blending, blended) To mix together, to mix pleasantly and successfully. **blender** *noun*.

bless *verb* (blesses, blessing, blessed) **1** To wish somebody well, to be good to someone. **2** To make something holy.

blessing *noun* (blessings) **1** A prayer, a grace before meals. **2** Something you are grateful for.

blight *noun* (blights) A disease, an evil influence.

blind¹ *adjective* **1** Unable to see. **2** Unable to understand. **3** Reckless, thoughtless. **blind alley** a road which has one end closed. **blindly** *adverb*, **blindness** *noun*.

blind² *verb* (blinds, blinding, blinded) To make blind.

blind³ *noun* (blinds) A kind of screen for windows.

blindfold *verb* (blindfolds, blindfolding, blindfolded) To cover someone's eyes so that they cannot see.

blink *verb* (blinks, blinking, blinked) To shut and open the eyes rapidly.

bliss *noun* Great happiness. **blissful** *adjective*, **blissfully** *adverb*.

blister *noun* (blisters) A swelling like a bubble under the skin.

blitz *noun* A sudden attack, usually from the air.

blizzard *noun* (blizzards) A severe windy snowstorm.

bloated *adjective* Swollen.

blob *noun* (blobs) A drop of liquid, a small round lump of something.

block¹ *noun* (blocks) **1** A solid lump of something. *a block of ice.* **2** A large building or a group of buildings. **block letters** capital letters.

block² *verb* (blocks, blocking, blocked) To stop something up, to obstruct. *to block the way.*

blockade *verb* (blockades, blockading, blockaded) To prevent people or supplies from going in or out of a place.

blockage *noun* (blockages) Something that blocks the way.

blockhead *noun* (blockheads) A slow, foolish person.

blond, blonde¹ *adjectives* Fair-haired. *a blond boy, a blonde girl.*

blonde² *noun* (blondes) A fair-haired woman.

blood *noun* The red liquid that flows through veins and arteries. *He has royal blood*, he has royal ancestors. **bloody** *adjective*.

bloodhound *noun* (bloodhounds) A large dog with a keen scent.

bloodshed *noun* Killing or wounding.

bloodshot *adjective* **bloodshot eyes** red eyes.

bloodstained *adjective* Stained with blood.

bloodthirsty *adjective* Eager for blood-shed.

bloom[1] *noun* (blooms) A flower.

bloom[2] *verb* (blooms, blooming, bloomed). **1** To produce flowers. **2** To be strong and healthy.

blossom[1] *noun* (blossoms) **1** A flower. **2** A mass of flowers.

blossom[2] *verb* (blossoms, blossoming, blossomed) To produce flowers.

blot[1] *noun* (blots) **1** A spot of ink. **2** An ugly mark, a flaw. *a blot on the landscape.*

blot[2] *verb* (blots, blotting, blotted) **1** To make a blot. **2** To dry wet ink with blot-ting-paper. **blot out** to cover, to hide.

blotch *noun* (blotches) A spot of colour.

blotting-paper *noun* A special paper which soaks up ink.

blouse *noun* (blouses) A loose garment for the top half of the body.

blow[1] *verb* (blows, blowing, blew, blown) **1** To make a movement of the air. *A gale is blowing.* **2** To be moved by the wind. *His hat blew away.* **3** To make something move by blowing. *She blew the dust away.* **4** To make

a sound produced by blowing. *The whistle blew.* **blow up 1** To force air into something. *to blow up a tyre.* **2** To explode, to destroy with explosives. **blower** *noun*.

blow[2] *noun* (blows) **1** A hard knock. **2** An unexpected misfortune.

blubber[1] *noun* Fat from a whale.

blubber[2] *verb* (blubbers, blubbering, blubbered) To weep noisily.

blue[1] *noun* A colour, the colour of a cloudless sky.

blue[2] *adjective* (bluer, bluest) **1** Blue in colour. **2** Feeling sad, depressed.

bluebell *noun* (bluebells) A blue wild flower.

bluebottle *noun* (bluebottles) A large fly.

blues *noun* A kind of slow sad jazz. **the blues** a state of depression.

bluff[1] *verb* (bluffs, bluffing, bluffed) To try to deceive somebody by pretend-ing to have the power to do some-thing.

bluff[2] *noun* Bluffing. *His bluff doesn't fool me.*

bluish *adjective* Rather blue.

blunder[1] *verb* (blunders, blundering, blundered) To stumble, to make a clumsy mistake.

blunder[2] *noun* (blunders) A clumsy mistake.

blunderbuss *noun* (blunderbusses) An old type of gun.

blunt *adjective* (blunter, bluntest) **1** Not sharp. **2** Speaking plainly, not very polite. **bluntly** *adverb*, **bluntness** *noun*.

blur *verb* (blurs, blurring, blurred) **1** To become confused or not clear. **2** To make something confused or not clear.

blurt *verb* (blurts, blurting, blurted) To speak suddenly and without think-ing.

blush[1] *verb* (blushes, blushing, blushed) To become red in the face.

blush[2] *noun* (blushes) A reddening of the face.

blustery *adjective* Windy.

boa-constrictor *noun* (boa-constrictors) A large snake which crushes its prey.

boar *noun* (boars) **1** A wild pig. **2** Any male pig.

board[1] *noun* (boards) **1** A plank. **2** A flat piece of wood or other material. **3** A board made for a special purpose, such as a notice-board. **board and lodging** meals and a place to sleep. **on board** on a ship or other form of transport.

board[2] *verb* (boards, boarding, boarded) **1** To go onto a ship or other form of transport. **2** To get board and lodging somewhere. **boarder** *noun*.

boarding-house *noun* (boarding-houses) A place where you can get board and lodging.

boarding-school *noun* (boarding-schools) A school where children live during the term.

boast[1] *verb* (boasts, boasting, boasted) To praise yourself or your own possessions.

boast[2] *noun* (boasts) Boasting talk. **boastful** *adjective*, **boastfully** *adverb*, **boastfulness** *noun*.

boat *noun* (boats) Something made to float on water as a toy or to carry people or goods.

boat-house *noun* (boat-houses) A building where boats are kept.

boating *noun* Going out in a boat.

boatman *noun* (boatmen) A man in charge of a boat.

boatswain *noun* (boatswains) A senior seaman.

bob *verb* (bobs, bobbing, bobbed) To move up and down like something floating.

bobsleigh *noun* (bobsleighs) A kind of racing sleigh.

bodice *noun* (bodices) The upper part of a woman's dress.

bodily *adverb* **1** To do with the human body. **2** As a whole.

body *noun* (bodies) **1** The physical part of a person. *Exercise develops a healthy body.* **2** A dead body, a corpse. **3** The main part of your body, not the head, arms, or legs. **4** The main part of anything. **5** A collection of things, people, or ideas. **heavenly bodies** suns, stars, and planets.

bodyguard *noun* (bodyguards) A guard for an important person.

bog *noun* (bogs) Wet and spongy ground, marsh. **boggy** *adjective*.

bogie *noun* (bogies) A set of wheels.

bogus *adjective* False, not real.

boil[1] *noun* (boils) An inflamed spot on the skin.

boil[2] *verb* (boils, boiling, boiled) **1** To bubble and give off steam. **2** To cook in boiling water. **3** To be very hot.

boiler *noun* (boilers) An apparatus for heating water.

boisterous *adjective* Wild, noisy, and cheerful. **boisterously** *adverb*.

bold *adjective* (bolder, boldest) **1** Fearless. **2** Cheeky, shameless. **3** Clearly seen. **boldly** *adverb*, **boldness** *noun*.

bolster *noun* (bolsters) A long pillow.

bolt[1] *noun* (bolts) **1** A type of fastening for a door. **2** A thick metal pin on which a nut can be screwed. **3** A short, heavy arrow fired from a crossbow.

bolt[2] *verb* (bolts, bolting, bolted) **1** To fasten with a bolt. **2** To run away suddenly. **3** To gulp food.

bomb[1] *noun* (bombs) An explosive device.

bomb[2] *verb* (bombs, bombing, bombed) To attack with a bomb or bombs. **bomber** *noun*.

bombard *verb* (bombards, bombarding, bombarded) **1** To attack with gunfire. **2** To fire questions at someone. **bombardment** *noun*.

bombshell *noun* (bombshells) A shattering surprise.

bond *noun* (bonds) Something which binds or ties.

bondage *noun* Slavery.

bone *noun* (bones) One of the parts of a skeleton. **bone dry** completely dry. **bony** *adjective*.

bonfire *noun* (bonfires) A large outdoor fire.

bongo *noun* (bongos) One of a pair of small drums played with your fingers.

bonnet *noun* (bonnets) **1** The hinged lid over a car's engine. **2** A kind of hat.

bonus *noun* (bonuses) An extra payment.

boo *verb* (boos, booing, booed) To show disapproval by shouting 'boo'.

booby *noun* (boobies) A silly person. **booby trap** a dangerous device designed to take an enemy by surprise.

book¹ *noun* (books) A set of sheets of paper fastened together inside a cover.

book² *verb* (books, booking, booked) **1** To record something in a book. **2** To reserve seats for a journey or an entertainment.

bookcase *noun* (bookcases) A piece of furniture designed to hold books.

bookie *noun* (bookies) (informal) A bookmaker.

booking-office *noun* (booking-offices) An office where you can book seats.

booklet *noun* (booklets) A small book.

bookmaker *noun* (bookmakers) A person whose business is taking bets.

boom¹ *verb* (booms, booming, boomed) To make a deep sound like a heavy gun or the low notes of an organ.

boom² *noun* (booms) **1** A booming sound. **2** A long pole holding a sail straight at the bottom.

boomerang *noun* (boomerangs) A curved stick thrown as a weapon, supposed to return to the person who threw it.

boost *verb* (boosts, boosting, boosted) To give something a push upwards, to increase something in size, value, or power. **booster** *noun*.

boot *noun* (boots) **1** A shoe that covers the ankle and sometimes also the leg. **2** The luggage space in a car.

bootee *noun* (bootees) A knitted boot for a baby.

booth *noun* (booths) A small enclosed space. *a telephone booth.*

booty *noun* Loot.

booze *noun* (informal) Alcoholic drink. **boozy** *adjective*.

border *noun* (borders) **1** An edge, a boundary, a frontier. **2** A flower bed.

bore¹ See **bear¹** and **bear²**

bore² *verb* (bores, boring, bored) **1** To make a narrow, round hole. **2** To make someone weary by being dull and uninteresting.

bore³ *noun* (bores) A dull, uninteresting person or thing. **boredom** *noun*.

born See **bear²**

borne See **bear¹**

borough *noun* (boroughs) An important town or district.

borrow *verb* (borrows, borrowing, borrowed) To use something which belongs to someone else and which must be returned. **borrower** *noun*.

bosom *noun* (bosoms) A person's breast.

boss *noun* (bosses). **1** The person in

control. **2** A knob like that at the centre of a shield.

bossy *adjective* (bossier, bossiest) Enjoying being in charge, giving tiresome orders. **bossily** *adverb*.

botany *noun* The scientific study of plants. **botanical** *adjective*, **botanist** *noun*.

both **1** The two. *You can have cake or a biscuit, but not both.* **2** *Both wise and rich*, not only wise but also rich.

bother[1] *noun* Trouble, worry. **bothersome** *adjective*.

bother[2] *verb* (bothers, bothering, bothered) **1** To cause trouble to someone. **2** To worry. **3** To take trouble.

bottle[1] *noun* (bottles) A narrow-necked container for liquids. **bottle bank** a bin in which you put bottles for recycling.

bottle[2] *verb* (bottles, bottling, bottled) To put something in a bottle, to keep it in a bottle.

bottle[3] *noun* (informal) Courage.

bottle-neck *noun* (bottle-necks) A narrow part of a road where traffic jams occur.

bottom *noun* (bottoms) **1** The lowest or farthest part of anything. *the bottom of the garden*, the end of the garden. **2** The part of the body on which you sit. **3** The ground under the water in a river, a lake, or the sea. **bottomless** *adjective*.

bough *noun* (boughs) A branch of a tree.

bought *See* **buy**

boulder *noun* (boulders) A large rock worn smooth by water or weather.

bounce *verb* (bounces, bouncing, bounced) **1** To jump back when thrown against something hard. **2** To move with jumps and jolts. **bouncy** *adjective*.

bouncer *noun* (bouncers) A ball bowled in cricket so that it bounces up near the batsman's head.

bound[1] *See* **bind**. **bound to 1** Certain

to. *bound to fail*. **2** Obliged to. *bound to pay for it.* **bound for** going somewhere. *bound for Spain*.

bound[2] *verb* (bounds, bounding, bounded) To leap, to bounce.

boundary *noun* (boundaries) **1** A line marking the edge of something. **2** A hit to the edge of a cricket field.

boundless *adjective* Unlimited.

bounds *noun* **out of bounds** where you are forbidden to go.

bounty *noun* (bounties) A generous gift, a payment. **bountiful** *adjective*.

bouquet *noun* (bouquets) A bunch of flowers.

bout *noun* (bouts) **1** A contest, a trial of strength. **2** An attack of an illness.

boutique *noun* (boutiques) A fashionable shop.

bow[1] *noun* (bows) **1** A weapon used to shoot arrows. **2** The stick with hair stretched along it used to play stringed instruments. **3** A knot made with loops. **bow window** a curved bay window.

bow[2] *or* **bows** *noun* The front part of a ship.

bow[3] *verb* (bows, bowing, bowed) To bend politely forward.

bowels *noun* **1** The lowest part of the digestive system in the body. **2** The deep inside part of something. *the bowels of the earth*.

bowl[1] *noun* (bowls) A basin.

bowl[2] *verb* (bowls, bowling, bowled) To send a ball for the batsman to play in cricket. **bowler** *noun*. **bowling alley** a place where you can play a kind of skittles.

bowls *noun* A game played by rolling large balls on a lawn or carpet.

box[1] *noun* (boxes) **1** A container. *a money-box*. **2** A hut or shelter. *a signal box*. **a box on the ears** a slap on the side of the face.

box[2] *verb* (boxes, boxing, boxed) To fight with fists. **boxer** *noun*.

Boxing Day The first weekday after Christmas Day.

boxing-gloves *noun* Padded gloves worn by boxers.

box-office *noun* (box-offices) A booking-office in a theatre or cinema.

boy *noun* (boys) A male child. **boyish** *adjective*.

boycott *verb* (boycotts, boycotting, boycotted) To refuse to have anything to do with somebody or something.

boy-friend *noun* (boy-friends) The boy with whom a girl usually goes out.

boyhood *noun* The time when you are a boy.

bra *noun* (bras) A woman's undergarment that supports her breasts.

brace *noun* 1 A pair. 2 (braces) A device to hold something in position. **braces** straps worn over the shoulders to keep trousers up.

bracelet *noun* (bracelets) An ornament worn round the wrist.

bracken *noun* A kind of fern.

bracket *noun* (brackets) A support for something, fastened to a wall. **brackets** punctuation marks like ( ) or [ ].

brackish *adjective* Slightly salt.

brag *verb* (brags, bragging, bragged) To boast.

brahmin *noun* (brahmins) A Hindu priest.

braid *noun* (braids) A kind of ribbon.

braille *noun* A method of writing or printing which blind people read by touch.

brain *noun* (brains) 1 The grey matter inside people's or animals' heads. **brains** intelligence. **brainy** *adjective*.

brainwash *verb* (brainwashes, brainwashing, brainwashed) To destroy someone's own way of thinking and force him or her to have new ideas.

brainwave *noun* (brainwaves) (informal) A sudden clever idea.

brake[1] *noun* (brakes) A device for slowing down or stopping a vehicle.

brake[2] *verb* (brakes, braking, braked) To use brakes.

bramble *noun* (brambles) A blackberry plant, with long trailing stems.

bran *noun* Husks of wheat or other grain.

branch[1] *noun* (branches) 1 Something that sticks out from a main part. *a branch of a tree.* 2 A part of a larger organization. *the local branch of a building society.*

branch[2] *verb* (branches, branching, branched) To form a branch.

brand[1] *noun* (brands) 1 A mark made by a red-hot iron. 2 A particular kind of goods. *the cheapest brand of butter.*

brand[2] *verb* (brands, branding, branded) To burn with a hot iron.

brandish *verb* (brandishes, brandishing, brandished) To wave about.

brand-new *adjective* Very new.

brandy *noun* A strong alcoholic drink.

brass *noun* 1 A yellow metal made by mixing copper and other metals. 2 Musical instruments often made of brass, such as trumpets and trombones. **brassy** *adjective*.

brat *noun* (brats) (informal) A child.

brave[1] *adjective* (braver, bravest) Able to face danger, pain, or difficulty without giving way to it. **bravely** *adverb*, **bravery** *noun*.

brave[2] *noun* (braves) A North American Indian warrior.

bravo Hurray! Well done!

brawl *noun* (brawls) A noisy quarrel.

brawn *noun* 1 Strength, muscle. **brawny** *adjective*. 2 A kind of cold meat.

bray *verb* (brays, braying, brayed) To make a harsh noise like a donkey.

brazen *adjective* 1 Made of brass. 2 Shameless.

brazier *noun* (braziers) A metal container for burning coals.

breach *noun* (breaches) A gap.

bread *noun* Food made by baking flour, water, and yeast.

breadth *noun* Width.

break[1] *verb* (breaks, breaking, broke, broken) **1** To divide in pieces, to smash, to snap, to pull apart. **2** To fail to keep to something. *You broke your promise.* **3** To change. *The weather broke.* **break a record** to do something better than anyone has done before. **break down** to collapse, to stop working properly. **break in** to enter a building illegally. **break off** to bring to an end. **break up 1** To destroy. **2** To fall to pieces. **3** To come to the end of term at school. **breakable** *adjective*, **breakage** *noun*.

break[2] *noun* (breaks) **1** A place where something is broken. **2** A gap, an interruption. **3** A short rest from work.

break-dancing *noun* An energetic style of street dancing.

breaker *noun* (breakers) A wave crashing on the shore.

breakfast *noun* (breakfasts) The first meal of the day.

breakneck *adjective* Dangerous. *breakneck speed.*

break-up *noun* The destruction or ending of something.

breakwater *noun* (breakwaters) A wall built out into the sea as a protection against heavy waves.

breast *noun* (breasts) **1** A person's or animal's chest. **2** One of the two parts of a woman's body where milk is produced.

breastplate *noun* (breastplates) Armour protecting the chest.

breast-stroke *noun* A way of swimming.

breath *noun* (breaths) **1** Air taken into and let out of the body. **out of breath** panting. **under your breath** in a whisper. **breathless** *adjective*, **breathlessly** *adverb*.

breathalyse *verb* (breathalyses, breathalysing, breathalysed) To test someone's breath for traces of alcohol. **breathalyser** *noun*.

breathe *verb* (breathes, breathing, breathed) To take air into the lungs or body and let it out again.

breather *noun* (breathers) A short rest, a break.

bred *See* **breed**[1]

breech *noun* (breeches) The closed end of the barrel of a gun.

breeches *noun* Trousers, usually fitting tightly at the knee.

breed[1] *verb* (breeds, breeding, bred) **1** To give birth to. **2** To keep animals to produce their young. **3** To bring up, to educate.

breed[2] *noun* A particular kind of animal. *What breed of dog is that?*

breeze *noun* (breezes) A wind. **breezy** *adjective*.

brew *verb* (brews, brewing, brewed) **1** To make tea or beer. **2** To develop. *Trouble is brewing.*

brewery *noun* (breweries) A place where beer is brewed.

bribe[1] *noun* (bribes) A gift offered to a person to tempt him or her to do someone a favour.

bribe[2] *verb* (bribes, bribing, bribed) To give someone a bribe. **bribery** *noun*.

brick *noun* (bricks) **1** A block of hard-baked clay used in building. **2** A toy building block.

bricklayer *noun* (bricklayers) Someone who builds with bricks.

bride *noun* (brides) A woman on her wedding day. **bridal** *adjective*.

bridegroom *noun* (bridegrooms) A man on his wedding day.

bridesmaid *noun* (bridesmaids) A girl or young woman who helps a bride at her wedding.

bridge *noun* (bridges) **1** A structure

which allows you to cross from one side of something to the other. **2** The high platform over a ship's deck. **3** The top bony part of the nose. **4** A card game.

bridle *noun* (bridles) The part of a horse's harness which goes on its head.

brief *adjective* (briefer, briefest) Short. **briefly** *adverb*.

briefs *noun* Short underpants or knickers.

brigade *noun* (brigades) **1** A unit in the army. **2** An organized body of people.

brigadier *noun* (brigadiers) A senior officer in the army, one rank above a colonel.

brigand *noun* (brigands) A bandit, a robber.

bright *adjective* (brighter, brightest) **1** Shining, giving a strong light. **2** Cheerful. **3** Clever. **brightly** *adverb*, **brightness** *noun*.

brighten *verb* (brightens, brightening, brightened) To make brighter, to become brighter.

brill *adjective* (informal) Brilliant, wonderful.

brilliant *adjective* **1** Very bright, sparkling. **2** (informal) Very good. **brilliantly** *adverb*, **brilliance** *noun*.

brim *noun* (brims) The edge of something. *The cup was full to the brim.* **brimming over** overflowing.

brine *noun* Salt water. **briny** *adjective*.

bring *verb* (brings, bringing, brought) To carry, to fetch, to take with you. *Bring your own sandwiches.* **bring something about** to cause it to happen. **bring someone round** to make someone conscious again. **bring up 1** To look after a child and educate it. **2** To introduce a subject in conversation. **3** To be sick.

brink *noun* The edge of a steep or dangerous place.

brisk *adjective* (brisker) Lively, moving quickly. **briskly** *adverb*.

bristle *noun* (bristles) A short stiff hair. **bristly** *adverb*.

British *adjective* Of or from Great Britain.

Briton *noun* (Britons) A native of Great Britain.

brittle *adjective* Hard but easily broken.

broad *adjective* (broader, broadest) **1** Wide, a long way from side to side. **2** Fully complete. *broad daylight.* **3** Not detailed. *a broad outline of a story.*

broadcast[1] *verb* (broadcasts, broadcasting, broadcast) **1** To send out by radio or television. **2** To take part in a broadcast.

broadcast[2] *noun* (broadcasts) A programme on radio or television.

broad-minded *adjective* Not easily shocked.

broadside *noun* (broadsides) The firing of all the guns on one side of a ship.

brochure *noun* (brochures) A pamphlet, an advertising leaflet.

brogue *noun* (brogues) **1** A strong shoe. **2** A way of talking in certain areas.

broke *See* **break**[1]

broken *See* **break**[1] **broken home** a home where the parents are separated.

broken-hearted *adjective* Desperately unhappy.

bronchitis *noun* A disease which makes breathing difficult.

bronco *noun* (broncos) A wild horse.

bronze *noun* **1** A metal, a mixture of copper and tin. **2** A reddish brown colour like bronze. **Bronze Age** the period when the best tools and weapons were made of bronze.

brooch *noun* (brooches) A piece of jewellery that can be pinned on a dress or blouse.

brood[1] *noun* (broods) A family of young birds.

brood[2] *verb* (broods, brooding, brooded). **1** To sit on eggs to hatch them. **2** To keep thinking about your troubles.

brook *noun* (brooks) A stream.

broom *noun* (brooms) **1** A long-handled brush for sweeping. **2** A shrub with yellow, white, or pink flowers.

broth *noun* A kind of soup.

brother *noun* (brothers) A son of the same parents as the person speaking or being spoken about.

brought *See* **bring**

brow *noun* (brows) **1** The forehead. **2** An eyebrow. **3** The top of a hill, the edge of a cliff.

brown¹ *noun* A colour, the colour of earth.

brown² *adjective* (browner, brownest) Brown in colour.

brown³ *verb* (browns, browning, browned) **1** To become brown. **2** To make something brown.

Brownie *noun* (Brownies) A junior Guide.

bruise¹ *noun* (bruises) A dark mark on the skin caused by a blow.

bruise² *verb* (bruises, bruising, bruised) To cause a bruise, to get a bruise.

brunette *noun* (brunettes) A woman with dark hair.

brush¹ *noun* (brushes) **1** A tool with bristles for painting, sweeping, or scrubbing. **2** A fox's tail.

brush² *verb* (brushes, brushing, brushed) To use a brush. **brush against** to touch something lightly. **brush up** to improve your knowledge of a subject.

Brussels sprouts A kind of green vegetable.

brutal *adjective* Cruel, beastly. **brutally** *adverb*, **brutality** *noun*.

brute *noun* (brutes) **1** An animal. **2** A stupid and cruel person.

bubble¹ *noun* (bubbles) **1** A small filmy ball of liquid filled with air. **2** A ball of air or gas in a liquid. **bubbly** *adjective*.

bubble² *verb* (bubbles, bubbling, bubbled) To send up bubbles, to make bubbles.

buccaneer *noun* (buccaneers) A pirate.

buck¹ *noun* (bucks) A male deer, hare, or rabbit.

buck² *verb* (bucks, bucking, bucked) To jump as if to throw off a rider. **buck up** to hurry.

bucket *noun* (buckets) A container for water or other things.

buckle¹ *noun* (buckles) A type of fastener for a belt or strap.

buckle² *verb* (buckles, buckling, buckled) **1** To fasten with a buckle. **2** To bend.

bud¹ *noun* (buds) A flower or leaf before it is fully open.

bud² *verb* (buds, budding, budded) **1** To grow buds. **2** To develop well. *Sarita is a budding dancer.*

Buddhism *noun* A religion based on the teachings of Gautama Buddha.

budge *verb* (budges, budging, budged) To move very slightly. *It won't budge.*

budgerigar *noun* (budgerigars) An Australian bird commonly kept as a pet.

budget *noun* (budgets) A plan for spending money wisely.

budgie *noun* (budgies) (informal) A budgerigar.

buffalo *noun* (buffaloes) A kind of wild ox.

buffer *noun* (buffers) A device designed to soften the blow when a railway engine or other vehicle hits something.

buffet *noun* (buffets) **1** A refreshment counter. **2** An informal meal.

bug *noun* (bugs) **1** An insect. **2** (informal) A germ. **3** A mistake in a computer program.

bugle *noun* (bugles) A musical instrument like a small trumpet.

build *verb* (builds, building, built) To make something by putting parts together. *to build a house.* **build up** to make or become stronger or bigger. **builder** *noun*.

building *noun* (buildings) Something built, such as a house, a church, or a block of flats.

bulb *noun* (bulbs) **1** An electric lamp. **2** The swollen underground part of certain plants. *a tulip bulb.*

bulge[1] *noun* (bulges) A swelling.

bulge[2] *verb* (bulges, bulging, bulged) To swell.

bulk *noun* Size, especially large size. **in bulk** in large quantities. **bulky** *adjective*.

bull *noun* (bulls) A male ox, elephant, or whale.

bulldog *noun* (bulldogs) A type of dog with a short thick neck.

bulldozer *noun* (bulldozers) A heavy tractor used to flatten land.

bullet *noun* (bullets) A round or pointed piece of metal shot from a rifle or pistol.

bulletin *noun* (bulletins) An official news announcement.

bulletproof *adjective* Able to stop bullets.

bull-fight *noun* (bull-fights) A contest between men and bulls.

bullfinch *noun* (bullfinches) A small bird with a pink breast.

bullfrog *noun* (bullfrogs) A large frog.

bullion *noun* Bars of gold or silver.

bullock *noun* (bullocks) A young bull.

bull's-eye *noun* (bull's-eyes) **1** The centre of a target. **2** A peppermint sweet.

bully[1] *verb* (bullies, bullying, bullied) To frighten and hurt a weaker person.

bully[2] *noun* (bullies) A person who bullies others.

bumble-bee *noun* (bumble-bees) A large kind of bee.

bump[1] *noun* (bumps) **1** A knock, a collision. **2** A lump or swelling.

bump[2] *verb* (bumps, bumping, bumped) **1** To give or receive a bump. **2** To go along with jerky up and down movements. **bumpy** *adjective*.

bumper[1] *noun* (bumpers) A buffer on a motor vehicle.

bumper[2] *adjective* Exceptionally large. *a bumper crop.*

bumptious *adjective* Full of your own importance. **bumptiously** *adverb*.

bun *noun* (buns) A small, round cake.

bunch[1] *noun* (bunches) **1** A number of things growing or fastened together. *a bunch of grapes, a bunch of flowers.* **2** (informal) A gang, a group.

bunch[2] *verb* (bunches, bunching, bunched) To make a bunch.

bundle[1] *noun* (bundles) A collection of things wrapped or tied together.

bundle[2] *verb* (bundles, bundling, bundled) **1** To make into a bundle. **2** To put away carelessly. **bundle off** to send someone away in a hurry.

bung[1] *noun* (bungs) A stopper, a large cork.

bung[2] *verb* (bungs, bunging, bunged) To stop something up, to clog it up.

bungalow *noun* (bungalows) A kind of house without any upstairs rooms.

bungle *verb* (bungles, bungling, bungled) To do a job badly or clumsily. **bungler** *noun*.

bunk *noun* (bunks) A kind of bed, often arranged one above another.

bunker *noun* (bunkers) **1** A place for storing fuel. **2** An underground stronghold or shelter.

buoy *noun* (buoys) A float used as a marker or as a mooring-place.

burden *noun* (burdens) **1** A load.

2 Anything hard to bear. **burdensome** *adjective*.

bureau *noun* (bureaux) **1** A writing-desk with drawers. **2** An office.

burger *noun* (burgers) A hamburger.

burglar *noun* (burglars) Someone who breaks into a building to steal something. **burglary** *noun*.

burgle *verb* (burgles, burgling, burgled) To break into a building as a burglar.

burial *noun* (burials) The burying of a dead person.

burka *noun* (burkas) A veil worn by Muslim women covering the whole body.

burly *adjective* Big and strong.

burn[1] *verb* (burns, burning, burned or burnt) **1** To be in flames, to be destroyed while giving out heat, flames, and smoke. *Asbestos won't burn.* **2** To use as fuel. *Our boiler burns gas.* **3** To damage by fire, heat, or acid. *Don't burn the toast.*

burn[2] *noun* (burns) **1** An injury caused by burning. **2** The firing of a rocket engine.

burn[3] *noun* (burns) (Scottish) A stream.

burner *noun* (burners) The part of a lamp or stove from which the flame comes.

burning *adjective* Intense, exciting.

burnished *adjective* Brightly polished.

burnt *adjective* Damaged or destroyed by fire. *burnt toast.*

burrow[1] *noun* (burrows) A hole in the ground, like those made by rabbits.

burrow[2] *verb* (burrows, burrowing, burrowed) To dig a burrow.

burst[1] *noun* (bursts) **1** An explosion. **2** A violent effort. **3** A number of shots fired continuously.

burst[2] *verb* (bursts, bursting, burst) To explode, to break apart, to force open. **burst in** to rush in.

bury *verb* (buries, burying, buried) To put something in the ground, to hide it away.

bus *noun* (buses) A large road vehicle for the public to travel in.

bush *noun* (bushes) A shrub. **bushy** *adjective*. **the bush** wild land in Africa and Australia.

busily *adverb* In a busy manner.

business *noun* (businesses) **1** A trade or occupation. *Jo's dad runs a taxi business.* **2** A responsibility, things you have to do. *I was just going about my business.* **3** A matter, a subject. *I'm tired of the whole business.*

businesslike *adjective* Well-organized, good at getting things done.

bus-stop *noun* (bus-stops) A place where you can catch a bus.

bust[1] *adjective* (informal) Broken.

bust[2] *noun* (busts) The measurement round a woman's chest.

bustle *verb* (bustles, bustling, bustled) To fuss about, to hurry.

busy *adjective* (busier, busiest) **1** Having a lot to do. **2** Full of activity.

busybody *noun* (busybodies) An interfering person.

but[1] *conjunction* On the other hand, however. *I called but he did not answer.*

but[2] *preposition* Except. *We were all there but Peter.*

butane *noun* A kind of gas used as fuel.

butcher *noun* (butchers) A person who prepares and sells the flesh of animals as food.

butler *noun* (butlers) A senior male servant in a large household.

butt[1] *noun* (butts) **1** The handle end of a tool or weapon. *the butt of a rifle.* **2** A large barrel. *a water butt.*

butt[2] *verb* (butts, butting, butted) To charge into something head first. **butt in** to interrupt.

butter *noun* A fatty food made from cream.

buttercup *noun* (buttercups) A yellow wild flower.

butterfingers *noun* A person who drops things.

butterfly *noun* (butterflies) An insect with large wings.

butterscotch *noun* A sweet made with butter and sugar.

buttocks *noun* The part of the body on which you sit.

button¹ *noun* (buttons) **1** A small disc sewn on clothes as a fastener or for decoration. **2** A small knob.

button² *verb* (buttons, buttoning, buttoned) To fasten with a button.

button-hole *noun* (button-holes) **1** A hole for a button. **2** A flower worn on the lapel of a coat.

buttress *noun* (buttresses) A support built against a wall.

buy *verb* (buys, buying, bought) To get something by paying for it. **buyer** *noun*.

buzz *verb* (buzzes, buzzing, buzzed) **1** To make a rough humming sound like a bee. **2** To annoy another aircraft by deliberately flying too close to it. **buzzer** *noun*.

buzzard *noun* (buzzards) A bird of prey.

by¹ *preposition* **1** Near. *Sit here by me.* **2** Through, along. *We came by the* main road. **3** Past. *Who has just gone by the window?* **4** During. *The sun shines by day and the moon by night.* **5** Not later than. *Let me know by tomorrow.* **6** Through the means of. *We cook by gas.* **7** According to. *It's two o'clock by my watch.*

by² *adverb* **1** Past. *I saw Lynn go by.* **2** Aside, in reserve. *Put it by for later.* **by and by** later.

bye *noun* (byes) A run made in cricket when the batsman has not hit the ball.

by-election *noun* (by-elections) An election in one particular area to replace a Member of Parliament who has died or resigned, not a general election.

bygone *adjective* Belonging to the past.

by-law *noun* (by-laws) A law which applies only to a particular town or district.

bypass *noun* (bypasses) A main road which goes round a town.

bystander *noun* (bystanders) A spectator.

byte *noun* (bytes) A fixed number of binary digits in a computer, often representing a single character.

C 100 in Roman numerals.

cab *noun* (cabs) **1** A taxi. **2** A compartment for the driver in a lorry, bus, or train.

cabaret *noun* (cabarets) An entertainment given in a restaurant or night-club.

cabbage *noun* (cabbages) A vegetable with large green or purple leaves.

cabin *noun* (cabins) **1** A hut. **2** A room or compartment in a ship or airliner.

cabinet *noun* (cabinets) A piece of furniture with shelves or drawers. **the Cabinet** the ministers chosen by the

Prime Minister to be responsible for government affairs.

cable *noun* (cables) **1** Thick strong rope, wire, or chain. **2** Heavy insulated wire for electricity or telephones. **3** A telegram. **cable television** a television service brought to people's homes along wires.

cache *noun* (caches) Hidden treasure or stores.

cackle¹ *noun* (cackles) **1** The sound made by a hen. **2** A noisy laugh.

cackle² *verb* (cackles, cackling, cackled) To make a cackle.

cactus *noun* (cacti) A prickly desert plant.

cadet *noun* (cadets) A young person being trained for service in the army, navy, air force, or police force.

cadge *verb* (cadges, cadging, cadged) To beg.

Caesarean *noun* An operation to take a baby out of its mother's womb.

café *noun* (cafés) A shop which serves meals or refreshments.

cafeteria *noun* (cafeterias) A café where customers fetch what they want from a counter.

caffeine *noun* A drug found in tea and coffee.

cage *noun* (cages) A framework of bars in which animals or birds are kept.

cagoule *noun* (cagoules) A waterproof covering for the top half of the body.

cairn *noun* (cairns) A pile of stones set up as a landmark or a monument.

cake *noun* (cakes) **1** A baked mixture of flour, eggs, butter, and other ingredi-

ents. **2** A solid shaped lump of something. *a cake of soap.*

caked *adjective* Covered with something that dries hard. *shoes caked with mud.*

calamity *noun* (calamities) A disaster. **calamitous** *adjective*.

calcium *noun* A chemical found in teeth, bones, and chalk.

calculate *verb* (calculates, calculating, calculated) **1** To find out by using mathematics. **2** To plan deliberately. *That was no accident: it was calculated.* **calculation** *noun*.

calculator *noun* (calculators) a small electronic calculating machine.

calendar *noun* (calendars) A list or table showing the dates in every month of a year.

calf *noun* (calves) **1** A young cow, whale, or elephant. **2** The part of your leg behind the shin.

call¹ *verb* (calls, calling, called) **1** To shout, to cry, to speak loudly. **2** To summon. *Call the next witness!* **3** To telephone. **4** To make a visit. *Mr Weston called today.* **5** To wake someone up. *Mum calls me at 7.30.* **6** To name. *What is your dog called?* **7** To describe as. *I would call him a good footballer.* **call someone names** to insult him or her. **caller** *noun*.

call² *noun* (calls) **1** A shout. **2** A command to appear. **3** A telephone conversation. **4** A visit.

calling *noun* (callings) A profession or trade.

calliper *noun* (callipers) A metal support for a weak leg.

callous *adjective* Hard, cruel. **callously** *adverb*.

calm¹ *adjective* (calmer, calmest) **1** Quiet, windless. *calm weather.* **2** Not excited, not panicky. *Keep calm.* **calmly** *adverb*.

calm² *verb* (calms, calming, calmed) To make or become calm.

calorie *noun* (calories) A measure of energy supplied by food.

calves *See* **calf**

camcorder *noun* (camcorders) An electronic camera for taking video pictures.

came *See* **come**

camel *noun* (camels) An animal with one or two humps on its back used in desert countries for carrying people and goods.

camera *noun* (cameras) An apparatus for taking still or moving pictures.

camouflage *verb* (camouflages, camouflaging, camouflaged) To disguise the appearance of something.

camp[1] *noun* (camps) A place where people live for a time in tents or huts.

camp[2] *verb* (camps, camping, camped) To make a camp, to live in a camp. **camper** *noun*.

campaign *noun* (campaigns) **1** A series of battles in a particular area. **2** A series of happenings planned for a particular purpose. *a road safety campaign*.

campsite *noun* (campsites) A place for camping.

campus *noun* (campuses) The grounds of a school, college, or university.

can[1] (could) **1** To be able to do something. *I can play the piano*. **2** To be allowed to do something. *Mum said we could play outside*.

can[2] *noun* (cans) A metal container for liquids or foods, a tin.

can[3] *verb* (cans, canning, canned) To put in a can. *canned drinks*.

canal *noun* (canals) An artificial water-way for boats, or for drainage or irrigation.

canary *noun* (canaries) A yellow song-bird.

cancel *verb* (cancels, cancelling, cancelled). **1** To say that something already arranged is not to take place. *He cancelled the party*. **2** To mark something to show that it must not be used again.

cancer *noun* A disease producing harmful growths in some part of the body.

candid *adjective* Honest, frank. **candidly** *adverb*.

candidate *noun* (candidates) **1** One of the people you can vote for in an election. **2** A person taking a test or examination.

candle *noun* (candles) A stick of wax with a wick through the centre used as a light.

candlestick *noun* (candlesticks) An upright holder for a candle.

candy-floss *noun* A fluffy mass of sugar.

cane *noun* (canes) A stick, usually of bamboo.

canister *noun* (canisters) A small container.

cannibal *noun* (cannibals) A person who eats human flesh. **cannibalism** *noun*.

cannon *noun* (cannons *or* cannon) **1** A large heavy gun. **2** A large machine-gun that fires shells.

cannonball *noun* (cannonballs) A metal ball fired from a cannon.

cannot can not.

canoe[1] *noun* (canoes) A light, narrow boat.

canoe[2] *verb* (canoes, canoeing, canoed) To travel by canoe.

can't (informal) Cannot.

canteen *noun* (canteens) **1** A restaurant for workers in a factory or offices. **2** A container for food or water. **3** A box holding cutlery.

canter *verb* (canters, cantering, cantered) To go at a gentle gallop.

canvas *noun* A kind of strong, coarse cloth.

canyon *noun* (canyons) A deep valley, usually with a river flowing along it.

cap¹ *noun* (caps) **1** A kind of hat. **2** A lid, a top covering. **3** A small explosive device, like those used in toy pistols.

cap² *verb* (caps, capping, capped) **1** To put a cap on, to cover. *a mountain capped with snow.* **2** To award a cap to a member of a games team.

capable *adjective* Gifted, able. *capable of something*, able to do it. **capably** *adverb*, **capability** *noun*.

capacity *noun* (capacities) **1** The amount something will hold. **2** A person's ability. *This is within my capacity*, I am able to do it.

cape *noun* (capes) **1** A short cloak. **2** A piece of land jutting into the sea.

caper *verb* (capers, capering, capered) To leap happily.

capital *noun* (capitals) **1** The chief city or town of an area. **2** The decorative top of a pillar. **3** Money invested to make more money. **capital letters** letters of this type: A, B, C, D. **capital punishment** punishment by putting to death.

capitulate *verb* (capitulates, capitulating, capitulated) To surrender. **capitulation** *noun*.

capsize *verb* (capsizes, capsizing, capsized) To overturn a boat in the water.

capsule *noun* (capsules) **1** A hollow pill containing medicine. **2** A container for crew or instruments fired into space on a rocket.

captain *noun* (captains) **1** A leader or commander, especially of a games team. **2** An army officer above a lieutenant. **3** A senior officer in the navy. **4** The person in charge of a ship. **5** The pilot of an airliner.

caption *noun* (captions). **1** A heading in a newspaper or magazine. **2** An explanation printed under a picture.

captivate *verb* (captivates, captivating, captivated) To fascinate.

captive *noun* (captives) A captured person or animal. **captivity** *noun*.

capture *verb* (captures, capturing, captured) To seize something, to take somebody prisoner.

car *noun* (cars) **1** A vehicle with an engine, usually for four or five people. **2** A railway carriage or other vehicle for passengers. *a dining car.*

caramel *noun* A kind of toffee.

caravan *noun* (caravans) **1** A covered cart or wagon for living in, a mobile home. **2** A company of people travelling together in the desert.

carbon *noun* A black chemical found in charcoal. **carbon paper** a kind of copying paper.

carburettor *noun* (carburettors) Part of a petrol engine where petrol is mixed with air.

carcass *noun* (carcasses) An animal's dead body.

card *noun* (cards) **1** Thick, stiff paper. **2** A piece of card or plastic made for a particular purpose. *a credit card, a Christmas card.* **3** A playing-card.

cardboard *noun* Thick card.

cardigan *noun* (cardigans) A knitted jacket.

cardinal *noun* (cardinals) One of the leading priests in the Roman Catholic Church.

care¹ *verb* (cares, caring, cared) To take

an interest, to have feelings about something, to feel concerned. **care for** to look after. **carer** noun.

care² noun (cares) **1** Caring. **2** Worry, anxiety. **in care** being looked after. **take care** to be careful. **take care of** to look after.

career¹ noun (careers) **1** A job, a profession, a settled way of earning your living. **2** Progress through life. *I shall watch your career with interest.*

career² verb (careers, careering, careered) To rush wildly along.

carefree adjective Free from worry.

careful adjective Cautious, caring. **carefully** adverb.

careless adjective Not caring, thoughtless. **carelessly** adverb.

caress verb (caresses, caressing, caressed) To touch gently and lovingly.

caretaker noun (caretakers) Someone who is paid to look after a building such as a school or church.

careworn adjective Worn out by worry.

cargo noun (cargoes) Goods carried in a ship or aircraft.

Caribbean adjective Of or from the West Indies.

carnage noun Slaughter, killing.

carnation noun (carnations) A garden flower.

carnival noun (carnivals) A festival.

carnivorous adjective Eating meat as food. *a carnivorous animal.*

carol noun (carols) A kind of song, especially one sung at Christmas.

carp noun (carp) A freshwater fish.

car-park noun (car-parks) A space where cars may be parked.

carpenter noun (carpenters) A man who makes things with wood. **carpentry** noun.

carpet noun (carpets) A thick, soft material used to cover floors.

carphone noun (carphones) A telephone that can be used in a vehicle.

carriage noun (carriages) **1** A horse-drawn vehicle. **2** A wagon for passengers on a train.

carrion noun Dead and decaying flesh.

carrot noun (carrots) A long orange-coloured root vegetable.

carry verb (carries, carrying, carried) **1** To lift and move something from one place to another. **2** To support. *The whole roof is carried on those two pillars, Samson.* **3** To reach. *The arrows carried easily to the target.* **carry the day** to be victorious. **carried away** too excited. **carry out** to finish something successfully. **carry on** to continue. **carrier** noun.

cart noun (carts) A vehicle, usually pulled by a horse or by a person.

cart-horse noun (cart-horses) A large horse bred for heavy work.

carton noun (cartons) A cardboard box.

cartoon noun (cartoons) **1** An amusing drawing. **2** A film made by photographing a series of drawings. **strip cartoon** a series of drawings which tell a story. **cartoonist** noun.

cartridge noun (cartridges) A small container such as is used to hold the film in a camera, the explosive in a bullet, or the ink in a pen.

cartwheel noun (cartwheels) A sideways somersault with arms and legs stretched out.

carve verb (carves, carving, carved) **1** To slice meat. **2** To cut something deliberately or artistically. **carver** noun.

case noun (cases) **1** A box, bag, or container to keep or carry things in. **2** An example or occurrence of something.

a case of measles. **3** A question to be decided in a lawcourt, the facts and arguments used on each side. *He has a strong case*, he has good evidence on his side.

cash *noun* Coins or paper money, ready money.

cashier *noun* (cashiers) A person in charge of cash in a bank, office, or shop.

casino *noun* (casinos) A public building for gambling and other entertainments.

cask *noun* (casks) A barrel.

casket *noun* (caskets) A small box for valuables.

cassava *noun* (cassavas) A tropical plant with roots used as food.

casserole *noun* (casseroles) **1** A kind of cooking dish. **2** Food cooked in a casserole.

cassette *noun* (cassettes) A plastic case containing recording tape.

cassock *noun* (cassocks) A long black robe worn by some Christian priests.

cast[1] *verb* (casts, casting, cast) **1** To throw. **2** To throw off. **3** To mould.

cast[2] *noun* (casts) **1** Something made in a mould. *a plaster cast*. **2** All the actors in a play.

castanets *noun* A percussion instrument which makes a clicking sound.

castaway *noun* (castaways) A ship-wrecked person.

caste *noun* (castes) One of the traditional divisions of Hindu society.

castle *noun* (castles) **1** A large building with fortifications. **2** A piece in chess, also called a rook.

castor *noun* (castors) A small wheel on a piece of furniture.

casual *adjective* **1** Not planned. *a casual meeting*. **2** Careless. *casual behaviour*. **3** Informal. *casual clothes*. **casually** *adverb*.

casualty *noun* (casualties) A person killed or injured in battle or in an accident. **casualty ward** a hospital ward for people injured in accidents.

cat *noun* (cats) A small furry domestic animal.

catacombs *noun* Underground burial chambers.

catalogue *noun* (catalogues) An orderly list.

catamaran *noun* (catamarans) A boat with two hulls.

catapult *noun* (catapults) **1** A device for shooting stones. **2** A device to help gliders or aeroplanes to take off.

cataract *noun* (cataracts) **1** A steep waterfall. **2** A growth on the eye.

catarrh *noun* Inflammation causing a blocked or runny nose.

catastrophe *noun* (catastrophes) A great disaster.

catch[1] *verb* (catches, catching, caught) **1** To stop something and prevent it from falling or escaping. *Catch the ball! I caught a mouse*. **2** To be in time for. *Will I catch the bus?* **3** To hear and understand. *I can't catch what you're saying*. **4** To hit. *I caught him on the chin*. **catch an illness** to become infected with it. **catch fire** to begin to burn. **catch on** to become popular. **catch up with** to move up and join someone.

catch[2] *noun* (catches) **1** The action of catching. **2** Something that has been caught. **3** A difficulty. *There's a catch in it somewhere*. **4** A device for keeping a door shut.

catching *adjective* Infectious.

catchy *adjective* Easily learnt and remembered. *a catchy tune*.

category *noun* (categories) A class, a group, a set.

cater *verb* (caters, catering, catered) To provide food. **caterer** *noun*.

caterpillar *noun* (caterpillars) **1** The larva of a butterfly or moth. **2** The endless track of a tank or a tractor.

cathedral *noun* (cathedrals) The chief church of a diocese.

Catherine-wheel *noun* (Catherine-wheels) A firework which spins on a pin.

Catholic 1 Belonging to all Christianity. *the Holy Catholic Church.* **2** Roman Catholic.

catkin *noun* (catkins) One of the fluffy flowers of willow, hazel, or some other trees.

Catseye *noun* (Catseyes) The trade name for a reflector fixed on the surface of a road to guide traffic.

cattle *noun* Cows or bulls.

catty *adjective* Sly, spiteful. **cattily** *adverb*.

caught *See* **catch**[1]

cauldron *noun* (cauldrons) A large pot for cooking.

cauliflower *noun* (cauliflowers) A vegetable with a head of hard white flowers.

cause[1] *noun* (causes) **1** A reason why something happens. **2** A purpose. *a good cause.*

cause[2] *verb* (causes, causing, caused) To make something happen.

causeway *noun* (causeways) A raised path or road across swampy land.

caution[1] *noun* **1** Being cautious. **2** A warning. *The judge let him off with a caution.*

caution[2] *verb* (cautions, cautioning, cautioned) To give somebody a warning.

cautious *adjective* Careful to avoid risks. **cautiously** *adverb*.

cavalcade *noun* (cavalcades) A procession of people on horseback.

Cavalier *noun* (Cavaliers) A supporter of King Charles I.

cavalry *noun* Soldiers who fight on horseback.

cave *noun* (caves) A hollow, underground place.

caveman *noun* (cavemen) A person who lived in a cave in ancient times.

cavern *noun* (caverns) A large, deep cave. **cavernous** *adjective*.

caviare *noun* A very expensive delicacy made from the roe of a fish called sturgeon.

cavity *noun* (cavities) A hole, a hollow space.

CB Citizens' Band, a system ordinary people can use for sending or receiving messages by radio.

cease *verb* (ceases, ceasing, ceased) To stop.

ceaseless *adjective* Never ending. **ceaselessly** *adverb*.

CD *abbreviation* Compact disc.

cedar *noun* (cedars) An evergreen tree.

Ceefax *noun* The trade name of a system showing information on TV screens.

ceiling *noun* (ceilings) The roof of a room.

celebrate *verb* (celebrates, celebrating, celebrated) To do something to show that a day or event is special. *to celebrate your birthday.* **celebrated** famous. **celebration** *noun*.

celebrity *noun* (celebrities) A famous person.

celery *noun* A vegetable with crisp white stems.

celestial *adjective* To do with the sky, heavenly.

cell *noun* (cells) **1** A small room in a prison or monastery. **2** A hole in a honeycomb. **3** An electrical battery. **4** A microscopic unit of living matter.

cellar *noun* (cellars) An underground room.

cello *noun* (cellos) A large stringed instrument played with a bow. **cellist** *noun.*

Cellophane *noun* A material as transparent as glass and as thin as paper.

cellular *adjective* Made with many holes or cells. *a cellular blanket.*

celluloid *noun* A transparent plastic material.

Celsius *adjective* Centigrade.

Celtic *adjective* Of the languages or inhabitants of Wales, Scotland, and Ireland.

cement *noun* **1** A grey powder used to make mortar and concrete. **2** A strong glue.

cemetery *noun* (cemeteries) A place where people are buried.

censor *verb* (censors, censoring, censored) To ban or edit something because it is thought to be harmful. **censorship** *noun.*

censure *noun* Disapproval.

census *noun* (censuses) An official counting of the inhabitants of a country or district.

cent *noun* (cents) A coin. In USA, Canada, and Australia 100 cents = 1 dollar. **per cent** in every hundred.

centenary *noun* (centenaries) The hundredth anniversary of something.

centigrade *adjective* Measuring temperature on a scale with the freezing-point of water at 0 degrees and the boiling-point at 100 degrees.

centimetre *noun* (centimetres) A unit of length, one hundredth of a metre.

centipede *noun* (centipedes) A small crawling creature with many legs.

central *adjective* At the centre, to do

with the centre. **centrally** *adverb.*
central heating a method of heating a building from one boiler.

centre *noun* (centres) **1** The middle of something. **2** A place designed for certain activities. *a youth centre. a shopping centre.*

centurion *noun* (centurions) A Roman army officer.

century *noun* (centuries) **1** A period of 100 years. **2** A score of 100.

cereal *noun* (cereals) **1** Grain crops used as food, such as wheat and maize. **2** A breakfast food made from cereals.

ceremony *noun* (ceremonies) A dignified public occasion. **ceremonial** *adjective*, **ceremonially** *adverb*, **ceremonious** *adjective.*

certain *adjective* **1** Unavoidable. *The damaged plane faced certain disaster.* **2** Sure. *I'm certain I'm right!* **a certain person** someone whom we are not going to mention by name. **certainly** *adverb.*

certainty *noun* (certainties) Something which is unavoidable.

certificate *noun* (certificates) A piece of paper which gives official proof of something. *a birth certificate.*

CFC *abbreviation* Chlorofluorocarbon, a gas which damages the ozone layer.

chador *noun* (chadors) A veil for the whole body as worn by women in certain Muslim countries.

chaff *noun* Dry husks, chopped straw or hay.

chaffinch *noun* (chaffinches) A small bird.

chain[1] *noun* (chains) **1** A row of metal rings, called links, passing through one another. **2** A line of people or things.

chain[2] *verb* (chains, chaining, chained) To fasten with chains.

chair *noun* (chairs) A seat with a back, for one person.

chalet *noun* (chalets) A wooden house or cottage.

chalk *noun* **1** Soft, white rock. **2** (chalks) A stick of a similar substance used for writing and drawing. **chalky** *adjective*.

challenge *verb* (challenges, challenging, challenged) **1** To demand an explanation or a password from someone. *The sentry challenged the stranger.* **2** To invite someone to play a game or fight a duel. **challenge, challenger** *nouns*.

chamber *noun* (chambers) A room. **chamber music** music for a small number of players.

champagne *noun* A bubbly French wine.

champion *noun* (champions) **1** Someone who has beaten all other competitors. **2** Someone who fights for a particular cause. **championship** *noun*.

chance *noun* (chances) **1** An accident. *It happened by chance.* **2** A possibility, a risk, an opportunity. *There's no chance of that!*

chancel *noun* (chancels) The eastern part of a church, containing the altar.

chancellor *noun* (chancellors) An important minister of a country. **Chancellor of the Exchequer** the minister in the British government who is responsible for the country's money affairs.

chancy *adjective* Taking risks.

chandelier *noun* (chandeliers) A hanging display of candles or electric lights.

change[1] *verb* (changes, changing, changed) **1** To make something different. *He changed direction.* **2** To become different. *The weather changed.* **3** To exchange. *The shop will change it if it doesn't work.* **4** To move from one train or bus to another. *Change at Shrewsbury for Central Wales.* **change into** to become. *The tadpoles changed into frogs.* **change your mind** to alter your opinion.

change[2] *noun* (changes) **1** The act of changing. **2** Something different from the usual. *Trout and chips will be a change.* **3** Money in small amounts. *Have you change for £5?* **4** Money given back when you have given more than is needed to pay for something.

changeable *adjective* Liable to change.

channel *noun* (channels) **1** A stretch of water joining two seas. *the English Channel.* **2** A way for water to flow along or for ships to travel along. **3** A radio or television wavelength.

chant *noun* (chants) A tune, especially a psalm tune.

chaos *noun* Utter disorder, complete confusion. **chaotic** *adjective*, **chaotically** *adverb*.

chapel *noun* (chapels) A place of worship.

chaplain *noun* (chaplains) A clergyman working for a particular organization. *a hospital chaplain.*

chapped *adjective* Rough and cracked.

chapter *noun* (chapters) A section of a book.

char *verb* (chars, charring, charred) To scorch.

character *noun* (characters) **1** A person, especially in a story or play. **2** The characteristics of someone or something. *He has a friendly character.* **3** A letter of the alphabet or a similar sign. **4** In computing, any symbol used to communicate information, such as 1, B, +, or $

characteristic[1] *noun* (characteristics) Something which makes one person or thing different from others.

characteristic[2] *adjective* Typical.

charades *noun* A party game in which words have to be guessed from short acted scenes.

charcoal *noun* A black substance made by burning wood slowly.

charge[1] *noun* (charges) **1** An accusation. **2** A fast and sudden attack. **3** The price asked for something. **4** A quantity of explosive. **5** Electricity stored in something. **in charge of** in command of something, responsible for it.

charge[2] *verb* (charges, charging, charged) **1** To accuse. **2** To rush forward, to attack. **3** To ask a price for something. **4** To fill something, especially to fill a battery with electric power.

chariot *noun* (chariots) A horse-drawn vehicle used in ancient times for racing or fighting. **charioteer** *noun*.

charismatic *adjective* **1** Having an exciting personality. **2** In Christianity, emphasizing the work of the Holy Spirit.

charity *noun* **1** Kindness, generosity. **charitable** *adjective* **2** (charities) A voluntary organization which helps those in need.

charm[1] *noun* (charms) **1** A magic spell. **2** Something worn for good luck. **3** Attractiveness.

charm[2] *verb* (charms, charming, charmed) **1** To put a spell on someone or something. **2** To delight. **charmer** *noun*.

charming *adjective* Attractive. **charmingly** *adverb*.

chart *noun* (charts) **1** A map, especially one used by sailors. **2** A diagram or list of information.

charter *verb* (charters, chartering, chartered) To hire. **charter flight** a journey on a chartered aircraft.

charwoman *noun* (charwomen) A woman paid to do housework.

chase *verb* (chases, chasing, chased) To run after, to try to overtake. **chase away** to chase a person or animal so that it runs away.

chasm *noun* (chasms) A deep opening in the ground.

chaste *adjective* Pure, virtuous. **chastely** *adverb*, **chastity** *noun*.

chat[1] *verb* (chats, chatting, chatted) To have a friendly talk.

château *noun* (châteaux) A French castle or mansion.

chat-show *noun* (chat-shows) A broadcast with interviews and discussions.

chatter *verb* (chatters, chattering, chattered) To talk quickly and continuously about unimportant things.

chatterbox *noun* (chatterboxes) Someone who chatters.

chauffeur *noun* (chauffeurs) A person paid to drive someone's car.

cheap *adjective* (cheaper, cheapest) **1** Not expensive, costing little money. **2** Of poor quality. **cheaply** *adverb*, **cheapness** *noun*.

cheat[1] *verb* (cheats, cheating, cheated) To play or act dishonestly, to trick someone.

cheat[2] *noun* (cheats) A person who cheats.

check[1] *verb* (checks, checking, checked) **1** To make sure that something is correct. *Check your answers.* **2** To stop something, or make it go slower.

check² *noun* (checks) **1** The checking of something. **2** A pattern of squares. **3** The situation in chess when a king could be taken.

checkmate *noun* The winning situation in chess when a king cannot move out of check.

check-out *noun* (check-outs) A counter in a supermarket where you pay for what you have bought.

cheek *noun* **1** (cheeks) The side of the face below the eye. **2** Cheeky behaviour.

cheeky *adjective* (cheekier, cheekiest) Impudent, cheerful but lacking respect. **cheekily** *adverb*.

cheer¹ *verb* (cheers, cheering, cheered) **1** To shout joyfully, to urge somebody on. **2** To encourage, to comfort. **cheer up** to make or become happier.

cheer² *noun* (cheers) A cry of encouragement or rejoicing.

cheerful *adjective* Happy. **cheerfully** *adverb*, **cheerfulness** *noun*.

cheese *noun* (cheeses) A solid food made from milk.

cheetah *noun* (cheetahs) A kind of leopard.

chef *noun* (chefs) A professional cook.

chemical¹ *adjective* Of chemistry.

chemical² *noun* (chemicals) A substance used in chemistry, such as an acid.

chemist *noun* (chemists) **1** An expert in chemistry. **2** A person who prepares and sells medicines.

chemistry *noun* The branch of science dealing with what substances are composed of and how they act upon each other.

cheque *noun* (cheques) A written instruction to a bank to pay money.

cherish *verb* (cherishes, cherishing, cherished) To care for, to look after.

cherry *noun* (cherries) A small red or yellow fruit with a stone.

chess *noun* A game played on a board with black and white squares.

chest *noun* (chests) **1** The upper part of the front of the body. **2** A strong box with a lid. *a treasure chest.* **chest of drawers** a piece of furniture with drawers.

chestnut *noun* (chestnuts) **1** A large tree which produces shiny brown nuts in spiky green cases. **2** Its nut.

chew *verb* (chews, chewing, chewed) To crush food with the teeth by continually moving your jaw.

chewing-gum *noun* A kind of sweet for chewing.

chick *noun* (chicks) A young bird.

chicken *noun* (chickens) A young fowl.

chicken-pox *noun* A disease causing red spots on the skin.

chief¹ *adjective* Most important.

chief² *noun* (chiefs) A leader, a ruler.

chiefly *adverb* **1** Above all. **2** Mainly. *It's built chiefly of stone.*

chieftain *noun* (chieftains) The leader of a tribe or gang.

chilblain *noun* (chilblains) A painful swelling, usually on a hand or foot, occurring in cold weather.

child *noun* (children) **1** A young boy or girl. **2** Someone's son or daughter.

childhood *noun* The time when you are a child.

childish *adjective* Like a child, immature. **childishly** *adverb*.

child-minder *noun* (child-minders) A person who looks after a child, usually in the daytime.

chill¹ *noun* **1** A feeling of coldness. **2** An illness which causes sickness and shivering.

chill[2] *verb* (chills, chilling, chilled) To make a person or thing cold.

chilly *adjective* (chillier, chilliest) **1** Rather cold. **2** Unfriendly. **chilliness** *noun*.

chime[1] *verb* (chimes, chiming, chimed) To make a sound like a bell.

chime[2] *noun* (chimes) The sound of a bell.

chimney *noun* (chimneys) A tall part of a building which carries smoke away from a fire.

chimney-pot *noun* (chimney-pots) A piece of pipe at the top of a chimney.

chimney-sweep *noun* (chimney-sweeps) A person who cleans chimneys.

chimpanzee *noun* (chimpanzees) An African ape.

chin *noun* (chins) The part of a person's face below the mouth.

china *noun* **1** A fine kind of pottery. **2** Cups, saucers, plates, and so on.

Chinese *adjective* Of China, from China.

chink *noun* (chinks) **1** A narrow crack or opening. **2** A sound like that of coins or glasses hitting each other.

chip[1] *noun* (chips) **1** A small piece broken off something. **2** A piece of fried potato. **3** A small piece of silicon with electrical circuits printed in it, used in various kinds of electronic equipment.

chip[2] *verb* (chips, chipping, chipped) To cut or break chips off something.

chirp *verb* (chirps, chirping, chirped) To make short sharp sounds like a bird.

chisel *noun* (chisels) A tool with a sharp end for cutting wood or stone.

chivalry *noun* **1** The rules and customs of knights in the Middle Ages. **2** Polite, helpful behaviour. **chivalrous** *adjective*.

chlorine *noun* A greenish-yellow gas, used as a disinfectant in water.

chocolate *noun* (chocolates) A sweet or drink made from cocoa powder.

choice *noun* (choices) **1** Choosing, the right or chance to choose. *I've had my choice, so now it's your turn.* **2** A variety of things to choose from. *There's a big choice on the menu.* **3** The person or thing you choose. *Who's your choice for captain?*

choir *noun* (choirs) A group of people trained to sing together.

choke[1] *verb* (chokes, choking, choked) **1** To be prevented from breathing properly. **2** To block somebody's breathing by squeezing his or her throat. **3** To block something up.

choke[2] *noun* (chokes) A device controlling the intake of air into a petrol engine.

cholera *noun* A serious infectious disease.

cholesterol *noun* A fatty substance that can clog your arteries.

choose *verb* (chooses, choosing, chose, chosen) **1** To take what you want from what is available. *Choose a sweet. Choose a partner.* **2** To make a decision. *You chose to stay at home.*

chop[1] *verb* (chops, chopping, chopped) To cut by hitting with an axe or a heavy knife.

chop[2] *noun* (chops) **1** A chopping blow. **2** A thick slice of meat.

chopper *noun* (choppers) **1** A small axe. **2** (informal) A helicopter.

chopsticks *noun* A pair of sticks for eating Chinese or Japanese food.

chop-suey *noun* A Chinese dish of meat and vegetables.

choral *adjective* Of or for a choir.

chord *noun* (chords) A number of musical notes sounded together.

chore *noun* (chores) A boring task.

chorus *noun* (choruses) **1** Music for a group of singers. **2** Part of a song which is repeated after every verse. **3** A choir.

chose, chosen *See* **choose**

christen *verb* (christens, christening, christened) **1** To baptize a child in a Christian church. **2** To give someone or something a name.

Christian *noun* (Christians) Someone who believes in Jesus Christ. **Christianity** *noun*.

Christmas Day December 25th, when Christians celebrate the birth of Jesus.

chromatic scale A scale using all the black and white notes on a piano.

chrome, chromium *nouns* A bright shiny silvery metal.

chronic *adjective* **1** Lasting a long time. **2** (informal) Bad.

chronicle *noun* (chronicles) A record of events.

chronological *adjective* In the order in which things happen or happened.

chrysalis *noun* (chrysalises) The form into which a caterpillar changes before it becomes a butterfly or moth.

chrysanthemum *noun* (chrysanthemums) A garden flower which blooms in autumn.

chub *noun* (chub) A small river fish.

chubby *adjective* Plump, rather fat.

chuck *verb* (chucks, chucking, chucked) (informal) To throw.

chuckle *verb* (chuckles, chuckling, chuckled) To laugh quietly.

chum *noun* (chums) A friend. **chummy** *adjective*.

chunk *noun* (chunks) A thick lump. **chunky** *adjective*.

chupatty *noun* (chupatties) A kind of bread made flat like a pancake.

church *noun* (churches) A building for Christian worship.

churchyard *noun* (churchyards) The graveyard round a church.

churn *noun* (churns) **1** A machine for making butter. **2** A large can for milk.

chutney *noun* A strong-tasting mixture of sweet and sour flavours sometimes eaten with meat.

cider *noun* An alcoholic drink made from apples.

cigar *noun* (cigars) A fat roll of tobacco leaf for smoking.

cigarette *noun* (cigarettes) Shredded tobacco rolled in paper for smoking.

cinder *noun* (cinders) A small piece of partly-burnt coal or wood.

cine-camera *noun* (cine-cameras) A camera for taking moving pictures.

cinema *noun* (cinemas) A building or room where films are shown.

circle¹ *noun* (circles) **1** A perfectly round, flat shape. **2** Something shaped like O. **3** A route or path which returns to where it started. **circular** *adjective*. **4** A balcony in a cinema or theatre.

circle² *verb* (circles, circling, circled) To travel in a circle, to go right round something.

circuit *noun* (circuits) **1** A circular race-course. **2** A circular journey. **3** The path followed by an electric current.

circulate *verb* (circulates, circulating, circulated) To send something round, to go round. **circulation** *noun*.

circumcision *noun* The cutting off of a piece of skin from the penis.

circumference *noun* (circumferences) **1** The boundary of a circle. **2** The distance round a circle.

circumstance *noun* (circumstances) A fact or detail connected with something. *You'll understand my mistake when you know the circumstances.*

circus *noun* (circuses) An entertainment given by clowns, acrobats, trained animals, and other performers.

cistern *noun* (cisterns) A water tank.

citadel *noun* (citadels) A fortress.

citizen *noun* (citizens) **1** A person who lives in a city or town. **2** A person having full rights in a particular country. **citizenship** *noun*.

citrus fruit A fruit such as an orange, lemon, or grapefruit.

city *noun* (cities) An important town.

civic *adjective* Of a city or its citizens.

civil *adjective* **1** To do with ordinary citizens, not the armed services. **2** Polite. *Be civil to our visitors.* **civilly** *adverb*. **the Civil Service** people employed by the government to run various parts of the country's affairs. **civil war** war between groups of people of the same country.

civilian *noun* (civilians) A person not in the armed forces.

civilized *adjective* Belonging to or suitable for an orderly, organized state. **civilization** *noun*.

clad *adjective* Clothed.

claim *verb* (claims, claiming, claimed) **1** To demand something because you have a right to it. *The winner claimed her prize.* **2** To declare something as a fact. *He claims that he was robbed.*

clam *noun* (clams) A large shellfish.

clamber *verb* (clambers, clambering, clambered) To climb by using the hands to help.

clammy *adjective* Damp, cold, and slimy.

clamour *noun* Shouting, confused noise.

clamp *noun* A device for holding things so that they do not move.

clan *noun* (clans) A family group, a tribe.

clang *verb* (clangs, clanging, clanged) To make a noisy, ringing sound.

clanger *noun* (clangers) (informal) An embarrassing mistake.

clank *verb* (clanks, clanking, clanked) To make the sound of heavy pieces of metal knocked together.

clap[1] *verb* (claps, clapping, clapped) To hit the palms of the hands together, especially to show that you approve of something.

clap[2] *noun* (claps) **1** The act of clapping. **2** A sudden noise. *a clap of thunder.*

clarify *verb* (clarifies, clarifying, clarified) To make clear. **clarification, clarity** *nouns*.

clarinet *noun* (clarinets) A woodwind instrument. **clarinettist** *noun*.

clash *verb* (clashes, clashing, clashed) **1** To make a noise like the sound of cymbals. **2** To collide, to fight.

clasp[1] *noun* (clasps) **1** A device for fastening a necklace, a belt, or some other object. **2** An embrace.

clasp[2] *verb* (clasps, clasping, clasped) **1** To fasten. **2** To hold something firmly.

class *noun* (classes) **1** A group of children or students who are taught together. **2** A group of people or things with something in common.

classic[1] *adjective* Generally agreed to be very good. *a classic Beatles song.*

classic[2] *noun* (classics) A classic book, play, film, or piece of music.

classical *adjective* Of or from the ancient Greeks or Romans. *classical architecture.* **classical music** the kind of music which includes symphonies, concertos, operas, and so on.

classify *verb* (classifies, classifying, classified) To arrange in sets, groups, or classes. **classification** *noun*.

classroom *noun* (classrooms) A room where a class is taught.

clatter *verb* (clatters, clattering, clattered) To make a confused rattling noise.

claustrophobia *noun* The fear of being shut in.

claw[1] *noun* (claws) One of the curved,

pointed nails on the feet of some creatures.

claw[2] *verb* (claws, clawing, clawed) To scratch or tear with claws or hands.

clay *noun* A stiff, sticky kind of earth. **clayey** *adjective*.

clean[1] *adjective* 1 Free from dirt. *clean clothes*. 2 Fresh, unused. *clean paper*. 3 Fair, without breaking the rules. *a clean game*. **cleanly** *adverb*, **cleanness, cleanliness** *nouns*.

clean[2] *adverb* Completely. *I clean forgot*.

clean[3] *verb* (cleans, cleaning, cleaned) To make or become clean. **cleaner** *noun*

cleanse *verb* (cleanses, cleansing, cleansed) To clean, to make pure.

clear[1] *adjective* (clearer, clearest) 1 Easy to see through. *clear water*. 2 Easy to see, to hear, or to understand. *a clear explanation*. 3 Free from doubt. *a clear memory*. 4 Free from obstacles or difficulties. *a clear road*. **clearly** *adverb*, **clearness** *noun*.

clear[2] *adverb* 1 Completely. *He got clear away*. 2 At a distance, not in contact. *Keep clear!*

clear[3] *verb* (clears, clearing, cleared) 1 To make a thing clear. 2 To become clear. 3 To go over or past something without touching it. *The horse cleared the fence*. **clearance** *noun*. **clear off** to go away. **clear out** 1 to empty. 2 to go away. **clear up** 1 to make things tidy. 2 to stop raining.

clearing *noun* (clearings) An open space in wooded country.

clef *noun* (clefs) A sign that labels a stave in music.

clemency *noun* Mercy.

clench *verb* (clenches, clenching, clenched) To close tightly. *clenched teeth*.

clergy *noun* People authorized to conduct services in a Christian Church. **clergyman** *noun*.

clerk *noun* (clerks) An office worker. **clerical** *adjective*.

clever *adjective* (cleverer, cleverest) 1 Quick to learn, skilful, intelligent. 2 Done or made with skill. *a clever trick*. **cleverly** *adverb*, **cleverness** *noun*.

click *verb* (clicks, clicking, clicked) To make a short sharp sound.

client *noun* (clients) A customer, a person who does business with a bank or other firm.

cliff *noun* (cliffs) A steep rock-face.

climate *noun* (climates) The normal weather conditions of a particular area. *a dry climate*.

climax *noun* (climaxes) The moment of greatest excitement, especially near the end of something.

climb *verb* (climbs, climbing, climbed) 1 To go up something. 2 To grow upwards. **climber** *noun*. **climb down** 1 to come down something steep. 2 to admit that you were wrong.

cling *verb* (clings, clinging, clung) To hold tightly to something.

clinic *noun* (clinics) A place where people go for medical advice or treatment. **clinical** *adjective*.

clink *verb* (clinks, clinking, clinked) To make a small ringing sound.

clip[1] *noun* (clips) 1 A fastening device. *a paper-clip*. 2 A short extract from a film or TV programme.

clip[2] *verb* (clips, clipping, clipped) 1 To fasten with a clip. 2 To cut with scissors or shears. *to clip a hedge*. **clippers** *noun*.

clipper *noun* (clippers) A fast sailing ship.

cloak *noun* (cloaks) An outer garment which hangs loose from the shoulders.

cloakroom *noun* (cloakrooms) 1 A place where people can leave their coats. 2 A lavatory.

clock *noun* (clocks) An instrument for measuring time.

clockwise *adverb* Moving round in the same direction as a clock's hands.

clockwork *adjective* Driven by a spring which has to be wound up. *a clockwork toy*.

clod *noun* (clods) A lump of earth.

clog[1] *noun* (clogs) A wooden shoe.

clog[2] *verb* (clogs, clogging, clogged) To block up.

cloister *noun* (cloisters) A covered walk round the inside of a quadrangle.

clone *noun* (clones) An animal or plant developed from cells of another animal or plant, and therefore exactly like it.

close[1] *verb* (closes, closing, closed) **1** To shut. **2** To end. **closure** *noun*. **close in 1** to move nearer. **2** to get shorter. *The days are closing in*.

close[2] *adjective* (closer, closest) **1** Near. *close neighbours*. **2** Careful, thorough. *close study*. **3** Tight. *a close fit*. **4** Stuffy, uncomfortably warm. *close weather*. **5** Mean, stingy. *close with your money*.

close-up *noun* (close-ups) A picture taken at short range.

clot[1] *noun* (clots) A lump formed when a liquid dries or thickens. *a clot of blood*.

clot[2] *verb* (clots, clotting, clotted) To form clots. *clotted cream*.

cloth *noun* **1** Material woven from wool, cotton, nylon, or other substances. **2** A piece of cloth used for a particular purpose. *a table-cloth*.

clothe *verb* (clothes, clothing, clothed or clad) To cover, to cover with clothes.

clothes, clothing *nouns* Things that you wear to keep warm or to cover yourself.

clothes-line *noun* (clothes-lines) A line on which washing is hung to dry.

cloud *noun* (clouds) A mass of tiny water-drops, smoke, or dust, floating in the air.

cloudless *adjective* Without clouds.

cloudy *adjective* (cloudier, cloudiest) **1** Covered with clouds, full of clouds.
cloudy sky. **2** Not clear, hard to see through. *cloudy water*.

clout *verb* (clouts, clouting, clouted) (informal) To hit.

clover *noun* A small plant with each leaf in three parts.

clown *noun* (clowns) The performer in a circus who does funny tricks.

club *noun* (clubs) **1** A heavy stick. **2** A stick with a head for use in golf. **3** A society of people who meet together. **4** A playing-card marked with ♣

cluck *verb* (clucks, clucking, clucked) To make a noise like a hen.

clue *noun* (clues) Something that helps to solve a puzzle or a mystery.

clump *noun* (clumps) A group of plants growing together.

clumsy *adjective* (clumsier, clumsiest) Lacking skill, not neat, not graceful. **clumsily** *adverb*, **clumsiness** *noun*.

clung *See* cling

cluster[1] *noun* (clusters) A bunch or group.

cluster[2] *verb* (clusters, clustering, clustered) To form a cluster.

clutch[1] *verb* (clutches, clutching, clutched) To hold something eagerly or tightly.

clutch[2] *noun* (clutches) **1** One of the controls in a motor car. **2** A set of eggs in a nest.

clutter *noun* (clutters) An untidy quantity of things.

coach[1] *noun* (coaches) **1** A bus. **2** A carriage with four wheels drawn by four horses. **3** A railway passenger carriage. **4** An instructor, especially in athletics or games.

coach[2] *verb* (coaches, coaching, coached) To train people, especially in sports.

coal *noun* (coals) A black solid fuel.

coalfield *noun* (coalfields) An area where coal is to be found.

coal-mine *noun* (coal-mines) A place where coal is dug from the earth.

coarse *adjective* (coarser, coarsest)
1 Rough, not smooth or delicate.
2 Indecent, rude. *coarse language*.
coarsely *adverb*, **coarseness** *noun*.

coast¹ *noun* (coasts) The sea-shore and the land close to it. **coastal** *adjective*.

coast² *verb* (coasts, coasting, coasted) To freewheel down a slope.

coat *noun* (coats) **1** A garment with sleeves, opening down the front.
2 The hair or fur on an animal's body.
3 A covering. *a coat of paint*.

coating *noun* (coatings) A covering.

coax *verb* (coaxes, coaxing, coaxed) To persuade very gently.

cobble *noun* (cobbles) A round, smooth stone. **cobbled** *adjective*.

cobbler *noun* (cobblers) A person whose business is mending shoes.

cobra *noun* (cobras) A poisonous snake.

cobweb *noun* (cobwebs) A spider's web.

cock¹ *noun* (cocks) **1** A male bird.
2 A male farmyard fowl.

cock² *verb* (cocks, cocking, cocked)
1 To make a gun ready for firing.
2 To raise. *The dog cocked its ears*.

cockerel *noun* (cockerels) A male farmyard fowl.

cock-eyed *adjective* (informal) **1** Not straight, crooked. **2** Absurd.

cockle *noun* (cockles) A kind of shellfish.

cockney *noun* (cockneys) **1** Someone born in East London. **2** A kind of English spoken in East London.

cockroach *noun* (cockroaches) A dark brown insect.

cocktail *noun* (cocktails) A mixed alcoholic drink.

cocky *adjective* (informal) Conceited, cheeky.

cocoa *noun* **1** A hot chocolate drink.
2 The powder from which this is made.

coconut *noun* (coconuts) A large brown nut which grows on palm-trees.

cocoon *noun* (cocoons) The covering of a chrysalis.

cod *noun* (cod) A large sea fish.

code *noun* (codes) **1** A set of rules. *The Highway Code*. **2** A secret language. *a message in code*. **3** A set of signals. *Morse code*.

coeducation *noun* The education of boys and girls together. **coeducational** *adjective*.

coffee *noun* **1** A kind of hot drink.
2 The roasted beans from which this is made.

coffin *noun* (coffins) A box in which dead bodies are buried or cremated.

cog-wheel *noun* (cog-wheels) A wheel with teeth round the edge.

coherent *adjective* **1** Sticking together.
2 Clear and logical. **coherently** *adverb*, **coherence** *noun*.

coil¹ *verb* (coils, coiling, coiled) To twist into a spiral.

coil² *noun* (coils) Something coiled. *a coil of rope*.

coin *noun* (coins) A piece of metal money.

coinage *noun* (coinages) A system of money.

coincide *verb* (coincides, coinciding, coincided) To happen at the same time or place as something else. **coincidence** *noun*.

coke *noun* A solid fuel made from coal.

cold[1] *adjective* (colder, coldest) **1** Not warm, low in temperature. *Winter days are short and cold.* **2** Unkind, unfeeling. *He had cold eyes.* **coldly** *adverb*, **coldness** *noun*.

cold[2] *noun* (colds) An illness of the nose and throat.

cold-blooded *adjective* **1** Cruel, without pity. **cold-bloodedly** *adverb*. **2** Having blood that changes temperature according to the surroundings. *Fish are cold-blooded animals.*

coleslaw *noun* A salad dish made from shredded cabbage.

colic *noun* Severe pain in the stomach and bowels.

collaborate *verb* (collaborates, collaborating, collaborated) To share work. **collaboration, collaborator** *nouns*.

collage *noun* (collages) A picture made from scraps of paper or other materials.

collapse *verb* (collapses, collapsing, collapsed) To fall down or in.

collapsible *adjective* Capable of being folded up.

collar *noun* (collars) **1** Part of the clothing that goes round the neck. **2** A band that goes round the neck of an animal.

collect *verb* (collects, collecting, collected) **1** To gather together, to bring to a central place. *Please collect the maths books.* **2** To get specimens of things to study or enjoy them. *David collects stamps.* **3** To come together. *A large crowd collected.* **4** To fetch. *Ruth's father collected her from school.* **collector, collection** *nouns*.

college *noun* (colleges) A place where people go for further study after leaving school.

collide *verb* (collides, colliding, collided) To crash together. **collision** *noun*.

collie *noun* (collies) A kind of sheepdog.

colliery *noun* (collieries) A coal-mine.

colon *noun* (colons) The punctuation mark **:**

colonel *noun* (colonels) An army officer of higher rank than a major.

colony *noun* (colonies) **1** A land which has been developed by settlers from another country and is not yet independent. **colonial** *adjective*, **colonist** *noun*. **2** A group of people, animals, or birds living together.

colossal *adjective* Huge, giant-like.

colour[1] *noun* (colours) **1** Any of the different effects of light you see in the appearance of things, like the different effects in the stripes of a rainbow. *Red, yellow,* and *blue* are all colours. **2** The use of colours, not just black and white. *The pictures in this book are in colour.* **colourful, colourless** *adjectives*. **3** The colour of a person's skin. **4** The flag of a ship or regiment.

colour[2] *verb* (colours, colouring, coloured) **1** To add colour to something. **2** To blush.

colour-blind *adjective* Unable to see the difference between certain colours.

coloured *adjective* Having various colours.

colt *noun* (colts) A young male horse.

column *noun* (columns) **1** A pillar. **2** Something which is long and narrow. *a column of smoke.*

coma *noun* (comas) An unnatural deep sleep.

comb[1] *noun* (combs) **1** A device with teeth for making your hair tidy. **2** The red crest on a chicken's head.

comb[2] *verb* (combs, combing, combed) **1** To tidy hair with a comb. **2** To search thoroughly.

combat *noun* (combats) A fight, a battle. **combatant** *noun*.

combine *verb* (combines, combining, combined) To join together. **combination** *noun*. **combine harvester** a machine that cuts and threshes corn.

combustion *noun* Burning. **internal combustion engine** a petrol or diesel engine.

come *verb* (comes, coming, came) **1** To move towards, to move near. **2** To arrive. *He came late.* **3** To happen. *No harm will come to you.* **4** To go with somebody. *May I come with you?* **5** To amount to something. *It came to a lot of money.* **6** To become. *Dreams sometimes come true.*

comedian *noun* (comedians) A performer who makes people laugh.

comedy *noun* (comedies) An amusing play.

comet *noun* (comets) A heavenly body which looks like a star with a tail of light.

comfort¹ *noun* **1** Freedom from pain or distress. **2** (comforts) A person or thing that gives you comfort.

comfort² *verb* (comforts, comforting, comforted) To give someone comfort.

comfortable *adjective* **1** Pleasant to use or wear, giving comfort. *comfortable chairs. comfortable clothes.* **2** Free from pain or distress. *Are you comfortable?* **comfortably** *adverb*.

comic¹ *adjective* Funny. **comical** *adjective*, **comically** *adverb*.

comic² *noun* (comics) **1** A paper for children with stories told in pictures. **2** A comedian.

comma *noun* (commas) The punctuation mark **,**

command¹ *noun* (commands) **1** A statement that something must be done. **2** Skill and ability. *a good command of English.* **in command** in authority, in control.

command² *verb* (commands, commanding, commanded) **1** To give a command. **commandment** *noun*. **2** To be in charge of. **commander, commandant** *nouns*.

commando *noun* (commandos) A soldier trained to take part in dangerous raids.

commence *verb* (commences, commencing, commenced) To begin. **commencement** *noun*.

commend *verb* (commends, commending, commended) To praise. **commendation** *noun*.

comment¹ *noun* (comments) A short explanation or opinion.

comment² *verb* (comments, commenting, commented) To give a comment.

commentary *noun* (commentaries) A description of what is going on.

commentator *noun* (commentators) A person giving a commentary.

commerce *noun* Trade.

commercial¹ *adjective* Concerned with selling things.

commercial² *noun* (commercials) An advertisement, especially on TV or radio.

commit *verb* (commits, committing, committed) To do, to perform. *to commit a crime.* **commit yourself** to promise to do something. **commitment** *noun*.

committee *noun* (committees) A group of people with the job of discussing and organizing something. *the Sports Day Committee.*

common¹ *adjective* (commoner, commonest) **1** Belonging to or shared by a lot of people. *Most British people share a common language.* **2** Ordinary, found in many places. *Sparrows are common birds.* **3** Rude, vulgar. *Don't be* *common!* **common sense** the kind of sensible thinking you expect of a normal person. **commonly** *adverb.*

common² *noun* (commons) An area of land which anyone can use.

commonplace *adjective* Ordinary.

commonwealth *noun* (commonwealths) A group of countries which co-operate and help each other.

commotion *noun* (commotions) An uproar.

communal *adjective* Shared by a number of people.

communicate *verb* (communicates, communicating, communicated) To pass on information, news, or feelings.

communication *noun* (communications) A message, something which has been communicated. **communications** ways of sending messages or of getting from one place to another.

communicative *adjective* Ready and willing to talk.

communion *noun* **Holy Communion** a church service in which consecrated bread and wine are given to Christian worshippers.

communiqué *noun* (communiqués) An official announcement.

communism *noun* A set of political beliefs, a political system like that in China. **communist** *noun.*

community *noun* (communities) The people living in one place.

commuter *noun* (commuters) A person who travels daily to work.

compact *adjective* Small and neat. **compactly** *adverb.* **compact disc**

a type of recorded disc played by an apparatus using a laser beam.

companion *noun* (companions) Someone who shares a journey or an interest with you. **companionship** *noun.*

company¹ *noun* 1 Being together with someone else. *to keep someone company, to part company.* 2 (informal) Visitors.

company² *noun* (companies) 1 A set of people who do things together. *a ship's company.* 2 A business firm. 3 A unit in the army.

compare *verb* (compares, comparing, compared) 1 To judge the similarity of two or more things. 2 To be similar to. *Robinson cannot compare with Jones,* he is not nearly so good. **comparable, comparative** *adjectives,* **comparison** *noun.*

compartment *noun* (compartments) A space divided off inside a vehicle or container.

compass *noun* (compasses) An instrument with a swinging needle that always points north. **compasses** an instrument for drawing circles.

compassion *noun* Pity. **compassionate** *adjective,* **compassionately** *adverb.*

compatible *adjective* Capable of living or working together. **compatibility** *noun.*

compel *verb* (compels, compelling, compelled) To force somebody to do something.

compensate *verb* (compensates, compensating, compensated) To give somebody something to make up for a loss or injury. **compensation** *noun.*

compère *noun* (compères) A person who introduces the performers in a variety show.

compete *verb* (competes, competing, competed) 1 To take part in a race or contest. 2 To try to win, to try to do better than other people. **competitive** *adjective,* **competitor** *noun.*

competent *adjective* Properly qualified

and quite able to do a particular job. *a competent driver.* **competently** *adverb,* **competence** *noun.*

competition *noun* (competitions) **1** A game or contest in which people compete with each other. **2** Competing.

compile *verb* (compiles, compiling, compiled) To put together. *John and Alan compiled this dictionary.* **compiler, compilation** *nouns.*

complacent *adjective* Self-satisfied, smug. **complacently** *adverb,* **complacency** *noun.*

complain *verb* (complains, complaining, complained) **1** To say that you are not satisfied with something. *We complained about the food.* **2** To say that you have an illness or pain. *She complained of a cold.* **complaint** *noun.*

complete¹ *verb* (completes, completing, completed) **1** To finish. **2** To make whole, to make up the full number. *The arrival of the last guest completed the party.* **completion** *noun.*

complete² *adjective* **1** Finished, completed. **2** Perfect. *a complete success.* **completely** *adverb.*

complex¹ *adjective* Complicated. **complexity** *noun.*

complex² *noun* (complexes) A set of buildings, shops, or things.

complexion *noun* (complexions) The natural colour and appearance of a person's skin.

complicated *adjective* Made up of many parts, hard to understand.

complication *noun* (complications) Something that makes something else complicated or difficult. *All was going well, but now there's a complication.*

compliment *noun* (compliments) An admiring remark. *She paid me a compliment,* she said something nice about me. **complimentary** *adjective.*

component *noun* (components) A part.

compose *verb* (composes, composing, composed) **1** To put together, to

make. *Our class is composed of 15 boys and 18 girls.* **2** To make up music. **composer, composition** *nouns.*

compost *noun* Decayed stalks, leaves, and similar stuff, used to fertilize the soil.

compound *noun* (compounds) **1** Something made of several parts or ingredients. **2** A fenced area in which buildings stand.

comprehend *verb* (comprehends, comprehending, comprehended) **1** To understand. **comprehensible** *adjective.* **2** To include.

comprehension *noun* Understanding.

comprehensive *adjective* Including all kinds or things. **comprehensive school** a secondary school providing education for all children in an area.

compress *verb* (compresses, compressing, compressed) To squeeze something into a smaller space than it would usually occupy. **compression** *noun.*

comprising *adjective* Consisting of, including.

compulsion *noun* Being compelled.

compulsory *adjective* Having to be done, not voluntary.

compute *verb* (computes, computing, computed) **1** To count, to calculate. **2** To use a computer.

computer *noun* (computers) An electronic machine which can be programmed to solve problems, to sort out information, to control machinery, and to do other tasks.

computerize *verb* (computerizes, computerizing, computerized) To make or adapt something so that it can be done by computer.

comrade *noun* (comrades) A good friend or companion. **comradeship** *noun.*

concave *adjective* Curved like the inside of a ball.

conceal *verb* (conceals, concealing,

concealed) To hide something. **concealment** *noun*.

conceited *adjective* Feeling too proud of yourself.

conceive *verb* (conceives, conceiving, conceived) **1** To become pregnant. **2** To form an idea or plan. **conceivable** *adjective*, **conceivably** *adverb*.

concentrate *verb* (concentrates, concentrating, concentrated) **1** To give full attention to something, to think hard. **2** To gather things together. **3** To make denser or thicker or stronger. **concentration** *noun*.

concentric circles Circles having the same centre.

concept *noun* (concepts) An idea.

conception *noun* Conceiving.

concern¹ *noun* (concerns) **1** Something a person is interested in or responsible for. *That's no concern of mine.* **2** A business. *a going concern,* a successful business. **3** Worry, anxiety.

concern² *verb* (concerns, concerning, concerned) **1** To affect, to interest, to be important to. *Road safety concerns everyone.* **2** To worry. *We're concerned about his health.*

concerning *preposition* About.

concert *noun* (concerts) A musical performance.

concerto *noun* (concertos) A musical composition for a solo instrument and orchestra.

concession *noun* (concessions) Something allowed as a right or privilege.

concise *adjective* Brief, using few words. **concisely** *adverb*.

conclude *verb* (concludes, concluding, concluded) **1** To finish. **2** To form an opinion. *After waiting 15 minutes, we concluded that we had missed the bus.* **conclusion** *noun*.

concoct *verb* (concocts, concocting, concocted) To invent, to make up. **concoction** *noun*.

concord *noun* Agreement, harmony.

concrete *noun* A mixture of cement, gravel, sand, and water which sets like rock.

concussion *noun* An injury to the brain caused by a hard knock on the head.

condemn *verb* (condemns, condemning, condemned) To say that someone has done wrong or that something is wrong. *We condemn cruelty to animals.* **condemn to gaol** to send someone to gaol as a punishment. **condemnation** *noun*.

condense *verb* (condenses, condensing, condensed) **1** To make shorter or denser. *condensed milk.* **2** To turn into water or liquid. *Steam condenses on a cold window.* **condensation** *noun*.

condescending *adjective* Kind in a superior sort of way.

condition *noun* **1** The state or fitness of someone or something. *out of condition,* in a bad state. **2** (conditions) Something you have to agree to. *I'll come on condition that you pay,* I'll come if you agree to pay. **conditions** circumstances. *It'll be an exciting game if the conditions are good.*

condom *noun* (condoms) A contraceptive in the form of a sheath for the penis.

conduct¹ *noun* Behaviour.

conduct² *verb* (conducts, conducting, conducted) **1** To guide. *We were conducted round the castle.* **2** To direct, to be in charge of. *She conducted the orchestra.* **3** To allow electricity to pass. *Copper wire conducts electricity.* **conduct yourself** to behave. *You conducted yourselves well.*

conductor *noun* (conductors) **1** A person who sells tickets on a bus or tram. **2** A person who conducts an orchestra. **3** Something which conducts electricity.

cone *noun* (cones) **1** An object which is round at one end and pointed at the other. **conical** *adjective*. **2** The fruit of certain evergreen trees. *pine cones.*

confederate *noun* (confederates) An ally.

conference *noun* (conferences) A meeting for discussion.

confess *verb* (confesses, confessing, confessed) To admit you have done something wrong. **confession** *noun*.

confetti *noun* Small pieces of paper showered on bride and bridegroom.

confide *verb* (confides, confiding, confided) To trust someone with a secret.

confidence *noun* (confidences) **1** Faith in somebody or something. **2** Faith in yourself. **3** A secret. *I'll take you into my confidence*, I'll tell you my secret.

confident *adjective* Having confidence. **confidently** *adverb*.

confidential *adjective* To be kept secret. **confidentially** *adverb*.

confine *verb* (confines, confining, confined) To imprison, to restrict.

confinement *noun* (confinements) **1** Imprisonment. *solitary confinement*. **2** Giving birth to a child.

confirm *verb* (confirms, confirming, confirmed) **1** To agree for certain. **2** To show the truth of. **be confirmed** to become a full member of a Christian church. **confirmation** *noun*.

confiscate *verb* (confiscates, confiscating, confiscated) To take something away from somebody as a punishment. **confiscation** *noun*.

conflagration *noun* (conflagrations) A big fire.

conflict[1] *noun* (conflicts) A fight, a struggle, a disagreement.

conflict[2] *verb* (conflicts, conflicting, conflicted) To be against or opposed, to disagree.

conform *verb* (conforms, conforming, conformed) To keep to the rules, to behave like other people.

confront *verb* (confronts, confronting, confronted) To bring face to face, to meet face to face. **confrontation** *noun*.

confuse *verb* (confuses, confusing, confused) To mix up, to muddle. **confusion** *noun*.

congealed *adjective* Frozen, stiffened, solid.

congested *adjective* Overcrowded, too full. **congestion** *noun*.

congratulate *verb* (congratulates, congratulating, congratulated) To tell someone that you are very pleased about their success or good fortune. **congratulation** *noun*.

congregate *verb* (congregates, congregating, congregated) To come together, to make a crowd.

congregation *noun* (congregations) A group of people attending a service in church.

congress *noun* (congresses) A meeting.

conical *adjective* Cone-shaped.

conifer *noun* (conifers) A tree on which cones grow, like pine or fir. **coniferous** *adjective*.

conjunction *noun* (conjunctions) A joining word, such as *and*, *but*. **in conjunction with** together with.

conjure *verb* (conjures, conjuring, conjured) To do clever tricks which seem magical. **conjurer** *noun*.

conker *noun* (conkers) (informal) The fruit of a horse-chestnut tree.

connect *verb* (connects, connecting, connected) To join, to link. **connection** *noun*.

conning-tower *noun* (conning-towers) The observation tower of a submarine.

conquer *verb* (conquers, conquering, conquered) To defeat, to overcome, to win by battle. **conqueror** *noun*.

conquest *noun* (conquests) Conquering, victory.

conscience *noun* (consciences) The knowledge of right and wrong, the feeling of being guilty when you have done wrong.

conscientious *adjective* Careful, honest, dutiful. **conscientiously** *adverb*.

conscious *adjective* Awake, aware of what is happening. **consciously** *adverb*, **consciousness** *noun*.

consecrate *verb* (consecrates, consecrating, consecrated) To make something holy.

consecutive *adjective* Following one after the other. **consecutively** *adverb*.

consent[1] *verb* (consents, consenting, consented) To give permission, to agree.

consent[2] *noun* Permission, agreement.

consequence *noun* (consequences) Something that follows as a result of something else. **consequently** *adverb*. **in consequence of** as a result of. **of no consequence** unimportant.

conservation *noun* Preservation and care, especially of natural things. **conservationist** *noun*.

conservative *adjective* Opposed to great and sudden change. **Conservative Party** one of the British political parties. **conservatism** *noun*.

conservatory *noun* (conservatories) A greenhouse attached to a house.

conserve *verb* (conserves, conserving, conserved) To preserve, to avoid spoiling or wasting something.

consider *verb* (considers, considering, considered) **1** To think about something. **2** To hold an opinion.

considerable *adjective* Fairly large. **considerably** *adverb*.

considerate *adjective* Kind and thoughtful. **considerately** *adverb*.

consideration *noun* **1** Thoughtful feelings for other people. **2** Careful thought. **3** Something needing careful thought.

consignment *noun* (consignments) A batch of things sent together.

consist *verb* (consists, consisting, consisted) To be made up of something.

consistent *adjective* **1** Regular. *He is*

a good and consistent supporter. **2** In agreement with. *That is not consistent with what you said yesterday.* **consistently** *adverb*.

console *verb* (consoles, consoling, consoled) To give comfort or sympathy. **consolation** *noun*.

consonant *noun* (consonants) Any letter of the alphabet except a, e, i, o, and u.

consort *noun* (consorts) The husband or wife of a queen or king.

conspicuous *adjective* Noticeable, very easily seen. **conspicuously** *adverb*.

conspire *verb* (conspires, conspiring, conspired) To plot, to get together for some evil purpose. **conspirator, conspiracy** *nouns*.

constable *noun* (constables) A police officer.

constabulary *noun* (constabularies) A police force.

constant *adjective* **1** Faithful. *a constant friend.* **2** Unchanging, continual. *a constant temperature.* **constantly** *adverb*.

constellation *noun* (constellations) A group of stars.

consternation *noun* Surprise and dismay.

constipated *adjective* Unable to empty the bowels easily and regularly. **constipation** *noun*.

constituency *noun* (constituencies) A district which elects a Member of Parliament.

constitute *verb* (constitutes, constituting, constituted) To form, to make up. *These 30 children constitute Class I.*

constitution *noun* (constitutions) **1** All the laws and rules according to which a country is governed. **2** General health. *He has a strong constitution,* he is very healthy. **constitutional** *adjective*.

construct *verb* (constructs, constructing, constructed) To make, to build. **constructor, construction** *nouns*.

a b **c** d e f g h i j k l m

constructive *adjective* Helpful. **constructively** *adverb*.

consul *noun* (consuls) An official who lives in a foreign town to help and protect people from his or her country.

consult *verb* (consults, consulting, consulted) To go to a person or book for information or advice. *We consulted our dictionary*. **consultation** *noun*.

consume *verb* (consumes, consuming, consumed) To eat, to use up. **consumption** *noun*.

consumer *noun* (consumers) A person who buys goods from shops.

contact[1] *noun* 1 Touching. 2 (contacts) A place where one thing touches another. **in contact with** communicating with, in touch with. **contact lenses** lenses you wear touching the eye to correct your eyesight.

contact[2] *verb* (contacts, contacting, contacted) To communicate with someone by letter, phone, or other means.

contagious *adjective* Infectious, caught by touching. *a contagious disease*.

contain *verb* (contains, containing, contained) To hold something inside, to include. **container** *noun*.

contaminate *verb* (contaminates, contaminating, contaminated) To make something dirty or unhealthy. **contamination** *noun*.

contemplate *verb* (contemplates, contemplating, contemplated) 1 To look thoughtfully at something. 2 To think deeply about something. **contemplation** *noun*.

contemporary *adjective* 1 Living or existing at the same time as somebody or something else. 2 Up-to-date, modern in style.

contempt *noun* Scorn, lack of respect.

contemptible *adjective* Unworthy of respect.

contemptuous *adjective* Scornful. **contemptuously** *adverb*.

contend *verb* (contends, contending, contended) 1 To compete. 2 To argue. **contender, contention** *nouns*.

content *adjective* Satisfied. **contentment** *noun*.

contented *adjective* Satisfied. **contentedly** *adverb*.

contents *noun* The things contained in something.

contest[1] *verb* (contests, contesting, contested) To contend, to fight. **contestant** *noun*.

contest[2] *noun* (contests) A fight, a competition.

continent *noun* (continents) One of the big land masses of the world, Africa, Antarctica, Asia, Australia, Europe, North America, and South America. **the Continent** the mainland of Europe, not including the British Isles.

continental *adjective* (for British people) On or from the mainland of Europe. *continental holidays, continental visitors*. **continental quilt** a warm covering for a bed, with a soft filling.

continual *adjective* Very frequent, happening again and again. *continual interruptions*. **continually** *adverb*.

continue *verb* (continues, continuing, continued) 1 To go on, to go further. 2 To remain unchanged. 3 To start again after an interruption. **continuation** *noun*.

continuous *adjective* Going on without a break. **continuously** *adverb*, **continuity** *noun*.

contortionist *noun* (contortionists) Someone who can twist his or her body into strange positions.

contour *noun* (contours) 1 An outline. 2 A line on a map joining all points at the same height above sea-level.

contraband *noun* Smuggled goods.

contraceptive *noun* (contraceptives) A device or drug which prevents a woman from becoming pregnant. **contraception** *noun*.

contract¹ *noun* (contracts) An official agreement.

contract² *verb* (contracts, contracting, contracted) **1** To make a contract. **contractor** *noun*. **2** To catch, to get. *to contract an illness*. **3** To make smaller, to become smaller. **contraction** *noun*.

contradict *verb* (contradicts, contradicting, contradicted) To say that something someone has said is not true, to say the opposite of what someone else has said. **contradictory** *adjective*, **contradiction** *noun*.

contraflow *noun* A system which allows traffic to travel in both directions on one side of a dual carriageway.

contralto (contraltos) A female singer with a low voice.

contraption *noun* (contraptions) A strange-looking device.

contrary *adjective* **1** Opposite. *a contrary wind*, an unfavourable wind. **2** Obstinate, unhelpful. *contrary behaviour*.

contrast¹ *verb* (contrasts, contrasting, contrasted) **1** To point out the differences when comparing things. **2** To be obviously different when compared. *Our red shirts contrasted with the visitors' blue shirts*.

contrast² *noun* (contrasts) **1** A very great difference. **2** Something that differs greatly.

contribute *verb* (contributes, contributing, contributed) **1** To give money or help to a particular cause. *We contributed to the swimming-pool fund*. **2** To play a part in. *His bowling contributed to his team's victory*. **3** To write a story or article for a magazine or newspaper. **contributor, contribution** *nouns*.

contrive *verb* (contrives, contriving, contrived) To invent, to find a way of doing something. **contrivance** *noun*.

control¹ *verb* (controls, controlling, controlled) **1** To make someone or something do what you want. *Control that dog!* **2** To hold something back. *Control your giggling!* **controllable** *adjective*, **controller** *noun*.

control² *noun* (controls) The ability to control people or things. *Our teacher has good control over the class*. **In control** in charge. **controls** the levers and instruments by which a machine is controlled.

controversy *noun* (controversies) A long argument. **controversial** *adjective*.

conundrum *noun* (conundrums) A riddle.

convalescent *adjective* Recovering after an illness. **convalescence** *noun*.

convector *noun* (convectors) A heater which makes warm air circulate.

convenience *noun* (conveniences) Something that is convenient. **at your convenience** as it suits you. **public conveniences** public lavatories.

convenient *adjective* Easy to use, easy to reach. **conveniently** *adverb*.

convent *noun* (convents) A house where nuns live and work.

convention *noun* (conventions) The usual or accepted way of doing a particular thing. **conventional** *adjective*.

converge *verb* (converges, converging, converged) To come together from different directions.

conversation *noun* (conversations) Talking between two or more people. **conversational** *adjective*.

convert *verb* (converts, converting, converted) **1** To alter something to make it suitable for a new purpose or for new conditions. **2** To make somebody change his or her beliefs. **convertible** *adjective*, **conversion** *noun*.

convex *adjective* Curved like the outside of a ball.

convey *verb* (conveys, conveying, conveyed) **1** To carry something. **2** To communicate, to mean. *This message conveys nothing to me*.

conveyor belt An endless belt on which goods can be moved along.

convict[1] *noun* (convicts) A convicted criminal.

convict[2] *verb* (convicts, convicting, convicted) To declare someone guilty.

conviction *noun* (convictions) **1** Being found guilty of a crime. *a conviction for speeding.* **2** A firm opinion or belief. *religious convictions.*

convince *verb* (convinces, convincing, convinced) To persuade someone of the truth of something.

convoy *noun* (convoys) A group of ships or vehicles travelling together.

convulsion *noun* (convulsions) A violent disturbance, a fit. **convulsive** *adjective*.

coo *verb* (coos, cooing, cooed) To make a soft murmuring sound.

cook[1] *verb* (cooks, cooking, cooked) To make food ready to eat by boiling, frying, baking, or some other method of heating.

cook[2] *noun* (cooks) Someone who cooks.

cooker *noun* (cookers) An oven or some other apparatus for cooking.

cookery *noun* Cooking.

cool[1] *adjective* (cooler, coolest) **1** Fairly cold. **2** Calm. *Keep cool, don't panic!* **3** Not enthusiastic. **coolly** *adverb*, **coolness** *noun*.

cool[2] *verb* (cools, cooling, cooled) To become cool, to make cool. **cooler** *noun*.

coop *noun* (coops) A kind of cage to keep chickens in.

co-operate *verb* (co-operates, co-operating, co-operated) To work helpfully together. **co-operative** *adjective*, **co-operation** *noun*.

coot *noun* (coots) A black water-bird.

cop *noun* (cops) (informal) A police officer.

cope *verb* (copes, coping, coped) To deal with something successfully. *Can you cope with that pile of books?*

copious *adjective* Plentiful. **copiously** *adverb*.

copper A reddish-brown metal. **coppers** coins made of copper or bronze.

coppice, copse *nouns* (coppices, copses) A clump of small trees.

copulate *verb* (copulates, copulating, copulated) To mate. **copulation** *noun*.

copy[1] *noun* (copies) **1** Something made to be like something else. **2** Something written out a second time. *I made a neat copy of my poem.* **3** One particular example of something issued in large numbers, such as a book, newspaper, or record. *Where's my copy of 'Treasure Island'?*

copy[2] *verb* (copies, copying, copied) **1** To make a copy. **copier** *noun*. **2** To do the same as someone else. *We sometimes copy our parents.*

coral *noun* A hard substance built up from the sea bed by small creatures.

cord *noun* (cords) A thin rope.

cordial[1] *adjective* Warm and friendly. **cordially** *adverb*.

cordial[2] *noun* (cordials) A sweet drink.

cordon *noun* (cordons) A line of troops or police acting as guards.

corduroy *noun* A thick cloth with raised velvet lines on its surface.

core *noun* (cores) The central part of something. *an apple core.*

cork *noun* **1** The light, thick bark of a tree called the cork-oak. **2** (corks) A piece of cork used to stop a bottle.

corkscrew *noun* (corkscrews) A tool for removing corks.

cormorant *noun* (cormorants) A large black diving bird.

corn[1] *noun* Grain, the seeds of wheat, barley, oats, and rye.

corn[2] (corns) A small lump of hardened skin on the foot.

corner[1] *noun* (corners) **1** The place where two walls, roads, or lines meet. **2** A kick taken from a corner of the field in football.

corner[2] *verb* (corners, cornering, cornered) **1** To turn a corner. **2** To trap someone or something in a corner.

cornet *noun* (cornets) **1** A cone-shaped wafer containing ice-cream. **2** A musical instrument rather like a trumpet.

cornflakes *noun* A breakfast cereal made from maize.

cornflour *noun* A fine flour used in cooking.

cornflower *noun* (cornflowers) A blue wild flower.

corny *adjective* (informal) Heard too often to be interesting. *a corny joke*.

coronation *noun* (coronations) The ceremony of crowning a king or queen.

coroner *noun* (coroners) An official who inquires into why people died.

coronet *noun* (coronets) A small crown.

corporal *noun* (corporals) A soldier below sergeant in rank. **corporal punishment** whipping or beating.

corporation *noun* (corporations) A group of people acting together to govern a city or to run a business.

corps *noun* A part of an army. *The Royal Army Medical Corps*.

corpse *noun* (corpses) A dead body.

corral *noun* (corrals) An enclosure for horses or cattle.

correct[1] *verb* (corrects, correcting, corrected) **1** To make correct. **2** To mark mistakes. **correction** *noun*.

correct[2] *adjective* Right, true, without mistakes. **correctly** *adverb*, **correctness** *noun*.

correspond *verb* (corresponds, corresponding, corresponded) **1** To exchange letters. *I correspond with a pen-friend in France*. **2** To be similar or equivalent to.

correspondence *noun* Letters, written messages.

correspondent *noun* (correspondents) **1** Someone who writes letters. **2** Someone who sends news to a newspaper.

corridor *noun* (corridors) A passage with doors leading into many rooms or compartments.

corrode *verb* (corrodes, corroding, corroded) To eat or be eaten away by the action of chemicals. **corrosive** *adjective*, **corrosion** *noun*.

corrugated *adjective* With wrinkles or folds. *corrugated iron*.

corrupt[1] *adjective* Dishonest, taking bribes. **corruptly** *adverb*.

corrupt[2] *verb* (corrupts, corrupting, corrupted) To make a person corrupt. **corruptible** *adjective*, **corruption** *noun*.

corset *noun* (corsets) An undergarment which fits tightly to make the waist and hips look slimmer.

cosmetics *noun* Substances used to make you prettier, such as lipstick and eye-shadow.

cosmonaut *noun* (cosmonauts) A Russian traveller in space.

a b **c** d e f g h i j k l m

cosmos *noun* The universe. **cosmic** *adjective*.

cost[1] *noun* (costs) The price of something. **at all costs** whatever the cost may be.

cost[2] *verb* (costs, costing, cost) **1** To be bought for a certain price. **2** To cause the loss of. *The mistake cost him his life.*

costly *adjective* Expensive, valuable.

costume *noun* (costumes) **1** A way of dressing, a style of clothing. **2** Clothes for actors in a play.

cosy *adjective* (cosier, cosiest) Warm and comfortable. **cosily** *adverb*, **cosiness** *noun*.

cot *noun* (cots) A child's bed with sides to prevent it falling out.

cottage *noun* (cottages) A small house.

cotton *noun* **1** A soft white substance from the seeds of the cotton plant. **2** Thread or cloth made from cotton. **cotton wool** clean, fluffy cotton used in nursing.

couch *noun* (couches) A long seat like a sofa.

cough[1] *noun* (coughs) An explosion of air from the lungs.

cough[2] *verb* (coughs, coughing, coughed) To make a cough.

could *See* **can**[1]

couldn't (informal) Could not.

council *noun* (councils) A group of people elected to plan and work together. **councillor** *noun*.

council-house (council-houses) A house rented from the local council.

count[1] *verb* (counts, counting, counted) **1** To say the numbers in order. *to count down*, to say the numbers backwards. **2** To add up. **3** To include in the total. *There were five of us not counting the driver*, there were six of us altogether. **count on** to rely on.

count[2] *noun* (counts) A nobleman in certain countries.

countenance *noun* (countenances) A face, the expression on a face.

counter *noun* (counters) **1** A small disc used for keeping count in games. **2** A long, narrow table at which customers are served in a shop, café, or bank.

counter-attack *noun* (counter-attacks) An attack in reply to an attack by the enemy.

counterfeit *verb* (counterfeits, counterfeiting, counterfeited) To forge, to copy something unlawfully.

counterpane *noun* (counterpanes) A quilt, a top covering for a bed.

countess *noun* (countesses) A noble woman, the wife of an earl or count.

countless *adjective* Too many to count easily.

country *noun* (countries) **1** A land inhabited by a particular nation. **2** A nation, the people who live in a country. **3** An area which is nearly all fields, woods, or open land. **countryside** *noun*.

countryman *noun* (countrymen) **1** Someone from your own nation. *my countrymen*. **2** Someone who lives in the country, not in the town.

county *noun* (counties) One of the divisions of Great Britain.

couple[1] *noun* (couples) **1** A pair. *a couple of things*, two things. **2** A husband and wife, or a boy-friend and girl-friend.

couple[2] *verb* (couples, coupling, coupled) To join together.

coupling *noun* (couplings) A device for joining two things together.

coupon *noun* (coupons) A piece of paper which gives you the right to do something or to receive something.

courage *noun* The ability to control your fear of pain or danger. **courageous** *adjective*, **courageously** *adverb*.

courier *noun* (couriers) A person who accompanies and helps holiday parties, especially abroad.

course *noun* (courses) **1** The direction taken by something or somebody. *the course of a river, a course of events.* **2** A race-course. **3** An area set out for playing golf. **4** A series. *a course of lessons.* **5** A part of a meal. *the meat course.* **in the course of** during. **in due course** at the proper time. **of course** certainly, naturally.

court¹ *noun* (courts) **1** A king or queen with his or her family and councillors, the place where these assemble officially. **courtly** *adjective.* **2** The place where cases are tried by a judge or magistrate. **3** An area marked out for tennis or other games. **court martial** a court where people in the armed forces accused of breaking military laws are tried.

court² *verb* (courts, courting, courted) To try to win someone's love or support. **courtship** *noun.*

courteous *adjective* Having good manners, polite. **courteously** *adverb*, **courtesy** *noun.*

courtier *noun* (courtiers) A person at the royal court.

courtyard *noun* (courtyards) A space surrounded by buildings or walls.

cousin *noun* (cousins) A child of your uncle or aunt.

cove *noun* (coves) A small bay.

coven *noun* (covens) An assembly of witches.

covenant *noun* (covenants) A solemn agreement. **The Covenant** the undertaking which God made to the Jews on Mount Sinai.

cover¹ *verb* (covers, covering, covered) **1** To place one thing over another to hide or protect it. *We covered the wall with white paint.* **2** To go over a certain area. *Will this paint cover that wall?* **3** To deal with. *An encyclopaedia covers many subjects.* **4** To aim a gun at

someone. *I've got you covered.* **coverage** *noun.*

cover² *noun* (covers) **1** Something that covers, such as a lid, a wrapper, or the binding of a book. **2** A shelter, a hiding-place.

covering *noun* (coverings) A layer that covers.

coverlet *noun* (coverlets) A bed cover.

cow *noun* (cows) A female animal kept by farmers for its milk.

coward *noun* (cowards) A person unable to control his or her fear. **cowardly** *adverb*, **cowardice** *noun.*

cowboy *noun* (cowboys) A man who looks after cattle in America.

cowed *adjective* Frightened.

cower *verb* (cowers, cowering, cowered) To crouch in fear.

cowslip *noun* (cowslips) A yellow wild flower.

cox, coxswain *nouns* (coxes, coxswains) A person who steers a boat.

coy *adjective* Pretending to be shy or embarrassed. **coyly** *adverb*, **coyness** *noun.*

crab *noun* (crabs) A shellfish with five pairs of legs.

crab-apple *noun* (crab-apples) A small sour kind of apple.

crack¹ *noun* (cracks) **1** A narrow gap or line where something is broken but has not come completely apart. *a crack in a cup.* **2** A sudden sharp noise. *the crack of a pistol shot.* **3** A sudden knock. *a crack on the head.*

crack² *verb* (cracks, cracking, cracked)

To get or make a crack. **crack a joke** to make a joke.

cracker noun (crackers) 1 A kind of firework. 2 A Christmas toy consisting of a paper tube which explodes when pulled apart. 3 A kind of biscuit.

crackle verb (crackles, crackling, crackled) To make small cracking sounds.

crackling noun The crisp skin of roast pork.

cradle noun (cradles) A cot for a baby.

craft[1] noun (crafts) 1 Skill, art, cunning. 2 A job which needs skill in the use of the hands.

craft[2] noun (craft) A vehicle for travelling on water, through air, or in space.

craftsman noun (craftsmen) Someone who is good at a craft. **craftsmanship** noun.

crafty adjective Cunning. **craftily** adverb, **craftiness** noun.

crag noun (crags) A steep, rough rock. **craggy** adjective.

cram verb (crams, cramming, crammed) To fill something to overflowing.

cramp[1] noun Painful tightening of the muscles, often caused by cold or too much work.

cramp[2] verb (cramps, cramping, cramped) 1 To keep in a small space. 2 To prevent from growing or developing.

crane noun (cranes) 1 A large wading bird. 2 A machine for lifting heavy weights.

crane-fly noun (crane-flies) A daddy-long-legs.

crank noun (cranks) 1 A bent rod. 2 (informal) A person with strange ideas. **cranky** adjective.

cranny noun (crannies) A crack, a narrow split.

crash[1] verb (crashes, crashing, crashed) 1 To fall, move, or hit something violently and noisily. *The elephant crashed through the jungle.* 2 To crash into something and be badly damaged. *The plane crashed.* 3 To cause something to crash. *Dad has crashed the car again.*

crash[2] noun (crashes) The act or sound of crashing.

crash-helmet noun (crash-helmets) A padded helmet worn to protect your head in a crash.

crash-landing noun (crash-landings) The landing of an aircraft in an emergency, often causing damage.

crate noun (crates) A large wooden box.

crater noun (craters) 1 The mouth of a volcano. 2 A big hole in the ground.

crawl[1] verb (crawls, crawling, crawled) 1 To move slowly, usually on hands and knees. 2 To be covered with crawling things. *The ground was crawling with ants.*

crawl[2] noun 1 A crawling movement. 2 A swimming stroke with each arm coming out of the water in turn.

crayon noun (crayons) A coloured drawing pencil.

craze noun (crazes) A temporary enthusiasm for something.

crazy adjective (crazier, craziest) Mad. **crazy paving** paving stones of odd shapes fitted together.

creak verb (creaks, creaking, creaked) To make a noise like a door whose hinges need oiling. **creaky** adjective.

cream noun 1 The thick fatty liquid which rises to the top of milk. 2 Its colour, between white and yellow. 3 Something that looks like cream. *face-cream.* **creamy** adverb, **creaminess** noun.

crease[1] noun (creases) 1 A line in a piece of paper or cloth caused by folding or pressing. 2 A line on a cricket pitch to show where the batsman should stand.

crease[2] verb (creases, creasing, creased) To make a crease in paper or cloth.

create verb (creates, creating, created) To make, to bring something into existence. **creative** adjective, **creatively** adverb, **creation** noun.

creator noun (creators) Someone who creates. **The Creator** God. **creativity** noun, **creative** adjective, **creatively** adverb.

creature noun (creatures) A living thing, especially an animal.

crèche noun (crèches) A nursery.

cred noun (informal) A quality that is admired as smart and modern.

credible adjective Believable. **credibly** adverb, **credibility** noun.

credit noun 1 Honour, good reputation. *You deserve the credit for our success.* 2 A person or thing that brings honour. *He was a credit to his parents.* **buy on credit** to be allowed to pay later. **credit card** a plastic card you can use to buy things on credit. **credits** a list of people who helped to make a film.

creditable adjective Praiseworthy. **creditably** adverb.

creed noun (creeds) 1 A statement of what you believe in. 2 A religion.

creek noun (creeks) 1 A narrow inlet in a coastline, shaped like the mouth of a river. 2 (Australian) A small stream.

creep verb (creeps, creeping, crept) 1 To move along close to the ground, to move stealthily. *He crept up on his victim.* 2 To come gradually. *Sleep crept over him.*

creeper noun (creepers) A plant that creeps or climbs.

creepy adjective Weird, frightening.

cremate verb (cremates, cremating, cremated) To burn a dead body. **cremation** noun.

crematorium noun (crematoria) A place where bodies are cremated.

creosote noun An oily liquid used to prevent wood from rotting.

crept See **creep**

crescendo noun (crescendos) An increase in the loudness of something.

crescent noun (crescents) A curved shape like a new moon.

cress noun A green plant used in salads.

crest noun (crests) 1 A tuft of feathers, skin, or hair on a creature's head. 2 A plume on a helmet. 3 A badge. 4 The top of a hill or wave.

crestfallen adjective Disappointed, downcast.

crevasse noun (crevasses) A deep crack in ice.

crevice noun (crevices) A crack, a narrow split.

crew noun (crews) All the people who work on a ship or aircraft.

crib[1] noun (cribs) 1 A baby's cot. 2 A rack from which animals eat hay.

crib[2] verb (cribs, cribbing, cribbed) To cheat by copying.

cricket noun 1 An outdoor game played with a ball, bats, and wickets. 2 (crickets) An insect like a grasshopper.

cried, crier, cries See **cry**[1, 2]

crime noun (crimes) An action which is against the law.

criminal noun (criminals) Someone who has committed a crime.

crimson noun and adjective Deep red.

cringe verb (cringes, cringing, cringed) To cower.

crinkle noun (crinkles) A small fold, a wrinkle.

cripple[1] noun (cripples) A lame person.

cripple[2] verb (cripples, crippling, crippled) 1 To make someone lame. 2 To damage something very badly.

crisis noun (crises) A time of particular danger, difficulty, or suspense.

crisp[1] adjective (crisper, crispest) 1 Hard, dry and easily broken. 2 *crisp weather*, dry, frosty weather. 3 Quick, definite, smart. **crisply** adverb.

crisp² *noun* (crisps) A crisp slice of fried potato.

criss-cross *adjective and adverb* With crossing lines.

critic *noun* (critics) **1** A person who writes about books, films, plays, music, and other arts. **2** Someone who finds fault with things and people.

critical *adjective* **1** Criticizing. **2** Very serious. *a critical illness*. **critically** *adverb*.

criticize *verb* (criticizes, criticizing, criticized) To point out faults in someone or something. **criticism** *noun*.

croak *verb* (croaks, croaking, croaked) To make a hoarse sound like a frog.

crochet *noun* A kind of knitting done with a hooked stick called a crochet-hook.

crockery *noun* Plates, cups, saucers, and other pottery dishes.

crocodile *noun* (crocodiles) A large river reptile.

crocus *noun* (crocuses) A spring flower.

croft *noun* (crofts) A small farm in Scotland. **crofter** *noun*.

crook *noun* (crooks) **1** A stick with a rounded hook, used by shepherds. **2** (informal) A criminal.

crooked *adjective* **1** Not straight, bent. **2** Dishonest. **crookedly** *adverb*, **crookedness** *noun*.

croon *noun* (croons, crooning, crooned) To sing softly. **crooner** *noun*.

crop¹ *verb* (crops, cropping, cropped) **1** To cut something short. *close-cropped hair*. **2** To produce a crop of plants. **crop up** to arise unexpectedly.

crop² *noun* (crops) **1** The yearly produce of agriculture, the plants in the field. **2** A kind of small whip.

croquet *noun* A garden game played with mallets and balls.

cross¹ *noun* (crosses) **1** A mark such as + or × **2** Anything made in such a shape. **the Cross** the gallows on which Jesus Christ was crucified. **3** An animal whose parents are of different breeds.

cross² *verb* (crosses, crossing, crossed) **1** To move from one side of something to the other. **2** *It crossed my mind*, it occurred to me. **3** To make a cross shape with something. *Cross your fingers!* **4** To pass somebody or something going in the opposite direction. **5** To annoy somebody. **cross out** to draw a line through something.

cross³ *adjective* (crosser, crossest) Bad-tempered, annoyed. **crossly** *adverb*.

crossbar *noun* (crossbars) A horizontal bar or beam.

crossbow *noun* (crossbows) An ancient weapon for shooting arrows.

cross-country *adjective and adverb* Across the countryside.

cross-examine *verb* (cross-examines, cross-examining, cross-examined) To question someone carefully, especially to check whether previous answers were true. **cross-examination** *noun*.

cross-eyed *adjective* Squinting.

crossfire *noun* The paths of bullets coming from several directions.

crossing *noun* (crossings) A place where people can cross a road or railway. *a zebra crossing*.

crossroads *noun* A place where two roads cross.

crossword *noun* (crosswords) A kind of puzzle in which letters forming words are put into numbered spaces.

crotchet *noun* (crotchets) A note in music. It is written ♩

crouch *verb* (crouches, crouching, crouched) To stoop, to bend.

crow¹ *noun* (crows) A large black bird. **crow's nest** a look-out position at the top of a ship's mast.

crow² *verb* (crows, crowing, crowed) **1** To make a noise like a cock. **2** To boast.

crowbar *noun* (crowbars) An iron bar used as a lever.

crowd¹ *noun* (crowds) A large number of people together in one place.

crowd² *verb* (crowds, crowding, crowded) **1** To make a crowd, to come together as a crowd. **2** To fill a space too full for comfort.

crown¹ *noun* (crowns) **1** The golden head-dress worn by a king or queen. **2** The top part of anything. *the crown of a hill.* **The crown** royal authority. *This land belongs to the crown,* this land belongs to the king or queen.

crown² *verb* (crowns, crowning, crowned) **1** To put a crown on a king or queen. **2** To form or cover the top part of something. **3** To reward. *His efforts were crowned with success.*

crucial *adjective* Very important.

crucifix *noun* (crucifixes) An image of Jesus Christ on the cross.

crucify *verb* (crucifies, crucifying, crucified) To put someone to death by fastening him to a cross. **crucifixion** *noun.*

crude *adjective* (cruder, crudest) **1** Raw, in a natural state. *crude oil.* **2** Rough, clumsy. *a crude carving.* **3** Rude, coarse. *crude manners.* **crudely** *adverb,* **crudity** *noun.*

cruel *adjective* (crueller, cruellest) **1** Deliberately causing pain or suffering. **2** Pleased by someone else's pain or suffering. **cruelly** *adverb,* **cruelty** *noun.*

cruise¹ *verb* (cruises, cruising, cruised) **1** To have a holiday on a ship, visiting various places. **2** To travel at a moderate, pleasant speed.

cruise² *noun* (cruises) A cruising holiday.

cruiser *noun* (cruisers) A kind of warship.

crumb *noun* (crumbs) A tiny piece of bread or cake. **crumby** *adjective.*

crumble *verb* (crumbles, crumbling, crumbled) To break into small pieces. **crumbly** *adverb.*

crumple *verb* (crumples, crumpling, crumpled) To crush into folds and creases, to become creased.

crunch *verb* (crunches, crunching, crunched) **1** To chew noisily. **2** To crush.

crusade *noun* (crusades) A holy war. **crusader** *noun.*

crush¹ *verb* (crushes, crushing, crushed) **1** To press and break something. *Don't crush the eggs!* **2** To defeat someone completely.

crush² *noun* (crushes) **1** A crowd. **2** A fruit drink.

crust *noun* (crusts) **1** The hard outer part of a loaf or a pie. **2** Any hard outer covering. **crusty** *adjective.*

crutch *noun* (crutches) A walking aid for a crippled person.

cry¹ *verb* (cries, crying, cried) **1** To weep. **2** To shout, to yell. **crier** *noun.*

cry² *noun* (cries) **1** A loud sound, an excited call. **2** A fit of weeping.

crypt *noun* (crypts) An underground room beneath a church.

crystal *noun* **1** A mineral which is hard and clear like glass. **2** A small, hard, shiny piece. *crystals of ice.*

crystallize *verb* (crystallizes, crystallizing, crystallized) To form crystals.

cub *noun* (cubs) A young lion, fox, bear, or other animal. **Cub Scout** a junior Scout.

cube *noun* (cubes) Something that has six square sides. **cubic** *adjective.*

cubicle *noun* (cubicles) A small room divided off from another one.

a b **c** d e f g h i j k l m

cuckoo *noun* (cuckoos) A bird that makes the sound 'cuckoo'.

cucumber *noun* (cucumbers) A vegetable used in salads.

cud *noun* The food which a cow brings up from its first stomach to chew again.

cuddle *verb* (cuddles, cuddling, cuddled) To hold someone closely and lovingly in your arms. **cuddly** *adjective*.

cudgel *noun* (cudgels) A short thick stick used as a weapon.

cue *noun* (cues) **1** A signal for an actor to say or do something. **2** A long stick used in snooker and billiards.

cuff[1] *verb* (cuffs, cuffing, cuffed) To slap, to hit with the hand.

cuff[2] *noun* (cuffs) The wrist end of a sleeve.

cul-de-sac *noun* A street you can enter or leave at one end only.

cull *verb* (culls, culling, culled) To pick out and kill certain animals from a flock or herd in order to control numbers.

culprit *noun* (culprits) A person who has done wrong.

cult *noun* (cults) A religion.

cultivate *verb* (cultivates, cultivating, cultivated) **1** To prepare the soil and grow crops. **cultivator** *noun*. **2** To try to make something grow or develop. *to cultivate a friendship.* **cultivated** having good manners and education. **cultivation** *noun*.

culture *noun* **1** Enjoyment of art, music, literature, science, and other forms of knowledge. **2** The traditions and ways of a particular group of people. *West Indian culture.* **cultural** *adjective*.

cultured *adjective* Well educated.

cumbersome *adjective* Heavy and awkward.

cunning *adjective* **1** Clever at deceiving others. **2** Skilful.

cup *noun* (cups) **1** A bowl with a handle, for drinking from. **2** A gold or silver bowl given as a prize or trophy.

cupboard *noun* (cupboards) A piece of furniture or a part of a room fitted with shelves and doors.

cup-tie *noun* (cup-ties) A match to decide which team goes on to the next round in a competition for a cup.

cur *noun* (curs) A worthless dog.

curate *noun* (curates) A minister who helps a vicar or rector.

curator *noun* (curators) A person in charge of a museum or art gallery.

curb *verb* (curbs, curbing, curbed) To keep something under control. *to curb your temper.*

curd *noun* (curds) A thick soft substance formed when milk goes sour.

curdle *verb* (curdles, curdling, curdled) To form into curds. **curdle a person's blood** to horrify him or her.

cure[1] *verb* (cures, curing, cured) **1** To bring somebody back to health. **2** To put an end to a problem. **3** To preserve food by smoking or salting it.

cure[2] *noun* (cures) **1** Curing, being cured. **2** A substance or treatment that cures someone.

curfew *noun* (curfews) An order that everybody must be indoors by a certain time.

curious *adjective* **1** Eager to learn about anything new. **2** Showing too much interest in other people's affairs. **3** Strange, unusual. **curiously** *adverb*, **curiosity** *noun*.

curl[1] *noun* (curls) A spiral or curved shape.

curl[2] *verb* (curls, curling, curled) To twist into a curl or curls. **curlers** *noun*.

curlew *noun* (curlews) A wading bird with a long curved bill.

curly *adjective* (curlier, curliest) Having curls.

currant *noun* (currants) **1** A small dried grape. **2** A small juicy fruit.

currency *noun* (currencies) Money.

current[1] *noun* (currents) **1** A stream of air or water. **2** The flow of electricity through a circuit.

current[2] *adjective* Happening at the present time. *current affairs.* **currently** *adverb*.

curriculum *noun* (curricula) A statement of what pupils are expected to learn, a course of study.

curry *noun* (curries) A hot-flavoured, spicy food.

curse[1] *noun* (curses) **1** A violent exclamation. **2** Words calling for destruction or injury to fall on a person or thing.

curse[2] *verb* (curses, cursing, cursed) To use a curse. **be cursed with** to suffer from.

cursor *noun* (cursors) A mark showing your position on a computer screen.

cursory *adjective* Hurried and careless.

curtail *verb* (curtails, curtailing, curtailed) To cut short. **curtailment** *noun*.

curtain *noun* (curtains) **1** A piece of cloth hung at a window or door. **2** The cloth screen across the front of a stage.

curtsy *verb* (curtsies, curtsying, curtsied) To make a respectful movement by bending the knees.

curve[1] *noun* (curves) A line which is not straight and which has no sharp angles.

curve[2] *verb* (curves, curving, curved) To move in a curve, to bend into a curve. **curvature** *noun*.

cushion *noun* (cushions) A bag filled with soft material for sitting on.

custard *noun* A sweet sauce eaten with fruit or puddings.

custodian *noun* (custodians) A keeper or guardian of something.

custody *noun* **in custody** under guard.

custom *noun* (customs) The usual way of doing things. *It is our custom to give presents on Christmas Day.* **customary** *adjective*.

customer *noun* (customers) A person who goes into a shop to buy something.

customs *noun* **1** Taxes which have to be paid on goods brought into a country. **2** The place where officials can examine your luggage when you come into a country.

cut[1] *verb* (cuts, cutting, cut) **1** To use a knife, axe, spade, or any other sharp instrument on something. *to cut string. to cut the grass.* **2** To make something by cutting. *to cut a channel.* **3** To make something smaller or shorter. *to cut someone's wages.* **4** To divide a pack of cards. **cut in** to overtake another car and then drive in front of it suddenly. **cut off** to stop, to interrupt.

cut[2] *noun* (cuts) **1** A small wound. **2** The result of cutting, damage caused by cutting. **short cut** a quicker way to somewhere.

cute *adjective* (cuter, cutest) **1** Quick and clever. **2** (informal) Attractive.

cutlass *noun* (cutlasses) A short sword with a wide curved blade.

cutlery *noun* Knives, forks, and spoons.

cutlet *noun* (cutlets) A thick slice of meat.

cut-price *adjective* At a reduced price.

cutter *noun* (cutters) **1** Someone or something that cuts. **2** A kind of sailing ship.

cutting *noun* (cuttings) **1** A steep-sided way cut through a hill for a road or railway. **2** Something cut out of a newspaper or magazine. **3** A piece cut off a plant and set in soil to grow.

cycle¹ *noun* (cycles) **1** A bicycle. **2** A series of events which keep on coming round in the same order. *the cycle of the seasons.*

cycle² *verb* (cycles, cycling, cycled) To ride on a bicycle. **cyclist** *noun*.

cyclone *noun* (cyclones) A violent windstorm.

cygnet *noun* (cygnets) A young swan.

cylinder *noun* (cylinders) **1** A tube-shaped thing. **2** Part of an engine in which a piston moves. **cylindrical** *adjective*.

cymbal *noun* (cymbals) A musical instrument, a brass plate which is struck against another cymbal or with a stick.

cypress *noun* (cypresses) An evergreen tree.

Dd
·····

D 500 in Roman numerals.

dab *verb* (dabs, dabbing, dabbed) To touch something lightly and quickly.

dabble *verb* (dabbles, dabbling, dabbled) **1** To splash something in and out of water. **2** To do something occasionally, usually as a hobby.

dachshund *noun* (dachshunds) A small dog with a long body and short legs.

dad, daddy *nouns* (dads, daddies) (informal) Father.

daddy-long-legs *noun* An insect with very long legs.

daffodil *noun* (daffodils) A yellow flower.

dagger *noun* (daggers) A knife used as a weapon.

daily *adjective and adverb* Happening every day, done every day.

dainty *adjective* (daintier, daintiest) Pretty, neat, and delicate. **daintily** *adverb*.

dairy *noun* (dairies) A place where milk and milk products such as butter and cheese are produced or sold.

daisy *noun* (daisies) A small flower.

dale *noun* (dales) A valley.

dally *verb* (dallies, dallying, dallied) To waste time.

Dalmatian *noun* (Dalmatians) A kind of spotted dog.

dam¹ *noun* (dams) A wall built across a river to hold back the water and make a reservoir.

dam² *verb* (dams, damming, dammed) To make a dam across a river or a lake.

damage¹ *noun* The breaking or spoiling of something. **damages** compensation for injury.

damage² *verb* (damages, damaging, damaged) To injure, to break, to spoil.

dame *noun* (dames) (old-fashioned or informal) A woman. **Dame** a woman's title corresponding to 'Sir'.

damn *verb* (damns, damning, damned) To condemn, to say that something is worthless or bad.

damp *adjective* (damper, dampest) Slightly wet, not quite dry. **dampness** *noun*.

dampen *verb* (dampens, dampening, dampened) To make a thing damp.

damsel *noun* (damsels) (old-fashioned) A girl.

damson *noun* (damsons) A small, sour plum.

dance¹ *verb* (dances, dancing, danced) **1** To move about to the rhythm of music. **2** To move in a lively way. *He danced for joy!* **dancer** *noun*.

dance² *noun* (dances) **1** A piece of music for dancing. **2** A special pattern of movements for dancing. **3** A party where dancing takes place.

dandelion *noun* (dandelions) A yellow wild flower.

dandruff *noun* Tiny white flakes of dead skin in the hair.

Dane *noun* (Danes) A Danish person.

danger *noun* (dangers) **1** The chance of being killed or injured. **2** Something which may cause misfortune or disaster. *The wreck is a danger to other ships.* **dangerous** *adjective*, **dangerously** *adverb*.

dangle *verb* (dangles, dangling, dangled) To hang or swing loosely.

Danish *adjective* Of Denmark, from Denmark.

dank *adjective* Unpleasantly damp.

dappled *adjective* Marked with patches of light and shade.

dare *verb* (dares, daring, dared) **1** To be brave enough or cheeky enough to do something. **2** To challenge someone to do something. *I dare you to hit me!*

daredevil *noun* (daredevils) Someone who does foolish and dangerous things.

dark *adjective* (darker, darkest) **1** With no light, with very little light. *a dark night.* **2** Nearly black. *dark hair.* **3** Having a deep, strong colour. *dark red.* **4** Secret. *Keep it dark!* **darkly** *adverb*, **darkness** *noun*.

darken *verb* (darkens, darkening, darkened) **1** To make something dark. **2** To become dark.

darling *noun* (darlings) Someone who is loved very much.

darn *verb* (darns, darning, darned) To mend a hole in clothing with crisscross stitches.

dart¹ *noun* (darts) A short arrow which is thrown in the game of darts.

dart² *verb* (darts, darting, darted) To move quickly and suddenly.

dartboard *noun* (dartboards) The target used in the game of darts.

dash¹ *verb* (dashes, dashing, dashed). **1** To throw something violently. *The ship was dashed against the rocks.* **2** To rush. *We dashed to catch the bus.*

dash² *noun* (dashes) **1** A sudden rush. *a dash to get out of the rain.* **2** A small quantity. *a dash of milk.* **3** The punctuation mark – .

data *noun* Facts, especially those used in a computer.

database *noun* (databases) A set of data organized for use in a computer.

date¹ *noun* (dates) **1** A way of naming a particular day or month or year. *The date of Alan's birthday is 10 August. 1066 is the date of the Battle of Hastings.* **2** A meeting, an engagement to go out with someone. **out of date** old-fashioned. **up to date** modern.

date² *noun* (dates) The small sweet brown fruit of a tree called the date-palm.

daughter *noun* (daughters) Someone's female child.

daunt *verb* (daunts, daunting, daunted) To discourage.

dawdle *verb* (dawdles, dawdling, dawdled) To be slow. **dawdler** *noun*.

dawn¹ *noun* (dawns) The first light of day.

dawn² *verb* (dawns, dawning, dawned) To begin to grow light. *It dawned on me*, it occurred to me.

day *noun* (days) **1** The period from sunrise to sunset. **2** A period of 24 hours. **3** A period of time. *the present day*.

daybreak *noun* Dawn.

day-dream *noun* (day-dreams) Idle and pleasant thoughts.

daylight *noun* Natural light during the day.

daze *noun* (dazes) **In a daze** dazed.

dazed *adjective* Bewildered, stunned.

dazzle *verb* (dazzles, dazzling, dazzled) To shine so brightly that people cannot see properly. *dazzling headlights*.

deacon *noun* (deacons) A kind of Christian minister, an official of a church. **deaconess** *noun*.

dead¹ *adjective* (deader, deadest) **1** Not living. **2** Not lively. *a dead party*. **3** Numb, without any feeling. *dead with cold*. **dead heat** the end of a race in which two or more runners finish exactly together.

dead² *adverb* Completely, suddenly. *She stopped dead*.

deaden *verb* (deadens, deadening, deadened) **deaden a pain** to make it less severe. **deaden noise** to make it less loud.

deadly *adjective* (deadlier, deadliest) Likely to cause death.

deaf *adjective* (deafer, deafest) Unable to hear properly. **deafness** *noun*.

deafen *verb* (deafens, deafening, deafened) To make so much noise that nothing else can be heard clearly.

deal¹ *verb* (deals, dealing, dealt) To give out, to distribute. *to deal cards*. **deal with** to be concerned with something, to manage or attend to it. **dealer** *noun*.

deal² *noun* (deals) A business agreement. **a great deal, a good deal** a large amount.

dean *noun* (deans) The senior minister in a cathedral.

dear *adjective* (dearer, dearest) **1** Loved. **2** The polite way of beginning a letter. *Dear Sir, Dear David*. **3** Expensive.

dearly *adverb* **1** At great cost. **2** Very much. *I should dearly like to come*.

death *noun* (deaths) The end of life, dying. **put to death** to kill.

deathly *adjective* Like death.

death's-head *noun* (death's-heads) A picture of a skull.

death-trap *noun* (death-traps) A very dangerous thing or place.

debate¹ *verb* (debates, debating, debated) **1** To have a sensible argument, to discuss something in public. **2** To think something over very carefully. *She debated whether to spend her money or save it*. **debatable** *adjective*.

debate² *noun* (debates) A discussion.

debris *noun* Scattered fragments, wreckage.

debt *noun* (debts) Money due to be paid to somebody, something owed to somebody. **debtor** *noun*.

début *noun* A person's first appearance in public.

decade *noun* (decades) A period of ten years.

decaffeinated *adjective* With the caffeine removed. *decaffeinated coffee*.

decapitate *verb* (decapitates, decapitating, decapitated) To cut off somebody's head. **decapitation** *noun*.

decathlon *noun* (decathlons) A series of ten athletic events. Competitors have to compete in all of them and the scores are added up.

decay¹ *verb* (decays, decaying, decayed) To go bad, to rot.

decay² *noun* The process of decaying.

deceased *adjective* Dead.

deceit *noun* Deceiving. **deceitful** *adjective*, **deceitfully** *adverb*, **deceitfulness** *noun*.

deceive verb (deceives, deceiving, deceived) To make somebody believe something that is not true.

December noun The last month of the year.

decent adjective 1 Modest. 2 (informal) Pleasant. **decently** adverb, **decency** noun.

deception noun (deceptions) A trick which deceives someone.

deceptive adjective Deceiving, misleading. **deceptively** adverb.

decide verb (decides, deciding, decided) To make up your mind about something, to make a choice.

deciduous adjective Losing its leaves in winter. a deciduous tree.

decimal adjective Using tens or tenths. **decimal currency** a system of money in which units are counted by tens. **decimal point** the dot in numbers like 2·5.

decipher verb (deciphers, deciphering, deciphered) To find the meaning of something badly written, or of something written in code.

decision noun (decisions) 1 Deciding. 2 What is decided.

decisive adjective 1 Deciding. a decisive battle, a battle that settles a war. 2 Able to decide. decisive people, people who are sure of what they want. **decisively** adverb, **decisiveness** noun.

deck noun (decks) One of the floors in a ship or bus.

deck-chair noun (deck-chairs) A kind of folding chair.

declare verb (declares, declaring, declared) 1 To make something known officially. to declare war. 2 To say something very definitely. 3 In cricket, to close an innings before the batsmen are all out. **declaration** noun.

decline verb (declines, declining, declined) 1 To refuse, to say no to something. 2 To become weaker, to become less.

decode verb (decodes, decoding, decoded) To work out the meaning of a message in code.

decompose verb (decomposes, decomposing, decomposed) To decay, to rot.

decorate verb (decorates, decorating, decorated) 1 To make something look more beautiful or colourful. 2 To improve a house with new paint or wall-paper. **decorator** noun. 3 To give someone a medal. He was decorated for bravery. **decorative** adjective, **decoratively** adverb, **decoration** noun.

decoy verb (decoys, decoying, decoyed) To tempt a person or an animal into a trap. **decoy** noun.

decrease[1] verb (decreases, decreasing, decreased) 1 To make something smaller or less. 2 To become smaller or less.

decrease[2] noun (decreases) A decreasing, the amount by which something decreases.

decree[1] noun (decrees) An official order.

decree[2] verb (decrees, decreeing, decreed) To make a decree.

decrepit adjective Old and worn out.

dedicated adjective Devoted. **dedication** noun.

deduct verb (deducts, deducting, deducted) To subtract a part of something.

deduction noun (deductions) 1 Something deducted. 2 Something worked out by reasoning.

deed noun (deeds) 1 An action, something which has been done. 2 A legal document.

deep adjective (deeper, deepest) 1 Going a long way down from the top. a deep hole. 2 Going a long way in from the front. a deep shelf. 3 Measuring from top to bottom or from front to back. one metre deep. 4 Requiring much thought. deep problems. 5 Dark and strong in colour. deep purple. 6 a deep note, a low note. **deeply** adverb.

deer *noun* (deer) A kind of wild animal. The male has horns called antlers.

deface *verb* (defaces, defacing, defaced) To spoil the surface of something.

defeat[1] *verb* (defeats, defeating, defeated) To conquer somebody, to win a victory over somebody.

defeat[2] *noun* (defeats) **1** Defeating someone. **2** Being defeated.

defect[1] *noun* (defects) A fault.

defect[2] *verb* (defects, defecting, defected) To go over and join the enemy. **defector** *noun*, **defection** *noun*.

defective *adjective* Faulty. **defectively** *adverb*.

defence *noun* (defences) **1** Defending. *He rushed to her defence*, he rushed to protect her. **2** A protection, something used for defending. **defensive** *adjective*, **defensively** *adverb*, **defenceless** *adjective*.

defend *verb* (defends, defending, defended) To guard, to protect, to speak on behalf of somebody.

defendant *noun* (defendants) A person accused of something in a court of law.

defer *verb* (defers, deferring, deferred) To put something off until later.

defiant *adjective* Defying. **defiantly** *adverb*, **defiance** *noun*.

deficient *adjective* Lacking. **deficiency** *noun*.

defile *verb* (defiles, defiling, defiled) To make a thing dirty. **defilement** *noun*.

define *verb* (defines, defining, defined) To explain exactly what something is, to explain what a word means. **definition** *noun*.

definite *adjective* Clear, certain. **definitely** *adverb*.

deforest *verb* (deforests, deforesting, deforested) To remove the trees from an area. **deforestation** *noun*.

deformed *adjective* Badly shaped, not naturally shaped. **deformity** *noun*.

defraud *verb* (defrauds, defrauding, defrauded) To cheat.

defrost *verb* (defrosts, defrosting, defrosted) To unfreeze, to remove ice and frost from something.

deft *adjective* Clever, skilful. **deftly** *adverb*.

defuse *verb* (defuses, defusing, defused) **1** To remove the fuse from a bomb. **2** To make something less dangerous.

defy *verb* (defies, defying, defied) **1** To resist boldly and openly. **2** To challenge. *I defy you to come any further.*

degenerate *verb* (degenerates, degenerating, degenerated) To become worse.

degree *noun* (degrees) **1** A unit for measuring angles. *There are 90 degrees (90°) in a right angle.* **2** A unit for measuring temperature. *Water boils at 100 degrees Celsius (100°C).* **3** An award given to someone who has passed an examination in a university or college. **by degrees** by stages, gradually.

dehydrated *adjective* Dried out, with all the water removed. **dehydration** *noun*.

de-ice *verb* (de-ices, de-icing, de-iced) To remove the ice from something.

deity *noun* (deities) A god.

dejected *adjective* Sad, gloomy. **dejectedly** *adverb*, **dejection** *noun*.

delay *verb* (delays, delaying, delayed) **1** To make someone or something late. **2** To put something off until later.

delete *verb* (deletes, deleting, deleted) To cross out. **deletion** *noun*.

deliberate *adjective* 1 Done on purpose. 2 Slow and careful. **deliberately** *adverb*, **deliberation** *noun*.

delicacy *noun* 1 Delicate quality. 2 (delicacies) A delicious food.

delicate *adjective* 1 Soft, tender, fine. *a delicate material*. 2 Easily damaged. *delicate machinery*. 3 Liable to become ill. *a delicate child*. 4 Needing great skill and care. *delicate work*. 5 Not strong, subtle. *a delicate flavour*. 6 Tactful. **delicately** *adverb*.

delicatessen *noun* (delicatessens) A shop which sells unusual foods, especially foreign foods.

delicious *adjective* Very good to eat. **deliciously** *adverb*.

delight¹ *verb* (delights, delighting, delighted) To give great pleasure to someone. **delight in** to enjoy.

delight² *noun* (delights) Pleasure, enjoyment. **delightful** *adjective*, **delightfully** *adverb*.

delinquent *noun* (delinquents) Someone who does wrong. **delinquency** *noun*.

delirious *adjective* 1 Wildly excited. 2 In a confused state of mind during an illness. **deliriously** *adverb*, **delirium** *noun*.

deliver *verb* (delivers, delivering, delivered) To take something to the place where it has to go. *to deliver a letter*. **deliver a baby** to help a mother at the birth of her child. **delivery** *noun*.

delta *noun* (deltas) The area between the branches of a river at its mouth.

delude *verb* (deludes, deluding, deluded) To deceive.

deluge *noun* (deluges) A great flood, violent rainfall.

delusion *noun* (delusions) A false idea or belief.

demand¹ *verb* (demands, demanding, demanded) To ask for something, especially in a forceful manner.

demand² *noun* (demands) 1 The act of demanding. 2 What is demanded. **in demand** asked for by many people.

demented *adjective* Mad. **dementedly** *adverb*.

demerara *noun* A kind of brown sugar.

demo *noun* (demos) A demonstration, a protest.

democracy *noun* (democracies) 1 A system of government by the people. 2 A country which is governed in this way. **democratic** *adjective*, **democratically** *adverb*, **democrat** *noun*.

demolish *verb* (demolishes, demolishing, demolished) To knock down. **demolition** *noun*.

demon *noun* (demons) A devil.

demonstrate *verb* (demonstrates, demonstrating, demonstrated) 1 To show. 2 To have a demonstration. **demonstrator** *noun*.

demonstration *noun* (demonstrations) 1 A display of how something should be done. 2 A public procession, a protest.

demonstrative *adjective* Showing your feelings.

demure *adjective* Quiet, modest. **demurely** *adverb*.

den *noun* (dens) 1 The home or hiding-place of a wild animal. 2 A private or secret place.

denial *noun* (denials) 1 A statement that something is not true. 2 A refusal.

denim *noun* A kind of cotton cloth. **denims** trousers or overalls made of this.

denomination *noun* (denominations) A branch of the Christian Church.

denounce *verb* (denounces, denouncing, denounced) To inform against someone. **denunciation** *noun*.

dense *adjective* (denser, densest) 1 Thick. *a dense fog*. 2 Packed close together. *a dense crowd*. 3 Stupid. *You are dense today!* **densely** *adverb*, **density** *noun*.

dent[1] *noun* (dents) A hollow made in a flat surface by hitting or pressing it.

dent[2] *verb* (dents, denting, dented) **1** To make a dent. **2** To become dented.

dental *adjective* Of the teeth. *a dental surgeon.*

dentist *noun* (dentists) A person who fills or removes bad teeth and fits artificial ones.

denture *noun* (dentures) A set of false teeth.

deny *verb* (denies, denying, denied) **1** To declare that something is not true. **2** To refuse.

deodorant *noun* (deodorants) Something that removes smells.

depart *verb* (departs, departing, departed) To go away, to leave. **departure** *noun*.

department *noun* (departments) A part of a big organization. **department store** a large shop which sells many kinds of goods. **departmental** *adjective*.

depend *verb* (depends, depending, depended) **depend on 1** To need, to rely on. **2** To be decided by. *Whether we buy it or not depends on the price.*

dependable *adjective* Reliable.

dependant *noun* (dependants) A person who depends on another.

dependent *adjective* Depending. **dependence** *noun*.

depict *verb* (depicts, depicting, depicted) **1** To paint, to draw, to show in a picture. **2** To describe.

deplorable *adjective* Regrettable. **deplorably** *adverb*.

deport *verb* (deports, deporting, deported) To send someone out of the country. **deportation** *noun*.

depose *verb* (deposes, deposing, deposed) To remove a monarch from the throne.

deposit[1] *verb* (deposits, depositing, deposited) **1** To put something down. **2** To pay money into a bank.

deposit[2] *noun* (deposits) **1** A first payment for something. **2** Money paid into a bank.

depot *noun* (depots) A base, a station. *a bus depot.*

depraved *adjective* Evil, bad. **depravity** *noun*.

depress *verb* (depresses, depressing, depressed) **1** To make somebody sad. **2** To press something down.

depression *noun* (depressions) **1** Low spirits. **2** An area of low air pressure which may bring rain. **3** A shallow hollow in the ground.

deprive *verb* (deprives, depriving, deprived) To take something away from somebody.

depth *noun* (depths) Measurement from top to bottom or from front to back. **in depth** thoroughly.

deputation *noun* (deputations) A small group of people representing others.

deputy *noun* (deputies) An official substitute for someone, an assistant. *a deputy sheriff.*

derail *verb* (derails, derailing, derailed) To cause a train to run off the rails. **derailment** *noun*.

deranged *adjective* Mad.

derelict *adjective* Abandoned, ruined.

derive *verb* (derives, deriving, derived) To obtain something from something else. **derivation** *noun*.

dermatitis *noun* A skin complaint.

derrick *noun* (derricks) **1** A type of crane as used for loading ships. **2** A device used to hold the drill when boring a well.

dervish *noun* (dervishes) A member of a Muslim religious group.

descant *noun* (descants) A tune sung or played above another tune. **descant recorder** a small recorder.

descend *verb* (descends, descending, descended) To come down, to go down. *They are descended from a French family*, their family has French origins. **descendant** *noun*, **descent** *noun*.

describe *verb* (describes, describing, described) To say what somebody or something is like. **descriptive** *adjective*, **descriptively** *adverb*, **description** *noun*.

desert¹ *noun* (deserts) A large area of very dry, often sandy, land. **desert island** an uninhabited island.

desert² *verb* (deserts, deserting, deserted) To abandon something or someone. *The soldiers deserted*, they left the army without permission. **deserter** *noun*, **desertion** *noun*.

deserts *noun* What someone deserves. *The thief got his just deserts.*

deserve *verb* (deserves, deserving, deserved) To be good enough or bad enough to receive something. *You deserve a prize.*

design¹ *noun* (designs) **1** A plan, a drawing which shows how something can be made. **2** A pattern. **3** The appearance of something when it is finished. *a smart design.*

design² *verb* (designs, designing, designed) To plan, to make a design.

designer¹ *noun* (designers) A person who designs things.

designer² *adjective* Made to look new and fashionable.

desire¹ *verb* (desires, desiring, desired) To want, to long for something. **desirable** *adjective*, **desirability** *noun*.

desire² *noun* (desires) A strong wish.

desk *noun* (desks) A piece of furniture for writing or reading at.

desktop *adjective* Made to stand on a table. **desktop publishing** preparing a book or magazine for publication on a computer.

desolate *adjective* Neglected, unhappy. **desolately** *adverb*, **desolation** *noun*.

despair¹ *noun* Hopelessness.

despair² *verb* (despairs, despairing, despaired) To lose hope.

desperate *adjective* **1** Without hope, in despair. **2** Very serious. *a desperate situation.* **3** Violent, dangerous. *a desperate criminal.* **desperately** *adverb*, **desperation** *noun*.

despise *verb* (despises, despising, despised) To have a very low opinion of someone or something, to regard as worthless. **despicable** *adjective*.

despite *preposition* In spite of.

despondent *adjective* Gloomy, unhappy. **despondently** *adverb*.

dessert *noun* Fruit served at the end of a meal.

dessert-spoon *noun* (dessert-spoons) A spoon used for eating puddings.

destination *noun* (destinations) The place to which someone or something is going.

destined *adjective* Intended, fated.

destiny *noun* Fate.

destitute *adjective* Without the necessities of life, very poor.

destroy *verb* (destroys, destroying, destroyed) To damage beyond repair. **destruction** *noun*.

destroyer *noun* (destroyers) A kind of warship.

destructive *adjective* Likely to cause damage. **destructively** *adverb*, **destructiveness** *noun*.

detach *verb* (detaches, detaching, detached) To unfasten and separate something. **detachable** *adjective*, **detachment** *noun*.

detached *adjective* **1** Separated. **detached house** one not joined to another. **2** Not taking sides, not involved.

detail *noun* (details) A small part of something, an item. *the details of something* all the facts about it.

detailed *adjective* Fully described.

detain *verb* (detains, detaining, detained) **1** To keep somebody waiting. **2** To keep somebody somewhere against his or her will.

detect *verb* (detects, detecting, detected) To discover. **detectable** *adjective*, **detector** *noun*, **detection** *noun*.

detective *noun* (detectives) A police officer who investigates crime.

detention *noun* Being kept in, temporary imprisonment.

deter *verb* (deters, deterring, deterred) To put somebody off from doing something.

detergent *noun* (detergents) A kind of washing powder or liquid.

deteriorate *verb* (deteriorates, deteriorating, deteriorated) To get worse. **deterioration** *noun*.

determined *adjective* Having made up your mind firmly. **determination** *noun*.

deterrent *noun* (deterrents) Something used to deter people.

detest *verb* (detest, detesting, detested) To hate. **detestable** *adjective*.

dethroned *adjective* Deposed.

detonate *verb* (detonates, detonating, detonated) To set off an explosion. **detonator** *noun*, **detonation** *noun*.

detour *noun* (detours) A roundabout route, a diversion.

deva *noun* One of the ancient Hindu gods.

devastate *verb* (devastates, devastating, devastated) To destroy a place, to make it uninhabitable. **devastation** *noun*.

develop *verb* (develops, developing, developed) **1** To become bigger or better or more important. **2** To make something bigger or better or more important. **develop a cold** to get a cold. **develop a film** to treat film with chemicals so that the pictures can be seen. **development** *noun*.

device *noun* (devices) An invention, something made for a particular purpose.

devil *noun* (devils) A wicked spirit. **The Devil** Satan, the enemy of God. **devilry** *noun*, **devilish** *adjective*.

devilment *noun* Mischief.

devious *adjective* **1** Indirect. **2** Rather dishonest.

devise *verb* (devises, devising, devised) To invent, to plan.

devoted *adjective* Loyal, loving, enthusiastic.

devotion *noun* Strong, deep love or loyalty.

devour *verb* (devours, devouring, devoured) To eat hungrily.

devout *adjective* Religious, sincere. **devoutly** *adverb*.

dew *noun* Tiny drops of water formed on cool surfaces out of doors during the night. **dewy** *adjective*.

dexterity *noun* Skill.

dhal *noun* An Indian food of curried lentils.

dharma *noun* (in Hinduism) Fate.

dhow *noun* (dhows) An Arab sailing ship.

diabetes *noun* A disease in which too much sugar is found in the blood. **diabetic** *noun and adjective*.

diabolical *adjective* Devilish. **diabolically** *adverb*.

diadem *noun* (diadems) A crown.

diagnose *verb* (diagnoses, diagnosing, diagnosed) To examine a patient and say what is wrong with him or her. **diagnostic** *adjective*, **diagnosis** *noun*.

diagonal *noun* (diagonals) A straight line across a square or oblong from one corner to the opposite one. **diagonally** *adverb*.

diagram *noun* (diagrams) A sketch or plan made to explain or illustrate something.

dial[1] *noun* (dials) The face of a clock or any similar-looking instrument.

dial[2] *verb* (dials, dialling, dialled) To

make a telephone call by pressing buttons or turning a dial.

dialect *noun* (dialects) The form of a language used by people living in a particular district. *a London dialect.*

dialogue *noun* (dialogues) A conversation, a discussion.

diameter *noun* (diameters) A line drawn from one side of a circle to the other passing through the centre.

diamond *noun* (diamonds) **1** A sparkling precious stone. **2** A shape which has four equal sides but which is not a square. **3** A playing card marked with ♦

diarrhoea *noun* An illness which makes a person go to the lavatory frequently.

diary *noun* (diaries) A book in which daily events are written down.

dice *noun* (dice) A small cube marked with dots (1 to 6) on the sides, used in various games.

dictate *verb* (dictates, dictating, dictated) To speak or read something aloud for somebody else to write down. **dictation** *noun.*

dictator *noun* (dictators) A ruler with absolute power. **dictatorial** *adjective,* **dictatorship** *noun.*

dictionary *noun* (dictionaries) A book that explains the meanings of words.

did *See* **do**

die *verb* (dies, dying, died) To cease to live, to come to an end. **die down, die away** to become weaker, to stop.

diesel *noun* (diesels) A kind of engine which uses oil as fuel.

diet *noun* (diets) **1** The food someone normally eats. **2** The food someone

has to eat for medical reasons or to lose weight.

differ *verb* (differs, differing, differed) **1** To be different. **2** To disagree.

difference *noun* (differences) **1** Being different. **2** The amount by which something is different. **3** A quarrel.

different *adjective* Unlike, not the same. **differently** *adverb.*

difficult *adjective* **1** Hard to do, not easy. *difficult work.* **2** Hard to please. *a difficult person.* **difficulty** *noun.*

dig *verb* (digs, digging, dug) **1** To break up earth with a spade or fork. **2** To make something by removing earth. *to dig a trench.* **3** To poke. *to dig someone in the ribs.* **digger** *noun.*

digest *verb* (digests, digesting, digested) To soften and change food in the stomach so that the body can absorb its goodness. **digestible** *adjective,* **digestive** *adjective,* **digestion** *noun.*

digit *noun* (digits) **1** A finger or a toe. **2** Any of the numbers 0 to 9.

digital *adjective* Using digits. *a digital watch,* one showing the time in numbers only.

dignified *adjective* Calm, serious, stately.

dignity *noun* Calm and serious behaviour.

dike *noun* (dikes) **1** A large ditch. **2** An earth wall, often made to prevent flooding.

dilapidated *adjective* Broken down. **dilapidation** *noun.*

dilemma *noun* (dilemmas) *To be in a dilemma,* to have to make a difficult choice.

diligent *adjective* Hard-working, careful. **diligently** *adverb,* **diligence** *noun.*

dilute *verb* (dilutes, diluting, diluted) To make a liquid weaker or thinner by adding water. **dilution** *noun.*

dim *adjective* (dimmer, dimmest) Not bright. **dimly** *adverb,* **dimness** *noun.*

dimension *noun* (dimensions) Measurement, size.

diminish *verb* (diminishes, diminishing, diminished) To make or become smaller.

diminutive *adjective* Very small.

din *noun* (dins) A loud noise.

dine *verb* (dines, dining, dined) To have dinner.

ding-dong *noun* The sound of a bell.

dinghy *noun* (dinghies) A small open boat.

dingo *noun* (dingoes) An Australian wild dog.

dingy *adjective* (dingier, dingiest) Dirty and depressing. **dingily** *adverb*, **dinginess** *noun*.

dining-room *noun* (dining-rooms) A room where meals are eaten.

dinner *noun* (dinners) The main meal of the day.

dinosaur *noun* (dinosaurs) A prehistoric animal like a huge lizard.

diocese *noun* (dioceses) The area looked after by a bishop. **diocesan** *adjective*.

dip¹ *verb* (dips, dipping, dipped) **1** To lower something into a liquid. **2** To make lower. *Dip your headlights.* **3** To become lower. *The road dips into the valley.* **dip into a book** to read here and there in it. **dip into something** to put a hand or spoon in to take something out.

dip² *noun* (dips) **1** Dipping. **2** A quick swim. **3** A downward slope.

diphtheria *noun* A disease of the throat.

diploma *noun* (diplomas) A certificate awarded for passing certain examinations.

diplomat *noun* (diplomats) A person whose job is to try to keep friendly relations with other countries.

diplomatic *adjective* **1** Having to do with diplomats. **2** Tactful. **diplomatically** *adverb*, **diplomacy** *noun*.

dire *adjective* (direr, direst) Extremely serious.

direct¹ *adjective* **1** As straight as possible. **2** Straightforward, without deception or hesitation. *a direct manner.* **directly** *adverb*, **directness** *noun*.

direct² *verb* (directs, directing, directed) **1** To show somebody the way. **2** To aim, to turn something or someone a certain way. **3** To manage, to control. **director** *noun*, **direction** *noun*.

directory *noun* (directories) A list of names, with other details. *a telephone directory.*

dirge *noun* (dirges) A mournful song or tune.

dirt *noun* Mud, dust, anything unclean.

dirty *adjective* (dirtier, dirtiest) **1** Covered with dirt, not clean. *dirty shoes.* **2** Unpleasant, nasty. *dirty stories.* **3** Unfair. *dirty play.* **dirtily** *adverb*, **dirtiness** *noun*.

disable *verb* (disables, disabling, disabled) To make someone unable to do something, to cripple. **disability** *noun*.

disadvantage *noun* (disadvantages) A difficulty, something that hinders.

disagree *verb* (disagrees, disagreeing, disagreed) **1** To have different opinions about something. **2** To have a bad effect on. *Onions disagree with me.* **disagreement** *noun*.

disagreeable *adjective* Unpleasant. **disagreeably** *adverb*.

disappear *verb* (disappears, disappearing, disappeared) To move or fade out of sight. **disappearance** *noun*.

disappoint *verb* (disappoints, disappointing, disappointed) To make someone sad by not doing what they expected or by not being as good as they hoped. **disappointingly** *adverb*, **disappointment** *noun*.

disapprove *verb* (disapproves, disapproving, disapproved) To have a low opinion of someone or something. **disapproval** *noun*.

disarm *verb* (disarms, disarming, disarmed) **1** To take away someone's weapons. **2** To reduce the power or number of your weapons. **disarmament** *noun*.

disaster *noun* (disasters) **1** A serious accident, a great misfortune. **2** (informal) A complete failure. *The cake I made was a disaster.* **disastrous** *adjective*, **disastrously** *adverb*.

disbelieve *verb* (disbelieves, disbelieving, disbelieved) Not to believe. **disbelief** *noun*.

disc *noun* (discs) **1** Anything flat and circular in shape. **2** A gramophone record. **disc jockey** a person who introduces and plays records. **3** A disc (often spelt **disk**) on which computer programs and data can be stored. **disc drive** an apparatus that uses such a disc.

discard *verb* (discards, discarding, discarded) To throw something away.

discern *verb* (discerns, discerning, discerned) To see clearly, to understand. **discernment** *noun*.

discharge *verb* (discharges, discharging, discharged) **1** To send someone away, to release someone from service. **2** To send out a liquid or gas.

disciple *noun* (disciples) A follower. *the disciples of Jesus Christ.*

discipline *noun* Good, well-trained behaviour. **disciplined** *adjective*.

disclaim *verb* (disclaims, disclaiming, disclaimed) To say that you are not responsible for something.

disclose *verb* (discloses, disclosing, disclosed) To make known, to uncover. **disclosure** *noun*.

disco *noun* (discos) (informal) **1** A place for dancing to popular music played on records. **2** A party with dancing to such music, introduced by a disc jockey. **3** A type of pop music. **4** A style of dancing.

discolour *verb* (discolours, discolouring, discoloured) To stain, to spoil the colour of something.

discomfort *noun* Uneasiness, lack of comfort.

disconnect *verb* (disconnects, disconnecting, disconnected) To remove a connection.

disconsolate *adjective* Unhappy. **disconsolately** *adverb*.

discontented *adjective* Not contented. **discontentedly** *adverb*.

discontinue *verb* (discontinues, discontinuing, discontinued) To stop doing something.

discord *noun* **1** Disagreement. **2** (discords) A clash of sounds in music. **discordant** *adjective*.

discount *noun* (discounts) An amount by which a price is reduced.

discourage *verb* (discourages, discouraging, discouraged) **1** To take away someone's confidence and enthusiasm. **2** To try to persuade someone not to do something. **discouragement** *noun*.

discourteous *adjective* Rude. **discourteously** *adverb*.

discover *verb* (discovers, discovering, discovered) To find something, to make something known for the first time. **discoverer** *noun*, **discovery** *noun*.

discreet *adjective* Careful and tactful. **discreetly** *adverb*, **discretion** *noun*.

discriminate *verb* (discriminates, discriminating, discriminated) **1** To be aware of the differences between things. **2** To treat people differently because of their race or sex or age or religion. **discrimination** *noun*.

discus *noun* (discuses) A heavy disc thrown in athletic sports.

discuss *verb* (discusses, discussing, discussed) To talk with other people about something. **discussion** *noun*.

disdain *verb* (disdains, disdaining, disdained) To scorn.

disease *noun* (diseases) Illness, sickness. **diseased** *adjective*.

disembark *verb* (disembarks, disembarking, disembarked) To land goods or people from a ship, to come ashore.

disentangle *verb* (disentangles, disentangling, disentangled) To untie, to untwist.

disfigure *verb* (disfigures, disfiguring, disfigured) To spoil the appearance of something or someone. **disfigurement** *noun*.

disgrace¹ *noun* **1** Shame. **2** A person or thing that causes shame. **in disgrace** out of favour, disapproved of.

disgrace² *verb* (disgraces, disgracing, disgraced) To bring disgrace upon something or someone. **disgraceful** *adjective*, **disgracefully** *adverb*.

disgruntled *adjective* Bad-tempered.

disguise¹ *verb* (disguises, disguising, disguised) To change the appearance of someone or something in order to deceive.

disguise² *noun* (disguises) Something you put on to disguise yourself.

disgust¹ *noun* A strong feeling of dislike.

disgust² *verb* (disgusts, disgusting, disgusted) To cause disgust.

dish *noun* (dishes) **1** A plate or bowl from which you serve food. **2** The food brought to the table in a dish. **3** A kind of aerial for receiving broadcasts by satellite.

dishearten *verb* (disheartens, disheartening, disheartened) To discourage.

dishevelled *adjective* With untidy hair or clothes.

dishonest *adjective* Not honest. **dishonestly** *adverb*, **dishonesty** *noun*.

dishonour *noun* Shame, disgrace. **dishonourable** *adjective*.

dishwasher *noun* (dishwashers) A machine for washing dishes.

disillusion *noun* (disillusions, disillusioning, disillusioned) To make someone aware of the sad truth about something. **disillusionment** *noun*.

disinclined *adjective* Unwilling. **disinclination** *noun*.

disinfect *verb* (disinfects, disinfecting, disinfected) To make a thing free from germs. **disinfectant** *noun*.

disintegrate *verb* (disintegrates, disintegrating, disintegrated) To break up into small pieces. **disintegration** *noun*.

disinterested *adjective* Not biased.

disjointed *adjective* Broken up into parts, not orderly or logical.

disk *See* **disc**

dislike¹ *verb* (dislikes, disliking, disliked) Not to like something or somebody.

dislike² *noun* A feeling of not liking something or somebody.

dislocate *verb* (dislocates, dislocating, dislocated) To put something out of place or out of order. **dislocation** *noun*.

dislodge *verb* (dislodges, dislodging,

dislodged) To move something from its place.

disloyal *adjective* Not loyal. **disloyalty** *noun*.

dismal *adjective* Sad and gloomy. **dismally** *adverb*.

dismantle *verb* (dismantles, dismantling, dismantled) To take parts off something, to take it to pieces.

dismay [1] *noun* A feeling of fear and discouragement.

dismay [2] *verb* (dismays, dismaying, dismayed) To fill someone with dismay.

dismiss *verb* (dismisses, dismissing, dismissed) 1 To send someone away. 2 To cease to employ someone. 3 To get the batsman out in cricket. 4 To stop thinking about something. *We dismissed his absurd idea.* **dismissal** *noun*.

dismount *verb* (dismounts, dismounting, dismounted) To get off a bicycle or a horse.

disobey *verb* (disobeys, disobeying, disobeyed) To refuse to obey. **disobedient** *adjective*, **disobediently** *adverb*, **disobedience** *noun*.

disorder *noun* (disorders) 1 Confusion. 2 Rioting. 3 An illness.

disorderly *adverb* 1 Untidy. 2 Badly-behaved.

disorganize *verb* (disorganizes, disorganizing, disorganized) To upset the order or system, to throw into confusion. **disorganization** *noun*.

disown *verb* (disowns, disowning, disowned) To declare that someone or something has nothing to do with you.

disparaging *adjective* Uncomplimentary, rude.

dispatch [1] *verb* (dispatches, dispatching, dispatched). 1 To send something off somewhere. 2 To kill.

dispatch [2] *noun* (dispatches) A message, a report.

dispensary *noun* (dispensaries) A place where medicines are dispensed.

dispense *verb* (dispenses, dispensing, dispensed) To prepare and give out medicines. **dispenser** *noun*. **dispense with** to do without.

disperse *verb* (disperses, dispersing, dispersed) To scatter in different directions. **dispersal** *noun*.

display [1] *noun* (displays) 1 An exhibition, a show. 2 Something shown on a screen or panel.

display [2] *verb* (displays, displaying, displayed) 1 To show something publicly. 2 To show something on a screen or panel.

displease *verb* (displeases, displeasing, displeased) To annoy. **displeasure** *noun*.

disposable *adjective* Made to be thrown away after use.

disposal *noun* Getting rid of what you do not want. **at your disposal** for you to use. **bomb disposal** making bombs safe and removing them.

dispose *verb* (disposes, disposing, disposed) **dispose of** to get rid of. **disposed to** willing to.

disposition *noun* (dispositions) Character, state of mind. *a kind disposition*.

disprove *verb* (disproves, disproving, disproved) To show that something is not true.

dispute *verb* (disputes, disputing, disputed) To argue, to quarrel.

disqualify *verb* (disqualifies, disqualifying, disqualified) To declare that someone is no longer fit or qualified for something. *disqualified from driving*. **disqualification** *noun*.

disregard *verb* (disregards, disregarding, disregarded) To pay no attention to something.

disreputable *adjective* Not respectable.

disrespect *noun* Rudeness, lack of respect. **disrespectful** *adjective*.

disrupt *verb* (disrupts, disrupting, disrupted) To break up, to interrupt the flow of something. **disruption** *noun*.

dissatisfied adjective Not satisfied. **dissatisfaction** noun.

dissect verb (dissects, dissecting, dissected) To cut something into pieces in order to examine it. **dissection** noun.

dissimilar adjective Not similar.

dissolve verb (dissolves, dissolving, dissolved) 1 To mix something with a liquid so that it becomes liquid too. 2 To disappear, to fade away.

dissuade verb (dissuades, dissuading, dissuaded) To persuade someone not to do something. **dissuasion** noun.

distance noun (distances) The amount of space between two places. **within walking distance** near enough to walk to. **in the distance** far away.

distant adjective Far away. **distantly** adverb.

distaste noun Dislike. **distasteful** adjective.

distended adjective Swollen.

distil verb (distils, distilling, distilled) To purify a liquid by boiling it and condensing the steam. **distiller** noun, **distillation** noun.

distinct adjective 1 Easily heard or seen. 2 Clearly separate. **distinctly** adverb.

distinction noun (distinctions) 1 A difference. 2 Excellence, honour. 3 An award for excellence. **distinctive** adjective, **distinctively** adverb.

distinguish verb (distinguishes, distinguishing, distinguished) 1 To notice the differences between things. 2 To make out, to recognize. **distinguished** famous. *a distinguished poet.* **distinguishable** adjective.

distort verb (distorts, distorting, distorted) To twist something out of shape. **distortion** noun.

distract verb (distracts, distracting, distracted) To take someone's attention away from what he or she is doing. **distraction** noun.

distress[1] noun Severe pain, sorrow, or difficulty.

distress[2] verb (distresses, distressing, distressed) To cause distress.

distribute verb (distributes, distributing, distributed) To share out, to give out. **distributor** noun, **distribution** noun.

district noun (districts) A part of a country, an area.

distrust[1] noun Lack of trust.

distrust[2] verb (distrusts, distrusting, distrusted) Not to trust, to be suspicious of someone or something. **distrustful** adjective, **distrustfully** adverb.

disturb verb (disturbs, disturbing, disturbed) 1 To spoil someone's rest or quiet. 2 To cause worry. 3 To move something from its proper position. **disturbance** noun.

disused adjective No longer used.

ditch noun (ditches) A narrow trench or channel.

dither verb (dithers, dithering, dithered) To fuss about aimlessly.

ditto noun The same as the thing just mentioned.

divan noun (divans) A kind of bed.

dive verb (dives, diving, dived) 1 To go head first into water. 2 To move quickly downwards.

diver noun (divers) 1 A person who dives. 2 A person who works under water in a special suit called a diving-suit.

diverge verb (diverges, diverging, diverged) To go in different directions.

diverse adjective Varied. **diversity** noun.

divert verb (diverts, diverting, diverted) 1 To change the direction of something. *to divert traffic.* 2 To entertain, to amuse. **diversion** noun.

divide verb (divides, dividing, divided) 1 To separate into smaller parts. *Divide into teams.* 2 To share out. *Divide the sweets between you.* 3 In arithmetic, to find out how often one number is contained in another. *36 divided by 3 = 12.* **4** To keep things apart, to separate. *a dividing fence.* **divisible** *adjective,* **division** *noun.*

dividers *noun* A mathematical measuring instrument.

divine *adjective* **1** Belonging to God, from God. **2** Like a god. **divinely** *adverb,* **divinity** *noun.*

diviner *noun* (diviners) Someone who claims to be able to find hidden water or minerals with a stick called a divining rod.

diving-board *noun* (diving-boards) A board you dive from at a swimming pool.

divorce *verb* (divorces, divorcing, divorced) To end a marriage legally.

divorcee *noun* (divorcees) A divorced person.

divulge *verb* (divulges, divulging, divulged) To make something known to somebody.

Diwali *noun* A festival celebrated by Sikhs and Hindus in October or November.

DIY *abbreviation* Do it yourself.

dizzy *adjective* Confused, giddy. **dizzily** *adverb.*

DJ (DJs) A disc jockey.

do *verb* (does, doing, did, done) **1** This word is used in questions, and in statements with 'not'. *Do you want this? I do not like it.* **2** To perform an action. *Do your duty.* **3** To deal with something. *I'll do the potatoes.* **4** To be suitable for something, to be enough. *That's enough, that will do.* **to do with** concerned or connected with. *Have nothing to do with him,* do not work or play with him. **can (could) do with** to want, to need. *I could do with a wash.* **do away with** to get rid of. **do up** to fasten. **do without** to manage without something. **doer** *noun.*

docile *adjective* Easily controlled, obedient.

dock¹ *noun* (docks) **1** A place where

ships may be loaded, unloaded, or repaired. **dry dock** a dock which can be emptied of water. **docker** *noun.* **2** The place for an accused person in a court of law. **3** A kind of weed with broad leaves.

dock² *verb* (docks, docking, docked) **1** To come into dock. **2** To join two spacecraft together in orbit.

dockyard *noun* (dockyards) A group of docks and surrounding buildings.

doctor *noun* (doctors) A person trained to heal sick people.

document *noun* (documents) An important paper, an official record. **documentation** *noun.*

documentary *noun* (documentaries) A film showing people and events in real life.

dodder *verb* (dodders, doddering, doddered) To move unsteadily like a very old person. **dodderer** *noun.*

dodge¹ *verb* (dodges, dodging, dodged) To move about quickly keeping out of someone's way. **dodger** *noun.*

dodge² *noun* (dodges) (informal) A plan, a trick.

dodgem *noun* (dodgems) A small car at a fun-fair designed for bumping into others.

doe *noun* (does) A female deer, rabbit, or hare.

doer, does *See* **do**

doesn't (informal) Does not.

dog *noun* (dogs) An animal that barks, often kept as a pet.

dogged *adjective* Obstinate, persistent. **doggedly** *adverb.*

dole *noun* Money paid to an unemployed person. **on the dole** receiving money from the government while out of work.

doleful *adjective* Dreary, sad. **dolefully** *adverb.*

doll *noun* (dolls) A toy baby or person.

dollar *noun* (dollars) A unit of money in the USA and other countries.

dollop *noun* (dollops) A shapeless lump of something.

dolphin *noun* (dolphins) A sea animal like a small whale.

dome *noun* (domes) A rounded roof.

domestic *adjective* Connected with the home. **domestic animals** tame animals.

domesticated *adjective* **1** Fond of home. **2** Tamed.

dominant *adjective* Most important, outstanding, ruling.

dominate *verb* (dominates, dominating, dominated) To have a strong influence over people or things, to be dominant. **domination** *noun*.

domineering *adjective* Tyrannical, bossy.

domino *noun* (dominoes) A flat, oblong piece of wood or plastic with dots (1 to 6) or a blank space at each end, used in the game of dominoes.

donate *verb* (donates, donating, donated) To give. **donation** *noun*.

done *See* **do**

donkey *noun* (donkeys) An animal of the horse family that brays.

donor *noun* (donors) A giver. *a blood donor.*

don't (informal) Do not.

doodle *verb* (doodles, doodling, doodled) To scribble absent-mindedly.

doom *noun* Ruin, death, fate. **doomed** *adjective*.

door *noun* (doors) **1** A device which opens and closes to let people into and out of a building or room. **2** Any similar device. *a cupboard door.* **out of**

doors in the open air. **next door** in the next house or room.

doorway *noun* (doorways) An opening for a door.

dope *noun* (dopes) (informal) **1** A drug. **2** A stupid person.

dormant *adjective* Sleeping.

dormitory *noun* (dormitories) A room arranged for several people to sleep in.

dormouse *noun* (dormice) A small hibernating animal.

dorsal *adjective* On the back. *A shark has a dorsal fin.*

dose[1] *noun* (doses) An amount of medicine taken at one time.

dose[2] *verb* (doses, dosing, dosed) To give someone a dose.

dot[1] *noun* (dots) A small spot.

dot[2] *verb* (dots, dotting, dotted) To mark with dots. *a dotted line.*

dote *verb* (dotes, doting, doted) **dote on** to love somebody or something.

dotty *adjective* (dottier, dottiest) (informal) Slightly mad. **dottiness** *noun*.

double[1] *verb* (doubles, doubling, doubled) **1** To make something twice as big. **2** To become twice as big. **3** To bend something over in two. **double back** to go back the way you came.

double[2] *adjective and adverb* **1** Twice as much; twice as many. *to see double.* **2** Suitable for two. *a double bed.* **3** Having two of something. *a double-barrelled shotgun.*

double[3] *noun* (doubles) Someone who looks very like someone else.

double-bass *noun* (double-basses) A deep-sounding stringed instrument.

double-cross *verb* (double-crosses, double-crossing, doubled-crossed) To cheat and betray someone.

double-decker *noun* (double-deckers) A bus with two decks.

doubt[1] *noun* (doubts) A feeling of being

unsure. **doubtful** *adjective*, **doubt-fully** *adverb*, **doubtless** *adjective*.

doubt² *verb* (doubts, doubting, doubted) To be unsure about something, to question the truth of it.

dough *noun* **1** A thick mixture of flour and water for making bread, buns, or cake. **2** (informal) Money.

doughnut *noun* (doughnuts) A sugar-covered cake of fried dough.

dove *noun* (doves) A kind of bird that makes a cooing sound.

dovecote *noun* (dovecotes) A pigeon-house.

dowdy *adjective* (dowdier, dowdiest) Shabby, badly dressed. **dowdily** *adverb*, **dowdiness** *noun*.

down¹ *adverb* **1** From a higher to a lower part of something. *The rain came down heavily.* **2** To a place of rest. *He lay down.* **3** Along. *I walked down to the shop.* **4** As a first payment. *We paid £10 down.* **down on** disapproving of, unfair to.

down² *preposition* Downwards into, or along, or through. *down the drain.*

down³ *adjective* Sad, ill. *She's feeling down today.*

down⁴ *noun* Soft, fluffy feathers or hair. **downy** *adjective*.

downcast *adjective* Down-hearted.

downfall *noun* (downfalls) **1** A shower of rain. **2** Ruin, a cause of ruin. *Pride was his downfall.*

down-hearted *adjective* Sad, depressed.

downhill *adverb* Down a slope.

downpour *noun* (downpours) A heavy shower of rain.

downs *noun* Gentle, grass-covered hills.

downstairs *adjective and adverb* **1** To a lower floor in a building. **2** On a lower floor.

downtrodden *adjective* Badly treated, oppressed.

downward, downwards *adverbs* Towards a lower position.

dowry *noun* (dowries) Money or property which a father gives to his daughter when she marries.

doze¹ *verb* (dozes, dozing, dozed) To sleep lightly, to be half asleep.

doze² *noun* (dozes) A light sleep. **dozy** *adjective*, **doziness** *noun*.

dozen *noun* (dozens) **a dozen** twelve. **in dozens** in sets of twelve. **dozens of** a lot of.

Dr. A short way of writing Doctor.

drab *adjective* Dull, not colourful. **drabness** *noun*.

drag *verb* (drags, dragging, dragged) **1** To pull something along. **2** To move slowly or painfully. **3** To search under water with hooks and nets. *to drag a canal.*

dragon *noun* (dragons) A fire-breathing monster.

dragon-fly *noun* (dragon-flies) A large flying insect.

drain¹ *noun* (drains) A pipe or ditch for taking away water or sewage. **drainage** *noun*.

drain² *verb* (drains, draining, drained) **1** To take away water by means of drains. **2** To empty liquid out of a container. *He drained his glass.* **3** *Put the plates to drain*, leave them so that the water will run off them. **4** To exhaust. *He was drained of strength.*

drake *noun* (drakes) A male duck.

drama *noun* **1** Acting, improvising, the study of plays. **2** (dramas) A play. **dramatist** *noun* **3** Excitement, an exciting event. **dramatic** *adjective*, **dramatically** *adverb*.

drank *See* **drink¹**

drape *verb* (drapes, draping, draped) To

hang up cloth in folds over something.

drapes *noun* Curtains, draped material.

drastic *adjective* Having a violent effect. **drastically** *adverb*.

draught *noun* (draughts) A current of air indoors. **draughty** *adjective*.

draughts *noun* A game played with counters on a chess-board.

draw¹ *verb* (draws, drawing, drew, drawn) 1 To use a pencil, a piece of chalk, or something similar, to make a picture, diagram, or pattern. 2 To pull. *We drew the boat out of the water.* 3 To take out. *I drew £10 from the bank.* 4 To attract. *The circus drew large crowds.* 5 To end a game with neither side having won or lost. 6 To move, to come. *Christmas is drawing near.* **draw out** to make something longer. **draw up** to stop. *The taxi drew up at the gate.*

draw² *noun* (draws) 1 A game which neither side has won. 2 A raffle. 3 An attraction.

drawback *noun* (drawbacks) A disadvantage.

drawbridge *noun* (drawbridges) A bridge that can be raised when a castle is attacked.

drawer *noun* (drawers) A tray which slides in and out of a piece of furniture.

drawers *noun* Knickers.

drawing *noun* (drawings) Something

drawn with pencil, chalk, or something similar.

drawing-board *noun* (drawing-boards) A flat board to put paper on while you draw.

drawing-pin *noun* (drawing-pins) A short pin with a large flat top.

dread¹ *verb* (dreads, dreading, dreaded) To fear greatly.

dread² *noun* Great fear. **dreadful** *adjective*, **dreadfully** *adverb*.

dreadlocks *noun* Hair tied in many thin ringlets.

dream¹ *noun* (dreams) 1 Things a person seems to see while asleep. 2 A mental picture. *a dream of wealth and happiness.* **dreamy** *adjective*, **dreaminess** *noun*.

dream² *verb* (dreams, dreaming, dreamed) To have a dream.

dreary *adjective* (drearier, dreariest) Sad, depressing. **drearily** *adverb*, **dreariness** *noun*.

dredge *verb* (dredges, dredging, dredged) To bring mud or other things up from the bottom of the sea or a river, especially to keep a channel clear. **dredger** *noun*.

dregs *noun* The unwanted bits left at the bottom of a bottle or other container.

drench *verb* (drenches, drenching, drenched) To make something or somebody thoroughly wet.

dress¹ *noun* (dresses) 1 A woman's or girl's garment with a skirt, covering the whole of the body. 2 Clothing. 3 Costume. *national dress, fancy dress.* **dress rehearsal** the final rehearsal in which actors wear their costumes.

dress² *verb* (dresses, dressing, dressed) 1 To put clothes on. **dress up** to put on special clothes. 2 To prepare something, to get it ready. 3 To attend to a wound and put a dressing on it.

dressage *noun* Skilful horse control.

dresser *noun* (dressers) A piece of furniture with shelves for plates and dishes.

dressing *noun* (dressings) **1** A bandage or some other covering for a wound. **2** A kind of sauce. *salad dressing.*

dressing-gown *noun* (dressing-gowns) A gown which can be worn over night clothes.

drew *See* **draw**[1]

dribble *verb* (dribbles, dribbling, dribbled) **1** To allow saliva to trickle out of the side of the mouth as babies do. **2** In football, to take the ball forward with short kicks.

dried, drier *See* **dry**[2]

drier, driest *See* **dry**[1]

drift[1] *noun* (drifts) **1** A heap of snow or sand piled up by the wind. **2** The general meaning of something.

drift[2] *verb* (drifts, drifting, drifted) **1** To make drifts. *drifting snow.* **2** To be carried along by gently moving air or water. *a drifting ship.* **3** To move about aimlessly.

drift-wood *noun* Wood washed up on the beach.

drill[1] *noun* (drills) **1** A tool for boring holes. **2** Marching or other exercises done as part of a soldier's training.

drill[2] *verb* (drills, drilling, drilled) To make a hole with a drill.

drink[1] *verb* (drinks, drinking, drank, drunk) **1** To swallow any kind of liquid. **2** To drink alcoholic drinks. **drink up, drink in** to soak up greedily or with pleasure. **drinkable** *adjective,* **drinker** *noun.*

drink[2] *noun* (drinks) **1** A liquid for drinking. **2** An alcoholic drink.

drip[1] *verb* (drips, dripping, dripped) **1** To fall in drops. **2** To let liquid fall in drops. *a dripping tap.*

drip[2] *noun* (drips) A falling drop of liquid.

drip-dry *adjective* Made of a material that dries quickly and needs no ironing.

dripping *noun* Fat which comes from roasting meat.

drive[1] *verb* (drives, driving, drove, driven) **1** To force someone or something to move in a certain direction. *The wind drove the ship on the rocks.* **2** To be in charge of the controls of something. *She is learning to drive a car.* **3** To take someone for a ride in a car. *Dad drove me to the station.* **4** To go for a ride in a car or other vehicle. *We drove to the seaside.* **5** To make something work. *The toy is driven by batteries.* **6** To hit a ball in cricket, golf, or tennis.

drive[2] *noun* (drives) **1** A journey in a vehicle. **2** A stroke in cricket or golf. **3** A road, a road up to a house. **4** Energy, enthusiasm.

drivel *noun* Nonsense.

driver *noun* (drivers) A person who drives.

drizzle[1] *noun* Fine misty rain.

drizzle[2] *verb* (drizzles, drizzling, drizzled) To rain with fine misty drops.

dromedary *noun* (dromedaries) A camel with one hump.

drone[1] *noun* (drones) **1** A male bee. **2** A low humming sound.

drone[2] *verb* (drones, droning, droned) **1** To make a low humming sound like bees. **2** To talk in a boring voice.

droop *verb* (droops, drooping, drooped) To hang down wearily.

drop[1] *noun* **1** A small spot of a liquid, a tiny quantity of something. **2** A kind of sweet. *acid drops.* **3** A fall. *a drop in prices.*

drop[2] *verb* (drops, dropping, dropped) To fall, to let something fall, to make it fall. **drop in** to visit.

drought *noun* (droughts) A period of continuous dry weather, a water shortage.

drove *See* **drive**[1]

drown *verb* (drowns, drowning, drowned) **1** To die or to kill by suffocation under water. **2** To make such a loud noise that another sound can no longer be heard.

drowsy *adjective* Sleepy. **drowsily** *adverb*, **drowsiness** *noun*.

drudgery *noun* Hard, boring work.

drug[1] *noun* (drugs) **1** A substance which can be used to cure diseases or to kill pain. **2** A substance which can produce effects rather like being drunk. *a drug addict.*

drug[2] *verb* (drugs, drugging, drugged) To give drugs to someone.

Druid *noun* (Druids) A pagan priest in ancient Britain.

drum[1] *noun* (drums) **1** A percussion instrument. **2** A cylindrical container. *an oil drum.*

drum[2] *verb* (drums, drumming, drummed) **1** To play a drum. **drummer** *noun*. **2** To tap or thump something.

drumstick *noun* (drumsticks) **1** A stick used to beat a drum. **2** A chicken's leg for eating.

drunk 1 *See* **drink**[1]. **2** In a helpless state through drinking too much alcohol.

drunkard *noun* (drunkards) A person who is frequently drunk.

drunken *adjective* **drunken man** a man who is drunk, a drunkard.

dry[1] *adjective* (drier, driest) **1** Not wet, without any moisture. **2** (informal) Thirsty. **3** Dull. *a dry book.* **dry cleaning** a method of cleaning clothes which does not use water. **drily** *adverb*, **dryness** *noun*.

dry[2] *verb* (dries, drying, dried) **1** To make something dry. **2** To become dry. **drier** *noun*.

dual *adjective* Double. **dual carriageway** a wide road divided down the middle.

dubious *adjective* Doubtful. **dubiously** *adverb*.

duchess *noun* (duchesses) The wife of a duke.

duck[1] *noun* (ducks) A common waterbird. **make a duck** to score 0 in cricket.

duck[2] *verb* (ducks, ducking, ducked) **1** To go or push someone suddenly under water. **2** To bend down quickly to avoid being hit or seen.

duckling *noun* (ducklings) A baby duck.

dud *adjective* (informal) Useless.

due[1] *adjective* **1** Owing, to be paid. *The money for the outing is now due.* **2** Expected, planned to happen. *The train is due in 10 minutes.* **3** Right, suitable. *You should show due respect to your teachers.* **due to** caused by.

due[2] *noun* The respect owing to someone. *Give him his due.* **dues** fees.

due[3] *adverb* Exactly. *due east.*

duel *noun* (duels) A fight between two people.

duet *noun* (duets) A piece of music for two performers.

duffle coat (duffle coats) A coat with a hood made of a thick coarse cloth.

dug-out *noun* (dug-outs) **1** A canoe made by hollowing out a tree trunk. **2** An underground shelter.

duke *noun* (dukes) A nobleman of high rank, next below a prince.

dull *adjective* (duller, dullest) **1** Slow to understand, stupid. *a dull boy.* **2** Uninteresting. *a dull programme.* **3** Not bright, gloomy. *a dull day.* **4** Not sharp. *a dull pain.* **dully** *adverb*, **dullness** *noun*.

duly *adverb* Rightly, as expected.

dumb *adjective* Unable to speak, silent. **dumbly** *adverb*.

dumbfounded *adjective* Struck dumb with surprise.

dummy *noun* (dummies) **1** An imitation, something made to look like a person or an object. **2** A rubber teat for a baby to suck.

dump¹ *noun* (dumps) **1** A place where rubbish or unwanted things may be left. **2** A military stores depot. *an ammunition dump.*

dump² *verb* (dumps, dumping, dumped) **1** To put something on a dump. **2** To put something down carelessly and untidily.

dumpling *noun* (dumplings) A lump of boiled or baked dough.

dunce *noun* (dunces) Someone who is slow at learning.

dune *noun* (dunes) A low hill of loose sand.

dung *noun* Manure.

dungarees *noun* Overalls.

dungeon *noun* (dungeons) A dark underground prison.

dupe *verb* (dupes, duping, duped) To deceive.

duplicate¹ *noun* (duplicates) An exact copy.

duplicate² *verb* (duplicates, duplicating, duplicated) To make a duplicate, to make copies. **duplicator, duplication** *nouns.*

durable *adjective* Lasting. **durability** *noun.*

duration *noun* The time something lasts.

during *preposition* **1** Throughout. *The sun shone during the whole match.* **2** At some moment in. *It happened during the night.*

dusk *noun* Dim evening light.

dust¹ *noun* Finely-powdered dry dirt.

dust² *verb* (dusts, dusting, dusted) **1** To clean away dust. **2** To sprinkle with dust or powder.

dustbin *noun* (dustbins) A container for household rubbish.

dustcart *noun* (dustcarts) A kind of lorry into which dustbins are emptied.

duster *noun* (dusters) A cloth used for dusting.

dustman *noun* (dustmen) A person who empties dustbins.

dusty *adjective* (dustier, dustiest) **1** Covered with dust. **2** Like dust.

Dutch *adjective* Of Holland, from Holland. **double Dutch** nonsense.

duty *noun* (duties) **1** What you must do, or ought to do. **dutiful** *adjective*, **dutifully** *adverb*. **2** What a person does as part of a job. **3** A kind of tax. *customs duty.*

duvet *noun* (duvets) A warm cover for a bed, filled with soft material.

dwarf¹ *noun* (dwarfs) A very small person or thing.

dwarf² *verb* (dwarfs, dwarfing, dwarfed) To make something look smaller.

dwell *verb* (dwells, dwelling, dwelt) To live somewhere. **dweller** *noun.*

dwelling *noun* (dwellings) A house or some other place to live in.

dwindle *verb* (dwindles, dwindling, dwindled) To get gradually smaller.

dye¹ *verb* (dyes, dyeing, dyed) To colour a material by soaking it in a special liquid.

dye² *noun* (dyes) A coloured substance used for dyeing material.

dying *See* **die**

dynamic *adjective* Energetic.

dynamite *noun* An explosive.

dynamo *noun* (dynamos) A machine for generating electricity.

dysentery *noun* A disease with severe diarrhoea.

dyslexic *adjective* Having unusual difficulty in reading and spelling. **dyslexia** *noun.*

Ee
• • • • •

each *adjective and pronoun* Every, every

a b c **d e** f g h i j k l m

one. *Jack and Jill love each other*, he loves her and she loves him.

eager *adjective* Showing or feeling great desire, keen. **eagerly** *adverb*, **eagerness** *noun*.

eagle *noun* (eagles) A large bird of prey.

ear *noun* (ears) The organ of the body with which we hear. **ear of corn** the cluster of grains at the top of the stalk.

earache *noun* An ache in the ear.

earl *noun* (earls) A nobleman of high rank.

early *adjective and adverb* (earlier, earliest) **1** Near the beginning of a period of time. *early in the day*. **2** Before the usual time, before the right time. *to go to bed early*. **earliness** *noun*.

earn *verb* (earns, earning, earned) To get something as a payment or reward for something you do. *I earn £4 a week delivering papers*.

earnest *adjective* Serious, determined. *in earnest*, not joking. **earnestly** *adverb*, **earnestness** *noun*.

earnings *noun* Wages, money earned.

earphone *noun* (earphones) A listening device fitting into or over the ear.

ear-ring *noun* (ear-rings) An ornament worn on the ear.

earshot *noun* Hearing distance. *within earshot*.

earth *noun* **1** The planet we live on. **earthly** *adjective*. **2** Ground, soil.

earthy *adjective*. **3** The hole where a fox or badger lives.

earthenware *noun* Pottery made of baked clay.

earthquake *noun* (earthquakes) A sudden violent shaking of the earth.

earthworm *noun* (earthworms) A worm which lives in the ground.

earwig *noun* (earwigs) An insect with pincers at the end of its body.

ease[1] *noun* **1** Freedom from pain or anxiety. **2** Rest, freedom from work.

ease[2] *verb* (eases, easing, eased) **1** To give ease to someone. *The drug eased her pain*. **2** To do something gradually and carefully. *The lame man eased himself into a chair*. **ease off** to become less severe.

easel *noun* (easels) A stand for a painting or a blackboard.

east[1] *noun* One of the points of the compass, the direction from which the sun rises.

east[2] *adjective and adverb* In or to the east. **east wind** wind blowing from the east.

Easter *noun* The day on which Christians celebrate Christ's rising from the dead.

easterly *adjective* To or from the east.

eastern *adjective* Of or in the east.

eastward *adjective and adverb* Towards the east. **eastwards** *adverb*.

easy *adjective* (easier, easiest) **1** Able to be done without trouble. **2** Free from pain or anxiety, comfortable. **easily** *adverb*, **easiness** *noun*.

easygoing *adjective* Not strict.

eat *verb* (eats, eating, ate, eaten) **1** To take food into the mouth and then swallow it. **2** To use up or destroy something a little at a time. *The river had eaten away the bank*. **eater** *noun*.

eatable *adjective* Fit to eat.

eaves *noun* The overhanging edges of a roof.

eavesdrop *verb* (eavesdrops, eavesdropping, eavesdropped) To listen secretly to a conversation. **eavesdropper** *noun*.

ebb[1] *noun* The going down of the tide.

ebb[2] *verb* (ebbs, ebbing, ebbed) To go down, to become less.

ebony *noun* A hard black wood.

EC *abbreviation* The European Community, a group of countries in Europe.

eccentric *adjective* Behaving oddly. **eccentricity** *noun*.

echo[1] *noun* (echoes) A sound which bounces back and is heard again.

echo[2] *verb* (echoes, echoing, echoed) **1** To send back an echo. *The walls echoed the sound*. **2** To cause echoes. *My shout echoed through the caves*.

éclair *noun* (éclairs) A cake of pastry with a chocolate top and cream inside.

eclipse[1] *noun* (eclipses) *an eclipse of the sun*, a time when the moon gets between the sun and the earth and blocks its light. *an eclipse of the moon*, a time when the earth's shadow falls on the moon.

eclipse[2] *verb* (eclipses, eclipsing, eclipsed) To cause an eclipse.

ecology *noun* The science which deals with living creatures in their surroundings. **ecological** *adjective*, **ecologist** *noun*.

economical *adjective* Careful in using money, avoiding waste. **economically** *adverb*.

economize *verb* (economizes, economizing, economized) To use less money or fewer things than before.

economy *noun* (economies) Careful use and control of money and resources.

ecstasy *noun* (ecstasies) An excited feeling of joy. **ecstatic** *adjective*.

ecu *noun* (ecus) A unit of money in the EC.

eddy *noun* (eddies) A circular movement of wind or water.

edge[1] *noun* **1** The sharp cutting part of a knife or other tool. **2** The place where something ends, the line which separates one thing from another. *the edge of a table*, *the edge of the sea*. **on edge** nervous.

edge[2] *verb* (edges, edging, edged) **1** To move slowly. **2** To make an edge.

edgeways *adverb* With the edge forwards or outwards.

edgy *adjective* Nervous, on edge.

edible *adjective* Fit to be eaten.

edifice *noun* (edifices) A building.

edit *verb* (edits, editing, edited) **1** To arrange or change parts of a book, film, or computer program. **2** To get a newspaper or magazine ready for publication. **editor** *noun*.

edition *noun* (editions) All the copies of a newspaper, magazine, or book issued at the same time.

editorial *noun* (editorials) An article written by the editor of a newspaper or magazine.

educate *verb* (educates, educating, educated) To teach, to train, to bring someone up. **educational** *adjective*, **educator**, **education** *nouns*.

eel *noun* (eels) A long, snake-like fish.

eerie *adjective* Strange, weird, frightening. **eerily** *adverb*.

effect *noun* (effects) **1** The result of something happening or being done. **2** A general impression. *a colourful effect*. **take effect** to produce results. **effective** *adjective*, **effectively** *adverb*.

effervescent *adjective* Giving off many little bubbles, fizzy. **effervescence** *noun*.

efficient *adjective* Competent, doing work well. **efficiently** *adverb*, **efficiency** *noun*.

effort *noun* (efforts) **1** Hard work, trying hard. **2** An attempt to do something.

effortless *adjective* Without hard work. **effortlessly** *adverb*.

egg[1] *noun* (eggs) **1** The round or oval object laid by a bird, insect, fish, or reptile in which her young begins its life. **2** A hen's egg used as food.

egg[2] *verb* (eggs, egging, egged) **egg on** to encourage.

eggshell *noun* (eggshells) The shell of an egg.

Egyptian *adjective* Of Egypt, from Egypt.

eiderdown *noun* (eiderdowns) A bed covering filled with feathers or other soft material.

eight (eights) The number 8. **eighth**.

eighteen The number 18. **eighteenth**.

eighty (eighties) The number 80. **eightieth**.

eisteddfod *noun* (eisteddfods) A Welsh musical festival.

either *adjective and pronoun* One of two people or things. *at either end*, at both ends.

eject *verb* (ejects, ejecting, ejected) To throw out. **ejector, ejection** *nouns*.

elaborate *adjective* Carefully planned, complicated, detailed. **elaborately** *adverb*.

elapse *verb* (elapses, elapsing, elapsed) To pass. *A long time elapsed before I saw her again.*

elastic *noun* A material which can stretch and go back to its original size afterwards. *an elastic band*.

elated *adjective* In high spirits. **elation** *noun*.

elbow *noun* (elbows) The joint in the middle of your arm.

elder[1] *adjective* Older.

elder[2] *noun* (elders) A small tree with black berries.

elderly *adjective* Rather old.

eldest *adjective* Oldest.

elect *verb* (elects, electing, elected) To choose.

election *noun* (elections) Choosing by voting. **elector** *noun*.

electric *adjective* **1** Producing electricity. *an electric battery*. **2** Using electricity as a source of power. *an electric train*. **3** Exciting. *an electric atmosphere*.

electrical *adjective* Worked by electricity, to do with electricity. **electrically** *adverb*.

electrician *noun* (electricians) A person trained to deal with electrical apparatus.

electricity *noun* A form of power or energy for lighting, heating, and working machinery, supplied by batteries or along wires from generators.

electrify *verb* (electrifies, electrifying, electrified) **1** To make or alter something so that it can be worked by electricity. *to electrify a railway*. **electrification** *noun*. **2** To excite, to thrill.

electrocute *verb* (electrocutes, electrocuting, electrocuted) To kill someone by means of electricity. **electrocution** *noun*.

electronic *adjective* **electronic devices** devices such as transistors or microprocessors which process and store electrical signals. Computers, TV sets, and automatic washing machines all use electronic devices.

electronics *noun* The science or industry concerned with the study or use of electronic devices.

elegant *adjective* Graceful, dignified, tasteful. **elegantly** *adverb*, **elegance** *noun*.

element *noun* (elements) **1** A substance which cannot be divided into simpler substances. **2** One of the parts of which something is made. *the elements of a subject*, the simplest parts of the subject which you learn first. **3** The coil of wire which gives out heat in an electric fire, kettle, or cooker. **the elements** the weather, especially bad weather.

elementary *adjective* Easy, simple, basic.

elephant *noun* (elephants) A large animal with a trunk.

elevate *verb* (elevates, elevating, elevated) To lift up. **elevator, elevation** *nouns.*

eleven (elevens) **1** The number 11. **2** A team in cricket, hockey, or association football. **eleventh**.

elf *noun* (elves) A small fairy.

eligible *adjective* Suitable, qualified. **eligibility** *noun*.

eliminate *verb* (eliminates, eliminating, eliminated) To remove someone or something. **elimination** *noun*.

Elizabethan *adjective* Belonging to the reign of Queen Elizabeth I.

elk *noun* (elks) A large North American deer.

ellipse *noun* (ellipses) An oval shape. **elliptical** *adjective*.

elm *noun* (elms) A tall tree with rough bark.

elongated *adjective* Lengthened.

elope *verb* (elopes, eloping, eloped) To run away from home with a lover. **elopement** *noun*.

eloquent *adjective* Speaking well and fluently. **eloquently** *adverb*, **eloquence** *noun*.

else *adverb* **1** Besides, as well. *Have you anything else to do?* **2** Otherwise. *Hurry, or else you'll be late.*

elsewhere *adverb* In another place, to another place.

elude *verb* (eludes, eluding, eluded) To avoid being caught by someone. **elusive** *adjective*.

elves *See* **elf**

emaciated *adjective* Thin, wasted away.

emancipate *verb* (emancipates, emancipating, emancipated) To set free. **emancipation** *noun*.

embankment *noun* (embankments) **1** A wall built to strengthen a river bank. **2** A bank made for a road or railway.

embark *verb* (embarks, embarking, embarked) To go on a ship, to start a sea voyage. **embarkation** *noun*. **embark on** to begin.

embarrass *verb* (embarrasses, embarrassing, embarrassed) To make someone feel awkward and self-conscious. **embarrassment** *noun*.

embassy *noun* (embassies) The place where an ambassador lives and works.

embedded *adjective* Firmly fixed in something.

embers *noun* Small pieces of smouldering material in a dying fire.

embittered *adjective* Made to feel bitter.

emblem *noun* (emblems) **1** A symbol. **2** A badge.

embrace *verb* (embraces, embracing, embraced) To hug, to put your arms lovingly round someone.

embroider *verb* (embroiders, embroidering, embroidered) To sew designs or pictures on cloth. **embroidery** *noun*.

embryo *noun* (embryos) A baby before it is born or a bird before it is hatched.

emerald *noun* (emeralds) A green jewel.

emerge *verb* (emerges, emerging, emerged) To come out, to appear.

emergency *noun* (emergencies) Sudden danger, a crisis.

emigrate *verb* (emigrates, emigrating, emigrated) To leave your own country and settle in another. **emigrant**, **emigration** *nouns*.

eminent *adjective* Famous, outstanding. *an eminent politician.*

emit *verb* (emits, emitting, emitted) To give out, to send out. *The engine emitted clouds of black smoke.* **emission** *noun*.

emotion *noun* (emotions) A feeling you have inside yourself, such as love, happiness, or hatred. **emotional** *adjective*, **emotionally** *adverb*.

emperor *noun* (emperors) A man who rules an empire.

emphasis *noun* (emphases) The emphasizing of something. **emphatic** *adjective*.

emphasize *verb* (emphasizes, emphasizing, emphasized) To show the special importance of something by saying it more loudly, by underlining it, or by other means.

empire *noun* (empires) A group of countries under one ruler.

employ *verb* (employs, employing, employed) **1** To pay someone to work for you. **2** To use. **employer**, **employment** *nouns*.

employee *noun* (employees) Someone who works for an employer.

empress *noun* (empresses) **1** The wife of an emperor. **2** A woman who rules an empire.

empties *noun* (informal) Empty bottles.

empty¹ *adjective* (emptier, emptiest) With nothing inside. **emptiness** *noun*.

empty² *verb* (empties, emptying, emptied) To make or become empty.

emu *noun* (emus) An Australian bird that cannot fly.

emulsion paint A kind of paint for walls and ceilings.

enable *verb* (enables, enabling, enabled) To make something possible for somebody.

enamel *noun* (enamels) **1** A coloured glass-like coating on metal. **2** A paint that dries with a hard, shiny surface.

enchant *verb* (enchants, enchanting, enchanted) **1** To charm, to delight. **2** To put a spell on somebody. **enchantment** *noun*.

encircle *verb* (encircles, encircling, encircled) To make a circle round.

enclose *verb* (encloses, enclosing, enclosed) **1** To shut something in, to put a wall or fence around it. **2** To put something into an envelope with a letter or card. *Auntie enclosed £5 with her birthday card.* **enclosure** *noun*.

encore *noun* (encores) An extra performance after the first has been applauded at a concert.

encounter¹ *noun* (encounters) An unexpected or unwelcome meeting.

encounter² *verb* (encounters, encountering, encountered) To have an encounter with someone or something.

encourage *verb* (encourages, encouraging, encouraged) To fill somebody with hope or confidence, to urge somebody on. **encouragement** *noun*.

encyclopaedia *noun* (encyclopaedias) A book of information on many different subjects.

end[1] *noun* (ends) **1** The point after which something no longer exists. *the end of a journey. the end of the world.* **2** The part near the end. *seats at the end of the row.* **3** The bit that is left after something has been used. *a cigarette end.* **4** A purpose. *for his own ends,* for his own purposes. **on end 1** Upright. *to stand something on its end.* **2** One after the other. *for days on end.*

end[2] *verb* (ends, ending, ended) **1** To come to an end. **2** To bring something to an end.

endanger *verb* (endangers, endangering, endangered) To cause danger to someone or something.

endearing *adjective* Causing love.

endeavour *verb* (endeavours, endeavouring, endeavoured) To try.

ending *noun* (endings) The end of something.

endless *adjective* Without an end. **endlessly** *adverb.*

endure *verb* (endures, enduring, endured) **1** To suffer or put up with something. **2** To last or continue. **endurable** *adjective,* **endurance** *noun.*

enemy *noun* (enemies) **1** Someone who hates and wishes to harm someone else. **the enemy** the opposing army or people in a war or conflict. **2** Something harmful. *Slugs are enemies to the gardener.*

energy *noun* **1** Strength and liveliness. **energetic** *adjective,* **energetically** *adverb.* **2** Something that animals and machines must have to enable them to do work. Food provides energy for animals, fuel provides it for machines.

enforce *verb* (enforces, enforcing, enforced) To force people to obey rules or laws. **enforcement** *noun.*

engage *verb* (engages, engaging, engaged) To put or come into a working position. *He engaged first gear.* **become engaged** to agree to get married. **be engaged in** to be busy doing something.

engagement *noun* (engagements) **1** An agreement between a man and woman that they will get married. **2** An appointment. **3** A battle.

engine *noun* (engines) **1** A machine which provides power. *a petrol engine.* **2** A railway locomotive.

engineer *noun* (engineers) A person who does engineering.

engineering *noun* The designing, building, and maintaining of machines, of constructions like roads and bridges, of electrical equipment, and so on.

English *adjective* Of England, from England. **Englishman, Englishwoman** *nouns.*

engrave *verb* (engraves, engraving, engraved) To cut pictures or writing on a metal, wood, or stone surface.

engulfed *adjective* Swallowed up.

enjoy *verb* (enjoys, enjoying, enjoyed) To take pleasure and delight in something. **enjoy yourself** to have a good time. **enjoyable** *adjective,* **enjoyment** *noun.*

enlarge *verb* (enlarges, enlarging, enlarged) To make a thing bigger.

enlargement *noun* (enlargements) A photograph printed larger than its negative.

enlist *verb* (enlists, enlisting, enlisted) To join one of the armed services.

enormous *adjective* Very large indeed. **enormously** *adverb.*

enough *adjective, noun, and adverb* As many or as much as necessary.

enquire *verb* (enquires, enquiring, enquired) To ask about something. **enquiry** *noun.*

enrage *verb* (enrages, enraging, enraged) To make someone very angry.

enrich *verb* (enriches, enriching, enriched) To make richer.

enrol *verb* (enrols, enrolling, enrolled) To enter a person's name on a list for something. **enrolment** *noun*.

ensemble *noun* (ensembles) A group of musicians. *a recorder ensemble*.

ensign *noun* (ensigns) A flag.

enslave *verb* (enslaves, enslaving, enslaved) To make someone a slave.

ensnare *verb* (ensnares, ensnaring, ensnared) To catch in a trap.

ensure *verb* (ensures, ensuring, ensured) To make certain.

entangle *verb* (entangles, entangling, entangled) To tangle up. **entanglement** *noun*.

enter *verb* (enters, entering, entered) **1** To go in, to come in. **2** To write something in a book. *Enter your names in the register.* **3** To become a competitor in a race, competition, or examination.

enterprise *noun* A spirit of adventure, willingness to try something difficult or risky.

enterprising *adjective* Showing enterprise.

entertain *verb* (entertains, entertaining, entertained) **1** To amuse someone, to give them enjoyment. **2** To have people as guests and give them food and drink. **entertainment** *noun*.

enthusiasm *noun* A strong and lively interest in something, keenness. **enthusiastic** *adjective*, **enthusiastically** *adverb*, **enthusiast** *noun*.

entice *verb* (entices, enticing, enticed) To tempt someone with something nice.

entire *adjective* Whole, complete, not broken. **entirely** *adverb*.

entitle *verb* (entitles, entitling, entitled) **1** To give you the right to something. *This coupon entitles you to a free gift.* **entitlement** *noun*. **2** To give

a title to something. *The book was entitled 'Heidi'.*

entrance[1] *noun* (entrances) **1** A way in. *Please pay at the entrance.* **2** Coming in. *We cheered the entrance of our team.*

entrance[2] *verb* (entrances, entrancing, entranced) To enchant.

entrant *noun* (entrants) Someone who enters a race, competition, or examination.

entreat *verb* (entreats, entreating, entreated) To ask very seriously.

entrust *verb* (entrusts, entrusting, entrusted) To give something to someone to look after. *I'm entrusting this money to you.*

entry *noun* (entries) **1** Entering. **2** A way in, an entrance.

entwine *verb* (entwines, entwining, entwined) To twist together.

envelop *verb* (envelops, enveloping, enveloped) To wrap something up.

envelope *noun* (envelopes) A paper wrapper with a flap such as is used to hold letters.

enviable *adjective* Liable to cause envy.

environment *noun* Our surroundings, the things around us which affect the way we live.

envy[1] *noun* A bitter feeling because of someone else's good fortune. **envious** *adjective*, **enviously** *adverb*.

envy[2] *verb* (envies, envying, envied) To feel envy.

epic *noun* (epics) **1** A heroic story. **2** A grand spectacular film.

epidemic *noun* (epidemics) A rapidly-spreading outbreak of illness.

epilepsy *noun* A disease causing fits. **epileptic** *adjective*.

epilogue *noun* (epilogues) Words spoken or written at the end of something.

episode *noun* (episodes) **1** One incident in a series of events. **2** One programme in a radio or television serial.

epistle *noun* (epistles) A letter, a written message. *the Epistles of St Paul*.

epitaph *noun* (epitaphs) The words written on a tomb.

equal[1] *adjective and noun* The same in number, size, or value. **equal to** capable of, able to do something. **equally** *adverb*.

equal[2] *verb* (equals, equalling, equalled) To be the same in number, size, or value. **equality** *noun*.

equalize *verb* (equalizes, equalizing, equalized) **1** To make equal. **2** To score the goal which makes the scores equal. **equalizer** *noun*.

equator *noun* An imaginary line round the earth half way between the North and South Poles. **equatorial** *adjective*.

equidistant *adjective* The same distance apart.

equilateral *adjective* With sides of equal length.

equilibrium *noun* Balance.

equip *verb* (equips, equipping, equipped) To provide someone or something with equipment.

equipment *noun* Things needed for a particular purpose. *deep-sea diving equipment*.

equivalent *adjective and noun* Equal in value or meaning. *'Merci' is the French equivalent of 'thank you'*.

era *noun* (eras) A period of history, an age.

eradicate *verb* (eradicates, eradicating, eradicated) To get rid of something completely.

erase *verb* (erases, erasing, erased) To rub out. **eraser** *noun*.

erect[1] *verb* (erects, erecting, erected) To build, to raise, to set up. **erection** *noun*.

erect[2] *adjective* Upright. **erectly** *adverb*.

erode *verb* (erodes, eroding, eroded) To wear away. **erosion** *noun*.

err *verb* (errs, erring, erred) To do wrong, to make mistakes.

errand *noun* (errands) A small job which a person is sent to do.

erratic *adjective* Not regular, liable to do unexpected things. **erratically** *adverb*.

error *noun* (errors) A mistake. **in error** by mistake.

erupt *verb* (erupts, erupting, erupted) To burst out. *The volcano erupted*, it poured out smoke and molten lava. **eruption** *noun*.

escalate *verb* (escalates, escalating, escalated) To become steadily greater or more serious.

escalator *noun* (escalators) A moving staircase.

escapade *noun* (escapades) A reckless or foolish adventure.

escape[1] *verb* (escapes, escaping, escaped) **1** To get out, to become free. **2** To avoid something. *to escape disaster*.

escape[2] *noun* (escapes) **1** The act of escaping. **2** A means of escaping. *a fire-escape*.

escort[1] *noun* (escorts) **1** A group of armed guards. **2** A companion, protector, or guard.

escort[2] *verb* (escorts, escorting, escorted) To act as an escort.

Eskimo *noun* (Eskimos) A member of a race living in the North American polar regions.

especially *adverb* Specially, particularly.

espionage *noun* Spying.

esplanade *noun* (esplanades) A promenade.

essay *noun* (essays) A short piece of writing on a subject.

essence *noun* (essences) **1** The essential part of something. **2** A concentrated flavouring.

essential *adjective* Absolutely necessary. **essentially** *adverb*.

essentials *noun* The essential things.

establish *verb* (establishes, establishing, established) To set something up, to get something generally accepted.

establishment *noun* (establishments) **1** The establishing of something. **2** A shop, office, or other place where business is carried out.

estate *noun* (estates) **1** An area of land on which houses, flats, or factories are built. *a housing estate.* **2** An area of land owned by one person. **3** A person's total possessions. *The dead man left his estate to his wife.* **estate agent** a person who arranges the buying and selling of houses and land. **estate car** a car with a van-shaped body and a door at the back.

esteemed *adjective* Highly valued.

estimate[1] *verb* (estimates, estimating, estimated) To guess, to calculate approximately. **estimation** *noun*.

estimate[2] *noun* (estimates) A guess or calculation.

estranged *adjective* No longer friendly or loving.

estuary *noun* (estuaries) A wide mouth of a river into which the tide flows.

etcetera (often shortened to **etc.**) And so on, and other things.

eternal *adjective* Never ending. **eternally** *adverb*.

eternity *noun* Time without end.

ethnic *adjective* Belonging to people of a particular race. *ethnic music.*

eucalyptus *noun* An Australian tree. It provides an oil which is used to treat colds.

Eurasian *adjective* (Eurasians) A person with one European parent and one Asian parent.

European *adjective* Of Europe, from Europe.

evacuate *verb* (evacuates, evacuating, evacuated) To move people out of an area. **evacuation** *noun*.

evacuee *noun* (evacuees) Someone who is evacuated in a war.

evade *verb* (evades, evading, evaded) To avoid. *He was fined for evading payment of his bus fare.* **evasion** *noun*, **evasive** *adjective*.

evangelist *noun* (evangelists) A preacher of Christianity. **evangelism** *noun*.

evaporate *verb* (evaporates, evaporating, evaporated). To change from liquid into steam or vapour, to dry up. **evaporated milk** thick unsweetened tinned milk. **evaporation** *noun*.

evasion, evasive See **evade**

eve *noun* (eves) The day before an important day. *Christmas Eve.*

even[1] *adverb* A word used for adding emphasis or showing surprise in such expressions as: *He was rude even to the headmaster. Even the teacher could not solve it.* **even if** although. **even so** nevertheless, in spite of this.

even[2] *adjective* **1** Smooth, flat. *even ground.* **2** Calm. *an even temper.* **3** Equal. *even scores.* **even number** a number that can be divided exactly by two. **evenly** *adverb*, **evenness** *noun*.

even[3] *verb* (evens, evening, evened) To make something smooth or equal.

evening *noun* (evenings) The time between the end of the afternoon and night.

event *noun* (events) **1** A happening, an occurrence of some importance. **2** A competition in an athletics programme.

eventually *adverb* Finally, at last.

ever *adverb* **1** At any time. *Nothing like that ever happens to me.* **2** Always. *ever faithful.* This word is also used for emphasis in expressions like: *He's ever so rich. Why ever not?*

evergreen *adjective* Having green leaves all the year round. *an evergreen tree.*

everlasting *adjective* Lasting for ever.

evermore *adverb* For all time.

every *adjective* Each. *Every child must go to school.* **everybody, everyone, everything** *pronouns.*

everyday *adjective* Ordinary.

everywhere *adverb* In all places.

evict *verb* (evicts, evicting, evicted) To make somebody move out of a house. **eviction** *noun.*

evidence *noun* Anything that gives you reason to believe something. **give evidence** to say what you know in a lawcourt.

evident *adjective* Plain, clear, obvious. **evidently** *adverb.*

evil[1] *adjective* Having or showing a bad character, immoral, wicked.

evil[2] *noun* (evils) An evil thing or quality.

evolution *noun* The process by which animals and plants are believed to have developed over many millions of years from very simple forms of life. **evolutionary** *adjective.*

evolve *verb* (evolves, evolving, evolved) To develop naturally and gradually.

ewe *noun* (ewes) A female sheep.

exact *adjective* Perfectly correct, accurate. **exactly** *adverb,* **exactness** *noun.*

exaggerate *verb* (exaggerates, exaggerating, exaggerated) To say that something is larger, better, worse, or in some other way more impressive than it really is. **exaggeration** *noun.*

exam *noun* (exams) (informal) An examination.

examination *noun* (examinations) **1** A test of your knowledge or skill. **2** A close inspection. *An examination of the wreckage revealed the cause of the crash.*

examine *verb* (examines, examining, examined) To give or make an examination. **examiner** *noun.*

example *noun* (examples) **1** Something which illustrates a general rule. **2** Something which shows what other similar things are like. *On Open Day we show examples of our work.* **set an example** to behave in a way which others ought to copy. **make an example of** to punish someone as a warning to others.

exasperate *verb* (exasperates, exasperating, exasperated) To irritate someone, to make someone angry. **exasperation** *noun.*

excavate *verb* (excavates, excavating, excavated) To dig out, to unearth. **excavator, excavation** *nouns.*

exceed *verb* (exceeds, exceeding, exceeded) **1** To be greater than something. **2** To do more than. *to exceed the speed limit.*

exceedingly *adverb* Very much, extremely.

excel *verb* (excels, excelling, excelled) To be very good at something.

excellent *adjective* Very good. **excellently** *adverb,* **excellence** *noun.*

except *preposition* Not including, with the exception of. *Everyone was ill except me!*

exception *noun* (exceptions) Someone or something that does not follow a general rule. **take exception to** to object to something.

exceptional *adjective* Unusual. **exceptionally** *adverb.*

excerpt *noun* (excerpts) A piece taken from a book, play, or film.

excess *adjective* Extra, too much.

excessive *adjective* Too great, more than necessary. **excessively** *adverb.*

exchange *verb* (exchanges, exchanging, exchanged) To give one thing and get another thing for it. **exchange** *noun*.

excite *verb* (excites, exciting, excited) To stir up somebody's feelings, to make somebody or something more lively and active. **excitable** *adjective*, **excitability, excitement** *nouns*.

exclaim *verb* (exclaims, exclaiming, exclaimed) To shout out. **exclamation** *noun*.

exclamation mark The punctuation mark !

exclude *verb* (excludes, excluding, excluded) **1** To keep out. **2** To consider something as not being part of the whole. *There are 32 of us, excluding the driver.* **exclusive** *adjective*, **exclusion** *noun*.

excrete *verb* (excretes, excreting, excreted) To pass waste matter out of the body. **excrement** *noun*.

excruciating *adjective* Very painful. **excruciatingly** *adverb*.

excursion *noun* (excursions) An outing.

excuse¹ *noun* (excuses) A reason you give to explain why you did something wrong.

excuse² *verb* (excuses, excusing, excused) **1** To allow somebody not to do something. *He was excused from swimming because of his cold.* **2** To say that somebody is not to be blamed for something. **excusable** *adjective*, **excusably** *adverb*.

execute *verb* (executes, executing, executed) **1** To carry something out. *We executed our orders.* **2** To kill somebody officially as a punishment. **executioner, execution** *nouns*.

executive *noun* (executives) A manager or other senior person in a business firm.

exercise¹ *noun* (exercises) Something you do to keep yourself fit or for practice or training. **take exercise** to do exercises to keep fit.

exercise² *verb* (exercises, exercising, exercised) **1** To do exercises. **exercise an animal** to make it do something active. **2** To use. *to exercise patience.*

exert *verb* (exerts, exerting, exerted) **exert yourself** to make an effort. **exertion** *noun*.

exhaust¹ *noun* **1** The fumes that are given out from an engine. **2** The pipe these fumes come out of.

exhaust² *verb* (exhausts, exhausting, exhausted) **1** To use something up completely. **2** To make somebody very tired. **exhaustion** *noun*.

exhaustive *adjective* Thorough.

exhibit¹ *verb* (exhibits, exhibiting, exhibited) To put something on show.

exhibit² *noun* (exhibits) Something which is put on show.

exhibition *noun* (exhibitions) A collection of things attractively arranged for people to look at.

exile¹ *verb* (exiles, exiling, exiled) To make someone live in exile.

exile² *noun* (exiles) A person who is in exile. **in exile** having to live away from your own country.

exist *verb* (exists, existing, existed) **1** To be, to be real, to have a form which people can know and understand. *Do ghosts exist?* **2** To keep going, to live. *You can't exist without food.* **existence** *noun*.

exit¹ *noun* (exits) A way out.

exit² *verb* He or she goes out.

exorbitant *adjective* Much too high. *exorbitant prices.*

exorcize *verb* (exorcizes, exorcizing, exorcized) To drive out evil spirits. **exorcist, exorcism** *nouns*.

expand *verb* (expands, expanding, expanded) **1** To become larger. **2** To make something larger. **expansion** *noun*.

expanse *noun* (expanses) A wide area.

expect *verb* (expects, expecting, expected) **1** To think that something ought to happen. *Dad expects us to be* good. **2** To think that someone will come or something will happen. *We're expecting visitors for tea. I expect it will rain.* **expecting a baby** pregnant. **expectant** *adjective*.

expedition *noun* (expeditions) A journey with a definite purpose.

expel *verb* (expels, expelling, expelled) To turn someone out, to send someone out by force. **expulsion** *noun*.

expenditure *noun* Spending.

expense *noun* (expenses) Cost. **expenses** money spent for a particular purpose. *holiday expenses.*

expensive *adjective* Costing a great deal of money. **expensively** *adverb*.

experience[1] *noun* (experiences) **1** Gaining knowledge or skill by doing and seeing things. **2** Something which happened to you which you remember for a particular reason. *a frightening experience.*

experience[2] *verb* (experiences, experiencing, experienced) To have something happen to you.

experienced *adjective* Skilled and knowledgeable.

experiment[1] *noun* (experiments) A test or trial made so that the results can be studied. **experimental** *adjective*, **experimentally** *adverb*.

experiment[2] *verb* (experiments, experimenting, experimented) To make an experiment.

expert[1] *adjective* Skilful, knowledgeable. **expertly** *adverb*.

expert[2] *noun* (experts) A person with special skill or training in something.

expire *verb* (expires, expiring, expired) **1** To come to an end. *Our TV licence expires next month.* **2** To die.

explain *verb* (explains, explaining, explained) To show the meaning of something, to say how or why something happens or is going to happen. **explanatory** *adjective*, **explanation** *noun*.

explode *verb* (explodes, exploding,

exploded) **1** To go off with a loud bang. **2** To set off an explosive.

exploit[1] *noun* (exploits) A bold, exciting adventure.

exploit[2] *verb* (exploits, exploiting, exploited) **1** To use something to the full. **2** To make selfish use of something or somebody. **exploitation** *noun*.

explore *verb* (explores, exploring, explored) To go through unknown areas in order to make discoveries. **explorer, exploration** *nouns*.

explosion *noun* (explosions) The exploding of something.

explosive[1] *noun* (explosives) A substance that will explode.

explosive[2] *adjective* Liable to explode. **explosively** *adverb*.

export[1] *noun* (exports) Something that is exported.

export[2] *verb* (exports, exporting, exported) To send goods abroad to be sold. **exporter** *noun*.

expose *verb* (exposes, exposing, exposed) To uncover, to let light fall on something. **exposure** *noun*.

express[1] *noun* (expresses) A fast train.

express[2] *verb* (expresses, expressing, expressed) To make something known by speech, writing, or actions. **express yourself** to say what you mean. **expressive** *adjective*.

expression *noun* (expressions) **1** A look on someone's face. **2** A word or a phrase. **with expression** in a way that shows the feeling or meaning of something. *She plays the piano with expression.* **expressionless** *adjective*.

expulsion See expel

exquisite *adjective* Very beautiful. **exquisitely** *adverb*.

extend *verb* (extends, extending, extended) **1** To lie or reach out at full length. **2** To make longer, to stretch out. **3** To offer. *We extend a warm welcome to all.*

extension *noun* (extensions) A part

added to make something longer or bigger.

extensive *adjective* Covering a large area. **extensively** *adverb*.

extent *noun* The distance something extends, its length or area. **to some extent** partly. **to a great extent** mostly, largely.

exterior *noun* (exteriors) The outside of something.

exterminate *verb* (exterminates, exterminating, exterminated) To destroy completely. **extermination** *noun*.

external *adjective* Outside. **externally** *adverb*.

extinct *adjective* **1** No longer in existence. *The dinosaur is extinct.* **2** No longer active. *an extinct volcano.*

extinguish *verb* (extinguishes, extinguishing, extinguished) To put out a fire or a light. **extinguisher** *noun*.

extra *adjective and adverb* Additional, more than usual.

extract¹ *verb* (extracts, extracting, extracted) To pull out, to take out. **extractor, extraction** *nouns*.

extract² *noun* (extracts) A short piece taken from a book, play, or film.

extraordinary *adjective* Remarkable, unusual. **extraordinarily** *adverb*.

extraterrestrial *adjective* Outside the earth and its atmosphere.

extravagant *adjective* Foolishly expensive, wasteful. **extravagantly** *adverb*, **extravagance** *noun*.

extreme¹ *adjective* **1** Farthest possible. *the extreme tip of the island.* **2** Not moderate, very strong, as much as possible. *extreme enthusiasm.*

extreme² *noun* (extremes) The furthest point of something. **extremes** opposites. *the extremes of heat and cold.* **in the extreme** very much.

extremely *adverb* Very.

exuberant *adjective* In high spirits, overflowing with life. **exuberantly** *adverb*, **exuberance** *noun*.

exult *verb* (exults, exulting, exulted) To rejoice, to triumph. **exultant** *adjective*, **exultantly** *adverb*, **exultation** *noun*.

eye¹ *noun* (eyes) **1** The organ of the body with which we see. **2** A small hole. *the eye of a needle.*

eye² *verb* (eyes, eyeing, eyed) To watch.

eyebrow *noun* (eyebrows) The curved line of hair growing above your eye.

eyelash *noun* (eyelashes) One of the short hairs which grow on an eyelid.

eyelid *noun* (eyelids) Either of the two coverings of skin that can move together to cover your eye.

eye-shadow *noun* Make-up for eyelids.

eyesight *noun* The power of seeing.

eyesore *noun* (eyesores) Something that is ugly to look at.

eyewitness *noun* (eyewitnesses) A person who actually saw the event he or she is describing.

eyrie *noun* (eyries) An eagle's nest.

Ff

fable *noun* (fables) A kind of short story with a moral, in which the characters are usually animals.

fabric *noun* (fabrics) Cloth, material.

fabulous *adjective* **1** Legendary, occurring in stories. *fabulous monsters.* **2** (informal) Wonderful. **fabulously** *adverb*.

face¹ *noun* (faces) **1** The front part of the head. **2** An expression on a person's face. *a straight face*, a serious expression. **3** The front surface of anything. *the face of a cliff.*

face² *verb* (faces, facing, faced) **1** To look in a certain direction, to have the front in a certain direction. *a house facing south.* **2** To look at something firmly or bravely. *to face danger.*

facetious *adjective* Trying to be funny. **facetiously** *adverb*.

fact *noun* (facts) Something that is known to be true. **factual** *adjective*.

factory *noun* (factories) A building where things are made by machinery.

fade *verb* (fades, fading, faded) **1** To lose colour or freshness. **2** To become fainter, to make fainter.

fag *noun* (fags) (informal) A cigarette.

Fahrenheit *adjective* Using a scale for measuring temperature with the freezing-point of water at 32 degrees and the boiling-point at 212 degrees.

fail *verb* (fails, failing, failed) **1** Not to do something you ought to do, or something you wanted to do. **2** Not to pass a test or examination. **3** To come to an end, to become weak or useless. *His strength failed.*

failing *noun* (failings) A fault, a weakness.

faint¹ *adjective* (fainter, faintest) **1** Weak, dim, not clear. *faint sounds. faint colours. faint shapes.* **2** Nearly unconscious, exhausted. *faint with hunger.* **faintly** *adverb*, **faintness** *noun*.

faint² *verb* (faints, fainting, fainted) To lose consciousness for a short time.

faint-hearted *adjective* Timid, cowardly.

fair¹ *noun* (fairs) **1** A group of outdoor entertainments such as roundabouts, stalls, and sideshows. **2** A market, bazaar, or exhibition.

fair² *adjective* (fairer, fairest) **1** Light in colour, blond. *fair hair.* **2** Honest, keeping to the rules. *a fair referee.* **3** Fairly, quite good. *a fair number.* **4** Favourable. *a fair wind.* **5** *a fair copy*, a neat, clean copy. **6** (old-fashioned) Beautiful. *a fair maiden.*

fairly *adverb* **1** Honestly, without cheating. **2** Moderately.

fairy *noun* (fairies) An imaginary creature who can do magic.

fairyland *noun* An imaginary country where fairies live.

fairy-tale *noun* (fairy-tales) A kind of folk tale including magical events.

faith *noun* (faiths) **1** Trust, strong belief. **2** A religion. *the Jewish faith.* **in good faith** sincerely, trustingly.

faithful *adjective* Loyal, true, reliable. **faithfully** *adverb*, **faithfulness** *noun*.

fake¹ *verb* (fakes, faking, faked) To make a copy of something valuable or interesting and pretend to others that it is real.

fake² *noun* (fakes) Something that is faked.

falcon *noun* (falcons) A kind of hawk. **falconer** *noun*, **falconry** *noun*.

fall¹ *verb* (falls, falling, fell, fallen) **1** To move downwards out of control, to come down. *Rain falls.* **2** To become lower. *The temperature falls at night.* **3** To be captured. *The city fell after a long siege.* **4** To die. *King Harold fell at the Battle of Hastings.* **5** To happen. *My birthday fell on a Sunday this year.* **fall back** to retreat. **fall behind** to fail to keep level. **fall ill** to become ill. **fall out** to quarrel. **fall through** not to happen.

fall² *noun* (falls) **1** The act of falling. **2** (American) Autumn. **falls** a waterfall.

fallacy *noun* (fallacies) A false idea.

fall-out *noun* Dangerous radioactive dust from a nuclear explosion.

false *adjective* **1** Not true, wrong. **2** Deceitful, treacherous. **3** Not genuine, not real. **falsely** *adverb*, **falseness** *noun*.

falsehood *noun* (falsehoods) A lie.

falter *verb* (falters, faltering, faltered) To move or speak in a hesitating manner.

fame *noun* **1** Being famous. **2** Reputation.

familiar *adjective* **1** Well known. Common. Friendly. **familiarly** *adverb*, **familiarity** *noun*.

family *noun* (families) **1** A parent or parents with a child or children. **2** A group of people who are closely related. **3** Any group of things or creatures which are in some way similar or related. **family planning** deciding how many babies to have and when to have them. **family tree** a diagram showing how people in a family are related.

famine *noun* (famines) A severe shortage of food.

famished *adjective* Very hungry.

famous *adjective* Well known, known to a lot of people.

fan[1] *noun* (fans) An enthusiastic supporter. *a football fan.* **fan club** an organized group of supporters.

fan[2] *noun* (fans) **1** A folding device for fanning yourself which can open out into a half circle. **2** A device for blowing air.

fan[3] *verb* (fans, fanning, fanned) **1** To send a draught of air on something. **fan out** to spread out like an open fan.

fanatic *noun* (fanatics) A person who is extremely enthusiastic about something. **fanatical** *adjective*, **fanatically** *adverb*.

fanciful *adjective* **1** Imagining things. **2** Unusual, imaginative.

fancy[1] *adjective* Decorated. *a fancy handkerchief.* **fancy dress** unusual clothes you sometimes wear for fun at a party.

fancy[2] *verb* (fancies, fancying, fancied) **1** To imagine. *I fancied I saw a ghost.* **2** To desire, to like the look of. *I fancy chicken for dinner.* **fancy yourself** to have a high opinion of yourself.

fancy[3] *noun* Imagination. **take a fancy to** to become fond of.

fanfare *noun* (fanfares) A short, loud burst of music on trumpets.

fang *noun* (fangs) A long sharp tooth.

fantastic *adjective* **1** Strange, unreal.

2 (informal) Wonderful. **fantastically** *adverb*.

fantasy *noun* (fantasies) Something imagined, something which is more like a dream than real life.

far[1] *adverb* **1** At or to a great distance. *Did you go far?* **2** Much, by a great amount. *That is far better.*

far[2] *adjective* (farther, farthest) Distant, remote. *the far horizon.* **the Far East** the countries of eastern Asia.

far-away *adjective* Distant, remote. *far-away places.*

farce *noun* (farces) A ridiculous comedy. **farcical** *adjective*.

fare *noun* (fares) The money paid by passengers who travel by public transport.

farewell Good-bye.

far-fetched *adjective* Hard to believe.

farm[1] *verb* (farms, farming, farmed) To look after a farm. **farmer, farming** *nouns*.

farm[2] *noun* (farms) An area of land used to grow crops, or to produce meat, milk, or eggs.

farmhouse *noun* (farmhouses) The house where a farmer lives.

farmyard *noun* (farmyards) The area round a farmhouse and its buildings.

farther, farthest *See* far[2]

farthing *noun* (farthings) A small old coin, a quarter of an old penny.

fascinate *verb* (fascinates, fascinating, fascinated) To charm, to be very attractive to someone. **fascination** *noun*.

fashion *noun* (fashions) **1** The way or style in which clothes or other things are made at a particular time. **fashionable** *adjective*, **fashionably** *adverb*. **2** A way of doing something. *Don't giggle in that silly fashion!*

fast[1] *adjective* (faster, fastest) **1** Quick. *a fast train. The clock is fast,* it is ahead of the proper time. **2** Fixed, not easy to remove. *fast colours.* **fast food** food that is prepared in advance so that it can be served quickly when needed. **fast** *adverb*.

fast² *verb* (fasts, fasting, fasted) To go without food.

fast³ *noun* (fasts) A period during which you eat no food.

fasten *verb* (fastens, fastening, fastened) To tie, to attach, to fix firmly. **fastener** *noun*.

fastidious *adjective* Choosing with very great care. **fastidiously** *adverb*.

fastwind *verb* (fastwinds, fastwinding, fastwound) To move a video or audio tape rapidly forwards.

fat¹ *noun* 1 The greasy, white substance in meat. 2 Any of the oily substances used in cooking, such as butter, margarine, and lard. **fatty** *adjective*.

fat² *adjective* (fatter, fattest) 1 Having too much flesh on the body. 2 Thick. 3 Oily, full of fat. **fatness** *noun*.

fatal *adjective* Causing death or disaster. **fatally** *adverb*.

fatality *noun* (fatalities) A death in an accident or in war.

fate *noun* 1 Something that is bound to happen. **fated** *adjective*. 2 Death or disaster. *What a terrible fate!*

father *noun* (fathers) A male parent.

fatherhood *noun* The state of being a father.

fatherly *adjective* Like a good father, kind.

fathom *noun* (fathoms) A unit for measuring the depth of water, 6 feet or nearly two metres.

fatigue *noun* Tiredness, weakness.

fatten *verb* (fattens, fattening, fattened) 1 To make fat. 2 To become fat.

fault *noun* (faults) A mistake, something which is not as it should be.

faultless *adjective* Without faults, perfect. **faultlessly** *adverb*.

faulty *adjective* Not in perfect condition, not working properly.

favour *noun* (favours) A kind deed. *to do someone a favour.* **be in favour of** to like something, to support it. **in my favour** to my advantage. **out of favour** unpopular. **favourable** *adjective*, **favourably** *adverb*.

favourite *adjective* Liked the best. **favouritism** *noun*.

fawn *noun* (fawns) 1 A young deer. 2 A light colour between yellow and brown.

fax *noun* A system which lets you put papers in a machine which sends signals by telephone or radio and prints identical papers at the other end.

fear¹ *noun* (fears) The feeling you have when you face danger or pain, being afraid. **fearful** *adjective*, **fearfully** *adverb*, **fearless** *adjective*, **fearlessly** *adverb*, **fearlessness** *noun*.

fear² *verb* (fears, fearing, feared) To feel fear.

fearsome *adjective* Frightful, dreadful.

feasible *adjective* Possible, able to be done.

feast *noun* (feasts) 1 A large meal for a number of people. 2 A religious anniversary.

feat *noun* (feats) A deed which requires courage, cleverness, or strength.

feather *noun* (feathers) One of the growths which cover a bird's skin.

feathery *adjective* Light and soft.

feature *noun* (features) 1 Any of the parts of the face, such as the eyes, nose, or chin. 2 An important or noticeable part of something. 3 A long or important film, television programme, or newspaper article.

February *noun* The second month of the year.

fee *noun* (fees) A payment, charge, or subscription.

feeble *adjective* (feebler, feeblest) Weak, not energetic. **feebly** *adverb*, **feebleness** *noun*.

feed *verb* (feeds, feeding, fed) 1 To give food to someone. *to feed a baby.* 2 To eat food. **3** To put something into a machine or container. *The results were fed into the computer.*

feel *verb* (feels, feeling, felt) **1** To touch. **2** To explore with the hands or fingers. *He felt his way round the dark room.* **3** To seem to the touch. *The cat's coat feels warm.* **4** To experience something. *She felt much pain.* **5** To think. *I feel that holidays should be longer.* **6** To have a certain feeling. *I feel happy*, I am aware of being happy. **7** *I feel like a cup of tea*, I should enjoy one.

feeler *noun* (feelers) A projecting part on the head of some insects, used for feeling with.

feeling *noun* (feelings) Something you are aware of in your mind or in your body. *a feeling of happiness*, *a feeling of pain*. **hurt someone's feelings** to offend or upset someone.

feet *See* **foot**

feign *verb* (feigns, feigning, feigned) To pretend.

fell¹ *See* **fall**¹

fell² *noun* (fells) Wild, hilly country in the north of England.

fell³ *verb* (fells, felling, felled) To cut down, to knock down.

fellow¹ *noun* (fellows) **1** (informal) A man or a boy. **2** A friend or companion.

fellow² *adjective* Of the same kind, belonging to the same group. *fellow travellers*.

fellowship *noun* A group that does things together.

felt¹ *See* **feel**

felt² *noun* A kind of thick woollen material. **felt-tipped pen** a pen with a stiff felt point.

female¹ *adjective* Of the sex which can give birth to babies or lay eggs.

female² *noun* (females) A female person or animal.

feminine *adjective* Belonging to women, suitable for women.

feminist *noun* (feminists) Someone who believes that women have the same rights as men. **feminism** *noun*.

fen *noun* (fens) An area of low, marshy ground.

fence¹ *noun* (fences) **1** A line of posts with wood or wire between them along the edge of a piece of ground. **2** A criminal who buys and sells stolen goods.

fence² *verb* (fences, fencing, fenced) **1** To put a fence round something. **2** To practise fighting with foils.

fend *verb* (fends, fending, fended) **fend off** to keep something away from you. **fend for yourself** to look after yourself.

fender *noun* (fenders) A low guard round a fireplace.

ferment *verb* (ferments, fermenting, fermented) To give off many tiny bubbles because of the action of substances such as yeast.

fern *noun* (ferns) A kind of plant, often with feathery leaves.

ferocious *adjective* Fierce, savage, cruel. **ferociously** *adverb*, **ferocity** *noun*.

ferret *noun* (ferrets) A small animal used for hunting rats and rabbits.

ferry¹ *verb* (ferries, ferrying, ferried) To carry people or goods across a river or channel.

ferry² *noun* (ferries) A ship or aircraft used for ferrying.

fertile *adjective* Fruitful, able to produce crops or babies. **fertility** *noun*.

fertilize *verb* (fertilizes, fertilizing, fertilized) To make fertile. **fertilizer** *noun*.

fervent *adjective* Very enthusiastic. **fervently** *adverb*, **fervour** *noun*.

fester *verb* (festers, festering, festered) To fill with poisonous pus. *a festering wound*.

festival *noun* (festivals) **1** A time when some event is celebrated. **2** A time when special exhibitions and entertainments are put on. **festive** *adjective*, **festivity** *noun*.

fetch *verb* (fetches, fetching, fetched) **1** To go for something and bring it back. **2** To be sold for a price. *How much would my watch fetch?*

fetching *adjective* Attractive, charming. **fetchingly** *adverb*.

fête *noun* (fêtes) A festival with side-shows, competitions, and entertainments.

fetters *noun* Prisoners' chains.

feud *noun* (feuds) A long-lasting quarrel.

fever *noun* (fevers) An illness with a high temperature and restlessness. **feverish** *adjective*, **feverishly** *adverb*.

few[1] *noun* **a few** some, a small number. **a good few, quite a few** a rather large number.

few[2] *adjective* (fewer, fewest) Not many.

fiancé *noun* (fiancés) A man engaged to be married.

fiancée *noun* (fiancées) A woman engaged to be married.

fiasco *noun* (fiascos) A complete failure.

fib[1] *noun* (fibs) (informal) A lie.

fib[2] *verb* (fibs, fibbing, fibbed) (informal) To tell a lie. **fibber** *noun*.

fibre *noun* **1** An essential part of our diet which encourages the intestines to work. **2** (fibres) A very thin thread. **3** A substance made up of very thin threads.

fibreglass *noun* A substance made from glass fibres.

fickle *adjective* Changeable.

fiction *noun* **1** Stories and novels. **fictional** *adjective*. **2** Something imagined or made up. **fictitious** *adjective*.

fiddle[1] *noun* (fiddles) A violin.

fiddle[2] *verb* (fiddles, fiddling, fiddled) **1** To play a fiddle. **2** To play with something with your fingers. **3** (informal) To cheat. **fiddler** *noun*.

fiddlesticks (informal) Nonsense.

fidelity *noun* Faithfulness.

fidget *verb* (fidgets, fidgeting, fidgeted) To move about nervously or restlessly.

field[1] *noun* (fields) **1** A piece of ground usually surrounded by a hedge or fence. *a corn field. a games field.* **2** A battlefield. **3** An area. **4** The runners in a race.

field[2] *verb* (fields, fielding, fielded) To catch or stop the ball in cricket and other games. **fielder, fieldsman** *nouns*.

field-glasses *noun* Binoculars for use out of doors.

fiend *noun* (fiends) A devil.

fierce *adjective* (fiercer, fiercest) Violent, cruel, angry. **fiercely** *adverb*, **fierceness** *noun*.

fiery *adjective* **1** Blazing, very hot, very red. **2** Easily becoming angry.

fifteen 1 The number 15. **fifteenth**. **2** (fifteens) A Rugby Union football team.

fifth *See* **five**

fifty (fifties) The number 50. **fiftieth**.

fifty-fifty (informal) **1** Half and half. **2** Shared equally.

fig *noun* (figs) A small soft pear-shaped fruit.

fight[1] *verb* (fights, fighting, fought) To try to hurt or destroy somebody who is trying to do the same to you.

fight[2] *noun* (fights) The act of fighting.

figure[1] *noun* (figures) **1** One of the signs we use to show how many. 3, 12, and 72 are all figures. **2** The shape of a person's body. **3** A diagram or illustration.

figure[2] *verb* (figures, figuring, figured) To work out, to calculate.

file *noun* (files) **1** A metal tool with a rough surface used for making things smooth. **2** A line of people one behind the other. *single file.* **3** A box or folder to keep papers in.

fill *verb* (fills, filling, filled) **1** To make something full. *to fill a hole.* **2** To become full. *The bath slowly filled.* **3** To block up. *The crowd filled the doorway.* **fill in a form** to write in all that is wanted. **fill out** to become larger or fatter, to make larger or fatter. **filling station** a place where petrol is sold.

fillet *noun* (fillets) A slice of meat or fish without bones.

filling *noun* (fillings) Something used to fill a hole or a gap.

film[1] *noun* (films) **1** A moving picture, such as those shown at cinemas. **2** The material used in a camera for taking photographs. **3** A very thin layer of something. *a film of oil on the water.* **filmy** *adjective.*

film[2] *verb* (films, filming, filmed) To make a moving picture.

filter[1] *noun* (filters) A device that removes dirt or other substances from liquid or smoke which passes through it.

filter[2] *verb* (filters, filtering, filtered) **1** To pass something through a filter. **2** To merge with another line of traffic at a road junction.

filth *noun* Disgusting dirt. **filthy** *adjective*, **filthily** *adverb*, **filthiness** *noun.*

fin *noun* (fins) **1** One of the parts of a fish's body used for swimming and steering. **2** A device shaped like a fin on an aircraft, rocket, or other machine.

final[1] *adjective* **1** At the end, coming last. *the final goal.* **2** Definite, unchangeable. *That's final!* **finally** *adverb*, **finality** *noun.*

final[2] *noun* (finals) The last race or game in a series. *the Cup Final.* **finalist** *noun.*

finance *noun* (finances) Money affairs. **financial** *adjective.*

finch *noun* (finches) A kind of small bird.

find *verb* (finds, finding, found) **1** To discover something, to come across it. **2** To know something from experience. *I find it pays to be honest.* **find out** to learn. **find someone out** to discover someone doing wrong. **find guilty** to declare that someone is guilty. **finder** *noun.*

fine[1] *noun* (fines) A sum of money which has to be paid as a punishment.

fine[2] *verb* (fines, fining, fined) To make someone pay a fine.

fine[3] *adjective* (finer, finest) **1** Of good quality, excellent. *fine weather*, bright weather without rain. **2** Very thin. *fine wire.* **3** In very tiny pieces. *fine sand.* **4** Delicate and beautiful. *fine embroidery.* **5** Pure. *fine gold.* **finely** *adverb.*

finery *noun* A smart, showy set of clothes.

finger[1] *noun* (fingers) **1** A part of the body at the end of the hand. **2** A narrow piece of anything. *fish fingers.*

finger[2] *verb* (fingers, fingering, fingered) To touch with the fingers.

finger-nail *noun* (finger-nails) The nail at the end of a finger.

fingerprint *noun* (fingerprints) The mark made by the tip of a person's finger.

finish[1] *verb* (finishes, finishing, finished) **1** To stop something, to bring it to an end. **2** To come to an end.

finish[2] *noun* The end, the final point.

Finn *noun* (Finns) A Finnish person.

Finnish *adjective* Of or from Finland.

fiord *noun* (fiords) A narrow inlet of the sea between high cliffs.

fir *noun* (firs) A kind of evergreen tree.

fir-cone *noun* (fir-cones) A cone growing on a fir-tree.

fire[1] *noun* (fires) **1** A mass of burning material. **2** Fuel used to provide heat. **3** An apparatus to be used to provide heat. **4** Shooting. **under fire** being shot at. **on fire** burning. **fire brigade** a team of people organized to fight fires.

fire[2] *verb* (fires, firing, fired) **1** To set something on fire. **2** To bake clay in a kiln or oven. **3** To shoot a bullet from a gun, to make it go off. **4** To dismiss someone from his or her job.

fire-alarm *noun* (fire-alarms) A warning sounded in case of fire.

firearms *noun* Small guns, rifles, and revolvers.

fire-engine *noun* (fire-engines) A vehicle used by a fire brigade.

fire-escape *noun* (fire-escapes) A ladder or extra stairs for use in case of fire.

fire-extinguisher *noun* (fire-extinguishers) An apparatus for putting out a fire.

fireman *noun* (firemen) **1** A member of a fire brigade. **2** The driver's assistant on a steam locomotive.

fireplace *noun* (fireplaces) A place for an indoor fire.

fireproof *adjective* Not damaged by fire or heat.

firework *noun* (fireworks) A device which burns attractively or noisily.

firm[1] *adjective* (firmer, firmest) Solid, fixed, steady. **firmly** *adverb*, **firmness** *noun*.

firm[2] *noun* (firms) A business. *My father works for a building firm.*

first[1] *adjective* Before all others, earliest, most important. **first aid** help given right away to an injured person. **first class**, **first rate** very good. **firstly** *adverb*.

first[2] *adverb* Before anything else.

first[3] *noun* A person or thing that comes first.

fish[1] *noun* (fish *or* fishes) A water animal which breathes with gills.

fish[2] *verb* (fishes, fishing, fished) To try to catch fish. **fisherman** *noun*.

fishing-rod *noun* (fishing-rods) A rod with a line and a hook for fishing.

fishmonger *noun* (fishmongers) A shopkeeper who sells fish.

fist *noun* (fists) A tightly closed hand.

fit[1] *adjective* (fitter, fittest) **1** Suitable, good enough. *Is this dress fit to wear?* **2** In good health, strong. *An athlete must be fit.* **fitness** *noun*. **3** Ready. *I'm so tired I'm fit to drop.*

fit[2] *verb* (fits, fitting, fitted) **1** To be the right size and shape. **2** To put something into place. *to fit new tyres.*

fit[3] *noun* The way something fits. *This is a good fit,* it is the right shape and size.

fit[4] *noun* (fits) **1** A sudden attack of illness causing violent movements or making a person unconscious. **2** An outburst. *a fit of coughing.*

fitting *adjective* Suitable. **fittingly** *adverb*.

five (fives) The number 5. **fifth.**

fiver *noun* (fivers) (informal) A five-pound note.

fix[1] *verb* (fixes, fixing, fixed) **1** To make something firm, to fasten it, to attach it. **2** To make something long-lasting or permanent. **3** To settle, to decide. *We've fixed a date for the party.* **4** To mend. *Can the garage fix the car?* **fix up** to arrange. **fix your eyes on** to look steadily at.

fix[2] *noun* A great difficulty. *to be in a fix.*

fixture *noun* (fixtures) A date fixed for a sports event such as a football match.

fizz *verb* (fizzes, fizzing, fizzed) To give off lots of little bubbles, to make a hissing, spluttering sound. **fizzy** *adjective*, **fizzily** *adverb*, **fizziness** *noun*.

fizzle *verb* (fizzles, fizzling, fizzled) To fizz. **fizzle out** (informal) to come to a feeble end.

flabby *adjective* (flabbier, flabbiest) Soft and feeble, not firm. **flabbily** *adverb*, **flabbiness** *noun*.

flag¹ *noun* (flags) A piece of cloth, often with a coloured pattern or design on it, used as a sign or signal.

flag² *verb* (flags, flagging, flagged) 1 To signal with a flag. 2 To become tired or weak.

flagship *noun* (flagships) The chief ship of a fleet, the admiral's ship.

flagstaff *noun* (flagstaffs) A pole from which a flag is flown.

flagstone *noun* (flagstones) A paving stone.

flak *noun* Anti-aircraft fire.

flake *noun* (flakes) A small, leaf-like piece of a substance. *soap-flakes. flakes of rust.* **flaky** *adjective*.

flame¹ *noun* (flames) A tongue of fire, a jet of burning gas.

flame² *verb* (flames, flaming, flamed) To give out flames, to burn.

flamingo *noun* (flamingos) A large, long-legged wading bird.

flan *noun* (flans) A kind of open tart.

flank *noun* (flanks) The side of something.

flannel *noun* (flannels) 1 A kind of soft cloth. 2 A piece of cloth used for washing yourself.

flap¹ *verb* (flaps, flapping, flapped) 1 To move a flat object up and down or from side to side. *The swan flapped its wings.* 2 To move like this. *The sail flapped in the breeze.*

flap² *noun* (flaps) A piece of material that hangs down from one edge, often to cover an opening. *the flap of an envelope.*

flare¹ *verb* (flares, flaring, flared) To burn with a bright, unsteady flame. **flare up** to become suddenly angry.

flare² *noun* (flares) A light or firework used as a signal.

flared *adjective* Widening gradually. *a flared skirt.*

flash¹ *noun* (flashes) A sudden short burst of flame or light. **in a flash** in an instant.

flash² *verb* (flashes, flashing, flashed) 1 To give out a flash or flashes. 2 To appear suddenly and disappear quickly. *The racing cars flashed past.*

flashy *adjective* Bright and gaudy. *a flashy tie.*

flask *noun* (flasks) A kind of bottle.

flat¹ *adjective* (flatter, flattest) 1 Smooth, having no lumps. *a flat surface.* 2 Horizontal, spread out. *flat on the floor.* 3 Dull, uninteresting, past its best.

flat² *adverb* 1 So as to be flat. *Lay it out flat.* 2 In music, below the right pitch. *Try not to sing flat!* 3 Exactly. *He finished in ten seconds flat.* **flat out** at top speed.

flat³ *noun* (flats) 1 Anything that is flat. 2 A set of rooms for living in, usually on one floor of a building. 3 The sign ♭ in music.

flatten *verb* (flattens, flattening, flattened) 1 To make flat. 2 To become flat.

flatter *verb* (flatters, flattering, flattered) 1 To praise someone more than he or she deserves. 2 To make someone seem better or more attractive than he or she really is. **flattery** *noun*.

flavour¹ *noun* (flavours) The taste of something.

flavour² *verb* (flavours, flavouring, flavoured) To give something a flavour.

flavouring *noun* (flavourings) Something added to food to alter its taste.

flaw *noun* (flaws) A weakness, a mistake, a crack.

flea *noun* (fleas) A small jumping insect that feeds on blood.

fledgeling *noun* (fledgelings) A young bird just ready to fly.

flee *verb* (flees, fleeing, fled) To run away.

fleece *noun* A sheep's woolly coat. **fleecy** *adjective*.

fleet *noun* (fleets) A number of ships, aircraft, or vehicles.

flesh *noun* The soft substances between the skin and bones of animals.

flew *See* **fly¹**

flex *noun* Insulated wire for electric current.

flexible *adjective* 1 Easy to bend. 2 Easy to change. **flexibility** *noun*.

flick *verb* (flicks, flicking, flicked) To hit something lightly but sharply.

flicker *verb* (flickers, flickering, flickered) To burn or shine unsteadily.

flight *noun* (flights) 1 Flying. 2 A journey in an aircraft. 3 A set of stairs. 4 An escape, running away.

flimsy *adjective* (flimsier, flimsiest) Thin, easily destroyed. **flimsily** *adverb*, **flimsiness** *noun*.

flinch *verb* (flinches, flinching, flinched) To make a sudden movement in fear.

fling *verb* (flings, flinging, flung) To throw something violently.

flint *noun* (flints) A kind of very hard stone.

flip *verb* (flips, flipping, flipped) To flick.

flipper *noun* (flippers) 1 A limb used by water animals for swimming. 2 A device you can wear on your foot to help you to swim.

flit *verb* (flits, flitting, flitted) To move quickly but quietly.

float¹ *verb* (floats, floating, floated) 1 To stay on the surface of a liquid or in the air. *Wood floats on water.* 2 To make something float.

float² *noun* (floats) 1 An object designed to float. *a fishing float.* 2 A kind of vehicle. *a milk-float.*

flock¹ *noun* (flocks) A large group of sheep or birds.

flock² *verb* (flocks, flocking, flocked) To gather or go in a large group.

floe *noun* (floes) A sheet of ice floating on the sea.

flog *verb* (flogs, flogging, flogged) To beat violently with a whip or a stick.

flood¹ *noun* (floods) 1 Water spreading over what is usually dry land. 2 A large quantity of anything.

flood² *verb* (floods, flooding, flooded) To cover with a flood, to fill too full.

floodlights *noun* Strong lamps used for lighting out of doors. **floodlit** *adjective*, **floodlighting** *noun*.

floor *noun* (floors) 1 The part of a building on which you walk. 2 All the rooms on one level in a building. *the ground floor, the first floor.*

flop *verb* (flops, flopping, flopped) 1 To drop down suddenly. 2 To droop.

floppy *adjective* (floppier, floppiest) Flexible, hanging loosely, not stiff. **floppy disc** a disc on which computer information is stored.

floral *adjective* Made of flowers.

florist *noun* (florists) A shopkeeper who sells flowers.

flounder *verb* (flounders, floundering, floundered) To struggle awkwardly and clumsily.

flour *noun* A fine white powder made from wheat, used to make bread and cakes.

flourish *verb* (flourishes, flourishing, flourished) **1** To grow strongly, to be successful. **2** To wave something about. *He flourished his sword threateningly*.

flow *verb* (flows, flowing, flowed) **1** To move along in a stream. **2** To hang loosely. *long flowing hair*.

flower[1] *noun* (flowers) **1** The part of a plant which usually has colourful petals. **2** A flowering plant. **flowery** *adjective*.

flower[2] *verb* (flowers, flowering, flowered) To produce flowers.

flown *See* **fly**[1]

flu *noun* Influenza.

fluent *adjective* Not hesitating, skilful at speaking. **fluently** *adverb*, **fluency** *noun*.

fluff *noun* Soft feathery or woolly stuff. **fluffy** *adjective*.

fluid *noun* (fluids) A substance that flows easily, as liquids and gases do.

fluke *noun* (flukes) (informal) A lucky accident.

flung *See* **fling**

fluorescent *adjective* Luminous.

fluoridation *noun* The addition of a chemical called fluoride to drinking water.

flush *verb* (flushes, flushing, flushed) **1** To wash out a lavatory or a drain with a flood of water. **2** To blush deeply.

flustered *adjective* Nervous and confused.

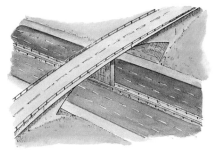

flute *noun* (flutes) A woodwind instrument played by blowing across a hole near the end.

flutter *verb* (flutters, fluttering, fluttered) To make quick flapping movements, to move restlessly.

fly[1] *verb* (flies, flying, flew, flown) **1** To go up in the air, to move along in the air, to be able to stay in the air. **2** To make something fly. *A pilot flies an aeroplane*. **3** To move very quickly. **4** To do something very suddenly. *He flew into a rage*. **5** To escape. **flyer** *noun*.

fly[2] *noun* (flies) A flying insect.

flyover *noun* (flyovers) A bridge carrying one road over another.

flywheel *noun* (flywheels) A heavy wheel used to regulate machinery.

foal *noun* (foals) A young horse.

foam[1] *noun* Froth. **foamy** *adjective*.

foam[2] *verb* (foams, foaming, foamed) To make foam, to bubble.

foam-rubber *noun* Spongy rubber.

fo'c'sle *See* **forecastle**

focus *verb* (focuses, focusing, focused) **1** To adjust the lens of a camera, projector, telescope, or similar instrument in order to get a clear, sharp picture. **2** To concentrate on something.

fodder *noun* Food for cattle or horses.

foe *noun* (foes) An enemy.

foetus *noun* (foetuses) An embryo.

fog *noun* (fogs) Thick mist. **foggy** *adjective*.

foil¹ *verb* (foils, foiling, foiled) To prevent.

foil² *noun* **1** (foils) A thin sword used in fencing. **2** A sheet of metal as thin as paper.

fold¹ *verb* (folds, folding, folded) To double over, to bend part of a thing back on itself. **fold your arms** to cross your arms in front of your body.

fold² *noun* (folds) **1** A line where something is folded. **2** An enclosure for sheep.

folder *noun* (folders) A cover for loose papers.

foliage *noun* Leaves on trees and plants.

folk *noun* People. **folk-dances, folk-songs, folk-tales** dances, songs, and tales handed down from long ago.

follow *verb* (follows, following, followed) **1** To come or go after someone or something. **follower** *noun*. **2** To take someone or something as a guide. *Follow this road.* **3** To understand. *Did you follow what I said?* **4** To take an interest in something, to support. *Which team do you follow?* **follow up** to continue with something and go on to the next stage.

folly *noun* Foolish behaviour.

fond *adjective* Loving. **be fond of** to like.

fondle *verb* (fondles, fondling, fondled) To touch lovingly.

fondly *adverb* **1** Lovingly. **2** Foolishly.

font *noun* (fonts) A basin on a stand to hold water for baptism in a church.

food *noun* (foods) Anything which a person, animal, or plant takes in to keep alive.

fool¹ *noun* (fools) **1** A stupid person. **2** A jester or clown.

fool² *verb* (fools, fooling, fooled) **1** To behave like a fool. **2** To trick or deceive someone.

foolish *adjective* Stupid, silly. **foolishly** *adverb*.

foolproof *adjective* So simple that even a fool cannot make a mistake.

foot *noun* (feet) **1** The part of the body on which people and animals walk. **2** The lowest part of anything. *the foot of a mountain.* **3** A measure of length, 12 inches or about 300 millimetres.

football *noun* A game played with a large, air-filled ball. **footballer** *noun*.

footlights *noun* A row of lights across the front of the stage in a theatre.

footman *noun* (footmen) A man servant.

footpath *noun* (footpaths) A path to walk along.

footplate *noun* (footplates) A platform for the driver and fireman on a steam locomotive.

footprint *noun* (footprints) The mark made by a foot on the ground.

footsteps *noun* The sound of a person walking.

for¹ *preposition* **1** Intended to belong to. *This letter is for you.* **2** In place of. *I offer you new lamps for old!* **3** In defence of, in favour of. *He fought for his country.* **4** As far as, as long as. *We walked for a mile. They waited for two hours.* **5** Towards. *They sailed for America.* **6** Because of. *They could not see for smoke.* **7** At a cost of. *I bought it for £5.*

for² *conjunction* Because, since.

forbid *verb* (forbids, forbidding, forbade, forbidden) **1** To tell someone not to do something. **2** Not to allow something.

forbidding *adjective* Stern, threatening. **forbiddingly** *adverb*.

force¹ *noun* (forces) **1** Strength, power, violence. **forceful** *adjective*, **forcefully** *adverb*. **2** An organized group of police or soldiers. **the forces** the army, navy, and air force.

force² *verb* (forces, forcing, forced) **1** To do something by strength or violence. **2** To use force to make someone do something.

forceps *noun* Special pincers used by a surgeon or dentist.

ford *noun* (fords) A shallow place where people can wade or drive across a river.

foreboding *noun* (forebodings) A feeling that trouble is coming.

forecast¹ *verb* (forecasts, forecasting, forecast) To make a forecast.

forecast² *noun* (forecasts) A statement of what is likely to happen. *the weather forecast.*

forecastle, fo'c'sle *nouns* (forecastles, fo'c'sles) **1** A raised deck at the bow of a ship. **2** The part of a ship near the bow, where the crew lives.

forefathers *noun* Ancestors.

foregone conclusion An ending or result that can easily be foreseen.

foreground *noun* The part of a view or picture nearest to you.

forehead *noun* (foreheads) The part of your face just above the eyebrows.

foreign *adjective* **1** Belonging to another country. **2** Strange, not familiar.

foreigner *noun* (foreigners) A person from another country.

foreleg *noun* (forelegs) A front leg.

foreman *noun* (foremen) A person in charge of a group of workers.

foremost *adjective* Most important.

foresee *verb* (foresees, foreseeing, foresaw, foreseen) To see in advance that something will happen. **foreseeable** *adjective*, **foresight** *noun*.

forest *noun* (forests) A large area of land covered with trees. **forester, forestry** *nouns*.

foretaste *noun* A small taste of what something is going to be like.

foretell *verb* (foretells, foretelling, foretold) To say what will happen in the future.

forethought *noun* Careful planning.

forfeit¹ *verb* (forfeits, forfeiting, forfeited) To pay a penalty because you have done wrong, or because of the rules of a game.

forfeit² *noun* (forfeits) Something forfeited as a penalty.

forgave *See* **forgive**

forge¹ *noun* (forges) A blacksmith's workshop.

forge² *verb* (forges, forging, forged) **1** To shape metal by heating and hammering. **2** To make a copy of something to deceive people. **forger, forgery** *nouns*. **forge ahead** to get ahead by making great efforts.

forget *verb* (forgets, forgetting, forgot, forgotten) To fail to remember something, to overlook it. **forget yourself** to behave in a rude, thoughtless way. **forgetful** *adjective*, **forgetfully** *adverb*, **forgetfulness** *noun*.

forget-me-not *noun* (forget-me-nots) A plant with small blue flowers.

forgive *verb* (forgives, forgiving, forgave, forgiven) To cease to be angry with someone. **forgiveness** *noun*.

fork *noun* (forks) **1** A device with points or prongs used in eating. **2** An instrument with prongs used for digging. **3** A place where something divides into branches. *a fork in the road.*

forked *adjective* Divided into branches.

forlorn *adjective* Unhappy. **forlornly** *adverb*.

form[1] *noun* (forms) **1** Shape, appearance. *The moth begins its life in the form of a grub.* **2** Kind, variety. *TV is a form of entertainment.* **3** A class in school. **4** A bench. **5** A printed paper with spaces to be filled in. **in form, on form** fit and successful.

form[2] *verb* (forms, forming, formed) **1** To give a shape to something, to make, to create. **2** To take shape, to develop.

formal *adjective* Stiff and proper, keeping to certain rules and customs. **formally** *adverb*.

formality *noun* **1** Formal behaviour. **2** (formalities) Something which has to be done because of the rules.

formation *noun* **1** The forming of something. **2** A carefully arranged order or pattern. *flying in formation.*

former *adjective* Of the past, earlier. *The garage restored the damaged car to its former condition.* **the former** the first of two things just mentioned.

formerly *adverb* In the past.

formless *adjective* Shapeless.

formula *noun* (formulas) A way of writing mathematical or scientific information using letters, numbers, and signs.

forsake *verb* (forsakes, forsaking, forsook, forsaken) To abandon, to give up.

fort *noun* (forts) A fortified building.

forth *adverb* Forwards, onwards.

forthcoming *adjective* About to come, coming soon.

forthwith *adverb* Immediately.

fortieth *See* **forty**

fortify *verb* (fortifies, fortifying, fortified) To make stronger, to build defences. **fortification** *noun*.

fortitude *noun* Bravery.

fortnight *noun* (fortnights) A period of two weeks.

fortress *noun* (fortresses) A fort, a fortified town.

fortune *noun* (fortunes) **1** Chance, luck. **fortunate** *adjective*, **fortunately** *adverb*. **2** A large amount of money. **tell fortunes** to tell people what is going to happen to them in the future.

fortune-teller *noun* (fortune-tellers) A person who claims to be able to tell fortunes.

forty (forties) The number 40. **fortieth**.

forward[1] *adjective and adverb* **1** Towards the front, in the front. **2** Eager, too eager. **forwardness** *noun*.

forward[2] *noun* (forwards) An attacking player in football and other games.

forwards *adverb* Onwards, towards the front.

fossil *noun* (fossils) The rock-like remains of a prehistoric animal or plant.

fossilized *adjective* Turned into a fossil.

foster *verb* (foster, fostering, fostered) To care for someone else's child as if it was a member of your own family.

foster-child *noun* (foster-children) A child who is fostered.

foster-parent *noun* (foster-parents) A person who fosters a child.

fought *See* **fight**[1]

foul[1] *adjective* (fouler, foulest) **1** Filthy, disgusting. **2** Stormy, violent, rough. *foul weather.* **3** Against the rules. *a foul stroke.* **foul play** murder. **foully** *adverb*, **foulness** *noun*.

foul[2] *noun* (fouls) A breaking of the rules of a game.

found[1] *See* **find**

found[2] *verb* (founds, founding, founded) To begin, to establish, to set up. *The school was founded 100 years ago.* **founder** *noun*.

foundation *noun* (foundations) **1** The founding of something. **2** The strong base on which something is built.

foundry *noun* (foundries) A place where metal or glass is melted and moulded.

fountain *noun* (fountains) A device which sends out jets of water. **fountain pen** a pen which can be filled with a supply of ink.

four (fours) The number 4. **fourth, fourthly.**

four-poster *noun* (four-posters) A bed with four tall posts and curtains round it.

fourteen The number 14. **fourteenth.**

fowl *noun* (fowls) A bird, usually a farmyard cock or hen.

fox *noun* (foxes) A wild animal of the dog family.

foxglove *noun* (foxgloves) A tall wild flower.

foxhound *noun* (foxhounds) A dog used for foxhunting.

foyer *noun* (foyers) An entrance hall in a cinema or some other large building.

fraction *noun* (fractions) **1** A small part of something. **2** In arithmetic, a number that is not a whole unit, such as $\frac{1}{2}, \frac{2}{3}, \frac{7}{8}$. **fractional** *adjective*, **fractionally** *adverb*.

fracture[1] *noun* (fractures) A break, a break in a bone.

fracture[2] *verb* (fractures, fracturing, fractured) To break, to crack.

fragile *adjective* Easily broken. **fragility** *noun*.

fragment *noun* (fragments) A broken piece, a small piece.

fragrant *adjective* Having a pleasant smell. **fragrantly** *adverb*, **fragrance** *noun*.

frail *adjective* (frailer, frailest) Weak, fragile. **frailty** *noun*.

frame[1] *noun* (frames) **1** A firm, rigid, structure made of rods, bars, or girders. *the frame of a tent.* **2** An edging for a picture. **the human frame** the body. **frame of mind** a state of mind.

frame[2] *verb* (frames, framing, framed) To put a picture in a frame.

framework *noun* (frameworks) **1** A frame. **2** A general plan or outline.

franc *noun* (francs) A unit of money in France and some other countries.

frank *adjective* (franker, frankest) Honest, outspoken. **frankly** *adverb*, **frankness** *noun*.

franked *adjective* Marked with a postmark.

frantic *adjective* Wildly excited. **frantically** *adverb*.

fraud *noun* (frauds) **1** Dishonesty. **2** A cheat. **fraudulent** *adjective*, **fraudulently** *adverb*.

fray *verb* (frays, fraying, frayed) To become ragged at the edges.

freak *adjective* Not normal, very unusual. *a freak storm.*

freckle *noun* (freckles) A small brown spot on the skin. **freckled** *adjective*.

free[1] *adjective* (freer, freest) **1** Able to do what you want to do, able to move without hindrance. **2** Not costing anything. *a free gift.* **3** Generous. *free with his money.* **4** Available, open. *Is the bathroom free?* **freely** *adverb*, **freedom** *noun*.

free[2] *verb* (frees, freeing, freed) To make free, to set free.

free-wheel *verb* (free-wheels, freewheeling, free-wheeled) To ride along on a bicycle without turning the pedals.

freeze *verb* (freezes, freezing, froze, frozen) **1** To change into ice, to become stiff and hard with cold. **2** To be very cold, to feel very cold. **3** To make something very cold. **4** To stand completely still.

freezer *noun* (freezers) A piece of equipment in which food is stored at very low temperatures.

freezing-point *noun* (freezing-points) The temperature at which a liquid freezes.

freight *noun* Goods, cargo.

French *adjective* Of or from France. **Frenchman, Frenchwoman** *nouns*. **French window** a long window which opens like a door.

frenzy *noun* Madness, wild excitement. **frenzied** *adjective*, **frenziedly** *adverb*.

frequent *adjective* Happening often, numerous. **frequently** *adverb*, **frequency** *noun*.

fresh *adjective* (fresher, freshest) **1** Newly made. *fresh bread.* **2** New or different. *a fresh page.* **3** Not tinned or preserved. *fresh fruit.* **4** Cool and clean. *fresh air.* **fresh water** water that is not salty. **5** Healthy-looking. *a fresh complexion.* **freshly** *adverb*, **freshness** *noun*.

freshen *verb* (freshens, freshening, freshened) To make something fresh, to become fresh.

fret *verb* (frets, fretting, fretted) To worry. **fretful** *adjective*, **fretfully** *adverb*.

fretsaw *noun* (fretsaws) A saw with a narrow blade for making fretwork.

fretwork *noun* Thin wood with patterns cut out of it.

friar *noun* (friars) A Christian man who has vowed to live a life of poverty.

friction *noun* **1** Rubbing. **2** Disagreement.

Friday *noun* (Fridays) The sixth day of the week.

fridge *noun* (fridges) (informal) A refrigerator.

friend *noun* (friends) **1** A person you like to talk to and go out with, a helpful, pleasant person. **2** Someone who is not an enemy. *Who goes there, friend or foe?* **friendly** *adverb*, **friendliness**, **friendship** *nouns*.

frieze *noun* (friezes) A strip of pictures or designs along a wall.

frigate *noun* (frigates) A fast warship.

fright *noun* Sudden fear, terror.

frighten *verb* (frightens, frightening, frightened) To fill someone with fear.

frightful *adjective* (informal) **1** Unpleasant. **2** Very great. **frightfully** *adverb*.

frill *noun* (frills) A decorative edging for clothes or curtains.

fringe *noun* (fringes) **1** A decorative edging with many threads hanging loosely down. **2** Front hair cut short and allowed to hang over the forehead. **3** The edge of something. *the fringe of a crowd.*

fringed *adjective* Having a fringe.

frisk *verb* (frisks, frisking, frisked) To move about playfully. **frisky** *adjective*, **friskily** *adverb*, **friskiness** *noun*.

fritter¹ *noun* (fritters) A slice of fruit or meat fried in batter.

fritter² *verb* (fritters, frittering, frittered) To waste something bit by bit.

frivolous *adjective* Silly, not serious. **frivolously** *adverb*, **frivolity** *noun*.

fro *adverb* **to and fro** backwards and forwards.

frock *noun* (frocks) A girl's or woman's dress.

frog *noun* (frogs) A small jumping animal which can live on land or in the water.

frogman *noun* (frogmen) A person with apparatus for under-water swimming.

from *preposition* This word is used in

many ways including: **1** To show where something starts. *I got a bus from town.* **2** To show where you get something. *The meat came from the market.* **3** To show where you start measuring or counting. *Fares go up from today.* **4** To show separation. *He took £5 from me.* **5** To show difference. *I can't tell one from the other.*

front[1] *noun* (fronts) **1** The most important side of a thing, the side which faces forwards. *the front of the house.* **2** The part of a thing or place which is furthest forward. *the front of a train.* **3** In a war, the place where the fighting is going on. **4** A road or promenade along the seashore.

front[2] *adjective* At or on the front.

frontal *adjective* At or from the front. *a frontal attack.*

frontier *noun* (frontiers) A boundary between two countries.

frost *noun* (frosts) **1** Freezing weather. **2** White, powdery ice which covers things in freezing weather. **frosty** *adjective*, **frostily** *adverb*, **frostiness** *noun*.

frostbite *noun* Injury done to a person's body by severe frost. **frostbitten** *adjective*.

froth *noun* Masses of tiny bubbles. **frothy** *adjective*.

frown *verb* (frowns, frowning, frowned) To wrinkle your forehead because you are angry or puzzled.

froze, frozen *See* **freeze**

fruit *noun* (fruit *or* fruits) **1** The part of a plant which contains the seeds and which is often used as food. **2** A result of something. *the fruit of all my work.* **fruit cake** a cake containing currants or other dried fruit.

fruitful *adjective* **1** Successful. **2** Bearing fruit.

fruitless *adjective* Unsuccessful.

frustrate *verb* (frustrates, frustrating, frustrated) To prevent someone from doing something. **frustration** *noun*.

fry *verb* (fries, frying, fried) To cook in hot fat. **fryer** *noun*.

frying-pan *noun* (frying-pans) A pan for frying food.

fudge *noun* A soft, sugary sweet.

fuel *noun* (fuels) Anything which is burnt to provide heat or power, such as coal, wood, or oil.

fug *noun* (informal) A stuffy atmosphere.

fugitive *noun* (fugitives) Someone who is running away.

fulfil *verb* (fulfils, fulfilling, fulfilled) **1** To carry something out successfully. *He fulfilled his promise.* **2** To satisfy. **fulfilment** *noun*.

full *adjective* (fuller, fullest) **1** Holding as much or as many as possible. *The cinema was full.* **2** Containing a large number or amount. *The room was full of people I did not know.* **3** Complete, with nothing left out. *Give me the full facts.* **4** The maximum, the greatest possible. *Full speed ahead!* **full skirt** a skirt with lots of material hanging in folds. **full moon** a moon that looks like a complete disc. **full stop** the punctuation mark which goes at the end of a sentence. **fully** *adverb*, **fullness** *noun*.

fumble *verb* (fumbles, fumbling, fumbled) To be clumsy with your hands.

fume *verb* (fumes, fuming, fumed) **1** To give off fumes. **2** To be very angry.

fumes *noun* Smelly gas or smoke.

fun *noun* Amusement, enjoyment. **make fun of** to make other people laugh at someone.

function[1] *noun* (functions) **1** The purpose or use of something. *The function of a knife is to cut.* **2** A public event.

function[2] *verb* (functions, functioning, functioned) To work. *The telephone is not functioning.* **functional** *adjective*.

fund *noun* (funds) A supply of money or other things, money to be used for a particular purpose.

fundamental *adjective* Basic. **fundamentally** *adverb*.

funeral *noun* (funerals) A ceremony held before a dead person is buried or cremated.

fun-fair *noun* (fun-fairs) A fair with amusements and side-shows.

fungus *noun* (fungi) A kind of plant such as a mushroom or a toadstool.

funk *verb* (funks, funking, funked) (informal) To try to avoid doing something you are afraid of.

funnel *noun* (funnels) 1 The chimney of a ship or steam-engine. 2 A device for pouring liquids into narrow openings.

funny *adjective* (funnier, funniest) 1 Amusing, comical. 2 Strange, odd. **funnily** *adverb*.

funny-bone *noun* (funny-bones) The sensitive part of your elbow.

fur¹ *noun* (furs) 1 The soft hair which covers certain animals. **furry** *adjective*. 2 Skin from these animals used for clothing.

fur² *noun* 1 A chalky substance found inside kettles and water-pipes. 2 A rough coating on the tongue when a person is ill. **furred** *adjective*.

furious *adjective* Very angry. **furiously** *adverb*.

furl *verb* (furls, furling, furled) To roll up a sail, an umbrella, or a flag.

furnace *noun* (furnaces) A special fireplace for making a great heat.

furnish *verb* (furnishes, furnishing, furnished) To provide furniture.

furniture *noun* Tables, chairs, beds, cupboards, and other things needed in a house, school, or other building.

furrow *noun* (furrows) 1 A cut made in the ground by a plough. 2 A groove, a wrinkle.

further *adjective and adverb* 1 To a greater distance, farther. *I can go no further.* 2 More, additional. *Can you give me any further information?* 3 Also, in addition.

furthermore *adverb* Moreover, besides.

furthermost *adjective* The most distant.

furthest *adjective and adverb* To the greatest distance, farthest.

furtive *adjective* Sly, stealthy. **furtively** *adverb*.

fury *noun* Wild anger, rage. **furious** *adjective*, **furiously** *adverb*.

fuse¹ *noun* (fuses) 1 A safety device in an electric circuit. 2 A device for setting off an explosive.

fuse² *verb* (fuses, fusing, fused) To be put out of action because a fuse has melted.

fuselage *noun* (fuselages) The body of an aircraft.

fuss *noun* Unnecessary excitement about unimportant things. **make a fuss about something** to complain. **make a fuss of someone** to do many kind things for them.

fussy *adjective* (fussier, fussiest) 1 Making a fuss. 2 Having too many details. *fussily adverb*.

futile *adjective* Useless. **futility** *noun*.

future *noun* 1 The time to come. 2 What is going to happen in the time to come. *No one can be sure about the future.*

fuzzy *adjective* (fuzzier, fuzziest) 1 Fluffy. 2 Blurred, indistinct.

Gg

gabble *verb* (gabbles, gabbling, gabbled) To talk quickly and indistinctly.

gable *noun* (gables) The triangular part of an outside wall between the ends of sloping roofs.

gadget *noun* (gadgets) A small useful tool or piece of machinery. *My penknife has a gadget for opening bottles.*

Gaelic *noun* An ancient language of Scotland and Ireland.

gag[1] *noun* (gags) **1** Something used to gag someone. **2** A joke.

gag[2] *verb* (gags, gagging, gagged) To stop up someone's mouth so that he or she cannot speak.

gaiety, gaily *See* **gay**

gain[1] *verb* (gains, gaining, gained) **1** To get something you did not have before. **2** To reach. *to gain the shore.* **gain on** to get nearer to someone in a race.

gain[2] *noun* (gains) Something gained, profit.

gala *noun* (galas) A fête, a day of sports and entertainments.

galaxy *noun* (galaxies) A large system or group of stars. **galactic** *adjective*.

gale *noun* (gales) A very strong wind.

gallant *adjective* Brave, chivalrous. **gallantly** *adverb*, **gallantry** *noun*.

galleon *noun* (galleons) A large ancient Spanish sailing ship.

gallery *noun* (galleries) **1** The highest balcony in a theatre. **2** A raised floor or platform over a part of a hall or church. **3** A long room or passageway. **art gallery** a building used for displaying works of art.

galley *noun* (galleys) **1** A boat rowed by slaves or criminals in ancient times. **2** A ship's kitchen.

gallon *noun* (gallons) A unit of measure for liquids, 8 pints or about 4.5 litres.

gallop[1] *noun* (gallops) **1** The fastest pace of a horse. **2** A fast ride on horseback.

gallop[2] *verb* (gallops, galloping, galloped) To go at a gallop.

gallows *noun* A wooden framework for executing criminals.

galvanized iron Iron with a coating of zinc.

gamble *verb* (gambles, gambling, gambled) **1** To play a game in the hope of winning money or a prize. **2** To take great risks.

game[1] *noun* (games) **1** A form of playing, especially with rules. *My favourite games are football and chess.* **2** A period of playing which ends after an agreed time or when someone wins. *We had two games of snooker.*

game[2] *noun* Wild animals or birds hunted for food or for sport.

game[3] *adjective* Brave, willing to go on.

gamekeeper *noun* (gamekeepers) A person employed to look after animals or birds which are to be hunted for sport.

gammon *noun* A kind of ham or bacon.

gander *noun* (ganders) A male goose.

gang *noun* (gangs) A set of people who do things together. *a gang of robbers.*

gangplank *noun* (gangplanks) A plank used for walking on or off a boat.

gangster *noun* (gangsters) A member of a gang of violent criminals.

gangway *noun* (gangways) **1** A way between rows of seats or people. **2** A moveable bridge between a ship and the shore.

gaol[1] *noun* (gaols) A prison.

gaol[2] *verb* (gaols, gaoling, gaoled) To put someone in gaol. **gaoler** *noun*.

gap *noun* (gaps) An empty place or time between two things or events.

gape *verb* (gapes, gaping, gaped) **1** To open your mouth wide. **2** To be wide open. **3** To stare in surprise.

garage *noun* (garages) **1** A building where motor vehicles are kept. **2** A place where cars are serviced or repaired.

garbage *noun* Waste food, rubbish.

garbled *adjective* Confused, misleading.

garden *noun* (gardens) A piece of ground for growing flowers, fruit, or vegetables. **gardener, gardening** *nouns*. **garden centre** a place where plants and garden tools are sold.

gargle *verb* (gargles, gargling, gargled) To make a gurgling sound through liquid held in the back of your mouth.

gargoyle *noun* (gargoyles) A spout to carry water off the roof of a church, often carved like an ugly head.

garland *noun* (garlands) A wreath of flowers.

garlic *noun* An onion-like plant.

garment *noun* (garments) An article of clothing.

garrison *noun* (garrisons) Troops stationed in a town or fortress to defend it.

garter *noun* (garters) A band used to keep a sock or stocking up.

gas¹ *noun* (gases) **1** Any air-like substance. **2** The inflammable gas which is used for heating and cooking.

gas² *verb* (gases, gassing, gassed) To overcome someone with a poisonous gas.

gash *noun* (gashes) A long, deep cut.

gasometer *noun* (gasometers) A large, round container storing inflammable gas.

gasp *verb* (gasps, gasping, gasped) To take short quick breaths, to breathe with difficulty.

gastric *adjective* Of the stomach. *gastric flu.*

gate *noun* (gates) **1** A barrier on hinges used to close a gap in a wall or hedge. **2** A gateway. **3** The number of people attending a football match.

gateway *noun* (gateways) An opening for a gate, an entrance.

gather *verb* (gathers, gathering, gathered) **1** To collect, to bring together. *We gathered flowers.* **2** To come together. *A crowd gathered.* **3** To understand. *I gather it's your birthday.*

gathering *noun* (gatherings) A group of people who have met for some purpose.

gaudy *adjective* (gaudier, gaudiest) Too bright and showy. **gaudily** *adverb*.

gauge *noun* (gauges) **1** Size or measurement, especially the measurement between the two rails of a railway track. **2** An instrument for measuring.

gaunt *adjective* Thin, lean.

gauntlet *noun* (gauntlets) A glove with a wide part that covers the wrist.

gauze *noun* Thin, transparent, net-like material.

gave *See* **give**

gay *adjective* (gayer, gayest) **1** Cheerful, light-hearted. **gaily** *adverb*, **gaiety** *noun*. **2** Homosexual.

gaze *verb* (gazes, gazing, gazed) To look steadily at something for a long time.

gear (gears) **1** One of a set of cogwheels, such as those in a car or bicycle by which power is transmitted to the wheels. **2** One of the positions in which a set of gears can be used for travelling at different speeds. *Paul's bike has six gears.* **3** Equipment, things needed for a particular purpose. *camping gear.*

geese *See* **goose**

Geiger counter An instrument which detects and measures radioactivity.

gel *noun* (gels) A substance like a slightly runny jelly. *hair gel.*

gelignite *noun* An explosive.

gem *noun* (gems) A jewel.

general¹ *adjective* **1** Belonging to everyone or everything, concerning everyone. *general knowledge. a general election.* **2** Not detailed. *a general impression.* **in general** generally.

general[2] *noun* (generals) An officer of high rank in the army.

generally *adverb* Usually, on the whole.

generate *verb* (generates, generating, generated) To bring something into existence. *to generate electricity.* **generator** *noun*.

generation *noun* **1** Generating. **2** (generations) A single stage in a family. *Three generations*, children, parents, grandparents. **3** All people who are about the same age. *My father's generation*, the people who are about the same age as my father.

generous *adjective* **1** Ready to give freely. *a generous person.* **2** Given freely. *a generous present.* **generously** *adverb*, **generosity** *noun*.

genes *noun* Molecules which pass on family likeness, the colour of hair and eyes, and other characteristics from parents to their children.

genial *adjective* Kindly, warm, cheerful. **genially** *adverb*, **geniality** *noun*.

genitals *noun* The sex organs of the body.

genius *noun* (geniuses) An unusually clever person.

gentile *noun* (gentiles) A person who is not a Jew.

gentle *adjective* (gentler, gentlest) **1** Quiet and kind, not rough. **2** Moderate, not severe. **gently** *adverb*, **gentleness** *noun*.

gentleman *noun* (gentlemen) **1** A polite word for a man. **2** A kind, well-mannered man. **gentlemanly** *adverb*.

genuine *adjective* True, not pretended or faked. *genuine feelings.* **genuinely** *adverb*, **genuineness** *noun*.

geo-board *noun* (geo-boards) A board with an arrangement of upright nails or pegs, for experimenting with shapes in mathematics.

geography *noun* The scientific study of the earth, its lands and seas, its climate, its peoples, what they grow, what they produce, and how they live. **geographical** *adjective*.

geology *noun* The scientific study of the rocks and other substances which make up the earth's crust. **geological** *adjective*, **geologist** *noun*.

geometry *noun* A branch of mathematics which deals with lines, angles, and shapes. **geometry set** a case of drawing instruments. **geometric**, **geometrical** *adjectives*.

geranium *noun* (geraniums) A plant with red, pink, or white flowers.

gerbil *noun* (gerbils) A small animal with long back legs.

germ *noun* (germs) A tiny living thing, sometimes causing diseases.

German *adjective* Of or from Germany.

germinate *verb* (germinates, germinating, germinated) To start to develop or grow. **germination** *noun*.

gesture *noun* (gestures) A movement or an action which helps to show what you mean or feel.

get *verb* (gets, getting, got) **1** To receive, to obtain, to earn, to win, to fetch. *Do you get pocket-money?* **2** To catch, to suffer from. *Sue got a cold.* **3** To persuade. *Get John to do it.* **4** To prepare. *I'll get tea now.* **5** (informal) To understand. *Do you get what I mean?* **6** To manage to go somewhere, to arrive. *Can you get here by tea-time?* **7** To manage to put something somewhere. *You won't get that big envelope in the postbox.* **8** To put yourself somewhere, to move. *Get on the bus quickly.* **get at** to reach. **get away** to escape. **get off** to be let off punishment. **get on with 1** To like a person. **2** To make progress with a job. **get over** to recover from an illness.

getaway *noun* (getaways) An escape.

geyser *noun* (geysers) A natural spring which sends up a column of hot water.

ghastly *adjective* (ghastlier, ghastliest) **1** Horrible, shocking. **2** Very pale, looking ill.

ghee *noun* A kind of Indian clear butter.

ghetto *noun* (ghettos) An area of a town where one group of people lives separated from others.

ghost *noun* (ghosts) The spirit of a dead person appearing to someone living. **ghostly** *adjective*, **ghostliness** *noun*.

ghoul *noun* (ghouls) **1** A person who enjoys horrors. **2** In Muslim stories, a spirit who robs graves and devours corpses.

giant[1] *noun* (giants) A huge man.

giant[2] *adjective* Huge. *a giant crane*.

gibberish *noun* Nonsense.

giddy *adjective* (giddier, giddiest) Having the feeling that everything is turning round, dizzy. **giddily** *adverb*, **giddiness** *noun*.

gift *noun* (gifts) **1** Something given to somebody, a present. **2** An ability, a talent. *a gift for music*.

gifted *adjective* Talented, clever.

gigantic *adjective* Huge, giant-like. **gigantically** *adverb*.

giggle *verb* (giggles, giggling, giggled) To laugh in a silly way.

gild *verb* (gilds, gilding, gilded) To cover something thinly with gold.

gill *noun* (gills) One of the parts of a fish's body with which it breathes.

gilt *adjective* Covered thinly with gold.

gimmick *noun* (gimmicks) A clever or unusual way of attracting people's attention to something.

gin *noun* A strong alcoholic drink.

ginger *noun* **1** A hot-tasting flavouring. **2** A reddish-yellow colour. **gingery** *adjective*.

gingerbread *noun* A cake made with ginger.

gingerly *adverb* Very cautiously.

gipsy *See* **gypsy**

giraffe *noun* (giraffes) A tall African wild animal with a long neck.

girder *noun* (girders) A long, thick bar of iron or steel.

girdle *noun* (girdles) **1** A belt tied round the waist. **2** A corset.

girl *noun* (girls) **1** A female child. **2** A young woman. **girlish** *adjective*.

girl-friend *noun* (girl-friends) The girl with whom a boy usually goes out.

girlhood *noun* The time when you are a girl.

giro *noun* **1** A system of banking. **2** (giros) (informal) A type of cheque.

girth *noun* (girths) **1** A band fastened round the belly of a horse to keep its saddle in place. **2** The measurement round something.

give *verb* (gives, giving, gave, given) **1** To hand something over to someone to use or keep. *Jamie gave me his old comics*. **2** To let someone have something, to provide. *Cally gave us a lovely dinner*. **3** To pay. *How much did you give for those stamps?* **4** To show, to tell. *Give me the facts*. **5** To collapse, to become less firm. *Will this branch give if I sit on it?* **6** To do something suddenly. *He gave a shout.* **give someone or something away** to betray someone or something. **give birth** to have a baby. **give chase** to pursue. **give in, give yourself up** to surrender. **give up** to stop doing or using something. **give way 1** To break, to collapse. **2** To let other traffic go first. **giver** *noun*.

glacier *noun* (glaciers) A slowly moving river of ice.

glad *adjective* Pleased, joyful. **gladly** *adverb*, **gladness** *noun*.

gladiator *noun* (gladiators) A man trained to fight at public entertainments in ancient Rome.

glamour *noun* Attractiveness, beauty. **glamorous** *adjective*.

glance[1] *verb* (glances, glancing, glanced) **1** To look briefly at something. **2** To slip or slide off something. *The ball glanced off the edge of the bat.*

glance[2] *noun* (glances) A brief look.

gland *noun* (glands) A kind of organ in the body that separates certain substances from the blood. **glandular** *adjective*.

glare[1] *noun* (glares) **1** A dazzling light. **2** An angry look.

glare[2] *verb* (glares, glaring, glared) To give a glare.

glass *noun* **1** The hard, clear substance used to make windows. **2** (glasses) A drinking cup made of this substance. **3** A mirror. **glasses** spectacles or binoculars. **magnifying glass** a lens which you can use to make things look bigger.

glass-house *noun* (glass-houses) A greenhouse.

glass-paper *noun* Paper covered with glass dust for smoothing wood.

glaze *verb* (glazes, glazing, glazed) **1** To fit glass into a window frame. **glazier** *noun*. **2** To put a shiny surface on something. *glazed pottery.*

gleam[1] *noun* (gleams) A ray of soft light.

gleam[2] *verb* (gleams, gleaming, gleamed) To give a gleam.

glee *noun* Happiness, delight. **gleeful** *adjective*, **gleefully** *adverb*.

glen *noun* (glens) A narrow valley.

glide *verb* (glides, gliding, glided) To move smoothly and steadily.

glider *noun* (gliders) A kind of aeroplane without an engine.

gliding *noun* Flying in a glider.

glimmer *verb* (glimmers, glimmering, glimmered) To give a faint light.

glimpse[1] *verb* (glimpses, glimpsing, glimpsed) To see something very briefly.

glimpse[2] *noun* (glimpses) A brief view of something.

glint *verb* (glints, glinting, glinted) To flash, to sparkle.

glisten *verb* (glistens, glistening, glistened) To shine like a wet surface.

glitter *verb* (glitters, glittering, glittered) To sparkle.

gloat *verb* (gloats, gloating, gloated) To be selfishly pleased about something.

global *adjective* Of the whole world.

globe *noun* (globes) **1** Any object shaped like a ball or sphere. **2** A sphere with a map of the earth on it.

glockenspiel *noun* (glockenspiels) A musical instrument with bells or bars played with hammers.

gloomy *adjective* (gloomier, gloomiest) **1** Nearly dark. **2** Sad. **gloomily** *adverb*, **gloom** *noun*.

glorious *adjective* Splendid, magnificent, very beautiful. **gloriously** *adverb*.

glory *noun* **1** Fame. **2** Great beauty.

gloss *noun* A shiny surface. **glossy** *adjective*.

glove *noun* (gloves) A covering for the hand.

glow[1] *verb* (glows, glowing, glowed)

1 To send out brightness and warmth without flames. **2** To look or feel warm or excited. *glowing with pride*.

glow² *noun* **1** Brightness. **2** Warmth.

glower *verb* (glowers, glowering, glowered) To scowl.

glow-worm *noun* (glow-worms) An insect. The female gives out a green light in the dark.

glucose *noun* A form of sugar.

glue¹ *noun* A substance used for sticking things together. **gluey** *adjective*.

glue² *verb* (glues, gluing, glued) To stick with glue.

glum *adjective* Sad, gloomy. **glumly** *adverb*.

glutton *noun* (gluttons) A greedy person. **gluttonous** *adjective*, **gluttony** *noun*.

gnarled *adjective* Twisted, knobbly.

gnat *noun* (gnats) A small fly which bites.

gnaw *verb* (gnaws, gnawing, gnawed) To keep on biting something.

gnome *noun* (gnomes) A goblin or dwarf, supposed to live underground.

go¹ *verb* (goes, going, went, gone) **1** To start, to move. *Ready, steady, go!* **2** To travel. *We went by bus.* **3** To reach, to extend. *How far does this road go?* **4** To work, to be in working order. *Is your watch going?* **5** To disappear, to die. *The light goes in the evening.* **6** To make your way somewhere, to pay a visit. *Do you go to church?* **7** To become. *Milk goes sour in warm weather.* **8** To break. *Look out, that branch is going!* **9** To have a proper or usual place. *The butter goes in the fridge.* **10** To be given. *The prize goes to the winner.* **11** To be sold. *The house went for a huge amount.* **12** To make a particular noise. *The gun went bang.* **go in for** to enjoy doing or having something. **go off 1** To explode. **2** To become unfit to eat.

go² *noun* **1** Energy. *full of go.* **2** (goes) An attempt. *to have a go!*

goal *noun* (goals) **1** The posts between which the ball has to be sent in football and other games. **2** The point scored when this is done. **3** A place you are trying to reach, a thing you are trying to achieve.

goalie *noun* (goalies) (informal) A goalkeeper.

goalkeeper *noun* (goalkeepers) The player who guards the goal.

goat *noun* (goats) A farm animal with horns.

gobble *verb* (gobbles, gobbling, gobbled) To eat quickly and greedily.

goblet *noun* (goblets) A kind of drinking-cup.

goblin *noun* (goblins) A mischievous demon.

god *noun* (gods) Someone or something that people worship. **God** the creator of the universe.

goddess *noun* (goddesses) A female god.

godparent *noun* (godparents) A person who promises when a child is baptized to see that it is brought up as a Christian. **godfather**, **godmother**, **godchild**, **god-daughter**, **godson** *nouns*.

goggles *noun* Large spectacles worn to protect the eyes.

go-kart *noun* (go-karts) A small simple racing car, often home-made.

gold *noun* **1** A precious metal. **2** Its yellowish colour. **golden** *adjective*.

goldfinch *noun* (goldfinches) A small, brightly coloured bird.

goldfish *noun* (goldfish) A small red fish.

goldsmith *noun* (goldsmiths) A person who makes things of gold.

golf *noun* An outdoor game in which a small, hard ball is struck with clubs into a series of holes. **golfer** *noun*.

golf-course *noun* (golf-courses) An area where you can play golf.

golfing *noun* Playing golf.

gondola *noun* (gondolas) A kind of boat used on the canals in Venice. **gondolier** *noun*.

gone *See* go¹.

gong *noun* (gongs) A large metal disc which makes an echoing sound when hit.

good¹ *adjective* (better, best) **1** Of the kind that people want, like, or approve of. *good friends, a good book.* **2** Well behaved, virtuous. *That's a good dog!* **3** Kind. *Would you be so good as to pass the salt?* **4** Healthy and nourishing. *Fresh vegetables are good for you.* **5** Quite large, considerable. *It's a good five kilometres*, it's at least five. **as good as** very nearly. **in good time** with time to spare. **good morning, good night** polite expressions used when meeting or leaving someone.

good² *noun* **1** Something that is good. *to do good.* **2** Advantage, benefit. *for the good of others.* **It's no good!** it's no use! **for good** for ever.

goodbye A word used when parting from someone.

good-humoured *adjective* Cheerful. **good-humouredly** *adverb*.

good-looking *adjective* Handsome, attractive.

good-natured *adjective* Kind, willing to help.

goodness *noun* **1** Kindness. **2** Any good quality.

goods *noun* **1** Things which are bought or sold in a shop or warehouse.

2 Things which are carried on lorries or trains.

good-tempered *adjective* Not easily made angry, gentle.

goodwill *noun* Friendliness.

goody-goody *noun* (goody-goodies) Someone who makes a great show of behaving well.

goose *noun* (geese) A large water-bird.

gooseberry *noun* (gooseberries) A small green fruit which grows on a prickly bush.

goose-pimples *noun* Little bumps on the skin caused by fear or cold.

gore *verb* (gores, goring, gored) To wound with horns.

gorge¹ *verb* (gorges, gorging, gorged) **gorge yourself** to eat greedily.

gorge² *noun* (gorges) A narrow opening between hills or mountains.

gorgeous *adjective* Colourful, beautiful, splendid. **gorgeously** *adverb*.

gorilla *noun* (gorillas) A large African ape.

gorse *noun* A prickly bush with yellow flowers.

gory *adjective* **1** Covered with blood. **2** With much bloodshed.

gosling *noun* (goslings) A young goose.

gospel *noun* The teachings of Jesus Christ. **The Gospels** the first four books of the New Testament, containing the story of Jesus Christ.

gossip¹ *noun* Gossiping.

gossip² *verb* (gossips, gossiping, gossiped) To chatter about other people.

got *See* **get**

gouge *verb* (gouges, gouging, gouged) to scoop out.

goulash *noun* A kind of stew.

govern *verb* (governs, governing, governed) To rule, to control, to manage. **governor** *noun*.

government *noun* (governments) The group of people who govern a country.

gown *noun* (gowns) **1** A woman's dress. **2** A loose, flowing garment.

grab *verb* (grabs, grabbing, grabbed) To seize suddenly and roughly, to snatch.

grace *noun* **1** Attractiveness, beauty of movement. **graceful** *adjective*, **gracefully** *adverb*. **2** God's loving mercy. **3** A short prayer before or after a meal. **with a good grace** without complaining. **with a bad grace** reluctantly, unwillingly.

gracious *adjective* **1** Kind, agreeable. **2** Merciful. **graciously** *adverb*.

grade¹ *noun* (grades) Quality, standard.

grade² *verb* (grades, grading, graded) To sort into grades.

gradient *noun* (gradients) A slope.

gradual *adjective* Happening slowly but steadily. **gradually** *adverb*.

graffiti *noun* Things written or drawn on a wall.

grain *noun* (grain *or* grains) **1** A seed of corn, wheat, rice, or similar plants. **2** A tiny piece of anything. *a grain of sand* **3** The arrangement of lines which can be seen in a piece of wood.

gram *noun* (grams) A unit of weight.

grammar *noun* Rules for the use of words. *bad grammar*, not using words properly. **grammatical** *adjective*. **grammar school** a kind of secondary school.

gramophone *noun* (gramophones) An old word for a record-player.

granary *noun* (granaries) A building for storing grain.

grand *adjective* (grander, grandest) Great, splendid, important. **grandly** *adverb*, **grandeur** *noun*.

grandad *noun* (grandads) Grandfather.

grandchild *noun* (grandchildren) A child of your son or daughter. **granddaughter**, **grandson** *nouns*.

grandfather *noun* (grandfathers) The father of your mother or father. **grandfather clock** a clock in a tall wooden case.

grandma *noun* (grandmas) Grandmother.

grandmother *noun* (grandmothers) The mother of your mother or father.

grandpa *noun* (grandpas) Grandfather.

grandparent *noun* (grandparents) A grandfather or grandmother.

grandstand *noun* (grandstands) A stand with seats for spectators at a racecourse or sports arena.

granite *noun* A hard, usually grey rock.

granny *noun* (grannies) Grandmother. **granny knot** a wrongly-tied reef-knot.

grant¹ *noun* (grants) An amount of money granted for a particular purpose.

grant² *verb* (grants, granting, granted) **1** To give or allow what is asked for. *to grant a request.* **take for granted** to assume that something is true or will always be available.

granulated sugar Sugar in the form of white grains.

grape *noun* (grapes) A small green or purple fruit which grows in clusters on vines.

grapefruit *noun* (grapefruit *or* grapefruits) A citrus fruit, like a large yellow orange.

graph *noun* (graphs) A diagram for comparing numbers or amounts.

graphics *noun* Pictures, patterns, or designs.

grapple *verb* (grapples, grappling, grappled) **1** To seize something, to wrestle with it. **2** To try to deal with something.

grasp[1] *verb* (grasps, grasping, grasped) **1** To hold something firmly. **2** To understand.

grasp[2] *noun* (grasps) The power to grasp.

grasping *adjective* Selfish, greedy for money.

grass *noun* (grasses) A green plant with narrow, pointed leaves. **grassy** *adjective*.

grasshopper *noun* (grasshoppers) A jumping, chirping insect.

grass-snake *noun* (grass-snakes) A kind of small, harmless snake.

grate[1] *noun* (grates) A metal frame for holding coal in a fireplace.

grate[2] *verb* (grates, grating, grated) **1** To shred into small pieces. *grated cheese.* **grater** *noun*. **2** To make an ugly, irritating noise.

grateful *adjective* Thankful for a person's help or kindness. **gratefully** *adverb*.

grating *noun* (gratings) A framework of criss-cross or parallel metal bars.

gratitude *noun* Being grateful.

grave[1] *adjective* (graver, gravest) Serious, solemn, important. **gravely** *adverb*.

grave[2] *noun* (graves) A hole dug in the ground for a dead body.

gravel *noun* Small stones and coarse sand. **gravelly** *adverb*.

gravestone *noun* (gravestones) A stone placed over a grave as a memorial.

graveyard *noun* (graveyards) A place where dead bodies are buried.

gravity *noun* **1** The force which attracts things towards the earth. **2** Seriousness.

gravy *noun* A brown sauce eaten with meat.

graze *verb* (grazes, grazing, grazed) **1** To feed on growing grass. *Cows graze in the fields.* **2** To scrape something. *I grazed my knee when I fell.*

grease *noun* Soft, sticky fat or thick oil. **greasy** *adjective*.

great *adjective* (greater, greatest) **1** Big, large. *a great sum of money.* **2** Important. *a great event.* **3** Unusually talented. *a great composer.* **4** Very good. *a great friend.* **great-grandparent** a grandparent of your mother or father.

greedy *adjective* (greedier, greediest) Wanting more food or money than you need. **greedily** *adverb*, **greed**, **greediness** *nouns*.

Greek *adjective* Of Greece, from Greece.

green[1] *noun* (greens) **1** A colour, the colour of grass. **2** An area of grass. *a village green.* **greens** green vegetables such as cabbage.

green[2] *adjective* (greener, greenest) **1** Having the colour green. **2** Not experienced, immature. **3** Concerned about nature and the conservation of our environment.

greenery *noun* Green plants and leaves.

greengage *noun* (greengages) A kind of green plum.

greengrocer *noun* (greengrocers) A shopkeeper who sells fresh fruit and vegetables.

greenhouse *noun* (greenhouses) A glass building for growing tender plants.

greenish *adjective* Rather green.

greet *verb* (greets, greeting, greeted) To say words of welcome to someone.

greeting *noun* (greetings) The first words used when meeting someone. **greetings** good wishes.

grenade *noun* (grenades) A small bomb thrown by hand.

grew *See* **grow**

grey[1] *noun* A colour between black and white, like clouds on a dull day.

grey[2] *adjective* (greyer, greyest) Grey in colour.

greyhound *noun* (greyhounds) A kind of dog used for racing.

grief *noun* Great sadness. **come to grief** to have an accident.

grievance *noun* (grievances) Something to complain about.

grieve *verb* (grieves, grieving, grieved) **1** To feel very sad. **2** To make someone very sad.

grill[1] *noun* (grills) **1** A device for grilling food. **2** A grating.

grill[2] *verb* (grills, grilling, grilled) To cook something under a flame or glowing electric element.

grim *adjective* (grimmer, grimmest) Stern, unfriendly, cruel. **grimly** *adverb*, **grimness** *noun*.

grimace[1] *noun* (grimaces) An ugly, twisted expression on the face.

grimace[2] *verb* (grimaces, grimacing, grimaced) To make a grimace.

grime *noun* A coating of dirt. **grimy** *adjective*.

grin[1] *noun* (grins) A broad smile.

grin[2] *verb* (grins, grinning, grinned) To smile broadly.

grind *verb* (grinds, grinding, ground) **1** To crush something into powder. *to grind coffee.* **2** To polish or sharpen something by rubbing it on a rough surface. *to grind scissors.* **grinder** *noun*.

grip[1] *verb* (grips, gripping, gripped) To take firm hold of something.

grip[2] *noun* (grips) **1** A hold, a grasp. **2** A handle. **3** A traveller's bag.

grisly *adjective* Horrible, frightful.

gristle *noun* Tough, rubbery lumps in meat. **gristly** *adjective*.

grit[1] *noun* **1** Tiny pieces of stone or sand. **2** Courage. **gritty** *adjective*, **grittiness** *noun*.

grit[2] *verb* (grits, gritting, gritted) To put grit on something. *to grit the roads.* **grit your teeth** to clench them.

grizzle *verb* (grizzles, grizzling, grizzled) (informal) To cry and whimper.

grizzly bear A large fierce North American bear.

groan[1] *verb* (groans, groaning, groaned) To make a deep sound of pain, sadness, or disapproval.

groan[2] *noun* (groans) A sound of groaning.

grocer *noun* (grocers) A shopkeeper who sells tea, sugar, jam, and other foods. **grocery, groceries** *nouns*.

groom[1] *noun* (grooms) **1** Someone whose job is to look after horses. **2** A bridegroom.

groom[2] *verb* (grooms, grooming, groomed) To clean and brush a horse.

groove *noun* (grooves) A long, narrow cut in the surface of something.

grope *verb* (gropes, groping, groped) To feel about, to search blindly.

gross[1] *noun* (gross) Twelve dozen, 144.

gross[2] *adjective* **1** Fat and ugly. **2** Coarse. **3** Obviously bad. *gross carelessness.* **grossly** *adverb*.

grotesque *adjective* Absurd, ugly. **grotesquely** *adverb*.

grotto *noun* (grottoes) A cave.

ground[1] *noun* (grounds) **1** The surface of the earth. *level ground.* **2** Soil. *fertile ground.* **3** A piece of land used to play on. *a football ground.* **grounds 1** The gardens of a large house. **2** Solid bits of coffee that sink to the bottom of the cup. **3** Reasons. *grounds for suspicion.*

ground[2] *See* **grind**

grounded *adjective* Prevented from flying. *All planes were grounded by fog.*

groundless *adjective* Without good cause or reasons.

groundsheet *noun* (groundsheets) A waterproof sheet which campers spread beneath them on the ground.

groundsman *noun* (groundsmen) A person employed to look after a sports ground.

group[1] *noun* (groups) A number of

people or things gathered together, people who do things together.

group² *verb* (groups, grouping, grouped) To make a group.

grouse¹ *noun* (grouse) A game bird.

grouse² *verb* (grouses, grousing, groused) To complain.

grove *noun* (groves) A small wood.

grovel *verb* (grovels, grovelling, grovelled) To make yourself too humble.

grow *verb* (grows, growing, grew, grown) **1** To become bigger, taller, or longer. **2** To develop. **3** To look after plants and help them grow. *to grow flowers.* **4** To become. *to grow older.* **grower** *noun.* **grow up** to become an adult.

growl *verb* (growls, growling, growled) To make a rough noise in the throat as an angry dog does.

grown-up *noun* (grown-ups) A fully grown person.

growth *noun* **1** Growing. **2** (growths) Something which is growing or has grown on something else.

grub *noun* (grubs) **1** A small wriggling creature, the larva of an insect. **2** (informal) Food.

grudge¹ *noun* (grudges) An unkind, resentful feeling against someone.

grudge² *verb* (grudges, grudging, grudged) To be unwilling to let someone have something.

gruelling *adjective* Exhausting.

gruesome *adjective* Horrible. **gruesomely** *adverb.*

gruff *adjective* (gruffer, gruffest) With a rough, unfriendly voice or manner. **gruffly** *adverb,* **gruffness** *noun.*

grumble *verb* (grumbles, grumbling, grumbled) **1** To complain. **2** To make a rumbling noise.

grumpy *adjective* (grumpier, grumpiest) Bad-tempered. **grumpily** *adverb,* **grumpiness** *noun.*

grunt *verb* (grunts, grunting, grunted) To make a noise like a pig.

guarantee¹ *noun* (guarantees) A promise to repair or replace something if it goes wrong.

guarantee² *verb* (guarantees, guaranteeing, guaranteed) **1** To give a guarantee. **2** To make a solemn promise.

guard¹ *noun* **1** Protection, watching. *Keep him under close guard.* **2** (guards) Someone watching or protecting. **3** A group of soldiers or police on duty as a guard. **4** A railway official in charge of a train. **5** A device to protect you from injury. *a fire guard.* **on guard** guarding.

guard² *verb* (guards, guarding, guarded) **1** To protect something or someone. **2** To watch over someone to prevent them escaping.

guardian *noun* (guardians) **1** Someone who is legally in charge of a child whose parents cannot look after him or her. **2** A keeper, a protector.

guava *noun* The orange-coloured fruit of a tropical American tree.

guerrilla *noun* (guerrillas) A fighter who wages war by ambushes and surprise attacks.

guess¹ *noun* (guesses) An opinion which is not based on certain knowledge or exact calculations.

guess² *verb* (guesses, guessing, guessed) To make a guess.

guesswork *noun* Guessing.

guest *noun* (guests) **1** A person paying a visit to someone else's house. **2** A person staying in a hotel.

guest-house *noun* (guest-houses) A kind of small hotel.

guide¹ *noun* (guides) **1** A person or a thing that shows the way or gives help. **2** A person or book that describes interesting sights for tourists. **Guide** a member of the Guides Association, an organization for girls.

guide² *verb* (guides, guiding, guided) To act as a guide. **guided missile** a rocket which can be controlled in its flight. **guidance** *noun.*

guide-dog *noun* (guide-dogs) A dog trained to guide a blind person.

guillotine *noun* (guillotines) **1** An instrument for cutting off people's heads. **2** An instrument for cutting paper.

guilt *noun* The fact that you have done wrong.

guilty *adjective* **1** Responsible for committing a crime. *The prisoner was found guilty.* **2** Aware of having done wrong. *He has a guilty conscience.* **guiltily** *adverb*.

guinea-pig *noun* (guinea-pigs) **1** A small, tailless animal often kept as a pet. **2** A person who is used in an experiment.

guitar *noun* (guitars) A musical instrument with strings which are plucked.

Gujarati *adjective* Of Gujarat, a state in western India.

gulf *noun* (gulfs) A large bay.

gull *noun* (gulls) A kind of seabird.

gullet *noun* (gullets) The throat.

gully *noun* (gullies) A narrow channel.

gulp *verb* (gulps, gulping, gulped) **1** To swallow hastily or greedily. **2** To gasp.

gum *noun* **1** A sticky substance used as glue. **gummed, gummy** *adjectives*. **2** Chewing-gum. **3** (gums) The firm pink flesh round the teeth.

gumboot *noun* (gumboots) A long rubber boot.

gum-tree *noun* (gum-trees) A eucalyptus tree.

gumption *noun* (informal) Common sense.

gun *noun* (guns) Any weapon which fires bullets, shells, or shot from a metal tube.

gunboat *noun* (gunboats) A small warship.

gunfire *noun* The firing of guns.

gunman *noun* (gunmen) An armed criminal.

gunner *noun* (gunners) A soldier in charge of a large gun. **gunnery** *noun*.

gunpowder *noun* Explosive powder.

gurdwara *noun* (gurdwaras) A Sikh temple.

gurgle *verb* (gurgles, gurgling, gurgled) To make a sound like bubbling water.

guru *noun* (gurus) A Hindu religious teacher.

gush *verb* (gushes, gushing, gushed) To flow out in a rush. **gusher** *noun*.

gust *noun* (gusts) A sudden rush of wind.

gut *verb* (guts, gutting, gutted) To remove the guts or inside of something.

guts *noun* **1** The insides of a person or animal. **2** (informal) Courage and determination.

gutter *noun* (gutters) A channel to carry away rain-water.

guy *noun* (guys) **1** The figure of Guy Fawkes burnt on 5 November. **2** (informal) A man. **guy ropes** the ropes which hold a tent up.

guzzle *verb* (guzzles, guzzling, guzzled) To eat or drink greedily.

gym *noun* (informal) **1** (gyms) A gymnasium. **2** Gymnastics.

gymkhana *noun* (gymkhanas) A sports display with pony-riding or horse-riding.

gymnasium *noun* (gymnasiums) A building with apparatus for gymnastics.

gymnastics *noun* Exercises for strengthening your body or displaying your skill. **gymnast** *noun*.

gypsy or **gipsy** *noun* (gypsies or gipsies) A member of a race of people who live in caravans and travel from place to place.

Hh

habit *noun* (habits) Something you do so often that you do it without thinking. **habitual** *adjective*, **habitually** *adverb*.

habitable *adjective* Fit to be lived in.

habitat *noun* (habitats) The natural home of an animal or plant.

hack *verb* (hacks, hacking, hacked) To chop, to cut roughly.

hack-saw *noun* (hack-saws) A saw for cutting metal.

had *See* **have**

haddock *noun* (haddock) A sea fish.

hadn't (informal) Had not.

hag *noun* (hags) An ugly old woman.

haggis *noun* A traditional Scottish food.

haggle *verb* (haggles, haggling, haggled) To argue about the price of something.

haiku *noun* (haiku) A poem with seventeen syllables arranged in three lines.

hail[1] *noun* Frozen raindrops.

hail[2] *verb* (hails, hailing, hailed) **1** *It is hailing*, hail is falling. **2** To greet someone, to call out to someone.

hailstone *noun* (hailstones) One of the frozen drops in a storm of hail.

hair *noun* **1** The fine, thread-like growths on skin, especially on a person's head or an animal's body. **2** (hairs) One of these. **hairless** *adjective*.

hairbrush *noun* (hairbrushes) A brush used on the hair.

haircut *noun* (haircuts) **1** Having your hair cut. **2** The style in which it is cut.

hairdresser *noun* (hairdressers) A person who cuts, washes, and arranges people's hair.

hairpin *noun* (hairpins) A piece of bent wire used to hold hair in place. **hairpin bend** a very sharp bend in a road.

hair-raising *adjective* Terrifying.

hairy *adjective* (hairier, hairiest) **1** Covered with hair. **2** (informal) Dangerous.

halal *adjective* As required by Muslim law.

half[1] *noun* (halves) One of the two equal parts into which something is or can be divided. Half of 6 is 3. Half of 1 is $\frac{1}{2}$.

half[2] *adverb* Partly, not completely. *This meat is only half cooked.*

half-hearted *adjective* Not very enthusiastic. **half-heartedly** *adverb*.

half-term *noun* (half-terms) A holiday in the middle of a term.

half-time *noun* An interval between the two halves of a game.

half-way *adjective and adverb* At a point half of the distance between two places.

half-wit *noun* (half-wits) A stupid person. **half-witted** *adjective*.

hall *noun* (halls) **1** A large room for concerts, assemblies, meetings, or other purposes. **2** The first room or passage inside the front door of a house. **3** A large house like a palace.

hallelujah Praise God!

hallo, hello, or **hullo 1** A greeting. **2** A word used to attract someone's attention.

hallowed *adjective* Holy, sacred.

Hallowe'en *noun* 31 October.

hallucination *noun* (hallucinations) Something which you think you can see but which does not really exist.

halo *noun* (haloes) A circle of light. In paintings, a halo is often shown over the head of a holy person.

halt *verb* (halts, halting, halted) To stop.

halter *noun* (halters) A rope or strap with a loop to hold a horse's head.

halve *verb* (halves, halving, halved) **1** To divide something into halves. **2** To reduce something to half its size.

halves *See* **half**

ham *noun* Meat from a pig's leg.

hamburger *noun* (hamburgers) A fried cake of chopped beef.

hamlet *noun* (hamlets) A tiny village.

hammer¹ *noun* (hammers) A hitting tool.

hammer² *verb* (hammers, hammering, hammered) **1** To hit with a hammer. **2** To hit hard. *to hammer on a door.*

hammock *noun* (hammocks) A hanging bed.

hamper¹ *noun* (hampers) A large basket with a lid.

hamper² *verb* (hampers, hampering, hampered) To hinder somebody, to make things difficult.

hamster *noun* (hamsters) A small rodent often kept as a pet.

hand¹ *noun* (hands) **1** The part of the body at the end of the arm, below the wrist. **2** A member of a ship's crew or a worker in a factory. **3** A pointer on a clock. **4** The cards dealt to a player in a card-game. **first hand** directly from the person concerned. **out of hand** out of control.

hand² *verb* (hands, handing, handed) To pass something with your hands. *Please hand me my overcoat.*

handbag *noun* (handbags) A small bag carried by a woman.

handcuffs *noun* A device for locking a prisoner's wrists together.

handful *noun* (handfuls) **1** An amount that fills a person's hand. **2** A small number. *a handful of people.* **3** (informal) A troublesome person.

handicap *noun* (handicaps) A disadvantage.

handicapped *adjective* **1** At a disadvantage. **2** Disabled.

handicraft *noun* (handicrafts) Skilful work done with the hands.

handiwork *noun* Work done by the hands. *Is this your handiwork? Did you do this?*

handkerchief *noun* (handkerchiefs) A square piece of cloth or tissue for wiping your nose.

handle¹ *noun* (handles) The part of a thing you hold it by.

handle² *verb* (handles, handling, handled) **1** To touch something with the hands. **2** To deal with something, to manage it. *You won't enjoy your ride if you can't handle the horse!*

handlebars *noun* The bar with handles which a cyclist uses to steer a bicycle.

handsome *adjective* **1** Attractive, good-looking. **2** Generous. *a handsome gift.* **handsomely** *adverb*.

handwriting *noun* Writing done by hand. **handwritten** *adjective*.

handy *adjective* (handier, handiest) **1** Convenient, not far away. **2** Useful. **3** Clever with your hands. *He's handy at carpentry*.

hang¹ *verb* (hangs, hanging, hung) **1** To fix something at the top and let it be free at the bottom. *We hung the picture on the wall.* **2** To float in the air. *A smell of cooking hung about the house.* **3** *To hang wallpaper*, to paste it to the wall. **hang about** to stand about doing nothing. **hang back** to hesitate. **hang on to** to hold something, to keep it.

hang² *verb* (hangs, hanging, hanged) To put someone to death by hanging him or her with a noose tied round the neck.

hang³ *noun* **get the hang of** to understand something.

hangar *noun* (hangars) A large shed for aeroplanes.

hanger *noun* (hangers) A device on which to hang things.

hang-glider *noun* (hang-gliders)

A large kind of kite in which a person can fly. **hang-gliding** *noun*.

hangman *noun* (hangmen) A man whose job is to put condemned criminals to death by hanging them.

hanker *verb* (hankers, hankering, hankered) **hanker after** to long for something.

Hanukka *noun* A Jewish festival of lights that takes place in December.

haphazard *adjective* Accidental, without planning.

happen *verb* (happens, happening, happened) **1** To occur, to take place. **2** *I happened to be there*, I was there by chance.

happening *noun* (happenings) An event, something which happens.

happy *adjective* (happier, happiest) **1** Pleased, glad, enjoying yourself. **2** Lucky. **happily** *adverb*, **happiness** *noun*.

harass *verb* (harasses, harassing, harassed) To trouble and worry someone. **harassment** *noun*.

harbour¹ *noun* (harbours) **1** A place where ships can shelter. **2** A place where ships unload.

harbour² *verb* (harbours, harbouring, harboured) To give shelter to someone or something.

hard¹ *adjective* (harder, hardest) **1** Firm, solid, not soft, not easily cut. *hard rock*. **2** Difficult. *a hard problem*. **3** Severe, harsh, cruel. *a hard frost*. **4** Severely. *to freeze hard*. **5** With great effort. *to try hard*. **hard up** poor, short of money. **hard of hearing** rather deaf.

hard² *adverb* **1** With great effort or intensity. **2** With great difficulty. **3** Severely. *It will freeze hard tonight*.

hardboard *noun* Board like very stiff, thick cardboard.

harden *verb* (hardens, hardening, hardened) To make hard, to become hard.

hard-hearted *adjective* Cruel, unfeeling.

hardly *adverb* Only just, only with difficulty. **hardly any** almost none.

hardship *noun* (hardships) Suffering.

hardware *noun* **1** Tools and other goods sold by an ironmonger. **2** Computer equipment.

hard-wearing *adjective* Not wearing out easily.

hardy *adjective* (hardier, hardiest) Able to bear cold and hardship.

hare *noun* (hares) An animal like a large rabbit.

hare-lip *noun* (hare-lips) A deformed upper lip.

harem *noun* (harems) **1** The women in a Muslim household. **2** The place where they live.

hark *verb* Listen!

harm¹ *verb* (harms, harming, harmed) To damage, to hurt.

harm² *noun* Damage, injury. **harmful**, **harmless** *adjectives*, **harmfully**, **harmlessly** *adverbs*.

harmonica *noun* (harmonicas) A mouth-organ.

harmony *noun* **1** Agreement. **2** (harmonies) A combination of musical notes sounding pleasantly together. **harmonious** *adjective*, **harmoniously** *adverb*.

harness¹ *noun* (harnesses) Straps and other equipment worn by a horse.

harness² *verb* (harnesses, harnessing, harnessed) **1** To put a harness on a horse. **2** To control something and use it.

harp noun (harps) A musical instrument with many strings. **harpist** noun.

harp verb (harps, harping, harped) **harp on** to keep on talking about something in a boring way.

harpoon noun (harpoons) A spear used in hunting whales.

harpsichord noun (harpsichords) A keyboard instrument in which strings are plucked.

harrow noun (harrows) A heavy frame with iron teeth towed behind a tractor for breaking up the soil.

harsh adjective (harsher, harshest) **1** Grating, unpleasant. *a harsh sound*. **2** Stern, cruel. *a harsh ruler*. **harshly** adverb, **harshness** noun.

harvest noun (harvests) **1** The gathering in of the corn or other crops. **2** The crop that is gathered in.

harvest verb (harvests, harvesting, harvested) To gather in the crops. **harvester** noun.

has See **have**

hash noun (hashes) A kind of stew. **make a hash of** to do something very badly.

hasn't (informal) Has not.

haste noun Hurry, being quick. **hasty** adjective, **hastily** adverb, **hastiness** noun.

hasten verb (hastens, hastening, hastened) To hurry.

hat noun (hats) A covering for the head.

hatch noun (hatches) **1** An opening in a wall, especially between a kitchen and a dining-room. **2** An opening in the deck of a ship.

hatch verb (hatches, hatching, hatched) **1** To keep an egg warm until a baby bird breaks out of it. **2** To break out of an egg. **hatch a plot** to plan it.

hatchback noun (hatchbacks) A car with a door at the back that lifts up.

hatchet noun (hatchets) A small axe.

hate verb (hates, hating, hated) To dislike someone or something very much.

hate or **hatred** noun Very great dislike. **hateful** adjective.

haughty adjective (haughtier, haughtiest) Proud of yourself and looking down on other people. **haughtily** adverb, **haughtiness** noun.

haul verb (hauls, hauling, hauled) To pull, to drag.

haunt verb (haunts, haunting, haunted) To visit a place often. **haunted** inhabited or visited by a ghost.

have verb (has, having, had) **1** To possess, to own. *We have two cats.* **2** To provide a place for something. *John has the telephone on his desk.* **3** To contain. *This book has coloured pictures.* **4** To enjoy. *We had a marvellous time.* **5** To suffer. *I had mumps.* **6** To be compelled. *We had to do the washing-up.* **7** To cause something to be done. *Is it worth having this watch repaired?* **8** To receive, to obtain. *She had a recorder for Christmas.*

haven noun (havens) A safe place.

haven't (informal) Have not.

haversack noun (haversacks) A bag worn on the back by soldiers and hikers.

havoc noun Great destruction.

hawk noun (hawks) A bird of prey.

hawser noun (hawsers) A thick rope, often made of steel.

hawthorn noun (hawthorns) A small

thorny tree which has red berries in winter.

hay *noun* Dried grass for feeding animals. **hay fever** irritation of the nose, throat, and eyes, caused by pollen.

haystack *noun* (haystacks) A stack of hay.

hazard *noun* (hazards) A risk, a danger. **hazardous** *adjective*, **hazardously** *adverb*.

haze *noun* A thin mist.

hazel *noun* (hazels) A small nut tree.

hazy *adjective* (hazier, haziest) **1** Misty. **2** Blurred, confused. **hazily** *adverb*.

he *pronoun* (him, himself) The male person or animal being talked about.

head[1] *noun* (heads) **1** The part of the body containing brains, eyes, and mouth. **2** A knob or swelling at the end of something. *the head of a nail.* **3** The top or front end of something. *the head of the stairs, the head of a queue.* **4** The chief, the person in charge. **head wind** a wind that blows directly towards you. **come to a head** to reach a crisis. **keep your head** to stay calm, not to panic. **use your head** to think, to use your intelligence.

head[2] *verb* (heads, heading, headed) **1** To hit with the head. *Gary headed the ball into the net.* **header** *noun*. **2** To be in charge of something, to lead it. **head for** to go towards a place.

headache *noun* (headaches) A pain in the head.

head-dress *noun* (head-dresses) Something worn on the head.

heading *noun* (headings) A headline, a title, words written at the top of a piece of writing.

headlight *noun* (headlights) A powerful light on the front of a car or other vehicle.

headline *noun* (headlines) Words in large print at the top of an article in a newspaper or magazine. **the headlines** the main points of the news.

headlong *adverb and adjective* **1** Head first. **2** Thoughtlessly and hurriedly.

head-on *adverb and adjective* Front to front. *a head-on collision.*

headphones *noun* A listening device which fits over your head.

headquarters *noun* A central office from which orders are sent out, a base.

headteacher *noun* (headteachers) The person in charge of a school. **headmaster, headmistress** *nouns*.

headway *noun* **make headway** to make progress.

heal *verb* (heals, healing, healed) **1** To become well again. *Has your wound healed?* **2** To make well again, to cure. **healer** *noun*.

health *noun* The condition of a person's body or mind. *Good health is a great blessing.* **health food** food which is supposed to be specially good for you.

healthy *adjective* (healthier, healthiest) **1** Strong and well, free from illness. **2** Good for your health. **healthily** *adverb*, **healthiness** *noun*.

heap[1] *noun* (heaps) A pile. **heaps** (informal) plenty.

heap[2] *verb* (heaps, heaping, heaped) To put into a heap.

hear *verb* (hears, hearing, heard) **1** To receive sounds through the ears. **2** To receive news. *We haven't heard from Harry lately.*

hearing *noun* The ability to hear.

hearse *noun* (hearses) A car for carrying a coffin to a funeral.

heart *noun* (hearts) **1** The organ that pumps the blood round your body. **2** Kind feelings, sympathy. **3** Courage, enthusiasm. *Don't lose heart!* **4** The middle of something, the core. *I was lost in the heart of the forest.* **5** A playing card marked with ♥. **break someone's heart** to make someone very unhappy. **learn by**

heart to learn to say something from memory.

heartbeat *noun* (heartbeats) The beat of the heart.

heartbreaking, heartbroken *adjectives* Very sad.

hearth *noun* (hearths) The floor of a fireplace.

heartless *adjective* Cruel. **heartlessly** *adverb*.

hearty *adjective* (heartier, heartiest) **1** Sincere and enthusiastic. *Hearty congratulations!* **2** Big, strong, healthy. *a hearty appetite*. **heartily** *adverb*.

heat[1] *noun* **1** Warmth, the feeling received from the sun, a fire, or a radiator. **2** (heats) A trial race to decide which runners are to take part in the final.

heat[2] *verb* (heats, heating, heated) **1** To make something hot. **2** To become hot.

heath *noun* (heaths) An area of waste land often covered with heather or bracken.

heathen[1] *noun* (heathen *or* heathens) A person who does not believe in God.

heathen[2] *adjective* Not religious.

heather *noun* A low-growing bush with purple or white flowers.

heat-wave *noun* (heat-waves) A long period of hot weather.

heave *verb* (heaves, heaving, heaved) **1** To pull or lift something with great effort. **2** (informal) To lift and throw. **heave to** to stop.

heaven *noun* **1** The home of God and the saints. **2** A happy place. **3** A feeling of happiness. **the heavens** the sky. **heavenly** *adverb*.

heavy *adjective* (heavier, heaviest) **1** Of great weight, hard to lift. **2** Serious, worse than usual. *heavy rain*. **3** Hard, difficult. *heavy work*. **4** Gloomy, dull. *a heavy sky*. **heavily** *adverb*, **heaviness** *noun*.

Hebrew *noun* The language of the Jews in Old Testament times and in modern Israel.

hectare *noun* (hectares) A measure of area of land, 10,000 square metres or about 2½ acres.

hectic *adjective* Excited and without rest.

hedge[1] *noun* (hedges) A row of bushes forming a kind of fence.

hedge[2] *verb* (hedges, hedging, hedged) **1** To make a hedge, to surround with a hedge. **2** To avoid giving a direct answer. **hedge in** to surround.

hedgehog *noun* (hedgehogs) A small animal covered with prickles.

hedgerow *noun* (hedgerows) A hedge.

heed[1] *verb* (heeds, heeding, heeded) To take notice of something.

heed[2] *noun* Care, attention. **heedless** *adjective*.

heel[1] *noun* (heels) **1** The back part of the foot. **2** The part of a sock round the heel, the part of a shoe under the heel.

heel[2] *verb* (heels, heeling, heeled) **1** To repair the heel of a shoe. **2** To kick with the heel. **3** To lean over to one side.

hefty *adjective* (heftier, heftiest) Big and strong.

heifer *noun* (heifers) A young cow.

height *noun* (heights) **1** The distance from the bottom of something to the top. **2** The highest, busiest, or most intense part. *the height of a storm*.

heir *nouns* (heirs) The person who will inherit someone's title or property.

heiress *noun* (heiresses) A female heir.

held *See* **hold**[1]

helicopter *noun* (helicopters) A kind of

aircraft with a large horizontal propeller.

hell *noun* **1** A place of punishment after death. **2** A very unpleasant place. **hellish** *adjective*.

he'll (informal) He will.

hello *See* **hallo**

helm *noun* (helms) The handle or wheel used to steer a ship. **helmsman** *noun*.

helmet *noun* (helmets) A tough covering to protect the head.

help[1] *verb* (helps, helping, helped) **1** To aid, to assist, to do something which makes someone's work easier, or their troubles less hard to bear. **helper** *noun*. **2** To avoid. *I can't help sneezing.*

help[2] *noun* **1** Aid, the act of helping someone. *I couldn't have done without your help.* **2** A person or thing that helps. *You were a great help.* **helpful** *adjective*, **helpfully** *adverb*.

helping *noun* (helpings) A portion of food put on your plate.

helpless *adjective* Unable to look after yourself. **helplessly** *adverb*.

help-line *noun* (help-lines) A telephone number where someone will answer and help you.

hem[1] *noun* (hems) The edge of a piece of cloth, the border made by turning the edge over and sewing it down.

hem[2] *verb* (hems, hemming, hemmed) To make a hem. **hem in** to surround.

hemisphere *noun* (hemispheres) Half the earth, half a globe.

hen *noun* (hens) **1** A female bird. **2** A farmyard chicken.

hence *adverb* From here, from this time.

henceforth *adverb* From now onwards.

her *See* **she**

herald *noun* (heralds) In former times, an official who made public announcements.

heraldry *noun* The study of the badges and emblems of old families. **heraldic** *adjective*.

herb *noun* (herbs) A plant used for flavouring or for medicines. **herbal** *adjective*.

herd[1] *noun* (herds) A number of cattle feeding or going about together.

herd[2] *verb* (herds, herding, herded) To crowd together.

here *adverb* **1** In this place, at this place, to this place. *Stand here! Look here! Come here!* **2** At this point. *Here he stopped for us to ask questions.* **3** This place. *We live quite near here.*

hereabouts *adverb* Near here.

hereditary *adjective* Passed on from parents to children. **heredity** *noun*.

heritage *noun* The things that we inherit from the past.

hermit *noun* (hermits) A person who lives quite alone.

hero, heroine *nouns* (heroes, heroines) **1** A very brave person. **2** The most important person in a play or story. *Juliet is the heroine, and Romeo is the hero.* **heroic** *adjective*, **heroically** *adverb*, **heroism** *noun*.

heroin *noun* A very strong drug.

heron *noun* (herons) A long-legged wading bird.

herring *noun* (herring *or* herrings) A sea fish.

hers Belonging to her.

herself *See* **she**. This word is used in various ways including: **1** *She hurt herself on the broken glass.* **2** *I heard the news from the headmistress herself.* **3** *She was by herself,* she was alone. **4** *She isn't herself today,* she isn't well.

he's (informal) **1** He is. **2** He has.

hesitate *verb* (hesitates, hesitating, hesitated) To pause uncertainly, when doing something or when speaking. **hesitant** *adjective*, **hesitantly** *adverb*, **hesitation** *noun*.

hew *verb* (hews, hewing, hewed, hewn) To chop, to cut with an axe or sword.

hexagon *noun* (hexagons) A shape with six sides. **hexagonal** *adjective*.

hibernate *verb* (hibernates, hibernating, hibernated) To stay sleepy and inactive through the winter. **hibernation** *noun*.

hiccup *verb* (hiccups, hiccuping, hiccuped) To make a sound like a sharp cough.

hide¹ *verb* (hides, hiding, hid, hidden)
1 To put something out of sight.
2 To go to a place where you cannot be seen.

hide² *noun* (hides) An animal's skin.

hide-and-seek *noun* A hiding game.

hideous *adjective* Very ugly. **hideously** *adverb*.

hide-out *noun* (hide-outs) A hiding-place.

hiding *noun* **give someone a hiding** to thrash someone.

hiding-place *noun* (hiding-places) A place where you hide.

hieroglyphics *noun* Picture-writing like that used by the ancient Egyptians.

hi-fi *noun* High-fidelity equipment.

higgledy-piggledy *adverb and adjective* Mixed up, in complete confusion.

high¹ *adjective* (higher, highest)
1 Going up a long way. *high hills.*
2 Measuring from top to bottom. *two metres high.* **3** Situated a long way above ground level or sea level. *high clouds.* **4** Above what is expected. *high prices.* **5** Very important. *a high rank in the army.* **6** Strong, intense, stormy. *a high wind.* **7** Favourable. *to have a high opinion of someone.* **8** Smelly, going bad. *This meat is high.* **in high spirits** cheerful, lively. **the high seas** the ocean. **high tea** an early evening meal with tea and cooked food. **high**

time fully time, past the proper time. *It's high time for bed.*

high² *adverb* at or to a high level, at or to a high place.

high-fidelity *adjective* Reproducing sound very clearly.

Highlander *noun* (Highlanders) Someone who lives in the Highlands of Scotland.

highlands *noun* Hilly or mountainous country.

highlight¹ *noun* (highlights) One of the most interesting or exciting parts of something.

highlight² *verb* (highlights, highlighting, highlighted) **1** To draw special attention to something. **2** To draw attention to words on a page by colouring them with a special pen. **highlighter** *noun*.

highly *adverb* **1** Very. **2** Favourably. *to think highly of someone.*

highly-strung *adjective* Nervous, easily upset.

Highness *noun* A title used for a member of a royal family. *His Royal Highness.*

highway *noun* (highways) A main road.

highwayman *noun* (highwaymen) A horseman who used to rob travellers on the highway.

hijack *verb* (hijacks, hijacking, hijacked) To seize control of a vehicle or aircraft during a journey. **hijacker** *noun*.

hike *verb* (hikes, hiking, hiked) To go for a long walk in the country. **hiker** *noun*.

hilarious *adjective* Very funny, very cheerful. **hilariously** *adverb*, **hilarity** *noun*.

hill *noun* (hills) **1** A high piece of land with sloping sides. **2** A slope. **hilly** *adjective*.

hillside *noun* (hillsides) The side of a hill.

hilltop *noun* (hilltops) The top of a hill.

hilt *noun* (hilts) The handle of a sword or dagger.

him *See* **he**

himself *See* **he.** This word is used in the same ways as **herself.**

hind *adjective* At the back. *The hind legs of a horse.*

hinder *verb* (hinders, hindering, hindered) To delay, to get in someone's way when he or she wants to do something. **hindrance** *noun*.

Hindi *noun* One of the languages of India.

Hindu *noun* (Hindus) A believer in Hinduism, one of the religions of India.

hinge *noun* (hinges) A device on which a door or gate swings when it opens. **hinged** *adjective*.

hint¹ *noun* (hints) A suggestion, a slight indication.

hint² *verb* (hints, hinting, hinted) To give a hint.

hip¹ *noun* (hips) The bony part on each side of the body just above the top of the legs.

hip² *noun* (hips) The fruit of the wild rose.

hippopotamus *noun* (hippopotamuses) A large African river-animal.

hire *verb* (hires, hiring, hired) To borrow or lend something in return for payment. *We hired a boat for £40 a day.*

hire-purchase *noun* Buying something by paying in instalments.

his Belonging to him.

hiss *verb* (hisses, hissing, hissed) To make a sound like the sound of *s*.

historian *noun* (historians) A person who studies history.

historic *adjective* Famous in history.

historical *adjective* Belonging to history, of the past. **historically** *adverb*.

history *noun* **1** The study of things which happened in the past. **2** (histories) A book or story about past events.

hit¹ *verb* (hits, hitting, hit) **1** To knock, to come into violent contact with something. *The car hit the gate.* **2** To move something by hitting it. *I hit the ball over the fence.* **3** To hurt, to damage. *The harvest was hit by bad weather.* **4** To reach. *The collection hit our target of £50.*

hit² *noun* (hits) **1** The act of hitting. **2** A success, a successful song.

hitch *verb* (hitches, hitching, hitched) **1** To pull up with a quick movement. *to hitch up your trousers.* **2** To fasten with a hook or a loop. **3** (informal) To hitch-hike.

hitch-hike *verb* (hitch-hikes, hitch-hiking, hitch-hiked) To beg a lift in a car or other vehicle. **hitch-hiker** *noun*.

hither *adverb* To this place. **hither and thither** in various directions.

hitherto *adverb* Up to now.

hive *noun* (hives) A beehive.

hoard *verb* (hoards, hoarding, hoarded) To gather things together and store them, to keep things in a miserly way.

hoarding *noun* (hoardings) A tall wooden fence covered with advertisements.

hoar-frost *noun* White frost.

hoarse *adjective* (hoarser, hoarsest) With a rough voice, husky, croaking. **hoarsely** *adverb*, **hoarseness** *noun*.

hoax¹ *noun* (hoaxes) A deceitful trick played on someone for a joke.

hoax² *verb* (hoaxes, hoaxing, hoaxed) To deceive someone by a hoax.

hobble *verb* (hobbles, hobbling, hobbled) To walk with a limp.

hobby *noun* (hobbies) Something you like doing in your spare time.

hockey *noun* **1** An outdoor game played with a ball and curved sticks. **2** In Canada, ice-hockey.

hoe *noun* (hoes) A tool for scraping up weeds.

hog *noun* (hogs) A male pig.

Hogmanay *noun* (in Scotland) New Year's Eve.

hoist *verb* (hoists, hoisting, hoisted) To lift up by means of ropes, pulleys, or other equipment.

hold¹ *verb* (holds, holding, held) **1** To grasp something, to have it firmly in the hands. *Hold the ladder while I climb.* **2** To possess, to keep. *My father holds a driving licence.* **3** To contain. *How much does this bottle hold?* **4** To keep someone captive. *The suspect was held for questioning by the police.* **5** To keep yourself in a certain position. *Hold yourself up straight!* **6** To keep something back, not to let it go. *Hold your breath!* **7** To cause something to take place. *The captain held a meeting.* **8** To continue. *How long will this weather hold?* **9** Not to break. *Will that rope hold?* **hold back** to hesitate. **hold out** to last, to continue. **hold someone up 1** To delay someone. **2** To stop and rob someone.

hold² *noun* (holds) **1** A grasp. **2** A place to hold on to. **3** The part of a ship below decks where the cargo is stored.

holdall *noun* (holdalls) A traveller's bag.

holder *noun* (holders) A person or thing that holds something.

hold-up *noun* (hold-ups) **1** A delay. **2** An attack by an armed robber.

hole *noun* (holes) **1** An opening, a gap, a space.

Holi *noun* A Hindu spring festival.

holiday *noun* (holidays) Time off from school or work.

holiday-maker *noun* (holiday-makers) A person on holiday.

hollow¹ *adjective* Not solid, having an empty space inside.

hollow² *noun* (hollows) **1** A hollow place. **2** A hole. **3** A small valley.

hollow³ *adverb* Completely. *We beat them hollow.*

hollow⁴ *verb* (hollows, hollowing, hollowed) To make something hollow.

holly *noun* An evergreen bush with prickly leaves.

hollyhock *noun* (hollyhocks) A very tall garden flower.

hologram *noun* (holograms) A picture produced by the use of lasers which gives a three-dimensional effect.

holster *noun* (holsters) A case for carrying a pistol.

holy *adjective* (holier, holiest) **1** Sacred, belonging to God. **2** Religious. **holiness** *noun*.

homage *noun* Great respect.

home¹ *noun* (homes) **1** The place where you live with your family. **2** A place where people live together and are cared for. *an old people's home.* **feel at home** to feel comfortable and relaxed. **homeless** *adjective*.

home² *adjective and adverb* At or of or to home. **home game** a game played on your own ground. **bring something home to someone** to make him or her realize it.

home-made *adjective* Made at home.

homesick *adjective* Sad at being away from home. **homesickness** *noun*.

homestead *noun* (homesteads) A farmhouse.

homeward *adjective and adverb* Going towards home. **homewards** *adverb*.

homework *noun* School work which has to be done at home.

homing *adjective* **homing pigeon** a pigeon trained to fly home. **homing**

missile a missile which can aim itself at its target.

homosexual *adjective* Sexually attracted to people of your own sex.

honest *adjective* Fair, not liable to steal or cheat or lie. **honestly** *adverb*, **honesty** *noun*.

honey *noun* A sweet, sticky food made by bees.

honeycomb *noun* (honeycombs) A structure made out of wax by bees for storing their honey and eggs.

honeymoon *noun* (honeymoons) A holiday taken by a newly married couple.

honeysuckle *noun* A climbing plant with sweet-smelling flowers.

honour[1] *noun* 1 Great respect. 2 A reputation for being good, loyal, and noble. 3 A person or thing that brings honour. *You are an honour to the school.* 4 (honours) A title, medal, certificate, or special reward given to a deserving person.

honour[2] *verb* (honours, honouring, honoured) To feel or show great respect towards someone. **honour a promise** to keep a promise.

honourable *adjective* Good and noble. **honourably** *adverb*.

hood[1] *noun* (hoods) 1 A covering for the head and neck like that on an anorak. 2 A folding roof or cover like that on a pram. **hooded** *adjective*.

hood[2] *verb* (hoods, hooding, hooded) To cover with a hood.

hoodwink *verb* (hoodwinks, hoodwinking, hoodwinked) To deceive, to trick.

hoof *noun* (hoofs *or* hooves) The horny part of a horse's foot.

hook[1] *noun* (hooks) A bent or curved piece of metal or other material, such as a fish-hook or a cup-hook.

hook[2] *verb* (hooks, hooking, hooked) 1 To catch something by means of a hook. 2 To attach or fasten something by means of a hook.

hooligan *noun* (hooligans) A rowdy disorderly person, a member of a street gang. **hooliganism** *noun*.

hoop *noun* (hoops) A large ring.

hoot *verb* (hoots, hooting, hooted) 1 To make a noise like the cry of an owl or the sound of a car horn. **hooter** *noun*. 2 To jeer.

Hoover[1] *noun* (Hoovers) The trade name of a kind of vacuum cleaner.

hoover[2] *verb* (hoovers, hoovering, hoovered) To use a vacuum cleaner.

hop[1] *noun* (hops) A climbing plant whose fruits are used to flavour beer.

hop[2] *verb* (hops, hopping, hopped) 1 To jump on one foot. 2 To move along by jumping. *The bird hopped across the lawn.*

hope[1] *noun* (hopes) 1 A feeling that something you want is likely to happen, confidence in the future. 2 A person or thing you hope will be successful.

hope[2] *verb* (hopes, hoping, hoped) To have hope.

hopeful *adjective* 1 Hoping. 2 Likely to turn out well. *The weather looks hopeful.* **hopefully** *adverb*, **hopefulness** *noun*.

hopeless *adjective* 1 Without hope. 2 Very bad. *I am hopeless at drawing.* **hopelessly** *adverb*, **hopelessness** *noun*.

hopscotch *noun* A game played by hopping and kicking a stone into squares marked on the ground.

horde *noun* (hordes) A crowd, a gang.

horizon *noun* (horizons) The line in the distance where the earth and sky seem to meet.

horizontal *adjective* Flat, level, parallel to the horizon. **horizontally** *adverb*.

hormone *noun* (hormones) A chemical which passes round the body in the blood and stimulates various organs to react.

horn *noun* (horns) 1 One of the hard, pointed growths on the heads of

· cattle and some other animals. **2** A kind of musical instrument played by blowing. **3** A device for making warning sounds. *a fog-horn.*

hornet *noun* (hornets) A large kind of wasp.

hornpipe *noun* (hornpipes) A lively sailor's dance.

horoscope *noun* (horoscopes) A forecast of future events by an astrologer.

horrible *adjective* Horrifying, shocking, unpleasant. **horribly** *adverb.*

horrid *adjective* Horrible. **horridly** *adverb.*

horrific *adjective* Causing horror. **horrifically** *adverb.*

horrify *verb* (horrifies, horrifying, horrified) To cause horror, to shock.

horror *noun* (horrors) **1** A feeling of great fear or dislike. **2** Something which causes this feeling.

horse *noun* (horses) **1** An animal used for riding or for pulling carts or other vehicles. **horseman, horsewoman** *nouns.* **2** A wooden framework for jumping over in gymnastics. **clotheshorse** a framework for drying clothes.

horseback *noun* **on horseback** riding a horse.

horse-box *noun* (horse-boxes) A trailer for carrying horses.

horse-chestnut *noun* (horse-chestnuts) A large tree on which conkers grow.

horsepower *noun* (horsepower) A unit for measuring the power of engines.

horseshoe *noun* (horseshoes) A U-shaped piece of iron nailed to a horse's hoof.

hosanna *noun* A cry of praise to God.

hose, hose-pipe *nouns* (hoses, hosepipes) A flexible tube through which water can pass.

hospitable *adjective* Friendly and welcoming to strangers and guests. **hospitably** *adverb,* **hospitality** *noun.*

hospital *noun* (hospitals) A place where doctors and nurses care for sick and injured people.

host *noun* (hosts) **1** A person who has guests and looks after them. **hostess** *noun.* **2** A crowd.

hostage *noun* (hostages) A person who is held captive and whose life is threatened unless certain demands are agreed to.

hostel *noun* (hostels) A building where certain people can get board and lodging. *a youth hostel.*

hostile *adjective* Unfriendly, belonging to an enemy. **hostility** *noun.*

hostilities *noun* Fighting, warfare.

hot *adjective* (hotter, hottest) **1** Very warm, giving off much heat. *a hot fire.* **2** Fiery, eager, angry. *a hot temper.* **3** Having a burning flavour like pepper or ginger. **hot dog** a bread roll with a hot sausage in it. **hotly** *adverb.*

hotel *noun* (hotels) A building where meals and rooms are provided for travellers and for people on holiday.

hotpot *noun* A kind of stew.

hound[1] *noun* (hounds) A dog kept for hunting.

hound[2] *verb* (hounds, hounding, hounded) To chase, to pursue.

hour *noun* (hours) **1** A unit of time, 60 minutes. **2** A time of day. *Why are you up at this hour?*

hourglass *noun* (hourglasses) An old-fashioned device for measuring the time.

hourly *adverb and adjective* Every hour, once an hour.

house[1] *noun* (houses) **1** A building for people to live in, usually for one family. **2** A building used by an official assembly, the assembly itself. *the Houses of Parliament.* **3** One of the divisions of children in a school, which compete against each other in games and so on.

house[2] *verb* (houses, housing, housed) To provide a house or shelter for someone or something.

houseboat *noun* (houseboats) A boat used as a home.

household *noun* (households) All the people who live in a house.

housekeeper *noun* (housekeepers) A person employed to be in charge of the housework. **housekeeping** *noun*.

house-proud *adjective* Very keen to keep the house clean and tidy.

house-trained *adjective* Trained to behave properly in the house.

housewife *noun* (housewives) A woman who does the housework for her husband and family.

housework *noun* All the work that has to be done in the house, such as cleaning and cooking.

hovel *noun* (hovels) A small dirty house.

hover *verb* (hovers, hovering, hovered) **1** To hang still in the air, to stay in one place in the air. *The kestrel hovered above the motorway.* **2** To loiter, to hang about.

hovercraft *noun* (hovercraft) A vehicle that travels above the surface of land or water on a current of air fanned downwards by its engines.

how *adverb* **1** In what way. *Show me how to do it.* **2** To what extent. *How certain are they?* **3** In what condition. *How are you?* **4** *How about a game of football?* Shall we play football?

however *adverb* **1** Nevertheless, in spite of this. **2** In whatever way, to whatever extent. *However hard she ran, she could not catch up.*

howl[1] *verb* (howls, howling, howled) To make a long, loud cry.

howl[2] *noun* (howls) A long, loud cry.

howler *noun* (howlers) A ridiculous mistake.

HP Hire-purchase.

hub *noun* (hubs) The centre of a wheel.

hubbub *noun* A confused noise.

huddle *verb* (huddles, huddling, huddled) To crowd together. **huddled up** curled up.

hue[1] *noun* (hues) Colour.

hue[2] *noun* **hue and cry** a general cry of alarm.

huff *noun* **in a huff** offended, in a bad mood.

hug[1] *verb* (hugs, hugging, hugged) **1** To clasp someone lovingly in your arms. **2** To keep close to something. *The ship hugged the shore.*

hug[2] *noun* (hugs) A loving clasp with your arms.

huge *adjective* Very large, enormous. **hugely** *adverb*.

hulking *adjective* Large, clumsy.

hull *noun* (hulls) The body or frame of a ship.

hullo *See* **hallo**

hum[1] *verb* (hums, humming, hummed) **1** To sing with closed lips. **2** To make a gentle murmuring sound like bees.

hum[2] *noun* (hums) A humming sound.

human *adjective* Of a man or a woman. **human beings** men and women.

humane *adjective* Kind-hearted. **humanely** *adverb*.

humanity *noun* **1** The human race. **2** Human nature. **3** Kind-heartedness.

humble[1] *adjective* (humbler, humblest) Modest, meek, not proud. **humbly** *adverb*.

humble[2] *verb* (humbles, humbling, humbled) To make someone less proud.

humbug¹ *noun* Dishonest talk or behaviour, nonsense.

humbug² *noun* (humbugs) A hard peppermint-flavoured sweet.

humid *adjective* Moist, damp. **humidity** *noun*.

humiliate *verb* (humiliates, humiliating, humiliated) To make someone feel ashamed. **humiliation** *noun*.

humility *noun* Being humble.

humour¹ *noun* **1** Amusement, being funny. *a sense of humour*. **humorous** *adjective*, **humorously** *adverb*, **humorist** *noun*. **2** A mood. *in a good humour*.

humour² *verb* (humours, humouring, humoured) To try to please someone.

hump¹ *noun* (humps) A bump, a round lump.

hump² *verb* (humps, humping, humped) **1** To make a hump. **2** To carry something on your back.

hunch¹ *noun* (hunches) **have a hunch** to believe you can guess what will happen.

hunch² *verb* (hunches, hunching, hunched) To bend, to make a hump.

hunchback *noun* (hunchbacks) Someone with a hump on the back. **hunchbacked** *adjective*.

hundred (hundreds) The number 100. **hundredth**.

hung *See* **hang¹**

hunger *noun* The feeling of wanting food.

hungry *adjective* (hungrier, hungriest) Feeling hunger. **hungrily** *adverb*.

hunk *noun* (hunks) A large shapeless piece of something.

hunt¹ *verb* (hunts, hunting, hunted) **1** To chase wild animals and game, to try to kill them. **hunter, huntsman** *nouns*. **2** To pursue something, to search for it.

hunt² *noun* (hunts) **1** A chase, a search, hunting. **2** A group of people hunting.

hurdle *noun* (hurdles) A framework for jumping over in hurdling.

hurdling *noun* A kind of racing in which competitors must jump over hurdles. **hurdler** *noun*.

hurl *verb* (hurls, hurling, hurled) To throw something as hard as possible.

hurrah or **hurray** A shout of happiness or approval.

hurricane *noun* (hurricanes) A very violent windy storm.

hurry¹ *noun* The wish to get something done quickly. **in a hurry** hurrying.

hurry² *verb* (hurries, hurrying, hurried) **1** To move quickly, to do something quickly. **2** To try to make someone be quick. **hurriedly** *adverb*.

hurt *verb* (hurts, hurting, hurt) To cause harm, pain, or distress.

hurtle *verb* (hurtles, hurtling, hurtled) To move along very quickly or violently.

husband *noun* (husbands) A married man.

hush *verb* (hushes, hushing, hushed) **1** To become silent. **2** To tell people to be silent. **hush up** to keep something secret.

husk *noun* (husks) The dry outer covering of a seed.

husky¹ *adjective* (huskier, huskiest) **1** Dry, hoarse. **2** Big and strong.

husky² *noun* (huskies) An Eskimo dog.

hustle *verb* (hustles, hustling, hustled) **1** To push roughly, to jostle. **2** To hurry.

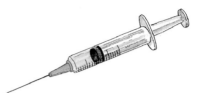
hut *noun* (huts) A small house or shelter.

hutch *noun* (hutches) A box for a pet rabbit to live in.

hyacinth *noun* (hyacinths) A sweet-smelling flower which grows from a bulb.

hydrant *noun* (hydrants) An outdoor water tap.

hydraulic *adjective* Worked by water or other liquid. *hydraulic brakes*.

hydroelectric *adjective* Producing electricity by water power.

hydrofoil, hydroplane *nouns* (hydrofoils, hydroplanes) A kind of boat which skims fast over the surface of the water.

hydrogen *noun* A very light inflammable gas.

hyena *noun* (hyenas) An animal like a wolf with a laugh-like cry.

hygiene *noun* Rules for keeping clean and healthy. **hygienic** *adjective*, **hygienically** *adverb*.

hymn *noun* (hymns) A song sung in a religious service.

hymn-book *noun* (hymn-books) A book of hymns.

hyphen *noun* (hyphens) The mark -. It is used in words like *wicket-keeper*, or when a word has to be divided at the end of a line.

hypnosis *noun* A condition like a deep sleep in which a person's actions may be controlled by someone else. **hypnotic** *adjective*.

hypnotize *verb* (hypnotizes, hypnotizing, hypnotized) To put someone into a state of hypnosis. **hypnotist** *noun*.

hypocrite *noun* (hypocrites) A person who pretends to be more virtuous than he or she really is. **hypocritical** *adjective*, **hypocritically** *adverb*, **hypocrisy** *noun*.

hypodermic syringe A device for giving injections.

hysteria *noun* Wild, uncontrollable excitement. **hysterical** *adjective*, **hysterically** *adverb*, **hysterics** *noun*.

Ii
···

I[1] One in Roman numerals.

I[2] (me, myself) A word you use when referring to yourself.

ice[1] *noun* **1** Frozen water. **2** (ices) An ice-cream.

ice[2] *verb* (ices, icing, iced) **1** To make something very cold. **2** To cover something with ice or icing.

iceberg *noun* (icebergs) A large floating lump of ice at sea.

ice-breaker *noun* (ice-breakers) A ship with strong bows for breaking through ice.

ice-cream *noun* (ice-creams) A creamy frozen food.

ice-hockey *noun* A kind of hockey played on ice by skaters.

ice-rink *noun* (ice-rinks) A building with an ice floor for skating.

icicle *noun* (icicles) A hanging piece of ice.

icing *noun* A sweet covering for a cake.

icy *adjective* (icier, iciest) Very cold, like ice, covered with ice. **icily** *adverb*.

I'd (informal) I had, I would.

idea *noun* (ideas) Something which exists in your mind, a thought, an opinion, a plan.

ideal *adjective* Just what is wanted, perfect. *ideal weather for a swim.* **ideally** *adverb.*

identical *adjective* The very same, similar in every detail. *identical twins.*

identify *verb* (identifies, identifying, identified) To discover who or what someone or something is. **identification** *noun.*

Identikit picture A picture of a wanted person put together from descriptions given to the police.

identity *noun* (identities) Who somebody is. *Can you prove your identity? Can you prove who you are?*

idiot *noun* (idiots) A stupid person, a fool. **idiotic** *adjective,* **idiotically** *adverb,* **idiocy** *noun.*

idle *adjective* (idler, idlest) **1** Not working. **2** Lazy. **3** Worthless. *idle gossip.* **idly** *adverb,* **idleness** *noun.*

idol *noun* (idols) **1** A statue worshipped as a god. **2** Someone who is greatly loved or admired.

idolize *verb* (idolizes, idolizing, idolized) To love or admire very much.

if 1 On condition that, supposing that. *You can come if you pay your own fare.* **2** Whenever. *If I don't wear my glasses I get a headache.* **3** Even though. *I'll finish this job if it kills me!* **4** Whether. *Do you know if dinner is ready?*

igloo *noun* (igloos) An Eskimo's dome-shaped snow hut.

ignite *verb* (ignites, igniting, ignited) **1** To set on fire. **2** To catch fire. **ignition** *noun.*

ignition-key *noun* (ignition-keys) The key used to start a car or other vehicle.

ignoramus *noun* (ignoramuses) An ignorant person.

ignorant *adjective* **1** Having no knowledge about something. **2** Uneducated, having little knowledge about anything. **ignorantly** *adverb,* **ignorance** *noun.*

ignore *verb* (ignores, ignoring, ignored) To take no notice of someone or something.

ill *adjective* **1** Sick, in bad health. **illness** *noun.* **2** Bad, harmful. *ill effects.*

I'll (informal) I will, I shall.

illegal *adjective* Against the law. **illegally** *adverb.*

illegible *adjective* Impossible to read, hard to read. **illegibly** *adverb.*

illegitimate *adjective* **illegitimate child** a child whose parents were not married to each other when it was born.

illiterate *adjective* Unable to read or write. **illiteracy** *noun.*

illogical *adjective* Not logical. **illogically** *adverb.*

ill-treat *verb* (ill-treats, ill-treating, ill-treated) To misuse, to treat someone or something badly.

illuminate *verb* (illuminates, illuminating, illuminated) To light something up, to decorate it with lights. **illumination** *noun.*

illusion *noun* (illusions) A false idea, a belief that something is real when it is not.

illustrate *verb* (illustrates, illustrating, illustrated) To help to explain something by using pictures, diagrams, or examples. **illustration** *noun.*

I'm (informal) I am.

image *noun* (images) **1** A picture or a carving of something. **2** A copy, a likeness.

imaginary *adjective* Not real, existing only in the mind.

imagination *noun* The power to imagine things.

imaginative *adjective* Having a strong imagination. **imaginatively** *adverb.*

imagine *verb* (imagines, imagining,

imagined) To form pictures in the mind. **imaginable** *adjective*.

imam *noun* (imams) A Muslim leader.

imbecile *noun* (imbeciles) An idiot.

imitate *verb* (imitates, imitating, imitated) To mimic, to copy. **imitation, imitator** *nouns*.

immature *adjective* Not mature, not fully grown-up. **immaturity** *noun*.

immeasurable *adjective* Too big to measure.

immediate *adjective* 1 Happening without delay. *I want an immediate answer.* 2 Next, nearest. *We talk to our immediate neighbours over the fence.*

immediately *adverb* At once, without delay.

immense *adjective* Very big, enormous. **immensely** *adverb*, **immensity** *noun*.

immerse *verb* (immerses, immersing, immersed) To put something completely in water or other liquid. **immersed in** very busy and interested in something.

immersion heater An electric water-heater in a hot-water tank.

immigrate *verb* (immigrates, immigrating, immigrated) To come into a country to live there. **immigrant, immigration** *nouns*.

immobile *adjective* Not movable, not moving.

immobilize *verb* (immobilizes, immobilizing, immobilized) To make something immobile and useless.

immoral *adjective* Wicked, not moral. **immorality** *noun*.

immortal *adjective* 1 Living for ever. 2 Famous for all time. **immortality** *noun*.

immovable *adjective* Not movable.

immune *adjective* Safe from the danger of catching a disease. **immunity** *noun*.

immunize *verb* (immunizes, immunizing, immunized) To make someone immune. **immunization** *noun*.

imp *noun* (imps) A small devil. **impish** *adjective*, **impishly** *adverb*.

impact *noun* (impacts) 1 A collision, a violent coming together. 2 A strong influence.

impale *verb* (impales, impaling, impaled) To stick a spear or spike through something or someone.

impartial *adjective* Fair, not biased. **impartially** *adverb*.

impassable *adjective* Impossible to travel along or through.

impatient *adjective* Not patient, restless. **impatiently** *adverb*, **impatience** *noun*.

impede *verb* (impedes, impeding, impeded) To hinder.

impediment *noun* (impediments) Something that hinders your speech, like stammering.

impenetrable *adjective* Unable to be penetrated.

imperative *adjective* Urgent, essential.

imperceptible *adjective* Very slight, not noticeable. **imperceptibly** *adverb*.

imperfect *adjective* Not perfect, not complete. **imperfectly** *adverb*, **imperfection** *noun*.

imperial *adjective* Of an empire or its rulers.

impersonal *adjective* Without personal feelings.

impersonate *verb* (impersonates, impersonating, impersonated) To pretend to be somebody else. **impersonation, impersonator** *nouns*.

impertinent *adjective* Rude, not respectful. **impertinently** *adverb*, **impertinence** *noun*.

impetigo *noun* A skin disease.

impetuous *adjective* Liable to act hastily without thinking. **impetuously** *adverb*.

implement *noun* (implements) A tool, an instrument.

implication *noun* (implications) What is implied or involved in something.

implore *verb* (implores, imploring, implored) To beg, to ask very earnestly.

imply *verb* (implies, implying, implied) To hint at something without actually saying it.

impolite *adjective* Rude, not polite. **impolitely** *adverb*.

import[1] *verb* (imports, importing, imported) To bring goods into a country from abroad.

import[2] *noun* (imports) Something which is imported.

important *adjective* **1** To be treated very seriously. *an important message*. **2** Well known and deserving respect. *an important visitor*. **importantly** *adverb*, **importance** *noun*.

impose *verb* (imposes, imposing, imposed) To make someone pay or suffer or do something. *to impose a penalty*. **impose on** to take unfair advantage of someone. **imposition** *noun*.

imposing *adjective* Looking important, large.

impossible *adjective* **1** Not possible. **2** Not to be put up with. **impossibly** *adverb*, **impossibility** *noun*.

impostor *noun* (impostors) A person pretending to be someone else.

impotent *adjective* Lacking the power or strength to do something. **impotence** *noun*.

impoverished *adjective* Poor.

impracticable *adjective* Not able to be put into practice.

impractical *adjective* Not practical, not easily done.

impregnable *adjective* Safe against attack. *an impregnable castle*.

impress *verb* (impresses, impressing, impressed) To fill someone with admiration. **impress something on someone** to fix it in his or her mind. **impressive** *adjective*.

impression *noun* (impressions) **1** A mark or idea or memory left behind by someone or something. **2** An imitation of another person. *I do impressions of pop stars*. **3** A vague idea. *I had the impression you might be unhappy*.

imprison *verb* (imprisons, imprisoning, imprisoned) To put somebody into prison. **imprisonment** *noun*.

improbable *adjective* Not likely. **improbably** *adverb*, **improbability** *noun*.

impromptu *adjective and adverb* Without preparation, without rehearsal.

improper *adjective* Not suitable, wrong, indecent. **improperly** *adverb*.

improve *verb* (improves, improving, improved) To make or become better. **improvement** *noun*.

improvise *verb* (improvises, improvising, improvised) **1** To make something up as you go along. **2** To make do with what is there when the proper materials are lacking. **improvisation** *noun*.

impudent *adjective* Rude, openly lacking in respect. **impudently** *adverb*, **impudence** *noun*.

impulse *noun* (impulses) A sudden desire to do something without previous planning. **impulsive** *adjective*, **impulsively** *adverb*.

impure *adjective* Not pure. **impurity** *noun*.

in *preposition* **1** At. *They live in London*. **2** Into. *I fell in the river*. **3** Inside, not outside. *We keep the butter in the fridge*. **4** During. *Ruth's birthday is in June*. **5** Consisting of. *The serial is in four episodes*.

inability *noun* Lack of ability.

inaccessible *adjective* Impossible to reach.

inaccurate *adjective* Not accurate. **inaccurately** *adverb*, **inaccuracy** *noun*.

inactive *adjective* Not active. **inactivity** *noun*.

inadequate *adjective* Not adequate, not enough. **inadequately** *adverb*, **inadequacy** *noun*.

inanimate *adjective* Lifeless.

inappropriate *adjective* Not appropriate, not suitable. **inappropriately** *adverb*.

inattentive *adjective* Not attentive, not taking proper notice. **inattentively** *adverb*, **inattention** *noun*.

inaudible *adjective* Not able to be heard. **inaudibly** *adverb*.

incalculable *adjective* Too great to be measured or calculated.

incapable *adjective* Not able to do something.

incautious *adjective* Not cautious, rash. **incautiously** *adverb*.

incendiary bomb A bomb which starts a fire.

incense[1] *noun* A substance which gives off a spicy smell when burning.

incense[2] *verb* (incenses, incensing, incensed) To make someone very angry.

incentive *noun* (incentives) An encouragement to do something.

incessant *adjective* Continual, not stopping. **incessantly** *adverb*.

inch *noun* (inches) A measure of length, 25.4 millimetres. Twelve inches make one foot.

incident *noun* (incidents) An event.

incidental *adjective* **1** Not very important. **incidental music** music for a play. **incidentally** *adverb*.

incinerate *verb* (incinerates, incinerating, incinerated) To destroy by burning. **incineration**, **incinerator** *nouns*.

incite *verb* (incites, inciting, incited) To stir people up, to rouse them to action. **incitement** *noun*.

inclination *noun* (inclinations) A readiness or desire to do something, a habit.

incline[1] *verb* (inclines, inclining, inclined) To lean, to slope. **be inclined** to have an inclination. *He's inclined to chatter.*

incline[2] *noun* (inclines) A slope.

include *verb* (includes, including, included) To count something as part of the whole. *The cost of the trip includes meals.* **inclusion** *noun*, **inclusive** *adjective*.

incognito *adjective and adverb* With your identity kept secret, not saying who you are.

incoherent *adjective* Muddled, confused. **incoherently** *adverb*.

income *noun* (incomes) Money which a person receives regularly for doing work or from investments.

incompatible *adjective* Not compatible, unable to get on well together.

incompetent *adjective* Unable to do a job properly. **incompetently** *adverb*, **incompetence** *noun*.

incomplete *adjective* Not complete. **incompletely** *adverb*.

incomprehensible *adjective* Not able to be understood.

inconceivable *adjective* Impossible to imagine.

inconclusive *adjective* **1** Not reaching a definite or satisfying end. **2** Not proving anything. **inconclusively** *adverb*.

incongruous *adjective* Out of place, absurd. **incongruously** *adverb*.

inconsiderate *adjective* Thoughtless, not caring about others. **inconsiderately** *adverb*.

inconsistent *adjective* Not consistent, contradictory. **inconsistently** *adverb*.

inconspicuous *adjective* Not easily noticed. **inconspicuously** *adverb*.

inconvenient *adjective* Not convenient. **inconveniently** *adverb*, **inconvenience** *noun*.

incorporate *verb* (incorporates, incorporating, incorporated) To include.

incorrect *adjective* Not correct, wrong, mistaken. **incorrectly** *adverb*.

increase[1] *verb* (increases, increasing,

increased) To make or become greater. **increasingly** *adverb*.

increase² *noun* (increases) The amount by which something increases.

incredible *adjective* Not credible, not to be believed. **incredibly** *adverb*.

incredulous *adjective* Not believing. *Dad was incredulous when I said I'd won first prize.* **incredulously** *adverb*.

incriminate *verb* (incriminates, incriminating, incriminated) To suggest that a person is guilty.

incubate *verb* (incubates, incubating, incubated) To hatch eggs by keeping them warm. **incubation** *noun*.

incubator *noun* (incubators) A box in which a premature baby is kept warm and safe from infection, or where eggs are placed until they hatch.

incurable *adjective* Not able to be cured. **incurably** *adverb*.

indebted *adjective* Owing money or gratitude to somebody.

indecent *adjective* Not decent, rude. **indecently** *adverb*, **indecency** *noun*.

indecipherable *adjective* Impossible to read.

indecisive *adjective* Unable to make up your mind. **indecisively** *adverb*.

indeed *adverb* Really.

indefinite *adjective* Vague, not clearly stated. **indefinitely** *adverb*.

indelible *adjective* Not easily rubbed out. **indelibly** *adverb*.

independent *adjective* Not controlled by others, free of other people's orders or influence. **independently** *adverb*, **independence** *noun*.

indescribable *adjective* Not able to be described. **indescribably** *adverb*.

indestructible *adjective* Not able to be destroyed.

index *noun* (indexes) A list in alphabetical order at the end of a book. **index finger** the finger you use for pointing.

Indian *adjective* **1** Of or from India. **2** Of the American Indians, the original inhabitants of North America.

indicate *verb* (indicates, indicating, indicated) **1** To point something out, to make it known. **2** To be a sign of something. *A red signal indicates danger.* **indication**, **indicator** *nouns*.

indifferent *adjective* **1** Not caring. **2** Not very good. **indifferently** *adverb*, **indifference** *noun*.

indigestible *adjective* Not easily digested.

indigestion *noun* A pain caused by difficulty in digesting food.

indignant *adjective* Angry and scornful. **indignantly** *adverb*, **indignation** *noun*.

indignity *noun* (indignities) Shameful treatment.

indigo *adjective* Deep blue.

indirect *adjective* **1** Not going the straightest way. *an indirect route.* **2** Not going straight to the point. *an indirect answer.* **indirectly** *adverb*.

indispensable *adjective* Necessary, essential.

indisposed *adjective* Unwell, poorly. **indisposition** *noun*.

indisputable *adjective* Not to be argued about, true. **indisputably** *adverb*.

indistinct *adjective* Not clear, confused, hazy. **indistinctly** *adverb*.

indistinguishable *adjective* Not able to be distinguished, exactly alike.

individual¹ *adjective* **1** For one person. *I bought myself an individual meat pie.* **2** Belonging to one person. *He has an individual style of bowling.* **3** Separate, on its own. *The judge considered each individual piece of evidence.* **individually** *adverb*.

individual² *noun* (individuals) (informal) A person.

indivisible *adjective* Not able to be divided. **indivisibly** *adverb*.

indoctrinate *verb* (indoctrinates, indoctrinating, indoctrinated) To fill someone else's mind with your ideas. **indoctrination** *noun*.

indoor *adjective* Happening or belonging inside a building.

indoors *adverb* Inside a building.

induce *verb* (induces, inducing, induced) **1** To persuade. **2** To cause something to happen.

indulge *verb* (indulges, indulging, indulged) To let someone have his or her way. **indulge in** to have or do something that you enjoy. **indulgent** *adjective*, **indulgence** *noun*.

industrial *adjective* To do with industries. **industrial action** action taken by workers, such as a strike.

industrialized *adjective* Having developed industries. *an industrialized country*.

industrious *adjective* Working hard. *an industrious worker*. **industriously** *adverb*.

industry *noun* **1** Hard work. **2** The making of things in factories and workshops. **3** (industries) A trade or business, especially one which employs many people.

inedible *adjective* Not suitable for eating.

ineffective *adjective* Useless, feeble. **ineffectively** *adverb*.

inefficient *adjective* Not capable of doing a job properly. **inefficiently** *adverb*, **inefficiency** *noun*.

inequality *noun* (inequalities) A lack of equality.

inescapable *adjective* Not to be avoided.

inevitable *adjective* Sure to happen. **inevitably** *adverb*, **inevitability** *noun*.

inexcusable *adjective* Very wrong, not to be excused. **inexcusably** *adverb*.

inexhaustible *adjective* Not able to be used up.

inexpensive *adjective* Not expensive, cheap. **inexpensively** *adverb*.

inexperienced *adjective* Not experienced.

inexplicable *adjective* Impossible to explain. **inexplicably** *adverb*.

infallible *adjective* Always right, never making a mistake. **infallibly** *adverb*, **infallibility** *noun*.

infamous *adjective* Wicked. **infamy** *noun*.

infant *noun* (infants) **1** A baby. **2** A young child. **infant school** a school for children aged about 5 to 7. **infancy** *noun*.

infantile *adjective* Childish.

infantry *noun* Soldiers trained to fight on foot.

infatuated *adjective* Madly in love. **infatuation** *noun*.

infect *verb* (infects, infecting, infected) **1** To give a disease to someone. **2** To make something unhealthy by spreading germs to it. **infection** *noun*.

infectious *adjective* **1** Catching, liable to be passed on from one person to another. **2** Suffering from an infectious disease.

inferior *adjective* **1** Less important. **2** Of poor quality. **inferiority** *noun*.

inferno *noun* (infernos) A terrifying fire.

infertile *adjective* Not fertile. **infertility** *noun*.

infested *adjective* Full of pests.

infidelity *noun* Unfaithfulness.

infiltrate *verb* (infiltrates, infiltrating,

infiltrated) To move into a place gradually without being noticed. **infiltration** noun.

infinite adjective Endless, too big to be imagined or understood. **infinitely** adverb.

infinity noun An infinite distance, an infinite number.

infirm adjective Weak, ill. **infirmity** noun.

infirmary noun (infirmaries) A hospital.

inflame verb (inflames, inflaming, inflamed) To make someone or something red or fiery or angry. **inflammation** noun.

inflammable adjective Easily set on fire.

inflate verb (inflates, inflating, inflated) To fill with air. **inflatable** adjective.

inflation noun A general rise in prices. **inflationary** adjective.

inflexible adjective Not able to be bent or altered. **inflexibly** adverb.

inflict verb (inflicts, inflicting, inflicted) To make somebody suffer something. to inflict a punishment. **infliction** noun.

influence[1] noun (influences) **1** The power to affect something. The weather has a big influence on the harvest. **2** The power to persuade someone to think or do something. How much influence should parents have over their children?

influence[2] verb (influences, influencing, influenced) To have influence over something or somebody.

influential adjective Having influence.

influenza noun An illness with high temperature, aching body, and catarrh.

inform verb (informs, informing, informed) To tell somebody something. **inform against** to report somebody to the police. **informer**, **informant** nouns.

informal adjective **1** Relaxed, free and easy, not formal. an informal party. **2** In this dictionary words marked 'informal' are normally used only in conversation. **informally** adverb, **informality** noun.

information noun Something told to someone, news or knowledge.

informative adjective Containing much information.

infrequent adjective Not frequent, rare. **infrequently** adverb.

infringe verb (infringes, infringing, infringed) To infringe the rules, to break the rules. **infringement** noun.

infuriate verb (infuriates, infuriating, infuriated) To make somebody very angry.

ingenious adjective Clever, skilful. **ingeniously** adverb, **ingenuity** noun.

ingot noun (ingots) A lump of metal.

ingrained adjective Deeply fixed.

ingratitude noun Not being thankful.

ingredient noun (ingredients) One of the things in a mixture, one of the things used in a recipe for cooking.

inhabit verb (inhabits, inhabiting, inhabited) To inhabit a place, to live there. **inhabitable** adjective, **inhabitant** noun.

inhale verb (inhales, inhaling, inhaled) To breathe air, smoke, or gas deeply into your lungs. **inhaler** noun.

inherit verb (inherits, inheriting, inherited) **1** To receive money, property, or a title from your parents when they are dead. The young duke inherited a large fortune. **2** To get certain qualities or characteristics from your parents. Alan has inherited his father's nose. **inheritor**, **inheritance** nouns.

inhospitable adjective Unwelcoming, not friendly to visitors.

inhuman adjective Cruel, without human feelings. **inhumanly** adverb.

initial[1] adjective Coming at the beginning. **initially** adverb.

initial[2] noun (initials) The first letter of a person's name.

initiate *verb* (initiates, initiating, initiated) 1 To start a plan or scheme working. 2 To admit someone into a group as a new member. **initiation** *noun*.

initiative *noun* **take the initiative** to make the first move. **use your initiative** to do something without being told to do it.

inject *verb* (injects, injecting, injected) To put a medicine or drug into someone's body through a hollow needle. **injection** *noun*.

injure *verb* (injures, injuring, injured) To hurt, to damage, to do wrong to someone. **injury** *noun*.

injustice *noun* (injustices) An unjust action, unfair treatment.

ink *noun* (inks) A black or coloured liquid used with a pen for writing or drawing. **inky** *adjective*.

inkling *noun* A faint idea.

inland *adjective and adverb* In the middle of a country, away from the coast.

inlet *noun* (inlets) A narrow strip of sea that goes a short way inland.

inmate *noun* (inmates) A person who lives in an institution with many other people.

inmost or **innermost** *adjectives* Furthest inside.

inn *noun* (inns) A public house, a small hotel.

inner *adjective* Inside. **inner tube** the inflatable tube inside a tyre.

innings *noun* (innings) In cricket, the time during which a team or a player is batting.

innocent *adjective* 1 Not guilty. 2 Harmless, knowing no evil. **innocently** *adverb*, **innocence** *noun*.

innocuous *adjective* Harmless. **innocuously** *adverb*.

innovation *noun* (innovations) Something recently invented or brought into use. **innovator** *noun*.

innumerable *adjective* Too many to count.

inoculate *verb* (inoculates, inoculating, inoculated) To inject someone to protect him or her from a disease. **inoculation** *noun*.

inoffensive *adjective* Not offensive, not nasty. **inoffensively** *adverb*.

input *noun* What is put into something.

inquest *noun* (inquests) An official inquiry after a death to discover why the person died.

inquire *verb* (inquires, inquiring, inquired) To make an inquiry. **inquirer** *noun*.

inquiry *noun* (inquiries) An investigation, especially an official one.

inquisitive *adjective* Curious, fond of asking questions. **inquisitively** *adverb*, **inquisitiveness** *noun*.

insane *adjective* (insaner, insanest) Mad, not sane. **insanely** *adverb*, **insanity** *noun*.

insanitary *adjective* Dirty and unhealthy.

inscribe *verb* (inscribes, inscribing, inscribed) To write or engrave words or letters on something. **inscription** *noun*.

insect *noun* (insects) A small six-legged animal with no backbone, such as a fly, an ant, or a bee.

insecticide *noun* (insecticides) A poison which kills insects.

insecure *adjective* Not safe, not secure, not firm. **insecurely** *adverb*, **insecurity** *noun*.

insensible *adjective* Unconscious, not aware. **insensibly** *adverb*, **insensibility** *noun*.

insensitive *adverb* Not sensitive, without feelings. **insensitively** *adverb*.

inseparable *adjective* Not to be separated. **inseparably** *adverb*.

insert *verb* (inserts, inserting, inserted) To put something into something else. *You insert a coin in a slot machine.* **insertion** *noun.*

inside[1] *noun* The inner or middle part of something. **insides** your stomach and other digestive organs. **inside out** with the inside turned to face outwards.

inside[2] *adjective* Nearest the middle, in the middle. *an inside forward.*

inside[3] *adverb* Enclosed in something, within it. *Stay inside,* stay in the house.

inside[4] *preposition* In the inside of something. *inside the house.*

insignificant *adjective* Not important, not significant. **insignificance** *noun.*

insincere *adjective* Not sincere. **insincerely** *adverb,* **insincerity** *noun.*

insist *verb* (insists, insisting, insisted) To say very firmly that something must happen or that something is true. *I insist on coming with you. The accused man insisted that he was innocent.* **insistent** *adjective,* **insistence** *noun.*

insolent *adjective* Insulting, cheeky. **insolently** *adverb,* **insolence** *noun.*

insoluble *adjective* 1 Impossible to solve. 2 Impossible to dissolve.

insomnia *noun* Sleeplessness.

inspect *verb* (inspects, inspecting, inspected) To examine something, to look very carefully at it. **inspection** *noun.*

inspector *noun* (inspectors) 1 An official who inspects places or things. 2 An officer in the police.

inspire *verb* (inspires, inspiring, inspired) To fill someone with good and exciting thoughts or feelings. *The beautiful scenery inspired us to make up a poem.* **inspiration** *noun.*

install *verb* (installs, installing, installed) To put something into place ready for use. *They installed a new heater in our classroom.* **installation** *noun.*

instalment *noun* (instalments) 1 *To pay by instalments,* to pay a small amount at a time. 2 An episode in a serial.

instance *noun* (instances) An example.

instant[1] *adjective* 1 Happening at once. **instantly** *adverb.* 2 Able to be made very quickly. *instant coffee.*

instant[2] *noun* (instants) 1 A precise point of time. 2 A moment. *I'll be back in an instant.*

instantaneous *adjective* Immediate, done in an instant. **instantaneously** *adverb.*

instead *adverb* As an alternative. *If you haven't got a large loaf, I'll take two small ones instead.* **instead of** in place of.

instep *noun* (insteps) The top of the foot between the toes and the ankle.

instinct *noun* (instincts) 1 A natural tendency to behave in a certain way. 2 A feeling, an intuition. **instinctive** *adjective,* **instinctively** *adverb.*

institute *noun* (institutes) A society or organization, its offices or buildings.

institution *noun* (institutions) 1 A custom, a habit, a law. 2 A building where people can live or work together.

instruct *verb* (instructs, instructing, instructed) 1 To teach somebody. 2 To give orders to somebody. 3 To inform somebody of something. **instructor, instruction** *nouns.*

instructional *adjective* Intended to teach you something.

instructive *adjective* Giving information.

instrument *noun* (instruments) 1 An object used to produce musical sounds. *musical instruments.* **instrumental** *adjective,* **instrumentalist** *noun.* 2 A piece of apparatus, a tool.

insubordinate *adjective* Disobedient, rebellious. **insubordination** *noun.*

insufficient *adjective* Not sufficient, not enough. **insufficiently** *adverb.*

insulate *verb* (insulates, insulating, insulated) 1 To cover something in order to prevent loss of heat. **2** To cover wires that carry electricity in order to prevent them touching by mistake. **insulator, insulation** *nouns*.

insult[1] *noun* (insults) A piece of hurtful rudeness.

insult[2] *verb* (insults, insulting, insulted) To be rude and unkind to someone.

insurance *noun* An arrangement by which you regularly pay money to a company which in return agrees to pay you in case of sickness, loss or damage of property, or other emergencies. **insurance policy** an agreement to do this.

insure *verb* (insures, insuring, insured) To make an insurance agreement. **insurer** *noun*.

intact *adjective* Untouched, undamaged.

intake *noun* (intakes) **1** An amount or number taken in. **2** A place where something is taken in.

integer *noun* (integers) A whole number.

integrate *verb* (integrates, integrating, integrated) To combine things or people into a complete whole or into a single group.

integration *noun* Getting different kinds of people to live happily together as equals.

integrity *noun* Honesty.

intellect *noun* A person's power of reasoning, the ability to understand things.

intellectual *adjective* **1** With a good intellect, keen on studying and learning. **2** Needing a good intellect, requiring hard study.

intelligence *noun* **1** Cleverness, the ability to use your mind well. **2** Secret information, spying.

intelligent *adjective* Clever. **intelligently** *adverb*.

intelligible *adjective* Able to be understood. **intelligibly** *adverb*.

intend *verb* (intends, intending, intended) To have a particular plan in mind. *I intend to go camping next holidays.*

intense *adjective* (intenser, intensest) Very great, violent. *intense heat, intense feelings.* **intensely** *adverb*, **intensity** *noun*.

intensive *adjective* Thorough, concentrated. *an intensive search.*

intent *adjective* Keen, eager. **intently** *adverb*.

intention *noun* (intentions) A purpose, a plan.

intentional *adjective* Deliberate, done on purpose. **intentionally** *adverb*.

intercept *verb* (intercepts, intercepting, intercepted) To attack or stop someone or something on its way from one place to another. **interceptor, interception** *nouns*.

interchange *noun* (interchanges) A place where people can change from one railway or motorway to another.

interchangeable *adjective* Easily changed one for another.

intercom *noun* (intercoms) (informal) A type of telephone communication system such as that used between the crew of an aircraft.

intercourse *noun* **1** Communication between people. **2** The sexual coming together of a man and a woman.

interest[1] *noun* (interests) **1** A state of wanting to know about something. *I have an interest in music.* **2** Something which interests you. *Music is one of my interests.* **3** *It is in your interest*, it is for your advantage or benefit. **4** Money which you get regularly in return for money you have invested.

interest[2] *verb* (interests, interesting, interested) To make someone curious about something, to hold someone's attention. **interestingly** *adverb*.

interfere *verb* (interferes, interfering, interfered) **1** To take part in something that is not your concern. **2** To get in the way and prevent something from being done. **interference** *noun*.

interior *noun* (interiors) The inside.

interlude *noun* (interludes) An interval of time, something to fill an interval.

intermediate *adjective* Coming between two stages, sizes, or times.

interminable *adjective* Endless, seeming to go on for ever. **interminably** *adverb*.

intermission *noun* (intermissions) An interval during a film or play.

intermittent *adjective* Stopping and starting at intervals. **intermittently** *adverb*.

intern *verb* (interns, interning, interned) To put somebody into a prison camp, usually in time of war. **internment** *noun*.

internal *adjective* Of or in the inside of something. **internal combustion engine** a petrol engine like that used in a motor car.

international *adjective* Between two or more nations, concerning two or more nations. *Interpol is an international police organization.* **internationally** *adverb*.

interplanetary *adjective* Between the planets.

interpret *verb* (interprets, interpreting, interpreted) 1 To make the meaning of something clear. 2 To translate from one language into another. **interpreter, interpretation** *nouns*.

interrogate *verb* (interrogates, interrogating, interrogated) To question someone closely. **interrogation** *noun*.

interrupt *verb* (interrupts, interrupting, interrupted) 1 To stop someone who is in the middle of saying or doing something. 2 To stop something for a time. *Rain interrupted the game.* **interruption** *noun*.

intersect *verb* (intersects, intersecting, intersected) To divide something by

passing through it or by crossing it. **intersection** *noun*.

interstellar *adjective* Between the stars.

interval *noun* (intervals) 1 A break, a gap. 2 A break between two parts of a concert, play, or film. **at intervals** from time to time, occasionally.

intervene *verb* (intervenes, intervening, intervened) 1 To come between. 2 To interrupt an argument or quarrel and try to settle it. **intervention** *noun*.

interview[1] *noun* (interviews) A meeting with someone to discuss a particular subject.

interview[2] *verb* (interviews, interviewing, interviewed) To be the person who asks the questions in an interview. **interviewer** *noun*.

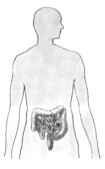

intestines *noun* The tube-like parts of your body through which food passes after it has gone through the stomach.

intimate *adjective* 1 Close, very friendly. *intimate friends.* 2 Private. *intimate secrets.* **intimately** *adverb*, **intimacy** *noun*.

intimidate *verb* (intimidates, intimidating, intimidated) To try to make a person do something by frightening him or her. **intimidation** *noun*.

into *preposition* To a place inside. *We ran into the garden.* **change into** to become. *The frog changed into a handsome prince.*

intolerable *adjective* Unbearable, not to be endured. **intolerably** *adverb*.

intolerant *adjective* Scornful of other people's views and opinions. **intolerantly** *adverb*, **intolerance** *noun*.

intoxicate *verb* (intoxicates, intoxicating, intoxicated) To make someone drunk, to make someone foolishly excited. **intoxication** *noun*.

intrepid *adjective* Fearless, brave. **intrepidly** *adverb*.

intricate *adjective* Complicated. **intricately** *adverb*.

intrigue[1] *noun* (intrigues) A secret plot or plan.

intrigue[2] *verb* (intrigues, intriguing, intrigued) **1** To arouse curiosity in someone, to interest deeply. *Her strange story intrigued me.* **2** To plot.

introduce *verb* (introduces, introducing, introduced) **1** To make somebody known to someone else. **2** To make an announcement before a performance. **3** To bring something into use. *They are introducing a new bus service.*

introduction *noun* (introductions) **1** The act of introducing someone or something. **2** A short section before the main part of something such as a book or piece of music. **introductory** *adjective*.

intrude *verb* (intrudes, intruding, intruded) To enter without being invited, to force a way in. **intruder**, **intrusion** *nouns*.

intuition *noun* (intuitions) The power of suddenly understanding something without having to think it out in every detail. **intuitive** *adjective*, **intuitively** *adverb*.

inundate *verb* (inundates, inundating, inundated) To flood. **inundation** *noun*.

invade *verb* (invades, invading, invaded) **1** To attack and enter a country. **2** To enter anything by force. **invader** *noun*.

invalid[1] *noun* (invalids) Someone suffering from a long illness. *He remained an invalid for the rest of his life.*

invalid[2] *adjective* Not valid. *Our old passport is invalid.*

invaluable *adjective* Very valuable, beyond price.

invariable *adjective* Unchangeable, that never changes. **invariably** *adverb*.

invasion *noun* (invasions) **1** Invading. **2** Being invaded.

invent *verb* (invents, inventing, invented) To plan, create, or make something that has not been thought of before. **inventive** *adjective*, **inventor**, **invention** *nouns*.

invert *verb* (inverts, inverting, inverted) To turn something upside down. **inversion** *noun*.

invest *verb* (invests, investing, invested) To put money into savings where it will gain interest, or to use it in some other profitable way. **investment** *noun*.

investigate *verb* (investigates, investigating, investigated) To look for information about something. **investigator**, **investigation** *nouns*.

invigorating *adjective* Strengthening, giving energy.

invincible *adjective* Not able to be conquered. **invincibly** *adverb*, **invincibility** *noun*.

invisible *adjective* Not able to be seen. **invisibly** *adverb*, **invisibility** *noun*.

invite *verb* (invites, inviting, invited) To tell people that you would like them to be present somewhere or to do something. *I'll invite you to my party. We've invited Jane to play the piano.* **invitation** *noun*.

inviting *adjective* Attractive. **invitingly** *adverb*.

involuntary *adjective* Done without thinking, deliberate. **involuntarily** *adverb*.

involve *verb* (involves, involving, involved) **1** To result in, to make necessary. *This job involves getting up* at 6.30. **2** To affect, to concern. *Road safety involves everyone*. **involved** complicated. **involvement** *noun*.

inward¹ *adjective* **1** On the inside. **2** Going in. *the inward journey*.

inward² *adverb* Inwards.

inwardly *adverb* In the mind, not speaking aloud.

inwards *adverb* Towards the inside.

iodine *noun* A chemical sometimes used as an antiseptic.

irascible *adjective* Easily made angry.

irate *adjective* Angry. **irately** *adverb*.

iris *noun* (irises) **1** The coloured part of the eyeball. **2** A flower with pointed leaves.

Irish *adjective* Of Ireland, from Ireland. **Irishman**, **Irishwoman** *nouns*.

iron¹ *noun* (irons) **1** A grey metal used in making steel. **2** A tool made of iron. **3** A flat piece of metal with a handle used for smoothing clothes after washing. **Iron Age** the period when the best tools and weapons were made of iron. **Irons** fetters.

iron² *verb* (irons, ironing, ironed) To smooth material with an iron.

ironing-board *noun* (ironing-boards) A folding table used when ironing.

ironmonger *noun* (ironmongers) A person who sells tools and other things. **ironmongery** *noun*.

irrational *adjective* Not reasonable, absurd. **irrationally** *adverb*.

irregular *adjective* **1** Not even, not regular, not equal. **2** Against the rules, not usual. **irregularly** *adverb*, **irregularity** *noun*.

irrelevant *adjective* Not on the subject. **irrelevantly** *adverb*, **irrelevance** *noun*.

irrepressible *adjective* Lively, impossible to discourage. **irrepressibly** *adverb*.

irresistible *adjective* Impossible to resist, very attractive. **irresistibly** *adverb*.

irresponsible *adjective* Stupid and careless, not trustworthy. **irresponsibly** *adverb*, **irresponsibility** *noun*.

irreverent *adjective* Not respectful. **irreverently** *adverb*, **irreverence** *noun*.

irrigate *verb* (irrigates, irrigating, irrigated) To supply dry land with water so that crops can grow. **irrigation** *noun*.

irritable *adjective* Easily irritated. **irritably** *adverb*.

irritate *verb* (irritates, irritating, irritated) **1** To annoy someone, to make someone angry. **2** To cause an itch. **irritation** *noun*.

is *See* **be**

Islam *noun* The religion of Muslims. **Islamic** *adjective*.

island *noun* (islands) A piece of land surrounded by water.

isle *noun* (isles) An island.

isn't (informal) Is not.

isolate *verb* (isolates, isolating, isolated) To separate someone or something from others. **isolation** *noun*.

Israeli *adjective* Of Israel, from Israel.

issue¹ *verb* (issues, issuing, issued) **1** To come out, to flow out. *Smoke issued from the chimney*. **2** To send out, to give out, to publish. *The weather office issued a gale warning*.

issue² *noun* (issues) **1** A matter for discussion. *We have several issues to talk about*. **2** A result, an outcome. *We await the issue of the trial*. **3** A magazine or other publication brought out at a particular time. *Have you seen this term's issue of the magazine?* **4** A set of stamps issued at a particular time. *a special issue for Christmas*.

Jj
· · ·

isthmus *noun* (isthmuses) A narrow neck of land joining two larger areas of land.

it (itself) The thing being talked about.

Italian *adjective* Of Italy, from Italy.

italics *noun* Printing that slopes *like this.*

itch¹ *noun* (itches) **1** A feeling which makes you want to scratch. **2** A desire to do something. **itchy** *adjective*.

itch² *verb* (itches, itching, itched) To have an itch.

item *noun* (items) **1** A single article in a list or collection. **2** A single piece of news in a newspaper or broadcast.

it'll (informal) It will.

its Of it.

it's (informal) It is.

itself *See* **it**. This word is used in the same ways as **herself**.

ITV Independent television.

ivory *noun* The substance of which elephants' tusks are made.

ivy *noun* (ivies) A climbing evergreen plant.

jab *verb* (jabs, jabbing, jabbed) To poke something roughly, to hit or stab it suddenly and sharply.

jabber *verb* (jabbers, jabbering, jabbered) To talk quickly in a confused way.

jack¹ *noun* (jacks) **1** A device for raising heavy objects from the ground. *a car jack.* **2** The card in a suit of playing cards next in value above the ten.

jack² *verb* (jacks, jacking, jacked) **jack up** to lift with a jack.

jackal *noun* (jackals) A wild animal of the dog family.

jackdaw *noun* (jackdaws) A kind of black bird.

jacket *noun* (jackets) **1** A coat which covers the top half of the body. **2** An outer covering.

jackpot *noun* (jackpots) An amount of prize money which keeps on increasing until someone wins it.

jade *noun* A valuable green, white, or blue stone used for ornaments.

jaded *adjective* Tired out, weary.

jagged *adjective* With sharp, uneven edges.

jaguar *noun* (jaguars) A large fierce cat-like animal.

jam¹ *verb* (jams, jamming, jammed) **1** To squeeze, to crush. *I jammed my fingers in the door.* **2** To become wedged, to become stuck tight. *The surging crowd jammed in the doorway.*

jam² *noun* (jams) **1** Food made by boiling fruit with sugar. **2** A tight and difficult situation. **traffic jam** traffic crowded so tightly together that it can hardly move.

jamboree *noun* (jamborees) **1** A large gathering of Scouts. **2** A celebration.

jangle *verb* (jangles, jangling, jangled) To make an unpleasant ringing noise.

January *noun* The first month of the year.

Japanese *adjective* Of or from Japan.

jar¹ *verb* (jars, jarring, jarred) **1** To strike against something harshly. **2** To have an unpleasant effect on someone's feelings.

jar² *noun* (jars) A kind of container, often made of glass.

jaundice *noun* An illness which makes a person's skin turn yellow.

jaunt *noun* (jaunts) An outing.

jaunty *adjective* (jauntier, jauntiest) Lively. **jauntily** *adverb*.

javelin *noun* (javelins) A kind of spear.

jaw *noun* (jaws) **1** The bones of the mouth, in which the teeth are set. **2** The lower part of the face.

jay *noun* (jays) A noisy, brightly-coloured bird.

jazz *noun* A kind of music first played and sung by black people in America. **jazzy** *adjective*.

jealous *adjective* **1** Envious, unhappy because of someone else's good fortune. **2** Afraid of losing something to someone else. **jealously** *adverb*, **jealousy** *noun*.

jeans *noun* Trousers usually made of blue cotton cloth.

Jeep *noun* (Jeeps) The trade name for a kind of motor vehicle for use on rough ground.

jeer *verb* (jeers, jeering, jeered) To laugh rudely at someone.

jelly *noun* (jellies) **1** A soft food which

melts in your mouth. **2** Any substance like jelly.

jellyfish *noun* (jellyfish) A sea animal which looks like jelly.

jerk¹ *noun* (jerks) A sudden unexpected movement or change of speed. **jerky** *adjective*, **jerkily** *adverb*.

jerk² *verb* (jerks, jerking, jerked) To make a jerk.

jersey *noun* (jerseys) A close-fitting woollen garment worn on the top half of the body.

jest¹ *noun* (jests) A joke.

jest² *verb* (jests, jesting, jested) To make jokes.

jester *noun* (jesters) In old times, a professional entertainer at a royal court.

jet¹ *noun* A hard, black substance used for making ornaments.

jet² *noun* (jets) **1** A strong stream of gas, liquid, or flame forced out of a small opening. **2** A small hole through which gas, liquid, or flame is forced. **3** An aircraft with jet engines. **jet engine** an engine which drives a vehicle or aircraft by sending out a powerful jet of gas.

jet-black *adjective* Absolutely black.

jetty *noun* (jetties) A small pier or landing-place.

Jew *noun* (Jews) A member of the race descended from the ancient tribes of Israel, or a believer in their religion. **Jewish** *adjective*.

jewel *noun* (jewels) **1** A precious stone. **2** An ornament made with precious stones.

jeweller *noun* (jewellers) A person who makes or sells jewellery.

jewellery *noun* Brooches, necklaces, and other ornaments made with jewels.

jig¹ *noun* (jigs) A lively dance.

jig² *verb* (jigs, jigging, jigged) **1** To dance a jig. **2** To move up and down quickly and jerkily.

jigsaw *noun* (jigsaws) **1** A jigsaw puzzle.

2 A kind of saw which can cut curved shapes. **jigsaw puzzle** a picture on card or plywood cut into curved shapes which you fit together to make the picture complete.

jihad *noun* In Islam, a holy war.

jingle¹ *verb* (jingles, jingling, jingled) To make a tinkling sound like the noise of small bells.

jingle² *noun* (jingles) A short catchy tune.

jittery *adjective* Nervous, jumpy.

job *noun* (jobs) **1** Work which a person does regularly to earn a living. **2** A particular task. **3** (informal) *That's a good job!* that's fortunate.

jobcentre *noun* (jobcentres) An office where you can find information about jobs.

jockey *noun* (jockeys) A person who rides a horse in a race.

jodhpurs *noun* Special trousers worn for riding fitting closely from knee to ankle.

jog *verb* (jogs, jogging, jogged) **1** To give something a slight knock. *to jog someone's elbow.* **2** To go for a gentle run. **jogger** *noun.* **jog someone's memory** to help him or her to remember.

join¹ *verb* (joins, joining, joined) **1** To put together, to come together, to fix together. **2** To become a member of a society or some other group. *He joined the navy.*

join² *noun* (joins) A place where something is joined.

joiner *noun* (joiners) A person who makes things with wood.

joint¹ *noun* (joints) **1** A join. **2** The place where two bones fit together. **3** A piece of meat big enough to feed several people.

joint² *adjective* Shared by two or more people. *a joint effort.*

joist *noun* (joists) A long beam which supports a ceiling or floor.

joke¹ *noun* (jokes) Something done or said to make people laugh.

joke² *verb* (jokes, joking, joked) To make jokes.

joker *noun* (jokers) **1** A person who makes jokes. **2** A playing-card with a picture of a jester.

jolly¹ *adjective* (jollier, jolliest) Joyful, cheerful. **jollity** *noun.*

jolly² *adverb* (informal) Very. *These cakes are jolly good!*

jolt¹ *verb* (jolts, jolting, jolted) To jerk.

jolt² *noun* (jolts) A jerk.

jostle *verb* (jostles, jostling, jostled) To push roughly or rudely.

jot *verb* (jots, jotting, jotted) To write quickly, to make notes.

jotter *noun* (jotters) A notebook.

journal *noun* (journals) **1** A newspaper or magazine. **2** A diary.

journalist *noun* (journalists) Someone who writes for a newspaper or magazine. **journalism** *noun.*

journey¹ *noun* (journeys) A distance travelled, an expedition.

journey² *verb* (journeys, journeying, journeyed) To make a journey, to travel.

joust *verb* (jousts, jousting, jousted) To fight on horseback with lances.

jovial *adjective* Merry, cheerful. **jovially** *adverb.*

joy *noun* Great happiness, great pleasure. **joyful** *adjective,* **joyfully** *adverb.*

joy-ride *noun* A drive in a stolen car. **joy-rider, joy-riding** *nouns.*

joystick *noun* (joysticks) A control lever that can be moved forwards, backwards, or sideways.

jubilee *noun* (jubilees) A special anniversary celebration.

judge¹ *noun* (judges) **1** A person who tries accused people in a lawcourt. **2** A person who decides the result of a contest or competition. **3** A person who is able to give an opinion about whether something is good or bad. *Our teacher is a good judge of character.*

judge² *verb* (judges, judging, judged)
1 To be a judge, to act as a judge. **2** To estimate, to make a guess about something. *The goalkeeper judged the speed of the ball perfectly.* **judgement** *noun*.

judo *noun* A Japanese way of wrestling.

jug *noun* (jugs) A container for liquids, with a handle and a lip.

juggernaut *noun* (juggernauts) A huge vehicle.

juggle *verb* (juggles, juggling, juggled) To perform such tricks as throwing many balls into the air and catching them. **juggler** *noun*.

juice *noun* (juices) Liquid from fruit, vegetables, or other food. **juicy** *adjective*.

juke-box *noun* (juke-boxes) A machine that plays a record when a coin is put in.

July *noun* The seventh month of the year.

jumble¹ *verb* (jumbles, jumbling, jumbled) To mix things up in confusion.

jumble² *noun* A muddle. **jumble sale** a sale of unwanted odds and ends and second-hand clothes.

jumbo *adjective* (informal) Very large. **jumbo jet** a very large jet airliner.

jump¹ *verb* (jumps, jumping, jumped) **1** To leap, to make yourself move through the air by pushing with the legs. **2** To go over something by jumping. *The horse jumped the fence.* **3** To move suddenly and quickly. *He jumped out of his chair.* **jump at** to accept eagerly.

jump² *noun* (jumps) The act of jumping.

jumper *noun* (jumpers) **1** A person or animal that jumps. **2** A jersey.

jump-jet *noun* (jump-jets) A jet aircraft that can take off or land without a runway.

junction *noun* (junctions) A place where roads or railway lines join.

June *noun* The sixth month of the year.

jungle *noun* (jungles) A dense, steamy forest.

junior *adjective* **1** Younger. **2** Less important, lower in rank. **junior school** a school for children aged about 7 to 11.

junk¹ *noun* Things of little value. **junk food** food which contains very little goodness.

junk² *noun* (junks) A Chinese sailing-boat.

jury *noun* (juries) A group of 12 people who have to listen to the evidence at a trial and then declare whether the accused person is guilty or not. **juror** *noun*.

just¹ *adverb* **1** Exactly. *It's just one o'clock.* **2** Hardly, barely. *I just caught the bus.* **3** Very recently. *He has just gone.* **4** Now, very soon. *They are just going.* **5** Only. *I just wanted a glass of water.*

just² *adjective* **1** According to the law, proper. **2** Fair, right, deserved. **justly** *adverb*.

justice *noun* **1** Just treatment, fairness. **2** The law. **3** A judge or magistrate. **bring someone to justice** to bring someone to trial. **do someone justice** to be fair to someone.

justify *verb* (justifies, justifying, justified) To show that something is right, reasonable, or proper. **justifiable** *adjective*, **justification** *noun*.

jut *verb* (juts, jutting, jutted) To stick out.

juvenile *adjective* Suitable for young people, to do with young people. **juvenile delinquent** a young person who breaks the law.

Kk
•••••

K Thousand, or precisely in computing 1024. *25K*, 25,000.

kale *noun* A green vegetable.

kaleidoscope *noun* (kaleidoscopes) A tube in which you can see colourful symmetrical patterns.

kangaroo *noun* (kangaroos) An Australian animal that jumps along.

karaoke *noun* **1** An entertainment, often in a pub or club, where customers sing to a recorded accompaniment. **2** The equipment used in this entertainment.

karate *noun* A Japanese method of using the hands and feet in self-defence.

kayak *noun* (kayaks) An Eskimo canoe.

kebab *noun* (kebabs) Small pieces of meat and other food cooked on a skewer.

keel *noun* (keels) The strip of wood or metal which runs along the middle of the bottom of a boat.

keen *adjective* (keener, keenest) **1** Eager, interested, enthusiastic. *a keen sportsman.* **2** Sharp. *a knife with a keen edge.*

3 Very cold. *a keen wind.* **keen on** very fond of. **keenly** *adverb*, **keenness** *noun*.

keep[1] *verb* (keeps, keeping, kept) **1** To have something and not give it away, to hold on to something. *If you've paid for it, you can keep it.* **2** To look after something. *Will you keep my watch while I go swimming?* **3** To stay, to continue. *Keep still!* **4** To do something repeatedly. *He keeps getting it wrong!* **5** To provide a home, food, and clothing for someone. *It costs a lot to keep a family.* **6** To make someone or something remain in a certain condition. *The fire will keep us warm.* **7** To remain good and usable. *Will the milk keep until tomorrow?* **8** To prevent. *Can't you keep your dog from barking?* **9** To hold, to detain. *He was kept in prison.* **keep goal** to defend the goal. **keep up** to go at the same speed as others. **keep watch** to be on the look-out. **keep your word** to do what you promise.

keep[2] *noun* (keeps) A strong tower in a castle.

keeper *noun* (keepers) A person who looks after someone or something.

keg *noun* (kegs) A small barrel.

kennel *noun* (kennels) A small hut for a dog to live in.

kept See **keep**[1]

kerb *noun* (kerbs) The stone edging of a path, pavement, or road.

kernel *noun* (kernels) The eatable part of a nut inside the shell.

kestrel *noun* (kestrels) A kind of hawk.

ketchup *noun* A kind of sauce.

kettle *noun* (kettles) A container specially designed for boiling water.

kettledrum *noun* (kettledrums) A drum with a skin stretched over a large metal hemisphere.

key *noun* (keys) **1** A device which you insert and turn to work a lock or to wind clockwork. **2** A clue or fact which explains or solves something. *the key to a problem.* **3** One of the buttons or levers which you press to work things such as typewriters and pianos. **4** A system of notes in music. *the key of C major.*

keyboard *noun* (keyboards) **1** A set of keys arranged in rows, such as those belonging to computers and pianos. **2** An electronic musical instrument with keys arranged as on a piano.

keyhole *noun* (keyholes) A hole for a key to go into a lock.

khaki *adjective* Dull yellowish brown.

kibbutz *noun* (kibbutzim) A group of people who live and work together in Israel.

kick¹ *verb* (kicks, kicking, kicked) **1** To hit with your foot. **2** To wave your legs about vigorously. **kicker** *noun*.

kick² *noun* (kicks) **1** The act of kicking. **2** (informal) Excitement, a thrill.

kick-off *noun* The start of a football match.

kid¹ *noun* (kids) **1** A young goat. **2** (informal) A child.

kid² *verb* (kids, kidding, kidded) (informal) To deceive or fool someone.

kidnap *verb* (kidnaps, kidnapping, kidnapped) To take someone away by force illegally. **kidnapper** *noun*.

kidney *noun* (kidneys) A part of your body which purifies the blood.

kill *verb* (kills, killing, killed) **1** To cause the death of someone or something. **killer** *noun*. **2** To destroy something, to spoil it completely.

kiln *noun* (kilns) A kind of oven or furnace.

kilo *noun* (kilos) A kilogram.

kilogram *noun* (kilograms) A unit of weight, 1000 grams or about 2.2 pounds.

kilometre *noun* (kilometres) A unit of length, 1000 metres or about 0.62 mile.

kilowatt *noun* (kilowatts) A unit of electrical power, 1000 watts.

kilt *noun* (kilts) A kind of skirt worn by men of the Scottish Highlands.

kimono *noun* (kimonos) A loose-fitting Japanese robe.

kin *noun* Family, relations. **next of kin** a person's closest relative. **kinsman** *noun*.

kind¹ *noun* (kinds) Sort, type. *What kind of sweet would you like?*

kind² *adjective* (kinder, kindest) Friendly, gentle, concerned for others. **kindness** *noun*.

kindergarten *noun* (kindergartens) A school for very young children.

kind-hearted *adjective* Kind.

kindle *verb* (kindles, kindling, kindled) **1** To set something on fire. **2** To catch fire.

kindling *noun* Small pieces of wood for starting a fire.

kindly¹ *adjective* (kindlier, kindliest) Kind. **kindliness** *noun*.

kindly² *adverb* **1** In a kind way. **2** Please. *Kindly pass the salt.*

king *noun* (kings) **1** A man who is the crowned ruler of a country. **2** A piece in chess.

kingdom *noun* (kingdoms) A country ruled over by a king or queen.

kingfisher *noun* (kingfishers) A brightly-coloured bird which lives by rivers.

kink *noun* (kinks) A twist in a rope or wire.

kinky *adjective* (kinkier, kinkiest) (informal) Peculiar, queer.

kiosk *noun* (kiosks) **1** A telephone-box. **2** A small hut or stall where you can buy newspapers, sweets, ice-creams, and so on.

kipper *noun* (kippers) A smoked salted herring.

kiss *verb* (kisses, kissing, kissed) To touch someone with your lips as a sign of affection. **kiss** *noun*.

kit *noun* (kits) **1** A set of tools, clothing, or other equipment. *sports kit.* **2** A set of all the things needed to make something. *a model aeroplane kit.*

kitchen *noun* (kitchens) A room where food is prepared and cooked.

kite *noun* (kites) A light frame covered with thin material, which can be made to fly at the end of a long string.

kitten *noun* (kittens) A young cat.

kiwi *noun* (kiwis) **1** A New Zealand bird which does not fly. **2** (informal) A person from New Zealand. **kiwi fruit** a fruit from a kind of vine.

knack *noun* A special skill you need to do something.

knapsack *noun* (knapsacks) A bag carried on the back by soldiers or hikers.

knead *verb* (kneads, kneading, kneaded) **1** To make dough ready for baking into bread by pressing, twisting, and turning it. **2** To work at any other soft substance in a similar way.

knee *noun* (knees) The joint half way up your leg.

kneecap *noun* (kneecaps). The bone at the front of your knee.

kneel *verb* (kneels, kneeling, knelt) **1** To go down on your knees. **2** To be on your knees.

knew *See* **know**

knickers *noun* A woman's or girl's

undergarment for the lower part of the body.

knife¹ *noun* (knives) A cutting instrument with a blade and a handle.

knife² *verb* (knifes, knifing, knifed) To stab with a knife.

knight *noun* (knights) **1** In the Middle Ages, a gentleman who fought on horseback for his lord or king. **2** A man with the title 'Sir'. *Sir Winston Churchill.* **3** A piece in chess.

knighthood *noun* (knighthoods) The honour of being a knight.

knit *verb* (knits, knitting, knitted *or* knit) To make wool into clothing with long needles or special machines.

knob *noun* (knobs) **1** A round handle. **2** A lump or swelling. **knobbly** *adjective*.

knock¹ *verb* (knocks, knocking, knocked) To hit something, to strike it, to bump into it. **knock out 1** To hit someone so that he or she becomes unconscious. **2** To defeat someone in a knock-out competition.

knock² *noun* (knocks) **1** A hit, a blow. **2** The sound of knocking.

knocker *noun* (knockers) A device for knocking on a door.

knock-kneed *adjective* Having knees that almost knock together when walking.

knock-out *adjective* **knock-out punch** a punch which makes someone unconscious. **knock-out competition** a competition in which the competitors have to drop out one by one.

knot¹ *noun* (knots) **1** The twists and loops where two pieces of string, rope, or something similar are tied together. **2** A lumpy tangle of string or something similar. **3** A small group. *a knot of people.* **4** A dark round hard lump in wood. **5** A unit for measuring the speed of ships or aircraft.

knot² *verb* (knots, knotting, knotted) **1** To tie a knot. **2** To tangle.

knotty *adjective* (knottier, knottiest)
1 Full of knots. **2** Puzzling. *a knotty problem.*

know *verb* (knows, knowing, knew, known) **1** To have something firmly in your mind. *We know the alphabet.* **2** To be able to remember or recognize someone or something. *How pleasant to know Mr Lear! Do you know London?* **3** To have experience or understanding of something, to have ideas about something. *Terry knows all about cars.*

know-all *noun* (know-alls) A person who thinks he or she knows everything.

know-how *noun* The skill and ability needed for a particular job.

knowing *adjective* Crafty, cunning.

knowingly *adverb* Deliberately.

knowledge *noun* Information, things that are known.

knowledgeable *adjective* Having much knowledge. **knowledgeably** *adverb*.

knuckle *noun* (knuckles) A joint in a finger.

koala *noun* (koalas) A small Australian animal.

kohl *noun* A powder used to darken the eyelids.

Koran *noun* The holy book of Islam.

Korean *adjective* Of Korea, from Korea.

kosher *adjective* As required by Jewish law. *kosher food.*

krill *noun* Tiny creatures in the sea which whales eat.

kung fu A Chinese form of karate.

Ll
· · · ·

L 50 in Roman numerals.

label[1] *noun* (labels) A piece of paper, card, plastic, or other material attached to something to tell you what it is, what it costs, who it belongs to, or where it is to be sent.

label[2] *verb* (labels, labelling, labelled) To put a label on something.

laboratory *noun* (laboratories) A room or building for scientific experiments.

labour[1] *noun* **1** (labours) Work, usually requiring strength and effort. **2** The time when a woman is giving birth to a baby. **laborious** *adjective*, **laboriously** *adverb*. **Labour Party** one of the British political parties.

labour[2] *verb* (labours, labouring, laboured) To work.

labourer *noun* (labourers) A person who does heavy work, usually out of doors.

labrador *noun* (labradors) A breed of dog.

labyrinth *noun* (labyrinths) A maze, a place with confusing passages and turnings.

lace *noun* **1** A material with decorative patterns of holes. **lacy** *adjective*. **2** (laces) A thin cord or string for tying up a shoe.

lack[1] *verb* (lacks, lacking, lacked) To be without something.

lack[2] *noun* The absence of something, a shortage of something.

lacquer *noun* Varnish or paint that dries with a hard shiny surface.

lad *noun* (lads) A boy.

ladder *noun* (ladders) **1** A climbing device of wood, metal, or rope with crosspieces called rungs. **2** A line running up or down a stocking from a hole or flaw.

laden *adjective* Carrying a large load.

ladle *noun* (ladles) A large spoon for serving soup or stew.

lady *noun* (ladies) A polite word for a woman. **Lady** the title of a noblewoman or of the wife of a knight or baronet. *Sir John and Lady Smith.*

ladybird *noun* (ladybirds) A small beetle, usually red with black spots.

ladylike *adjective* Behaving like a lady.

lag *verb* (lags, lagging, lagged) **1** To fall behind in a race or on a journey. **2** To wrap up pipes to protect them from frost or to prevent loss of heat.

lager *noun* (lagers) A kind of light beer.

lagoon *noun* (lagoons) A salt-water lake separated from the sea by coral, rocks, or sandbanks.

laid *See* **lay**²

lain *See* **lie**³

lair *noun* (lairs) The den or home of a wild beast.

laird *noun* (lairds) In Scotland, a landowner.

lake *noun* (lakes) A large area of water surrounded by land.

lama *noun* (lamas) A monk of Tibetan Buddhism.

lamb *noun* **1** (lambs) A young sheep. **2** The meat from young sheep.

lame *adjective* **1** Crippled, unable to walk properly. **2** Feeble. *What a lame excuse!* **lamely** *adverb*, **lameness** *noun*.

laminated *adjective* Made of thin layers stuck tightly together.

lamp *noun* (lamps) A source of artificial light. *an oil lamp.*

lamppost *noun* (lampposts) A post with a street-light.

lance *noun* (lances) A spear, as used by a warrior on horseback.

land¹ *noun* (lands) **1** A country. **2** Dry land, not the sea. **3** Ground for building or farming.

land² *verb* (lands, landing, landed) **1** To come to land from sea or air. **2** To put goods or passengers on land from a ship or aircraft.

landing *noun* (landings) The floor space at the top of a flight of stairs.

landing-strip *noun* (landing-strips) A space cleared for aircraft to land.

landlady *noun* (landladies) **1** A woman who takes in lodgers. **2** A female landlord.

landlord *noun* (landlords) **1** A man who rents a house or land to someone else. **2** A keeper of a public house.

landmark *noun* (landmarks) An object in a landscape easily seen from a distance.

landowner *noun* (landowners) Someone who owns a large amount of land.

landscape *noun* (landscapes) A view or picture of the countryside.

landslide *noun* (landslides) The sliding down of earth or rock from a cliff or mountain.

lane *noun* (lanes) **1** A narrow country road. **2** A name given to some streets in towns. **3** A division of a road marked out to keep streams of traffic separate.

language *noun* (languages) **1** The use of speech or written words in communication. **2** A system of symbols used in computer programs.

lanky *adjective* (lankier, lankiest) Awkwardly tall and thin.

lantern *noun* (lanterns) A box with transparent sides through which a light shines.

lap¹ *noun* (laps) **1** The tops of the thighs of a person sitting down, or the clothes covering them. **2** Going once round a race-track.

lap² *verb* (laps, lapping, lapped) **1** To drink by scooping with the tongue as a cat does. **2** To make a sound like lapping. *The little waves lapped gently on the shore.*

lapel *noun* (lapels) The folded-back part of the front of a coat.

lapse *noun* (lapses) **1** A fall from your usual good behaviour. **2** Passing of time.

laptop *noun* (laptops) A light portable computer.

lapwing *noun* (lapwings) A bird of the plover family.

larch *noun* (larches) A kind of tree.

lard *noun* A kind of fat used in cooking.

larder *noun* (larders) A cool room or cupboard used for storing food.

large *adjective* (larger, largest) Great in size, big. **largeness** *noun*.

largely *adverb* Mostly.

lark *noun* (larks) A small song-bird, in particular the skylark.

larva *noun* (larvae) The grub or caterpillar form of an insect.

lasagne *noun* A dish made with pasta.

laser *noun* (lasers) A device that sends out a narrow beam of intensely concentrated light. **laser disc** a video or other recording on a disc.

lash¹ *noun* (lashes) **1** A whip. **2** An eyelash.

lash² *verb* (lashes, lashing, lashed) **1** To whip. **2** To make a sudden violent movement. **3** To bind tightly with cord or twine.

lass *noun* (lasses) A girl.

lasso *noun* (lassos) A rope with a noose used by cowboys for catching cattle.

last¹ *adjective and adverb* **1** Coming after all others. *the last bus.* **2** Most recent. *The last time we played we won.*

last² *noun* **1** Someone who is last. **2** The end. *It was a good game to the last.* **at last, at long last** finally.

last³ *verb* (lasts, lasting, lasted) To continue, to go on being used.

lastly *adverb* Finally.

latch *noun* (latches) A type of fastening for a gate or door.

late *adjective and adverb* (later, latest *or* last) **1** Coming after the proper time. *I'll be late for dinner.* **2** Near the end of the day or some other period of time. *It's getting late.* **3** Recently dead. *the late king.* **the latest, the latest news** the most recent news. **of late** recently.

lately *adverb* Recently, not long ago.

lathe *noun* (lathes) A machine for making rounded objects in wood or metal.

lather *noun* White froth, like that caused by soap and water in washing.

Latin *noun* The language of the ancient Romans.

latitude *noun* (latitudes) **lines of latitude** lines drawn from east to west on a map.

latter the latter The second of two things or people just mentioned.

laugh *verb* (laughs, laughing, laughed) To make the sound we make when we are amused or happy or scornful. **laugh, laughter** *nouns*.

launch¹ *noun* (launches) A motor boat.

launch² *verb* (launches, launching, launched) **1** To slide a ship into the water. **2** To fire off a rocket.

launderette *noun* (launderettes) A shop fitted with washing-machines where you can go to do your washing.

laundry *noun* **1** Clothes to be washed. **2** (laundries) A place where clothes are sent to be washed.

lava *noun* The fiery liquid that pours from a volcano and cools into rock.

lavatory *noun* (lavatories) **1** An apparatus which gets rid of the waste products from a person's body cleanly and hygienically. **2** A room containing this apparatus.

lavender *noun* **1** A sweet-smelling shrub. **2** The pale purple colour of its flowers.

lavish *adjective* Generous, giving plenty.

law *noun* **1** (laws) A general rule. **2** The set of rules which govern the way we behave in society. *We must obey the law.* **the Law** (informal) the police.

law-abiding *adjective* Keeping to the law.

lawcourt *noun* (lawcourts) A court where legal cases are tried.

lawful *adjective* Legal, allowed by law. **lawfully** *adverb*.

lawless *adjective* Disorderly, not obeying the law. **lawlessly** *adverb*, **lawlessness** *noun*.

lawn *noun* (lawns) An area of mown grass in a garden or a park.

lawyer *noun* (lawyers) A barrister or a solicitor, and expert in the laws of a country.

lay¹ *See* **lie**³

lay² *verb* (lays, laying, laid) **1** To put something down in a particular place or in a particular way. **2** To make something lie down. *The crops were laid flat by the heavy rain.* **3** To arrange, to prepare. *Lay the table, please.* **4** To produce an egg. **lay off** to stop. **lay on** to provide. *They laid on a big tea.*

lay-by *noun* (lay-bys) A space for vehicles to stop beside a main road.

layer *noun* (layers) A thickness of some material laid on or inside some other material. *a layer of icing on a cake.*

lazy *adjective* (lazier, laziest) Not willing to work, idle. **lazily** *adverb*, **laziness** *noun*.

lbw *abbreviation* Leg before wicket.

L-driver *noun* (L-drivers) A person learning to drive a car.

lead¹ *noun* **1** A heavy soft grey metal. **leaden** *adjective*. **2** The black or grey substance in the middle of a pencil.

lead² *verb* (leads, leading, led) **1** To guide someone, especially by going in front. *The star led the wise men.* **2** To take someone away by force. *Lead the prisoner away!* **3** To go first, to be first. *Liz led all the way.* **4** To be in charge of something, to be the most important person in a group. *to lead an expedition.* **leader, leadership** *nouns*. **5** To stretch, to extend. *This road leads to the harbour.*

lead³ *noun* (leads) **1** An example to be followed. **2** The first or most important position in something. **3** An electric wire. **4** A strap for leading a dog.

leaf *noun* (leaves) **1** One of the usually flat and green growths on a tree or other plant. **leafy, leafless** *adjectives*.

2 One of the sheets of paper in a book. **3** A flat sheet of something.

leaflet *noun* (leaflets) A printed paper with information or instructions.

league *noun* (leagues) A group of sports clubs which play matches against each other. **in league with** working closely with.

leak[1] *noun* (leaks) A hole or crack through which liquid or gas can get in or out. **leaky** *adjective*.

leak[2] *verb* (leaks, leaking, leaked) **1** To pass through a leak. *The oil is leaking.* **2** To have a leak. *The pipe leaks.*

lean[1] *adjective* (leaner, leanest) **1** Thin. **2** Without fat. *lean meat.*

lean[2] *verb* (leans, leaning, leaned, leant) **1** To be in a sloping position, to put something in a sloping position. *He leant the ladder against the wall.* **2** To support yourself on something. *He leant on the table.*

leaning *noun* (leanings) A tendency, an inclination.

leap[1] *verb* (leaps, leaping, leaped, leapt) To jump, to jump over something.

leap[2] *noun* (leaps) An act of leaping. **leap year** a year in which February has 29 days.

leap-frog *noun* A game in which each player jumps with legs apart over the bended backs of the others.

learn *verb* (learns, learning, learnt, learned) To get knowledge and skill by studying or by practising or by being taught. **learner** *noun*.

leash *noun* (leashes) A dog's lead.

least[1] *adjective and adverb* Smallest, very small in amount.

least[2] *noun* The smallest amount, the smallest part. *That's the least of our worries.*

leather *noun* A material made from animal skins. **leathery** *adjective*.

leave[1] *verb* (leaves, leaving, left) **1** To go away from somewhere. **2** To put something somewhere and allow it to stay there. *I left my coat upstairs.* **3** To

cause or allow something to remain. *Two from six leaves four.* **4** To give something to somebody in a will. *She left him £10,000.*

leave[2] *noun* (leaves) A time when a person has permission to be off duty. **on leave** on holiday.

leaves *See* **leaf**

lectern *noun* (lecterns) A stand for a reading book.

lecture[1] *noun* (lectures) A talk to an audience by a teacher or an expert.

lecture[2] *verb* (lectures, lecturing, lectured) To give a lecture. **lecturer** *noun*.

led *See* **lead**[2]

ledge *noun* (ledges) A shelf, a narrow surface that sticks out like a shelf.

leek *noun* (leeks) An onion-like vegetable.

leer *verb* (leers, leering, leered) To look at someone unpleasantly and evilly.

leeward *adjective* On the sheltered side away from the wind.

left[1] *adjective and adverb* Of or on the side opposite the right. *Most people write with the right hand but some write with the left hand.* **left-handed** *adjective*.

left[2] *noun* The left-hand side. *In Britain we drive on the left.*

left[3] *See* **leave**[1]

leg *noun* (legs) **1** One of the parts of the body used in standing, walking, and running. **2** One of the supports of a chair or other piece of furniture. **3** One of a pair of matches between the same opponents.

legacy *noun* (legacies) A piece of property or sum of money left to someone in a will.

legal *adjective* **1** To do with the law. **2** Required or allowed by the law. **legally** *adverb*, **legality** *noun*.

legalize *verb* (legalizes, legalizing, legalized) To make something legal.

legend *noun* (legends) An old story handed down from the past.

legendary *adjective* **1** Known only in legends. **2** Famous.

legible *adjective* Clearly written, easy to read. **legibly** *adverb*, **legibility** *noun*.

legion *noun* (legions) A division of the ancient Roman army. **Foreign Legion** a unit of foreign volunteers in the French army.

legislate *verb* (legislates, legislating, legislated) To make laws. **legislator**, **legislation** *nouns*.

legitimate *adjective* Lawful. **legitimately** *adverb*, **legitimacy** *noun*.

leisure *noun* Spare time.

leisurely *adjective* Not hurried.

lemon *noun* (lemons) A yellow citrus fruit with very sour juice.

lemonade *noun* A drink flavoured with lemons.

lend *verb* (lends, lending, lent) To let someone have something for a certain time, after which it is to be returned. **lend a hand** to help.

length *noun* (lengths) **1** The distance or time from the beginning of something to the end. **2** A piece of something which you usually measure by length. *a length of string.* **at length 1** After a long time. **2** For a long time.

lengthen *verb* (lengthens, lengthening, lengthened) To make or become longer.

lengthy *adjective* (lengthier, lengthiest) Long.

lenient *adjective* Not severe. **leniently** *adverb*.

lens *noun* (lenses) A piece of glass with a slightly curved surface used to focus rays of light, as in spectacles or a camera.

Lent *noun* The period of six and a half weeks before Easter.

lent *See* **lend**

leopard *noun* (leopards) A spotted wild animal.

leotard *noun* (leotards) A garment worn by dancers when practising.

leper *noun* (lepers) A person who has leprosy.

leprosy *noun* A disease in which parts of the body waste away.

lesbian *noun* (lesbians) A homosexual woman.

less[1] *adjective and adverb* Smaller in amount, not so much. *less noise, a less exciting game.*

less[2] *noun* The smaller amount, the smaller part.

lessen *verb* (lessens, lessening, lessened) To make or become smaller.

lesson *noun* (lessons) **1** A period of time during which something is taught. **2** Something to be learnt. **3** A passage from the Bible read in church.

let *verb* (lets, letting, let) **1** To allow something to happen, to permit someone to do something. **2** To cause something to happen. *Let the music begin!* **3** To allow someone to use a place in return for payment. *We let our caravan to holidaymakers.* **let someone down** to disappoint someone by not doing what you promised. **let off 1** To let someone go without being punished or without doing what they were supposed to do. **2** To explode. *We let off fireworks.*

lethal *adjective* Deadly.

letter *noun* (letters) **1** One of the signs used to make up words in writing. **2** A written message, especially one sent by post.

letter-box *noun* (letter-boxes) **1** A slot in a door for the postman to deliver letters. **2** A postbox.

lettuce *noun* (lettuces) A green vegetable used in salads.

leukaemia *noun* A serious disease of the blood.

level¹ *adjective* **1** Smooth, flat, horizontal. *You need a level field for playing cricket.* **2** Even, equal. *The scores were level at half-time.* **level crossing** a place where a road and a railway cross at the same level.

level² *noun* (levels) Height. **at eye level** at the same height as the eyes. **on the level** honest.

level³ *verb* (levels, levelling, levelled) To make something level.

level-headed *adjective* Sensible.

lever¹ *noun* (levers) **1** A bar or other tool used to help lift a heavy weight or to force something open. **2** A handle which helps you work a machine. *a gear lever.*

lever² *verb* (levers, levering, levered) **1** To use a lever. **2** To move something with a lever.

liable *adjective* **liable to** likely to. **liable for** legally responsible for. **liability** *noun*.

liar *noun* (liars) Someone who tells lies.

liberal *adjective* **1** Generous. **liberality** *noun*. **2** Broad-minded, not prejudiced, not too strict. **Liberal Democrats** one of the British political parties.

liberate *verb* (liberates, liberating, liberated) To set free. **liberator, liberation** *nouns*.

liberty *noun* (liberties) Freedom, being able to do what you want and go where you want.

librarian *noun* (librarians) A person who looks after a library.

library *noun* (libraries) A place where books are kept and where people may go to read them or borrow them.

lice *See* **louse**

licence *noun* (licences) An official document giving permission for something.

license *verb* (licenses, licensing, licensed) To grant a licence to someone.

lichen *noun* (lichens) A plant that grows on rocks and trees.

lick *verb* (licks, licking, licked) **1** To pass the tongue along something, to touch something with the tongue. **2** (informal) To defeat.

lid *noun* (lids) A cover for a box, jar, or other container.

lido *noun* (lidos) An outdoor swimming pool or a recreation area by a lake or pool.

lie¹ *noun* (lies) A deliberately untrue statement.

lie² *verb* (lies, lying, lied) To tell a lie.

lie³ *verb* (lies, lying, lay, lain) **1** To be in a flat position. **2** To remain in a certain place. *The ship lay at anchor.* **lie low** to keep yourself hidden.

lieu *noun* **in lieu of** instead of.

lieutenant *noun* (lieutenants) An officer in the army or navy.

life *noun* **1** Being alive, the ability to exist by breathing and feeding as animals and plants do. **2** Living things. *Is there life on Mars?* **3** Energy, cheerfulness, liveliness. *The party didn't have any life.* **4** (lives) The time between birth and death. *Some insects have short lives.* **5** The story of a person's life.

lifeboat *noun* (lifeboats) A boat for rescuing people at sea.

life-guard *noun* (life-guards) A person whose job it is to rescue swimmers.

life-jacket *noun* (life-jackets) A safety

jacket to keep a person afloat in the water.

lifeless *adjective* **1** Dead. **2** Never alive. **3** Dull. **lifelessly** *adverb*.

lifelike *adjective* Looking like a real person.

lifelong *adjective* Lasting all your life.

life-size *adjective* Having the same size as the real thing.

lifetime *noun* The time during which a person is alive.

lift¹ *verb* (lifts, lifting, lifted) **1** To raise something to a higher level. **2** To rise, to go higher. *The plane lifted off the ground.* **3** To pick something up.

lift² *noun* **1** An apparatus for taking people or goods from one floor to another. **2** A free ride in someone else's car or other vehicle.

light¹ *noun* (lights) **1** That which makes it possible to see things, the opposite of darkness. *There was not enough light to read by.* **2** A thing which provides light or flame.

light² *verb* (lights, lighting, lit) **1** To cause something to shine or burn. *He lit the fire.* **2** To start shining or burning. *The fire would not light.* **3** To give light to someone or something. *The castle was lit by floodlights.*

light³ *adjective* (lighter, lightest) **1** Having plenty of light. **2** Pale-coloured.

light⁴ *adjective* (lighter, lightest) **1** Not heavy, having little weight. *a light suitcase.* **2** Easy, not needing much effort. *light work.* **3** Gentle, not violent. *a light wind.* **4** Lively, not serious. *light music.* **lightly** *adverb*, **lightness** *noun*.

lighten *verb* (lightens, lightening, lightened) **1** To make a thing lighter. **2** To become lighter.

lighter *noun* (lighters) A device for producing a flame.

light-hearted *adjective* Free from troubles, not serious. **light-heartedly** *adverb*, **light-heartedness** *noun*.

lighthouse *noun* (lighthouses) A tower with a bright flashing light to guide and warn ships.

lightning *noun* A flash of bright light in the sky during a thunderstorm.

lightning-conductor *noun* (lightning-conductors) A safety device to prevent buildings from being damaged by lightning.

lightship *noun* (lightships) An anchored ship with a bright flashing light to guide and warn other ships.

light-year *noun* (light-years) The distance travelled by light in one year.

like¹ *preposition* **1** Similar to, resembling. *He is like me.* **2** In the manner of. *We fought like tigers.* **3** This word is often used as a suffix to make such words as *fish-like, monster-like, coffin-like*.

like² *verb* (likes, liking, liked) **1** To be fond of someone or something. **2** To approve of something. **3** *I should like an ice-cream,* I wish to have one. **likeable** *adjective*.

likely *adjective* (likelier, likeliest) **1** Probable, to be expected. **2** Suitable. **very likely** probably. **likelihood** *noun*.

likeness *noun* (likenesses) A similarity, a resemblance.

likewise *adverb* Similarly.

lilac *noun* (lilacs) A shrub with purple or white flowers.

lily *noun* (lilies) A kind of flower that grows from a bulb.

limb *noun* (limbs) One of the parts of the body used for movement or handling things. **limbless** *adjective*.

lime¹ *noun* A fine white chalky powder.

lime² *noun* (limes) **1** A kind of tree. **2** A fruit rather like a lemon.

lime-juice *noun* The juice of limes used as a drink.

limelight *noun* **in the limelight** receiving great publicity.

limerick *noun* (limericks) A light-hearted poem of five lines.

limestone *noun* A kind of rock.

limit¹ *noun* (limits) A line or point that marks the edge of something, a point that should not or cannot be passed.

limit² *verb* (limits, limiting, limited) To restrict something, to keep it within limits. **limitation** *noun*.

limousine *noun* (limousines) A big luxurious car.

limp¹ *verb* (limps, limping, limped) To walk unevenly as when one leg or foot is injured.

limp² *noun* A limping movement.

limp³ *adjective* Not stiff, hanging loosely.

limpet *noun* (limpets) A shellfish that sticks itself firmly to rocks.

linctus *noun* Cough mixture.

line¹ *noun* (lines) **1** A length of thread, string, rope, or wire. **2** A long thin mark. **3** A row of people or things. **4** Something written or printed in one straight row. **5** Something spoken in a play. *Have you learnt your lines?* **6** A railway, a length of railway track. **on the right lines** doing a thing the right way.

line² *verb* (lines, lining, lined) **1** To mark something with a line or lines. **2** To form into lines. **3** To provide a border for something. *Cheering crowds lined the royal route.* **4** To provide a lining. *My boots are lined with fur.*

linen *noun* **1** A kind of cloth used to make sheets, table-cloths, and hand-kerchiefs. **2** Articles made from this cloth.

liner *noun* (liners) A large passenger ship.

linesman *noun* (linesmen) In football or tennis, an official who helps the referee or umpire.

linger *verb* (lingers, lingering, lingered) **1** To remain somewhere for a long time. **2** To be slow to depart.

lingerie *noun* Woman's underclothes.

linguist *noun* (linguists) An expert in foreign languages.

lining *noun* (linings) A layer of material on the inside of something.

link¹ *noun* (links) **1** One ring in a chain **2** A person or thing which links people or things together.

link² *verb* (links, linking, linked) To join, to connect.

links *noun* A golf course.

lino, linoleum *nouns* A kind of shiny floor-covering.

lint *noun* A soft material for covering wounds.

lion *noun* (lions) A large powerful wild animal. **lioness** *noun*.

lip *noun* (lips) **1** One of the edges of the mouth. **2** The edge of something hollow such as a cup or a crater.

lipstick *noun* A substance used for colouring the lips.

liquid *noun* (liquids) Any substance that can flow like water or oil.

liquidize *verb* (liquidizes, liquidizing, liquidized) To make into liquid or to become liquid. **liquidizer** *noun*.

liquor *noun* Alcoholic drink.

liquorice *noun* A strong-tasting black substance.

lisp *verb* (lisps, lisping, lisped) To make the sound of *th* instead of *s* when speaking.

list¹ *noun* (lists) A number of things or names written down.

list² *verb* (lists, listing, listed) To make a list.

list³ *verb* (lists, listing, listed) To lean over to one side in the water. *The ship listed after the collision.*

listen *verb* (listens, listening, listened) To pay attention in order to hear something. **listener** *noun*.

listless *adjective* Tired and not interested. **listlessly** *adverb*.

lit *See* **light²**

literally *adverb* **1** Word for word, exactly. **2** (informal) Without exaggeration.

literate *adjective* Able to read and write. **literacy** *noun*.

literature *noun* Novels, plays, poetry, and other writings.

litmus *noun* A blue substance that can be turned red by acid.

litre *noun* (litres) A unit of measure for liquids, about 1.75 pints.

litter¹ *noun* Untidy things left lying about. **litter lout** someone who leaves litter lying about.

litter² *verb* (litters, littering, littered) To scatter things untidily.

litter³ *noun* (litters) A family of baby animals born at one time.

little *adjective* **1** (littler, littlest) Small in size. *Jo's baby sister is very little.* **2** (less, least) Small in quantity. *She got little thanks for her hard work.* **a little** some, a small quantity of something. *Have a little sugar.*

live¹ *adjective* Living.

live² *verb* (lives, living, lived) **1** To have life, to remain alive. *Giant tortoises live to a great age.* **2** To have your home somewhere. *We live near London.* **3** To pass your life in a certain way. *He lived a life of luxury.* **live on** to eat something as your usual food. *The budgie lives on seed.* **live in** to sleep where you work or go to school.

lively *adjective* (livelier, liveliest) Full of life, cheerful, bright, exciting. **liveliness** *noun*.

liver *noun* (livers) One of the organs of the body.

livery *noun* (liveries) A kind of uniform worn by a servant.

livestock *noun* Farm animals.

livid *adjective* **1** Having a bluish colour like a bruise. **2** Very angry.

living¹ *adjective* Alive, having life.

living² *noun* **earn your living, make a living** to earn enough money for your needs. **standard of living** the way a person can afford to live.

living-room *noun* (living-rooms) A sitting-room.

lizard *noun* (lizards) A reptile with four legs and a scaly skin.

llama *noun* (llamas) A South American animal like a camel without a hump.

load¹ *noun* (loads) **1** Something to be carried, a burden. **2** The amount usually carried by something. *a truckload of coal.*

load² *verb* (loads, loading, loaded) **1** To put a load or weight on something. **2** To put something into a device for it to use. *to load a camera with film, to load a gun.*

loaf¹ *noun* (loaves) A mass of bread which has been baked in one piece.

loaf² *verb* (loafs, loafing, loafed) To wait about doing nothing useful. **loafer** *noun*.

loam *noun* Good fertile soil.

loan¹ *noun* (loans) Something which is lent to a person. **have the loan of** to borrow.

loan² *verb* (loans, loaning, loaned) To lend.

loathe *verb* (loathes, loathing, loathed) To hate, to detest.

loathsome *adjective* Disgusting, horrible.

lob *verb* (lobs, lobbing, lobbed) To send a ball slowly high in the air.

lobby *noun* (lobbies) An entrance hall.

lobster *noun* (lobsters) A large shellfish with feet and claws.

local[1] *adjective* 1 Belonging to a particular place or area. *local radio.* 2 Covering or affecting a small area. *local showers.* **locally** *adverb*.

local[2] *noun* (locals) (informal) A public house near your home.

locality *noun* (localities) A place, a district.

locate *verb* (locates, locating, located) To discover the exact position of something. **located** situated.

location *noun* (locations) The place where something is situated. **make a film on location** to make it in natural surroundings, not in a studio.

loch *noun* (lochs) (Scottish) 1 A lake. 2 A creek.

lock[1] *noun* (locks) 1 A mechanism to fasten a door so that it can be opened only with a key. 2 A section of a canal or river between gates where boats are raised or lowered to a different water level. **lock of hair** hairs that naturally hang together.

lock[2] *verb* (locks, locking, locked) 1 To fasten with a lock. 2 To keep somebody or something in a certain place by means of a lock. 3 To become fixed in a certain position. *The front wheel locked when he put the brakes on too hard.*

locker *noun* (lockers) A small cupboard.

locket *noun* (lockets) A tiny case for a picture or a lock of hair, worn round the neck on a chain.

locomotive *noun* (locomotives) A railway engine.

locust *noun* (locusts) An insect that flies in great swarms and destroys everything that grows.

lodge[1] *noun* (lodges) 1 A small house. 2 A room or house by the gate of a larger house.

lodge[2] *verb* (lodges, lodging, lodged) 1 To give someone a place to sleep. 2 To stay somewhere as a lodger. 3 To become fixed somewhere. *The ball lodged in the branches.*

lodger *noun* (lodgers) A person who pays to stay in someone else's house.

loft *noun* (lofts) A room in the roof of a house.

lofty *adjective* (loftier, loftiest) High. **loftily** *adverb*.

log *noun* (logs) 1 A rough piece of tree that has been cut down. 2 A record of a ship's voyage.

logic *noun* Reasoning, sound thinking. **logical** *adjective*, **logically** *adverb*.

logo *noun* (logos) A printed design for a company or other organization.

loiter *verb* (loiters, loitering, loitered) To linger, to hang about. **loiterer** *noun*.

lollipop *noun* (lollipops) A sweet on a stick.

lolly *noun* (lollies) Flavoured ice on a stick.

lonely *adjective* (lonelier, loneliest) 1 Without friends or companions.

2 Sad because of being alone. **3** Isolated, a long way from towns or villages. *a lonely farmhouse.* **loneliness** *noun.*

long¹ *adjective* (longer, longest) **1** Measuring a great distance. *a long road.* **2** Lasting a great time. *a long life.* **3** From one end to the other. *A cricket pitch is 22 yards long.* **4** From beginning to end. *The summer holidays are 6 weeks long.*

long² *adverb* **1** For a long time. *Have you waited long?* **2** A long time. *It happened long ago.* **as long as** on condition that.

long³ *verb* (longs, longing, longed) **long for** to want something very much.

long-bow *noun* (long-bows) A powerful bow for shooting arrows.

longitude *noun* **lines of longitude** lines drawn from north to south on a map.

long-winded *adjective* Using too many words, going on too long.

loo *noun* (loos) (informal) A lavatory.

look¹ *verb* (looks, looking, looked) **1** To turn your eyes towards something. **2** To face in a certain direction. *Our front windows look over the park.* **3** To seem. *It looks stormy.* **look after** to be in charge of something. **look down on** to have a poor opinion of someone. **look for** to search for. **look forward to** to wait for something eagerly. **look out for** to stay alert and try to see something. **Look out!** take care!

look² *noun* **1** The act of looking. **2** The appearance of a person's face. **good looks** attractiveness.

look-alike *noun* (look-alikes) Someone who looks very like someone else.

looking-glass *noun* (looking-glasses) A mirror.

look-out *noun* (look-outs) **1** Someone whose job it is to keep watch. **2** A place from which a person can keep watch.

loom¹ *noun* (looms) A machine for weaving cloth.

loom² *verb* (looms, looming, loomed) To appear large and threatening.

loop¹ *noun* (loops) **1** A shape made by a line curving round and crossing itself. **2** Anything formed into such a shape, like part of a knot.

loop² *verb* (loops, looping, looped) To make a loop.

loophole *noun* (loopholes) **1** A narrow gap, a small hole. **2** A way of avoiding a rule.

loose¹ *adjective* (looser, loosest) **1** Not tight, not firm. *My tooth is loose.* **2** Free from captivity. *The lion is loose!* **loosely** *adverb.*

loose² *verb* (looses, loosing, loosed) To set free, to untie.

loosen *verb* (loosens, loosing, loosened) **1** To make something become loose. **2** To become loose.

loot¹ *noun* Things taken away by thieves.

loot² *verb* (loots, looting, looted) To steal goods in a riot or battle. **looter** *noun.*

lop *verb* (lops, lopping, lopped) To cut, to chop off.

lop-sided *adjective* Unevenly balanced.

lord *noun* (lords) **1** A nobleman, a person allowed to use the title 'Lord' in front of his name. **2** A person in great authority. **Our Lord** for Christians, Jesus Christ.

lordly *adjective* Grand, proud, magnificent.

lorry *noun* (lorries) A truck, a goods vehicle.

lose *verb* (loses, losing, lost) **1** To have something taken away from you. **2** To be unable to find something. **3** To fail to catch something. *We lost the train.* **4** To be defeated. *We lost by six goals!* **5** *This clock loses five minutes a day,* it gets five minutes slower every day. **lose your way, be lost** not to know where you are. **loser** *noun.*

loss *noun* (losses) Losing. **at a loss** puzzled.

lot *noun* (lots) **a lot** a large number, a large amount. **the lot** everything, the whole number. **lots** plenty, a great amount. **draw lots** to make a choice by some method which relies on chance.

lotion *noun* (lotions) A liquid to rub on the skin.

lottery *noun* (lotteries) A gambling game in which numbered tickets are sold and then drawn by lot.

loud *adjective* (louder, loudest) Easily heard, noisy. **loudly** *adverb*, **loudness** *noun*.

loud-hailer *noun* (loud-hailers) A device to make your voice heard in the open air.

loudspeaker *noun* (loudspeakers) The device which produces the sound in a radio, record-player, or similar apparatus.

lounge[1] *noun* (lounges) A sitting-room.

lounge[2] *verb* (lounges, lounging, lounged) To stand about lazily, to do nothing in particular.

louse *noun* (lice) An insect, a pest.

lousy *adjective* (lousier, lousiest) **1** Full of lice. **2** (informal) Very bad.

lout *noun* (louts) A clumsy bad-mannered person.

love[1] *noun* A strong warm feeling of liking someone or something. **be in love with** to love someone very much.

love[2] *verb* (loves, loving, loved) To feel love for someone or something. **lovable** *adjective*, **lover** *noun*.

love[3] In tennis and other games, no score.

lovely *adjective* (lovelier, loveliest) **1** Beautiful. **2** (informal) Pleasing, enjoyable. **loveliness** *noun*.

low[1] *adjective* (lower, lowest) The opposite of high. **lowness** *noun*.

low[2] *adverb* Not high. *They flew low over the dam.*

low[3] *verb* (lows, lowing, lowed) To make a noise like a cow.

lower *verb* (lowers, lowering, lowered) **1** To let something down. *Lower the boats!* **2** To make something less high. *Lower your heads.* **3** To become less, to make something less. *Please lower your voice.*

lowly *adjective* Humble. **lowliness** *noun*.

loyal *adjective* To be relied on and trusted. **loyally** *adverb*, **loyalty** *noun*.

lozenge *noun* (lozenges) A small medicine tablet to be sucked like a sweet.

LP *abbreviation* A long-playing vinyl disc played on a record-player at $33\frac{1}{3}$ turns a minute.

L-plate *noun* (L-plates) A sign on a car driven by someone learning to drive.

lubricate *verb* (lubricates, lubricating, lubricated) To put oil or grease on something to make it run more smoothly. **lubrication** *noun*.

lucid *adjective* Clear and easy to understand. **lucidly** *adverb*, **lucidity** *noun*.

luck *noun* Chance, fortune. **luckless** *adjective*.

lucky *adjective* (luckier, luckiest) Having good luck, bringing good luck. **luckily** *adverb*.

ludicrous *adjective* Ridiculous.

lug *verb* (lugs, lugging, lugged) To pull something, to drag it.

luggage *noun* Suitcases, trunks, bags, and boxes used for packing when making a journey.

lugubrious *adjective* Gloomy. **lugubriously** *adverb*.

lukewarm *adjective* Moderately warm.

lull[1] *verb* (lulls, lulling, lulled) To make someone quiet. *She lulled the baby to sleep.*

lull[2] *noun* (lulls) An interval of quiet in a storm.

lullaby *noun* (lullabies) A song for sending a baby to sleep.

lumbago *noun* A pain in the back.

lumber[1] *verb* (lumbers, lumbering,

lumbered) To move along in a clumsy way.

lumber² *noun* **1** Rough timber. **2** Useless property stored untidily away.

luminous *adjective* Shining in the dark.

lump¹ *noun* (lumps) **1** A shapeless mass. **2** A swelling. **lumpy** *adjective*.

lump² *verb* (lumps, lumping, lumped) To put things together.

lunacy *noun* Madness.

lunar *adjective* Belonging to the moon, to do with the moon.

lunatic *noun* (lunatics) An insane person.

lunch *noun* (lunches) The midday meal.

lung *noun* (lungs) One of the inner parts of the body used in breathing.

lunge *verb* (lunges, lunging, lunged) **1** To thrust forward with a sword. **2** To move forward suddenly.

lupin *noun* (lupins) A garden flower.

lurch¹ *verb* (lurches, lurching, lurched) To lean suddenly to one side.

lurch² *noun* **leave someone in the lurch** to desert them at a time when they need help.

lure *verb* (lures, luring, lured) To tempt a person or an animal into a trap.

lurid *adjective* **1** Unpleasantly bright. **2** Violent and shocking. **luridly** *adverb*.

lurk *verb* (lurks, lurking, lurked) To stay hidden, to lie in wait.

luscious *adjective* Rich and sweet in taste or smell.

lush *adjective* (lusher, lushest) Growing plentifully.

lust *noun* (lusts) Strong or violent desire. **lustful** *adjective*.

lustre *noun* Brilliance, gloss.

lusty *adjective* Strong and healthy. **lustily** *adverb*.

lute *noun* (lutes) A plucked stringed musical instrument.

luxury *noun* **1** (luxuries) Something which a person enjoys but does not really need. **2** The enjoyment of luxuries. **luxurious** *adjective*, **luxuriously** *adverb*.

lying *See* lie², ³

lynch *verb* (lynches, lynching, lynched) To put someone to death without a proper trial by the action of a mob.

lyre *noun* (lyres) An ancient musical instrument like a small harp.

lyric *noun* (lyrics) Words for a song.

Mm

M 1,000 in Roman numerals.

mac *noun* (macs) (informal) A mackintosh.

macaroni *noun* A food made of flour paste formed into tubes.

machine *noun* (machines) An apparatus designed to do a job. *a sewing machine, a mowing machine*.

machine-gun *noun* (machine-guns) A gun that fires long bursts when the trigger is pulled.

machinery *noun* **1** Machines, especially large ones used in factories. **2** The moving parts of a machine.

Mach number A measurement of the speed of aircraft. Mach one is the speed of sound.

macho *adjective* Showing off masculine qualities.

mackerel *noun* (mackerel) A sea fish.

mackintosh *noun* (mackintoshes) A waterproof coat.

mad *adjective* (madder, maddest) **1** Mentally ill, not sane. **2** (informal) Wildly excited or angry. **like mad** wildly, with great haste. **madly** *adverb*, **madness** *noun*.

madam *noun* A polite title used when speaking to a woman.

madden *verb* (maddens, maddening, maddened) To make mad. **maddeningly** *adverb*.

made *See* **make**[1]

madman *noun* (madmen) A mad person.

Mafia *noun* An Italian criminal organization.

magazine *noun* (magazines) **1** A publication, usually with stories, articles, and pictures, that comes out regularly. **2** The part of a gun that holds cartridges. **3** A store for arms and ammunition.

maggot *noun* (maggots) The larva of some types of fly. **maggoty** *adjective*.

magic *noun* **1** The pretended art of controlling nature or spirits, witchcraft. **2** Any unexplained power. **3** The art of doing conjuring tricks. **magical** *adjective*, **magically** *adverb*, **magician** *noun*.

magistrate *noun* (magistrates) A person who acts as a judge in local courts.

magnet *noun* (magnets) A piece of metal which has the power of attracting pieces of iron. **magnetic** *adjective*, **magnetism** *noun*.

magnetize *verb* (magnetizes, magnetizing, magnetized) **1** To make a piece of metal into a magnet. **2** To attract like a magnet.

magnificent *adjective* **1** Looking grand or important. **2** (informal) Very good. **magnificently** *adverb*, **magnificence** *noun*.

magnify *verb* (magnifies, magnifying, magnified) To make something seem larger or more important than it really is. **magnification** *noun*.

magnitude *noun* Greatness, size, importance.

magpie *noun* (magpies) A black and white bird.

mahogany *noun* A reddish-brown wood.

maid *noun* (maids) **1** (old-fashioned) A girl. **2** A female servant.

maiden[1] *noun* (maidens) (old-fashioned) A girl.

maiden[2] *adjective* Unmarried. **maiden over** an over in cricket in which no runs are scored. **maiden voyage** a ship's first voyage.

mail[1] *noun* Armour made of metal rings fastened together.

mail[2] *noun* Letters and other things sent by post.

mail[3] *verb* (mails, mailing, mailed) To send something by post.

maim *verb* (maims, maiming, maimed) To cripple.

main[1] *adjective* Most important, very important.

main[2] *noun* (mains) The main pipes and wires which carry water or gas or electricity to people's houses.

mainland *noun* The main area of a country or continent, not the islands around it.

mainly *adverb* **1** Almost completely. *The stew was mainly gravy.* **2** Most importantly. *We were upset mainly because we'd lost Mum's money.* **3** Usually. *The rain falls mainly in the plain.*

maintain *verb* (maintains, maintaining, maintained) **1** To keep something in good working order. **maintenance** *noun*. **2** To keep to an opinion. *He maintained that he was innocent.*

maize *noun* A type of corn with large seeds.

majesty *noun* Stateliness, royal appearance and authority. **Your Majesty** the polite way to speak to a king or a queen. **majestic** *adjective*, **majestically** *adverb*.

major¹ *noun* (majors) An officer in the army next above captain.

major² *adjective* Greater, more important.

majority *noun* (majorities) The greater number, the larger part. *The majority voted to play rounders.*

make¹ *verb* (makes, making, made) **1** To construct or produce something, to bring it into existence. *A baker makes bread and cakes.* **2** To cause something to happen. *The mouse made Ann scream.* **3** To cause someone or something to become something else. *They made him king.* **4** To earn. *She makes £5 a week washing cars.* **5** To become. *In time you will make a good cricketer.* **6** To behave in a certain way. *He made as if to steal the jewels.* **7** To reach. *The survivors were lucky to make the shore.* **8** To come to an answer about something. *What time do you make it?* **9** To score something in a game. *I made 20 runs today.* **make a bed** to tidy a bed after sleeping. **make for** to go towards. *He made for the door.* **make out 1** To see or hear clearly. *I can't make out who it is.* **2** To succeed in understanding. *I can't make out what this book is about.* **3** To suggest, to pretend. *He made out that he was ill.* **make something up** to

invent it. **make up your mind** to decide. **make it up** to end a quarrel. **make up to** to try to win someone's favour. **make up** to put make-up on. **maker** *noun*.

make² *noun* (makes) A sort of goods made by a particular manufacturer. *What make of car is that?*

make-believe *adjective* Pretended.

makeshift *adjective* Used because nothing better is available.

make-up *noun* **1** Lipstick, face-powder, and other cosmetics. **2** Materials used by an actor to change his or her appearance.

malady *noun* (maladies) An illness.

malaria *noun* A fever spread by mosquitoes.

Malay or **Malayan** *adjective* Of or from Malaya.

male *noun* (males) **1** A man, a boy. **2** Any creature of the sex that does not give birth to babies or lay eggs.

malevolent *adjective* Spiteful, evilly inclined. **malevolently** *adverb*, **malevolence** *noun*.

malice *noun* A desire to harm other people. **malicious** *adjective*, **maliciously** *adverb*.

malignant *adjective* **1** Harmful. **2** Malicious. **malignantly** *adverb*.

mallet *noun* (mallets) A wooden hammer.

malnutrition *noun* Lack of good food.

malt *noun* A food made from barley.

Maltese *adjective* Of Malta, from Malta.

mammal *noun* (mammals) Any of those animals, including human beings, which feed their young with milk from the breast.

mammoth¹ *noun* (mammoths) A large extinct kind of elephant.

mammoth² *adjective* Huge.

man¹ *noun* (men) **1** A human being. **2** Human beings in general. **3** A grown-up male human being. **4** A piece in a game of chess or draughts.

man² *verb* (mans, manning, manned) To supply something with the people needed to work it. *Man the pumps!*

manage *verb* (manages, managing, managed) **1** To be in charge of something, to control it. **2** To be able to do something which is rather difficult. *Could you manage to carry this pile of books?* **manageable** *adjective*, **manager, manageress, management** *nouns*.

mane *noun* (manes) The long hair on the back of the neck of a horse, lion, or other animal.

manger *noun* (mangers) A trough for horses or cattle to feed from.

mangle¹ *noun* (mangles) A device for squeezing water out of wet clothes.

mangle² *verb* (mangles, mangling, mangled) **1** To use a mangle. **2** To crush or cut something roughly.

mango *noun* (mangoes) A yellow tropical fruit.

manhandle *verb* (manhandles, manhandling, manhandled) **1** To move something using human strength alone. **2** To treat someone roughly.

manhole *noun* (manholes) A hole through which a person may go to inspect a drain or machinery.

manhood *noun* The state of being a grown-up man.

mania *noun* Madness.

maniac *noun* (maniacs) A mad person.

manifesto *noun* (manifestos) A statement of what you believe in and intend to do.

manipulate *verb* (manipulates, manipulating, manipulated) To control something, to handle it skilfully. **manipulator, manipulation** *nouns*.

mankind *noun* The human race.

manly *adjective* Brave, strong. **manliness** *noun*.

man-made *adjective* Artificial.

manner *noun* The way a thing is done, how it happens. **manners** ways of behaving with other people. *It is bad manners to stare.*

manœuvre¹ (manœuvres) An awkward, complicated, or cunning movement. **manœuvres** a big training exercise for troops.

manœuvre² (manœuvres, manœuvring, manœuvred) To make a manœuvre.

manor *noun* (manors) The main house in a village or country estate.

manse *noun* (manses) The house where the minister of a church lives.

mansion *noun* (mansions) A grand house.

manslaughter *noun* Killing a person unlawfully but without meaning to.

mantelpiece *noun* (mantelpieces) A shelf over a fireplace.

manual¹ *adjective* Worked or done by hand. **manually** *adverb*.

manual² *noun* (manuals) A book of information or instructions.

manufacture *verb* (manufactures, manufacturing, manufactured) To make things by machine in a factory. **manufacturer** *noun*.

manure¹ *noun* Waste excreted by animals and other stuff used to fertilize the soil.

manure² *verb* (manures, manuring, manured) To put manure on the soil.

manuscript *noun* (manuscripts) Something written by hand or typed, not printed.

Manx *adjective* Of or from the Isle of Man.

many *adjective* (more, most) Large in number, numerous. **a good many** a large number.

Maori *noun* (Maoris) A member of the race which originally inhabited New Zealand.

map¹ *noun* (maps) A drawing showing the shape of a continent, country, or area, including marks for roads, rivers, hills, and other features.

map² *verb* (maps, mapping, mapped) To make a map of a place. **map out** to plan something.

maple *noun* (maples) A kind of tree whose leaf is the emblem of Canada.

mar *verb* (mars, marring, marred) To spoil.

Marathon *noun* (Marathons) A 26-mile race for runners.

marauder *noun* (marauders) A person who makes raids in search of plunder.

marble *noun* (marbles) **1** A small glass ball used in various games. **2** A kind of stone, often used for sculptures.

March¹ *noun* The third month of the year.

march² *verb* (marches, marching, marched) **1** To walk as soldiers do, with regular steps. **2** To compel someone to walk somewhere. *They marched him off to prison.*

march³ *noun* (marches) **1** A time spent marching. **2** A piece of music for marching.

mare *noun* (mares) A female horse or donkey.

margarine *noun* A food which can be used instead of butter.

margin *noun* (margins) **1** An edge, a border, a blank space round the edge of a page of writing. **2** An amount to spare. *He won by a small margin.*

marigold *noun* (marigolds) A golden flower.

marijuana *noun* A kind of drug.

marina *noun* (marinas) A centre for pleasure boats.

marine¹ *adjective* To do with the sea.

marine² *noun* (marines) A soldier trained to serve on a ship.

mariner *noun* (mariners) A sailor.

mark¹ *noun* (marks) **1** Something on a surface which is different in colour or appearance from the rest of the surface. *a dirty mark.* **2** A number or letter put on a piece of work to indicate how good it is. *10 out of 10 is full marks.*

mark² *verb* (marks, marking, marked) **1** To put a mark on something. *My dirty shoes marked the new carpet.* **2** To go through a pupil's work and give marks to it. **3** To pay attention to something. *Mark my words!* **4** To keep close to an opposing player in football and other games. **mark time** to move your feet up and down without moving forward. **marker** *noun*.

mark³ *noun* (marks) A unit of money in Germany.

market¹ *noun* (markets) A place where things are bought and sold, often in the open air.

market² *verb* (markets, marketing, marketed) To sell. **marketable** *adjective*.

marking *noun* (markings) A mark.

marksman *noun* (marksmen) An expert in shooting.

marmalade *noun* A kind of jam made from oranges or other citrus fruit.

maroon¹ *adjective* Very dark red.

maroon² *verb* (maroons, marooning, marooned) To abandon somebody in a deserted place.

marquee *noun* (marquees) A large tent.

marriage *noun* (marriages) **1** The state of being married. **2** A wedding.

marrow *noun* **1** (marrows) A large watery vegetable. **2** The soft substance inside bones.

marry *verb* (marries, marrying, married) **1** To become someone's husband or wife. **2** To join two people together as husband and wife.

marsh *noun* (marshes) Wet, low ground. **marshy** *adjective*.

marshal *noun* (marshals) **1** An official. **2** In the USA, an officer of the law.

marsupial *noun* (marsupials) An animal such as a kangaroo with a pouch for carrying its young ones.

martial *adjective* Warlike. **martial law** government controlled by the armed forces. **martial arts** fighting sports such as judo and karate.

Martian *adjective* Of or from the planet Mars.

martyr¹ *noun* (martyrs) A person who is killed or suffers because of his or her beliefs. **martyrdom** *noun*.

martyr² *verb* (martyrs, martyring, martyred) To make someone a martyr.

marvel¹ *noun* (marvels) A wonderful or astonishing thing. **marvellous** *adjective*, **marvellously** *adverb*.

marvel² *verb* (marvels, marvelling, marvelled) To be filled with wonder or astonishment.

Marxism *noun* A type of Communism based on the ideas of the writer Karl Marx. **Marxist** *noun*.

marzipan *noun* A sweet substance made with ground almonds.

mascot *noun* (mascots) An object which is supposed to bring good luck.

masculine *adjective* Belonging to men, suitable for men.

mash *verb* (mashes, mashing, mashed) To crush something up into a soft shapeless form. *mashed potatoes.*

mask¹ *noun* (masks) **1** A covering for the face, a disguise. **2** A model of a face.

mask² *verb* (masks, masking, masked) **1** To cover the face with a mask. **2** To conceal something.

mason *noun* (masons) A stone-cutter, a builder in stone.

masonry *noun* Stonework, parts of a building made of stone.

mass¹ *noun* (masses) A lump, a large quantity, a heap.

mass² *verb* (masses, massing, massed) To collect into a mass.

mass³ *adjective* For or involving many people. *a mass meeting.* **mass production** manufacturing goods in large quantities.

mass⁴ *noun* (masses) The Holy Communion Service.

massacre *noun* (massacres) Cruel slaughter of large numbers of people.

massage *verb* (massages, massaging, massaged) To rub and press the body to make it less stiff or less painful.

massive *adjective* Large and heavy. **massively** *adverb*.

mast *noun* (masts) An upright pole used to hold up sails, radio aerials, or flags.

master¹ *noun* (masters) **1** A male teacher in a school. **2** The male owner of a dog or horse. **3** The captain of a merchant ship. **4** A great artist or composer.

master² *verb* (masters, mastering, mastered) **1** To learn to do something perfectly. **2** To overcome something or somebody. **mastery** *noun*.

masterful *adjective* **1** Dominating. **2** Skilful.

masterly *adjective* Skilful.

mastermind *noun* (masterminds) **1** A

very clever person. **2** A person who plans something and carries it out.

masterpiece *noun* (masterpieces) Something done with the greatest skill.

mastiff *noun* (mastiffs) A kind of dog.

mastodon *noun* (mastodons) A large extinct animal like an elephant.

mat *noun* (mats) **1** A small piece of carpet or other floor covering. **2** A piece of material used on a table to prevent damage when you put something down.

matador *noun* (matadors) The man who has to kill the bull in a bull-fight.

match¹ *noun* (matches) A small stick with a head which bursts into flame when rubbed along a rough surface.

match² *noun* (matches) **1** A game or contest between two teams or players. **2** A marriage. **3** A person or thing which matches another person or thing.

match³ *verb* (matches, matching, matched) To be equal or similar in some important way to another person or thing.

mate¹ *noun* (mates) **1** A friend, someone who works or plays with another person. **2** One of a pair of animals who have mated. **3** One of the officers on a ship.

mate² *verb* (mates, mating, mated) To come together as a pair to fertilize the female.

mate³ *noun and verb* Checkmate.

material *noun* (materials) **1** Any substance you can use to make things. *building materials.* **2** Cloth. *material for a dress.*

materialize *verb* (materializes, materializing, materialized) To appear, to come into existence.

maternal *adjective* **1** Motherly. **2** Of or belonging to a mother.

maternity *noun* Motherhood. **a maternity ward** a part of a hospital where

a woman may go when it is time for her baby to be born.

mathematics *noun* The science which deals with numbers, quantities, and shapes. **mathematical** *adjective*, **mathematically** *adverb*, **mathematician** *noun*.

maths *noun* (informal) Mathematics.

matinée *noun* (matinées) An afternoon performance of a play or film.

matrimony *noun* Marriage. **matrimonial** *adjective*.

matron *noun* (matrons) **1** An old name for the woman in charge of nurses in a hospital. **2** A woman in charge of living arrangements in a boarding-school.

matt *adjective* Not shiny. *matt paint.*

matted *adjective* Tangled.

matter¹ *noun* (matters) **1** A substance, anything which can be seen and touched. **2** A subject thought about or discussed or done. *John has several matters to deal with today.* **3** *What is the matter with Alan?* what is wrong with him?

matter² *verb* (matters, mattering, mattered) To be important.

matting *noun* A rough kind of floor covering.

mattress *noun* (mattresses) A large flat oblong pad for sleeping on.

mature *adjective* (maturer, maturest) **1** Ripe, ready for use. **2** Sensible, like an adult.

maul *verb* (mauls, mauling, mauled) To cause damage by rough or careless handling.

mauve *adjective* Pale purple.

maximum¹ *adjective* Greatest. *maximum speed.*

maximum² *noun* (maxima) The greatest number, the greatest amount. *10 out of 10 is the maximum.*

may¹ *verb* (might) This word is used in various ways: **1** To show possibility. *I may come tomorrow.* **2** To ask or give permission. *May I come in?* **3** To indicate a hope or wish. *Long may she reign.* **4** To express purpose. *He died that we might live.* **5** *We might as well go,* it would be sensible to go.

may² *noun* Hawthorn blossom.

May³ *noun* The fifth month of the year.

maybe *adverb* Perhaps.

mayonnaise *noun* A dressing for salad.

mayor *noun* (mayors) The head of a city or district council.

mayoress *noun* (mayoresses) A mayor's wife or a lady officially assisting the mayor.

maze *noun* (mazes) A complicated and puzzling arrangement of lines or paths.

me *See* I²

meadow *noun* (meadows) A field of grass.

meagre *adjective* Thin, scanty. **meagrely** *adverb*, **meagreness** *noun*.

meal *noun* (meals) **1** An occasion when food is eaten. **2** The food that is eaten. *a good meal of fish and chips.*

mean¹ *verb* (means, meaning, meant) **1** To intend to show or pass on some idea or information, to indicate, to signify. *A red light means stop. The word 'maybe' means 'perhaps'.* **2** To plan. *He means mischief.*

mean² *adjective* (meaner, meanest) Not generous. **meanly** *adverb*, **meanness** *noun*.

meaning *noun* (meanings) What is meant. *The meaning is clear.*

means *noun* **1** A method, a way of doing something. **2** Income, money.

meantime *noun* **In the meantime** meanwhile.

meanwhile *adverb* During the same time.

measles *noun* An infectious disease causing red spots on the body.

measly *adjective* (informal) Very small, worthless.

measure¹ *noun* (measures) **1** A unit used for measuring. **2** A particular size or quantity. *two measures of flour to one of sugar.* **3** A device used in measuring. *a tape-measure.* **4** An action with a particular purpose. *measures to prevent crime.* **made to measure** made the particular size you want.

measure² *verb* (measures, measuring, measured) **1** To find the size or amount of something. **2** To be a certain size. *A cricket pitch measures 22 yards.* **measure out 1** To mark out a certain distance. **2** To put aside a certain quantity. *We measured out equal shares for all.* **measurable** *adjective*, **measurably** *adverb*, **measurement** *noun*.

meat *noun* Animal flesh used as food.

meaty *adjective* (meatier, meatiest) Full of meat.

mechanic *noun* (mechanics) A person who repairs machines.

mechanical *adjective* **1** Of machines. **2** Done by machine. **mechanically** *adverb*.

mechanism *noun* (mechanisms) A machine, or the working parts of a machine.

medal *noun* (medals) A piece of metal shaped like a coin or a cross or a star, awarded for winning a race, for bravery, or for some other achievement.

medallist *noun* (medallists) A person who has been awarded a medal.

meddle *verb* (meddles, meddling, meddled) To interfere. **meddler** *noun*.

media *noun* **the media** ways of communicating with large numbers of people, such as radio, TV, and newspapers.

medical *adjective* To do with the treatment of sick people. **medically** *adverb*.

medicine *noun* (medicines) A liquid or tablet taken to improve your health. **medicinal** *adjective*.

medieval *adjective* Of the Middle Ages.

mediocre *adjective* Not very good, not very bad.

meditate *verb* (meditates, meditating, meditated) To think about things. **meditation** *noun*.

Mediterranean *adjective* Of or from or in the area near the Mediterranean Sea.

medium *adjective* Average. *medium size, middle size*.

medley *noun* (medleys) A mixture.

meek *adjective* Obedient and gentle, not proud. **meekly** *adverb*, **meekness** *noun*.

meet *verb* (meets, meeting, met) To come together with someone or something.

meeting *noun* (meetings) **1** A coming together. **2** A group of people gathered for a particular purpose.

mega *adjective* (informal) Very large or important.

megastar *noun* (megastars) (informal) A very famous and successful performer.

melancholy *adjective* Sad.

mellow *adjective* Soft, ripe, pleasant.

melodious *adjective* Tuneful. **melodiously** *adverb*.

melody *noun* (melodies) A tune.

melon *noun* (melons) A large round juicy fruit.

melt *verb* (melts, melting, melted) **1** To change something into liquid by warming it. *The sun melted the snow.* **2** To become liquid by being warmed. *The snow melted in the sun.* **3** To go away slowly, to fade.

member *noun* (members) A person who belongs to a club or group. **membership** *noun*.

memorable *adjective* Easy to remember. **memorably** *adverb*.

memorial *noun* (memorials) Something to remind you of a person or an event. *a war memorial*.

memorize *verb* (memorizes, memorizing, memorized) To learn by heart.

memory *noun* (memories) **1** The ability to remember. *Jo has a good memory.* **2** Something that you remember. *I have happy memories of our holiday.* **3** The part of a computer which holds information ready for use. **in memory of** as a memorial to.

men *See* **man**[1]

menace *verb* (menaces, menacing, menaced) To threaten. **menacingly** *adverb*.

mend *verb* (mends, mending, mended) **1** To put something back into good condition. **2** To get better.

mending *noun* Clothes which are being mended.

menstruation *noun* The time when the lining of a woman's womb is shed, which happens once a month except when she is pregnant.

mental *adjective* In the mind, to do with the mind. **mentally** *adverb*.

mention *verb* (mentions, mentioning, mentioned) To speak or write about someone or something briefly.

menu *noun* (menus) A list of the food to be served at a meal.

mercenary[1] *adjective* Working only for money.

mercenary[2] *noun* (mercenaries) A soldier who will fight for any country that will pay him or her.

merchandise *noun* Goods to be bought and sold.

merchant *noun* (merchants) A trader. *a timber merchant.* **merchant navy** ships which carry goods.

merciful *adjective* Showing mercy. **mercifully** *adverb*.

merciless *adjective* Without mercy. **mercilessly** *adverb*.

mercury *noun* A silver-coloured liquid metal.

mercy *noun* (mercies) **1** Kindness and forgiveness towards someone you have the power to hurt or punish. *The king showed mercy and spared the traitor's life.* **2** A piece of good fortune. *Be thankful for small mercies.*

mere *adjective* Not more than. *She's a mere baby,* she's only a baby.

merely *adverb* Simply, only.

merge *verb* (merges, merging, merged) To become part of something else, to become joined together.

merger *noun* (mergers) The joining together of two firms, schools, or other organizations.

meringue *noun* (meringues) A sweet brittle cake made from white of egg and sugar.

merit[1] *noun* (merits) Something that deserves praise, a good quality.

merit[2] *verb* (merits, meriting, merited) To deserve.

mermaid *noun* (mermaids) A legendary creature, part woman and part fish.

merry *adjective* (merrier, merriest) Happy, cheerful, bright. **merrily** *adverb*, **merriment** *noun*.

merry-go-round *noun* (merry-go-rounds) An amusement at a fun-fair.

mesh *noun* (meshes) One of the spaces in a net.

mess[1] *noun* (messes) **1** An untidy or dirty state of things. **messy** *adjective*, **messily** *adverb*. **2** A place where soldiers or sailors eat their meals. **make a mess of** to do something badly.

mess[2] *verb* (messes, messing, messed) **mess up** to do something badly. **mess about** to do things with no definite purpose, to misbehave.

message *noun* (messages) A piece of information or a request sent from one person to another.

messenger *noun* (messengers) Someone who carries a message.

Messiah *noun* A name used of Jesus Christ.

met *See* **meet**

metal *noun* (metals) One of a type of

substances such as iron, gold, silver, tin, copper, and lead. **metallic** *adjective*.

meteor *noun* (meteors) A shooting star.

meteorite *noun* (meteorites) A meteor that has fallen to the earth.

meteorology *noun* The scientific study of the weather. **meteorological** *adjective*, **meteorologist** *noun*.

meter *noun* (meters) A measuring instrument. *gas meter, electricity meter,* instruments for measuring the amount of gas or electricity you use.

method *noun* **1** (methods) A way of doing something. **2** A sensible way of doing something.

methodical *adjective* Careful, using a sensible method. **methodically** *adverb*.

Methodist *adjective* Of the Methodist Church, a Christian denomination.

methylated spirits or **meths** *noun* A liquid fuel.

meticulous *adjective* Very careful and precise. **meticulously** *adverb*.

metre *noun* (metres) The main unit of length in the metric system.

metric system A decimal measuring system using metres, litres, and grams as the basic units.

metro *noun* (metros) A railway system in certain cities.

miaow *verb* (miaows, miaowing, miaowed) To make a sound like a cat.

mice *See* **mouse**

micro *noun* (micros) (informal) A microcomputer.

microbe *noun* (microbes) A microscopic living creature.

microchip *noun* (microchips) A small piece of silicon with electrical circuits printed in it, used in various kinds of electronic equipment.

microcomputer *noun* (microcomputers) A small computer using a microprocessor.

microfiche *noun* (microfiche) A sheet of microfilm.

microfilm *noun* (microfilms) A strip of film with photographs of documents or pages of a book reduced to very small size.

microlight *noun* (microlights) A small aircraft, like a large kite with an engine.

microphone *noun* (microphones) An instrument for picking up sound waves for recording, amplifying, or broadcasting.

microprocessor *noun* (microprocessors) A small electronic device consisting of one or more microchips, used in microcomputers, to control automatic machines, and for other purposes.

microscope *noun* (microscopes) An instrument for magnifying tiny things.

microscopic *adjective* Very small, invisible except through a microscope.

microwave *noun* (microwaves) A kind of oven which heats food very quickly.

mid *adjective* The middle of something. *The engine failed in mid Atlantic.*

midday *noun* Twelve o'clock in the middle of the day.

middle¹ *noun* (middles) **1** The point which is an equal distance from the ends or edges of something. **2** Your waist.

middle² *adjective* In the middle between two other things. *the middle stump.* **middle-aged** no longer young but not yet old. **Middle Ages** the period in European history from about AD 1000 to about 1500. **Middle East** the countries from the eastern end of the Mediterranean Sea to Iran. **middle school** a school for children aged about 9 to 13.

middling *adjective* Moderately good or well.

midge *noun* (midges) A small insect such as a gnat.

midget *noun* (midgets) An exceptionally short person.

midland *adjective* Of the Midlands. **The Midlands** the middle part of England.

midnight *noun* Twelve o'clock at night.

midshipman *noun* (midshipmen) A young person training to be a naval officer.

midsummer *noun* The period of summer when the days are longest.

midway *adverb* Half-way.

midwife *noun* (midwives) A person trained to give help when a baby is born.

might¹ *See* **may**

might² *noun* Great power, great strength. **mighty** *adjective*, **mightily** *adverb*.

migraine *noun* (migraines) A very severe kind of headache.

migrate *verb* (migrates, migrating, migrated) To go to live in another country. *Swallows migrate every spring and autumn.* **migratory** *adjective*, **migrant**, **migration** *nouns*.

mihrab *noun* (mihrab) A niche in the wall of a mosque showing the direction of Mecca.

mike *noun* (mikes) (informal) A microphone.

mild *adjective* (milder, mildest) Gentle, not severe, not harsh. **mildly** *adverb*, **mildness** *noun*.

mildew *noun* A stain or growth that forms in warm damp places.

mile *noun* (miles) A measure of distance, 1,760 yards or 1.61 kilometres.

mileage *noun* Number of miles travelled.

milestone *noun* (milestones) One of a series of stones placed along a road in old times marking the miles between towns.

militant *adjective* Ready to fight. **militancy** *noun*.

military *adjective* Of soldiers.

milk¹ *noun* A white liquid food which comes from cows and other mammals.

milk² *verb* (milks, milking, milked) To get the milk from a cow or other animal.

milkman *noun* (milkmen) A person who delivers milk to people's houses.

milky *adjective* (milkier, milkiest) White, like milk.

mill¹ *noun* (mills) **1** A building where corn is ground into flour. **2** A factory or workshop. *a steel mill*. **3** A grinding machine. *a coffee mill*.

mill² *verb* (mills, milling, milled) To grind something in a mill. **miller** *noun*. **mill about** to move about in a confused crowd.

milligram *noun* (milligrams) 0.001 of a gram.

millilitre *noun* (millilitres) 0.001 of a litre.

millimetre *noun* (millimetres) 0.001 of a metre.

million (millions) The number 1,000,000. **millionth** *adjective*.

millionaire *noun* (millionaires) An extremely rich person.

millipede *noun* (millipedes) A very small creature with many legs.

millstone *noun* (millstones) A heavy stone used to grind flour in a mill.

milometer *noun* (milometers) An instrument which shows how many miles you have travelled.

mime *verb* (mimes, miming, mimed) To tell a story by using gestures but no words.

mimic¹ *noun* (mimics) A person who is good at imitating other people. **mimicry** *noun*.

mimic² *verb* (mimics, mimicking, mimicked) To imitate someone or something.

minaret *noun* (minarets) A tall slender tower connected with a mosque.

mince¹ *verb* (minces, mincing, minced) To cut food into very small pieces.

mince² *noun* Minced meat. **mince pie** a small pie filled with mincemeat.

mincemeat *noun* A mixture of dried fruits.

mind¹ *noun* **1** The ability of your brain to think, feel, understand, and remember. **2** Your opinions or feelings. **make up your mind** to decide what to do. **presence of mind** the ability to cope with emergencies.

mind² *verb* (minds, minding, minded) **1** To look after something or somebody. *Mind the baby for a moment, please.* **2** To watch out for something. *Mind the step.* **3** To object to something, to dislike it. *Do you mind if I open the window?*

a b c d e f g h i j k l **m**

minder *noun* (minders) A person employed to look after somebody else.

mine¹ Belonging to me.

mine² *noun* (mines) **1** A hole dug to get coal or other minerals from the ground. **2** An explosive hidden underground or in the sea to destroy enemies when they pass.

mine³ *verb* (mines, mining, mined) **1** To dig mineral ore from a mine. **miner** *noun*. **2** To lay mines in land or in the sea.

minefield *noun* (minefields) An area where mines have been laid.

mineral *noun* (minerals) **1** Any substance other than a vegetable substance which can be dug from the ground. Rocks, coal, oil, and iron are minerals. **2** A fizzy soft drink. **mineral water** drinking water from some special source.

mingle *verb* (mingles, mingling, mingled) To mix.

mingy *adjective* (mingier, mingiest) (informal) Mean, stingy.

miniature *adjective* Very small, made on a small scale.

minibus *noun* (minibuses) A small bus.

minim *noun* (minims) A note in music. It is written ♩

minimum¹ *adjective* Smallest, least.

minimum² *noun* The smallest number, the smallest amount.

miniskirt *noun* (miniskirts) A very short skirt.

minister *noun* (ministers) **1** A member of the clergy. **2** A person in charge of a government department.

ministry *noun* (ministries) **1** The job done by a minister of religion. **2** A government department.

mink *noun* (minks) **1** A small water animal. **2** Its fur.

minnow *noun* (minnows) A small freshwater fish.

minor *adjective* **1** Smaller, less important. **2** Not very important.

minority *noun* (minorities) The smaller number, the smaller part.

minstrel *noun* (minstrels) A wandering musician.

mint¹ *noun* **1** A plant with scented leaves used in cooking. *mint sauce.* **2** A peppermint sweet.

mint² *noun* A place where coins are made. **in mint condition** in perfect condition, unused.

minuet *noun* (minuets) A slow graceful dance.

minus *preposition*. Less. In arithmetic, the sign −. *Five minus three leaves two* $(5 - 3 = 2)$.

minute¹ *noun* (minutes) **1** A unit of time. *There are 60 minutes in one hour.* **2** A short time. *Ready in a minute!*

minute² *adjective* **1** Tiny. **2** Very detailed. **minutely** *adverb*.

miracle *noun* (miracles) A wonderful happening which seems to be caused by supernatural or magical powers. **miraculous** *adjective*, **miraculously** *adverb*.

mirage *noun* (mirages) A trick of the light which makes pools of water seem to be present, or which creates some other illusion.

mirror *noun* (mirrors) A glass or metal surface which reflects things clearly.

mirth *noun* Happy laughter.

misadventure *noun* (misadventures) An unfortunate accident.

misbehave *verb* (misbehaves, misbehaving, misbehaved) To behave badly. **misbehaviour** *noun*.

miscalculate *verb* (miscalculates, miscalculating, miscalculated) To calculate wrongly. **miscalculation** *noun*.

miscarriage *noun* (miscarriages) The birth of a baby before it has developed enough to stay alive.

miscellaneous *adjective* Of mixed sorts.

mischance *noun* (mischances) A piece of bad luck.

mischief *noun* Naughty behaviour.
mischievous *adjective*,
mischievously *adverb*.

misconception *noun* (misconceptions)
A misunderstanding.

misconduct *noun* Bad behaviour.

misdeed *noun* (misdeeds) A crime,
a wicked act.

miser *noun* (misers) A person who
stores up money and spends as little
as possible. **miserly** *adverb*,
miserliness *noun*.

miserable *adjective* Unhappy and
wretched. **miserably** *adverb*.

misery *noun* Feeling miserable.

misfire *verb* (misfires, misfiring,
misfired) To fail to work or go off as
intended. *The joke misfired.*

misfit *noun* (misfits) Something or
someone that does not fit.

misfortune *noun* (misfortunes)
1 An unlucky event. **2** Bad luck.

misgiving *noun* (misgivings) A doubt.

misguided *adjective* Mistaken, foolish.
misguidedly *adverb*.

mishandle *verb* (mishandles, mis-
handling, mishandled). To handle
something roughly or clumsily.

mishap *noun* (mishaps) An unlucky
accident.

misinformed *adjective* Given the
wrong information.

misjudge *verb* (misjudges, misjudging,
misjudged) To judge someone or
something wrongly.

mislay *verb* (mislays, mislaying, mis-
laid) To lose something for a time.

mislead *verb* (misleads, misleading,
misled) To deceive someone.

misprint *noun* (misprints) A mistake
made in the printing of a book.

miss¹ *verb* (misses, missing, missed)
1 To fail to hit, reach, meet, find,
catch, or see something or someone.
2 To realize that something has gone.
*I must have lost my pen on Friday, but
I didn't miss it until Monday.* **3** To be

sad because you are parted from
someone or something. *I missed
mum when she was in hospital.*

Miss² *noun* A word used before the
name of a girl or unmarried woman
when speaking to her politely or
addressing a letter.

missile *noun* (missiles) **1** A weapon or
object which is thrown. **2** A weapon
which is sent to its target in a rocket.

missing 1 *See* **miss¹ 2** *adjective* Lost, not
in the proper place.

mission *noun* (missions) **1** A journey
with a special purpose. **2** Special work
which you feel you ought to do. **3** A
place where missionaries work.

missionary *noun* (missionaries) A person who goes somewhere to spread
his or her religion.

misspell *verb* (misspells, misspelling,
misspelt or misspelled) To spell
wrongly.

mist *noun* (mists) A cloud of very fine
water drops floating in the air.
misty *adjective*, **mistily** *adverb*,
mistiness *noun*.

mistake¹ *noun* (mistakes) Something
wrongly thought or done.

mistake² *verb* (mistakes, mistaking,
mistook, mistaken) **1** Misunderstand.
I mistook her meaning. **2** To identify
wrongly. *We mistook him for the
manager.*

mistaken *adjective* Wrong, unwise.
mistakenly *adverb*.

mistletoe *noun* A plant that grows on
trees.

mistook *See* **mistake**[2]

mistress *noun* (mistresses) **1** A female teacher in a school. **2** The female owner of a dog or horse.

mistrust *verb* (mistrusts, mistrusting, mistrusted) Not to trust somebody or something.

misunderstand *verb* (misunderstands, misunderstanding, misunderstood) To understand something wrongly.

misunderstanding *noun* (misunderstandings) A failure to understand something correctly.

misuse *verb* (misuses, misusing, misused) To use something wrongly, to treat it badly.

mite *noun* (mites) A tiny insect-like creature.

mitten *noun* (mittens) A kind of glove.

mix *verb* (mixes, mixing, mixed) **1** To put things together and stir or shake them. **2** To get together in a single group. **mix up** to confuse. **mixture** *noun*.

moan[1] *verb* (moans, moaning, moaned) **1** To make a long low sound. **2** (informal) To complain.

moan[2] *noun* (moans) The sound of moaning.

moat *noun* (moats) A deep ditch round a castle.

mob[1] *noun* (mobs) An unruly and dangerous crowd.

mob[2] *verb* (mobs, mobbing, mobbed) To crowd round somebody.

mobile[1] *adjective* Moving, movable. **mobility** *noun*.

mobile[2] *noun* (mobiles) A hanging decoration designed to move in the air.

mobilize *verb* (mobilizes, mobilizing, mobilized) To collect together to work or fight.

mock[1] *verb* (mocks, mocking, mocked) To make fun of someone or something. **mockery** *noun*.

mock[2] *adjective* Not real, imitation.

mode *noun* (modes) A way in which something is done.

model[1] *noun* (models) **1** A small-scale version of something. *I made a model aeroplane.* **2** A particular version of something. *We saw the latest models at the motor show.* **3** A thing or person to be copied. *Jane's handwriting is a model of neatness.* **4** A person who poses for an artist or photographer. **5** A person whose job it is to wear and display new clothes.

model[2] *verb* (models, modelling, modelled) **1** To make a model, especially with clay or plasticine. **2** To work as a model. **model yourself on** to try to be like someone you admire.

moderate *adjective* Not too little and not too much, fairly good. **moderately** *adverb*, **moderation** *noun*.

modern *adjective* In the style used in present and recent times, not old.

modernize *verb* (modernizes, modernizing, modernized) To make a thing modern. **modernization** *noun*.

modest *adjective* **1** Not boasting, not showing off. **2** Shy. **3** Proper, not rude. **4** Moderate. **modestly** *adverb*, **modesty** *noun*.

modify *verb* (modifies, modifying, modified) To alter something. **modification** *noun*.

module *noun* (modules) A part which can be used either on its own or fitted to other parts. *The lunar module returned to the spacecraft.* **modular** *adjective*.

moist *adjective* Slightly wet, damp. **moisture** *noun*.

moisten *verb* (moistens, moistening, moistened) To make or become moist.

mole *noun* (moles) **1** A small dark spot on a person's skin. **2** A small burrowing animal. **3** (informal) A spy.

molecule *noun* (molecules) The smallest group of atoms that a particular substance can consist of.

molehill *noun* (molehills) A small pile of earth thrown up by a mole.

molest *verb* (molests, molesting, molested) To pester someone, to touch someone in an unwelcome way.

mollusc *noun* (molluscs) A small animal with a soft body and usually a hard shell, such as snails, oysters, and mussels.

molten *adjective* Melted, usually by great heat. *molten metal.*

moment *noun* (moments) **1** A very brief period of time. *Wait a moment.* **2** A particular point of time. *He arrived at the last moment.*

momentary *adjective* Lasting only for a moment. **momentarily** *adverb*.

momentous *adjective* Serious, important.

monarch *noun* (monarchs) A king, queen, or emperor. **monarchy** *noun*.

monastery *noun* (monasteries) A building where monks live and work. **monastic** *adjective*.

Monday *noun* (Mondays) The second day of the week.

money *noun* Metal coins or paper notes which have value for buying and selling.

money-box *noun* (money-boxes) A box to keep money in.

mongoose *noun* (mongooses) A small animal that fights snakes.

mongrel *noun* (mongrels) A dog of mixed breeds.

monitor *noun* (monitors) **1** A television receiver. **2** A boy or girl given a particular job in a school.

monk *noun* (monks) A man who is a member of a religious community.

monkey *noun* (monkeys) An animal with long arms and hands with thumbs.

mono *noun* **in mono** not in stereo, needing only one loudspeaker.

monopolize *verb* (monopolizes, monopolizing, monopolized) To get control over something so that nobody else has a chance. **monopoly** *noun*.

monorail *noun* (monorails) A railway using only one rail.

monotonous *adjective* Dull, with no change of tone. **monotonously** *adverb*, **monotony** *noun*.

monsoon *noun* (monsoons) A wind which blows in the region of the Indian Ocean, bringing heavy rains in the summer.

monster *noun* (monsters) **1** A large, frightening creature. **2** A huge thing.

monstrous *adjective* **1** Like a monster. **2** Very shocking or wrong. **monstrously** *adverb*, **monstrosity** *noun*.

month *noun* (months) **1** Any of the 12 parts into which the year is divided, such as January, February, and March. **2** A period of four weeks.

monthly *adjective and adverb* Once a month, every month.

monument *noun* (monuments) A memorial.

moo *verb* (moos, mooing, mooed) To make a noise like a cow.

mood *noun* (moods) A state of mind. *in a good mood, in a bad mood.*

moody *adjective* (moodier, moodiest) Gloomy, liable to become bad-tempered. **moodily** *adverb*, **moodiness** *noun*.

moon *noun* The small planet which circles round the earth.

moonless *adjective* With the moon not shining.

a b c d e f g h i j k l

moonlight *noun* The light from the moon. **moonlit** *adjective*.

moor[1] *noun* (moors) An area of rough waste land often covered with heather.

moor[2] *verb* (moors, mooring, moored) To tie a boat to a quay or buoy.

moorhen *noun* (moorhens) A black water-bird.

moorings *noun* **1** A place to moor a boat. **2** Things used to moor a boat.

moose *noun* (moose) A large North American deer.

mop[1] *noun* (mops) A bundle of strings or other material fastened to the end of a stick for cleaning things.

mop[2] *verb* (mops, mopping, mopped) To clean with a mop.

mope *verb* (mopes, moping, moped) To be sad.

moped *noun* (mopeds) A small motor cycle.

moral[1] *adjective* **1** Concerned with right and wrong. *a moral problem*.

2 Virtuous, good. *moral behaviour*. **morally** *adverb*, **morality** *noun*.

moral[2] *noun* (morals) The moral lesson taught by a story or event. **morals** standards of behaviour.

morale *noun* Spirit. *Their morale was high*, they were cheerful.

morbid *adjective* **1** Thinking too much about sad things. **2** Unhealthy. **morbidly** *adverb*.

more *adjective and adverb* **1** *See* **many 2** *See* **much**. **once more** again. **more or less** approximately, almost.

moreover *adverb* Besides.

morning *noun* (mornings) The early part of the day, before noon.

moron *noun* (morons) A stupid person.

morose *adjective* Sullen, gloomy. **morosely** *adverb*.

morphine *noun* A drug used to relieve pain.

Morse *noun* A code in which letters are represented by dots and dashes.

morsel *noun* (morsels) A small piece of something, a mouthful.

mortal *adjective* **1** Liable to die. *We are all mortal*. **2** Causing death. *She received a mortal wound*. **mortally** *adverb*, **mortality** *noun*.

mortar[1] *noun* The cement mixture used to hold bricks or stones together in building.

mortar[2] *noun* (mortars) A short gun which shoots shells high in the air.

mortgage *noun* (mortgages) An arrangement to borrow money to buy a house.

mortuary *noun* (mortuaries) A place where dead bodies are kept for a time.

mosaic *noun* (mosaics) A picture or design made of many different coloured pieces of glass, stone, or other material.

mosque *noun* (mosques) A building where Muslims worship.

mosquito *noun* (mosquitoes) A blood-sucking insect.

moss *noun* (mosses) A plant which grows in damp places. **mossy** *adjective*.

most *adjective* **1** See **many** **2** See **much**

mostly *adverb* Usually, chiefly.

motel *noun* (motels) A hotel for motorists.

moth *noun* (moths) **1** An insect which usually flies at night-time. **2** A small moth whose larvae feed on cloth.

moth-ball *noun* (moth-balls) A small ball of chemical to keep moths out of clothes.

moth-eaten *adjective* **1** Damaged by moths. **2** Old and untidy-looking.

mother¹ *noun* (mothers) A female parent. **motherless** *adjective*.

mother² *verb* (mothers, mothering, mothered) To act like a mother to someone.

motherhood *noun* The state of being a mother.

motherly *adjective* Like a good mother, kind.

motion *noun* (motions) Movement. **motionless** *adjective*.

motive *noun* (motives) A reason for doing something.

motor¹ *noun* (motors) **1** An engine. **2** A car. **motor bike, motor cycle** a two-wheeled vehicle with a petrol engine. **motor boat** a boat with a petrol engine.

motor² *verb* (motors, motoring, motored) To travel in a car. **motorist** *noun*.

motorway *noun* (motorways) A modern road for fast traffic.

MOT test *noun* A test to make sure that a vehicle is safe to go on the roads.

mottled *adjective* Marked with spots.

motto *noun* (mottoes) **1** A short saying with a moral. **2** A short verse found in a Christmas cracker.

mould¹ *noun* A growth like fur on something that has gone bad in the damp. **mouldy** *adjective*, **mouldiness** *noun*.

mould² *noun* (moulds) A container in which some liquid is put to set in the required shape. *a jelly mould.*

mould³ *verb* (moulds, moulding, moulded) To give something its particular shape and character.

moult *verb* (moults, moulting, moulted) To lose feathers or hair.

mound *noun* (mounds) A small hill.

mount¹ *noun* (mounts) **1** A mountain. **2** Something on which a picture or object is mounted to display it. *a mount for a photograph.* **3** An animal on which someone is riding.

mount² *verb* (mounts, mounting, mounted) **1** To climb, to go up. *We mounted the stairs.* **2** To put a picture or an object on something designed to display or carry it. *I mounted my photos on card.* **3** To get on a horse or bicycle. **4** To increase. *Tension mounted when we scored.*

mountain *noun* (mountains) A high hill, a large mass of land rising to a peak. **mountain bike** a kind of bicycle with several gears, suitable for riding over rough country. **mountainous** *adjective*.

mountaineer *noun* (mountaineers) Someone who climbs mountains.

mountaineering *noun* Climbing mountains.

mourn *verb* (mourns, mourning, mourned) To feel sorrow because someone has died. **mourner** *noun*.

mournful *adjective* Sad. **mournfully** *adverb*.

mouse *noun* (mice) **1** A small animal with a long tail. **2** A small device you move about on your desk to control the cursor on a computer screen.

mousetrap *noun* (mousetraps) A trap for catching mice.

mousse *noun* A flavoured cream, served cold.

moustache *noun* (moustaches) Hair growing on a man's upper lip.

mouth *noun* (mouths) **1** The opening in the face through which people and animals take in food. **2** An opening, an outlet. *the mouth of a river*.

mouthful *noun* (mouthfuls) An amount you can put in your mouth.

mouth-organ *noun* (mouth-organs) A musical instrument played by blowing and sucking.

mouthpiece *noun* (mouthpieces) Part of something which is designed to be put in or near your mouth.

move¹ *verb* (moves, moving, moved) **1** To change from one position to another, to go or to take something from one place to another. **moveable** *adjective*. **2** To affect somebody's feelings. *We were moved to tears by their distress.*

move² *noun* (moves) **1** An action of moving. **2** A turn in a game. *Whose move is it next?*

movement *noun* (movements) **1** Moving or being moved. **2** A group of people organized for a particular cause. **3** A separate section of a piece of music. *the slow movement of a symphony.*

movie *noun* (movies) A film shown in the cinema or on TV.

mow *verb* (mows, mowing, mowed, mown) To cut grass. **mower** *noun*. **mow down** to knock down or kill in large numbers.

much¹ *noun* A large amount of something.

much² *adjective* (more, most) Great, existing in a large amount. *much noise.*

much³ *adverb* **1** Greatly, by a large amount. *I feel much happier.* **2** To a large extent, approximately. *She feels much the same.*

muck¹ *noun* **1** Dirt, filth. **2** Farmyard manure. **mucky** *adjective*.

muck² *verb* (mucks, mucking, mucked) (informal) **muck up** to make a mess of something. **muck about** to play about, to waste time.

mud *noun* Wet, soft soil. **muddy** *adjective*.

muddle¹ *noun* Confusion, disorder, mess.

muddle² *verb* (muddles, muddling, muddled) **1** To confuse, to bewilder. **2** To mix things up. **muddle through** to complete a job in spite of muddle.

mudguard *noun* (mudguards) A device to stop mud splashing up from the wheels of a vehicle.

muesli *noun* A food consisting of cereals, dried fruit, nuts, and other ingredients.

muffle *verb* (muffles, muffling, muffled) **1** To wrap something up for warmth. **2** To deaden the sound of something.

mug¹ *noun* (mugs) **1** A kind of drinking cup. **2** (informal) A face. **3** (informal) A fool.

mug² *verb* (mugs, mugging, mugged) To attack and rob someone, usually in the street. **mugger** *noun*.

muggy *adjective* (muggier, muggiest) Unpleasantly warm and damp.

mule *noun* (mules) A cross between a horse and an ass.

multilateral *adjective* Involving many sides.

multiple *adjective* Having many parts.

multiply *verb* (multiplies, multiplying, multiplied) **1** To find the answer when a certain number or quantity is taken a given number of times. *Three multiplied by four equals twelve (3×4=12).* **multiplication** *noun*. **2** To increase in number, to breed. *Rabbits multiply rapidly.*

multiracial *adjective* Made up of many races or peoples.

multi-storey *adjective* Having many floors.

multitude *noun* (multitudes) A great crowd.

mum *noun* (mums) (informal) Mother.

mumble *verb* (mumbles, mumbling, mumbled) To speak indistinctly.

mummy *noun* (mummies) **1** (informal) Mother. **2** The body of a person preserved after death as was the custom in ancient Egypt.

mumps *noun* A contagious disease causing swellings in the neck.

munch *verb* (munches, munching, munched) To chew with much movement of the jaw.

municipal *adjective* To do with a town or city.

mural *noun* (murals) A picture painted on a wall.

murder[1] *noun* (murders) The crime of deliberately killing someone. **murderous** *adjective*, **murderously** *adverb*.

murder[2] *verb* (murders, murdering, murdered) To commit murder. **murderer** *noun*.

murky *adjective* (murkier, murkiest) Dark and gloomy.

murmur[1] *noun* (murmurs) A low monotonous sound.

murmur[2] *verb* (murmurs, murmuring, murmured) To make a murmur.

muscle *noun* (muscles) One of the parts of the body used to produce movement.

muscular *adjective* Having powerful muscles.

museum *noun* (museums) A place where interesting objects are displayed for people to see.

mushroom *noun* (mushrooms) An edible fungus.

music *noun* **1** Pleasing or interesting sounds made by singing or playing various instruments. **2** The signs representing these sounds on paper.

musical[1] *adjective* **1** Fond of music, good at music. **2** Pleasant to listen to. **3** To do with music, for use in music making. **musically** *adverb*.

musical[2] *noun* (musicals) A play or film with much music and singing.

musician *noun* (musicians) A person who makes music.

musket *noun* (muskets) A soldier's gun used before rifles were invented. **musketeer** *noun*.

Muslim *noun* (Muslims) A believer in Islam, a follower of Muhammad.

muslin *noun* A thin fine cotton cloth.

mussel *noun* (mussels) A kind of shellfish.

must *verb* **1** To be obliged to, to feel that you ought to. *I must go home soon.* **2** To be certain to. *You must be tired,* I am sure that you are tired.

mustard *noun* **1** A yellow substance used to add a hot flavour to food. **2** *Mustard and cress,* small green plants eaten as salad.

muster *verb* (musters, mustering, mustered) To gather together.

musty *adjective* (mustier, mustiest) Stale, damp, and mouldy. **mustiness** *noun*.

mute *adjective* Silent, dumb. **mutely** *adverb*.

muted *adjective* Muffled, made quieter.

mutilate *verb* (mutilates, mutilating, mutilated) To damage something by tearing or breaking or cutting off a part. **mutilation** *noun*.

mutineer *noun* (mutineers) Someone who takes part in a mutiny.

mutinous *adjective* Rebellious. **mutinously** *adverb*.

mutiny[1] *noun* (mutinies) A rebellion, especially by sailors against the captain of their ship.

mutiny[2] *verb* (mutinies, mutinying, mutinied) To take part in a mutiny.

mutter *verb* (mutters, muttering, muttered) To murmur, to grumble.

mutton *noun* The meat from sheep.

mutual *adjective* Shared.

muzzle *noun* (muzzles) **1** An animal's nose and mouth. **2** A device put over an animal's muzzle to prevent it from biting. **3** The open end of a gun.

my Belonging to me.

myself *See* **I**[2] This word is used in the same ways as **herself**.

mystery *noun* (mysteries) Something that cannot be explained. **mysterious** *adjective*, **mysteriously** *adverb*.

myth *noun* (myths) A tale about gods and goddesses handed down from ancient times. **mythical** *adjective*.

Nn

nab *verb* (nabs, nabbing, nabbed) (informal) To catch someone doing wrong.

nag[1] *noun* (nags) (informal) A horse.

nag[2] *verb* (nags, nagging, nagged) To complain unceasingly, to scold.

nail[1] *noun* (nails) **1** The hard covering on the tip of a finger or a toe. **2** A short metal spike used in carpentry to fasten pieces of wood together. **nail varnish** a kind of varnish for your finger and toe nails.

nail[2] *verb* (nails, nailing, nailed) To fasten with a nail.

naked *adjective* Not wearing clothes, uncovered. **with the naked eye** without the use of instruments to see through. **nakedly** *adverb*, **nakedness** *noun*.

namaste *noun* A Hindu greeting made by pressing the palms of your hands together.

name[1] *noun* (names) The word by which something or somebody is known.

name[2] *verb* (names, naming, named) **1** To give somebody a name. **2** To say the name of somebody or something.

nameless *adjective* Having no name, not to be named.

namely *adverb* That is to say.

nan *noun* A traditional Indian or Pakistani bread.

nanny *noun* (nannies) (informal) **1** A child's nurse. **2** A grandmother.

nanny-goat *noun* (nanny-goats) A female goat.

nap *noun* (naps) A short sleep.

napalm *noun* Petrol jelly used as a weapon in fire bombs.

napkin *noun* (napkins) **1** A piece of cloth or paper used to keep yourself clean during a meal. **2** A piece of cloth or other material worn round a baby's bottom.

nappy *noun* (nappies) A baby's napkin.

narcotic *noun* (narcotics) A drug which produces sleep or unconsciousness.

narrate *verb* (narrates, narrating, narrated) To tell a story. **narrator**, **narration** *nouns*.

narrow *adjective* (narrower, narrowest) Thin, small in width.

narrowly *adverb* Only just. *He narrowly escaped being run over.*

narrow-minded *adjective* Not sympathetic towards other people's beliefs or views.

nasty *adjective* (nastier, nastiest) **1** Unpleasant, disagreeable. **2** Dirty. **3** Ill-natured, spiteful. **nastily** *adverb*, **nastiness** *noun*.

nation *noun* (nations) **1** A country and the people who live there. **2** A large number of people who have the same language and customs and history.

national *adjective* Belonging to a nation.

nationalist *noun* (nationalists) An enthusiastic supporter of his or her nation.

nationality *noun* (nationalities) Being a member of a nation. *What is his nationality?* what nation does he belong to?

nationalize *verb* (nationalizes, nationalizing, nationalized) To make something the property of the nation. **nationalization** *noun*.

nation-wide *adjective and adverb* Extending over the whole nation.

native[1] *adjective* **1** Natural, possessed from birth. *native wit.* **2** Connected with a person's birth. *my native land*, the land where I was born.

native[2] *noun* (natives) **1** A person born in the place mentioned. *He is a native of Russia*, he was born in Russia. **2** One of the original inhabitants of a country.

Nativity *noun* The birth of Jesus Christ.

NATO North Atlantic Treaty Organization.

natural[1] *adjective* **1** Made by nature, to do with nature. **2** Normal, ordinary, to be expected. **naturally** *adverb*.

natural[2] *noun* The sign ♮ in music.

naturalist *noun* (naturalists) A person who studies animals and plants.

nature[1] *noun* **1** The things in the universe that are not made by people, such as animals and plants, the sea and earth, the weather, and so on. **2** The powers that exist in these

things. **nature study** the study of animals and plants.

nature[2] *noun* (natures) **1** The general qualities or characteristics of a person or thing. *Angela has a kind nature.* **2** Sort, type. *things of that nature*, things of that sort.

naughty *adjective* (naughtier, naughtiest) Badly behaved. **naughtily** *adverb*, **naughtiness** *noun*.

nauseating *adjective* Disgusting, sickening.

nautical *adjective* To do with ships and sailors.

naval *adjective* Belonging to the navy.

navel *noun* (navels) The small hollow in the middle of the surface of your stomach.

navigate *verb* (navigates, navigating, navigated) **1** To direct and control the course of a ship or plane. **2** To sail a ship. **navigable** *adjective*, **navigator, navigation** *nouns*.

navy[1] *noun* (navies) A fleet of ships and the people who sail in them. **navy blue** dark blue.

Nazi *noun* (Nazis) A member of the German National Socialist Party in Hitler's time.

NB *abbreviation* Note carefully.

near[1] *adjective and adverb* (nearer, nearest) Not far away, at a short distance in space or time.

near[2] *preposition* Close to, not far from.

near[3] *verb* (nears, nearing, neared) To come or go near something.

nearby *adjective* Near. *We live in nearby houses.*

nearly *adverb* **1** Almost. *It's nearly dark.* **2** Closely. *nearly related.* **not nearly** far from. *There was not nearly enough food.*

neat *adjective* (neater, neatest) **1** Tidy. **2** Cleverly done. **3** Small and attractive. **neatly** *adverb*, **neatness** *noun*.

necessary *adjective* Having to be done,

essential, unavoidable. **necessarily** *adverb*.

necessity *noun* (necessities) Something which is necessary.

neck *noun* (necks) **1** The part of the body which joins the head and shoulders. **2** Something like a neck in shape. *the neck of a bottle*.

necklace *noun* (necklaces) An ornament worn round the neck.

nectar *noun* A sweet liquid collected by bees from plants.

née *adjective* Born with the name of. *Mrs Weston née Hambleton*.

need[1] *noun* (needs) **1** A want, a requirement. **2** An essential reason. *There's no need to go home yet.* **in need** in poverty and misfortune.

need[2] *verb* (needs, needing, needed) **1** To be without something which is necessary. *I need a handkerchief.* **2** To be obliged to do something, to have to do it. *You need not go.*

needle *noun* (needles) **1** A thin pointed instrument. *a knitting-needle.* **2** The pointer in a compass or a meter.

needlework *noun* Sewing or embroidery.

needy *adjective* (needier, neediest) Very poor.

ne'er *adverb* (old-fashioned) Never.

negative *noun* (negatives) **1** The word *no* or the word *not*. **2** A sentence which denies or refuses something. **3** In mathematics, a figure with a minus sign in front of it. **4** In photography, a film for printing in which the colours or light and dark areas are reversed. **5** In electricity, one of the terminals of a battery. **negative** *adjective*, **negatively** *adverb*.

neglect *verb* (neglects, neglecting, neglected) **1** To fail to look after someone or something properly. *Our neighbours neglect their garden.* **2** To fail to do something. *Don't neglect your homework.* **neglectful** *adjective*, **neglectfully** *adverb*.

negligent *adjective* Careless. **negligently** *adverb*, **negligence** *noun*.

negligible *adjective* Not important, not worth considering.

negotiate *verb* (negotiates, negotiating, negotiated) **1** To discuss and try to come to an agreement about something. **2** To get past or over something. **negotiator, negotiation** *nouns*.

neigh *verb* (neighs, neighing, neighed) To make a noise like a horse.

neighbour *noun* (neighbours) A person who lives near another.

neighbourhood *noun* The surrounding district. **neighbourhood watch** a scheme for neighbours to keep watch against crime near their homes.

neighbouring *adjective* Near, close by.

neighbourly *adverb* Friendly and helpful.

neither[1] *adjective* Not either. *Neither of them could come.*

neither[2] *adverb and conjunction* **1** Neither this nor that, not this and not that. **2** Nor. *If my friend can't go, neither will I.*

neon light A kind of light used in advertisements.

nephew *noun* (nephews) The son of your brother or sister.

nerve *noun* (nerves) **1** A thread-like organ of the body which carries messages between the brain and other parts of the body. *to suffer from nerves*, to get easily excited or upset. **2** Rudeness, cheek. *She's got a nerve!* **get on someone's nerves** to annoy someone. **keep your nerve** to be calm and brave.

nervous *adjective* **1** Connected with the nerves. *a nervous disease.* **2** Timid, fearful. *a nervous animal.* **nervously** *adverb*, **nervousness** *noun*.

nervy *adjective* (informal) Timid, easily upset.

nest[1] *noun* (nests) **1** The place where

a bird lays its eggs. **2** The home of certain animals and insects.

nest² *verb* (nests, nesting, nested) To make a nest, to have a nest.

nestle *verb* (nestles, nestling, nestled) To cuddle, to get comfortably settled.

nestling *noun* (nestlings) A baby bird.

net¹ *noun* (nets) **1** Material containing a large number of holes in a criss-cross pattern of strings, threads, or wires. **2** Something made of this material. *a fishing net.*

net² *verb* (nets, netting, netted) To catch in a net.

netball *noun* A team game in which a ball has to be thrown into a high net.

netting *noun* Material for nets.

nettle *noun* (nettles) A wild plant. *a stinging nettle.*

network *noun* (networks) **1** A net. **2** A criss-cross pattern of lines. **3** A system consisting of many lines or parts. *a railway network, a computer network.*

neuralgia *noun* Pain in the nerves of the face.

neurotic *adjective* Suffering from a nervous illness.

neuter *adjective* Neither masculine nor feminine.

neutral *adjective* **1** Not taking sides. **neutrality** *noun.* **2** Having nothing distinctive about it. *The ship was painted a neutral shade of grey.* **3** A position of gears in which they do not transmit power from the engine.

neutralize *verb* (neutralizes, neutralizing, neutralized) To remove the power or special qualities of something.

never *adverb* At no time.

nevermore *adverb* Never again.

nevertheless *adverb* In spite of that, however.

new *adjective* (newer, newest) Appearing for the first time, just discovered,

just bought or made, recent. **newly** *adverb*, **newness** *noun.*

news *noun* **1** Information about recent events. **2** A broadcast of news.

newsagent *noun* (newsagents) A shopkeeper who sells newspapers and magazines.

newspaper *noun* (newspapers) A daily or weekly publication of news on large sheets of paper folded but not fixed together.

newt *noun* (newts) A small animal like a lizard.

next *adjective* Closest, nearest, following immediately after.

nib *noun* (nibs) The pointed part of a pen which writes on the paper.

nibble *verb* (nibbles, nibbling, nibbled) To take tiny bites at something.

nice *adjective* (nicer, nicest) **1** Pleasant, kind, friendly. **2** Precise, exact. **nicely** *adverb.*

nick¹ *verb* (nicks, nicking, nicked) **1** To cut a notch in something. **2** (informal) To steal.

nick² *noun* (nicks) A notch. **in the nick of time** at the last possible moment.

nickel *noun* A silver-coloured metal.

nickname *noun* (nicknames) A name used instead of someone's proper name.

nicotine *noun* A poisonous substance found in tobacco.

niece *noun* (nieces) The daughter of your brother or sister.

night *noun* (nights) The dark time between sunset and sunrise.

night-club *noun* (night-clubs) A place open at night for drink, food, and entertainment.

nightdress *noun* (nightdresses) A garment worn at night by a girl or woman.

nightfall *noun* The coming of night.

nightingale *noun* (nightingales) A small song-bird.

night-life *noun* Amusements available late at night.

nightly *adjective and adverb* Every night.

nightmare *noun* (nightmares) A frightening dream. **nightmarish** *adjective*.

night-watchman *noun* (night-watchmen) A person employed to look after a place at night.

nil *noun* Nothing.

nimble *adjective* (nimbler, nimblest) Quick, lively, agile. **nimbly** *adverb*.

nine (nines) The number 9. **ninth.**

nineteen The number 19. **nineteenth.**

ninety (nineties) The number 90. **ninetieth.**

nip¹ *verb* (nips, nipping, nipped) **1** To pinch, to bite sharply. **2** (informal) To hurry along.

nip² *noun* (nips) A small quick pinch or bite. **nip in the air** a feeling of frost.

nipper *noun* (nippers) (informal) A small boy.

nipple *noun* (nipples) The round, pinkish area or point in the centre of a person's breast.

nippy *adjective* (nippier, nippiest) (informal) **1** Quick. **2** Cold.

nirvana *noun* In Buddhism, final and complete happiness.

nit *noun* (nits) **1** The egg of a kind of louse, sometimes found in the hair. **2** (informal) A stupid person.

nitrogen *noun* One of the gases in the air we breathe.

nitwit *noun* (nitwits) (informal) A stupid person.

no 1 Not one, not any. *We have no money.* **2** A word used when refusing, disagreeing, denying, or saying that something is not so.

noble¹ *adjective* (nobler, noblest) **1** Of high rank. **2** Having a very good character. **3** Splendid. **nobly** *adverb*, **nobility** *noun*.

noble² *noun* (nobles) A person of high rank, such as a duke or a duchess. **nobleman, noblewoman** *nouns*.

nobody No person, not anyone.

nocturnal *adjective* **1** Active at night. *nocturnal animals.* **2** Of or in the night.

nod¹ *verb* (nods, nodding, nodded) **1** To bow the head to show agreement or to greet somebody. **2** To let the head fall forward in sleep.

no-go area A place where some people are prevented from going.

noise *noun* (noises) **1** A loud sound. **2** A sound of any sort. *Did you hear a noise?* **noisy, noiseless** *adjectives*, **noisily, noiselessly** *adverbs*, **noisiness** *noun*.

nomad *noun* (nomads) A member of a wandering tribe.

no-man's-land *noun* The area between armies fighting each other.

nominate *verb* (nominates, nominating, nominated) To put forward somebody's name for an election. **nomination** *noun*.

nondescript *adjective* Hard to describe, uninteresting.

none *pronoun* **1** Not one, not any. *I told none of them.* **2** No one. *None can tell.*

none² *adverb* Not at all. *After all he said I'm none the wiser.*

non-existent *adjective* Not existing.

nonplussed *adjective* Amazed.

nonsense *noun* **1** Words that do not mean anything. **2** Foolish, pointless talk or behaviour. **nonsensical** *adjective*.

non-stick *adjective* Covered with a material to prevent food sticking.

non-stop *adjective* Without stopping.

noodles *noun* A food rather like spaghetti.

nook *noun* (nooks) A quiet corner.

noon *noun* Twelve o'clock in the middle of the day.

no one No person, not anyone.

noose *noun* (nooses) A loop in a rope which becomes tighter when the rope is pulled.

nor *conjunction* And not.

normal *adjective* Usual, typical, ordinary. **normally** *adverb*, **normality** *noun*.

north¹ *noun* One of the points of the compass, the direction to the left of you when you face east.

north² *adjective and adverb* In or to the north. **north wind** wind blowing from the north.

northerly *adjective* To or from the north.

northern *adjective* Of or in the north.

northward *adjective and adverb* Towards the north. **northwards** *adverb*.

Norwegian *adjective* Of Norway, from Norway.

nose¹ *noun* (noses) 1 The part of your face which sticks out over your mouth. 2 The sense of smell. 3 The front end of a thing.

nose² *verb* (noses, nosing, nosed) 1 To push your nose into or against something. 2 To search, to pry.

nosedive *noun* (nosedives) The movement of falling or flying steeply downwards nose first.

nosey *adjective* (nosier, nosiest) (informal) Inquisitive, prying. **nosily** *adverb*.

nostalgia *noun* A longing for old times. **nostalgic** *adjective*.

nostril *noun* (nostrils) One of the two openings in the nose.

not *adverb* A word which alters the meaning of a statement to its opposite.

notable *adjective* Remarkable. **notably** *adverb*.

notch *noun* (notches) A V-shaped cut in something.

note¹ *noun* (notes) 1 Something written down to help the memory. 2 A short letter or written message. 3 In music, a single sound of a particular pitch. 4 A quality, a sound, a tone. *There was a note of satisfaction in his voice.* 5 Notice. *Take note of what I say.* 6 Paper money. *a five-pound note.*

note² *verb* (notes, noting, noted) 1 To pay attention to something, to notice it. 2 To make a note of something.

notebook *noun* (notebooks) A book to make notes in.

notepaper *noun* Paper used for writing letters.

nothing *noun* Not anything.

notice¹ *verb* (notices, noticing, noticed) To observe something.

notice² *noun* (notices) 1 A written announcement put up somewhere to be read by other people. 2 A warning. 3 Attention. *Take no notice*, pay no attention.

notice-board *noun* (notice-boards) A board for displaying notices.

notify *verb* (notifies, notifying, notified) To tell somebody about something formally. **notification** *noun*.

notion *noun* (notions) An idea, an opinion.

notorious *adjective* Well known for bad reasons. **notoriously** *adverb*, **notoriety** *noun*.

nougat *noun* A sweet made from nuts and sugar.

nought *noun* 1 Nothing. 2 (noughts) The figure 0.

noun *noun* (nouns) A naming word. *David*, *Oxford*, *nursery*, and *zoo* are all nouns.

nourish *verb* (nourishes, nourishing, nourished) To keep somebody alive and well by feeding. **nourishment** *noun*.

novel[1] *adjective* New and strange. **novelty** *noun*.

novel[2] *noun* (novels) A long story which fills a whole book.

novelist *noun* (novelists) A person who writes novels.

November *noun* The eleventh month of the year.

novice *noun* (novices) A beginner.

now[1] *adverb* **1** At this time. **2** By this time. **3** Immediately. *Do it now.* **now and again, now and then** occasionally.

now[2] *conjunction* Since. *Now we are all ready, we can start.*

now[3] *noun* This moment. *They will all be gone by now.*

nowadays *adverb* In these days.

nowhere[1] *adverb* **1** No place. **2** In no place, to no place.

nowhere[2] *noun* No place. *Nowhere is as good as home.*

nozzle *noun* (nozzles) A spout, a piece fitted to the end of a hose-pipe.

nuclear *adjective* To do with atomic energy, the great energy released when the nuclei of atoms are split or combined. **nuclear disarmament** giving up nuclear weapons.

nucleus *noun* (nuclei) A centre round which other parts are grouped.

nude *adjective* Naked. **nudity** *noun*.

nudist *noun* (nudists) A person who enjoys wearing no clothes.

nugget *noun* (nuggets) A lump of gold.

nuisance *noun* (nuisances) A thing or person that causes trouble.

numb[1] *adjective* Without the power to feel or move. **numbly** *adverb*, **numbness** *noun*.

numb[2] *verb* (numbs, numbing, numbed) To make numb.

number[1] *noun* (numbers) **1** A word or figure which shows how many. 1, 3, and 37 are all numbers. **2** A word or figure used to name things in a series. *In most streets the houses are given numbers.* **3** A quantity or amount. *a large number of people.* **4** A song or dance performed as one item in a programme. **5** One issue of a newspaper or magazine.

number[2] *verb* (numbers, numbering, numbered) **1** To count. **2** To put a number on something.

numberless *adjective* Too many to count.

numeral *noun* (numerals) A figure, a number.

numerous *adjective* Many, consisting of a large number.

nun *noun* (nuns) A woman who is a member of a religious community.

nurse[1] *noun* (nurses) A person who is trained to look after sick people or young children.

nurse[2] *verb* (nurses, nursing, nursed) **1** To feed or look after a baby. **2** To look after sick or elderly people. **nursing home** a small hospital.

nursery *noun* (nurseries) **1** A room or building for young children. **2** A place where young plants and trees are grown. **nursery rhyme** a song or poem popular with young children. **nursery school** a school for children too young to go to an infant school.

nut *noun* (nuts) **1** A piece of metal designed to be screwed on a bolt. **2** A type of fruit with a hard shell. **nutty** *adjective*.

nutcrackers *noun* An instrument for breaking the shell of a nut.

nutritious *adjective* Nourishing.

nutshell *noun* (nutshells) The shell of a nut.

nuzzle *verb* (nuzzles, nuzzling, nuzzled) To press against something with the nose.

nylon *noun* A manufactured substance used to make clothes and many other things.

nymph *noun* (nymphs) A kind of goddess in ancient Greek stories.

Oo

oak *noun* (oaks) A large tree that produces acorns.

oar *noun* (oars) A pole with a flat blade used to row a boat.

oasis *noun* (oases) A green and fertile place in a desert.

oath *noun* (oaths) **1** A solemn promise. **2** A swearword.

oatmeal *noun* Oats ground into a powder.

oats *noun* A kind of cereal crop.

obey *verb* (obeys, obeying, obeyed) To do what you are told to do. **obedient** *adjective*, **obediently** *adverb*, **obedience** *noun*.

object¹ *noun* (objects) **1** A thing that can be seen or touched. **2** A purpose. *What is the object of the expedition?*

object² *verb* (objects, objecting, objected) To say that you are not in favour of something. **objector**, **objection** *nouns*.

objectionable *adjective* Unpleasant.

objective *noun* (objectives) A place you are trying to reach or a thing you are trying to do.

obligation *noun* (obligations) A duty, something you ought to do.

oblige *verb* (obliges, obliging, obliged) To help someone, to do someone a favour. *Will you oblige me by shutting the door?* **be obliged 1** To have a duty

to do something. **2** To be grateful to someone.

obliging *adjective* Helpful. **obligingly** *adverb*.

oblong *noun* (oblongs) A rectangle, a shape like a door or the page of a book.

obnoxious *adjective* Hateful, very unpleasant. **obnoxiously** *adverb*.

oboe *noun* (oboes) A woodwind instrument played with a double reed.

obscene *adjective* (obscener, obscenest) Indecent, disgusting. **obscenely** *adverb*, **obscenity** *noun*.

obscure¹ *adjective* (obscurer, obscurest) **1** Dim, not clear. **2** Hard to understand. **3** Not well known. **obscurely** *adverb*, **obscurity** *noun*.

obscure² *verb* (obscures, obscuring, obscured) To make something obscure, to cover it up.

observant *adjective* Quick at noticing things.

observation *noun* **1** (observations) A remark. **2** Observing, watching. **observation post** a place from which to keep watch.

observatory *noun* (observatories) A building from which the stars and planets are observed through telescopes.

observe *verb* (observes, observing, observed) **1** To see, to notice, to watch carefully. **2** To comment. **3** To obey a rule, to follow a custom. **observer** *noun*.

obsess *verb* (obsesses, obsessing, obsessed) To occupy the mind continually. **obsession** *noun*.

obsolete *adjective* Out of date, not in use any more.

obstacle *noun* (obstacles) Something that gets in the way.

obstinate *adjective* Difficult to persuade or deal with, inflexible. **obstinately** adverb, **obstinacy** noun.

obstreperous adjective Noisy, rough and unruly. **obstreperously** adverb.

obstruct verb (obstructs, obstructing, obstructed) To get in the way, to put something in the way. **obstruction** noun.

obtain verb (obtains, obtaining, obtained) To buy, to get, to be given something. **obtainable** adjective.

obtuse adjective Stupid. **obtuse angle** an angle between 90° and 180°.

obvious adjective Plain to see, understood at once. **obviously** adverb.

occasion noun (occasions) **1** A particular or suitable time. **2** A special event, the time when this takes place.

occasional adjective Happening only sometimes, not continuous, not regular. *occasional showers.* **occasionally** adverb.

occult adjective Mysterious, supernatural.

occupation noun (occupations) **1** A job. **2** A pastime. **3** The occupying of a place or a territory.

occupy verb (occupies, occupying, occupied) **1** To live in something. *to occupy a flat.* **occupier, occupant** nouns. **2** To take up space. **3** To keep someone busy. **4** To capture and keep territory in a war.

occur verb (occurs, occurring, occurred) **1** To happen, to take place. **2** To exist, to be found. **3** To come into the mind. *A brilliant idea occurred to me.* **occurrence** noun.

ocean noun (oceans) **1** The sea. **2** A great area of sea, such as the Atlantic or Pacific Ocean.

o'clock adverb By the clock. *School begins at nine o'clock.*

octagon noun (octagons) A shape with eight sides. **octagonal** adjective.

octave noun (octaves) A musical note together with the next note of the same name above or below it.

October noun The tenth month of the year.

octopus noun (octopuses) A sea animal with eight arms.

oculist noun (oculists) A specialist in the treatment of eye diseases.

odd adjective **1** (odder, oddest) Strange, queer. **oddly** adverb, **oddness** noun. **2** Remaining, spare, left over. *an odd sock.* **3** Of various sorts. *odd jobs.* **odd numbers** numbers which cannot be divided exactly by two, such as 1, 3, and 7.

oddity noun (oddities) A strange thing.

oddments noun Odds and ends.

odds noun Chances, likelihood. *The odds are against it,* it is not likely. **odds and ends** various bits and pieces.

ode noun (odes) A kind of poem.

odious adjective Hateful, repulsive.

odour noun (odours) A smell.

of preposition This word has many meanings including the following: **1** From. *a native of China.* **2** Concerning. *news of Granny.* **3** Belonging to. *the home of the Prime Minister.*

off adverb and preposition This word has many uses including the following: **1** Not on, no longer on. *Her glasses fell off.* **2** Away. *They ran off when the police arrived.* **3** Not working or operating. *The heating is off.* **4** Away or down from. *Keep off the grass! The cat jumped off the table.*

offence noun **1** (offences) A crime, the breaking of a law or rule or custom. **2** Hurt feelings. *to cause offence.*

offend verb (offends, offending,

offended) **1** To commit an offence or crime. **offender** *noun*. **2** To hurt someone's feelings.

offensive *adjective* **1** Unpleasant, causing hurt feelings. **2** Used for attacking. *an offensive weapon.* **offensively** *adverb*.

offer¹ *verb* (offers, offering, offered) **1** To say or indicate that someone can have or use something. *She offered me her pen.* **2** To say that you are willing to do something. *We offered to wash up.* **3** To suggest a price you are willing to pay for something. *He offered £10 for my old bike.*

offer² *noun* (offers) A statement offering something. **on offer** offered for sale at a specially reduced price.

offering *noun* (offerings) Something offered, something given.

office *noun* (offices) **1** A room where clerks and secretaries work, a room where business is done. **2** A government department. *the Foreign Office.* **hold office** to have an important job.

officer *noun* (officers) **1** A person who commands others in the services. **2** A senior person in some other jobs. **3** One of the people responsible for running a club or society. **police officer** a policeman or policewoman.

official¹ *adjective* **1** Done or made by someone with authority. *an official document.* **2** Having the authority to do something. *the official scorer.* **officially** *adverb*.

official² *noun* (officials) A person who has the right to give orders.

officious *adjective* Too eager with advice and help.

off-licence *noun* (off-licences) A shop which is allowed to sell alcoholic drinks.

offside *adjective* In football and some other games, in a position where it is against the rules to play the ball.

offspring *noun* (offspring) A person's child, or an animal's young one.

often *adverb* Frequently, many times.

ogre *noun* (ogres) A cruel giant.

oh A cry of surprise or some other sudden feeling.

oil¹ *noun* (oils) A liquid which does not mix with water. Oil is used as fuel, to lubricate machinery, to fry food, and for other purposes.

oil² *verb* (oils, oiling, oiled) To put oil on something to make it run more smoothly.

oil-can *noun* (oil-cans) A can with a long spout used for oiling.

oil-colours *noun* Paints made with oil.

oil-field *noun* (oil-fields) An area where crude oil is found.

oil-fired *adjective* Using oil as fuel.

oil-painting *noun* (oil-paintings) A painting done in oil-colours.

oil-rig *noun* (oil-rigs) A structure used in drilling an oil-well at sea.

oilskins *noun* A waterproof suit worn over other clothes.

oil-tanker *noun* (oil-tankers) A ship or a large truck used to transport oil.

oil-well *noun* (oil-wells) A well drilled for oil.

oily *adjective* (oilier, oiliest) **1** Like oil. **2** Covered in oil.

ointment *noun* (ointments) A soft greasy substance used for healing cuts and sores.

OK or **okay** (informal) **1** All right, yes. **2** Satisfactory. *Is everything OK?*

old *adjective* (older, oldest) **1** Having lived or existed for a long time. *an old castle.* **2** Known for a long time. *an old friend.* **3** 10 years old, born or made ten years previously. **4** Of the past. *in the old days.* **5** Used, out of date. *an old ticket.*

olden *adjective* **olden days** in past times.

old-fashioned *adjective* Out of date, not suitable for modern times.

olive *noun* (olives) A tree which bears a bitter-tasting fruit. **olive oil** oil obtained from this fruit.

Olympic Games or **Olympics** *noun* International athletic sports held once every four years.

omelette *noun* (omelettes) A food made of beaten eggs cooked in a frying-pan.

omen *noun* (omens) A sign of things to come.

ominous *adjective* Threatening. **ominously** *adverb*.

omit *verb* (omits, omitting, omitted) **1** To leave something out. **2** To fail to do something. **omission** *noun*.

omnibus *noun* (omnibuses) **1** (old-fashioned) A bus. **2** A collection of stories in a book.

omnipotent *adjective* Having power over everything. **omnipotence** *noun*.

on *preposition* **1** Situated at the top of, covering the top of. *Tea is on the table.* **2** To a position over or at the top of. *The cat jumped on the table.* **3** At, by, near. *The shops are on the right-hand side of the road.* **4** Attached to. *The picture is on the wall.* **5** Concerning, about. *He gave us a talk on computers.*

on *adverb* **1** So as to be on or over something. *Put your coat on.* **2** Forwards. *We must move on to the next place.* **3** Working, operating. *Is the heating on?*

once *adverb* **1** On one occasion, at one time. *We play netball once a week.* **2** At some time in the past. *Once there were dinosaurs.* **at once** immediately.

once *conjunction* As soon as, when. *Once you can swim, you never forget.*

oncoming *adjective* Coming towards you.

one The number 1. **first**.

one *pronoun* (oneself) **1** A single person, any person. **2** *one another*, each other. *They love one another.*

one-off *adjective* Once only, not repeated.

oneself *See* **one**. The word is used to refer to the person speaking or to people in general. *It's nice to give oneself a treat.*

one-sided *adjective* Favouring one side unfairly.

one-way *adjective* For going in one direction only. *a one-way street.*

onion *noun* (onions) A strong-tasting vegetable.

onlooker *noun* (onlookers) A spectator.

only *adjective* Single, the one person or thing of a kind. *Simon was the only boy to get full marks.* **only child** a child who has no brothers or sisters.

only *adverb* No more than, at the most. *I'll only be a minute.* **only too** very. *Jo is only too happy to help.*

only *conjunction* But then, however. *He'd like to play, only he's busy.*

onslaught *noun* (onslaughts) A fierce attack.

onward *adjective and adverb* Forward. **onwards** *adverb*.

ooze *verb* (oozes, oozing, oozed) To leak slowly through narrow openings.

opal *noun* (opals) A precious stone.

opaque *adjective* Not allowing light to pass through.

open *adjective* **1** Not closed, allowing people or things to pass through. *an open door.* **2** Not enclosed, not fenced in. *open country. in the open air*, out of doors. **3** Not covered over. *an open boat.* **4** Spread out, unfolded. *open arms.* **5** Ready for business. *open to visitors.* **6** Honest, not hiding secrets. *an open face.* **7** Not concealed. *open rebellion.*

open *verb* (opens, opening, opened) **1** To make a thing open. **2** To become open. **3** To start. *My story opens in a dark forest.* **opener** *noun*.

opencast *adjective* **opencast mine** a mine where earth and minerals are removed from the surface of the ground, not from underground.

opening *noun* (openings) **1** A space. **2** A beginning.

openly *adverb* Not secretly. **openness** *noun*.

open-plan *adjective* Built with few dividing walls.

opera *noun* (operas) A kind of play where most or all of the words are sung. **operatic** *adjective*.

operate *verb* (operates, operating, operated) **1** To work, to act. *The lift is not operating today.* **2** To cause something to work. *can you operate this lift?* **3** To perform a surgical operation on someone. **operator** *noun*.

operation *noun* (operations) **1** The working of something. *in operation*, working. **operational** *adjective*. **2** Treatment by a surgeon, involving the cutting of the patient's body. **3** A planned movement of troops and equipment in a war. **4** Any carefully planned activity.

opinion *noun* (opinions) An idea or belief which is not proved.

opium *noun* A kind of drug.

opponent *noun* (opponents) A person who is fighting or playing or arguing on the opposite side.

opportunity *noun* (opportunities) A good chance, a convenient occasion to do something.

oppose *verb* (opposes, opposing, opposed) To fight or argue or play against someone or something. **opposition** *noun*.

opposite[1] *adjective* **1** Facing. *the opposite wall.* **2** Entirely different, as different as can be. *opposite opinions.*

opposite[2] *noun* (opposites) One of two things which are entirely different. *Black is the opposite of white.*

oppress *verb* (oppresses, oppressing, oppressed) **1** To govern cruelly, to treat people unjustly. **2** To weigh

down with worry or sorrow. **oppressor, oppression** *nouns*.

oppressive *adjective* **1** Cruel, unjust. **2** *oppressive weather*, hot, close weather. **oppressively** *adverb*.

opt *verb* (opts, opting, opted) To choose. **opt out** to choose not to join in something, to choose to be independent.

optical *adjective* To do with the eyes or with seeing.

optician *noun* (opticians) A person who supplies spectacles.

optimist *noun* (optimists) An optimistic person. **optimism** *noun*.

optimistic *adjective* Feeling that all will turn out right in the end, expecting the best, hopeful. **optimistically** *adverb*.

option *noun* (options) A choice.

optional *adjective* Not compulsory.

or *conjunction* A word which shows that a choice is available. *You can have a bun or a sandwich.*

oral *adjective* **1** Spoken. **2** Done or taken by the mouth. **orally** *adverb*.

orange[1] *noun* (oranges) A round, juicy fruit with reddish-yellow peel.

orange[2] *adjective* Reddish-yellow.

orangeade *noun* A drink flavoured with oranges.

orbit[1] *noun* (orbits) The path followed by one planet or satellite moving round another in space. **in orbit** moving in an orbit.

orbit[2] *verb* (orbits, orbiting, orbited) To move round in orbit.

orbital *adjective* Going round something in a circle. *an orbital motorway.*

orchard *noun* (orchards) A field of fruit trees.

orchestra *noun* (orchestras) A large number of musicians who play together. *a symphony orchestra.* **orchestral** *adjective*.

orchid *noun* (orchids) A kind of flower.

ordeal *noun* (ordeals) A severe test of your strength or courage.

order¹ *noun* (orders) **1** A statement that you must do something. *The boss gives the orders.* **2** A request for something to be supplied. *The waiter took our order.* **3** Good behaviour. *Our teacher restored order.* **4** Tidiness. *Mum wants some order in my room.* **5** Arrangement. *Put the words in alphabetical order.* **6** Condition. *Keep your bike in good order.* **7** Kind, sort. *She showed skill of the highest order.* **in order that** so that. **in order to** for the purpose of.

order² *verb* (orders, ordering, ordered) **1** To give an order to someone. **2** To ask someone to supply something. *We ordered two cups of tea.*

orderly *adjective* **1** Well arranged. **2** Well behaved.

ordinary *adjective* Normal, usual, of the kind that you often find or would expect. *ordinary food, ordinary people.* **ordinarily** *adverb*.

ore *noun* (ores) A rock or mineral from which metal can be obtained. *iron ore.*

organ *noun* (organs) **1** A part of an animal's body with a particular job to do. *Ears are organs of hearing.* **2** A keyboard instrument which makes sounds either electronically or by blowing air through pipes.

organism *noun* (organisms) A living animal or plant.

organist *noun* (organists) A person who plays the organ.

organization *noun* (organizations) **1** The organizing of something. **2** A group of people working together.

organize *verb* (organizes, organizing, organized) **1** To make the arrangements for something. **2** To get people working together in an orderly way. **organizer** *noun*.

orgy *noun* (orgies) A wild, drunken party.

oriental *adjective* Of the East, especially of China or Japan.

orienteering *noun* A sport involving cross-country running and map-reading.

origami *noun* The Japanese art of folding paper into interesting shapes.

origin *noun* (origins) The point where something began.

original *adjective* **1** Earliest, first, existing from the beginning. **originally** *adverb*. **2** Not a copy, not an imitation. *an original painting.* **3** Able to produce new ideas. *an original thinker.* **originality** *noun*.

originate *verb* (originates, originating, originated) To begin. **originator** *noun*.

ornament *noun* (ornaments) An object or decoration intended to make something more beautiful. **ornamental** *adjective*.

ornithology *noun* The scientific study of birds. **ornithologist** *noun*.

orphan *noun* (orphans) A child whose parents are dead.

orphanage *noun* (orphanages) A home for orphans.

orthodox *adjective* Generally accepted. *orthodox opinion.* **the Eastern Orthodox Church** the Christian Churches of Eastern Europe.

osteopath *noun* (osteopaths) A person who treats patients by manipulating parts of their bodies.

ostrich *noun* (ostriches) A large bird that runs swiftly but cannot fly.

other Somebody or something different from the one just mentioned. *This egg is all right but the other was bad.* **the other day** a few days ago.

otherwise *adverb* **1** In another way, in a different way. **2** Or else. *Be careful, otherwise you'll fall.*

otter *noun* (otters) An animal that lives by rivers or streams.

ouch A cry of pain.

ought *verb* Should, must. *It ought to be ready by now. You ought to go.*

oughtn't (informal) Ought not.

ounce *noun* (ounces) A unit of weight, 28.3 grams. 16 ounces make one pound.

our, ours Belonging to us. *Our house. This house is ours.*

ourselves *See* we

out *adverb* **1** Away from its place inside something. *Take the cork out.* **2** Not at home. *The doctor is out.* **3** In the open. *The secret is out.* **4** Published. *There's a new book out.* **5** Finished. *The fire is out.* **6** Unconscious. *The boxer was out for an hour.* **7** No longer entitled to play, especially in a cricket innings. *Out first ball!* **8** At full length. *Stretch out your hand.* **9** To be used or seen. *Lay your work out on the table.* **10** To be heard. *Speak out.* **out of 1** Away from. *out of bed.* **2** From. *made out of wood. six out of ten* six from a possible total of ten. **3** Without. *out of work.* **out of date** no longer valid, old-fashioned. **out of the way** remote, unusual.

outback *noun* In Australia, the remote inland parts of a country.

outboard motor An engine fitted on the stern of a small boat.

outbreak *noun* (outbreaks) The beginning of something unpleasant or violent. *an outbreak of measles.*

outburst *noun* (outbursts) A sudden burst of something, an outbreak.

outcast *noun* (outcasts) A person disowned by society.

outcome *noun* (outcomes) A result.

outcry *noun* (outcries) A protest, an angry shout.

outdo *verb* (outdoes, outdoing, outdid, outdone) To do more, or to do better, than someone else.

outdoor *adjective* Done outdoors, for outdoors.

outdoors *adverb* Not inside any building or shelter, in the open air.

outer *adjective* Near the outside, further from the centre. **outer space** space beyond the earth's atmosphere.

outfit *noun* (outfits) All the clothes or equipment needed for a particular purpose.

outgrow *verb* (outgrows, outgrowing, outgrew, outgrown) **1** To grow too big or too old for something. **2** To grow larger than someone or something. *Susan has outgrown her brother.*

outhouse *noun* (outhouses) A shed or other small building near a main building.

outing *noun* (outings) A pleasure trip.

outlaw[1] *noun* (outlaws) A bandit.

outlaw[2] *verb* (outlaws, outlawing, outlawed) To make something illegal.

outlet *noun* (outlets) A way out.

outline[1] *noun* (outlines) **1** The shape of something. **2** A simple drawing which shows only the shape of a thing without any details or shading. **3** A summary.

outline[2] *verb* (outlines, outlining, outlined) To draw an outline, to give an outline.

outlive *verb* (outlives, outliving, outlived) To live longer than someone else.

outlook *noun* (outlooks) **1** A view. **2** A forecast.

outlying *adjective* Distant, far from a town or city.

outnumber *verb* (outnumbers, outnumbering, outnumbered) To be greater in number than something else.

out-patient *noun* (out-patients) A person who visits a hospital for treatment but does not sleep there.

outpost *noun* (outposts) A distant settlement.

output *noun* 1 The quantity of things produced. *the output of a factory*. 2 The results of running a computer program.

outrage *noun* (outrages) Something that shocks many people. **outrageous** *adjective*, **outrageously** *adverb*.

outright *adverb* Completely, altogether.

outside¹ *noun* (outsides) The outer part of something, the part furthest from the middle. **at the outside** at the most.

outside² *adjective* 1 Furthest from the middle. 2 Of the outside, coming from the outside. 3 Remote, unlikely. *an outside chance*.

outside³ *adverb* 1 On the outer side, to the outer side. *Please go outside*. 2 Outdoors. *It's warm enough to play outside*.

outsider *noun* (outsiders) 1 A person who is not a member of a particular group. 2 A horse with no obvious chance of winning a race.

outsize *adjective* Of larger than normal size.

outskirts *noun* The suburbs of a town.

outspoken *adjective* Saying what you think.

outstanding *adjective* 1 Easily noticed. 2 Very good. **outstandingly** *adverb*. 3 Still requiring attention.

outstretched *adjective* Stretched out.

outward *adjective* 1 On the outside. *outward appearances*. **outwardly** *adverb*. 2 Going out. *the outward journey*.

outwards *adverb* Towards the outside.

outwit *verb* (outwits, outwitting, outwitted) To defeat others by being cleverer than they are.

outworn *adjective* Worn out, used up.

oval *adjective* Egg-shaped, shaped like an 0.

oven *noun* (ovens) The part of a cooking stove into which food is put for baking or roasting.

over¹ *preposition* 1 On, above, covering. *Fog lay over the city*. 2 Across, to the other side of. *I climbed over the wall*. 3 More than. *There were over a dozen left*. 4 Concerning. *They fought over the bone*.

over² *adverb* 1 From an upright position, off the top or edge of something. *Mind you don't fall over!* 2 From showing one side upwards to the other. *Turn the record over, please*. 3 From beginning to end, thoroughly. *Think it over*. 4 Across, to a place. *Come over here*. 5 Remaining. *3 into 11 goes 3 and 2 over*. 6 Ended. *The quarrel was soon over*.

over³ *noun* (overs) In cricket, a number of balls bowled one after the other from the same end of the pitch.

overall *noun* (overalls) A loose-fitting garment worn over your clothes to keep them clean.

overbalance *verb* (overbalances, overbalancing, overbalanced) To fall over.

overboard *adverb* Over the side of a ship into the water.

overcast *adjective* Cloudy.

overcoat *noun* (overcoats) A warm outer coat.

overcome *verb* (overcomes, overcoming, overcame) 1 To defeat someone. 2 To make someone weak or helpless.

overcrowd *verb* (overcrowds, overcrowding, overcrowded) To crowd too many people or things together.

overdo *verb* (overdoes, overdoing, overdid, overdone) To do something too much.

overdose *noun* (overdoses) A dose which is too large.

overdue *adjective* Late, past the proper time.

overflow *verb* (overflows, overflowing, overflowed) To flood, to spill over.

overgrown *adjective* Covered with unwanted plants.

overhang *verb* (overhangs, overhanging, overhung) To jut out over something as a shelf does.

overhaul *verb* (overhauls, overhauling, overhauled) **1** To examine something thoroughly and repair it if necessary. **2** To overtake.

overhead *adjective and adverb* Above your head, in the sky.

overhear *verb* (overhears, overhearing, overheard) To hear something accidentally.

overjoyed *adjective* Delighted, very pleased.

overland *adjective and adverb* Across the land.

overlap *verb* (overlaps, overlapping, overlapped) To lie across part of something. *overlapping tiles*.

overleaf *adverb* On the other side of the paper.

overload *verb* (overloads, overloading, overloaded) To put too big a load on something.

overlook *verb* (overlooks, overlooking, overlooked) **1** To have a view of something from above. **2** To fail to notice something. **3** To let some wrong action pass without punishment.

overnight *adjective and adverb* Through the night, for a night. *We travelled overnight*.

overpower *verb* (overpowers, overpowering, overpowered) To overcome someone.

overrated *adjective* Valued too highly.

overrun *verb* (overruns, overrunning, overran, overrun) **1** To spread over an area and occupy it. **2** To use up more than the time allowed. **3** To go on too far.

overseas *adverb* Beyond the sea, across the sea.

oversight *noun* (oversights) A mistake made because something was not noticed.

oversleep *verb* (oversleeps, oversleeping, overslept) To go on sleeping too long.

overtake *verb* (overtakes, overtaking, overtook, overtaken) **1** To pass another moving vehicle and drive on in front of it. **2** To come upon somebody suddenly. *A storm overtook us*.

overthrow *verb* (overthrows, overthrowing, overthrew, overthrown) To defeat.

overtime *noun* Time spent at work after the usual hours. *overtime pay*.

overture *noun* (overtures) A piece of orchestral music to be performed at the beginning of a concert or opera.

overturn *verb* (overturns, overturning, overturned) To turn something over.

overweight *adjective* Too heavy.

overwhelm *verb* (overwhelms, overwhelming, overwhelmed) **1** To overcome completely. **2** To bury or submerge something.

ovulate *verb* (ovulates, ovulating, ovulated) To produce egg-cells inside the body.

owe *verb* (owes, owing, owed) **1** To have a duty to pay money to someone. *I owe John £10*. **2** To have something as a result of someone's action or ability. *I owe my life to her skill*.

owing to Because of, caused by.

owl *noun* (owls) A bird of prey which flies at night.

own¹ A word used to emphasize who owns something. *This pen is my own*, it belongs to me and no one else. **on your own** without anyone else.

own² (owns, owning, owned) **1** To possess something, to have the right to keep it. **2** To admit. **own up** to confess.

owner *noun* (owners) The person who owns something. **ownership** *noun*.

ox *noun* (oxen) A male animal of the cow family.

oxtail *noun* (oxtails) The tail of an ox, used to make soup.

oxygen *noun* One of the gases in the air. Animals and plants need it in order to live.

oyster *noun* (oysters) A kind of shellfish.

ozone *noun* A form of oxygen with a sharp smell. **ozone layer** a layer of ozone high above the earth which protects us from harmful amounts of the sun's rays.

Pp
•••••

pace¹ *noun* (paces) **1** The distance a person covers when taking a single step in walking. **2** Speed. *He walked at a brisk pace.*

pace² *verb* (paces, pacing, paced) **1** To walk with slow or regular steps. **2** To measure a distance in paces.

pacemaker *noun* (pacemakers) **1** The person who sets the speed in a race. **2** A device to regulate the speed of the heart.

pacifist *noun* (pacifists) A person who believes that war is always wrong. **pacifism** *noun*.

pacify *verb* (pacifies, pacifying, pacified) To make peaceful, to make calm.

pack¹ *noun* (packs) **1** A bundle or box of things packed together. **2** A group of hounds or wolves. **3** A set of playing-cards. **4** The forwards in rugby football.

pack² *verb* (packs, packing, packed) **1** To wrap things up or put them in containers. **2** To crowd together.

package *noun* (packages) A parcel or bundle. **package holiday** a holiday in which the fare and the accommodation are included in the price.

packet *noun* (packets) A small parcel.

packing *noun* Material used to pack goods in.

pact *noun* (pacts) A solemn agreement.

pad¹ *noun* (pads) **1** A piece of padding. **2** A set of sheets of paper held together at one edge. *a writing pad.* **3** A protection for the batsman's legs in cricket.

pad² *verb* (pads, padding, padded) **1** To fill or cover with padding. **2** To walk softly.

padding *noun* Soft material used to make something more comfortable or to change its shape.

paddle¹ *verb* (paddles, paddling, paddled) **1** To move a boat along with a paddle. **2** To walk with bare feet in shallow water.

paddle² *noun* (paddles) **1** A short oar. **2** A time spent paddling.

paddock *noun* (paddocks) A small field.

paddy-field *noun* (paddy-fields) A rice-field.

padlock¹ *noun* (padlocks) A lock with a curved bar which forms a loop when closed.

padlock² *verb* (padlocks, padlocking, padlocked) To fasten something with a padlock.

pagan *adjective* (pagans) Heathen.

page *noun* (pages) **1** A sheet of paper in a book or magazine. **2** One side of a sheet of paper. **3** A boy servant.

pageant *noun* (pageants) **1** An entertainment based on historic events and people. **2** A grand procession. **pageantry** *noun*.

pagoda *noun* (pagodas) A kind of sacred tower in the Far East.

paid *See* **pay**¹

pail *noun* (pails) A bucket.

pain *noun* (pains) An unpleasant feeling in a part of your body caused by injury or illness, suffering. **painful**, **painless** *adjectives*, **painfully**, **painlessly** *adverbs*. **take pains** to be careful and thorough.

paint¹ *noun* (paints) A substance which is put on something to colour it.

paint² *verb* (paints, painting, painted) **1** To put paint on something. **2** To make a picture with paints.

paintbox *noun* (paintboxes) A box containing paints.

paintbrush *noun* (paintbrushes) A brush for paint.

painter *noun* (painters) **1** Someone who paints. **2** A rope for tying up a boat.

painting *noun* (paintings) A painted picture.

pair *noun* (pairs) **1** Two things of the same kind which go together. *a pair of shoes*. **2** A single thing with two similar parts. *a pair of trousers*.

Pakistani *adjective* Of or from Pakistan.

pal *noun* (pals) (informal) A friend.

palace *noun* (palaces) **1** The official home of the ruler of a country, or of a bishop. **2** A large and splendid house.

pale *adjective* (paler, palest) **1** Having little colour, whitish. **2** Dim, faint, not bright. **palely** *adverb*, **paleness** *noun*.

palette *noun* (palettes) A board on which an artist mixes paints.

paling *noun* (palings) A wooden fence.

palisade *noun* (palisades) A fence made of pointed wooden sticks.

pall¹ *noun* (palls) A dark covering.

pall² *verb* (palls, palling, palled) To become tiresome or boring.

palm¹ *noun* (palms) The inside part of a person's hand between the wrist and the fingers.

palm² *noun* (palms) A kind of tree with no branches and a mass of large leaves at the top, growing in hot countries. *a date-palm, a coconut-palm*. **Palm Sunday** the Sunday before Easter.

pampas-grass *noun* A tall feathery plant of the grass family.

pamper *verb* (pampers, pampering, pampered) To take too much care of someone.

pamphlet *noun* (pamphlets) A thin paper-bound booklet.

pan *noun* (pans) **1** A flat dish, often without a cover. *a frying-pan*. **2** Anything dish-shaped.

pancake *noun* (pancakes) A food made from fried batter.

panda *noun* (pandas) **giant panda** a black and white animal from China. **panda car** a police patrol car.

pandemonium *noun* A scene of confused uproar and disorder.

pane *noun* (panes) A sheet of glass in a window.

panel[1] *noun* (panels) **1** A flat piece of board, metal, or other substance forming part of a wall or other surface. **2** A group of people chosen to take part in a quiz or to decide something.

panel[2] *verb* (panels, panelling, panelled) To cover something with panels. *a panelled wall.*

pang *noun* (pangs) A sudden feeling of sadness or pain.

panic[1] *noun* Sudden infectious fear. **panicky** *adjective*.

panic[2] *verb* (panics, panicking, panicked) To give way to panic.

pannier *noun* (panniers) One of a pair of baskets or bags hung over the rear wheel of a bicycle.

panorama *noun* (panoramas) A wide view.

pansy *noun* (pansies) A plant whose flowers have large velvety petals.

pant *verb* (pants, panting, panted) To take many short quick breaths, to gasp.

panther *noun* (panthers) A leopard.

panties *noun* Knickers.

pantomime *noun* (pantomimes) A Christmas entertainment usually based on a fairy-tale.

pantry *noun* (pantries) A room or cupboard where food is kept.

pants *noun* **1** Underpants. **2** Trousers.

paper[1] *noun* (papers) **1** A substance made in thin flexible sheets. It is used to write on, to make books, to wrap things in, and so on. **2** A newspaper. **paper-boy**, **paper-girl** someone who delivers newspapers. **papers** official or important documents.

paper[2] *verb* (papers, papering, papered) To paste wallpaper on a wall.

paperback *noun* (paperbacks) A book with paper covers.

papier-mâché *noun* Paper made into pulp and used for making models and other objects.

papyrus *noun* A kind of paper which was made out of reeds in ancient Egypt.

parable *noun* (parables) A story which teaches a moral.

parachute[1] *noun* (parachutes) An umbrella-shaped apparatus used for dropping safely from an aircraft.

parachute[2] *verb* (parachutes, parachuting, parachuted) To use a parachute. **parachutist** *noun*.

parade[1] *noun* (parades) **1** A procession. **2** A display of people moving past the spectators. **3** An assembly of soldiers for inspection and drill.

parade[2] *verb* (parades, parading, paraded) **1** To assemble for a parade. **2** To go in a parade.

paradise *noun* Heaven, a place of complete happiness.

paraffin *noun* An oil used as a fuel.

paragraph *noun* (paragraphs) A division of a piece of writing. Each paragraph starts on a new line.

parallel *adjective* Always the same distance apart, like the rails of a railway track.

paralyse *verb* (paralyses, paralysing, paralysed) To make helpless and unable to move.

paralysis *noun* A state of being unable to move or feel anything.

paranoid *adjective* Excessively anxious

about something, imagining that something is wrong or that someone is not to be trusted.

parapet *noun* (parapets) A low wall, like the wall along the side of a bridge.

paraphernalia *noun* Numerous pieces of equipment or other possessions.

paraplegic *noun* (paraplegics) A person paralysed in the legs and part of the body.

parasite *noun* (parasites) An animal or plant that grows and feeds on another. **parasitic** *adjective*.

paratroops *noun* Troops trained to drop by parachute. **paratrooper** *noun*.

parcel *noun* (parcels) Something wrapped up for carrying or posting.

parch *verb* (parches, parching, parched) To make something become hot and dry.

parchment *noun* A material for writing on, made from the skin of a goat or sheep.

pardon[1] *noun* (pardons) Forgiveness.

pardon[2] *verb* (pardons, pardoning, pardoned) To forgive, to excuse, to overlook. **pardonable** *adjective*.

parent *noun* (parents) A father or mother, a person who has produced a child. **parental** *adjective*.

parish *noun* (parishes) A small division of a county, an area with its own church.

park[1] *noun* (parks) **1** A public garden, an area of ground for public use. **2** An area of grassland with trees round a large country house. **3** A place where cars or other vehicles may be left for a time. *a car park*. **National Park** a large area of beautiful countryside protected by the government.

park[2] *verb* (parks, parking, parked) To leave a vehicle for a time in a car park or other suitable place.

parka *noun* (parkas) A kind of outdoor jacket with a hood.

parking-meter *noun* (parking-meters) An instrument which measures the length of time a car is parked in a street.

parliament *noun* (parliaments) A gathering of people responsible for making the laws of their country. **parliamentary** *adjective*.

parlour *noun* (parlours) A sitting-room.

parole *noun* **on parole** released from prison before the proper date on condition that you behave well.

parrot *noun* (parrots) A tropical bird often kept as a pet.

parry *verb* (parries, parrying, parried) To fend off a blow.

parsley *noun* A green herb.

parsnip *noun* (parsnips) A pointed white or yellow root vegetable.

parson *noun* (parsons) A Christian minister.

part[1] *noun* (parts) **1** Some but not all. *We saw part of the film.* **2** A share in something. *He was fined for his part in the crime.* **3** A piece of something. *Mum keeps spare parts in her car.* **4** An area or district. *John moved to another part of the country.* **5** A character in a play, or the words spoken by the character. **part of speech** any of the groups into which you can divide words in grammar (adjective, adverb, conjunction, exclamation or interjection, noun, preposition, pronoun, verb).

part[2] *verb* (parts, parting, parted) To separate or divide. **part with** to give something up, to give it away.

partial *adjective* Only in part, incomplete. **partially** *adverb*. **partial to** fond of.

participate *verb* (participates, participating, participated) To have a share in something, to take part in it. **participation** *noun*.

particle *noun* (particles) A tiny piece of something.

particular *adjective* **1** Outstanding,

a b c d e f g h i j k l m

special, important. *this particular example*, this one and no others. **2** Fussy, hard to please. **in particular** specially. **particularly** *adverb*.

particulars *noun* Details.

parting *noun* (partings) **1** Leaving, separation. **2** The line where some people part their hair.

partisan *noun* (partisans) **1** A strong or violent supporter. **2** A guerrilla.

partition *noun* (partitions) A dividing wall.

partly *adverb* In part, not completely.

partner *noun* (partners) One of a pair of people who share things or do things together. **partnership** *noun*.

partridge *noun* (partridges) A game bird.

part-time *adjective* Working for only part of the time.

party *noun* (parties) **1** A group of people who have met to enjoy themselves. *a birthday party*. **2** A group with similar political opinions. *the Labour Party*. **3** A group of people working or travelling together. *a party of tourists*. **4** Someone involved in a legal case. *the guilty party*.

pass¹ *verb* (passes, passing, passed) **1** To go past. *We passed your house today.* **2** To move, to go, to travel. *They passed along a narrow lane.* **3** To give, to hand over. *Please pass the jam.* **4** To disappear. *The pain will soon pass.* **5** To be successful in something. *Did Robert pass his test?* **6** To spend, to use. *How shall we pass the time?* **pass away** to die. **pass off** to take place. *The concert passed off successfully.*

pass² *noun* (passes) **1** The act of passing. **2** A narrow way between hills or mountains. **3** A permit. *a bus pass.*

passable *adjective* **1** Acceptable, satisfactory. **2** *The road is passable*, it can be travelled over.

passage *noun* (passages) **1** A long narrow way between walls, a corridor. **2** A way through. **3** A journey by sea or air. **4** A short extract from a piece of writing or music. **5** Passing. *the passage of time.*

passenger *noun* (passengers) **1** A person travelling by public transport. **2** A person being driven in a car.

passer-by *noun* (passers-by) A person who happens to be going past.

passion *noun* (passions) A strong feeling, an enthusiasm. **passionate** *adjective*, **passionately** *adverb*.

passive *adjective* Not resisting, not active. **passively** *adverb*.

Passover *noun* A Jewish festival.

passport *noun* (passports) An official document you carry when travelling abroad to show who you are.

password *noun* (passwords) A secret word which enables somebody to be recognized.

past¹ *noun* The time before the present. *Granny has lots of stories about the past.*

past² *adjective* Belonging to the past. *during these past weeks.*

past³ *preposition* **1** After. *It's past midnight.* **2** Beyond. *The shops are just past the school.* **3** Up to and beyond. *He walked straight past me.*

past⁴ *adverb* To a position further on. *The bus went past without stopping.*

pasta *noun* A mixture of flour and other ingredients used to make food like macaroni or noodles.

paste¹ *noun* (pastes) **1** A damp mixture used for sticking papers together or for hanging wallpaper. **2** Any soft damp mixture. *fish paste.*

paste² *verb* (pastes, pasting, pasted) To stick with paste.

pastel *noun* (pastels) A coloured chalk crayon.

pasteurize *verb* (pasteurizes, pasteurizing, pasteurized) To kill germs in milk by a heating process.

pastille *noun* (pastilles) A lozenge, a kind of sweet. *throat pastilles.*

pastime *noun* (pastimes) A game, anything done for recreation.

pastor *noun* (pastors) A minister of religion.

pastry *noun* (pastries) A mixture of flour, fat, and other ingredients baked in an oven.

pasture *noun* (pastures) Grassland for sheep or cattle.

pasty[1] *adjective* (pastier, pastiest) Pale.

pasty[2] *noun* (pasties) A kind of pie.

pat *verb* (pats, patting, patted) To hit gently with the open hand or with something flat.

patch[1] *noun* (patches) **1** A piece of material put over a hole or damaged place. **2** A small area of ground. **3** Part of a surface different from the rest.

patch[2] *verb* (patches, patching, patched) To put a patch on something. **patch up** to repair something roughly.

patchwork *noun* A piece of material made up of a variety of small pieces of cloth stitched together.

patchy *adjective* Made up of odds and ends, uneven in quality. **patchily** *adverb*, **patchiness** *noun*.

pâté *noun* A kind of meat or fish paste.

paternal *adjective* **1** Fatherly. **2** Of or belonging to a father.

path *noun* (paths) **1** A way to walk or ride along. **2** A line along which something moves.

pathetic *adjective* **1** Sad, causing pity. **2** (informal) Feeble. **pathetically** *adverb*.

pathway *noun* (pathways) A path.

patience *noun* **1** The ability to endure pain or trouble or inconvenience without complaining. **2** A card game for a single player.

patient[1] *adjective* Having patience. **patiently** *adverb*.

patient[2] *noun* (patients) A person treated by a doctor or a nurse.

patio *noun* (patios) A paved area beside a house.

patriot *noun* (patriots) A person who loves his or her country and is ready to defend it. **patriotic** *adjective*, **patriotism** *noun*.

patrol[1] *verb* (patrols, patrolling, patrolled) To go about to see that all is well.

patrol[2] *noun* (patrols) **1** A group of people, ships, vehicles, or aircraft patrolling an area. **2** A group of Scouts. **on patrol** patrolling. **patrol car** a car used by police on patrol.

patron *noun* **1** A regular customer. **2** Someone who supports a good cause by giving money or other help. **patron saint** a saint thought of as the special protector of a church or a particular group of people.

patter *verb* (patters, pattering, pattered) To make repeated light tapping sounds.

pattern *noun* (patterns) **1** Something which is to be copied, something which shows how a thing should be made. *a dress pattern.* **2** A pleasing arrangement of lines, shapes, or colours.

pauper *noun* (paupers) A very poor person.

pause[1] *noun* (pauses) A short stop or interval.

pause[2] *verb* (pauses, pausing, paused) To make a pause.

pave *verb* (paves, paving, paved) To cover an area with a surface of flat stones.

pavement *noun* (pavements) A path for pedestrians at the side of a road.

pavilion *noun* (pavilions) A building at a sports ground for the use of players or spectators.

paw[1] *noun* (paws) The foot of an animal with claws.

paw[2] *verb* (paws, pawing, pawed) To touch something with a hand or foot.

pawn[1] *noun* (pawns) One of the small, least valuable pieces in chess.

pawn[2] *verb* (pawns, pawning, pawned)

To leave something with a pawn-broker in order to borrow money.

pawnbroker *noun* (pawnbrokers) A shopkeeper who lends money to people who leave articles until they repay the loan.

pay¹ *verb* (pays, paying, paid) **1** To hand over to someone money which you owe. *We pay the milkman on Saturdays.* **2** To be profitable. *It pays to be honest.* **3** To suffer for something you have done. *I'll make you pay for this!* **pay attention** to give your attention to someone or something. **pay back 1** To give someone what you owe. **2** To take revenge on someone.

pay² *noun* Wages, money which has been earned.

payment *noun* (payments) **1** Paying. **2** Money which is to be paid.

pea *noun* (peas) A plant with pods containing round seeds which are used as a vegetable.

peace *noun* **1** Freedom from war, the absence of disorder or violence. **2** Quiet, calm, rest. **peaceful** *adjective*, **peacefully** *adverb*, **peacefulness** *noun*.

peach *noun* (peaches) A juicy round fruit with a large stone.

peacock *noun* (peacocks) A male bird with a long tail which it can spread like a fan. **peahen** *noun*.

peak *noun* (peaks) **1** The pointed tip of something, the highest point of something. **2** The front brim of a cap.

peal¹ *noun* (peals) **1** A loud ringing of bells. **2** An outburst of sound. *a peal of laughter.*

peal² *verb* (peals, pealing, pealed) To ring out loudly.

peanut *noun* (peanuts) A kind of nut.

pear *noun* (pears) A fruit which is narrower at the stalk end.

pearl *noun* (pearls) A small round silvery-white stone sometimes found in oyster shells and used as a jewel.

peasant *noun* (peasants) In some countries, a person who works on the land.

peat *noun* A substance dug from the ground used as a fuel or in gardening.

pebble *noun* (pebbles) A small rounded stone.

peck *verb* (pecks, pecking, pecked) To strike at something with the beak.

peckish *adjective* (informal) Hungry.

peculiar *adjective* **1** Odd, unusual, strange. **2** Particular, special. **peculiarly** *adverb*, **peculiarity** *noun*.

pedal¹ *noun* (pedals) A part of a machine worked by the foot.

pedal² *verb* (pedals, pedalling, pedalled) To use a pedal, to move by the use of pedals. *Timothy pedalled along on his bicycle.*

pedalo *noun* (pedalos) A small kind of boat driven by pedals.

pedestrian *noun* (pedestrians) A person walking along the street. **pedestrian crossing** a place where pedestrians can cross the street.

pedigree *noun* (pedigrees) A list of a person's or animal's parents and ancestors. **pedigree animal** one bred from known parents and ancestors.

pedlar *noun* (pedlars) A person who used to go from place to place with goods for sale.

peel¹ *noun* The skin or rind of a fruit or vegetable.

peel² *verb* (peels, peeling, peeled) **1** To take the skin or covering off something. **2** To lose a skin or covering. **3** To come off in thin layers.

peep *verb* (peeps, peeping, peeped)

1 To look through a narrow opening.
2 To take a short quick look.

peer¹ *verb* (peers, peering, peered) To look at something closely.

peer², **peeress** *nouns* (peers, peeresses) A noble.

peevish *adjective* Irritable, cross. **peevishly** *adverb*.

peewit *noun* (peewits) A bird of the plover family.

peg¹ *noun* (pegs) 1 A clip for fixing washed clothes to a line. 2 A wooden or metal rod for fastening things or for hanging things on.

peg² *verb* (pegs, pegging, pegged) To fasten with pegs.

Pekingese *noun* (Pekingese) A kind of dog with short legs and a flat face.

pelican *noun* (pelicans) A bird with a huge bill.

pellet *noun* (pellets) A tiny ball of something.

pelt *verb* (pelts, pelting, pelted) 1 To attack someone by throwing many things at him or her. 2 To rain hard.

pen¹ *noun* (pens) 1 An instrument for writing with ink.

pen² *noun* (pens) An enclosed space for sheep or other animals.

penalize *verb* (penalizes, penalizing, penalized) 1 To punish. 2 In games, to give a penalty against someone. 3 To take away marks or points.

penalty *noun* (penalties) 1 A punishment. 2 In games, an advantage given to the other side when a player breaks a rule. 3 A goal scored as the result of a penalty.

pence *See* **penny**

pencil¹ *noun* (pencils) An instrument containing a thin stick of lead for drawing or writing.

pendant *noun* (pendants) An ornament hung round the neck.

pendulum *noun* (pendulums) A wire or rod with a weight on the end which can swing to and fro.

penetrate *verb* (penetrates, penetrating, penetrated) To make or find a way into or through something, to pierce. **penetration** *noun*.

pen-friend *noun* (pen-friends) A friend made and kept by writing letters to him or her.

penguin *noun* (penguins) A bird of the Antarctic.

penicillin *noun* A substance valuable for curing certain infections.

peninsula *noun* (peninsulas) An area of land almost surrounded by water.

penis *noun* (penises) The tail-like part at the front of the body which males have and females do not have.

penitent *adjective* Sorry, regretful. **penitence** *noun*.

penknife *noun* (penknives) A small folding pocket-knife.

penniless *adjective* Very poor, without any money.

penny *noun* (pennies *or* pence) A bronze coin. In Great Britain, 100 pence equal one pound.

penny-farthing *noun* (penny-farthings) An early type of bicycle with a large front wheel and a small rear one.

pension *noun* (pensions) A regular payment made to someone who is old or who has retired from work or service. **pensioner** *noun*.

pensive *adjective* Deep in thought. **pensively** *adverb*.

pentagon *noun* (pentagons) A shape with five sides.

pentathlon *noun* (pentathlons) An athletic contest consisting of five separate events.

Pentecost *noun* a Christian festival, the seventh Sunday after Easter.

Pentecostal *noun* (Pentecostals) A member of one of the Christian denominations.

peony *noun* (peonies) A garden plant with large flowers.

people *noun* 1 Men, women, and children. 2 (peoples) The inhabitants of a country, the members of a nation.

pepper *noun* (peppers) 1 A hot-tasting spice used for flavouring food. **peppery** *adjective*. 2 A bright green or red vegetable.

peppermint *noun* 1 A kind of mint. 2 (peppermints) A sweet which tastes of peppermint.

per *preposition* For each, in each. *per litre*, for each litre. *per hour*, in each hour. **per cent** in each hundred. *ten per cent (10%)*, ten in each hundred.

perceive *verb* (perceives, perceiving, perceived) To notice something, to become aware of it, to understand it. **perception** *noun*.

percentage *noun* (percentages) A number of people or things out of every hundred. *What percentage of the children come to school by bus?*

perceptible *adjective* Noticeable, able to be perceived. **perceptibly** *adverb*.

perceptive *adjective* Quick to notice things. **perceptively** *adverb*.

perch¹ *noun* (perch) A fresh-water fish.

perch² *noun* (perches) A bird's resting place.

perch³ *verb* (perches, perching, perched) 1 To sit or rest on something. 2 To put something on a high place. *The house was perched on the edge of a cliff.*

percolator *noun* (percolators) An apparatus for making coffee.

percussion instrument *noun* A musical instrument played by hitting or shaking, such as a drum, a cymbal, or a tambourine.

perennial *adjective* Lasting for many years.

perfect *adjective* 1 Complete, without faults. 2 Exact, precise. *a perfect fit.* **perfectly** *adverb*, **perfection** *noun*.

perforate *verb* (perforates, perforating, perforated) To make a hole or holes through something. **perforation** *noun*.

perform *verb* (performs, performing, performed) 1 To do something, to carry it out. *to perform your duty.* 2 To do something in front of an audience, such as acting in a play, singing, or playing a musical instrument. **performer, performance** *nouns*.

perfume *noun* (perfumes) 1 A sweet smell. 2 A liquid with a beautiful smell.

perhaps *adverb* Possibly, it may be.

peril *noun* (perils) Serious danger. **perilous** *adjective*, **perilously** *adverb*.

perimeter *noun* (perimeters) A boundary.

period *noun* (periods) 1 A length of time. 2 The time when the lining of a woman's womb is shed, which happens once a month except when she is pregnant.

periodical *noun* (periodicals) A magazine which is published at regular intervals.

peripatetic *adjective* **peripatetic teacher** a teacher who visits various schools.

periscope *noun* (periscopes) A device with mirrors to enable you to see things which would be out of sight without it.

perish *verb* (perishes, perishing, perished) 1 To die. 2 To rot. *The tyres are perished and must be changed.* 3 (informal) *I'm perished*, I'm very cold. **perishable** *adjective*.

perky *adjective* (perkier, perkiest) Lively. **perkily** *adverb*, **perkiness** *noun*.

perm *noun* (perms) (informal) A permanent wave.

permanent *adjective* Going on for a long time, intended to last for ever. **permanently** *adverb*, **permanence** *noun*. **permanent wave** a way of curling the hair so that it stays curly for a long time.

permissible *adjective* Allowable.

permission *noun* A statement that something is allowed. *We had permission to go out.*

permissive *adjective* Allowing, not objecting.

permit[1] *noun* (permits) Written permission to go somewhere or to do something.

permit[2] *verb* (permits, permitting, permitted) To say that something may be done, to allow. *Smoking is not permitted.*

permutation *noun* (permutations) One of the possible arrangements of a set of figures.

perpendicular *adjective* Exactly upright, at right angles to the base. **perpendicularly** *adverb*.

perpetual *adjective* **1** Unending, going on for ever. **2** Frequently repeated. **perpetually** *adverb*.

perplex *verb* (perplexes, perplexing, perplexed) To bewilder, to puzzle, to confuse. **perplexity** *noun*.

persecute *verb* (persecutes, persecuting, persecuted) To keep on worrying someone, to treat someone cruelly. **persecutor**, **persecution** *nouns*.

persevere *verb* (perseveres, persevering, persevered) To continue in spite of difficulties. **perseverance** *noun*.

persist *verb* (persists, persisting, persisted) To persevere, to last. **persistent** *adjective*, **persistently** *adverb*, **persistence** *noun*.

person *noun* (persons) A human being, an individual.

personal *adjective* **1** Belonging to a particular person. *These tools are my personal property.* **2** Done or made by the person himself or herself. *I got a personal letter from the headmaster.* **personally** *adverb*. **3** About a person's looks or qualities. *You should not make personal remarks.*

personality *noun* (personalities) **1** The qualities that make up a person's character. *a friendly personality.* **2** A well-known person. *a television personality.*

personnel *noun* The people employed in a business or in the armed forces.

perspective *noun* The art of drawing a picture so as to give an impression of depth and distance. **get something in perspective** to give it its proper importance.

Perspex *noun* The trade name of a tough glass-like plastic.

perspire *verb* (perspires, perspiring, perspired) To sweat. **perspiration** *noun*.

persuade *verb* (persuades, persuading, persuaded) To cause someone to do something or to believe something. **persuasion** *noun*.

persuasive *adjective* Able to persuade, convincing. **persuasively** *adverb*.

perturb *verb* (perturbs, perturbing, perturbed) To worry or alarm someone.

perverse *adjective* **1** Tiresome, unreasonable. **2** Deliberately choosing to do wrong. **perversely** *adverb*, **perversity** *noun*.

pervert *verb* (perverts, perverting, perverted) **1** To turn something to a wrong use. **perversion** *noun*. **2** To cause somebody to do wrong.

peseta *noun* (pesetas) A unit of money in Spain.

pessimist *noun* (pessimists) A person who expects the worst to happen. **pessimism** *noun*.

pessimistic *adjective* Gloomy, expecting the worst. **pessimistically** *adverb*.

pest *noun* (pests) **1** A troublesome or destructive animal or insect. **2** A nuisance.

pester *verb* (pesters, pestering, pestered) To bother somebody repeatedly.

pesticide *noun* (pesticides) A poison for killing pests.

pet¹ *noun* (pets) **1** An animal kept as a companion. **2** A person treated as a favourite.

pet² *verb* (pets, petting, petted) To fondle.

petal *noun* (petals) One of the coloured leaf-like parts of a flower. *a rose petal.*

petition *noun* (petitions) A request, especially a written one signed by many people.

petrel *noun* (petrels) A kind of sea bird.

petrify *verb* (petrifies, petrifying, petrified) To paralyse somebody with terror.

petrol *noun* A fuel used to drive motor-car engines.

petticoat *noun* (petticoats) A women's garment worn under a dress.

petty *adjective* Small, unimportant. **pettiness** *noun*.

pew *noun* (pews) A long bench with a back, used in churches.

pewter *noun* An alloy of lead and tin.

phantom *noun* (phantoms) A ghost, an apparition.

phase *noun* (phases) A particular stage in the development or progress of something.

pheasant *noun* (pheasants) A game bird.

phenomenal *adjective* Remarkable, amazing. **phenomenally** *adverb*.

phenomenon *noun* (phenomena) A thing or a happening, especially a remarkable or unusual thing or happening.

philosophical *adjective* **1** Connected with philosophy. **2** Calm, able to accept hardship without worrying. *John was philosophical about his accident.* **philosophically** *adverb*.

philosophy *noun* **1** The study of the meaning of existence. **2** (philosophies) A particular way of thinking about things. *James has an unusual philosophy of life.* **philosopher** *noun*.

phobia *noun* (phobias) A great fear of something.

phone¹ *verb* (phones, phoning, phoned) To telephone.

phone² *noun* (phones) A telephone.

phoney *adjective* (informal) Not genuine, false.

phosphorescent *adjective* Luminous, glowing. **phosphorescence** *noun*.

photo *noun* (photos) (informal) A photograph.

photocopier *noun* (photocopiers) A machine for copying written or printed papers.

photocopy *verb* (photocopies, photocopying, photocopied) To make a copy on a photocopier.

photograph¹ *noun* (photographs) A picture made on film by the use of a camera and then printed on paper. **photographic** *adjective*.

photograph² *verb* (photographs, photographing, photographed) To take photographs. **photographer, photography** *nouns*.

phrase *noun* (phrases) **1** A small group of words. **2** A part of a tune.

phylactery *noun* (phylacteries) A leather container for written prayers worn by Jews while praying.

physical *adjective* **1** Able to be touched and seen. **2** Of the body. *physical education.* **physically** *adverb*.

physician *noun* (physicians) A doctor.

physics *noun* The branch of science which includes the study of heat, light, and sound.

physiotherapy *noun* Medical treatment by massage, heat, and exercises. **physiotherapist** *noun*.

pianist *noun* (pianists) A person who plays the piano.

piano *noun* (pianos) A keyboard instrument with strings that are struck by felt-covered hammers.

piccolo *noun* (piccolos) A small flute.

pick¹ *noun* (picks) A pickaxe.

pick² *verb* (picks, picking, picked) **1** To choose, to take, to gather. *to pick a partner*. **2** To take something out of a hole or cavity. *to pick someone's pocket*. **3** *to pick fruit or flowers*, to separate them from the plant on which they grew. **4** *to pick a bone*, to take all the meat off it. **5** *to pick a lock*, to open it without using the key. **picker** *noun*. **pick holes in something** to find faults in it.

pick³ *noun* **1** A choice. *Take your pick*. **2** The best one in a group. *Go on, take the pick of the bunch*.

pickaxe *noun* (pickaxes) A heavy tool for breaking up hard ground.

picket *noun* (pickets) A group of strikers who try to prevent others from working.

pickle¹ *noun* (pickles) A strong-tasting food made mainly from vegetables and vinegar.

pickle² *verb* (pickles, pickling, pickled) To preserve something in vinegar or salt water. *pickled onions*.

pickpocket *noun* (pickpockets) Someone who steals from people's pockets.

pick-up *noun* (pick-ups) **1** The part of a record-player holding the stylus. **2** An open truck for carrying small loads.

picnic¹ *noun* (picnics) A meal eaten out of doors.

picnic² *verb* (picnics, picnicking, picnicked) To have a picnic. **picnicker** *noun*.

pictorial *adjective* Shown in pictures, with pictures. **pictorially** *adverb*.

picture¹ *noun* (pictures) **1** A drawing, painting, or photograph of something. **2** A description of something. **the pictures** the cinema.

picture² *verb* (pictures, picturing, pictured) To imagine.

picturesque *adjective* Attractive to look at. **picturesquely** *adverb*.

pie *noun* (pies) Meat or fruit covered with pastry and baked in a deep dish.

piebald *adjective* Having light and dark patches.

piece *noun* (pieces) **1** A part or bit of something. *a piece of cake*. **2** An instance, an example. *an interesting piece of news*. **3** A single object, especially one of a set. *a chess piece*. **4** Something which has been composed or created. *a piece of poetry*.

piecemeal *adjective and adverb* Piece by piece.

pier *noun* (piers) **1** A long structure built out into the sea. **2** One of the pillars that support a bridge.

pierce *verb* (pierces, piercing, pierced) To bore a hole in something, to go through it.

piercing *adjective* Very loud. *a piercing scream*.

pig *noun* (pigs) **1** An animal kept by farmers for its meat. **2** (informal) A grubby, greedy, or unpleasant person.

pigeon *noun* (pigeons) A bird of the dove family.

piggy-bank *noun* (piggy-banks) A kind of money-box.

pigsty *noun* (pigsties) A building for pigs.

pigtail *noun* (pigtails) A plait of hair.

pike *noun* (pikes) **1** A very long and heavy spear. **2** A large fierce fresh-water fish.

pilchard *noun* (pilchards) A small sea-fish.

pile¹ *noun* (piles) **1** A number of things one on top of the other, a heap. **2** A heavy beam driven straight down into the ground as a support for a building or other structure.

pile² *verb* (piles, piling, piled) To make or become a heap.

pilfer *verb* (pilfers, pilfering, pilfered) To steal things in small amounts. **pilferer** *noun*.

pilgrim *noun* (pilgrims) A person who makes a journey to a holy place.

pilgrimage *noun* (pilgrimages) A journey to a holy place.

pill *noun* (pills) A small pellet of medicine. **the pill** a contraceptive in the form of a pill.

pillar *noun* (pillars) A tall, upright support for part of a building, a column.

pillar-box *noun* (pillar-boxes) A box standing in a street in which letters are posted.

pillion *noun* (pillions) A seat for a second person behind the rider of a motor cycle.

pillow *noun* (pillows) A cushion for a person's head to rest on, especially in bed.

pillowcase, pillowslip *nouns* (pillow-cases, pillowslips) A cover for a pillow.

pilot¹ *noun* (pilots) **1** The person who controls an aircraft while it is flying. **2** A person who guides ships in and out of harbour. **3** A guide.

pilot² *verb* (pilots, piloting, piloted) To act as a pilot.

pilot-light *noun* (pilot-lights) A small flame in a gas cooker or heater which lights the main jets.

pimple *noun* (pimples) A small inflamed spot on the skin. **pimply** *adjective*.

pin¹ *noun* (pins) A device with a sharp point, used for fastening things.

pin² *verb* (pins, pinning, pinned) To fasten with a pin.

pinafore *noun* (pinafores) A kind of apron.

pin-board *noun* (pinboards) A board for pictures and notices.

pincers *noun* A tool for gripping things.

pinch¹ *verb* (pinches, pinching, pinched) **1** To squeeze between thumb and finger. **2** To squeeze painfully. *I pinched my fingers in the door.* **3** (informal) To steal.

pinch² *noun* (pinches) **1** A painful squeeze. **2** An amount which can be picked up with the thumb and finger. *a pinch of salt.*

pincushion *noun* (pincushions) A soft pad for sticking pins into to keep them ready for use.

pine¹ *noun* (pines) A kind of evergreen tree.

pine² *verb* (pines, pining, pined) To become ill with longing or regret.

pineapple *noun* (pineapples) A tropical fruit.

ping *verb* (pings, pinging, pinged) To make a short, high ringing sound.

ping-pong *noun* (informal) Table-tennis.

pin-hole *noun* (pin-holes) A tiny round hole.

pink[1] *adjective* (pinker, pinkest) Pale red.

pink[2] *noun* (pinks) A garden flower.

pinnacle *noun* (pinnacles) The highest peak of something.

pint *noun* (pints) A unit of measure for liquids, one eighth of a gallon or 0.57 litre.

pioneer[1] *noun* (pioneers) **1** A person who is the first to do something, an explorer. **2** A person who is among the first to settle in a new country.

pioneer[2] *verb* (pioneers, pioneering, pioneered) To be a pioneer.

pip *noun* (pips) A seed of certain fruit such as apples and oranges. **the pips** the sound of a time-signal on a radio.

pipe[1] *noun* (pipes) **1** A tube. *a water-pipe*. **2** A small tube with a bowl at one end, used for smoking tobacco. **3** A simple flute.

pipe[2] *verb* (pipes, piping, piped) **1** To pass something along pipes or wires. **2** To play a pipe.

pipeline *noun* (pipelines) A line of pipes to carry oil or other substances over long distances.

piper *noun* (pipers) **1** A person who plays a pipe. **2** A person who plays the bagpipes.

piping *adjective* Thin, high. *a piping voice*. **piping hot** very hot.

pirate[1] *noun* (pirates) **1** A person who robs at sea. **2** A person who uses someone else's material illegally.

pistol *noun* (pistols) A small gun for use with one hand.

piston *noun* (pistons) The part of an engine which moves inside the cylinder.

pit *noun* (pits) **1** A deep hole. **2** A coal-mine. **3** A place by the track where racing cars are serviced.

pitch[1] *noun* A black, sticky substance like tar. **pitch black, pitch dark** too dark to see anything.

pitch[2] *noun* (pitches) **1** The lowness or highness of a musical note. **2** Intensity. *Excitement was at a high pitch*. **3** An area of ground marked out for playing a game. *a football pitch*.

pitch[3] *verb* (pitches, pitching, pitched) **1** To put up a tent. **2** To throw. **3** To fall. *He pitched forward.* **4** To rise and fall as a ship does in a storm. **pitch a note** to sing on the exact note.

pitcher *noun* (pitchers) A large jug.

pitchfork *noun* (pitchforks) A long fork with two prongs for haymaking.

piteous *adjective* Pitiful. **piteously** *adverb*.

pitfall *noun* (pitfalls) An unsuspected danger.

pitiful *adjective* **1** Causing pity. **2** Causing contempt. **pitifully** *adverb*.

pitiless *adjective* Showing no pity. **pitilessly** *adverb*.

pitta *noun* A kind of flat bread.

pitted *adjective* Marked with small holes or scars.

pity[1] *noun* **1** A feeling of sorrow for someone's troubles or sufferings. **2** Something that makes a person feel sorrow or regret. *It is a pity you can't come.* **take pity on** to help someone in trouble.

pity[2] *verb* (pities, pitying, pitied) To feel pity for someone.

pivot *noun* (pivots) A point on which something turns.

pizza *noun* (pizzas) A layer of dough baked with various ingredients such as cheese and tomatoes on top.

placard *noun* (placards) A poster.

place[1] *noun* (places) **1** Any particular part of space, any particular area, spot, or position. **2** Somewhere to sit, a seat. *Are there any spare places?* **take place** to happen. **in place of** as a substitute for.

place[2] *verb* (places, placing, placed) To put something in a certain place.

placid *adjective* Peaceful, calm. **placidly** *adverb*.

plague[1] *noun* (plagues) **1** A deadly,

infectious disease. **2** Anything which causes great trouble by coming in large quantities. *a plague of locusts*.

plague² *verb* (plagues, plaguing, plagued) To pester, to worry continually.

plaice *noun* (plaice) A flat sea-fish.

plain¹ *adjective* (plainer, plainest) **1** Easy to see, hear, or understand. *a plain signal*. **2** Simple, not decorated. *a plain dress*. **3** Honest, straightforward. *the plain truth*. **4** Not beautiful. **plainly** *adverb*, **plainness** *noun*.

plain² *noun* (plains) A large flat area of country.

plaintive *adjective* Sounding sad, mournful. **plaintively** *adverb*.

plait¹ *noun* (plaits) A rope-like length of hair or other material made by twisting strands together.

plait² *verb* (plaits, plaiting, plaited) To twist into a plait.

plan¹ *noun* (plans) **1** An arrangement made in advance. *Have you any plans for half-term?* **2** A map or diagram.

plan² *verb* (plans, planning, planned) To make a plan. **planner** *noun*.

plane¹ *noun* (planes) **1** An aeroplane. **2** A tool used for smoothing wood. **3** A kind of tree.

plane² *verb* (planes, planing, planed) To smooth wood with a plane.

planet *noun* (planets) A heavenly body which travels in orbit round a sun, such as Earth and Mars.

plank *noun* (planks) A long flat piece of wood.

plant¹ *noun* (plants) **1** Any living thing which is not an animal. Trees, flowers, and vegetables are all plants. **2** Industrial machinery and buildings.

plant² *verb* (plants, planting, planted) **1** To set plants in the ground to grow. **2** To put something firmly into place. **planter** *noun*.

plantation *noun* (plantations) An area

of land planted with trees or with a crop such as tea, cotton, or sugar.

plaster¹ *noun* (plasters) **1** A dressing for a wound. *sticking plaster*. **2** A mixture of lime, sand, water, or other minerals used to cover walls and ceilings. **3** A white powder that sets when mixed with water, also called plaster of Paris.

plaster² *verb* (plasters, plastering, plastered) **1** To cover a surface with plaster. **plasterer** *noun*. **2** To cover anything thickly.

plastic *noun* (plastics) A manufactured substance made from chemicals. **plastic surgery** surgery to repair or alter the surface of a person's face or body.

plasticine *noun* A soft substance used for modelling.

plate¹ *noun* (plates) **1** An almost flat dish. **2** A flat thin sheet of metal. **3** The thin piece of plastic to which false teeth are fixed.

plate² *verb* (plates, plating, plated) To cover a metal with a thin coating of a more valuable metal.

plateau *noun* (plateaux) An area of high but level land.

plate-glass *noun* Thick glass used for shop windows.

platform *noun* (platforms) **1** The raised surface alongside the lines at a railway station. **2** A stage in a hall. **3** Any flat raised surface.

platinum *noun* A very valuable silver-coloured metal.

platoon *noun* (platoons) A group of soldiers, part of a company.

platypus *noun* (platypuses) An Australian mammal which lays eggs.

plausible *adjective* Seeming to be right or reasonable. **plausibly** *adverb*, **plausibility** *noun*.

play[1] *verb* (plays, playing, played) **1** To have fun, to move about in a lively, happy way. **2** To take part in a game, to do something in a game. **3** To perform something. *I played the part of Joseph in the Nativity play*. **4** To perform on something. *John can play the piano*. **play up** to behave badly. **player** *noun*.

play[2] *noun* (plays) A story performed by actors on a stage or on television.

playback *noun* The playing of something that you have recorded.

playful *adjective* Lively, not serious. **playfully** *adverb*, **playfulness** *noun*.

playground *noun* (playgrounds) An area of ground where children may play.

playgroup *noun* (playgroups) A class for children too young to go to school.

playing-card *noun* (playing-cards) One of a set of cards used in various games.

playing-field *noun* (playing-fields) A field for playing games.

playtime *noun* (playtimes) A time when schoolchildren may go out to play.

playwright *noun* (playwrights) A person who writes plays.

plea *noun* (pleas) **1** A request. **2** An excuse.

plead *verb* (pleads, pleading, pleaded) **1** To ask earnestly. **2** To offer something as an excuse. **plead guilty** to admit that you are guilty.

pleasant *adjective* Agreeable, friendly, enjoyable. **pleasantly** *adverb*.

please[1] *verb* A polite word used when making a request. *Please come in*.

please[2] *verb* (pleases, pleasing, pleased) **1** To make someone feel happy or satisfied. **2** To like, to think suitable. *Do as you please*.

pleasure *noun* **1** A feeling of being pleased. **2** (pleasures) Something that brings you happiness.

pleat *noun* (pleats) A fold made in cloth. **pleated** *adjective*.

pledge[1] *noun* (pledges) An agreement, a promise.

pledge[2] *verb* (pledges, pledging, pledged) To make a pledge.

plenty *noun* As much or more than is necessary, a large quantity. **plentiful** *adjective*.

pliable *adjective* Bent easily, flexible.

pliers *noun* A tool for gripping things.

plight *noun* (plights) A serious condition.

plimsoll *noun* (plimsolls) A light shoe with a rubber sole.

plod *verb* (plods, plodding, plodded) To walk slowly and heavily. **plodder** *noun*.

plop *noun* (plops) The sound of an object dropping into water.

plot[1] *noun* (plots) **1** A secret plan. **2** The outline of what happens in a story. **3** A piece of ground for a house or garden.

plot[2] *verb* (plots, plotting, plotted) To make a secret plan. **plotter** *noun*.

plough[1] *noun* (ploughs) A farming tool for turning over the soil.

plough[2] *verb* (ploughs, ploughing,

ploughed) To use a plough. **plough-man** *noun*.

plover *noun* (plovers) A kind of wading bird.

pluck[1] *noun* (informal) Courage. **plucky** *adjective*, **pluckily** *adverb*.

pluck[2] *verb* (plucks, plucking, plucked) **1** To pull the feathers off a bird. **2** To pick flowers or fruit. **3** To snatch. **4** To sound a string on a musical instrument by pulling it and letting it go.

plug[1] *noun* (plugs) **1** Something used to stop up a hole. **2** A device which fits into an electric socket. **3** A sparking-plug.

plug[2] *verb* (plugs, plugging, plugged) **1** To stop up a hole. **2** (informal) To keep on mentioning something to advertise it. **plug in** to put an electric plug into a socket.

plum *noun* (plums) A soft juicy fruit with a stone in the middle.

plumage *noun* Feathers growing on a bird.

plumber *noun* (plumbers) A person who fits and repairs water-pipes in buildings.

plumbing *noun* **1** The job of a plumber. **2** The water-pipes and water-tanks in a building.

plume *noun* (plumes) A large feather.

plump *adjective* (plumper, plumpest) Rounded, slightly fat. **plumpness** *noun*.

plunder *verb* (plunders, plundering, plundered) To loot.

plunge *verb* (plunges, plunging, plunged) **1** To dip or dive suddenly or violently. **2** To thrust violently.

plural *noun* (plurals) The form of a word used when referring to more than one. *Men* is the plural of *man*. *Girls* is the plural of *girl*.

plus *preposition* With the addition of. In arithmetic, the sign +. *Two plus two equals four* $(2 + 2 = 4)$.

plywood *noun* A sheet of wood made of thin layers glued together.

p.m. The abbreviation for Latin *post meridiem*, after midday. *We go home from school at 4 p.m.*

pneumatic *adjective* **1** Filled with air. *pneumatic tyres.* **2** Worked by compressed air. *a pneumatic drill.*

pneumonia *noun* A serious illness of the lungs.

poach *verb* (poaches, poaching, poached) **1** To cook something in gently boiling water. **2** To hunt illegally on somebody else's land. **poacher** *noun*.

pocket[1] *noun* (pockets) A bag-shaped part of a garment, designed for carrying things.

pocket[2] *verb* (pockets, pocketing, pocketed) To put things in your pocket.

pocket-knife *noun* (pocket-knives) A small folding knife.

pocket-money *noun* Money given to a child to spend as he or she pleases.

pod *noun* (pods) A long seed container which grows on various plants.

podgy *adjective* (podgier, podgiest) Short and fat.

poem *noun* (poems) A piece of poetry.

poet *noun* (poets) A person who writes poetry.

poetry *noun* Writing arranged in lines, usually with a regular rhythm and often with a pattern of rhymes. **poetic** *adjective*.

point[1] *noun* (points) **1** The sharp end or tip of something. **2** A dot. *a decimal point.* **3** A mark on a scale or dial. *points of the compass.* **4** A position. *the half-way point.* **5** A unit used in scoring in a game or competition. *a penalty point.* **6** The main idea or the purpose of something. *the point of a lesson.* **points** a device for switching a train from one track to another.

point[2] *verb* (points, pointing, pointed) **1** To make a sign towards something, especially with one finger. **2** To aim. **3** To sharpen something. **point out** to draw attention to something. **pointer** *noun*.

point-blank *adjective* At very close range.

pointless *adjective* Without aim or purpose. **pointlessly** *adverb*.

poise¹ *verb* (poises, poising, poised) To balance. *She poised on the edge before diving in.*

poise² *noun* An appearance of quiet self-confidence.

poison¹ *noun* (poisons) A substance causing death or serious illness. **poisonous** *adjective*, **poisonously** *adverb*.

poison² *verb* (poisons, poisoning, poisoned) To give poison to somebody, to put poison in something. **poisoner** *noun*.

poke *verb* (pokes, poking, poked) To push at or into something with a finger, stick, or other long thin object. **poke fun at** to make fun of someone. **poker** *noun*.

poky *adjective* (pokier, pokiest) Small and inconvenient.

polar *adjective* To do with the North or South Pole. **polar bear** a large white bear which lives in the Arctic.

Polaroid *noun* The trade name of a type of camera that makes prints very quickly.

pole¹ *noun* (poles) **1** *North Pole, South Pole*, the two points on the earth's surface furthest away from the equator. **2** One of the two ends of a magnet.

pole² *noun* (poles) A long piece of wood or other material, a tall post.

pole-vault *noun* (pole-vaults) A jump made with the help of a long pole.

police *noun* The organization which has the job of keeping order and of catching criminals. **policeman, policewoman** *nouns*. **police station** the office of the local police.

policy *noun* (policies) A plan of action. **insurance policy** an insurance agreement.

polio *noun* (informal) Poliomyelitis.

poliomyelitis *noun* A disease which can cause paralysis.

Polish *adjective* Of or from Poland.

polish¹ *noun* **1** A substance used for polishing. **2** Smoothness, a shine.

polish² *verb* (polishes, polishing, polished) To make something smooth and shiny. **polisher** *noun*. **polish off** to finish something.

polite *adjective* (politer, politest) Having good manners. **politely** *adverb*, **politeness** *noun*.

political *adjective* To do with the governing of a country and the organizing of its affairs. **politically** *adverb*.

politician *noun* (politicians) A person who is involved in politics.

politics *noun* Political matters.

poll *noun* (polls) Voting at an election. **opinion poll** an attempt to find out what the public thinks by putting questions to a number of people.

pollen *noun* A fine powder in flowers which can fertilize other flowers.

pollinate *verb* (pollinates, pollinating, pollinated) To fertilize with pollen.

polling-station *noun* (polling-stations) A place where people vote in an election.

pollute *verb* (pollutes, polluting, polluted) To make a thing dirty or impure. **pollution** *noun*.

polo *noun* A game in some ways like hockey, played on horseback.

poltergeist *noun* (poltergeists) A mischievous and destructive ghost.

polyester *noun* An artificial fabric.

polygamy *noun* Having more than one wife at the same time.

polystyrene *noun* A kind of plastic material.

polytechnic *noun* (polytechnics) A college where people study for degrees and other qualifications, the old name of some universities.

polythene *noun* A kind of plastic.

pomp *noun* Grand and dignified display.

pompom *noun* (pompoms) A ball-shaped decoration made of wool or other material.

pompous *adjective* Self-important. **pompously** *adverb*, **pomposity** *noun*.

poncho *noun* (ponchos) A square garment with a central hole for the head.

pond *noun* (ponds) An area of water, a small lake.

ponder *verb* (ponders, pondering, pondered) To consider something, to think it over.

ponderous *adjective* Heavy, bulky. **ponderously** *adverb*.

pontoon[1] *noun* A card game.

pontoon[2] *noun* (pontoons) A flat-bottomed boat. **pontoon bridge** a temporary bridge resting on pontoons.

pony *noun* (ponies) A small breed of horse.

pony-trekking *noun* Touring on a horse.

poodle *noun* (poodles) A kind of dog with curly hair.

pool *noun* (pools) **1** An area of water, a pond, a puddle. **2** A swimming-pool. **3** A game rather like snooker. **the pools** a kind of gambling, usually on the result of football matches.

poop *noun* (poops) The raised deck at the stern of a ship.

poor *adjective* (poorer, poorest) **1** Having very little money. **2** Small in quantity. *a poor crop of beans.* **3** Low in quality. *poor work.* **4** Unfortunate. *He finished last, poor boy!* **poorly** *adverb*.

poorly *adjective* Unwell, ill. *I felt poorly after eating too much.*

pop[1] *noun* (pops) **1** A sharp explosive sound. **2** A bottled fizzy drink. **3** Popular music.

pop[2] *verb* (pops, popping, popped) **1** To make a sharp explosive sound. **2** To move or do something quickly.

popcorn *noun* Maize heated so that it forms irregular-shaped pieces, eaten as a snack.

Pope *noun* The head of the Roman Catholic Church.

poplar *noun* (poplars) A tall, straight tree.

poppadam *noun* (poppadams) A kind of thin biscuit eaten with Indian food.

poppy *noun* (poppies) A flower, usually with red petals.

popular *adjective* Liked by many people. **popularly** *adverb*, **popularity** *noun*.

populate *verb* (populates, populating, populated) **1** To inhabit. **2** To fill with people.

population *noun* (populations) The total number of people living in a particular place.

porcelain *noun* Fine china.

porch *noun* (porches) A small shelter outside the entrance to a building.

porcupine *noun* (porcupines) A small animal covered with long prickles.

pore *noun* (pores) A tiny opening in the skin through which sweat passes.

pork *noun* Meat from a pig.

porn *noun* (informal) Pornography.

pornography *noun* Indecent books, magazines, or pictures. **pornographic** *adjective*.

porous *adjective* Full of tiny holes, allowing liquid to pass through.

porpoise *noun* (porpoises) A sea animal like a small whale.

porridge *noun* A food made from boiled oatmeal.

port[1] *noun* **1** (ports) A harbour, or a town with a harbour. **2** The left-hand side of a ship looking forward towards the bows. **3** A kind of rich red wine.

portable *adjective* Easy to carry.

portcullis *noun* (portcullises) An iron grating which could be lowered in a castle gateway to keep attackers out.

porter *noun* (porters) **1** A person whose job is to carry luggage. **2** A door-keeper.

porthole *noun* (portholes) A small round window in the side of a ship.

portion *noun* (portions) **1** A part or share of something. **2** An amount of food suitable for one person.

portly *adjective* Stout, fat.

portrait *noun* (portraits) A painting, drawing, or photograph of a person.

portray *verb* (portrays, portraying, portrayed) To make a picture of somebody or something.

Portuguese *adjective* Of or from Portugal.

pose *verb* (poses, posing, posed) **1** To get into position to be photographed or painted. **2** To show off. **3** To put a question for discussion. **pose as** to

pretend to be some particular person. **poser** *noun*.

posh *adjective* (informal) Smart, elegant.

position *noun* (positions) **1** A place where something is or should be. **2** The way someone or something is placed or arranged. *He was in an uncomfortable crouching position.* **3** A condition, or situation, or attitude. *I am in no position to help.* **4** A regular job.

positive 1 Definite, sure. *I'm positive he was here this morning. a positive answer*, an answer that says 'yes'. **2** In mathematics, a figure greater than zero. **3** In electricity, one of the terminals of a battery. **positively** *adverb*, **positiveness** *noun*.

posse *noun* (posses) A band of men summoned to help a sherriff.

possess *verb* (possesses, possessing, possessed) To have something, to own it, to control it. **possessor** *noun*.

possessed *adjective* Mad, appearing to be controlled by an evil spirit.

possession *noun* **1** (possessions) Something owned. **2** The possessing of something.

possessive *adjective* Wanting to keep things for yourself. **possessively** *adverb*.

possible *adjective* Able to exist, able to happen, able to be done. **possibility** *noun*.

possibly *adverb* **1** In a possible manner. **2** Perhaps.

post[1] *noun* (posts) **1** An upright piece of wood, metal, or concrete. **2** A job. **3** A position where you are placed to do your duty.

post[2] *noun* The collecting, conveying, and delivering of letters and parcels. **post office** a place where postal business is done.

post[3] *verb* (posts, posting, posted) **1** To send something through the post. **2** To put up a notice.

postage *noun* The charge made for sending something by post. *a postage stamp.*

postal *adjective* To do with the post. **postal order** a document you buy so that you can send money by post.

postbox *noun* (postboxes) A box where you put letters for posting.

postcard *noun* (postcards) A card for sending by post.

postcode *noun* (postcodes) A group of letters and figures put at the end of your address to help the post office when they are sorting mail.

poster *noun* (posters) A large sheet of paper with pictures or printing for display on a wall.

posterity *noun* Descendants, people yet to be born.

postman, postwoman *nouns* (postmen, postwomen) A person who delivers letters.

postmark *noun* (postmarks) An official mark stamped over the postage stamp on an envelope.

post-mortem *noun* (post-mortems) An examination of a dead person to find out why he or she died.

postpone *verb* (postpones, postponing, postponed) Not to do something now but say that you will do it later.

postscript *noun* (postscripts) Something added to a letter or book after the main part has been finished.

posture *noun* (postures) The way you stand or sit.

posy *noun* (posies) A small bunch of flowers.

pot[1] *noun* (pots) A round container such as a jam-pot, a teapot, or a flower-pot.

pot[2] *verb* (pots, potting, potted) 1 To put something into a pot. 2 To hit a ball into a pocket in snooker or billiards.

potato *noun* (potatoes) A vegetable often eaten as part of a main course.

potent *adjective* Powerful. **potency** *noun*.

potential *adjective* Possible at some time in the future. **potentially** *adverb*.

pothole *noun* (potholes) 1 A deep natural hole in the ground. 2 A hole in a road.

potholing *noun* The sport of exploring potholes. **potholer** *noun*.

potion *noun* (potions) A drink of medicine, or poison, or magical liquid.

potter *noun* (potters) A maker of pots or pottery.

pottery *noun* Pots or other articles made of baked clay.

potty[1] *adjective* (informal) Slightly mad.

potty[2] *noun* (potties) (informal) A pot that can be used instead of a lavatory.

pouch *noun* (pouches) A small bag for carrying things, a pocket.

pouffe *noun* (pouffes) A large cushion for sitting on.

poultice *noun* (poultices) A hot pad put on a sore part of the body.

poultry *noun* Hens, ducks, geese, and other farmyard birds.

pounce *verb* (pounces, pouncing, pounced) To swoop and attack something.

pound[1] *noun* (pounds) 1 A unit of weight, 16 ounces or 0.45 kilogram. 2 A unit of money, 100 pence.

pound[2] *verb* (pounds, pounding, pounded) 1 To thump repeatedly. 2 To crush in this way.

pour *verb* (pours, pouring, poured) 1 To make something flow. 2 To flow. 3 To rain heavily. *It poured all day.*

pout *verb* (pouts, pouting, pouted) To push out your lips when you are annoyed.

poverty *noun* The state of being poor.

poverty-stricken *adjective* Very poor.

powder[1] *noun* Very small particles,

anything crushed or ground into dust. **powdery** *adjective*.

powder² *verb* (powders, powdering, powdered) **1** To make into powder. **2** To cover with powder.

power *noun* **1** The ability to do something. *The magician had the power to turn the frog back into a prince.* **2** The right, the authority. *The government has the power to increase taxes.* **3** Strength, force, energy. *electric power.* **power tool** a tool with a motor. **power point** a socket for electricity. **powerful, powerless** *adjectives*, **powerfully** *adverb*.

power-boat *noun* (power-boats) A small boat with a powerful motor.

powered *adjective* Fitted with an engine. **powered by** driven by. **high-powered** very powerful.

power-station *noun* (power-stations) A building where electric power is generated.

practicable *adjective* Capable of being done or used.

practical *adjective* **1** Concerned with doing or making something. *practical difficulties.* **2** Clever at doing or making things. **3** Useful, usable. *a practical gift.* **practical joke** a trick played on someone.

practically *adverb* **1** In a practical way. **2** Almost. *We are practically ready.*

practice *noun* **1** Practising. **2** The doing of something. **3** (practices) A doctor's or lawyer's business.

practise *verb* (practises, practising, practised) **1** To do something repeatedly in order to become skilful at it. **2** To do something as a habit. **3** To work as a doctor or a lawyer.

prairie *noun* (prairies) A large area of flat grass-covered land in North America.

praise¹ *verb* (praises, praising, praised) To say that someone or something is very good.

praise² *noun* (praises) The act of praising.

praiseworthy *adjective* Deserving praise.

pram *noun* (prams) A small four-wheeled vehicle to carry a baby.

prance *verb* (prances, prancing, pranced) To leap about happily.

prank *noun* (pranks) A practical joke.

prattle *verb* (prattles, prattling, prattled) To talk about unimportant things.

prawn *noun* (prawns) A kind of shellfish like a large shrimp.

pray *verb* (prays, praying, prayed) **1** To talk to God. **2** To ask earnestly.

prayer *noun* (prayers) **1** The act of praying. **2** What you say when you pray.

preach *verb* (preaches, preaching, preached) To give a religious or moral talk. **preacher** *noun*.

precarious *adjective* Not secure, liable to fall. **precariously** *adverb*.

precaution *noun* (precautions) An action taken to avoid harm in the future. *precautions against fire.*

precede *verb* (precedes, preceding, preceded) To come or go in front of someone or something.

precinct *noun* (precincts) An area round a cathedral. **pedestrian precinct** an area for pedestrians only.

precious *adjective* Very valuable, worth a lot of money.

precipice *noun* (precipices) The steep face of a cliff or rocky mountain.

precipitous *adjective* Very steep. **precipitously** *adverb*.

precise *adjective* Correct, exact. **precisely** *adverb*, **precision** *noun*.

predator *noun* (predators) An animal that hunts prey. **predatory** *adjective*.

predecessor *noun* (predecessors) A person who was there before you.

predicament *noun* (predicaments) A difficult, unpleasant, or dangerous situation.

predict *verb* (predicts, predicting, predicted) To foretell, to forecast, to prophesy. **predictable** *adjective*, **predictably** *adverb*, **prediction** *noun*.

predominantly *adverb* Mostly.

preen *verb* (preens, preening, preened) To make the feathers clean and tidy with the beak.

prefab *noun* (prefabs) (informal) A prefabricated house.

prefabricated *adjective* Made in sections and assembled later.

preface *noun* (prefaces) A piece at the beginning of a book written to introduce it to the reader.

prefect *noun* (prefects) A school pupil who is given certain duties to perform.

prefer *verb* (prefers, preferring, preferred) To like one thing better than another. **preferable** *adjective*, **preferably** *adverb*, **preference** *noun*.

prefix *noun* (prefixes) A word or syllable joined to the front of another word to alter its meaning, as in *un*happy, *re*play, and *dis*order.

pregnant *adjective* Having an unborn baby growing inside the body. **pregnancy** *noun*.

prehistoric *adjective* Belonging to the very early times before written records were kept.

prejudice *noun* (prejudices) A fixed opinion which is not based on a fair examination of the facts. **prejudiced** *adjective*.

preliminary[1] *adjective* Introductory, preparing for what follows.

preliminary[2] *noun* (preliminaries) The first stage in a series of events.

prelude *noun* (preludes) **1** An introduction. **2** A short piece of music.

premature *adjective* Too early. **premature baby** a baby that is born before the proper time. **prematurely** *adverb*.

premeditate *verb* (premeditates, premeditating, premeditated) To think something out beforehand. **premeditation** *noun*.

premier *noun* (premiers) A Prime Minister.

première *noun* (premières) A first performance.

premium *noun* (premiums) An amount of money paid regularly to an insurance company. **Premium Bond** a kind of savings certificate which has a chance of winning a money prize.

premonition *noun* (premonitions) A feeling that something is going to happen. *a premonition of disaster*.

preoccupied *adjective* Completely absorbed in something. **preoccupation** *noun*.

prep *noun* (informal) School work to be done in the evening.

preparatory school or **prep school** *noun* A school for children who may later go to public schools.

prepare *verb* (prepares, preparing, prepared) To get ready, to make ready. **be prepared** be ready. **preparatory** *adjective*, **preparation** *noun*.

preposition *noun* (prepositions) A word put before a noun to show such things as position, direction, method, or time. *On the shelf. To London. By hand. After tea.*

preposterous *adjective* Ridiculous.

Presbyterian *noun* (Presbyterians) A member of one of the Christian denominations.

prescribe *verb* (prescribes, prescribing, prescribed) **1** To say what is to be done. **2** To give a prescription.

prescription *noun* (prescriptions)

A doctor's order to a chemist to prepare a certain medicine.

presence *noun* Being present. **in the presence of** in the place where someone is.

present[1] *adjective* **1** In a particular place, here, there. *Were you present at the scene of the crime?* **2** Existing at this moment. *Do you know David's present address?*

present[2] *noun* The time now passing, the present time.

present[3] *noun* (presents) A gift. *a birthday present.*

present[4] *verb* (presents, presenting, presented) **1** To give, to offer. **2** To show, to reveal. **3** To put on a play or other entertainment. **presentation** *noun*.

presentable *adjective* Fit to be seen. **presentably** *adverb*.

presently *adverb* Soon.

preservative *noun* (preservatives) A substance used for preserving things.

preserve[1] *verb* (preserves, preserving, preserved) **1** To keep something safe. **2** To keep something in good condition. **preserver, preservation** *nouns*.

preserve[2] *noun* (preserves) Jam.

president *noun* (presidents) **1** The head of a republic. *the President of the United States.* **2** The person in charge of a club, business, or other organization. **presidential** *adjective*.

press[1] *verb* (presses, pressing, pressed) **1** To push, to squeeze, to squash. **2** To make something flat or smooth. **3** To urge, to persuade, to compel.

press[2] *noun* (presses) **1** The act of pressing. **2** A device for pressing things. **3** A printing machine, a printing or publishing business. *Oxford University Press.* **the press** the newspapers. **press conference** an interview with a group of reporters.

pressing *adjective* Urgent, needing attention.

pressure *noun* (pressures) **1** A force which presses or pushes. **2** Strong persuasion. *to put pressure on someone.* **3** Speed, urgency. *to work at high pressure.*

prestige *noun* Good reputation.

presume *verb* (presumes, presuming, presumed) **1** To suppose something to be true. *I presume you would like some cake?* **presumably** *adverb*. **2** To dare. *I would not presume to contradict a professor!* **presumption** *noun*.

presumptuous *adjective* Too confident, too bold.

pretend *verb* (pretends, pretending, pretended) **1** To behave as if things are not as they really are. *Let's pretend that you are a princess.* **2** To claim. *I don't pretend to be a good footballer.* **pretender, pretence** *nouns*.

pretext *noun* (pretexts) An excuse.

pretty[1] *adjective* (prettier, prettiest) Pleasant, attractive. **prettily** *adverb*, **prettiness** *noun*.

pretty[2] *adverb* (informal) Fairly, moderately. *We won pretty easily.*

prevailing *adjective* Usual, normal.

prevalent *adjective* Common, widespread.

prevent *verb* (prevents, preventing, prevented) To stop or hinder something. **preventive** *adjective*, **prevention** *noun*.

preview *noun* (previews) A showing of something before it is generally available.

previous *adjective* Earlier in time.

prey[1] *noun* An animal hunted, killed, and eaten by another. **bird of prey** a bird that lives by hunting.

prey[2] *verb* (preys, preying, preyed) **prey on** to hunt.

price[1] *noun* (prices) The sum of money for which something is to be bought.

price[2] *verb* (prices, pricing, priced) To fix a price on something.

priceless *adjective* **1** Very valuable. **2** (informal) Very amusing.

pricey *adjective* (informal) Expensive.

prick *verb* (pricks, pricking, pricked) **1** To make a hole in something with a pointed instrument. **2** To cause sharp pain. **prick up your ears** to pay special attention.

prickle *noun* (prickles) A thorn, a spike. **prickly** *adjective*.

pride¹ *noun* **1** A satisfied or conceited feeling because of what you have done. **2** Somebody or something which makes you feel pride. *Her baby was her pride and joy.* **pride of lions** a group of lions.

pride² *verb* (prides, priding, prided) **pride yourself on** to be pleased and satisfied about something.

pried, pries *See* **pry**

priest *noun* (priests) **1** A member of the clergy. **2** A person who leads others in worship.

prig *noun* (prigs) A person pleased with his or her own goodness. **priggish** *adjective*, **priggishly** *adverb*.

prim *adjective* (primmer, primmest) Disliking anything rough and rude. *prim and proper*. **primly** *adverb*.

primarily *adverb* Chiefly, in the first place.

primary *adjective* First. **primary school** a school for young children. **primary colours** red, blue, and yellow.

prime¹ *adjective* Chief, most important. **prime minister** the leader of a government.

prime² *verb* (primes, priming, primed) **1** To prepare something. **2** To put on a special first coat of paint. **primer** *noun*.

primitive *adjective* **1** At an early stage of development. **2** Simple, not complicated.

primrose *noun* (primroses) A pale yellow spring flower.

prince *noun* (princes) **1** The son of a king or other ruler. **2** A male member of a royal family.

princess *noun* (princesses) **1** The daughter of a king or other ruler. **2** A female member of a royal family.

principal¹ *adjective* Chief, most important. **principally** *adverb*.

principal² *noun* (principals) The head of a school or college.

principle *noun* (principles) A general rule about something.

print¹ *verb* (prints, printing, printed) **1** To put words or pictures on paper by means of a machine called a printing press or some other device which leaves a print. **2** To write in letters rather like those in a printed book. **3** To make a photograph on special paper from a negative.

print² *noun* (prints) **1** A mark made by pressing or stamping. **2** A printed picture or photograph.

printer *noun* (printers) **1** A person whose job is printing. **2** A machine used for printing.

printout *noun* (printouts) Printed paper from a computer.

prior *adjective* Earlier. **prior to** before.

priority *noun* (priorities) The right to be first, the right to have or do something before others.

priory *noun* (priories) A building where monks or nuns live or lived.

prism *noun* (prisms) A block of glass that breaks up white light into the colours of the rainbow.

prison *noun* (prisons) A place where criminals are kept locked up. **prisoner** *noun*.

private¹ *noun* (privates) An ordinary soldier.

private² *adjective* **1** Belonging to one person or one group of people. *a private road.* **2** Not to be known or talked about by everyone. *a private letter.* **3** Quiet, secluded. *a private place for a picnic.* **4** Not organized by the government. **privately** *adverb*, **privacy** *noun*.

privatize *verb* (privatizes, privatizing, privatized) To change an industry from government to private control.

privet *noun* An evergreen shrub used for garden hedges.

privilege *noun* (privileges) An advantage, or a right to do something, which only certain people have. **privileged** *adjective*.

prize¹ *noun* (prizes) 1 Something given to the winner of a game or competition, something given as a reward. 2 Something captured from the enemy in war.

prize² *verb* (prizes, prizing, prized) 1 To value something very highly. 2 To lever something open.

probable *adjective* Likely to be so, likely to happen. **probably** *adverb*, **probability** *noun*.

probation *noun* Testing a person's character or abilities. **probation officer** a person appointed to supervise the behaviour of someone who has been found guilty of a crime. **on probation** under the supervision of a probation officer.

probe¹ *verb* (probes, probing, probed) To go into something or to put an instrument into something to examine or explore it.

probe² *noun* (probes) An instrument used for probing. **space probe** an unmanned spacecraft for exploring space.

problem *noun* (problems) A question to be solved, a difficulty to be overcome.

procedure *noun* (procedures) The regular way of doing something.

proceed *verb* (proceeds, proceeding, proceeded) To go on, to continue forwards.

proceedings *noun* Actions, happenings.

proceeds *noun* The profits from something.

process¹ *noun* (processes) A series of actions for making or doing something.

process² *verb* (processes, processing, processed) 1 To treat or change something by a series of actions. *processed cheese*. 2 To put data through a computer. **processor** *noun*.

procession *noun* (processions) A line of people or vehicles moving steadily forwards.

proclaim *verb* (proclaims, proclaiming, proclaimed) To announce something publicly. **proclamation** *noun*.

procure *verb* (procures, procuring, procured) To obtain something.

prod *verb* (prods, prodding, prodded) To poke.

prodigal *adjective* Wasteful, foolishly extravagant.

produce¹ *noun* Things produced. *garden produce*.

produce² *verb* (produces, producing, produced) 1 To make something or bring it into existence. 2 To bring something into view. *He produced a handkerchief.* 3 To get a play ready for performance. **producer, production** *nouns*.

product *noun* (products) Something produced.

productive *adjective* Producing a lot of things, successful. **productivity** *noun*.

profession *noun* (professions) An occupation for which a person must study for a long time, such as being a lawyer or a doctor.

professional¹ *adjective* 1 Connected with a profession. 2 Doing something as a regular job, or for money. *a professional footballer.* 3 Expertly done, as if by a professional. *a professional job.* **professionally** *adverb*.

professional² *noun* (professionals)

A person who is paid to do something, not an amateur.

professor *noun* (professors) One of the senior teachers in a university.

proficient *adjective* Skilled. **proficiently** *adverb*, **proficiency** *noun*.

profile *noun* (profiles) A side view of a face.

profit¹ *noun* (profits) **1** Money gained in doing business. **2** An advantage, a benefit, a gain.

profit² *verb* (profits, profiting, profited) To gain profit from something. **profitable** *adjective*, **profitably** *adverb*.

profound *adjective* (profounder, profoundest) **1** Requiring much thought. **2** Very great. *profound silence*. **profoundly** *adverb*.

profuse *adjective* Plentiful. **profusely** *adverb*, **profusion** *noun*.

program¹ *noun* (programs) A set of instructions to a computer.

program² *verb* (programs, programming, programmed) **1** To write a program. **2** To control something with a program. **programmer** *noun*.

programme *noun* (programmes) **1** A play, entertainment, or other item on radio or television. **2** A list of events which are to take place. **3** A printed leaflet giving details of a play, football match, or some other event.

progress¹ *noun* **1** A forward movement, an advance. **2** Development, improvement.

progress² *verb* (progresses, progressing, progressed) To make progress. **progressive** *adjective*, **progressively** *adverb*, **progression** *noun*.

prohibit *verb* (prohibits, prohibiting, prohibited) To forbid. **prohibition** *noun*.

project¹ *verb* (projects, projecting, projected) **1** To stick out, to jut out. **2** *to project a film or slide*, to make the picture shine on a screen. **projector**, **projection** *nouns*.

project² *noun* (projects) **1** The task of studying a topic and discovering what you can about it. **2** A plan, a scheme, an undertaking.

projectile *noun* (projectiles) Something thrown or shot through the air.

prolific *adjective* Producing a great quantity.

prologue *noun* (prologues) An introduction to something.

prolong *verb* (prolongs, prolonging, prolonged) To make something longer.

prom *noun* (proms) (informal) A promenade concert.

promenade *noun* (promenades) An area set aside for walking or riding, especially by the seaside. **promenade concert** a concert at which some of the audience stand.

prominent *adjective* **1** Easily seen, jutting out. **2** Important. **prominently** *adverb*, **prominence** *noun*.

promise¹ *noun* (promises) A statement that you agree to do something, or not to do something. **show promise** to give evidence of being likely to succeed in the future.

promise² *verb* (promises, promising, promised) **1** To make a promise. **2** To show promise. **promisingly** *adverb*.

promote *verb* (promotes, promoting, promoted) **1** To move somebody to a higher rank or position. **2** To encourage the growth of something. **3** To organize the selling of a new product. **4** To organize a public entertainment. **promoter**, **promotion** *nouns*.

prompt¹ *adjective* Without delay. **promptly** *adverb*, **promptness** *noun*.

prompt² *verb* (prompts, prompting, prompted) **1** To urge or cause somebody to do something. *Greed prompted him to steal.* **2** To help an actor who forgets what to say. **prompter** *noun*.

prone *adjective* Lying stretched out with your face downwards. **prone to** likely to do or suffer something. *He's prone to catch colds.*

prong *noun* (prongs) One of the spikes of a fork.

pronoun *noun* (pronouns) A word used instead of a noun. *She, it, you,* and *them* are all pronouns.

pronounce *verb* (pronounces, pronouncing, pronounced) **1** To speak a word in a particular way, to speak the sounds of a language. *Right* and *write* are pronounced the same. **pronunciation** *noun.* **2** To make a serious announcement, to declare something officially. **pronouncement** *noun.*

pronounced *adjective* Obvious.

proof¹ *noun* Evidence that makes you believe for certain that something is true.

proof² *adjective* Safe against something. *bullet-proof glass.*

prop¹ *noun* (props) A support.

prop² *verb* (props, propping, propped) To support something or somebody.

propaganda *noun* Spreading ideas and information in order to make people believe something.

propel *verb* (propels, propelling, propelled) To make something move forward. **propulsion** *noun.*

propeller *noun* (propellers) A device which turns rapidly to propel a ship or aircraft.

proper *adjective* **1** Right, correct, suitable. **2** Respectable. **3** (informal) Great, complete. *We got into a proper muddle!* **properly** *adverb.*

property *noun* (properties) **1** A person's possessions. **2** Land or buildings belonging to someone. **3** A special quality belonging to something.

prophecy *noun* (prophecies) A prediction, a statement about what will happen in the future.

prophesy *verb* (prophesies, prophesying, prophesied) To make a prophecy.

prophet *noun* (prophets) **1** A great religious teacher. **2** A person who prophesies. **the Prophet** Muhammad. **prophetic** *adjective,* **prophetically** *adverb.*

proportion *noun* (proportions) **1** The relationship of one thing to another in quantity or size or importance. **2** A part, a share. *If you work for us, we'll give you a proportion of our profits.* **proportions** size, measurements. **proportional** *adjective.*

propose *verb* (proposes, proposing, proposed) **1** To suggest a plan. *I propose we go fishing.* **proposition** *noun.* **2** To ask a person to marry you. **proposal** *noun.*

proprietor *noun* (proprietors) An owner.

propulsion *See* **propel**

prose *noun* Any piece of writing which is not in the form of verse.

prosecute *verb* (prosecutes, prosecuting, prosecuted) To take legal action against somebody. **prosecutor, prosecution** *nouns.*

prospect¹ *noun* (prospects) **1** A wide view. **2** Something you look forward to, a hope.

prospect² *verb* (prospects, prospecting, prospected) To search for gold or some other mineral. **prospector** *noun.*

prospectus *noun* (prospectuses) A brochure describing and advertising a school or a business company.

prosper *verb* (prospers, prospering, prospered) To do well, to succeed. **prosperous** *adjective*, **prosperously** *adverb*, **prosperity** *noun*.

protect *verb* (protects, protecting, protected) To keep safe, to guard. **protective** *adjective*, **protectively** *adverb*, **protector**, **protection** *nouns*.

protein *noun* (proteins) A substance in food which is necessary to build up the body.

protest[1] *noun* (protests) An objection, something you do or say to show that you do not approve.

protest[2] *verb* (protests, protesting, protested) To make a protest.

Protestant *noun* (Protestants) A Christian not of the Roman Catholic or Orthodox Churches.

prototype *noun* (prototypes) The first example made to test the design of a new thing.

protractor *noun* (protractors) An instrument for measuring angles.

protrude *verb* (protrudes, protruding, protruded) To stick out.

proud *adjective* (prouder, proudest) **1** Having a proper pride or dignity. **2** Conceited. **3** Causing pride. *It was a proud moment when I got my prize.* **proudly** *adverb*.

prove *verb* (proves, proving, proved) **1** To show that something is really true, to establish it beyond doubt. **2** To turn out to be, to be found to be. *My pen proved to be useless.*

proverb *noun* (proverbs) A short, well-known saying which gives general advice, such as 'Look before you leap'. **proverbial** *adjective*.

provide *verb* (provides, providing, provided) **1** To supply, to give. **provider** *noun*. **2** To prepare for something. **providing that, provided that** on condition that.

providence *noun* God's loving care. **providential** *adjective* happening by good luck. **providentially** *adverb*.

province *noun* (provinces) A part of a country. **the provinces** the parts of a country away from the capital. **provincial** *adjective*.

provisional *adjective* Temporary. **provisionally** *adverb*.

provisions *noun* Supplies of food and drink.

provoke *verb* (provokes, provoking, provoked) **1** To make someone angry. **2** To arouse someone or something. **provocative** *adjective*, **provocatively** *adverb*, **provocation** *noun*.

prow *noun* (prows) The front end of a boat or ship, the bows.

prowess *noun* Bravery, skill.

prowl *verb* (prowls, prowling, prowled) To go about stealthily. **prowler** *noun*.

prudent *adjective* Careful, wise. **prudently** *adverb*, **prudence** *noun*.

prudish *adjective* Too easily shocked by anything that is rude or improper. **prudishly** *adverb*.

prune[1] *noun* (prunes) A dried plum.

prune[2] *verb* (prunes, pruning, pruned) To cut unwanted twigs or branches off a tree or shrub.

pry *verb* (pries, prying, pried) To look inquisitively into something.

PS A postscript.

psalm *noun* (psalms) One of the hymns or songs collected in the Bible. **psalmist** *noun*.

psychiatry *noun* The treatment of mental illness. **psychiatric** *adjective*, **psychiatrist** *noun*.

psychic *adjective* Having the power to be aware of supernatural things.

psychology *noun* The study of the mind and how it works. **psychological** *adjective*, **psychologist** *noun*.

pub *noun* (pubs) A building with public rooms where alcoholic drinks are served.

puberty *noun* The stage of life when young people begin to become adult, so that they are able to be mothers or fathers.

public *adjective* **1** Belonging to people in general, for general use. *a public place*. **2** Generally known. *public knowledge*. **public house** a pub. **public school** a kind of secondary school where you pay fees. **in public** not in secret, where anyone can see. **the public** people in general.

publication *noun* **1** Publishing. **2** (publications) Something published.

publicity *noun* **1** Making a thing public, advertising. **2** Being made public.

public-spirited *adjective* Ready to do things for the general good of other people.

publish *verb* (publishes, publishing, published) **1** To have something printed and put it on sale. **2** To announce something publicly. **publisher** *noun*.

puck *noun* (pucks) The rubber disc used instead of a ball in ice-hockey.

pudding *noun* (puddings) **1** A food made with flour and other ingredients, often steamed or baked. *Yorkshire pudding*. **2** The sweet course of a meal.

puddle *noun* (puddles) A small pool, usually of rain-water.

puff¹ *noun* (puffs) **1** A short spurt of air, smoke, or steam. **2** A small cloud of something. **puff pastry** a light flaky pastry.

puff² *verb* (puffs, puffing, puffed) **1** To make puffs, to come out in puffs, to gasp. **2** To make something swell. *He puffed out his chest*.

puffin *noun* (puffins) A sea bird with a large bill.

pug *noun* (pugs) A small dog with a flat face.

pugnacious *adjective* Fond of fighting. **pugnaciously** *adverb*.

pull *verb* (pulls, pulling, pulled) **1** To take hold of something and try to move it towards yourself. *to pull a rope*. **2** To make something move along behind you. *to pull a cart*. **pull a face** to make a funny face. **pull someone's leg** to play a joke on someone. **pull something off** to do it successfully. **pull out** to move out, to withdraw. **pull round, pull through** to recover after an illness. **pull yourself together** to get control of yourself. **pull up** to stop.

pullet *noun* (pullets) A young hen.

pulley *noun* (pulleys) A wheel with a groove in the rim for a rope to run over, used for lifting things.

pullover *noun* (pullovers) A knitted garment which covers the top part of the body.

pulp¹ *noun* A soft, wet mass of something.

pulp² *verb* (pulps, pulping, pulped) To make into pulp.

pulpit *noun* (pulpits) A small enclosed platform used by the preacher in church.

pulse *noun* (pulses) **1** The regular beat of a person's arteries as the blood is pumped through them. **2** A steady throbbing. **3** One of a series of electrical signals sent down a wire.

pumice *noun* A kind of light stone, or lava, used for cleaning.

pump¹ *noun* (pumps) **1** A machine for forcing air or liquid into or out of something, or along pipes. **2** A soft, light shoe.

pump[2] *verb* (pumps, pumping, pumped) To use a pump.

pumpkin *noun* (pumpkins) A large, round, yellow fruit.

pun *noun* (puns) A witty use of words which sound alike but which have different meanings.

punch[1] *noun* A hot drink made from wine.

punch[2] *noun* (punches) **1** A blow with the fist. **2** An instrument for making holes in paper, leather, metal, or other substances.

punch[3] *verb* (punches, punching, punched) **1** To hit with the fist. **2** To make a hole with a punch.

punctual *adjective* Exactly on time, prompt. **punctually** *adverb*, **punctuality** *noun*.

punctuate *verb* (punctuates, punctuating, punctuated) To put full stops, commas, and other marks into a piece of writing. **punctuation** *noun*.

puncture[1] *verb* (punctures, puncturing, punctured) To make a hole in something with a sharp object.

puncture[2] *noun* (punctures) A hole in a pneumatic tyre.

punish *verb* (punishes, punishing, punished) To make somebody suffer because he or she has done something wrong. **punishment** *noun*.

punk *noun* **1** A type of pop music. **2** (punks) A person who uses weird clothes, hair-styles, and jewellery to shock other people.

punt[1] *noun* (punts) A small flat-bottomed boat pushed along by a long pole.

punt[2] *verb* (punts, punting, punted) **1** To move a punt along with a pole, to go in a punt. **2** To drop a ball and kick it before it touches the ground.

puny *adjective* (punier, puniest) Small and feeble.

pup *noun* (pups) A puppy.

pupil *noun* (pupils) **1** A person learning from a teacher. **2** The circular opening in the middle of the eye.

puppet *noun* (puppets) A kind of doll that can be made to move by wires or strings. **glove puppet** a doll which fits over your hand so that your fingers can move it.

puppy *noun* (puppies) A young dog.

purchase[1] *noun* (purchases) **1** The buying of something. **2** Something bought.

purchase[2] *verb* (purchases, purchasing, purchased) To buy.

pure *adjective* (purer, purest) Clean, clear, not mixed with anything else. **purely** *adverb*, **purity** *noun*.

purge *verb* (purges, purging, purged) To get rid of an unwanted part or thing.

purify *verb* (purifies, purifying, purified) To make a thing pure. **purification** *noun*.

purple *adjective* Deep reddish-blue.

purpose *noun* (purposes) Something that a person means to do, a plan, an intention. **on purpose** deliberately. **purposeful, purposeless** *adjectives*.

purposely *adverb* On purpose.

purr *verb* (purrs, purring, purred) To make a gentle murmuring sound as a contented cat does.

purse *noun* (purses) A small bag to keep money in.

pursue *verb* (pursues, pursuing, pursued) **1** To chase, to try to catch up with someone or something. **2** To do something for a considerable time. *to pursue a hobby*. **pursuer, pursuit** *nouns*.

pus *noun* A whitish liquid which forms in boils and septic wounds.

push *verb* (pushes, pushing, pushed) **1** To use force to try to move something away from yourself. **2** To make your way by pushing. **3** To press something. *Push the bell*.

push-chair *noun* (push-chairs) A chair on wheels to carry a young child.

pussy *noun* (pussies) (informal) A cat or kitten.

put *verb* (puts, putting, put) **1** To place something in a certain position, to move something to a certain position. **2** To express something in words. *He put it very tactfully.* **put off** to postpone. **put someone off** to make someone less interested in something. **put a fire out** to make it stop burning. **put someone up** to give someone a place to sleep. **put up with something** to suffer it patiently. **put an end to something** to finish it. **put someone to death** to execute someone. **put up prices** to make prices higher.

putrid *adjective* Rotten and smelly.

putt *verb* (putts, putting, putted) In golf, to strike a ball gently towards a hole. **putter** *noun*.

putty *noun* A substance used to set glass in window frames.

puzzle¹ *noun* (puzzles) **1** A problem or question that is difficult to solve. **2** A kind of pastime or game which requires skill. *a jigsaw puzzle.*

puzzle² *verb* (puzzles, puzzling, puzzled) **1** To make someone think deeply. **2** To think deeply.

PVC A kind of plastic.

pyjamas *noun* A thin coat and trousers for sleeping in.

pylon *noun* (pylons) A steel tower used to carry electric cables.

pyramid *noun* (pyramids) **1** A structure with a square base and four sloping sides which come to a point. **2** An ancient Egyptian monument like this.

pyre *noun* (pyres) A large pile of wood for burning a corpse.

python *noun* (pythons) A large snake that crushes its prey.

Qq

quack *verb* (quacks, quacking, quacked) To make a noise like a duck.

quad *noun* (quads) (informal) **1** A quadrangle. **2** A quadruplet.

quadrangle *noun* (quadrangles) A courtyard or lawn with buildings all round it.

quadrilateral *noun* (quadrilaterals) A shape with four sides.

quadruped *noun* (quadrupeds) An animal with four feet.

quadruple *adjective* **1** Made up of four parts. **2** Multiplied by four.

quadruplet *noun* (quadruplets) One of four babies born to the same mother at one time.

quagmire *noun* (quagmires) A bog, a marsh.

quail¹ *noun* (quails) A small bird of the partridge family.

quail² *verb* (quails, quailing, quailed) To flinch, to show fear.

quaint *adjective* (quainter, quaintest) Attractive in an old-fashioned or unusual way. **quaintly** *adverb*, **quaintness** *noun*.

quake *verb* (quakes, quaking, quaked) To shake, to tremble.

Quaker *noun* (Quakers) A person who belongs to a Christian group called the Society of Friends.

qualify *verb* (qualifies, qualifying, qualified) To reach an acceptable standard, usually by an examination or test. **qualified** properly trained. **qualification** *noun*.

quality *noun* **1** The goodness or lack of goodness in something. *good quality,* *poor quality*. **2** (qualities) A characteristic of someone or something, a feature of a person's character.

qualm *noun* (qualms) A feeling of doubt or uneasiness.

quantity *noun* (quantities) An amount, a certain number of things, a certain measure of something.

quarantine *noun* A period when a person or animal is separated from others to prevent the spread of a disease.

quarrel¹ *noun* (quarrels) An angry or violent disagreement. **quarrelsome** *adjective*.

quarrel² *verb* (quarrels, quarrelling, quarrelled) To have a quarrel.

quarry *noun* (quarries) **1** A place where stone or slate is dug out of the ground. **2** A hunted animal or bird.

quart *noun* (quarts) A unit of measure for liquids, 2 pints or 1.14 litres.

quarter¹ *noun* (quarters) **1** One of the four equal parts into which something is, or can be, divided. A quarter of 4 is 1. A quarter of 1 is $\frac{1}{4}$. **2** A period of three months. **3** *a quarter past four*, 15 minutes past four o'clock. **4** A district in a town. **quarters** lodgings. **at close quarters** close together.

quarter² *verb* (quarters, quartering, quartered) **1** To divide into quarters. **2** To place troops in lodgings.

quarter³ Mercy *The enemy gave no quarter*.

quarterly *adjective and adverb* Once every three months.

quartet *noun* (quartets) A group of four musicians.

quaver¹ *noun* (quavers) A note in music. It is written ♪

quaver² *verb* (quavers, quavering, quavered) To shake, to tremble.

quay *noun* (quays) A harbour wall or pier where ships tie up to unload.

queasy *adjective* Feeling sick.

queen *noun* (queens) **1** A woman who is the crowned ruler of a country. **2** The wife of a king. **3** A piece in chess.

queer *adjective* (queerer, queerest) **1** Strange, unusual. **2** Unwell. *to feel queer*. **queerly** *adverb*, **queerness** *noun*.

quell *verb* (quells, quelling, quelled) To suppress, to overcome.

quench *verb* (quenches, quenching, quenched) **1** To satisfy a thirst. **2** To put out a fire.

query¹ *noun* (queries) **1** A question. **2** A question mark.

query² *verb* (queries, querying, queried) To question.

quest *verb* (quests) A long search for something.

question¹ *noun* (questions) Something which is asked, something which has to be decided. **in question** being discussed. **out of the question** impossible.

question² *verb* (questions, questioning, questioned) **1** To put questions to somebody. *The police questioned the suspect*. **2** To say that you have doubts about something. *We questioned the price*. **question mark** the punctuation mark ?

question-master *noun* (question-masters) The person who asks the questions in a quiz.

questionnaire *noun* (questionnaires) A list of questions to be answered.

queue¹ *noun* (queues) A line of people or vehicles waiting for something.

queue² *verb* (queues, queuing, queued) To be in a queue.

quiche *noun* (quiches) A tart with a savoury filling.

quick *adjective* (quicker, quickest) **1** Moving at speed. **2** Soon done. **3** Lively, bright, clever. **quickly** *adverb*, **quickness** *noun*.

quicken *verb* (quickens, quickening, quickened) To become quicker.

quicksand *noun* (quicksands) An area

of loose, wet sand which can swallow up anyone who walks on it.

quicksilver *noun* Mercury.

quid *noun* (quid) (informal) A pound (£1).

quiet *adjective* (quieter, quietest) **1** Without sound, silent. **2** Without movement, peaceful. **keep something quiet** to keep it secret. **quietly** *adverb*, **quietness** *noun*.

quieten *verb* (quietens, quietening, quietened) To make or become quieter.

quill *noun* (quills) A large feather, especially one used as a pen.

quilt *noun* (quilts) A cover for a bed, filled with feathers or soft material.

quin *noun* (quins) (informal) A quintuplet.

quintet *noun* (quintets) A group of five musicians.

quintuplet *noun* (quintuplets) One of five babies born to the same mother at one time.

quit *verb* (quits, quitting, quitted or quit) To go away, to leave.

quite *adverb* **1** Completely. *Have you quite finished?* **2** Rather, to some extent. *It's quite a good record, but not their best.*

quits *adjective* **be quits** to have paid someone back.

quiver¹ *noun* (quivers) A case for holding arrows.

quiver² *verb* (quivers, quivering, quivered) To tremble, to shake.

quiz *noun* (quizzes) A set of questions which test your knowledge.

quoits *noun* A game in which you throw a ring called a quoit.

quota *noun* (quotas) A share or amount which is allowed.

quotation *noun* (quotations) Words quoted from what someone has spoken or written. **quotation marks** the punctuation marks " " or ' ' which you put round quotations.

quote *verb* (quotes, quoting, quoted) To repeat words which were first spoken or written by someone else.

Rr
• • • • •

rabbi *noun* (rabbis) A Jewish religious leader.

rabbit *noun* (rabbits) An animal which lives in a burrow.

rabble *noun* (rabbles) A disorderly crowd.

rabies *noun* A disease which causes madness in dogs.

race¹ *noun* (races) **1** A group of people with the same origin, the same characteristics, and the same colour of skin. **racial** *adjective*. **human race** human beings. **race relations** relationships between people of different races.

race² *noun* (races) A competition in which competitors try to be the first to reach a certain point.

race³ *verb* (races, racing, raced) **1** To have a race. **2** To move very fast. **racer** *noun*.

racecourse *noun* (racecourses) A ground set out for horse-racing.

race-horse *noun* (race-horses) A horse bred for racing.

race-track *noun* (race-tracks) A track for racing.

racial *adjective* Concerned with race. *racial discrimination.*

racist *noun* (racists) A person who treats other people unfairly because of their race or colour.

rack *noun* (racks) **1** A framework for supporting things. *a plate-rack.* **2** An instrument of torture.

racket *noun* (rackets) **1** An uproar, a wild noise. **2** A light bat such as is used in playing tennis. **3** (informal) A dishonest way of making money.

radar *noun* A radio system or apparatus that detects objects which come within its range.

radiant *adjective* **1** Bright, shining. **2** Joyful, happy. **radiantly** *adverb*, **radiance** *noun*.

radiate *verb* (radiates, radiating, radiated) **1** To send out rays of light or heat or other energy. **radiation** *noun*. **2** To be arranged like the spokes of a wheel.

radiator *noun* (radiators) **1** An apparatus that radiates heat. **2** An apparatus that keeps a car engine cool.

radio *noun* **1** Broadcasting, sending and receiving sound through the air by means of electrical waves. **2** (radios) An apparatus for receiving radio transmissions or programmes. **radio telescope** a telescope for astronomy using radio waves instead of light waves.

radioactive *adjective* Giving out atomic rays. **radioactivity** *noun*.

radiography *noun* X-ray photography. **radiographer** *noun*.

radiotherapy *noun* Treatment by X-rays.

radish *noun* (radishes) A small red vegetable eaten in salads.

radius *noun* (radii) A straight line from the centre of a circle to the circumference.

RAF The Royal Air Force.

raffia *noun* Long fibres used to make baskets, mats, and other things.

raffle *noun* (raffles) A way of raising money by selling numbered tickets which may win prizes.

raft *noun* (rafts) A flat floating platform of logs or other materials.

rafter *noun* (rafters) One of the sloping beams of wood supporting a roof.

rag *noun* (rags) A torn piece of cloth.

rage[1] *noun* (rages) Violent anger.

rage[2] *verb* (rages, raging, raged) To be full of rage.

ragged *adjective* **1** Badly torn. *ragged clothes.* **2** Dressed in rags. *a ragged beggar.* **3** Rough, jagged. *ragged rocks.*

raid[1] *noun* (raids) A sudden attack.

raid[2] *verb* (raids, raiding, raided) To make a raid. **raider** *noun*.

rail *noun* (rails) **1** A long horizontal or sloping bar or rod. *a towel rail, a banister rail.* **2** A steel bar forming part of a railway track. **by rail** by railway.

railings *noun* A fence made with rails.

railway *noun* (railways) A system of transport using tracks made of steel rails on which trains run.

rain[1] *noun* Water falling in drops from the sky. **rainy** *adjective*.

rain[2] *noun* (rains, raining, rained) **1** *It is raining*, rain is falling. **2** To come down or send down like rain.

rainbow *noun* (rainbows) The curve of

many colours seen in the sky when the sun shines through rain.

raincoat noun (raincoats) A waterproof coat.

raindrop noun (raindrops) A drop of rain.

rainfall noun The amount of rain which falls at a certain place in a certain time.

rain-gauge noun (rain-gauges) An instrument for measuring rainfall.

raise verb (raises, raising, raised) **1** To lift something, to make it rise. **2** To bring up young children or animals. **3** To manage to get something. *to raise a loan*. **raise a siege** to end it.

raisin noun (raisins) A dried grape.

rajah noun (rajahs) An Indian prince.

rake[1] noun (rakes) A tool with many teeth used in gardening.

rake[2] verb (rakes, raking, raked) **1** To use a rake. **2** To search through something.

rally[1] verb (rallies, rallying, rallied) To recover, to revive.

rally[2] noun (rallies) **1** A recovery. **2** In tennis, an exchange of several hits before a point is scored. **3** A large gathering of people for a particular purpose. **4** A competition to test skill in driving.

ram[1] noun (rams) **1** A male sheep. **2** A heavy beam for hammering with great force. *a battering ram*.

ram[2] verb (rams, ramming, rammed) To push forcefully, to strike heavily.

Ramadan noun The month when Muslims fast during the day.

ramble verb (rambles, rambling, rambled) To walk for pleasure, to wander. **rambler** noun.

ramp noun (ramps) A slope joining two levels.

rampage verb (rampages, rampaging, rampaged) To rush wildly and violently about.

rampart noun (ramparts) A broad wall built as a defence.

ramshackle adjective In a bad state of repair.

ran See **run**[1]

ranch noun (ranches) A large cattle-farm in America. **rancher** noun.

rancid adjective Stale, unpleasant-tasting.

random noun and adjective **at random** without any particular aim, plan, or pattern. **random numbers** numbers chosen at random.

ranee noun (ranees) An Indian princess.

rang See **ring**[3]

range[1] noun (ranges) **1** A line or series of things. *a range of mountains*. **2** A varied collection of things. *a wide range of goods*. **3** Ability, scope. *a task outside my range*. **4** The distance over which something can operate. *the range of a gun*. **5** An area of ground with targets for shooting. *a rifle range*. **6** A kitchen fireplace with ovens for cooking in.

range[2] verb (ranges, ranging, ranged) **1** To vary between two limits. *Prices ranged from £18 to £25*. **2** To wander. *Tigers ranged about the jungle*. **3** To set in a line, to arrange.

Ranger Guide A senior Guide.

rank[1] noun (ranks) **1** A line of people or things. *a taxi-rank*. **2** A person's position in the forces or in society. *to hold a high rank in the army*, to be a senior officer in the army.

rank[2] verb (ranks, ranking, ranked) To arrange in order.

ransack verb (ransacks, ransacking, ransacked) **1** To search thoroughly. **2** To rob, to plunder.

ransom[1] noun (ransoms) A sum of money demanded so that a captive may be set free. **hold to ransom** to keep someone captive and demand a ransom.

ransom[2] verb (ransoms, ransoming, ransomed) To pay a ransom.

rap¹ *verb* (raps, rapping, rapped) To knock sharply but lightly.

rap² *noun* A kind of pop music in which verse is recited in time with the beat.

rape *verb* (rapes, raping, raped) To force someone to have sexual intercourse. **rape, rapist** *nouns*.

rapid *adjective* Quick, speedy. **rapidly** *adverb*, **rapidity** *noun*.

rapids *noun* A part of a river where the water flows rapidly over rocks.

rapier *noun* (rapiers) A long narrow sword.

rapture *noun* (raptures) Great delight. **rapturous** *adjective*, **rapturously** *adverb*.

rare *adjective* (rarer, rarest) Unusual, uncommon. **rarely** *adverb*, **rarity** *noun*.

rascal *noun* (rascals) A dishonest, naughty, or mischievous person.

rash¹ *adjective* (rasher, rashest) Too hasty, reckless. **rashly** *adverb*, **rashness** *noun*.

rash² *noun* (rashes) A number of tiny red spots on the skin.

rasher *noun* (rashers) A slice of bacon.

raspberry *noun* (raspberries) A small soft red fruit.

rasping *adjective* Harsh, grating.

Rastafarian *noun* (Rastafarians) A member of a religious group that started in Jamaica.

rat *noun* (rats) An animal like a large mouse.

rate¹ *noun* (rates) **1** Speed. *He drove off at a great rate.* **2** Quality or standard. *first-rate, second-rate.* **3** The money charged for something. **at any rate** whatever happens.

rate² *verb* (rates, rating, rated) To regard, to put a value on someone or something. *How do you rate her as a tennis player?*

rather *adverb* **1** Fairly, somewhat. *I was rather tired.* **2** More truly. *He ran, or rather staggered, to the finishing line.* **3** Preferably. *I would rather not come.*

ratio *noun* (ratios) A relationship between two numbers or quantities.

ration¹ *noun* (rations) An amount of something allowed to a person in a time of shortage.

ration² *verb* (rations, rationing, rationed) To share something out in fixed quantities.

rational *adjective* Reasonable, sensible, sane. **rationally** *adverb*.

rattle¹ *verb* (rattles, rattling, rattled) To make a rapid series of short sharp sounds.

rattle² *noun* (rattles) **1** A rattling noise. **2** A baby's toy which rattles.

rattlesnake *noun* (rattlesnakes) A poisonous American snake which makes a rattling noise with its tail.

ratty *adjective* (informal) Annoyed, angry.

raucous *adjective* Sounding harsh. **raucously** *adverb*.

ravage *verb* (ravages, ravaging, ravaged) **1** To plunder. **2** To do widespread damage.

rave¹ *verb* (raves, raving, raved) To talk or behave wildly or enthusiastically.

rave² *noun* (raves) A very big party.

raven *noun* (ravens) A large black bird like a crow.

ravenous *adjective* Very hungry. **ravenously** *adverb*.

ravine *noun* (ravines) A deep narrow valley.

raw *adjective* (rawer, rawest) **1** Not cooked. *raw food.* **2** In the natural state, not yet prepared for use. *raw materials.* **3** Not experienced. *a raw recruit.* **4** Damp and cold. *a raw wind.* **5** Sore, with the skin rubbed off. *a raw place on my heel.* **rawness** *noun*.

ray *noun* (rays) A narrow line of light, heat, or other form of energy.

rayon *noun* An artificial silky material.

raze *verb* (razes, razing, razed) To destroy a building or town completely, to knock it to the ground.

razor *noun* (razors) A sharp instrument used for shaving.

reach¹ *verb* (reaches, reaching, reached) **1** To stretch out the hand. *He reached for another chocolate.* **2** To get to somewhere or something. *They reached home. We reached a decision.*

reach² *noun* (reaches) **1** The distance a person can reach with an arm. **2** A convenient distance for travelling. *My uncle lives within reach of the sea.* **3** A straight stretch of a river.

react *verb* (reacts, reacting, reacted) To have a reaction.

reaction *noun* (reactions) A feeling or action caused by some thing, person, or event.

reactor *noun* (reactors) An apparatus for producing atomic power.

read *verb* (reads, reading, read) **1** To look at something which is written or printed and understand it. **2** To have certain words written on it. *The sign read 'Stop'.* **readable** *adjective*.

reader *noun* (readers) **1** A person who reads. **2** A school book used when you are learning to read.

readily *adverb* **1** Willingly. **2** Easily.

ready *adjective* (readier, readiest) **1** Able and willing to do something without delay. *ready for bed.* **2** Prepared for use. *ready answers.*

real *adjective* **1** Existing, not imaginary. **reality** *noun*. **2** Genuine, not fake.

realistic *adjective* Like the real thing. **realistically** *adverb*.

realize *verb* (realizes, realizing, realized) To come to understand something. *I realize this job will take a long time.* **realization** *noun*.

really *adverb* Truly, without doubt.

realm *noun* (realms) A kingdom.

reap *verb* (reaps, reaping, reaped) To cut and gather grain crops. **reaper** *noun*.

reappear *verb* (reappears, reappearing, reappeared) To appear again. **reappearance** *noun*.

rear¹ *noun* The back of something, the part furthest from the front.

rear² *adjective* Situated at the back. *the rear window.*

rear³ *verb* (rears, rearing, reared) **1** To bring up children or young animals. **2** To rise up on hind legs.

rearguard *noun* Troops protecting the rear of an army.

reason¹ *noun* (reasons) **1** An explanation or excuse. **2** A cause. *What is the reason for that?* **3** The ability to think things out. **4** Good sense. *It's against all reason to start in this weather.*

reason² *verb* (reasons, reasoning, reasoned) **1** To think. **2** To argue sensibly.

reasonable *adjective* **1** Sensible. **2** Moderate, fair. *reasonable prices.* **reasonably** *adverb*.

reassure *verb* (reassures, reassuring, reassured) To remove a person's doubts and fears. **reassurance** *noun*.

rebel¹ *verb* (rebels, rebelling, rebelled) To refuse to obey someone in authority. **rebellious** *adjective*, **rebelliously** *adverb*, **rebellion** *noun*.

rebel² *noun* (rebels) Someone who rebels.

rebound *verb* (rebounds, rebounding, rebounded) To bounce back.

rebuild *verb* (rebuilds, rebuilding, rebuilt) To build again.

rebuke[1] *verb* (rebukes, rebuking, rebuked) To speak severely to someone for doing wrong.

rebuke[2] *noun* (rebukes) Words spoken in rebuking someone.

recall *verb* (recalls, recalling, recalled) **1** To call back. **2** To remember.

recapture *verb* (recaptures, recapturing, recaptured) To capture again.

recede *verb* (recedes, receding, receded) To go back. *When the rain stopped, the flood receded.*

receipt *noun* (receipts) **1** The act of receiving something. **2** Written proof that a payment has been received.

receive *verb* (receives, receiving, received) **1** To accept or take in something which is given or sent. *to receive a letter.* **2** To welcome someone. *to receive a guest.* **receiver** *noun*.

recent *adjective* Made a short time ago, having happened a short time ago. **recently** *adverb*.

receptacle *noun* (receptacles) A container.

reception *noun* (receptions) **1** A welcome. **2** A party where people are given an official welcome. **3** An office in a garage, hotel, or other place where people are received when they arrive. **receptionist** *noun*.

receptive *adjective* Quick to receive new ideas.

recipe *noun* (recipes) Directions for cooking food.

recital *noun* (recitals) A concert given by a small number of performers.

recite *verb* (recites, reciting, recited) To speak aloud from memory. **recitation** *noun*.

reckless *adjective* Not thinking or caring about the consequences. **recklessly** *adverb*, **recklessness** *noun*.

reckon *verb* (reckons, reckoning, reckoned) **1** To calculate. **2** To consider.

reclaim *verb* (reclaims, reclaiming, reclaimed) To bring something back into profitable use. *reclaimed land.* **reclamation** *noun*.

recline *verb* (reclines, reclining, reclined) To lean or lie back.

recognize *verb* (recognizes, recognizing, recognized) **1** To realize that you know somebody or something. **2** To acknowledge. *I do not recognize your authority.* **recognizable** *adjective*, **recognition** *noun*.

recoil *verb* (recoils, recoiling, recoiled) To spring back, to move backwards.

recollect *verb* (recollects, recollecting, recollected) To remember. **recollection** *noun*.

recommend *verb* (recommends, recommending, recommended) **1** To suggest. **2** To speak well of someone or something. **recommendation** *noun*.

recompense *verb* (recompenses, recompensing, recompensed) To repay somebody for something.

reconcile *verb* (reconciles, reconciling, reconciled) To make people become friends again, to settle a difference. **reconcile yourself to** to accept or agree to something you do not really want. **reconciliation** *noun*.

recondition *verb* (reconditions, reconditioning, reconditioned) To put something into good working order again.

reconnaissance *noun* (reconnaissances) An advance into enemy territory to gather information.

reconsider *verb* (reconsiders, reconsidering, reconsidered) To think again about something.

reconstruct *verb* (reconstructs, reconstructing, reconstructed) To rebuild.

record[1] *verb* (records, recording, recorded) **1** To write something down for future reference. **2** To store sounds or pictures on a tape or disc.

record² *noun* (records) **1** A written account of things that have happened or things that have been done. **2** A disc on which sounds or pictures have been recorded. **3** The best performance of its kind.

recorder *noun* (recorders) **1** Someone who writes down a record of events. **2** A tape-recorder. **3** A musical instrument played by blowing into one end.

recording *noun* (recordings) Sounds or pictures recorded on a disc or tape.

record-player *noun* (record-players) An apparatus for playing records.

recount *verb* (recounts, recounting, recounted) To tell.

re-count *noun* (re-counts) A second counting of something.

recover *verb* (recovers, recovering, re-covered) **1** To return to normal health and strength. **2** To get back something which was lost. **recovery** *noun*.

re-cover *verb* (re-covers, re-covering, re-covered) To cover something again.

recreation *noun* (recreations) Games, hobbies, or other things which you do in your leisure time. **recreation ground** a playing-field.

recruit¹ *noun* (recruits) A person who has just joined the armed forces or some other organization.

recruit² *verb* (recruits, recruiting, recruited) To get recruits.

rectangle *noun* (rectangles) A shape with four straight sides and four right angles. **rectangular** *adjective*.

rectify *verb* (rectifies, rectifying, rectified) To put something right.

rector *noun* (rectors) A minister in charge of a parish.

rectory *noun* (rectories) A rector's house.

recuperate *verb* (recuperates, recuperating, recuperated) To get better after an illness. **recuperation** *noun*.

recur *verb* (recurs, recurring, recurred) To happen again, to be repeated. **recurrent** *adjective*, **recurrence** *noun*.

recycle *verb* (recycles, recycling, recycled) To treat waste material so that it can be used again.

red¹ *noun* A colour, the colour of blood.

red² *adjective* (redder, reddest) Red in colour. **Red Cross** an international organization caring for the injured and for the relief of suffering.

redden *verb* (reddens, reddening, reddened) **1** To become red. **2** To make something red.

reddish *adjective* Rather red.

redeem *verb* (redeems, redeeming, redeemed) **1** To buy something back. **2** To save someone from their wicked ways. **redeeming feature** a quality that makes up for someone's bad qualities. **redeemer, redemption** *nouns*.

red-handed *adjective* In the act of committing a crime. *to catch someone red-handed*.

red-hot *adjective* Glowing with heat.

reduce *verb* (reduces, reducing, reduced) **1** To become or make something less or smaller. **2** To bring somebody or something down to a different state. *reduced to poverty*. **reduction** *noun*.

redundant *adjective* No longer needed, liable to be disposed of. *to make someone redundant*. **redundancy** *noun*.

reed *noun* (reeds) **1** A plant which grows in or near water. **2** A piece of this plant or of plastic used to make the sound in an oboe, bagpipe, or similar musical instrument. **reedy** *adjective*.

reef *noun* (reefs) A line of rock or coral just below or just above the surface of the sea.

reef-knot *noun* (reef-knots) A kind of knot.

reek *verb* (reeks, reeking, reeked) To give off an unpleasant smell.

reel[1] *noun* (reels) **1** A cylinder or other device on which cotton, fishing-line, film, or other things may be wound. **2** A lively Scottish dance.

reel[2] *verb* (reels, reeling, reeled) **1** To stagger. **2** To be dizzy.

re-enter *verb* (re-enters, re-entering, re-entered) To come back into somewhere. **re-entry** *noun*.

refer *verb* (refers, referring, referred) **refer to 1** To mention. **2** To be connected with. **3** To go to someone or something for information or help. *I often refer to my dictionary.* **4** To tell a person to go to someone or something for information or help. *When I ask my teacher how to spell a word he refers me to the dictionary.*

referee[1] *noun* (referees) A person whose job is to see that a game is played according to the rules.

referee[2] *verb* (referees, refereeing, refereed) To act as a referee.

reference *noun* (references) **1** Words referring to or mentioning something. **2** A written recommendation. *a reference for a job.* **reference book** a book you can refer to for information. **with reference to** concerning, about.

referendum *noun* (referendums) An opportunity for the whole population to vote about something.

refill *verb* (refills, refilling, refilled) To fill something again.

refine *verb* (refines, refining, refined) To purify, to process a raw material such as oil or sugar to make it suitable for use. **refinery** *noun*.

refined *adjective* With good manners. **refinement** *noun*.

reflect *verb* (reflects, reflecting, reflected) **1** To throw back light. *Sunlight was reflected off the windscreens.* **reflector** *noun*. **2** To show an image as in a mirror. *Her face was reflected in the water.* **3** To consider, to think something over. **reflection** *noun*, **reflective** *adjective*.

reflex *noun* (reflexes) An action that you do without thinking. **reflex camera** one in which the scene to be photographed is viewed through the lens.

reform *verb* (reforms, reforming, reformed) To improve by putting right what is wrong. **reformer**, **reformation** *nouns*.

refrain[1] *noun* (refrains) The chorus of a song.

refrain[2] *verb* (refrains, refraining, refrained) To hold yourself back from doing something.

refresh *verb* (refreshes, refreshing, refreshed) To give new strength, to make fresh.

refreshments *noun* Something to eat or drink.

refrigerate *verb* (refrigerates, refrigerating, refrigerated) To make something cold or frozen.

refrigerator *noun* (refrigerators) An apparatus for keeping food cool and fresh.

refuel *verb* (refuels, refuelling, refuelled) To fill with more fuel.

refuge *noun* (refuges) A place of shelter.

refugee *noun* (refugees) A person who has had to leave home or country because of some emergency.

refund *verb* (refunds, refunding, refunded) To pay back money.

refuse[1] *verb* (refuses, refusing, refused) To say 'no' to something, not to do what you are asked to do. **refusal** *noun*.

refuse[2] *noun* Rubbish.

regain *verb* (regains, regaining, regained) **1** To get something back. **2** To reach somewhere again.

regal *adjective* To do with a king or queen, royal. **regally** *adverb*.

regard[1] *verb* (regards, regarding, regarded) **1** To look closely at something. **2** To consider. *Janet was regarded as our best singer.*

regard² *noun* (regards) **1** A look, a gaze. **2** Concern, care, respect. **kind regards** kind wishes.

regarding *preposition* Concerning, about.

regardless *adverb* Without paying attention, without caring.

regatta *noun* (regattas) A meeting for boat or yacht races.

regent *noun* (regents) A person who rules a country at a time when the king or queen cannot do so.

reggae *noun* A West Indian style of popular music.

regiment *noun* (regiments) A unit in the army **regimental** *adjective*.

region *noun* (regions) An area, a part of a country, a part of the world. **regional** *adjective*.

register¹ *noun* (registers) A book or file in which information is recorded. *an attendance register.*

register² *verb* (registers, registering, registered) **1** To record information officially. *to register a new car.* **2** To show, to indicate. *The thermometer registered 100 °C.* **3** *To register a letter,* to have the details recorded at the post office for safety. **registration** *noun*.

registrar *noun* (registrars) The official in charge of a registry office.

registry office A place where births, marriages, and deaths are officially recorded.

regret¹ *verb* (regrets, regretting, regretted) To be sad or sorry about something. **regretful, regrettable** *adjectives*, **regretfully, regrettably** *adverbs*.

regret² *noun* (regrets) A sorrowful feeling.

regular *adjective* **1** Evenly spaced, coming or happening at equal intervals. *the regular ticking of the clock.* **2** Nor-

mal, correct, proper. **regularly** *adverb*, **regularity** *noun*.

regulate *verb* (regulates, regulating, regulated) **1** To control. **2** To adjust something to make it work at the right speed. **regulator** *noun*.

regulation *noun* (regulations) **1** The regulating of something. **2** A rule, a law.

rehearse *verb* (rehearses, rehearsing, rehearsed) To practise something which is to be performed. **rehearsal** *noun*.

rehouse *verb* (rehouses, rehousing, rehoused) To provide somebody with a new place to live.

reign¹ *noun* (reigns) The period during which a king or queen governs a country.

reign² *verb* (reigns, reigning, reigned) To be a king or queen, to rule.

rein *noun* (reins) A narrow strap used to guide a horse.

reindeer *noun* (reindeer) A kind of deer that lives in cold regions.

reinforce *verb* (reinforces, reinforcing, reinforced) To make something stronger.

reinforcements *noun* Extra forces brought up when necessary.

reject *verb* (rejects, rejecting, rejected) **1** To throw something away. **2** To refuse to accept something. **rejection** *noun*.

rejoice *verb* (rejoices, rejoicing, rejoiced) To feel and show great happiness.

relapse[1] *verb* (relapses, relapsing, relapsed) To fall back into a former condition. *He said a few words, then relapsed into silence.*

relapse[2] *noun* Relapsing. **have a relapse** to become ill again after improving.

relate *verb* (relates, relating, related) **1** To tell a story, to give an account of something. **2** To connect in some way, to have reference to something. **be related** to belong to the same family.

relation *noun* (relations) **1** A relative. **2** A relationship.

relationship *noun* (relationships) The connection between people or things.

relative[1] *adjective* Comparative. **relatively** *adverb*.

relative[2] *noun* (relatives) A person to whom you are related.

relax *verb* (relaxes, relaxing, relaxed) **1** To become less stiff, less tense, or less strict. **2** To rest. **relaxation** *noun*.

relay *verb* (relays, relaying, relayed) To pass on a message or a radio or television broadcast. **relay race** a race in which members of a team each run part of the course.

release *verb* (releases, releasing, released) To set free, to allow out, to unfasten.

relegate *verb* (relegates, relegating, relegated) To put a team down into a lower division of a league. **relegation** *noun*.

relent *verb* (relents, relenting, relented) To become less stern, to begin to show mercy.

relentless *adjective* Without pity, apparently unending. **relentlessly** *adverb*.

relevant *adjective* Connected with the matter being discussed. **relevantly** *adverb*, **relevance** *noun*.

reliable *adjective* Trustworthy, to be relied on. **reliably** *adverb*, **reliability** *noun*.

reliant *adjective* Relying, trusting. **reliance** *noun*.

relic *noun* (relics) Something which has survived from a past age.

relief *noun* **1** The ending of pain, worry, or trouble. **2** Help, assistance, something which brings relief. **relief map** a map which shows hills and valleys.

relieve *verb* (relieves, relieving, relieved) To bring relief. **relieve someone of** to take something away from him or her.

religion *noun* (religions) A set of beliefs about God or about gods, the worship of God or gods. **religious** *adjective*, **religiously** *adverb*.

relish *verb* (relishes, relishing, relished) To enjoy.

reluctant *adjective* Unwilling to do something. **reluctantly** *adverb*, **reluctance** *noun*.

rely *verb* (relies, relying, relied) **rely on** to trust, to depend on.

remain *verb* (remains, remaining, remained) **1** To be left over. **remainder** *noun*. **2** To stay, to continue.

remains *noun* **1** Something left over. **2** Ruins. **3** A dead body.

remand *noun* **on remand** waiting in custody for trial in a court of law.

remark[1] *noun* (remarks) Something said about something or somebody.

remark[2] *verb* (remarks, remarking, remarked) To make a remark.

remarkable *adjective* Worth noticing, unusual. **remarkably** *adverb*.

remedy *verb* (remedies, remedying, remedied) To cure something, to put it right.

remember *verb* (remembers, remembering, remembered) To keep something in your mind, to be able to bring something back to your mind. **remembrance** *noun*.

remind *verb* (reminds, reminding, reminded) To help someone to remember something, to make someone think of something. **reminder** *noun*.

remnant *noun* (remnants) A small amount left over.

remorse *noun* Deep regret for something that you have done wrong. **remorseful** *adjective*.

remote *adjective* (remoter, remotest) Far away. **remotely** *adverb*, **remoteness** *noun*.

removal *noun* (removals) The removing of something. **removal van** a van for carrying furniture.

remove *verb* (removes, removing, removed) 1 To move somebody or something from one place to another. 2 To get rid of somebody or something. **removable** *adjective*, **remover** *noun*.

rend *verb* (rends, rending, rent) To tear.

render *verb* (renders, rendering, rendered) 1 To give something. 2 To perform something. 3 To change something into a new state or form. *She was rendered helpless by terror.*

rendezvous *noun* (rendezvous) 1 A meeting place. 2 An appointment to meet somebody somewhere.

renegade *noun* (renegades) A traitor.

renew *verb* (renews, renewing, renewed) To make new, to restore, to replace. **renewal** *noun*.

renounce *verb* (renounces, renouncing, renounced) To declare that you are giving something up. **renunciation** *noun*.

renovate *verb* (renovates, renovating, renovated) To restore something to good condition. **renovation** *noun*.

renown *noun* Fame.

renowned *adjective* Famous.

rent[1] *noun* (rents) A regular payment for the use of a thing or a place.

rent[2] *verb* (rents, renting, rented) To pay rent for something.

rental *noun* (rentals) Rent.

repair[1] *verb* (repairs, repairing, repaired) To mend.

repair[2] *noun* (repairs) 1 The act of repairing something. 2 Condition. *in good repair, in bad repair.*

repay *verb* (repays, repaying, repaid) To pay back. **repayment** *noun*.

repeat *verb* (repeats, repeating, repeated) 1 To say or do something again. 2 To happen again. **repeatable** *adjective*.

repeatedly *adverb* Again and again.

repel *verb* (repels, repelling, repelled) 1 To drive someone or something away. 2 To cause a feeling of dislike. **repellent** *adjective and noun*.

repent *verb* (repents, repenting, repented) To be sorry for what you have done. **repentant** *adjective*, **repentance** *noun*.

repetition *noun* 1 Repeating something. 2 (repetitions) Something that is repeated.

replace *verb* (replaces, replacing, replaced) 1 To put something back in its place. 2 To take the place of someone or something. 3 To put a new thing in the place of an old one. **replacement** *noun*.

replay *noun* (replays) 1 A football match played again after a draw. 2 The playing of a recording. *an action replay.*

replica *noun* (replicas) An exact copy.

reply[1] *noun* (replies) An answer.

reply[2] *verb* (replies, replying, replied) To answer.

report[1] *verb* (reports, reporting, reported) 1 To give an account of something, to give information about something. 2 To go to someone and say that you have come or that you are ready for work. *Competitors for the next race should report to the starter.* **report someone** to tell a person in authority what he or she has done.

report[2] *noun* (reports) **1** An account of something that has happened. **2** An explosion, a bang.

reporter *noun* (reporters) A person who collects news for a newspaper or radio or television.

repose *noun* Rest, peacefulness.

reprehensible *adjective* Deserving blame or disapproval. **reprehensibly** *adverb*.

represent *verb* (represents, representing, represented) **1** To be a picture or model of something or somebody. **2** To be an example of something. *This work represents the best I can do.* **3** To act on somebody else's behalf. *We are here to represent the school.* **representation**, **representative** *nouns*.

reprieve *verb* (reprieves, reprieving, reprieved) To postpone or cancel somebody's punishment.

reprimand[1] *verb* (reprimands, reprimanding, reprimanded) To speak severely to somebody for doing wrong.

reprimand[2] *noun* (reprimands) Words spoken in reprimanding someone.

reprisal *noun* (reprisals) An act of revenge.

reproach[1] *verb* (reproaches, reproaching, reproached) To find fault with someone, to scold someone.

reproach[2] *noun* (reproaches) Words spoken in reproaching someone.

reproduce *verb* (reproduces, reproducing, reproduced) **1** To cause something to happen again, to produce a copy of something. **2** To produce children or young animals. **reproductive** *adjective*, **reproduction** *noun*.

reptile *noun* (reptiles) A cold-blooded animal that creeps or crawls, such as a snake or a lizard.

republic *noun* (republics) A country which has an elected government but no king or queen.

repulse *verb* (repulses, repulsing, repulsed) To resist an attack, to drive back an enemy.

repulsive *adjective* Disgusting. **repulsively** *adverb*.

reputation *noun* (reputations) A widely-held opinion about somebody or something.

request[1] *verb* (requests, requesting, requested) To ask for something politely.

request[2] *noun* (requests) **1** Requesting. **2** Something requested. **request stop** a place where a bus stops when requested.

requiem *noun* (requiems) A church service for the dead.

require *verb* (requires, requiring, required) **1** To need. **2** To order someone to do something. **requirement** *noun*.

rescue *verb* (rescues, rescuing, rescued) To get someone safely away from captivity or danger. **rescuer** *noun*.

research *noun* (researches) Careful searching for information, a scientific investigation.

resemble *verb* (resembles, resembling, resembled) To be like someone or something. **resemblance** *noun*.

resent *verb* (resents, resenting, resented) To feel bitter or angry about something. **resentful** *adjective*, **resentfully** *adverb*, **resentment** *noun*.

reserve[1] *verb* (reserves, reserving, reserved) To put something aside for one particular person or for a special use, to order something. **reservation** *noun*.

reserve[2] *noun* (reserves) **1** A person or thing kept back to be used later if necessary. **2** An area which is set aside for certain people or animals to live in. **in reserve** for use when needed.

reserved *adjective* Shy, not talkative.

reservoir *noun* (reservoirs) An artificial lake where water is stored.

reside *verb* (resides, residing, resided)

To live in a particular place, to have your home there. **resident, residence** nouns.

resign verb (resigns, resigning, resigned) To give up your job or position. **resign yourself to** to decide to endure something patiently. **resignation** noun.

resist verb (resists, resisting, resisted) To oppose something, to try to stop it, to refuse to give in to it. **resistant** adjective, **resistance** noun.

resolute adjective Firm, determined. **resolutely** adverb, **resolution** noun.

resolve verb (resolves, resolving, resolved) To make a decision about something.

resort noun (resorts) A place where people go for holidays.

resound verb (resounds, resounding, resounded) To echo.

resource noun (resources) A useful or valuable person or thing.

resourceful adjective Clever at finding ways of doing things. **resourcefully** adverb, **resourcefulness** noun.

respect[1] noun 1 An admiration for somebody's good qualities or important position. 2 Serious consideration, care. We should have respect for the needs of others. 3 A detail, a particular point or aspect. It was a good game in some respects. **respectful** adjective, **respectfully** adverb.

respect[2] verb (respects, respecting, respected) To have respect for somebody or something.

respectable adjective Deserving respect or admiration. **respectably** adverb, **respectability** noun.

resplendent adjective Splendid, shining.

respond verb (responds, responding, responded) 1 To answer, to reply. 2 To react.

response noun (responses) 1 A reply. 2 A reaction.

responsible adjective 1 Having the duty of looking after something. 2 Deserving the praise or blame for something. 3 Trustworthy. a responsible boy. 4 Needing a responsible person. a responsible job. **responsibly** adverb, **responsibility** noun.

rest[1] noun (rests) 1 A period of quiet, freedom from work or other activities. 2 A support. an arm-rest. **restful** adjective, **restfully** adverb.

rest[2] verb (rests, resting, rested) 1 To have a rest. 2 To give a rest. to rest the horses. 3 To support something on something. 4 To be supported on something. 5 To remain, to be left.

rest[3] noun **the rest** the remainder, the others. Half of us got on the bus, but the rest walked.

restaurant noun (restaurants) A place where meals can be bought and eaten.

restless adjective Never still, fidgeting. **restlessly** adverb, **restlessness** noun.

restore verb (restores, restoring, restored) 1 To give or put something back. 2 To repair something, to make it as it was before. **restorer, restoration** nouns.

restrain verb (restrains, restraining, restrained) To hold back, to keep someone or something under control. **restraint** noun.

restrict verb (restricts, restricting, restricted) To keep someone or something within certain limits. **restriction** noun.

result[1] noun (results) 1 Something which happens because of certain actions or events. 2 The final score in a game, the final order of competitors in a competition. 3 The answer to a sum or problem.

result[2] verb (results, resulting, resulted) To happen because of certain other actions or events. **result in** to have as a result.

resume verb (resumes, resuming, resumed) To begin again after stopping for a time. **resumption** noun.

resurrection *noun* Rising from the dead.

retail *verb* (retails, retailing, retailed) To sell goods to the public. **retailer** *noun*.

retain *verb* (retains, retaining, retained) **1** To keep something. **2** To hold something in place.

retaliate *verb* (retaliates, retaliating, retaliated) To pay someone back for an unkind action. **retaliation** *noun*.

reticent *adjective* Not saying all that you know or feel. **reticence** *noun*.

retinue *noun* (retinues) A number of servants or attendants belonging to an important person.

retire *verb* (retires, retiring, retired) **1** To give up work, usually when you are getting older. **retirement** *noun*. **2** To move back, to withdraw. **3** To go to bed.

retort *verb* (retorts, retorting, retorted) To make a quick reply.

retrace *verb* (retraces, retracing, retraced) To go back over something again.

retreat[1] *verb* (retreats, retreating, retreated) To move back after a defeat, to move away.

retreat[2] *noun* (retreats) **1** Retreating. **2** A quiet peaceful place.

retribution *noun* A punishment that has been deserved.

retrieve *verb* (retrieves, retrieving, retrieved) To bring back, to get back. **retrievable** *adjective*.

retriever *noun* (retrievers) A kind of dog which can retrieve birds that have been shot.

retro-rocket *noun* (retro-rockets) A rocket used for manœuvring a spacecraft.

retrospect *noun* **in retrospect** as you look back in time. **retrospective** *adjective*.

return[1] *verb* (returns, returning, returned) **1** To come or go back somewhere. **2** To send back, to give back. *Please return my book soon.* **returnable** *adjective*.

return[2] *noun* (returns) Returning. **return match** a second match between two teams who have recently played each other. **return ticket** a ticket to go somewhere and come back. **many happy returns** a birthday greeting.

reunion *noun* (reunions) A coming together again after a separation.

rev *verb* (revs, revving, revved) (informal) To speed up the engine of a motor vehicle.

Rev or **Revd** Reverend.

reveal *verb* (reveals, revealing, revealed) **1** To allow something to be seen. **2** To make something known. **revelation** *noun*.

revel *verb* (revels, revelling, revelled) To make merry. **reveller, revelry** *nouns*. **revel in** to enjoy something greatly.

revenge[1] *noun* (revenges) An injury done to somebody in return for what he or she has done. **have revenge, take revenge** to perform an action of revenge, to retaliate.

revenge[2] *verb* (revenges, revenging, revenged) **revenge yourself, be revenged** to take revenge.

revenue *noun* (revenues) Income, especially the annual income of a state.

reverberation *noun* (reverberations) An echoing sound.

revere *verb* (reveres, revering, revered) To respect deeply, to honour. **reverent** *adjective*, **reverently** *adverb*, **reverence** *noun*.

Reverend noun The title of a clergy-man. *The Reverend John Mark.*

reverie noun (reveries) A day-dream.

reverse[1] adjective Opposite to what is normal or expected, reversed. **reverse gear** the gear which enables you to drive a vehicle backwards.

reverse[2] noun 1 The reverse way of doing something. 2 The reverse side or back of something. **in reverse** 1 Using reverse gear. 2 The opposite way round.

reverse[3] verb (reverses, reversing, reversed) 1 To turn something the other way round. 2 To go backwards, to drive a vehicle backwards. **reversible** adjective, **reversal** noun.

review[1] noun (reviews) 1 A survey, an inspection. 2 An account of what a person thinks about a book, or a play, or a concert. **reviewer** noun.

review[2] verb (reviews, reviewing, reviewed) 1 To examine or consider something. 2 To write a review.

revise verb (revises, revising, revised) 1 To read something through and make alterations if necessary. 2 To get ready for a test or examination by going over your work and learning it thoroughly. **revision** noun.

revive verb (revives, reviving, revived) 1 To come back to life, to become conscious again. 2 To bring someone or something back to life or con-sciousness. **revival** noun.

revolt verb (revolts, revolting, revolted) 1 To rebel. 2 To fill someone with disgust or horror.

revolution noun (revolutions) 1 A rebellion which overthrows the government. 2 A complete change of circumstances. 3 A full turn of a wheel or other round object.

revolutionary adjective 1 Rebellious. 2 Causing or encouraging great changes.

revolve verb (revolves, revolving, revolved) To turn as a wheel does.

revolver noun (revolvers) A pistol with a revolving cylinder of cartridges.

revulsion noun A sudden feeling of disgust.

reward[1] noun (rewards) Something promised or given to someone for behaving well or for doing a good deed.

reward[2] verb (rewards, rewarding, rewarded) To give someone a reward.

rewrite verb (rewrites, rewriting, rewrote, rewritten) To write some-thing again.

rheumatism noun A disease causing pain and swollen joints. **rheumatic** adjective.

rhinoceros noun (rhinoceroses) A large animal with either one or two horns on its nose.

rhododendron noun (rhododendrons) A flowering evergreen shrub.

rhubarb noun A plant with large leaves whose stalks are eaten as fruit.

rhyme[1] noun (rhymes) 1 A similarity of sound in the endings of words, as in *wall* and *fall*, or *fix* and *tricks*. 2 A short rhyming poem.

rhyme[2] verb (rhymes, rhyming, rhymed) To have rhymes at the ends of words or lines.

rhythm noun (rhythms) 1 A regular pattern of sounds or movements, as in the ticking of a clock or the mov-ing of a dancer's feet. 2 A regular beat or pattern in music or poetry. **rhyth-mic**, **rhythmical** adjectives, **rhythmi-cally** adverb.

rib noun (ribs) One of the curved bones round the upper part of the body.

ribbon noun (ribbons) A narrow length of silk or other material.

rice *noun* A white grain used as food.

rich *adjective* (richer, richest) **1** Having a lot of money or property. **2** Splendid, costly. **3** Specially full of goodness and colour. *rich creamy milk.* **richly** *adverb*, **richness** *noun*.

riches *noun* Wealth.

rick *noun* (ricks) A large neat stack of hay.

rickety *adjective* Unsteady, liable to fall down.

rickshaw *noun* (rickshaws) A two-wheeled carriage pulled by a person.

ricochet *verb* (ricochets, ricocheting, ricocheted) To bounce off something. *The bullet ricocheted off the rocks.*

rid *verb* (rids, ridding, rid) To make yourself free of something. **get rid of** to remove. **riddance** *noun*.

riddle *noun* (riddles) **1** A puzzling question. **2** A sieve.

ride¹ *verb* (rides, riding, rode, ridden) **1** To sit on and be carried along on something such as a horse or a bicycle. **2** To travel in a vehicle. **rider** *noun*.

ride² *noun* (rides) Riding, a time spent in riding.

ridge *noun* (ridges) A raised line where two sloping surfaces meet. *the ridge of a roof.*

ridicule *verb* (ridicules, ridiculing, ridiculed) To make fun of somebody or something.

ridiculous *adjective* Absurd, deserving to be laughed at. **ridiculously** *adverb*.

rifle *noun* (rifles) A kind of gun fired from the shoulder.

rift *noun* (rifts) A split, a crack.

rig¹ *verb* (rigs, rigging, rigged) To provide a ship with sails and rigging. **rig up** to put something up, to make something out of available materials.

rig² *noun* (rigs) **1** A framework of girders used to support drilling equipment. *an oil rig.* **2** Equipment for CB radio.

rigging *noun* The ropes used to support a ship's masts and sails.

right¹ *adjective* Of or on the same side as the right hand, which is the hand which most people use when writing.

right² *noun* The right-hand side. *In most European countries people drive on the right.*

right³ *adjective* **1** Good, proper, just. *It is not right to steal.* **2** Correct, true. *What's the right time?* **right angle** an angle of 90 degrees, like any of the angles in a square. **rightly** *adverb*.

right⁴ *noun* **1** That which is right. **2** Something you are allowed to do or have because it is legal or normal. **in the right** with the law on your side. **rightful** *adjective*.

right⁵ *adverb* **1** Straight, directly. *Go right on.* **2** Completely. *Turn right round.* **3** Exactly. *Stand right in the middle.* **4** *It serves you right*, it is just what you deserve.

righteous *adjective* Law-abiding, virtuous. **righteously** *adverb*, **righteousness** *noun*.

rigid *adjective* **1** Stiff, not able to be bent. **2** Strict, harsh. **rigidly** *adverb*.

rim *noun* (rims) The outer edge of a wheel or other round object.

rind *noun* (rinds) A hard outer skin or covering.

ring¹ *noun* (rings) **1** A circle. **2** Any object shaped like a circle. **3** The space where a circus performs. **4** A platform where boxing matches are fought. **ring road** a road which enables traffic to go round a town.

ring² *verb* (rings, ringing, ringed) To put or make a ring round something.

ring³ *verb* (rings, ringing, rang, rung) **1** To cause a bell to sound. **2** To make a sound like a bell. **3** To make a telephone call.

ringleader *noun* (ringleaders) The leader of a gang, a person who encourages others to do mischief.

rink *noun* (rinks) A place made for ice-skating.

rinse *verb* (rinses, rinsing, rinsed) To wash something in clean water.

riot[1] *noun* (riots) Noisy, violent behaviour by a crowd.

riot[2] *verb* (riots, rioting, rioted) To take part in a riot. **riotous** *adjective*, **riotously** *adverb*, **rioter** *noun*.

rip *verb* (rips, ripping, ripped) To tear violently.

ripe *adjective* (riper, ripest) Ready for harvesting, ready for eating. *ripe fruit.* **ripeness** *noun*.

ripen *verb* (ripens, ripening, ripened) **1** To become ripe. **2** To make ripe.

ripple *verb* (ripples, rippling, rippled) To make tiny waves. *The surface of the pond rippled in the breeze.*

rise[1] *verb* (rises, rising, rose, risen) **1** To get up. **2** To go upwards. **3** To rebel.

rise[2] *noun* (rises) **1** An upward slope. **2** An increase in a wage or a price.

rising *noun* (risings) A rebellion.

risk[1] *noun* (risks) The chance of meeting danger or of suffering injury or loss. **risky** *adjective*.

risk[2] *verb* (risks, risking, risked) To take a risk.

risotto *noun* (risottos) An Italian food made with rice.

rissole *noun* (rissoles) A fried ball of minced meat with other ingredients.

rite *noun* (rites) A ceremony.

ritual *noun* (rituals) A rite which is regularly repeated.

rival[1] *noun* (rivals) A competitor, a person who is competing with someone else. **rivalry** *noun*.

rival[2] *verb* (rivals, rivalling, rivalled) To be a rival.

river *noun* (rivers) A stream of water flowing into the sea or into a lake or into another river.

rivet *noun* (rivets) A fastening for metal plates.

road *noun* (roads) A level way with a hard surface for the use of traffic.

roadworthy *adjective* Safe to be used on public roads.

roam *verb* (roams, roaming, roamed) To wander.

roar *verb* (roars, roaring, roared) To make a loud deep sound, to shout noisily. **roaring trade** a brisk, successful trade.

roast *verb* (roasts, roasting, roasted, roast) To cook in an oven or over a fire.

rob *verb* (robs, robbing, robbed) To steal something from somebody or somewhere. **robber, robbery** *nouns*.

robe *noun* (robes) A long loose garment.

robin *noun* (robins) A small bird with a red breast.

robot *noun* (robots) **1** An automatic machine, especially in a factory. **2** A machine made to act like a person.

robust *adjective* Strong and healthy. **robustly** *adverb*.

rock[1] *noun* (rocks) **1** A large stone. **2** A large mass of stone. *The house is built on solid rock.* **3** A kind of hard sweet made in the shape of a stick.

rock[2] *verb* (rocks, rocking, rocked) **1** To move gently to and fro. **2** To sway, to shake.

rock[3] *noun* A kind of popular music.

rock-climbing *noun* Climbing rocky hills as a sport.

rockery *noun* (rockeries) A part of a garden where plants grow between large stones.

rocket *noun* (rockets) **1** A firework or signal which shoots high into the air. **2** A tube-shaped device filled with fast-burning fuel which is used to launch a missile or a spacecraft.

rock-garden *noun* (rock-gardens) A rockery.

rocking-chair *noun* (rocking-chairs) A chair which can be rocked by a person sitting in it.

rocking-horse *noun* (rocking-horses) A toy horse on which a child can sit and rock to and fro.

rocky *adjective* (rockier, rockiest) **1** Full of rocks, like rocks. **2** Unsteady.

rod *noun* (rods) A straight slender stick or bar.

rode *See* ride¹

rodent *noun* (rodents) An animal that gnaws things, such as rats and squirrels.

rodeo *noun* (rodeos) A display by cowboys of horse-riding and rounding up cattle.

roe *noun* (roes) A mass of eggs from a fish.

rogue *noun* (rogues) A rascal. **roguish** *adjective*, **roguishly** *adverb*, **roguery** *noun*.

role *noun* (roles) An actor's part in a play or film.

roll¹ *noun* (rolls) **1** A piece of paper or other material curled into a tube shape. **2** A small bun-shaped loaf of bread. **3** A list of names, a register.

roll² *verb* (rolls, rolling, rolled) **1** To turn over and over like a ball or wheel running along the ground. **2** To turn something over and over to make a ball or a tube shape. **3** To make something flat and smooth by rolling a rounded object over it. *We rolled the cricket pitch.* **4** To sway from side to side. **5** To make a long drawn out rumbling or rattling round. *The drums rolled.*

roller *noun* (rollers) A cylinder-shaped tool or device for rolling.

roller-skate *noun* (roller-skates) A set of wheels fixed under a shoe or boot for skating on a smooth surface.

rolling-pin *noun* (rolling-pins) A long cylinder for rolling pastry.

rolling-stock *noun* Railway wagons and coaches.

Roman *adjective* Of Rome, from Rome.

Roman Catholic Belonging to that part of the Christian Church which has the Pope as its head.

romance *noun* (romances) **1** The relationship between two people who are in love with each other. **2** A love story. **romantic** *adjective*.

romp *verb* (romps, romping, romped) To play rather roughly and noisily.

rompers *noun* A child's garment made in one piece.

roof *noun* (roofs) The top covering of a building, shelter, or vehicle.

roofed *adjective* Covered with a roof. *roofed with tiles*, having a roof made of tiles.

rook *noun* (rooks) **1** A large black bird. **2** A piece in chess, also called a castle.

room *noun* (rooms) **1** A division of a building with walls and a ceiling and a floor. **2** Space for somebody or something. *Is there room for me?*

roomy *adjective* (roomier, roomiest) Having plenty of space.

roost *noun* (roosts) A bird's resting place.

rooster *noun* (roosters) A male farmyard fowl.

root *noun* (roots) **1** The part of a plant which grows under the ground. **2** A basis or source from which something grows. **take root** to grow roots, to become established.

rope[1] *noun* (ropes) A thick cord made of twisted strands.

rope[2] *verb* (ropes, roping, roped) To tie something with a rope.

rope-ladder *noun* (rope-ladders) A ladder with sides made of rope.

rosary *noun* (rosaries) A string of beads used while saying prayers.

rose[1] *See* **rise**[1]

rose[2] *noun* (roses) A beautiful flower with a thorny stem.

rosette *noun* (rosettes) A kind of large circular badge.

rosewood *noun* A dark tropical timber.

rosy *adjective* (rosier, rosiest) 1 Pink. 2 Cheerful. **rosily** *adverb*, **rosiness** *noun*.

rot[1] *verb* (rots, rotting, rotted) To become soft or crumbly and unfit for use, to go bad.

rot[2] *noun* 1 Rotting in wood or other material. 2 (informal) Nonsense.

rotary *adjective* Rotating.

rotate *verb* (rotates, rotating, rotated) 1 To turn round as a wheel does. 2 To come round again and again, to come round in turn. **rotation** *noun*.

rotor *noun* (rotors) The large horizontal propeller on a helicopter.

rotten *adjective* 1 Rotted, unfit for use. *rotten wood.* 2 Nasty and unfriendly. *a rotten trick.* **rottenness** *noun*.

rough *adjective* (rougher, roughest) 1 Uneven, not smooth. *a rough road.* 2 Stormy, violent. *a rough wind.* 3 Harsh, unpleasant. *a rough voice.* 4 Done or made quickly and not exact. *a rough sketch, a rough guess.* **roughly** *adverb*, **roughness** *noun*.

roughen *verb* (roughens, roughening, roughened) 1 To make something rougher. 2 To become rougher.

round[1] *adjective* (rounder, roundest) Shaped like a circle or a ball. **roundness** *noun*.

round[2] *noun* (rounds) 1 A round shape. 2 One stage in a competition or contest. 3 A series of visits like those made by a doctor, postman, or milkman. 4 A whole slice of bread, or a sandwich made from two whole slices. 5 A single bullet or shell.

round[3] *preposition* 1 Surrounding. *There's a hedge round the garden.* 2 To every part of. *We walked round the garden.* 3 In a curve about. *The earth travels round the sun.* 4 Beyond. *Our house is round the corner.*

round[4] *adverb* 1 In a circle. *A wheel spins round.* 2 By a curving or bending route. *Go round to the back.* 3 In a new direction. *She looked round when I called.* 4 In every direction. *I've looked round but I can't see it.* 5 To someone's home or to the place where someone is. *I'll come round after tea.*

roundabout[1] *adjective* Not going the shortest way.

roundabout[2] *noun* (roundabouts) 1 A road junction where vehicles must go round a circle. 2 An amusement at a fun-fair.

rounders *noun* A team game played with a bat and ball.

Roundhead *noun* (Roundheads) An opponent of King Charles I.

roundish *adjective* Nearly round.

round-shouldered *adjective* With shoulders permanently bent forwards.

rouse *verb* (rouses, rousing, roused) 1 To wake. 2 To make somebody more energetic or fierce.

rout *verb* (routs, routing, routed) To defeat the enemy and make them run away.

route *noun* (routes) A way from one place to another.

routine *noun* (routines) A settled and regular way of doing things.

rove *verb* (roves, roving, roved) To roam, to wander. **rover** *noun*.

row¹ *noun* (rows) A number of people or things in a line.

row² *verb* (rows, rowing, rowed) To move a boat along with oars. **rower** *noun*.

row³ *noun* (rows) **1** A tiresome and disturbing noise. **2** A noisy or violent quarrel.

rowdy *adjective* (rowdier, rowdiest) Rough and noisy. **rowdily** *adverb*.

rowing-boat *noun* (rowing-boats) A boat moved along by oars.

royal *adjective* To do with a king or queen. **royally** *adverb*, **royalty** *noun*.

rub *verb* (rubs, rubbing, rubbed) To move something backwards and forwards on something else. *The cat rubbed her back against my legs.* **rub out** to remove something by rubbing.

rubber *noun* (rubbers) **1** A substance used to make tyres, bouncing balls, elastic bands, and other products. **2** A piece of rubber or plastic for rubbing out pencil marks. **rubbery** *adjective*.

rubbish *noun* **1** Waste material. **2** Nonsense.

rubble *noun* Broken bits of brick, stone, or rock.

ruby *noun* (rubies) A deep red jewel.

rucksack *noun* (rucksacks) A bag worn strapped on the back by walkers and climbers.

rudder *noun* (rudders) A flat hinged piece at the back of a ship or aircraft, used for steering.

ruddy *adjective* (ruddier, ruddiest) Red and healthy-looking.

rude *adjective* (ruder, rudest) **1** Not polite, not respectful. **2** Not decent,

vulgar. **rudely** *adverb*, **rudeness** *noun*.

rueful *adjective* Sorrowful. **ruefully** *adverb*.

ruffian *noun* (ruffians) A violent brutal person.

ruffle *verb* (ruffles, ruffling, ruffled) To disturb the smoothness of something.

rug *noun* (rugs) **1** A thick blanket. **2** A floor mat.

rugby *noun* A kind of football in which the ball may be carried.

rugged *adjective* Rough, uneven.

rugger *noun* (informal) Rugby football.

ruin¹ *noun* (ruins) **1** Destruction, serious damage. **2** The remains of an old building.

ruin² *verb* (ruins, ruining, ruined) To spoil something completely. **ruinous** *adjective*, **ruinously** *adverb*.

rule¹ *noun* (rules) **1** A law, a regulation, a custom which ought to be followed. **2** Government. **as a rule** usually.

rule² *verb* (rules, ruling, ruled) **1** To govern. **2** To make a decision. *The referee ruled that the player was offside.* **rule a line** to draw a straight line with the help of a ruler.

ruler *noun* (rulers) **1** A person who governs. **2** A strip of wood or metal, often marked with inches or centimetres, used for measuring or drawing straight lines.

rum *noun* A strong alcoholic drink.

rumble *verb* (rumbles, rumbling, rumbled) To make a deep continuous sound like thunder.

rummage *verb* (rummages, rummaging, rummaged) To turn things over and make them untidy while looking for something.

rummy *noun* A card game.

rumour *noun* (rumours) Something which is passed around as news but which may not be true.

rump *noun* (rumps) The tail end of an animal.

rumple *verb* (rumples, rumpling, rumpled) To crease, to crumple.

rumpus *noun* (informal) A noisy disturbance.

run[1] *verb* (runs, running, ran, run) **1** To move with quick steps. **2** To go, to travel. *The bus runs every hour.* **3** To flow. *Blood ran down his face.* **4** To manage something, to look after it. *Alan's uncle ran a grocery business.* **5** *to run a computer program,* to set it working. **run a risk** to take a chance. **run over** to knock someone down with a car or other moving vehicle. **run out of something** to have none left when you need it.

run[2] *noun* (runs) **1** A time spent running. *to go for a run.* **2** An enclosure for animals. *a chicken run.* **3** A series of events coming together. *a run of good luck.* **4** A point scored in cricket when the batsmen run between the wickets. **5** A line running up or down a stocking from a hole or flaw.

runaway *adjective* Escaped, hard to stop.

rung[1] *See* **ring**[3]

rung[2] *noun* (rungs) One of the cross-bars used as steps on a ladder.

runner *noun* (runners) **1** A person or animal that runs, especially in a race. **2** A long strip on which something moves. *the runners of a sledge.* **runner bean** a kind of climbing bean.

runny *adjective* (runnier, runniest) Flowing like a liquid.

runway *noun* (runways) A track which aircraft use when taking off or landing.

rural *adjective* Belonging to the countryside.

ruse *noun* (ruses) A deceitful trick.

rush[1] *verb* (rushes, rushing, rushed) **1** To move with force and speed. **2** To capture something by rushing. **3** To make somebody or something rush. *Don't rush me.*

rush[2] *noun* (rushes) The act of rushing. **rush hour** a busy time of day when people are travelling to or from work.

rush[3] *noun* (rushes) A plant which grows in or near water.

rusk *noun* (rusks) A kind of biscuit for a baby.

Russian *adjective* Of or from Russia.

rust[1] *noun* The reddish-brown substance which forms on iron when it has been wet.

rust[2] *verb* (rusts, rusting, rusted) **1** To become rusty. **2** To make something become rusty.

rustic *adjective* Rural.

rustle *verb* (rustles, rustling, rustled) **1** To make a gentle sound such as that of a light wind through trees. **2** To steal cattle or other animals. **rustler** *noun.*

rusty *adjective* (rustier, rustiest) Covered with rust.

rut *noun* (ruts) A groove made by the passing of the wheels of vehicles over the ground.

ruthless *adjective* Cruel, without pity. **ruthlessly** *adverb*, **ruthlessness** *noun.*

rye *noun* A kind of cereal plant.

Ss

sabbath *noun* (sabbaths) A weekly day of rest and prayer.

sabotage *noun* Damage done on purpose to machinery or equipment.

sabre *noun* (sabres) A sword with a slightly curved blade.

saccharine *noun* A sweet substance used instead of sugar.

sack[1] *noun* (sacks) A large oblong bag made of strong material. **get the sack** (informal) to be dismissed from your job.

sack[2] *verb* (sacks, sacking, sacked) To dismiss someone from his or her job.

sacking *noun* Rough cloth from which sacks are made.

sacrament *noun* (sacraments) An important Christian ceremony, such as Baptism or Holy Communion.

sacred *adjective* Holy, religious.

sacrifice[1] *noun* (sacrifices) **1** The killing of a person or animal as an offering to a god. **2** The giving up of something valuable or enjoyable for some special purpose. **3** Something sacrificed.

sacrifice[2] *verb* (sacrifices, sacrificing, sacrificed) To offer or give something as a sacrifice.

sacrilege *noun* Disrespectful treatment of something sacred. **sacrilegious** *adjective*.

sad *adjective* (sadder, saddest) Unhappy, sorrowful. **sadly** *adverb*, **sadness** *noun*.

sadden *verb* (saddens, saddening, saddened) To make someone sad.

saddle[1] *noun* (saddles) A seat for the rider of a horse or a bicycle.

saddle[2] *verb* (saddles, saddling, saddled) To put a saddle on a horse.

sadhu *noun* (sadhus) A Hindu holy man.

sadist *noun* (sadists) A person who enjoys being cruel. **sadistic** *adjective*, **sadistically** *adverb*, **sadism** *noun*.

safari *noun* (safaris) An expedition to see or hunt big game. **safari park** a park where big wild animals are kept.

safe[1] *adjective* (safer, safest) **1** Free from risk or danger, secure. **2** Not dangerous. **safely** *adverb*.

safe[2] *noun* (safes) A strong box or cupboard in which valuables can be locked for safety.

safeguard *verb* (safeguards, safeguarding, safeguarded) To protect.

safety *noun* Being safe, freedom from danger.

safety-belt *noun* (safety-belts) A seat-belt.

safety-pin *noun* (safety-pins) A pin looped over with a clip to guard the point.

safety-valve *noun* (safety-valves) A device for preventing pressure rising above danger level.

sag *verb* (sags, sagging, sagged) To curve down in the middle because of weight or pressure.

saga *noun* (sagas) **1** An old story of heroes. **2** A long story.

sage *noun* A kind of herb used for flavouring things.

said *See* **say**

sail[1] *noun* (sails) **1** A sheet of material hung from a mast to catch the wind and move a boat forwards. **2** An arm of a windmill. **3** A trip in a boat.

sail[2] *verb* (sails, sailing, sailed) **1** To be moved along by a sail. **2** To start a voyage, to make a voyage. *When does the ship sail?* **3** To control a boat.

sailor *noun* (sailors) A member of a navy or of a ship's crew.

saint *noun* (saints) A holy or very good person. **saintly** *adverb*, **saintliness** *noun*.

sake *noun* (sakes) **for the sake of** in order to please or help someone or something. *Do it for my sake*, do it to help me.

salaam *noun* (salaams) A Muslim greeting, the Arabic for 'peace'.

salad *noun* (salads) A mixture of raw or cold vegetables. **salad cream, salad dressing** sauces used on salads. **fruit salad** a mixture of pieces of fruit.

salary *noun* (salaries) Regular pay. *a salary of £19,000 a year.*

sale *noun* (sales) **1** The selling of something. **on sale, for sale** to be sold. **2** A time when goods are sold at lower prices.

salesman, saleswoman *nouns* (salesmen, saleswomen) A person whose job it is to sell things. **salesmanship** *noun*.

saliva *noun* The liquid which is always present in a person's mouth.

salmon *noun* (salmon) A large fish with pink flesh.

saloon *noun* (saloons) **1** A car seating four or five people, with a fixed roof. **2** A bar, a public room.

salt¹ *noun* (salts) The substance which gives sea water its taste and which is used for flavouring food.

salt² *verb* (salts, salting, salted) To use salt to flavour or preserve food.

salt-cellar *noun* (salt-cellars) A small dish or pot for salt.

salty *adjective* (saltier, saltiest) Tasting of salt.

salute¹ *noun* (salutes) Something done to welcome somebody or to show respect, especially by raising your hand smartly to your forehead.

salute² *verb* (salutes, saluting, saluted) To make a salute.

salvage *verb* (salvages, salvaging, salvaged) **1** To save waste or damaged material which can be used again. **2** To save a damaged ship.

salvation *noun* The saving of someone or something.

salvo *noun* (salvoes) The firing of a number of guns at the same time.

Samaritan *noun* (Samaritans) Someone who helps you in time of trouble.

same¹ *adjective* **1** Not different, being of one kind, value, size, or quality. *They were wearing the same uniform.* **2** Not changed. *The tickets are still at the same prices.*

same² *pronoun* **the same** the same thing. *We both had the same for dinner.* **all the same** in spite of that.

sameness *noun* Dullness, monotony.

samosa *noun* (samosas) An Indian triangular pastry.

sample *noun* (samples) A specimen, a part of something used for testing.

sanctuary *noun* (sanctuaries) A place of safety. *a bird sanctuary.*

sand *noun* Tiny grains of stone such as are found on the seashore or in deserts. **sands** a sandy area.

sandal *noun* (sandals) A kind of shoe with straps that go round the foot.

sandbag *noun* (sandbags) A sack filled with sand used as a defence.

sand-dune *noun* (sand-dunes) A hill of sand.

sandpaper *noun* Glass-paper.

sand-pit *noun* (sand-pits) A shallow hole with sand for children to play in.

sand-storm *noun* (sand-storms) A storm in which clouds of sand are blown in the wind.

sandwich *noun* (sandwiches) Two slices of bread with meat, cheese, or some other filling between them.

sandy *adjective* **1** Covered with sand. **2** Coloured like sand, light brown.

sane *adjective* (saner, sanest) Healthy in the mind, not mad. **sanely** *adverb*, **sanity** *noun*.

sang *See* **sing**

sangat *noun* (sangats) A congregation of Sikhs.

sanitary *adjective* Free from dirt and germs. **sanitary towel** a pad worn during menstruation.

sanitation *noun* Drainage and other arrangements for making things sanitary.

sank *See* **sink**¹

sap¹ *noun* The liquid that rises in a plant.

sap² *verb* (saps, sapping, sapped) To weaken someone's energy and strength.

sapling *noun* (saplings) A young tree.

sapphire *noun* (sapphires) A blue jewel.

sarcastic *adjective* Amusing but likely

to hurt someone's feelings. **sarcast-ically** adverb, **sarcasm** noun.

sardine noun (sardines) A small fish, usually sold in tins.

sari noun (saris) A garment worn by Indian women.

sash noun (sashes) A strip of cloth worn round the waist or over one shoulder.

sat See **sit**

Satan noun The Devil.

satchel noun (satchels) A bag which hangs from the shoulder, for carrying books.

satellite noun (satellites) **1** A small planet which moves in orbit round a larger one. **2** A spacecraft travelling in orbit round a planet.

satin noun A material with a silky, shiny front side and a dull back.

satire noun A piece of writing which ridicules someone or something. **satirical** adjective, **satirist** noun.

satisfactory adjective Adequate, good enough. **satisfactorily** adverb.

satisfy verb (satisfies, satisfying, satisfied) **1** To make someone pleased or contented. **2** To be enough for someone's needs. **3** To get rid of someone's doubts. **satisfaction** noun.

satsuma noun (satsumas) A kind of small sweet orange.

saturate verb (saturates, saturating, saturated) To soak thoroughly. **saturation** noun.

Saturday noun (Saturdays) The last day of the week.

sauce noun **1** (sauces) A liquid flavouring for food. *tomato sauce.* **2** (informal) Cheek, impertinence.

saucepan noun (saucepans) A metal cooking pan with a lid and a handle.

saucer noun (saucers) A small curved dish on which you put a cup.

saucy adjective (saucier, sauciest) Cheeky, cheerfully rude. **saucily** adverb, **sauciness** noun.

sauna noun (saunas) A kind of steam bath.

saunter verb (saunters, sauntering, sauntered) To walk in a leisurely way.

sausage noun (sausages) Minced meat and other ingredients in a tube of skin.

sausage-roll noun (sausage-rolls) A piece of sausage cooked in a roll of pastry.

savage[1] adjective **1** Fierce, cruel. **2** Not civilized. **savagely** adverb, **savagery** noun.

savage[2] noun (savages) An uncivilized person.

save verb (saves, saving, saved) **1** To make safe. *The sailors were saved from the wreck.* **2** To keep safe. *His seat-belt saved him.* **3** To keep money or other things for use later. **4** To avoid wasting something. *You'll save time if you go by bus.* **5** To prevent a ball going into the goal. **saver** noun.

savings noun Money saved up.

saviour noun (saviours) A person who saves somebody or something.

savoury adjective Tasty but not sweet.

saw[1] See **see**

saw[2] noun (saws) A cutting tool with a zigzag edge.

saw[3] verb (saws, sawing, sawn, sawed) To cut with a saw.

sawdust noun Wood dust produced when sawing.

saxophone *noun* (saxophones) A kind of wind instrument.

say *verb* (says, saying, said) **1** To produce words with the voice, to speak. **2** To give an opinion.

saying *noun* (sayings) A well-known remark, a proverb.

scab *noun* (scabs) A crust of dried blood which forms over a wound.

scabbard *noun* (scabbards) A sheath for a sword or dagger.

scaffolding *noun* A structure of poles and planks for workers to stand on.

scald *verb* (scalds, scalding, scalded) **1** To injure with hot liquid or steam. **2** To clean something with boiling water.

scale¹ *noun* (scales) **1** The series of marks used for measuring on a ruler, thermometer, or similar instrument. **2** A system of units for measuring. *the metric scale.* **3** A series of musical notes going up or down one step at a time. **4** Proportion, relative size. *The scale of the map is one centimetre to the kilometre*, one centimetre on the map represents one kilometre on the ground. **5** Size. *on a large scale.*

scale² *verb* (scales, scaling, scaled) To climb.

scale³ *noun* (scales) One of the thin flakes covering the skin of fish and other creatures. **scaly** *adjective*.

scales *noun* An instrument for weighing.

scalp¹ *noun* (scalps) The skin on the top of the head where the hair grows.

scalp² *verb* (scalps, scalping, scalped) To cut off someone's scalp.

scalpel *noun* (scalpels) A surgeon's knife.

scamp *noun* (scamps) A rascal.

scamper *verb* (scampers, scampering, scampered) To run hastily or playfully.

scampi *noun* A seafood like large shrimps.

scan *verb* (scans, scanning, scanned) To look at all parts of a thing. **scanner** *noun*.

scandal *noun* (scandals) **1** A shameful or disgraceful action. **2** Unkind gossip. **scandalous** *adjective*, **scandalously** *adverb*.

Scandinavian *adjective* Of or from Scandinavia, of or from Norway, Sweden, Finland, or Denmark.

scanty *adjective* (scantier, scantiest) Barely enough, small. **scantily** *adverb*, **scantiness** *noun*.

scapegoat *noun* (scapegoats) A person blamed for somebody else's wrongdoing.

scar¹ *noun* (scars) A mark that remains after injury or damage.

scar² *verb* (scars, scarring, scarred) To mark with a scar.

scarce *adjective* (scarcer, scarcest) Rare, in short supply. **scarcity** *noun*.

scarcely *adverb* Hardly, barely.

scare *verb* (scares, scaring, scared) To frighten.

scarecrow *noun* (scarecrows) A figure dressed in old clothes and set up in a field to scare birds off the crops.

scarf *noun* (scarves) A strip of material you wear round the neck.

scarlet *adjective* Bright red.

scary *adjective* (informal) Frightening.

scatter *verb* (scatters, scattering, scattered) **1** To throw things in various directions. **2** To move away in various directions.

scatter-brained *adjective* Careless, liable to do things in a disorganized way.

scavenger *noun* (scavengers) An animal or bird that feeds on refuse.

scene *noun* (scenes) **1** The place where something has happened. *the scene of a crime.* **2** An exciting, noisy, or quarrelsome happening. *Dad made a scene because the potatoes were burnt.* **3** Part of a play or film. **4** A view. **5** (informal) A way of behaving, something you like. *Cricket isn't my scene.*

scenery *noun* **1** A view of the countryside. **2** Things used to set a scene on a stage.

scenic *adjective* Picturesque, with attractive scenery.

scent¹ *noun* (scents) **1** Smell. **2** A liquid with a beautiful smell.

scent² *verb* (scents, scenting, scented) **1** To smell. **2** To give something a beautiful smell.

sceptical *adjective* Not ready to believe things.

schedule *noun* (schedules) A timetable, a list of details.

scheme¹ *noun* (schemes) A plan.

scheme² *verb* (schemes, scheming, schemed) To make plans, to plot.

scholar *noun* (scholars) **1** A pupil. **2** A person who studies a great deal.

scholarship *noun* (scholarships) An award made to someone to help to pay his or her school or college fees.

school *noun* (schools) **1** A place where children are educated. **2** All the children who attend a particular school. **3** The time when pupils should be at school. **4** A place or organization for teaching. *a driving school.* **5** A large number of whales or fish swimming together.

schoolchild *noun* (schoolchildren) A pupil in a school. **schoolboy, schoolgirl** *nouns*.

schoolteacher *noun* (schoolteachers) A teacher in a school. **schoolmaster, schoolmistress** *nouns*.

schooner *noun* (schooners) A kind of sailing ship.

science *noun* (sciences) **1** Knowledge which has been collected and arranged by people who observe things carefully and make experiments. **2** A particular branch of science such as astronomy, biology, or geology. **scientific** *adjective*, **scientifically** *adverb*. **science fiction** stories about space travel or other exciting scientific developments.

scientist *noun* (scientists) An expert in science.

scissors *noun* A cutting instrument with two hinged blades.

scoff *verb* (scoffs, scoffing, scoffed) To mock or jeer at something.

scold *verb* (scolds, scolding, scolded) To speak crossly to someone because he or she has done wrong.

scone *noun* (scones) A small bun.

scoop¹ *noun* (scoops) **1** A device like a shovel or ladle. *an ice-cream scoop.* **2** The amount taken up in one scooping movement.

scoop² *verb* (scoops, scooping, scooped) To pick up something or make a hole with a scoop.

scooter *noun* (scooters) **1** A child's toy with two wheels and a platform for the feet. **2** A kind of small motor cycle.

scope *noun* The opportunity or ability to do something.

scorch *verb* (scorches, scorching, scorched) To darken the surface of something by burning or heating.

score¹ *noun* (scores) **1** The number of points made in a game. **2** Twenty.

score² *verb* (scores, scoring, scored) **1** To make a score. **2** To keep a record of a score. **scorer** *noun*. **3** To scratch the surface of something.

score-board *noun* (score-boards) A board showing the score in a game.

scorn¹ *noun* A low opinion of someone or something, treating someone or something as worthless or not deserving respect.

scorn² *verb* (scorns, scorning, scorned) To feel or show scorn for someone or something.

scornful *adjective* Feeling or showing scorn. **scornfully** *adverb*.

scorpion *noun* (scorpions) A kind of spider with a dangerous sting in the tail.

Scot *noun* (Scots) A person from Scotland.

Scottish *adjective* Of or from Scotland.

scoundrel *noun* (scoundrels) A wicked person.

scour *verb* (scours, scouring, scoured) **1** To rub a thing clean and bright. *to scour a saucepan*. **2** To search every part of a place thoroughly.

scourge *noun* (scourges) A heavy whip.

scout¹ *noun* (scouts) A person sent out to get information. **Scout** a member of the Scout Association, an organization for boys and girls.

scout² *verb* (scouts, scouting, scouted) To act as a scout.

scowl *verb* (scowls, scowling, scowled) To have a bad-tempered look on your face.

scraggy *adjective* Thin and bony.

scramble¹ *verb* (scrambles, scrambling, scrambled) **1** To climb or crawl awkwardly. **2** To struggle with others who all want the same thing. **scrambled eggs** eggs beaten with milk and cooked.

scramble² *noun* (scrambles) **1** The

action of scrambling. **2** A motor-cycle race over rough country.

scrap¹ *adjective* Rubbish, waste. *scrap metal*.

scrap² *noun* (scraps) **1** A small piece of something. **2** (informal) A fight.

scrap³ *verb* (scraps, scrapping, scrapped) **1** To throw away useless things. **2** (informal) To fight.

scrap-book *noun* (scrap-books) A book in which you stick pictures, newspaper cuttings, and so on.

scrape¹ *verb* (scrapes, scraping, scraped) **1** To rub with something hard or sharp. **2** To do something by scraping. *I scraped the mud off my shoes*. **3** To damage by scraping. *The gate-post scraped the car*. **4** To manage with difficulty to do something. *I scraped into the first team this week*. **scrape things together** to collect them together with difficulty.

scrape² *noun* (scrapes) **1** The act or sound of scraping. **2** A place which has been scraped. **3** An awkward or dangerous situation.

scrappy *adjective* Made of scraps.

scratch¹ *verb* (scratches, scratching, scratched) **1** To mark or damage a surface with something sharp. **2** To scrape with claws or finger-nails.

scratch² *noun* (scratches) **1** A mark caused by scratching. **2** The act or sound of scratching. **scratchy** *adjective*.

scrawl *verb* (scrawls, scrawling, scrawled) To write hurriedly and untidily.

scream¹ *noun* (screams) A loud shrill cry.

scream² *verb* (screams, screaming, screamed) To give a scream.

scree *noun* Loose stones covering a mountain side.

screech *verb* (screeches, screeching, screeched) To make a harsh shrill sound.

screen¹ *noun* (screens) **1** The piece of

glass on which TV pictures or the output from a computer may be displayed. **2** A smooth surface on which films or slides may be projected. **3** A framework covered with material used to protect people from draughts or heat, or to hide something. *a fire screen.* **4** Anything which gives shelter or protection. *a smoke screen.*

screen² *verb* (screens, screening, screened) **1** To shelter, to hide from view. **2** To show pictures on a screen.

screw¹ *noun* (screws) **1** A device like a nail with a spiral groove cut into it. **2** A twist, a turn. **3** A propeller.

screw² *verb* (screws, screwing, screwed) **1** To use a screw to fix something. **2** To twist.

screwdriver *noun* (screwdrivers) A tool for turning a screw.

scribble *verb* (scribbles, scribbling, scribbled) **1** To write hurriedly and carelessly. **2** To make meaningless marks with a pen or pencil.

script *noun* (scripts) The words of a play or a broadcast.

scripture *noun* (scriptures) Sacred writings such as the Bible or the Koran.

scroll *noun* (scrolls) A roll of paper or parchment with writing on it.

scrounge *verb* (scrounges, scrounging, scrounged) (informal) To get things you want without paying for them. **scrounger** *noun*.

scrub *verb* (scrubs, scrubbing, scrubbed) To wash briskly with a stiff brush.

scruffy *adjective* Dirty, untidy.

scrum *noun* (scrums) A knot of players struggling for the ball in rugby football.

scrupulous *adjective* Careful, very attentive to small details. **scrupulously** *adverb*.

scrutinize *verb* (scrutinizes, scrutinizing, scrutinized) To examine carefully. **scrutiny** *noun*.

scuffle *verb* (scuffles, scuffling, scuffled) To have a rough confused struggle.

scull *noun* (sculls) A kind of oar.

scullery *noun* (sculleries) A small room where the washing-up is done.

sculptor *noun* (sculptors) An artist who makes things in stone, wood, or other materials.

sculpture *noun* (sculptures) Something made by a sculptor.

scum *noun* Dirty froth floating on a liquid. **scummy** *adjective*.

scurvy *noun* A disease caused by lack of fresh fruit and vegetables.

scuttle *verb* (scuttles, scuttling, scuttled) **1** To sink your own ship deliberately. **2** To run with short steps.

scythe *noun* (scythes) A tool with a long curved blade for cutting grass or corn.

sea *noun* (seas) **1** The salt water which covers most of the earth's surface. **2** A particular part of the sea, a large expanse of water. **3** A large area of something. *a sea of mud.*

seafaring *adjective* Travelling on the sea. **seafarer** *noun*.

seafood *noun* Fish or shellfish from the sea, used as food.

seagull *noun* (seagulls) A kind of sea bird.

seal¹ *noun* (seals) A sea animal often hunted for its fur.

seal² *noun* (seals) **1** A design stamped on wax, lead, or other material to show that a thing is genuine. **2** A device for stamping a seal.

seal³ *verb* (seals, sealing, sealed) **1** To put a seal on something. **2** To close something and fasten it firmly. **3** To make a thing airtight.

sealing-wax *noun* A coloured wax used for sealing letters or parcels.

sea-lion *noun* (sea-lions) A kind of large seal.

seam *noun* (seams) **1** A line where two pieces of material are sewn together. **2** A layer of coal underground.

seaman *noun* (seamen) A sailor.

seamanship *noun* The skill needed to sail a ship.

seaplane *noun* (seaplanes) An aeroplane designed to land on water.

search[1] *verb* (searches, searching, searched) To look carefully for something, to examine a person or place thoroughly in order to find something.

search[2] *noun* (searches) The act of searching.

searchlight *noun* (searchlights) A powerful spotlight for use out of doors.

search-warrant *noun* (search-warrants) An official document allowing the police to search a building.

sea-shore *noun* The land at the edge of the sea.

seasick *adjective* Sick because of the movement of a ship. **seasickness** *noun*.

seaside *noun* A place by the sea where people go for holidays.

season *noun* (seasons) **1** One of the four divisions of the year, namely spring, summer, autumn, and winter. **2** Any period during the year. *the cricket season*. **season ticket** a ticket that can be used many times during a certain period. **seasonal** *adjective*.

seasoning *noun* Salt, pepper, and other things used for flavouring.

seat[1] *noun* (seats) Something to sit on. **take a seat** to sit down.

seat[2] *verb* (seats, seating, seated) To have seats for a certain number of people. *The bus seats 50.* **be seated, seat yourself** to sit down.

seat-belt *noun* (seat-belts) A strap to keep you in your seat for greater safety in a car or aircraft.

seaweed *noun* Plants which grow in the sea.

seaworthy *adjective* In a suitable condition for a sea voyage.

secateurs *noun* A tool used for pruning.

secluded *adjective* Quiet, away from others.

second[1] *adjective* **1** Next after the first. *the second house on the left.* **secondly** *adverb*. **2** Another. *a second helping*.

second[2] *noun* (seconds) **1** A unit of time. Sixty seconds make one minute. **2** A moment. **3** A helper for a fighter in a boxing-match or duel.

second[3] *verb* (seconds, seconding, seconded) To support somebody in a fight or a debate.

secondary school *noun* A school for older children.

second-hand *adjective* Not new, having already been owned by someone else.

second-rate *adjective* Not of the best quality.

secret[1] *adjective* **1** Not to be made known. *secret information.* **2** Hidden, not generally known. *a secret garden*.

secret agent a spy. **secretly** *adverb*, **secrecy** *noun*.

secret² *noun* (secrets) Something which is secret. **in secret** secretly.

secretary *noun* (secretaries) A person whose job is to write letters, to look after papers, and to make business arrangements for another person, or for some organization. **secretarial** *adjective*.

secretive *adjective* In the habit of keeping things secret.

section *noun* (sections) A part or division of something.

sector *noun* (sectors) A part of a town, country, or area.

secure¹ *adjective* (securer, securest) **1** Safe, not in danger. **2** Firmly fixed. **securely** *adverb*, **security** *noun*.

secure² *verb* (secures, securing, secured) To make a thing secure.

sedate *adjective* Calm, serious. **sedately** *adverb*.

sedative *noun* (sedatives) A drug intended to make you calm or sleepy. **sedation** *noun*.

sediment *noun* Solid matter which settles at the bottom of a liquid.

seductive *adjective* Tempting, attractive. **seductively** *adverb*.

see *verb* (sees, seeing, saw, seen) **1** To use the eyes in order to recognize or get to know things. **2** To understand. *Do you see what I mean?* **3** To experience something. *We've seen many changes lately.* **4** To visit or meet or have an interview with someone. *The head wants to see you.* **5** To accompany. *Let me see you home.* **6** To imagine. *I can't see us winning.* **see to** to attend to something. **see something through** not to give it up until it is finished.

seed *noun* (seeds) A small part of a plant which can be sown to produce new plants.

seedling *noun* (seedlings) A young plant.

seek *verb* (seeks, seeking, sought) To try to find something or somebody.

seem *verb* (seems, seeming, seemed) To give the impression of being, to appear to be. *You seem cheerful.*

seen *See* **see**

seep *verb* (seeps, seeping, seeped) To trickle, to ooze.

see-saw *noun* (see-saws) A plank balanced in the middle on which two people can sit and make the ends move up and down.

seethe *verb* (seethes, seething, seethed) To boil, to be agitated.

segment *noun* (segments) A section.

segregate *verb* (segregates, segregating, segregated) To keep separate from others. **segregation** *noun*.

seize *verb* (seizes, seizing, seized) To take hold of something eagerly or violently. **seize up** to become jammed. **seizure** *noun*.

seldom *adverb* Rarely, not often.

select¹ *verb* (selects, selecting, selected) To choose. **selective** *adjective*, **selectively** *adverb*, **selection**, **selector** *nouns*.

select² *adjective* Carefully chosen. *a select group of friends.*

self *noun* (selves) A person's own nature or desires.

self-catering *adjective* Catering for yourself, not having food provided.

self-confident *adjective* Believing in your own ability to do things. **self-confidence** *noun*.

self-conscious *adjective* Worried about what other people think of you, shy or embarrassed. **self-consciously** *adverb*, **self-consciousness** *noun*.

self-control *noun* The ability to control your own behaviour.

self-defence *noun* Defending yourself.

self-employed *adjective* Working for yourself, not employed by someone else.

self-explanatory *adjective* Not needing any explanation.

self-important *adjective* Having too high an opinion of your own importance.

selfish *adjective* Not concerned about others, wanting things only for yourself. **selfishly** *adverb*, **selfishness** *noun*.

self-portrait *noun* (self-portraits) An artist's portrait of himself or herself.

self-preservation *noun* The desire to stay alive and safe.

self-raising flour Flour which will make cakes rise during cooking.

self-respect *noun* A feeling of respect for yourself.

self-righteous *adjective* Thinking too much of your own good qualities.

self-satisfied *adjective* Having too high an opinion of yourself. **self-satisfaction** *noun*.

self-service *adjective* Where customers serve themselves. *a self-service café.*

sell *verb* (sells, selling, sold) To hand over goods or property in exchange for money.

Sellotape *noun* The trade name of a kind of transparent sticky tape.

semaphore *noun* A kind of signalling using arms or flags.

semibreve *noun* (semibreves) A note in music, written o

semicircle *noun* (semicircles) A half circle. **semicircular** *adjective*.

semicolon (semicolons) The punctuation mark ;

semi-detached house A house joined to one other house of similar design.

semi-final *noun* (semi-finals) A match played to decide who shall take part in the final.

semiquaver *noun* (semiquavers) A note in music.

semolina *noun* Hard round grains of wheat, used to make milk puddings.

send *verb* (sends, sending, sent) To cause someone or something to move somewhere. **send for** to ask somebody to come. **send up** (informal) to make fun of someone or something.

senile *adjective* Sick and feeble because of being very old.

senior *adjective* 1 Older. 2 More important in rank. **seniority** *noun*. **senior citizen** an elderly person.

sensation *noun* (sensations) 1 Feeling. *a warm sensation.* 2 A very exciting happening. **sensational** *adjective*, **sensationally** *adverb*.

sense[1] *noun* (senses) 1 Any of the five ways by which you can be aware of things, namely sight, hearing, smell, taste, and touch. 2 A feeling, an awareness. *She's got a nice sense of humour.* 3 The power to think and make wise decisions. *If you have any sense you'll go before it rains.* 4 Meaning. *The message doesn't make sense.* **common sense** the kind of sensible thinking you except from a normal person. **out of your senses** mad.

sense[2] *verb* (senses, sensing, sensed) To be vaguely aware of something. *We sensed that a storm was brewing.*

senseless *adjective* 1 Foolish, pointless. 2 Unconscious. **senselessly** *adverb*, **senselessness** *noun*.

sensible *adjective* 1 Wise, able to make good decisions. 2 Practical, useful. *sensible clothes.* **sensibly** *adverb*.

sensitive *adjective* 1 Easily hurt, delicate. *a sensitive skin.* 2 Quick to react. *sensitive to other people's feelings.* **sensitively** *adverb*, **sensitivity** *noun*.

sensor *noun* (sensors) An electronic device which is sensitive to heat, light, sound, or other stimuli.

sent *See* **send**

sentence[1] *noun* (sentences) **1** A group of words beginning with a capital letter and ending with a full stop, question mark, or exclamation mark. **2** A punishment given to a criminal in a lawcourt.

sentence[2] *verb* (sentences, sentencing, sentenced) To announce a sentence in a lawcourt.

sentiment *noun* (sentiments) A thought or feeling.

sentimental *adjective* **1** Showing your feelings too easily, too soft-hearted. **2** Liable to make people sentimental. *a sentimental love story.* **sentimentally** *adverb*, **sentimentality** *noun*.

sentinel *noun* (sentinels) A sentry.

sentry *noun* (sentries) A soldier on guard.

sentry-box *noun* (sentry-boxes) A small shelter for a sentry.

separate[1] *adjective* Divided from others, not joined to others. **separately** *adverb*.

separate[2] *verb* (separates, separating, separated) To make or become separate. **separation** *noun*.

September *noun* The ninth month of the year.

septic *adjective* Infected, poisoned.

sepulchre *noun* (sepulchres) A tomb.

sequel *noun* (sequels) **1** Something that follows as a result of something else. **2** A book which continues the story of an earlier book.

sequence *noun* (sequences) A number of things which follow one another in a particular order.

sequin *noun* (sequins) A tiny disc sewn on clothes to make them glitter.

serene *adjective* Peaceful, calm.

sergeant *noun* (sergeants) A rank in the army or police force.

serial *noun* (serials) A story told or presented in several episodes.

series *noun* (series) **1** A sequence. **2** A number of things which are connected with each other. *a series of TV programmes.*

serious *adjective* **1** Solemn, not smiling or laughing. *a serious face.* **2** Very bad, severe. *a serious accident.* **3** Keen and careful. *a serious worker.* **seriously** *adverb*, **seriousness** *noun*.

sermon *noun* (sermons) A talk given by a preacher.

serpent *noun* (serpents) A snake.

servant *noun* (servants) **1** A person employed to do housework. **2** A person who serves others.

serve *verb* (serves, serving, served) **1** To do a particular job, to do your duty. *to serve in the army.* **2** To give food to someone at a meal. **3** To look after the needs of customers in a shop. **4** In tennis, to set the ball in play by hitting it towards the court beyond the net. **5** *It serves him right*, he deserves it. **server** *noun*.

service[1] *noun* (services) **1** Doing your duty, working for others, acting as a servant. **2** An arrangement to provide something regularly for people to use if they wish. *a bus service.* **3** A gathering for the worship of God. *a church service.* **4** A set of crockery. *a dinner service.* **5** Serving the ball in tennis. **6** The servicing of a car or other machine. **armed services** the army, navy, and air force. **service area, service station** a place where people travelling by road can find fuel, refreshments, and lavatories.

service[2] *verb* (services, servicing, serviced) To examine a car or other machine and put it into good working order.

serviceable *adjective* Useful, hard-wearing.

serviette *noun* (serviettes) A napkin to use during a meal.

session *noun* (sessions) A time spent at a particular activity.

set[1] *verb* (sets, setting, set) **1** To put, to lay, to arrange, to fix, to establish.

2 To become stiff or hard. *Has the jelly set?* **3** To go down below the horizon. *The sun sets.* **set about something** to start doing it. **set off, set out** to begin a journey. **set something off 1** to start it. **2** to make it explode. **set on someone** to attack someone. **set fire to, set on fire** to cause something to start burning. **set sail** to begin a voyage.

set² *noun* (sets) **1** A group of people or things of a similar kind. **2** A group of things that go together. *a train set.* **3** An apparatus for receiving radio or television programmes. **4** The scenery on a stage.

set-back *noun* (set-backs) Something which checks or hinders progress.

set-square *noun* (set-squares) A geometry instrument in the shape of a triangle with one of the angles a right angle.

settee *noun* (settees) A kind of sofa.

settle *verb* (settles, settling, settled) **1** To go and live somewhere. **2** To rest somewhere for a time. **3** To make somebody or something steady or comfortable. **4** To become steady or comfortable. **5** To decide, to agree. *to settle a problem.* **6** To pay a bill. *to settle a debt.* **settler, settlement** *nouns.*

set-up *noun* (set-ups) (informal) An arrangement, the organization of something.

seven (sevens) The number 7. **seventh.**

seventeen The number 17. **seventeenth.**

seventy (seventies) The number 70. **seventieth.**

sever *verb* (severs, severing, severed) To cut, to break.

several *adjective and noun* Three or more but not very many.

severe *adjective* **1** Strict. *a severe father.* **2** Serious, violent. *a severe storm.* **severely** *adverb*, **severity** *noun.*

sew *verb* (sews, sewing, sewed, sewn) To work with a needle and thread. **sewer** *noun.*

sewage *noun* Waste liquid carried away in drains.

sewer *noun* (sewers) A drain for sewage.

sex *noun* **1** (sexes) Being male or female. *Can you tell the sex of my kitten?* **2** The instinct which causes male and female to be attracted to each other. **3** Sexual intercourse.

sexism *noun* Unfairness because of someone's sex. **sexist** *adjective.*

sextant *noun* (sextants) An instrument used in navigation.

sextuplet *noun* (sextuplets) One of six babies born to the same mother at one time.

sexual *adjective* To do with sex. **sexual intercourse** the coming together of two people to make love, by the male putting his penis into the female's vagina.

sexy *adjective* (informal) **1** Attractive to people of the opposite sex. **2** Much concerned with sex.

shabby *adjective* (shabbier, shabbiest) **1** Nearly worn out. **2** Mean, unfair. *a shabby trick.* **shabbily** *adverb*, **shabbiness** *noun.*

shack *noun* (shacks) A rough hut.

shackles *noun* Fetters, chains.

shade¹ *noun* (shades) **1** An area sheltered from bright light. **2** Something that shuts out bright light, something that makes light less bright. **3** A colour, the quality or depth of a colour. *John painted his door a nice shade of blue.* **4** A slight difference. *This word has several shades of meaning.*

shade² *verb* (shades, shading, shaded) **1** To keep strong light away from something. **2** To provide a shade for a light or lamp. **3** To make parts of a picture darker with many pencil or crayon marks.

shadow¹ *noun* (shadows) **1** An area of shade. **2** The dark shape that appears on the ground or on a wall when an object is between it and a light. **shadowy** *adjective.*

shadow[2] *verb* (shadows, shadowing, shadowed) **1** To darken. **2** To follow someone secretly.

shady *adjective* (shadier, shadiest) **1** Giving shade. **2** Situated in shade. **3** (informal) Not to be trusted. *a shady character.*

shaft *noun* (shafts) **1** A long thin rod or pole. **2** A long narrow space going straight up and down. *a lift-shaft.* **3** A ray of light.

shaggy *adjective* (shaggier, shaggiest) Rough and hairy. **shagginess** *noun.*

shake[1] *verb* (shakes, shaking, shook, shaken) **1** To move something to and fro or up and down. *We shook hands.* **2** To tremble. *I was shaking with cold.* **3** To shock. *They were shaken by the bad news.* **shaky** *adjective*, **shakily** *adverb*, **shakiness** *noun.*

shall *verb* A word used in sentences which refer to the future. *We shall arrive at tea-time tomorrow.*

shallow *adjective* (shallower, shallowest) Not deep.

sham *verb* (shams, shamming, shammed) To pretend.

shamble *verb* (shambles, shambling, shambled) To walk in a tired or lazy way.

shambles *noun* A place of bloodshed or confusion.

shame *noun* **1** A guilty feeling caused by something foolish, awkward, or wrong. **2** Something you are very sorry about. *What a shame to cut down those trees!* **shameful**, **shameless** *adjectives*, **shamefully**, **shamelessly** *adverbs.*

shampoo *noun* (shampoos) A liquid for washing your hair.

shamrock *noun* (shamrocks) A plant like clover.

shandy *noun* (shandies) A mixture of beer and lemonade or other soft drink.

shan't (informal) Shall not.

shanty *noun* (shanties) **1** A roughly-made hut. **2** A sailors' song.

shape[1] *noun* (shapes) The outline or form of something. *Balls are round in shape.* **shapeless** *adjective.*

shape[2] *verb* (shapes, shaping, shaped) To make something into a particular shape. The word *shaped* is often used as a suffix meaning 'in shape', in words such as *diamond-shaped* or *heart-shaped.*

shapely *adjective* (shapelier, shapeliest) Attractive in shape. **shapeliness** *noun.*

share[1] *noun* (shares) One of the parts into which something is divided among several people.

share[2] *verb* (shares, sharing, shared) **1** To divide something, to give part of it to others. **2** To use something which other people also use.

Shariah *adjective* The holy law of Islam.

shark *noun* (sharks) A large fierce sea fish.

sharp[1] *adjective* (sharper, sharpest) **1** Having a thin cutting edge or piercing point. **2** Clever, bright. **3** Tasting slightly sour. **4** Sudden, severe. *a sharp bend.* **sharply** *adverb*, **sharpness** *noun.*

sharp[2] *adverb* **1** In a sharp way. **2** Exactly. *Be there at six o'clock sharp.* **3** Above the proper pitch. *Do not sing sharp.*

sharp[3] *noun* (sharps) The sign ♯ in music.

sharpen *verb* (sharpens, sharpening, sharpened) To make sharper.

shatter *verb* (shatters, shattering, shattered) To break suddenly and violently in pieces.

shave *verb* (shaves, shaving, shaved) **1** To make the skin smooth by cutting off the hairs. **2** To cut a thin slice off something. **shaver** *noun.*

shavings *noun* Thin curling slices shaved off wood.

shawl *noun* (shawls) A piece of cloth worn round the shoulders or wrapped round a baby.

she *pronoun* (her, herself) The female person or animal being talked about.

sheaf *noun* (sheaves) A bundle of corn stalks tied together after reaping.

shear *verb* (shears, shearing, sheared, shorn) **1** To cut the wool off a sheep. **2** To cut with shears or some other sharp tool.

shears *noun* A cutting tool like a large pair of scissors.

sheath *noun* (sheathes) **1** A case for the blade of a sword or dagger. **2** Any similar close-fitting cover.

sheathe *verb* (sheathes, sheathing, sheathed) To put something into a sheath.

shed¹ *noun* (sheds) A small building to keep things in.

shed² *verb* (sheds, shedding, shed) To let something fall or flow.

sheen *noun* A shine on a surface.

sheep *noun* (sheep) An animal bred for wool and meat.

sheepdog *noun* (sheepdogs) A dog trained to help look after sheep.

sheepish *adjective* Shy and embarrassed. **sheepishly** *adverb*.

sheer *adjective* **1** Complete. *sheer nonsense.* **2** Straight up and down. *a sheer precipice.*

sheet *noun* (sheets) **1** One of the pieces of smooth cloth between which you sleep in bed. **2** A flat thin piece of something. *a sheet of paper.* **3** A flat area of something. *a sheet of water.*

sheikh *noun* (sheikhs) An Arab leader.

shelf *noun* (shelves) **1** A length of board fitted to a wall or in a piece of furniture to put things on. **2** A flat level surface that sticks out like a shelf.

shelf-life *noun* The length of time it is safe to store food before using it.

shell¹ *noun* (shells) **1** A hard outer covering. Eggs, nuts, snails, crabs, and tortoises have shells. **2** The outer walls of a building. *After the fire only the shell of the building remained.* **3** A large hollow bullet filled with explosive. **shell suit** a track suit with a showerproof cover over a warm lining.

shell² *verb* (shells, shelling, shelled) **1** To take something out of its shell. **2** To fire shells at something.

shellfish *noun* (shellfish) A sea animal with a shell.

shelter¹ *noun* (shelters) **1** Protection. **2** A small building that gives protection.

shelter² *verb* (shelters, sheltering, sheltered) To protect, cover, or hide somebody or something.

shelve *verb* (shelves, shelving, shelved) **1** To put something on a shelf. **2** To slope.

shepherd *noun* (shepherds) A person who looks after sheep.

sherbet *noun* A fizzy powder or drink.

sheriff *noun* (sheriffs) A law officer.

sherry *noun* (sherries) A kind of wine.

shield¹ *noun* (shields) **1** A piece of armour carried to protect the body. **2** A protection.

shield[2] *verb* (shields, shielding, shielded) To guard, to protect.

shift[1] *verb* (shifts, shifting, shifted) To move.

shift[2] *noun* (shifts) **1** A change of position. **2** A group of workers who work together during a particular period of the day or night.

shifty *adjective* (shiftier, shiftiest) Tricky, deceitful. **shiftily** *adverb*, **shiftiness** *noun*.

shilling *noun* (shillings) A former British coin. Twenty shillings equalled one pound.

shin *noun* (shins) The front of the leg below the knee.

shine *verb* (shines, shining, shone) To be bright, to give out light.

shingle *noun* Pebbles on the beach.

shiny *adjective* (shinier, shiniest) Polished.

ship[1] *noun* (ships) A large sea-going vessel.

ship[2] *verb* (ships, shipping, shipped) To send something by ship.

shipping *noun* Ships.

shipshape *adjective* Tidy, in good order.

shipwreck *noun* (shipwrecks) The wreck of a ship.

shipyard *noun* (shipyards) A place where ships are built.

shirk *verb* (shirks, shirking, shirked) To avoid doing something you do not like. **shirker** *noun*.

shirt *noun* (shirts) A thin garment worn on the upper part of the body.

shiver *verb* (shivers, shivering, shivered) To tremble with cold or fear. **shivery** *adjective*.

shoal (shoals) A large number of fish swimming together.

shock[1] *noun* (shocks) **1** A sudden unpleasant surprise. **2** A violent knock or jolt. **3** The pain caused by electricity passing through the body.

shock[2] *verb* (shocks, shocking, shocked) **1** To give someone a shock. **2** To fill someone with disgust. **shockingly** *adverb*.

shoddy *adjective* (shoddier, shoddiest) Of poor quality.

shoe[1] *noun* (shoes) **1** An outer covering worn on the foot. **2** A U-shaped piece of iron nailed to a horse's hoof.

shoe[2] *verb* (shoes, shoeing, shod) To fit with shoes. *to shoe a horse.*

shoemaker *noun* (shoemakers) A person who makes or mends shoes.

shone *See* **shine**

shook *See* **shake**[1]

shoot[1] *verb* (shoots, shooting, shot) **1** To send a bullet or shell from a gun, to send off any kind of missile. **2** To wound or kill by shooting. **3** To move very quickly. **4** To grow quickly. **5** To take a photograph, to film. **6** To kick or hit the ball at the goal in football and other games. **shooting star** a heavenly body moving quickly across the sky.

shoot[2] *noun* (shoots) The young tip of a growing plant.

shop[1] *noun* (shops) **1** A building where you can buy things. **2** A workshop. **shop steward** a trade union official in a factory or other place of work.

shop[2] *verb* (shops, shopping, shopped) To go to buy things in a shop. **shopper** *noun*.

shopkeeper *noun* (shopkeepers) A person who looks after a small shop.

shoplifter *noun* (shoplifters) A person who steals things from a shop while pretending to be a customer. **shoplifting** *noun*.

shore *noun* (shores) The land at the edge of the sea or of a lake.

shorn *See* **shear**

short[1] *adjective* (shorter, shortest) **1** Measuring a small distance, not long. *a short walk.* **2** Not tall. *a short person.* **3** Not lasting very long. *a short visit.* **4** Less than the amount or number or distance required. *Our team was* *two players short.* **5** Bad-tempered. *Your mother was a bit short this morning.* **shortness** *noun.*

short² *adverb* Abruptly, suddenly. *He stopped short.*

shortage *noun* (shortages) A lack of supplies.

shortbread, shortcake *nouns* A kind of rich sweet biscuit.

shortcoming *noun* (shortcomings) A fault.

shorten *verb* (shortens, shortening, shortened) To make or become shorter.

shorthand *noun* A way of writing very quickly by using special signs.

shortly *adverb* **1** Soon. **2** Briefly.

shorts *noun* Short trousers.

short-sighted *adjective* Unable to see distant objects clearly.

short-tempered *adjective* Easily made angry.

shot¹ *See* **shoot¹**

shot² *noun* (shots) **1** The firing of a gun. **2** Something fired from a gun. **3** A person judged by his or her skill in shooting. *She's a good shot,* she shoots well. **4** A photograph or film scene. **5** An attempt to do something. **6** An injection. **7** A heavy iron ball thrown in an athletic contest.

shotgun *noun* (shotguns) A gun that fires many small lead balls.

should *verb* Ought to.

shoulder *noun* (shoulders) The part of your body where your arm joins the trunk.

shoulder-blade *noun* (shoulder-blades) A flat bone near the top of the back.

shouldn't (informal) Should not.

shout¹ *noun* (shouts) A loud cry.

shout² *verb* (shouts, shouting, shouted) To speak very loudly, to cry out.

shove *verb* (shoves, shoving, shoved) To push.

shovel¹ *noun* (shovels) A tool like a spade with raised edges. **shovelful** *noun.*

shovel² *verb* (shovels, shovelling, shovelled) To move something with a shovel.

show¹ *verb* (shows, showing, showed, shown) **1** To allow something to be seen, to bring it into view, to point it out. **2** To be visible. *The damage won't show.* **3** To guide somebody somewhere. *Show him in.* **4** To make something clear. *This book shows you how to do it.* **show off** to try to impress other people.

show² *noun* (shows) **1** A showing of something. **2** An exhibition, a display. **3** An entertainment.

shower¹ *noun* (showers) **1** A brief fall of rain or snow. **showery** *adjective.* **2** Water falling like rain. **3** A device which sprays water on your body so that you can wash all over. **4** A washing of your body under a shower. **5** A number of things coming down together.

shower² *verb* (showers, showering, showered) **1** To come or send down in a shower. **2** To wash under a shower.

show-jumping *noun* A riding display in which horses jump over fences and other obstacles. **show-jumper** *noun.*

showy *adjective* (showier, showiest) Likely to catch your attention, bright, gaudy. **showily** *adverb.*

shrank *See* **shrink**

shrapnel *noun* Pieces of metal scattered from an exploded shell.

shred¹ *verb* (shreds, shredding, shredded) To cut or tear into thin strips.

shred² *noun* (shreds) A thin strip.

shrew *noun* (shrews) A small mouse-like animal.

shrewd *adjective* (shrewder, shrewdest) Wise, clever. **shrewdly** *adverb,* **shrewdness** *noun.*

shriek *verb* (shrieks, shrieking, shrieked) To scream.

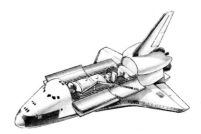
shrill *adjective* (shriller, shrillest) Making a high piercing sound. **shrilly** *adverb*, **shrillness** *noun*.

shrimp *noun* (shrimps) A small shellfish.

shrink *verb* (shrinks, shrinking, shrank, shrunk, shrunken) **1** To become smaller, to make a thing smaller. **shrinkage** *noun*. **2** To move back because of fear or embarrassment.

shrivel *verb* (shrivels, shrivelling, shrivelled) To become or to make something dry and wrinkled.

shroud *verb* (shrouds, shrouding, shrouded) To cover, to hide.

shrub *noun* (shrubs) A plant like a small tree.

shrubbery *noun* (shrubberies) Part of a garden where shrubs grow.

shrug *verb* (shrugs, shrugging, shrugged) To lift the shoulders slightly.

shrunk, shrunken *See* **shrink**

shudder *verb* (shudders, shuddering, shuddered) To shake.

shuffle *noun* (shuffles, shuffling, shuffled) **1** To walk without raising the feet properly. **2** To mix a pack of playing-cards before dealing them.

shunt *verb* (shunts, shunting, shunted) To move railway wagons from one track to another. **shunter** *noun*.

shut *verb* (shuts, shutting, shut) **1** To move something like a door, lid, or cover so that it closes a gap or puts something out of sight. *Shut the window. Shut your books.* **2** To become shut or closed. *The door shut behind him.* **shut out** to keep someone out. **shut up** (informal) to stop talking.

shutter *noun* (shutters) **1** A panel or screen which can be closed over a window. **2** A device in a camera which opens and closes when you take a photograph.

shuttle *noun* (shuttles) **1** Part of a loom or some other device that moves to and fro. **2** A plane, bus, or train going to and fro between two places. **3** A space shuttle.

shuttlecock *noun* (shuttlecocks) The object you hit to and fro in the game of badminton.

shy *adjective* (shyer, shyest) **1** Reluctant to meet other people. **2** Easily frightened. **shyly** *adverb*, **shyness** *noun*.

sick *adjective* Unwell, ill. **be sick** to throw up food through the mouth. **sick of** tired of. **sickness** *noun*.

sicken *verb* (sickens, sickening, sickened) **1** To become ill. **2** To make someone feel sick.

sickly *adjective* (sicklier, sickliest) **1** Weak, pale, unhealthy. **2** Liable to make you sick.

side *noun* (sides) **1** One of the flat, or fairly flat, surfaces of something such as a box, a sheet of paper, or a hill. *A cube has six sides.* **2** An edge of something, an area near an edge. *Robin lived on the other side of Nottingham.* **3** One of the two sides of somebody or something which is not the front or the back. *The cars were parked side by side.* **4** One of two opposing teams or armies.

sideboard *noun* (sideboards) A piece of dining-room furniture with drawers and cupboards.

side-car *noun* (side-cars) A small vehicle with one wheel, fixed beside a motor cycle.

side-show *noun* (side-shows) An entertainment at a fun-fair.

sideways *adverb and adjective* **1** Towards the side. **2** From the side. **3** Edge first.

siding *noun* (sidings) A short railway track by the side of a main line.

siege *noun* (sieges) The besieging of a castle or a town.

sieve *noun* (sieves) A network of wire or plastic in a round frame, used to separate dust or small pieces from larger pieces.

sift *verb* (sifts, sifting, sifted) To shake through a sieve.

sigh[1] *noun* (sighs) A sad sound made by breathing out.

sigh[2] *verb* (sighs, sighing, sighed) To make a sigh.

sight[1] *noun* (sights) **1** The ability to see. *He lost his sight in a terrible fire.* **2** The seeing of something. *The sight of blood makes me feel ill.* **3** Something you can see. *The lake is a lovely sight.* **4** A device on a gun used to aim it at something. **in sight** in a position to be seen. **out of sight** in a position not to be seen.

sight[2] *verb* (sights, sighting, sighted) To see something, to observe it.

sightseer *noun* (sightseers) A person who visits a place to see the interesting things. **sightseeing** *noun*.

sign[1] *noun* (signs) **1** A special mark, sound, action, or design which conveys a meaning or gives information. *Red is a sign of danger. The whistle is a sign to stop playing. A kiss is a sign that you love someone.* **2** A board which gives you information simply and quickly.

sign[2] *verb* (signs, signing, signed) **1** To make a sign. **2** To write your signature, especially on a formal document. **3** To get someone to sign a formal document. *Our team has signed a new goalkeeper.*

signal[1] *noun* (signals) **1** A sign. **2** A set of lights or some other sign used to give instructions to drivers. **3** A message sent in code. **4** A message sent by electronic equipment. *radio signals.*

signal[2] *verb* (signals, signalling, signalled) To give a signal. **signaller** *noun*.

signal-box *noun* (signal-boxes) A building from which railway signals are controlled.

signalman *noun* (signalmen) A person who controls railway signals.

signature *noun* (signatures) Your name written in your normal handwriting.

significant *adjective* Important, full of meaning. **significantly** *adverb*, **significance** *noun*.

signpost *noun* (signposts) A sign at a road junction showing directions and distances to places.

Sikh *noun* (Sikhs) A believer in Sikhism, one of the religions of India.

silage *noun* A food for cattle, made from grass.

silence *verb* (silences, silencing, silenced) To make someone or something silent.

silencer *noun* (silencers) A device for making an engine or gun quieter.

silent *adjective* Not talking, not making a sound, without sound. **silently** *adverb*, **silence** *noun*.

silhouette *noun* (silhouettes) A dark shadow seen against a light background.

silicon *noun* A mineral used in making microchips.

silk *noun* A kind of fine thread used to make a delicate fabric. **silky** *adjective*.

silkworm *noun* (silkworms) A kind of caterpillar which produces silk.

sill *noun* (sills) The shelf along the bottom of a window or door.

silly *adjective* (sillier, silliest) Foolish, thoughtless. **silliness** *noun*.

silo *noun* (silos) **1** A pit or tower for storing such things as grain or silage. **2** An underground place where a missile is kept ready for firing.

silver *noun* **1** A valuable shiny white

metal. **silvery** *adjective*. **2** Coins made of silver-coloured metal.

silver-plated *adjective* Covered with a thin coating of silver.

similar *adjective* Of the same sort, alike in some way. **similarly** *adverb*, **similarity** *noun*.

simile *noun* (similes) A comparison, often introduced by *as* or *like*. For example, *white as snow* or *run like the wind*.

simmer *verb* (simmers, simmering, simmered) To keep a liquid just boiling.

simple *adjective* (simpler, simplest) Plain, easy, not complicated. **simply** *adverb*, **simplicity** *noun*.

simplify *verb* (simplifies, simplifying, simplified) To make a thing simpler.

simultaneous *adjective* Taking place at the same time. **simultaneously** *adverb*.

sin[1] *noun* (sins) An act which you know to be wrong, the breaking of a religious or moral law. **sinful** *adjective*.

sin[2] *verb* (sins, sinning, sinned) To commit a sin. **sinner** *noun*.

since[1] *conjunction* Because. *I can't drive, since I'm too young.*

since[2] *preposition* Between the time mentioned and now. *I haven't eaten since breakfast.*

sincere *adjective* (sincerer, sincerest) Genuine, true, honest. **sincerely** *adverb*, **sincerity** *noun*.

sing *verb* (sings, singing, sang, sung) **1** To make music with the voice. **2** To make a pleasant continuous noise.

singe *verb* (singes, singeing, singed) To burn something slightly.

single[1] *adjective* **1** One, not more than one. *in single file.* **singly** *adverb*. **2** Not married. **3** For the use of one person. *a single bed.* **single ticket** a ticket for a journey to a place but not back again.

single[2] *noun* (singles) **1** A pop record with one piece of music on each side. **2** A single ticket.

single-handed *adjective* Without helpers.

singlet *noun* (singlets) A garment like a vest.

singular *adjective* **1** Referring to one person or thing. **2** Extraordinary.

sinister *adjective* Evil-looking.

sink[1] *verb* (sinks, sinking, sank, sunk, sunken) **1** To go down, to go down into something. **2** To cause a thing to sink. **3** To become weaker.

sink[2] *noun* (sinks) A basin fitted with a drain to take away water, used for washing dishes.

sip *verb* (sips, sipping, sipped) To drink by taking a tiny amount into the mouth at a time.

sir *noun* **1** A word sometimes used when talking politely to a man. **2** *Sir,* the title of a knight or baronet. *Sir Robert Peel.*

siren *noun* (sirens) A device which makes a loud hooting sound.

sister *noun* (sisters) **1** A daughter of the same parents as the person speaking or being spoken about. **2** A senior nurse in a hospital. **3** A nun.

sit *verb* (sits, sitting, sat) **1** To take up a position in which the body rests on the buttocks. **2** To put somebody in a sitting position. **sitter** *noun*. **3** To be situated, to stay.

sitar *noun* (sitars) An Indian musical instrument with strings.

site *noun* (sites) **1** A place for a building. **2** A place where something interesting happens or happened. *the site of a battle.*

sitting-room *noun* (sitting-rooms) A room with comfortable chairs.

situated *adjective* Placed.

situation *noun* (situations) **1** A place, a position. *Their house is in a nice situation.* **2** A condition, a state. *I was in an awkward situation when I lost my bus-fare.*

six (sixes) The number 6. **sixth**.

sixteen The number 16. **sixteenth**.

sixty (sixties) The number 60. **sixtieth**.

size noun (sizes) **1** The largeness or smallness of something, its height, length, volume, or weight. **2** A particular measurement. *a size seven shoe.*

sizeable adjective Fairly large.

sizzle verb (sizzles, sizzling, sizzled) To make a hissing and crackling sound.

skate¹ noun (skates) **1** A steel blade fixed under a boot for sliding over ice. **2** A roller-skate.

skate² verb (skates, skating, skated) To move on skates. **skater** noun.

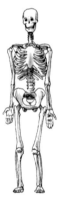

skeleton noun (skeletons) The framework of bones inside human beings and other animals.

sketch¹ noun (sketches) **1** A rough drawing. **2** A short amusing play.

sketch² verb (sketches, sketching, sketched) To make a rough drawing.

skewer noun (skewers) A pointed stick used to hold meat for cooking.

ski¹ noun (skis) A strip of wood or plastic fastened to the foot for sliding over snow.

ski² verb (skis, skiing, ski'd) To move on skis. **skier** noun.

skid verb (skids, skidding, skidded) To slip or slide accidentally.

skilful adjective **1** Having skill. *a skilful player.* **2** Done or made with skill. *a skilful performance.*

skill noun (skills) The ability to do something well or expertly.

skilled adjective Trained, experienced.

skim verb (skims, skimming, skimmed) **1** To remove something from the surface of a liquid. **2** To move quickly and lightly over a surface.

skin¹ noun (skins) **1** The outer layer of the body of a person or animal. **2** The outer layer of a fruit or vegetable. **3** A layer of thin material covering something.

skin² verb (skins, skinning, skinned) To remove the skin from something.

skin-diving noun The sport of diving using flippers and breathing apparatus. **skin-diver** noun.

skinhead noun (skinheads) A person with hair shaved off or cut very short.

skinny adjective (skinnier, skinniest) Very thin.

skip¹ verb (skips, skipping, skipped) **1** To move along hopping on each foot in turn. **2** To jump over a rope which is being turned over the head and under the feet. **3** To leave something out.

skip² noun (skips) **1** A skipping movement. **2** A large container for taking away rubbish in big quantities.

skipper noun (skippers) A captain.

skipping-rope noun (skipping-ropes) A rope with a handle at each end used in skipping.

skirt¹ noun (skirts) A woman's garment that hangs from the waist.

skirt² verb (skirts, skirting, skirted) To go round the edge of something.

skittle noun (skittles) A bottle-shaped piece of wood to be knocked over by a ball in the game of skittles.

skive verb (skives, skiving, skived) (informal) To avoid doing your work.

skull noun (skulls) The bony framework of the head.

skunk *noun* (skunks) A North American animal which sends out a bad-smelling liquid when attacked.

sky *noun* (skies) The space above our heads when we are in the open air.

sky-diving *noun* The sport of diving through the air from an aircraft. **sky-diver** *noun*.

skylark *noun* (skylarks) A small bird which sings as it hovers high in the air.

skylight *noun* (skylights) A window in a roof.

skyline *noun* (skylines) The shape of things seen on the horizon.

skyscraper *noun* (skyscrapers) A very tall building.

slab *noun* (slabs) A thick flat piece of something.

slack *adjective* (slacker, slackest) **1** Lazy. **2** Loose. **slackly** *adverb*, **slackness** *noun*.

slacken *verb* (slackens, slackening, slackened) **1** To make or become looser. **2** To make or become less. *to slacken speed*.

slacks *noun* Trousers.

slain *See* **slay**

slam *verb* (slams, slamming, slammed) **1** To shut violently. **2** To hit violently.

slang *noun* Words used in informal speech but not normally in writing or on important occasions.

slant *verb* (slants, slanting, slanted) To slope.

slap *verb* (slaps, slapping, slapped) To smack.

slapdash *adjective* Careless.

slash *verb* (slashes, slashing, slashed) To make big cuts in something.

slat *noun* (slats) A thin strip of wood or other material.

slate *noun* **1** A grey rock that splits easily into smooth flat pieces. **2** (slates) A flat piece of slate used for roofs.

slaughter *verb* (slaughters, slaughtering, slaughtered) **1** To kill an animal for food. **2** To kill many animals or people on the same occasion.

slaughterhouse *noun* (slaughterhouses) A place where animals are killed for food.

slave[1] *noun* (slaves) A servant who belongs to another person and has no rights of his or her own. **slavery** *noun*.

slave[2] *verb* (slaves, slaving, slaved) To work very hard.

slay *verb* (slays, slaying, slew, slain) To kill. **slayer** *noun*.

sledge *noun* (sledges) A vehicle for travelling over snow, with runners instead of wheels.

sledge-hammer *noun* (sledge-hammers) A very large heavy hammer.

sleek *adjective* (sleeker, sleekest) Soft, smooth, and glossy.

sleep[1] *noun* (sleeps) The state of complete rest and unconsciousness such as people normally enjoy each night in bed. **sleepless** *adjective*.

sleep[2] *verb* (sleeps, sleeping, slept) To have a sleep.

sleeper *noun* (sleepers) **1** Someone who is sleeping. **2** One of the beams of wood or concrete on which railway lines are laid. **3** A sleeping-car.

sleeping-bag *noun* (sleeping-bags) A warm bag for sleeping in when camping.

sleeping-car *noun* (sleeping-cars)
A railway carriage with beds.

sleepy *adjective* (sleepier, sleepiest)
Ready for sleep. **sleepily** *adverb*.

sleet *noun* A mixture of rain and hail.

sleeve *noun* (sleeves) Part of a garment
to cover an arm. **sleeveless** *adjective*.

sleigh *noun* (sleighs) A sledge.

slender *adjective* (slenderer, slenderest)
Narrow, slim, thin.

slew *See* **slay**

slice¹ *noun* (slices) A thin piece cut off
something.

slice² *verb* (slices, slicing, sliced) **1** To
cut into slices. **2** To cut easily.

slick¹ *adjective* (slicker, slickest) Clever,
quick, cunning. **slickly** *adverb*.

slick² *noun* (slicks) A patch of oil floating on water.

slide¹ *verb* (slides, sliding, slid) To move
smoothly over the surface of some-
thing, to slip.

slide² *noun* (slides) **1** The act of sliding.
2 A slippery surface or a smooth slope
for sliding on. **3** A picture which can
be projected on a screen. **4** A small
piece of glass on which you put
things to be examined under a microscope. **5** A device for keeping hair
tidy.

slight *adjective* (slighter, slightest)
Small, not important. **slightly**
adverb.

slim¹ *adjective* (slimmer, slimmest)
Thin, slender.

slim² *verb* (slims, slimming, slimmed)
To try to make yourself slimmer.

slime *noun* Any unpleasant slippery
substance. **slimy** *adjective*.

sling¹ *noun* (slings) **1** A device for
throwing stones. **2** A piece of material tied round the neck to support an
injured arm.

sling² *verb* (slings, slinging, slung) **1** To
throw something. **2** To hang some-
thing up.

slink *verb* (slinks, slinking, slunk) To
move stealthily.

slip¹ *verb* (slips, slipping, slipped) **1** To
slide accidentally. **2** To escape from
someone's grasp. **3** To move without
attracting attention. *She slipped out of
the room.* **4** To do something with
a smooth easy motion. *She slipped
her coat on.*

slip² *noun* (slips) **1** A slide, a fall. **2** A
mistake. **3** A garment worn under
a dress. **4** A piece of paper. **5** A fielder
in cricket who stands close to the
batsman. **give someone the slip**, to
escape from him or her.

slipper *noun* (slippers) A light shoe to
wear indoors.

slippery *adjective* Smooth, liable to slip
or cause slipping. **slipperiness** *noun*.

slip-road *noun* (slip-roads) A short road
for vehicles joining or leaving
a motorway.

slit¹ *noun* (slits) A long narrow opening.

slit² *verb* (slits, slitting, slit) To make
a slit in something.

slither *verb* (slithers, slithering,
slithered) To slide, to slip.

slithery *adjective* Slippery.

slog *verb* (slogs, slogging, slogged) **1** To
hit hard and wildly. **2** To work hard.

slogan *noun* (slogans) A motto,
a phrase used in advertising.

slop *verb* (slops, slopping, slopped) To
spill carelessly.

slope¹ *noun* (slopes) A line or surface
which goes gradually upwards or
downwards.

slope² *verb* (slopes, sloping, sloped)
1 To have a slope. **2** To make a slope.

sloppy *adjective* (sloppier, sloppiest)
1 Wet, runny. **2** Careless. *sloppy work.*
3 (informal) Sentimental. *a sloppy
love-story.* **sloppily** *adverb*, **sloppi-
ness** *noun*.

slot *noun* (slots) A narrow opening to
put things in.

slot-machine *noun* (slot-machines)

A machine which works when you put a coin in a slot.

slouch *verb* (slouches, slouching, slouched) To sit, stand, or move in a lazy way.

slovenly *adjective* Untidy, careless. **slovenliness** *noun*.

slow[1] *adjective* (slower, slowest) **1** Taking a long time, not fast. **2** Behind the correct time. *The clock is five minutes slow*. **slowly** *adverb*, **slowness** *noun*.

slow[2] *verb* (slows, slowing, slowed) **slow up**, **slow down** to move more slowly.

slug *noun* (slugs) A small slimy creature.

sluggish *adjective* Slow, lazy. **sluggishly** *adverb*, **sluggishness** *noun*.

slum *noun* (slums) An area of old, overcrowded houses.

slumber *verb* (slumbers, slumbering, slumbered) To sleep.

slump *verb* (slumps, slumping, slumped) To fall suddenly and heavily.

slung *See* **sling**[2]

slunk *See* **slink**

slush *noun* Melting snow. **slushy** *adjective*.

sly *adjective* (slyer, slyest) Cunning, deceitful. **slyly** *adverb*, **slyness** *noun*.

smack[1] *verb* (smacks, smacking, smacked) To hit hard, especially to hit someone with the palm of your hand.

smack[2] *noun* (smacks) **1** The act of smacking. **2** A kind of fishing boat.

small *adjective* (smaller, smallest) Below the usual or expected size, not large. **smallness** *noun*. **small arms** guns small enough to be carried in the hands.

smallpox *noun* A serious disease with spots that can leave scars.

smart[1] *adjective* (smarter, smartest) **1** Neatly and cleanly dressed. **2** Clever. **3** Fast. *a smart pace*.

4 Painful. *a smart blow*. **smartly** *adverb*, **smartness** *noun*.

smart[2] *verb* (smarts, smarting, smarted) To feel a sharp pain.

smash *verb* (smashes, smashing, smashed) **1** To break something in a violent or spectacular way. **2** To hit violently.

smear[1] *noun* (smears) A sticky or dirty mark. **smeary** *adjective*.

smear[2] *verb* (smears, smearing, smeared) To make a smear.

smell[1] *verb* (smells, smelling, smelled or smelt) **1** To use the nose in order to recognize or get to know things. **2** To give out a smell. *Bad eggs smell*.

smell[2] *noun* **1** The ability to smell. *Dogs have a keen sense of smell*. **2** The quality of a thing that you can smell. *Roses have a nice smell*. **3** (smells) Something you can smell. *There are nasty smells in the cellar*. **smelly** *adjective*.

smile[1] *noun* (smiles) A pleased, happy, or amused expression on the face.

smile[2] *verb* (smiles, smiling, smiled) To make a smile.

smirk *noun* (smirks) A silly smug smile.

smith *noun* (smiths) A person who works with metals. *a silversmith*.

smithereens *noun* Small fragments.

smock *noun* (smocks) A loose garment.

smoke[1] *noun* The mixture of gas and sooty particles that goes up when something is burnt. **smoky**, **smokeless** *adjectives*.

smoke[2] *verb* (smokes, smoking, smoked) **1** To give out smoke. **2** To suck in tobacco smoke through the mouth and breathe it out again. **smoker** *noun*.

smoke-screen *noun* (smoke-screens) A screen of dense smoke.

smooth[1] *adjective* (smoother, smoothest) **1** Having a surface without any lumps, scratches, or other marks that can be felt. *a smooth sheet of ice*. **2** Not bumpy. *a smooth ride*.

3 Without lumps. *a smooth creamy mixture.* **smoothly** *adverb*, **smoothness** *noun*.

smooth² *verb* (smoothes, smoothing, smoothed) To make a thing smooth.

smother *verb* (smothers, smothering, smothered) **1** To suffocate somebody. **2** To cover something thickly. *chips smothered in ketchup.*

smoulder *verb* (smoulders, smouldering, smouldered) To burn slowly without a flame.

smudge *noun* (smudges) A dirty mark.

smug *adjective* (smugger, smuggest) Thoroughly pleased with yourself. **smugly** *adverb*, **smugness** *noun*.

smuggle *verb* (smuggles, smuggling, smuggled) To move goods illegally from one country to another. **smuggler** *noun*.

smut *noun* (smuts) A piece of dirt. **smutty** *adjective*.

snack *noun* (snacks) A small meal.

snack-bar *noun* (snack-bars) A place where you can buy snacks.

snag *noun* (snags) A difficulty, an obstacle.

snail *noun* (snails) A kind of small soft creature with a shell.

snake *noun* (snakes) A long reptile without legs.

snaky *adjective* Twisting, snake-like.

snap¹ *verb* (snaps, snapping, snapped) **1** To make a quick or sudden bite. **2** To say something quickly and angrily. **snappy** *adjective*, **snappily** *adverb*. **3** To break with a sudden sharp noise. **4** To take a snapshot of something.

snap² *noun* (snaps) **1** The act or sound of snapping. **2** A snapshot. **3** A card game.

snapshot *noun* (snapshots) A simple photograph taken without special preparations.

snare *noun* (snares) A trap.

snarl *verb* (snarls, snarling, snarled) To growl and show the teeth as a fierce dog does. **snarled up** confused, tangled.

snatch *verb* (snatches, snatching, snatched) To take hold of something quickly and unexpectedly.

sneak¹ *verb* (sneaks, sneaking, sneaked) **1** To move quietly and secretly. **2** (informal) To tell tales. **sneaky** *adjective*, **sneakily** *adverb*.

sneak² *noun* (sneaks) (informal) A person who tells tales.

sneer¹ *verb* (sneers, sneering, sneered) To make a scornful expression or remark.

sneer² *noun* (sneers) A scornful expression or remark.

sneeze¹ *verb* (sneezes, sneezing, sneezed) To have an uncontrollable outburst of air through the mouth and nose as you often do when you have a cold.

sneeze² *noun* (sneezes) The act or sound of sneezing.

sniff *verb* (sniffs, sniffing, sniffed) **1** To draw air in noisily through the nose. **2** To smell something by sniffing.

snigger *verb* (sniggers, sniggering, sniggered) To laugh quietly or slyly.

snip *verb* (snips, snipping, snipped) To cut with scissors or shears.

snipe *verb* (snipes, sniping, sniped) To shoot at people from a hiding place. **sniper** *noun*.

snippet *noun* (snippets) A small piece of something.

snivel *verb* (snivels, snivelling, snivelled) To weep and whine.

snob *noun* (snobs) A person who thinks it is important to have wealth or possessions or influence and who looks down on people without them. **snobbish** *adjective*, **snobbishly** *adverb*, **snobbery** *noun*.

snooker *noun* A game played with coloured balls and cues on a special table.

snoop *verb* (snoops, snooping, snooped) To pry into other people's affairs. **snooper** *noun*.

snooze *verb* (snoozes, snoozing, snoozed) To have a short sleep.

snore¹ *verb* (snores, snoring, snored) To breathe roughly and noisily while sleeping.

snore² *noun* (snores) The sound of snoring.

snorkel *noun* (snorkels) A tube which supplies air to someone swimming under water.

snort *verb* (snorts, snorting, snorted) To make a short loud noise by forcing air violently through the nose.

snout *noun* (snouts) The nose of an animal.

snow¹ *noun* Frozen drops of water falling from the air in white flakes.

snow² *verb* (snows, snowing, snowed) To send down snow. *It is snowing,* snow is falling.

snowball *noun* (snowballs) A ball of snow pressed together.

snowdrift *noun* (snowdrifts) A bank of deep snow.

snowdrop *noun* (snowdrops) A small white flower.

snowflake *noun* (snowflakes) A flake of snow.

snowman *noun* (snowmen) A figure of a man made of snow.

snowplough *noun* (snowploughs) A device for pushing or throwing snow off roads or railways.

snowy *adjective* **1** Covered with snow. **2** Very white.

snub *verb* (snubs, snubbing, snubbed) To say or do something unkind to a person who wants to be friendly.

snub-nosed *adjective* Having a short nose.

snuff¹ *noun* Powdered tobacco sniffed up the nose.

snuff² *verb* (snuffs, snuffing, snuffed) To put out a candle by pinching the wick.

snug *adjective* Warm and comfortable. **snugly** *adverb*.

snuggle *verb* (snuggles, snuggling, snuggled) To cuddle up.

so *adverb* **1** To such an extent. *He was so ill that he went home.* **2** In that way, just like that. *I told you so.* **3** Very. *I'm so glad you came.* **4** Also. *Peter is going and so am I.* **or so** or about that number. *A dozen or so friends came to my party.* **so far** up till now. **so that** in order that. **so what?** (informal) who cares?

soak *verb* (soaks, soaking, soaked) To make something very wet. **soak up** to take moisture into numerous tiny holes or spaces.

soap *noun* A substance used with water for washing. **soapy** *adjective*.

soar *verb* (soars, soaring, soared) To rise in the air, to fly.

sob[1] *verb* (sobs, sobbing, sobbed) To gasp noisily while crying.

sob[2] *noun* (sobs) The act or sound of sobbing.

sober *adjective* **1** Not drunk. **2** Serious.

so-called *adjective* Wrongly called. *A so-called friend cheated me.*

soccer *noun* (informal) Association football.

sociable *adjective* Friendly, enjoying the company of others.

social *adjective* **1** Living in groups or societies. *Ants are social creatures.* **2** Concerned with society, for the benefit of people living in society. *a social worker.* **3** Giving people an opportunity to meet others. *a social club.*

socialism *noun* A set of political beliefs. **socialist** *noun*.

society *noun* (societies) **1** People living together, a community. *a civilized society.* **2** An organized group of people, a club. *a secret society.* **3** Being together with others, company. *I enjoy his society.*

sock *noun* (socks) A garment which covers the foot and lower part of the leg.

socket *noun* (sockets) A hole into which something fits.

soda *noun* Whitish crystals sometimes used in cleaning.

soda-water *noun* A fizzy water used in cold drinks.

sodden *adjective* Soaked, wet through.

sofa *noun* (sofas) A long comfortable seat with raised ends and back.

soft *adjective* (softer, softest) **1** Easily pressed into a new shape, easily cut, not hard. *as soft as butter.* **2** Smooth, pleasant to touch. *as soft as fur.* **3** Gentle, mild. *a soft breeze.* **softly** *adverb*, **softness** *noun*. **soft drinks** cold drinks such as lemonade or ginger beer.

soften *verb* (softens, softening, soft-ened) To make or become softer. **softener** *noun*.

soft-hearted *adjective* Kind, sympathetic.

software *noun* Computer programs, stored on disc or tape.

soggy *adjective* (soggier, soggiest) Soaked.

soil[1] *noun* The ground, the top layer of the earth in which plants grow.

soil[2] *verb* (soils, soiling, soiled) To stain with dirt.

solar *adjective* Of or from the sun, using the sun's rays. *solar energy.*

sold *See* **sell**

solder[1] *noun* An alloy which melts easily, used for joining metals.

solder[2] *verb* (solders, soldering, soldered) To join metals with solder.

soldier *noun* (soldiers) A member of an army, a person paid to fight on land.

sole[1] *adjective* Single, one and only. **solely** *adverb*.

sole[2] *noun* (soles) **1** The bottom of a person's foot. **2** The bottom of a sock or shoe. **3** A kind of flat fish.

solemn *adjective* Serious, thoughtful. **solemnly** *adverb*, **solemnity** *noun*.

solicitor *noun* (solicitors) A kind of lawyer.

solid *adjective* **1** Not hollow, having no space inside. **2** Hard, not like liquid or gas. *solid ice.* **3** Strong, firm. *a solid piece of furniture.* **solidly** *adverb*, **solidity** *noun*.

solidarity *noun* Unity, keeping together as a group.

solitary *adjective* **1** Alone, lonely. **2** One only.

solitude *noun* Being on your own.

solo[1] *adjective and adverb* On your own. *to fly solo.*

solo[2] *noun* (solos) A piece of music performed by one person. **soloist** *noun*.

soluble *adjective* **1** Able to be solved. **2** Able to be dissolved in a liquid.

solution *noun* (solutions) **1** An answer to a problem. **2** Something dissolved in a liquid.

solve *verb* (solves, solving, solved) To find the answer to a problem. **solvable** *adjective*.

sombre *adjective* Dark, gloomy. **sombrely** *adverb*.

some¹ *adjective* **1** A few, a little. *some sweets, some jam.* **2** One, a, an unknown. *Some person has taken my coat.* **3** Approximately. *There were some dozen people present.*

some² *pronoun* A few but not all, an amount but not the whole. *I'll just take some.*

somebody *pronoun* Some person, any person.

somehow *adverb* In some way.

someone *pronoun* Some person, any person.

somersault *noun* (somersaults) The action of jumping and turning heels over head before landing on the feet.

something *noun* Some thing, any thing.

sometimes *adverb* At some times.

somewhat *adverb* Rather, to some extent.

somewhere *adverb* In some place, to some place.

son *noun* (sons) Someone's male child.

sonar *noun* A system for detecting objects by reflecting sound waves.

song *noun* (songs) **1** A short piece of music for singing, something which is sung. **2** Words for a song.

song-bird *noun* (song-birds) A bird that sings.

sonic boom The bang heard when an aircraft goes faster than the speed of sound.

soon *adverb* (sooner, soonest) **1** Not long after. **2** In a short time. **3** Early. *Have we come too soon?* **4** Willingly. *If there are no apples I would just as soon have a banana.*

soot *noun* The black powder left inside a chimney by smoke. **sooty** *adjective*.

soothe *verb* (soothes, soothing, soothed) To make calm.

sophisticated *adjective* **1** Complicated. *sophisticated machinery.* **2** Done or made in a fashionable grown-up way. *sophisticated clothes.*

sopping *adjective* Soaked, very wet.

soppy *adjective* (informal) Foolish, silly.

soprano *noun* (sopranos) A female or boy singer with a high voice.

sorcerer *noun* (sorcerers) A wizard. **sorcery** *noun*.

sordid *adjective* Dirty, unpleasant.

sore¹ *adjective* (sorer, sorest) **1** Painful. **2** Annoyed. **sorely** *adverb*, **soreness** *noun*.

sore² *noun* (sores) A painful or inflamed place on the body.

sorrow *noun* Sadness, unhappiness, the heavy feeling you have when something happens that you do not want. **sorrowful** *adjective*, **sorrowfully** *adverb*.

sorry *adjective* (sorrier, sorriest) Feeling sorrow or pity.

sort¹ *noun* (sorts) A particular kind or type. **sort of** (informal) rather, to some extent. *The film was sort of scary.*

sort² *verb* (sorts, sorting, sorted) To arrange things into groups. **sorter** *noun*. **sort out** to deal with, to put in order.

SOS An urgent request for help.

soufflé *noun* (soufflés) A light food made with eggs.

sought *See* **seek**

soul *noun* **1** The part of you that is believed to go on after death. **2** Your mind and feelings. **3** (souls) A person. *I won't tell a soul.* **soul music** a kind of pop music.

sound¹ *adjective* (sounder, soundest) **1** Healthy, in good condition. **2** Reliable. **3** Reasonable, correct.

4 Thorough. **soundly** *adverb*, **soundness** *noun*.

sound[2] *noun* (sounds) Something that can be heard. **soundless** *adjective*, **soundlessly** *adverb*. **sound barrier** a resistance in the air that hinders anything going faster than the speed of sound.

sound[3] *verb* (sounds, sounding, sounded) **1** To make a sound. **2** To give an impression by means of a sound. *He sounds angry.* **sound out** to try to find out someone's feelings about something.

sound-effects *noun* Noises used in a play or film.

sound-proof *adjective* Not allowing sound to pass through.

sound-track *noun* (sound-tracks) The sound recorded on a film.

soup *noun* (soups) A liquid food usually made from meat or vegetables.

sour *adjective* (sourer, sourest) **1** Having a taste like that of vinegar, lemons, or unripe apples. **2** Bad-tempered. **sour milk** bad milk. **sourly** *adverb*, **sour-ness** *noun*.

source *noun* (sources) The place from which something starts.

south[1] *noun* One of the points of the compass, the direction to the right of you when you face east.

south[2] *adjective and adverb* In or to the south. **south wind** wind blowing from the south.

southerly *adjective* To or from the south.

southern *adjective* Of or in the south.

southward *adjective and adverb* Towards the south. **southwards** *adverb*.

souvenir *noun* (souvenirs) A thing which reminds you of a person, place, or event.

sou'wester *noun* (sou'westers) A waterproof hat with a wide flap at the back.

sovereign *noun* (sovereigns) **1** A reigning king or queen. **2** An old coin once worth £1.

sow[1] *verb* (sows, sowing, sowed, sown) To plant seeds.

sow[2] *noun* (sows) A female pig.

soya *noun* A kind of bean.

space[1] *noun* (spaces) **1** The immeasurable regions in which the planets and stars move. **2** A distance between two or more things. **3** An empty gap, an unused area. **4** A period of time. **space shuttle** a spacecraft which can be brought back to Earth to be used again.

space[2] *verb* (spaces, spacing, spaced) **space out** to arrange things neatly with spaces between.

spacecraft, spaceship *nouns* (spacecraft, spaceships) A vehicle for travelling in space.

spacesuit *noun* (spacesuits) Special clothing worn in space.

spacious *adjective* With plenty of space. **spaciously** *adverb*, **spaciousness** *noun*.

spade *noun* (spades) **1** A tool for digging. **2** A playing-card marked with ♠

spaghetti *noun* A kind of pasta.

span[1] *noun* (spans) **1** The part of a bridge between supports. **2** A length of time. **3** The length across something. *the span of a bird's wing.*

span[2] *verb* (spans, spanning, spanned) To stretch from one side of something to the other.

Spaniard *noun* (Spaniards) A Spanish person.

spaniel *noun* (spaniels) A kind of dog with long ears.

Spanish *adjective* Of Spain, from Spain.

spank *verb* (spanks, spanking, spanked) To smack somebody as a punishment.

spanner *noun* (spanners) A tool for turning nuts.

spare[1] *verb* (spares, sparing, spared)

1 To allow someone or something to go unharmed. **2** To be able to supply or provide something. *Have you a sandwich to spare?*

spare² *adjective* In reserve for use when needed. *a spare tyre.*

sparing *adjective* Making economical use of something. **sparingly** *adverb.*

spark *noun* (sparks) A glowing speck, a small bright flash.

sparking-plug, spark-plug *nouns* (sparking-plugs, spark-plugs) A device which ignites the fuel in a petrol engine.

sparkle *verb* (sparkles, sparkling, sparkled) To send out sparks.

sparkler *noun* (sparklers) A kind of firework which sparkles.

sparrow *noun* (sparrows) A common small bird.

sparse *adjective* Thinly scattered. **sparsely** *adverb.*

spasm (spasms) A sudden fit or jerk.

spasmodic *adjective* Occasional. **spasmodically** *adverb.*

spastic *noun* (spastics) A person suffering from a condition called cerebral palsy which makes it difficult to control the body.

spat *See* **spit**¹

spate *noun* A rushing flood.

spatter *verb* (spatters, spattering, spattered) To splash, to sprinkle.

spawn *noun* The eggs of fish, frogs, and other water animals.

speak *verb* (speaks, speaking, spoke, spoken) **1** To use the voice to produce words. **2** To know a language. *I speak French a little.* **speaker** *noun.*

spear *noun* (spears) A weapon with a metal point on a long pole.

special *adjective* **1** Of a rare or unusual kind. **2** For a particular person or occasion. **3** Important. **specially** *adverb.*

specialist *noun* (specialists) An expert in a particular subject.

specialize *verb* (specializes, specializing, specialized) To give particular attention to one subject, to be a specialist.

species *noun* (species) A number of animals or plants which are alike in certain ways.

specific *adjective* Detailed, definite. **specifically** *adverb.*

specimen *noun* (specimens) An example of something.

speck *noun* (specks) A small spot or piece.

speckled *adjective* Covered with specks.

spectacle *noun* (spectacles) **1** An exciting or impressive display. **spectacular** *adjective.* **2** Something you see. *a strange spectacle.*

spectacles *noun* A pair of glass lenses in a frame to help you see more clearly.

spectator *noun* (spectators) A person who watches something happen.

spectre *noun* (spectres) A ghost.

speech *noun* **1** Speaking. **2** (speeches) A talk given in public.

speechless *adjective* Unable to speak. **speechlessly** *adverb.*

speed¹ *noun* **1** Quickness, the ability to move from one place to another in a comparatively short time. **2** The measurement of speed, the rate at which something moves. *a speed of 50 miles an hour.* **at speed** quickly, with great speed.

speed² *verb* (speeds, speeding, sped) To move at great speed.

speed-boat *noun* (speed-boats) A fast motor boat.

speeding *noun* Driving too fast.

speedometer *noun* (speedometers) An instrument which measures a vehicle's speed.

speedway *noun* (speedways) A track for motor-cycle racing.

speedy *adjective* Moving at speed. **speedily** *adverb.*

spell¹ *verb* (spells, spelling, spelled,

spelt) To put letters in the right order to make a word.

spell² *noun* (spells) **1** A length of time. *a spell of good weather.* **2** A saying supposed to have magic power. *a witch's spell.*

spellbound *adjective* Enchanted.

spend *verb* (spends, spending, spent) **1** To pay out money. **2** To use something up. *He spends his time daydreaming.* **3** To pass time. *We spent a day by the sea.*

sperm *noun* The cells produced by a male which can fertilize the female's egg during sexual intercourse to produce a baby.

sphere *noun* (spheres) A globe, something which appears round whatever way you look at it. **spherical** *adjective.*

spice *noun* (spices) A substance, such as ginger or cloves, used to flavour food. **spicy** *adjective.*

spick-and-span *adjective* Bright and tidy.

spider *noun* (spiders) A creature with eight legs that spins webs.

spied *See* **spy²**

spike *noun* (spikes) A sharp point. **spiky** *adjective.*

spill *verb* (spills, spilling, spilled, spilt) **1** To flow over the side of a container. **2** To cause something to do this.

spin *verb* (spins, spinning, spun) **1** To turn round and round very fast. **2** To twist into a thread. **3** (of a spider) To make a web out of threads from its body.

spina bifida A disease of the spine.

spinach *noun* A green vegetable.

spin-drier *noun* (spin-driers) A machine which spins washing round so that the water is squeezed out.

spine *noun* (spines) **1** The series of bones along the middle of the back of people and many animals, the back-bone. **spinal** *adjective.* **2** A sharp spike like a needle.

spineless *adjective* Feeble.

spinning-wheel *noun* (spinning-wheels) A device for spinning wool into a continuous thread.

spinster *noun* (spinsters) An unmarried woman.

spiral *adjective* Winding round and round, like a clockwork spring or the thread of a screw.

spire *noun* (spires) A pointed structure on top of a church tower.

spirit *noun* (spirits) **1** The soul. **2** A ghost. **3** Courage, liveliness. *The team showed great spirit.* **4** A feeling, a quality. *We entered into the spirit of the occasion.* **5** A liquid used as fuel or for cleaning, such as methylated spirit. **6** A strong alcoholic drink. **in high spirits** cheerful. **in low spirits** sad.

spirited *adjective* Brave, lively.

spiritual¹ *adjective* Of the soul, religious. **spiritually** *adverb.*

spiritual² *noun* (spirituals) A traditional religious song of American Black people.

spit¹ *verb* (spits, spitting, spat) To send liquid forcefully out of the mouth.

spit² *noun* (spits) A rotating rod on which meat is roasted.

spite *noun* A desire to hurt someone. **spiteful** *adjective,* **spitefully** *adverb.* **in spite of** although it has happened or is happening.

splash¹ *verb* (splashes, splashing, splashed) **1** To make liquid fly about in drops. *Baby enjoys splashing in the bath.* **2** To fly about in drops. *The bath water splashed on the floor.* **3** To make something wet by splashing. *The bus splashed us as it went past.*

splash² *noun* (splashes) The act or sound of splashing.

splendid *adjective* Magnificent, excellent, impressive. **splendidly** *adverb,* **splendour** *noun.*

splint *noun* (splints) A strip of wood or

other material used to keep a broken bone straight while it heals.

splinter *noun* (splinters) A sharp broken piece of wood or metal.

split[1] *verb* (splits, splitting, split) **1** To divide or cut something. **2** To come apart, to form separate pieces or groups.

split[2] *noun* (splits) A crack, a separation.

splutter *verb* (splutters, spluttering, spluttered) To make quick repeated spitting sounds.

spoil *verb* (spoils, spoiling, spoilt) **1** To make a thing less valuable, useful, or pleasant. **2** To make a person selfish by giving him or her what he or she wants all the time.

spoke[1], **spoken** *See* **speak**

spoke[2] *noun* (spokes) One of the wires or rods joining the rim of a wheel to its hub.

sponge[1] *noun* (sponges) **1** A sea creature full of holes that soak up water. **2** A lump of some soft substance like a sponge, used in washing. **3** A kind of light soft cake. **spongy** *adjective*.

sponge[2] *verb* (sponges, sponging, sponged) To wash with a sponge.

sponsor *verb* (sponsors, sponsoring, sponsored) To support a person or a group of people, especially by giving money. **sponsorship** *noun*.

spontaneous *adjective* Happening or done quite naturally. **spontaneously** *adverb*.

spook *noun* (spooks) (informal) A ghost. **spooky** *adjective*.

spool *noun* (spools) A reel on which something is wound. *a spool of film.*

spoon *noun* (spoons) An instrument used in serving and eating food. **spoonful** *noun*.

spoor *noun* (spoors) The track of an animal.

sport *noun* (sports) An amusement or game, especially one done out of doors such as football, running, or

fishing. **sports car** a fast car, usually for two people and with a soft roof.

sportsman *noun* (sportsmen) A man who is good at sport. **sportsmanship** *noun*.

sportswoman *noun* (sportswomen) A woman who is good at sport.

spot[1] *noun* (spots) **1** A small round mark. **2** A pimple. **3** A small quantity. *just a spot of sugar.* **4** A place. *a good spot for a picnic.* **on the spot** immediately, in that very place. **spot check** an examination or search made on the spot without warning.

spot[2] *verb* (spots, spotting, spotted) **1** To mark with spots. **2** To see or recognize someone or something. **spotter** *noun*.

spotless *adjective* Perfectly clean. **spotlessly** *adverb*.

spotlight *noun* (spotlights) A strong light which can shine in a beam.

spotty *adjective* (spottier, spottiest) Covered in spots.

spout[1] *noun* (spouts) **1** A pipe or mouth out of which liquid pours. **2** A jet of liquid.

spout[2] *verb* (spouts, spouting, spouted) **1** To send out or come out in a jet. **2** (informal) To talk in a pompous or boring way.

sprain *verb* (sprains, spraining, sprained) To injure a joint by twisting it.

sprang *See* **spring**[2]

sprawl *verb* (sprawls, sprawling, sprawled) **1** To sit or lie with arms and legs carelessly spread out. **2** To spread out carelessly or irregularly.

spray[1] *noun* (sprays) **1** A shower of small drops of liquid. **2** A tool or device for spraying. **3** A small bunch of flowers.

spray[2] *verb* (sprays, spraying, sprayed) To scatter in small drops.

spread[1] *verb* (spreads, spreading, spread) **1** To lay something out flat, to stretch something out, to make something cover a surface. **2** To make something move outwards over a wide area. *He spread a rumour.* **3** To move outwards over a wide area. *The rumour spread.*

spread² *noun* (spreads) **1** The spreading out of something. **2** (informal) A lot of food set out for a meal. **3** A soft food for spreading on bread.

sprightly *adjective* Lively, brisk. **sprightliness** *noun.*

spring¹ *verb* (springs, springing, sprang, sprung) **1** To jump suddenly, to move upwards suddenly. **2** To make something happen without warning. *He sprang a surprise on me.*

spring² *noun* (springs) **1** The act of springing. **2** A place where water flows out of the ground. **3** A springy device made of metal or wire. **4** The season between winter and summer.

spring-board *noun* (spring-boards) A board from which you jump when diving.

springy *adjective* (springier, springiest) Able to bend and spring back, or to stretch like elastic.

sprinkle *verb* (sprinkles, sprinkling, sprinkled) To scatter drops or tiny pieces. **sprinkler** *noun.*

sprint *verb* (sprints, sprinting, sprinted) To run a short distance very fast.

sprout¹ *verb* (sprouts, sprouting, sprouted) To begin to grow, to develop.

sprout² *noun* (sprouts) A shoot from a seed or plant. **sprouts** Brussels sprouts.

spruce¹ *adjective* Neat and smart.

spruce² *noun* (spruces) A kind of fir tree.

sprung See **spring²**

spud *noun* (spuds) (informal) A potato.

spun See **spin**

spur¹ *noun* (spurs) A sharp device fixed to a rider's heel for urging a horse to go faster.

spur² *verb* (spurs, spurring, spurred) To urge on.

spurt *noun* (spurts, spurting, spurted) **1** To gush out. **2** To speed up suddenly.

spy¹ *noun* (spies) A person who tries to discover secret information.

spy² *verb* (spies, spying, spied) **1** To be a spy. **2** To see, to observe.

squabble *verb* (squabbles, squabbling, squabbled) To have a noisy little quarrel.

squad *noun* (squads) A small group of trained people.

squadron *noun* (squadrons) A unit in an army, navy, or air force.

squall *noun* (squalls) A sudden wind. **squally** *adjective.*

squalor *noun* Dirt, filth. **squalid** *adjective.*

squander *verb* (squanders, squandering, squandered) To waste money or other resources.

square¹ *noun* (squares) **1** A shape with four equal sides and four right angles. **2** An open space in a town with buildings on all four sides.

square² *adjective* **1** In the shape of a square. *a square room.* **2** Having a right angle. *a square corner.* **3** Honest, fair. *a square deal.* **4** *a square metre*, an area equal to that of a square with sides one metre long.

squash¹ *verb* (squashes, squashing, squashed) To crush, to squeeze.

squash² *noun* **1** A fruit drink. **2** A game played with rackets and a small ball on an indoor court.

squat¹ *adjective* (squatter, squattest) Short and thick.

squat² *verb* (squats, squatting, squatted) **1** To sit on your heels. **2** To move in and live somewhere without permission. **squatter** *noun.*

squaw *noun* (squaws) A North American Indian woman.

squawk *verb* (squawks, squawking, squawked) To make a loud harsh cry.

squeak¹ *noun* (squeaks) A high shrill noise. **squeaky** *adjective*, **squeakily** *adverb*.

squeak² *verb* (squeaks, squeaking, squeaked) To make a squeak.

squeal¹ *noun* (squeals) A long shrill cry.

squeal² *verb* (squeals, squealing, squealed) To make a long shrill cry.

squeamish *adjective* Liable to feel sick. **squeamishly** *adverb*.

squeeze *verb* (squeezes, squeezing, squeezed) **1** To press something from opposite sides, to crush it. **2** To get the liquid out of something by squeezing it. **3** To force something into or through a gap. **squeezer** *noun*.

squib *noun* (squibs) A kind of firework.

squid *noun* (squids) A sea creature with ten arms.

squint *verb* (squints, squinting, squinted) **1** To have eyes looking in different directions. **2** To peep at something, to look through half-shut eyes.

squirm *verb* (squirms, squirming, squirmed) To wriggle and twist.

squirrel *noun* (squirrels) A small animal which lives in trees.

squirt *verb* (squirts, squirting, squirted) To send out a jet of liquid.

Sri Lankan *adjective* Of Sri Lanka.

stab *verb* (stabs, stabbing, stabbed) To push a knife or other sharp instrument into somebody or something.

stabilize *verb* (stabilizes, stabilizing, stabilized) To make something steady or stable. **stabilizer** *noun*.

stable¹ *adjective* (stabler, stablest) Steady, firmly fixed, not changeable. **stability** *noun*.

stable² *noun* (stables) A building in which horses are kept.

stack¹ *noun* (stacks) **1** A pile, a heap. **2** The part of a chimney which sticks up above the roof.

stack² *verb* (stacks, stacking, stacked) To pile things up.

stadium *noun* (stadiums) A sports ground with stands and seats for spectators.

staff *noun* (staffs) The people who are paid to work for a school or other organization.

stag *noun* (stags) A male deer.

stage *noun* (stages) **1** A raised platform in a hall or theatre. **2** A point or step in the development of something, part of a journey, process, or activity.

stage-coach *noun* (stage-coaches) A horse-drawn coach which used to carry people and goods on a regular route.

stagger *verb* (staggers, staggering, staggered) **1** To walk unsteadily. **2** To shock and confuse.

stagnant *adjective* Not flowing. **stagnation** *noun*.

stain¹ *verb* (stains, staining, stained) **1** To colour something. **2** To spoil something with dirty marks.

stain² *noun* (stains) **1** A mark that stains something. **2** A liquid used to colour wood or other things.

stair *noun* (stairs) One of a series of steps going from one floor of a building to another.

staircase *noun* (staircases) A series of stairs.

stake *noun* (stakes) **1** A strong pointed stick to be driven into the ground. **2** A sum of money bet on something.

stalactite *noun* (stalactites) A stony spike hanging from the roof of a cave.

stalagmite *noun* (stalagmites) A stony spike rising from the floor of a cave.

stale *adjective* (staler, stalest) Not fresh. *stale bread, stale news.*

stalemate *noun* **1** The situation in chess when no further move is possible. **2** A situation in which people cannot agree and further action is impossible.

stalk[1] *noun* (stalks) A stem.

stalk[2] *verb* (stalks, stalking, stalked) To hunt stealthily.

stall[1] *noun* (stalls) **1** A table or counter where things are sold. *market stalls.* **2** A space for one animal in a stable or building for cattle. **stalls** seats on the ground floor of a theatre or cinema.

stall[2] *verb* (stalls, stalling, stalled) To stop accidentally. *The engine stalled.*

stallion *noun* (stallions) A male horse.

stamina *noun* The power to keep going.

stammer *verb* (stammers, stammering, stammered) To hesitate and repeat sounds while talking.

stamp[1] *verb* (stamps, stamping, stamped) **1** To bring the foot heavily down on to the ground. **2** To print a mark with a stamp. **3** To put a postage stamp on to a letter or parcel.

stamp[2] *noun* (stamps) **1** A small device for printing words or marks. *a date stamp.* **2** Words or marks printed with this device. **3** A small piece of paper which you stick on a letter or parcel before it is posted. *a postage stamp.* **stamp collector** a person who collects postage stamps.

stampede *noun* (stampedes) A sudden rush by a crowd of people or animals.

stand[1] *verb* (stands, standing, stood) **1** To be upright on the feet. **2** To be in an upright position, to move to an upright position. **3** To put something down in an upright position. **4** To remain unchanged or unmoved. **5** To

put up with something, to endure it. *I can't stand hot weather.* **stand for** to represent something, to be a sign for it. *What do your initials stand for?* **stand out** to be easily seen, to stick out. **stand up to** to be ready to oppose someone. **stand up for** to support or defend someone.

stand[2] *noun* (stands) **1** A support to stand things in or on. *a music stand.* **2** A stall where things are sold or displayed. **3** A structure with rows of seats for spectators at games or races.

standard[1] *adjective* Of the usual kind, of the normal quality.

standard[2] *noun* (standards) **1** A flag, a banner. **2** A degree of skill or success. *The standard of work in this class is very high.* **3** Something used for comparison when making judgements. *That's not expensive by modern standards.* **standard lamp** a tall lamp that stands on the floor.

stand-by *noun* Something ready to be used when needed.

stand-in *noun* (stand-ins) A person acting as a substitute.

stand-offish *adjective* Not friendly.

standpoint *noun* (standpoints) A point of view.

standstill *noun* A halt, a stop.

stank *See* stink[2]

stanza *noun* (stanzas) A verse in a poem.

staple *noun* (staples) **1** A U-shaped nail sharpened at both ends. **2** A kind of wire clip for fastening through papers. **stapler** *noun*.

star[1] *noun* (stars) **1** One of the heavenly bodies seen at night as specks of light. **starry, starless** *adjectives*. **2** A shape with five or six points. **3** A famous and popular entertainer.

star[2] *verb* (stars, starring, starred) **1** To take one of the chief parts in a film or play. **2** To have as a star. *The film starred Charlie Chaplin.* **3** To mark something with a ★

starboard *noun* The right-hand side of a ship looking towards the bows.

starch *noun* A substance in foods such as bread and potatoes. **starchy** *adjective*.

stare *verb* (stares, staring, stared) To look continuously at somebody or something.

starfish *noun* (starfishes *or* starfish) A sea animal shaped like a five-pointed star.

starlight *noun* The light from the stars.

starling *noun* (starlings) A common bird.

start[1] *verb* (starts, starting, started) **1** To begin, to make the first move, to take the first step. **2** To set something going. **starter** *noun*. **3** To move suddenly. *He started up in anger.*

start[2] *noun* (starts) **1** The act of starting. **2** The place where something starts. **3** An advantage which a person has at the beginning of something.

startle *verb* (startles, startling, startled) To surprise somebody by doing something suddenly. **startlingly** *adverb*.

starve *verb* (starves, starving, starved) **1** To suffer or die because of lack of food. **2** To make someone starve. **starvation** *noun*.

state[1] *noun* (states) **1** Condition. *The road was in a bad state after the storm.* **2** A community organized under one government, either as a separate country such as the State of Israel, or as part of a republic such as the United States of America.

state[2] *adjective* To do with a country or its government or its ruler. *state secrets.*

state[3] *verb* (states, stating, stated) To make a statement.

stately *adjective* Dignified, imposing.

statement *noun* (statements) Something you say or write down clearly and formally.

statesman *noun* (statesmen) A person who plays an important part in governing a country.

static *adjective* Not moving.

station[1] *noun* (stations) **1** A stopping place for trains or buses with buildings for passengers and staff. **2** A place where fire officers, police officers, soldiers, or others are stationed. **3** A place which broadcasts radio or television programmes.

station[2] *verb* (stations, stationing, stationed) To put someone in a particular place to do a particular job.

stationary *adjective* Not moving.

stationery *noun* Paper and all kinds of writing materials.

statistics *noun* Facts given in the form of figures.

statue *noun* (statues) A figure made of stone, metal, or other materials.

status *noun* A person's rank.

stave *noun* (staves) One of the sets of five parallel lines for writing music.

stay *verb* (stays, staying, stayed) **1** To keep still in the same place, to continue in the same condition. **2** To live somewhere as a visitor. *We stayed in a farmhouse for our holidays.*

steady[1] *adjective* (steadier, steadiest) **1** Firm, not shaking. **2** Regular, continuous. **steadily** *adverb*, **steadiness** *noun*.

steady[2] *verb* (steadies, steadying, steadied) To make something steady.

steak *noun* (steaks) A thick slice of meat or fish.

steal *verb* (steals, stealing, stole, stolen) **1** To take and keep something which belongs to somebody else. **2** To move stealthily. *I stole out of the room.*

stealthy *adjective* (stealthier, stealthiest) Quiet and secret. **stealthily** *adverb*.

steam¹ *noun* The vapour produced by boiling water. **steamy** *adjective*.

steam² *verb* (steams, steaming, steamed) **1** To give out steam. **2** To move under steam power. **3** To cook in steam.

steam-engine *noun* (steam-engines) A locomotive driven by steam.

steamroller *noun* (steamrollers) A machine used to flatten the surface when making roads.

steed *noun* (steeds) A horse.

steel *noun* A strong metal made of iron and other minerals. **steel band** a West Indian type of band using various sizes of steel drums.

steep *adjective* (steeper, steepest) Rising or falling sharply. **steeply** *adverb*, **steepness** *noun*.

steeple *noun* (steeples) A church spire and its tower.

steeplechase *noun* (steeplechases) **1** A race across country. **2** A long race over hurdles.

steeplejack *noun* (steeplejacks) A person who works on very high buildings.

steer¹ *noun* (steers) A young bull raised for beef.

steer² *verb* (steers, steering, steered) To control the direction in which something is to move.

steering-wheel *noun* (steering-wheels) The wheel a driver turns to steer a vehicle.

stem¹ *noun* (stems) **1** The part of a plant growing up from the ground. **2** A part of a plant that joins a leaf, fruit, or flower to its stalk or branch.

stem² *verb* (stems, stemming, stemmed) To stop something flowing. **stem from** to arise from. *That all stems from being so untidy*.

stench *noun* (stenches) A bad smell.

stencil *noun* (stencils) A device used for duplicating or simple printing.

step¹ *noun* (steps) **1** A complete movement forward with one foot when walking. **2** The sound you make putting down your foot when walking. **3** A flat place to put your foot when walking from one level to another. **4** One of a series of actions in making or doing something.

step² *verb* (steps, stepping, stepped) To make a step, to walk. **step up** to increase something.

stepbrother, stepsister *nouns* (stepbrothers, stepsisters) A child of your stepfather or stepmother.

stepdaughter, stepson *nouns* (stepdaughters, stepsons) Someone who is not your child but is the child of the person now married to you.

stepfather, stepmother *nouns* (stepfathers, stepmothers) Someone who is not your natural parent but who is now married to her or him.

step-ladder *noun* (step-ladders) A folding ladder with steps.

stepping-stone *noun* (stepping-stones) One of a series of flat stones placed to help people cross a stream.

stereo¹ *adjective* Stereophonic.

stereo² *noun* (stereos) Equipment for playing stereo tapes or records. **in stereo** using stereophonic equipment.

stereophonic *adjective* Giving the impression that sound is coming from several different directions at the same time.

sterile *adjective* **1** Barren, not fertile. **2** Free from germs.

sterilize *verb* (sterilizes, sterilizing, sterilized) To make sterile. **sterilizer, sterilization** *nouns*.

sterling *noun* British money.

stern[1] *adjective* (sterner, sternest) **1** Strict, keen on discipline. **2** Unkind, grim. **sternly** *adverb*, **sternness** *noun*.

stern[2] *noun* (sterns) The back end of a ship.

stethoscope *noun* (stethoscopes) An instrument used by doctors to listen to patients' heartbeats and breathing.

stew[1] *verb* (stews, stewing, stewed) To cook slowly in water or gravy or juice.

stew[2] *noun* (stews) Meat stewed with vegetables.

steward *noun* (stewards) **1** A person who attends to the needs of passengers on a ship or aircraft. **stewardess** *noun*. **2** An official.

stick[1] *noun* (sticks) **1** A thin length of a branch of a tree. **2** A long thin piece of wood made for a particular purpose. *a walking-stick.* **3** A rod-shaped piece of anything. *a stick of rock.*

stick[2] *verb* (sticks, sticking, stuck) **1** To push or be pushed into something. *I stuck a pin in the board.* **2** To fix or be fixed, especially with glue. *I stuck stamps on my letter.* **3** To be unable to move. *The ship stuck on a sandbank.* **4** To stay, to remain. *Stick at your work!* **5** (informal) To put up with something. *I can't stick that music!* **stick out, stick up** to be higher than the surrounding area, to be easily noticed. **stick to** to be faithful to, to keep to. *He stuck to his story.* **stick up for** to support or defend someone.

stickleback *noun* (sticklebacks) A small freshwater fish.

sticky *adjective* (stickier, stickiest) Covered with glue or any substance that sticks to your hands.

stiff *adjective* (stiffer, stiffest) **1** Not easily bent, stirred, or moved. **2** Difficult. *a stiff test.* **3** Strong. *a stiff wind.* **stiffly** *adverb*, **stiffness** *noun*.

stiffen *verb* (stiffens, stiffening, stiffened) To make or become stiffer.

stifle *verb* (stifles, stifling, stifled) To suffocate.

stile *noun* (stiles) A step or steps for climbing over a fence.

still[1] *adjective* **1** Without movement. **2** Silent. **3** Not fizzing. *still lemonade.* **stillness** *noun*.

still[2] *adverb* **1** Not moving. *Do stand still.* **2** Up to this time, up to that time. *Are you still there?* **3** Even. *I shall be still better at French next year.* **4** Nevertheless, on the other hand. *Still, I did try.*

still[3] *verb* (stills, stilling, stilled) To make quiet or motionless.

still-born *adjective* Born dead.

stilts *noun* A pair of poles used to walk on as an amusement.

stimulate *verb* (stimulates, stimulating, stimulated) To arouse interest or excitement.

stimulus *noun* (stimuli) Something that stimulates.

sting[1] *noun* (stings) **1** The part of the body which certain small creatures use to attack with. *a bee's sting.* **2** A painful wound caused by poison in the sting of certain creatures or plants.

sting[2] *verb* (stings, stinging, stung) **1** To use a sting to give a wound. **2** To feel or cause pain as if from a sting.

stingy *adjective* (stingier, stingiest) Mean, not generous. **stingily** *adverb*, **stinginess** *noun*.

stink[1] *noun* (stinks) A bad smell.

stink[2] *verb* (stinks, stinking, stank, stunk) To have a bad smell.

stir *verb* (stirs, stirring, stirred) **1** To move a liquid or soft substance round and round. *to stir a cup of tea.* **2** To move slightly. *to stir in your sleep.*

3 To excite. *stirring music.*
stirringly adverb.

stirrup noun (stirrups) A metal loop for the rider's foot, hanging from a horse's saddle.

stitch[1] noun (stitches) **1** A loop of thread made in stitching or knitting. **2** A pain in the side caused by running.

stitch[2] verb (stitches, stitching, stitched) To move a threaded needle in and out of cloth in sewing.

stoat noun (stoats) An animal like a weasel.

stock[1] noun (stocks) **1** A number of things kept ready to be used or to be sold, a supply. **2** The animals kept on a farm, livestock. **3** A liquid made by stewing bones, vegetables, or other things.

stock[2] verb (stocks, stocking, stocked) To keep a supply of something.

stockade noun (stockades) A wall of upright stakes.

stock-car noun (stock-cars) An ordinary car used for racing.

stocking noun (stockings) A garment which covers a person's foot and leg.

stockist noun (stockists) A shopkeeper who stocks certain goods.

stocks noun A wooden framework in which criminals were once locked as a punishment.

stocky adjective (stockier, stockiest) Short and strong. **stockily** adverb, **stockiness** noun.

stodgy adjective (stodgier, stodgiest) Dull, heavy.

stoke verb (stokes, stoking, stoked) To put fuel into a furnace. **stoker** noun.

stole, stolen See **steal**

stomach noun (stomachs) **1** The organ of the body in which food is digested. **2** The middle of the front of a person's body.

stone[1] noun (stones) **1** Rock, solid mineral which is not metal. **2** A piece of stone or rock of any kind. **3** A jewel. **4** The large hard seed of such fruits as the plum and apricot. **5** A unit of weight, 14 pounds or 6.35 kilograms. **Stone Age** The period when tools and weapons were made of stone.

stone[2] verb (stones, stoning, stoned) **1** To throw stones at somebody or something. **2** To take the stones from fruit.

stone-deaf adjective Completely deaf.

stony adjective (stonier, stoniest) **1** Full of stones. **2** Like stone. **stonily** adverb.

stood See **stand**[1]

stool noun (stools) A seat without a back.

stoop verb (stoops, stooping, stooped) To bend forwards and downwards.

stop[1] verb (stops, stopping, stopped) **1** To come to an end, to cease. **2** To bring something to an end, to put an end to its movement or progress. **3** To prevent, to hinder. **4** To come to rest, to stay somewhere for a while. **5** To fill a hole or crack.

stop[2] noun (stops) **1** The act of stopping. **2** A place to stop. *a bus-stop.*

stoppage noun (stoppages) The stopping of something.

stopper noun (stoppers) Something which fits into the top of a bottle to close it.

stop-watch noun (stop-watches) A kind of watch used for timing races and other activities.

storage noun The storing of goods.

store[1] noun (stores) **1** A collection of things kept for future use. **2** A place where things are stored. **3** A shop. **in store** coming in the future. *There's a surprise in store for you.*

store[2] verb (stores, storing, stored) To put something safely away for future use.

storey noun (storeys) All the rooms on one floor of a building.

stork *noun* (storks) A long-legged bird.

storm[1] *noun* (storms) **1** A period of violent windy weather. **2** A sudden violent attack. *They took the town by storm.* **stormy** *adjective*.

storm[2] *verb* (storms, storming, stormed) To attack suddenly and violently.

story *noun* (stories) **1** Words which tell of real or imaginary happenings, an account of something. *the story of my life.* **2** A lie. *Don't tell stories!*

stout *adjective* (stouter, stoutest) **1** Strong and thick. **2** Rather fat. **3** Brave. **stoutly** *adverb*, **stoutness** *noun*.

stove *noun* (stoves) An apparatus used for heating or cooking.

stow *verb* (stows, stowing, stowed) To pack or store something away.

stowaway *noun* (stowaways) A person who hides in a ship or aircraft in order to travel without paying.

straggle *verb* (straggles, straggling, straggled) **1** To fall behind, to lag. **straggler** *noun*. **2** To be spread out untidily. *a straggling village.*

straight *adjective* (straighter, straightest) **1** Not bending, not curving. *a straight road.* **2** Honest, direct. *a straight answer.* **3** Tidy, correctly placed. *Put the room straight before tea.*

straighten *verb* (straightens, straight-ening, straightened) To make or become straighter.

straightforward *adjective* **1** Not complicated. **2** Honest. **straightforwardly** *adverb*.

strain[1] *verb* (strains, straining, strained) **1** To stretch, to pull hard. *The dog strained at the leash.* **2** To make the greatest possible effort with something. *We strained our ears to hear the faint cries.* **3** To injure something by stretching it or making it work too hard. *She strained a muscle.* **4** To put something into a sieve or other device to separate the liquid from the solid parts. **strainer** *noun*.

strain[2] *noun* (strains) **1** Straining, stretching. *The rope broke under the strain.* **2** An injury caused by straining. **3** A severe test of a person's courage, strength, or endurance.

strait *noun* (straits) A narrow area of water joining two larger areas.

strand *noun* (strands) One of the threads or fibres twisted together to make rope.

stranded *adjective* Left in a difficult, awkward, or dangerous position. *a stranded ship.*

strange *adjective* (stranger, strangest) Unusual, queer, previously unknown. **strangely** *adverb*, **strangeness** *noun*.

stranger *noun* (strangers) **1** A person you do not know. **2** A person in a place he or she does not know. *Sorry, I'm a stranger here.*

strangle *verb* (strangles, strangling, strangled) To kill by squeezing the throat. **strangler**, **strangulation** *nouns*.

strap[1] *noun* (straps) A strip of leather or other material with a buckle. *a watch strap.*

strap[2] *verb* (straps, strapping, strapped) To fasten with straps.

strategy *noun* (strategies) A plan for doing something important, especially in war. **strategic** *adjective*, **strategist** *noun*.

stratosphere *noun* A layer of air high above the earth's surface.

stratum *noun* (strata) A layer.

straw *noun* 1 Dry cut stalks of corn. 2 (straws) A thin tube for drinking through.

strawberry *noun* (strawberries) A juicy red fruit.

stray *verb* (strays, straying, strayed) To wander, to become lost.

streak¹ *noun* (streaks) A long thin line. **streaky** *adjective*.

streak² *verb* (streaks, streaking, streaked) 1 To mark with streaks. 2 To move very quickly.

stream¹ *noun* (streams) 1 Water which moves in a particular direction along a channel. 2 Anything which flows along like a stream.

stream² *verb* (streams, streaming, streamed) 1 To move or flow like a stream. 2 To send out a stream.

streamer *noun* (streamers) A long ribbon or strip of paper.

street *noun* (streets) A road in a town with houses along it.

strength *noun* 1 Being strong. 2 Power.

strengthen *verb* (strengthens, strengthening, strengthened) To make or become stronger.

strenuous *adjective* Needing great effort. **strenuously** *adverb*.

stress¹ *noun* (stresses) 1 Pressure, strain. 2 Great anxiety. 3 An emphasis.

stress² *verb* (stresses, stressing, stressed) To emphasize.

stretch¹ *verb* (stretches, stretching, stretched) 1 To make something wider or longer or tighter. 2 To become wider or longer. *Elastic stretches.* 3 To put out, to extend. *He stretched his hand towards the fire.*

stretch² *noun* (stretches) 1 The act of stretching. 2 A continuous length of time or space. *a stretch of road.*

stretcher *noun* (stretchers) A frame-work with handles at each end for carrying a sick or injured person.

strewn *adjective* Scattered.

strict *adjective* (stricter, strictest) 1 Stern, keen on discipline. *a strict teacher.* 2 Exact. *the strict truth.* **strictly** *adverb*, **strictness** *noun*.

stride¹ *verb* (strides, striding, strode) To walk with long steps.

stride² *noun* (strides) A long step in walking or running.

strife *noun* Fighting, conflict.

strike¹ *verb* (strikes, striking, struck) 1 To hit. 2 To attack suddenly. 3 To do something with a single stroke. *I struck a match.* 4 To sound. *The clock struck twelve.* 5 To come into your mind, to make an impression on you. *She struck me as being unhappy.* 6 To refuse to work as a protest. 7 To find. *They struck oil.* **strike camp** to take down your tents and leave. **strike out** to cross out.

strike² *noun* (strikes) 1 A hit, an attack, a sudden movement. 2 A time when workers are on strike. **on strike** refusing to work as a protest.

striker *noun* (strikers) 1 A person on strike. 2 A footballer placed at the front of the team to score goals.

striking *adjective* Interesting and impressive.

string¹ *noun* (strings) 1 Thin cord used for tying things. 2 A length of stretched wire or thread used to sound a note in a musical instrument. *a guitar string. The strings,* stringed instruments. 3 A series of things coming one after another. *a string of disasters.*

string² *verb* (strings, stringing, strung) 1 To put strings on something. 2 To put things on a string.

stringed *adjective* **stringed instrument** a musical instrument with strings that are either plucked or played with a bow.

stringy *adjective* Having tough fibres.

strip[1] *verb* (strips, stripping, stripped) **1** To undress. **2** To take the covering off something. **3** To deprive somebody of something.

strip[2] *noun* (strips) A long narrow piece of something.

stripe *noun* (stripes) A long narrow mark. *Zebras have black and white stripes.*

striped *adjective* Having stripes.

strive *verb* (strives, striving, strove, striven) To struggle, to try very hard.

strode *See* **stride**[1]

stroke[1] *noun* (strokes) **1** A hit, a movement. **2** A sudden serious illness.

stroke[2] *verb* (strokes, stroking, stroked) To move your hand gently along something.

stroll *verb* (strolls, strolling, strolled) To walk at a comfortable pace.

strong *adjective* (stronger, strongest) **1** Having great power, not easily broken or damaged, able to resist. **2** Very noticeable. *a strong smell, a strong personality.* **strong drink** alcoholic drink. **strongly** *adverb*.

stronghold *noun* (strongholds) A fortress.

strove *See* **strive**

struck *See* **strike**[1]

structure *noun* (structures) **1** A thing which has been built or put together. **2** The way a thing is built or put together. **structural** *adjective*, **structurally** *adverb*.

struggle *verb* (struggles, struggling, struggled) To make violent or strenuous efforts to do something.

strum *verb* (strums, strumming, strummed) To play a piano, guitar, or other instrument monotonously or unskilfully.

strung *See* **string**[2]

strut[1] *verb* (struts, strutting, strutted) To walk proudly or stiffly.

strut[2] *noun* (struts) A bar of wood or metal used as part of a framework.

stub[1] *verb* (stubs, stubbing, stubbed) To hit your toe against something.

stub[2] *noun* (stubs) A short piece of something which remains when the rest has been used up. *a pencil stub.*

stubble *noun* **1** The short stalks left in the ground when corn has been cut. **2** Short hairs visible on a man's chin when he has not shaved recently. **stubbly** *adjective*.

stubborn *adjective* Obstinate. **stubbornly** *adverb*, **stubbornness** *noun*.

stuck *See* **stick**[2]

stuck-up *adjective* (informal) Conceited.

stud *noun* (studs) **1** A short nail with a thick head. **2** One of the knobs on the sole of a football boot.

student *noun* (students) A person who studies.

stud farm *noun* A farm which breeds horses.

studio *noun* (studios) **1** An artist's or photographer's work-room. **2** A place for making films, or radio or television broadcasts.

studious *adjective* Keen on studying. **studiously** *adverb*.

study[1] *verb* (studies, studying, studied) To spend time learning about something.

study[2] *noun* (studies) **1** The studying of something. **2** A private room used for reading and writing.

stuff[1] *noun* Any kind of material or substance. *What's this stuff stuck to my shoe?*

stuff[2] *verb* (stuffs, stuffing, stuffed) To fill something with stuffing.

stuffing *noun* **1** Soft material used to fill such things as cushions or cuddly toys. **2** A mixture of various ingredients put inside poultry or meat before cooking.

stuffy *adjective* (stuffier, stuffiest) Badly ventilated, without fresh air.

stumble *verb* (stumbles, stumbling,

stumbled) **1** To strike your foot against something and almost fall over. **2** To move or speak in a hesitating way.

stump¹ *noun* (stumps) **1** The bottom of the trunk left in the ground when a tree is cut down. **2** One of the three upright sticks used as a wicket in cricket.

stump² *verb* (stumps, stumping, stumped) **1** To get a batsman out in cricket by touching the stumps with the ball while he or she is out of the crease. **2** (informal) To be too difficult for somebody. *The question stumped me.*

stumpy *adjective* (stumpier, stumpiest) Short and thick.

stun *verb* (stuns, stunning, stunned) **1** To knock somebody unconscious. **2** To amaze.

stung *See* **sting**²

stunk *See* **stink**²

stunt *noun* (stunts) Something difficult or dangerous done as part of a film or to attract people's attention.

stupendous *adjective* Amazing.

stupid *adjective* Foolish, not intelligent. **stupidly** *adverb*, **stupidity** *noun*.

sturdy *adjective* (sturdier, sturdiest) Strong, healthy. **sturdily** *adverb*, **sturdiness** *noun*.

stutter *verb* (stutters, stuttering, stuttered) To stammer. **stutterer** *noun*.

sty *noun* (sties) **1** A pigsty. **2** An inflamed swelling on the edge of the eyelid.

style *noun* (styles) The way in which something is done, or made, or written.

stylish *adjective* Smart, fashionable. **stylishly** *adverb*.

stylus *noun* (styluses) The point in a pick-up, used to play records.

subaqua *adjective* Taking place under water.

subdue *verb* (subdues, subduing, sub-dued) **1** To overcome, to conquer. **2** To make quieter.

subject¹ *noun* (subjects) **1** A member of a particular country. *British subjects can have a British passport.* **2** The person, thing, or idea being talked or written about. *What's the subject of your book?* **3** Something you can study at school or college. *Science is Jo's favourite subject.*

subject² *verb* (subjects, subjecting, subjected) To make someone suffer something. *They subjected her to torture.*

submarine *noun* (submarines) A kind of ship which can travel under the surface of the sea.

submerge *verb* (submerges, submerging, submerged) **1** To go under water. **2** To cause something to go under water.

submit *verb* (submits, submitting, submitted) **1** To surrender. **2** To put yourself under somebody else's control. **3** To hand something in, to put something forward for consideration. **submission** *noun*.

subordinate *adjective* Lower in rank, less important.

subscribe *verb* (subscribes, subscribing, subscribed) To pay a subscription. **subscriber** *noun*.

subscription *noun* (subscriptions) **1** A regular contribution or payment to something. **2** A membership fee.

subsequent *adjective* Later, following,

next. *the subsequent day.* **subsequently** *adverb.*

subside *verb* (subsides, subsiding, subsided) **1** To sink. **2** To become quiet. **subsidence** *noun.*

subsidize *verb* (subsidizes, subsidizing, subsidized) To provide money to keep the price of something low. **subsidy** *noun.*

substance *noun* (substances) Any kind of matter or material, anything which can be seen, or touched, or used in the making of something.

substantial *adjective* **1** Strongly made. **2** Considerable, large.

substitute¹ *noun* (substitutes) A person or thing which can be used instead of another.

substitute² *verb* (substitutes, substituting, substituted) To use a substitute. **substitution** *noun.*

subtle *adjective* (subtler, subtlest) **1** Clever, ingenious. *a subtle argument.* **2** Faint but pleasing. *a subtle flavour.* **subtly** *adverb*, **subtlety** *noun.*

subtract *verb* (subtracts, subtracting, subtracted) To take one number or amount away from another. **subtraction** *noun.*

suburb *noun* (suburbs) An area of houses on the edge of a town or city. **suburban** *adjective.*

subway *noun* (subways) A tunnel for pedestrians.

succeed *verb* (succeeds, succeeding, succeeded) **1** To do what you set out to do. **2** To do well. **3** To come after, to take the place of another person. *When the King died, the Prince succeeded him.*

success *noun* (successes) **1** Doing what you set out to do, doing well. **2** A person or event that does well. *Was your party a success?* **successful** *adjective*, **successfully** *adverb.*

succession *noun* (successions) A number of things coming one after the other.

successor *noun* (successors) A person who succeeds another person.

such *adjective* **1** Of this kind, of that kind, of the same kind. *Such kindness should be rewarded.* **2** So great. *The shock was such that he never got over it.* **3** Truly, really. *She's such a good player!*

suck *verb* (sucks, sucking, sucked) **1** To draw in liquid or air. *to suck milk through a straw.* **2** To keep something in the mouth and lick it and squeeze it with the tongue. *to suck a sweet.*

suction *noun* Sucking.

sudden *adjective* Happening or done quickly and unexpectedly. **suddenly** *adverb*, **suddenness** *noun.*

suds *noun* Froth on soapy water.

sue *verb* (sues, suing, sued) To claim compensation from somebody in a court of law.

suede *noun* A kind of soft leather.

suet *noun* A kind of hard fat used in cooking.

suffer *verb* (suffers, suffering, suffered) **1** To feel pain, to have a loss or other unpleasant experience. **2** To put up with something, to have to experience it.

sufficient *adjective* Enough. **sufficiently** *adverb*, **sufficiency** *noun.*

suffix *noun* (suffixes) A word or syllable joined to the end of another word to alter its meaning or use, as in sudden*ly*, sudden*ness*.

suffocate *verb* (suffocates, suffocating, suffocated) **1** To kill or choke somebody by stopping his or her breathing. **2** To have difficulty in breathing. **suffocation** *noun.*

sugar *noun* A sweet substance obtained from plants such as sugarbeet or sugarcane. **sugary** *adjective.*

suggest *verb* (suggests, suggesting, suggested) **1** To put forward an idea. *I suggest we have a picnic.* **2** To give an impression of something. *The tracks* *suggest that an animal was here recently.* **suggestion** *noun*.

suicide *noun* Killing yourself deliberately. *to commit suicide*. **suicidal** *adjective*.

suit[1] *noun* (suits) **1** A set of clothes of the same material and colour. **2** One of the four sets in a pack of playing-cards, namely clubs, diamonds, hearts, and spades.

suit[2] *verb* (suits, suiting, suited) To be suitable for somebody or something.

suitable *adjective* What is wanted, right for the occasion or for the person. **suitably** *adverb*.

suitcase *noun* (suitcases) A case for carrying clothes and other things.

suite *noun* (suites) **1** A set of furniture. **2** A set of rooms.

suitor *noun* (suitors) (old-fashioned) A man courting a woman.

sulk *verb* (sulks, sulking, sulked) To be silent and bad-tempered. **sulky** *adjective*, **sulkily** *adverb*, **sulkiness** *noun*.

sullen *adjective* Gloomy, dismal, bad-tempered. **sullenly** *adverb*, **sullenness** *noun*.

sulphur *noun* A yellow chemical.

sultan *noun* (sultans) A Muslim ruler.

sultana *noun* (sultanas) A kind of raisin.

sultry *adjective* (sultrier, sultriest) Hot and damp.

sum[1] *noun* (sums) **1** The total you get when numbers are added together. **2** A problem to be solved in arithmetic. **3** An amount of money.

sum[2] *verb* (sums, summing, summed) **sum up** to give a summary at the end of a talk or discussion.

summarize *verb* (summarizes, summarizing, summarized) To make a summary.

summary *noun* (summaries) A short version giving the main points of something said or written.

summer *noun* (summers) The warm season between spring and autumn. **summery** *adjective*.

summit *noun* (summits) **1** The top of something. *the summit of a hill*. **2** An important meeting between the leaders of countries.

summon *verb* (summons, summoning, summoned) To command someone to appear.

summons *noun* (summonses) A command to appear in a lawcourt.

sumptuous *adjective* Magnificent, splendid. **sumptuously** *adverb*.

sun *noun* **1** The heavenly body from which the earth gets warmth and light. **2** The warmth or light from the sun.

sunbathe *verb* (sunbathes, sunbathing, sunbathed) To sit or lie in the sun.

sunburn *noun* A brown or red colour of the skin caused by the sun. **sunburnt** *adjective*.

Sunday *noun* (Sundays) The first day of the week.

sundial *noun* (sundials) A device which shows the time by a shadow cast by the sun on the face of a dial.

sunflower *noun* (sunflowers) A large yellow flower.

sung *See* **sing**

sun-glasses *noun* Dark glasses which protect a person's eyes from the sun.

sunk, sunken *See* **sink**[1]

sunlamp *noun* (sunlamps) A kind of electric lamp which makes artificial sunlight.

sunless *adjective* Without sunshine.

sunlight *noun* The light from the sun.

sunny *adjective* (sunnier, sunniest) With the sun shining.

sunrise *noun* The rising of the sun.

sunset *noun* The going down of the sun.

sunshine *noun* Light shining directly from the sun.

sunstroke *noun* An illness caused by too much heat from the sun.

suntan *noun* A brown colour of the skin caused by the sun.

super *adjective* (informal) Excellent, splendid.

superb *adjective* Magnificent. **superbly** *adverb*.

superficial *adjective* Not deep, on the surface. **superficially** *adverb*.

superfluous *adjective* More than is needed.

superhuman *adjective* Having more than normal human power or ability.

superintendent *noun* (superintendents) **1** A senior officer in the police. **2** A supervisor.

superior¹ *adjective* **1** Greater, higher, better. **2** Proud of yourself. **superiority** *noun*.

superior² *noun* (superiors) A person higher in rank than another. **Mother Superior** a nun in charge of a convent.

supermarket *noun* (supermarkets) A large self-service shop.

supernatural *adjective* Not to be explained by natural laws, to do with gods, ghosts, fairies, or other mysterious beings.

superpower *noun* (superpowers) One of the very powerful nations of the world.

supersonic *adjective* Faster than the speed of sound.

superstar *noun* (superstars) A very famous performer.

superstition *noun* (superstitions) An idea or an action based on a belief in supernatural happenings. **superstitious** *adjective*, **superstitiously** *adverb*.

supertanker *noun* (supertankers) A very large ship designed to carry oil.

supervise *verb* (supervises, supervising, supervised) To look after the organization of something. **supervisor**, **supervision** *nouns*.

supper *noun* (suppers) An evening meal.

supple *adjective* (suppler, supplest) Easy to bend, bending easily.

supplement *noun* (supplements) An extra part or amount, added to make something better, more interesting, or up to date. **supplementary** *adjective*.

supply¹ *verb* (supplies, supplying, supplied) To provide what is wanted. **supplier** *noun*.

supply² *noun* (supplies) **1** The supplying of something. **2** Something which is supplied. **3** A stock of something, an amount which can be supplied when needed.

support *verb* (supports, supporting, supported) **1** To hold something up, to keep it in place, to keep it going. **2** To give help or encouragement to someone. *to support a football team*, to take a special interest in it. **support**, **supporter** *nouns*.

suppose *verb* (supposes, supposing, supposed) To guess, to think. *Why do you suppose he did that?* **be supposed to** to be expected to do something, to have to do it. **supposition** *noun*.

suppress *verb* (suppresses, suppressing, suppressed) **1** To put an end to something. **2** To prevent something becoming generally known. **suppressor**, **suppression** *nouns*.

supreme *adjective* Highest in rank, greatest. **supremely** *adverb*, **supremacy** *noun*.

sure *adjective* (surer, surest) **1** Certain, having no doubts, confident. **2** Reliable. **surely** *adverb*.

surf *noun* White foaming waves breaking on the shore.

surface¹ *noun* (surfaces) **1** The outside of something. **2** A flat area on the top or on the outside of something. *A cube has six surfaces.* **3** A layer covering the surface of something.

surface[2] *verb* (surfaces, surfacing, surfaced) **1** To come to the surface. **2** To put a layer of something on a surface.

surfboard *noun* (surfboards) A board used to ride the surf in the sport of surf-riding.

surge *verb* (surges, surging, surged) To rush forwards or upwards.

surgeon *noun* (surgeons) A doctor who performs operations.

surgery *noun* **1** The performing of an operation. *His illness can be cured by surgery*. **2** (surgeries) A room where a doctor or dentist sees patients. **3** A time when you can visit a surgery.

surly *adjective* (surlier, surliest) Rude and bad-tempered. **surliness** *noun*.

surname *noun* (surnames) A person's last name, the name which all members of a family have.

surpass *verb* (surpasses, surpassing, surpassed) To do better or be better than others.

surplice *noun* (surplices) A white garment sometimes worn by priests or members of church choirs.

surplus *noun* (surpluses) An amount left over when the required amount has been taken or used.

surprise[1] *noun* (surprises) **1** Something which was not expected. **2** The feeling you have about something which was not expected.

surprise[2] *verb* (surprises, surprising, surprised) **1** To give someone a surprise, to cause a surprise. **surprisingly** *adverb*. **2** To attack or come upon someone unexpectedly.

surrender *verb* (surrenders, surrendering, surrendered) **1** To let yourself be captured, to give in. **2** To hand something over to someone.

surround *verb* (surrounds, surrounding, surrounded) To be round someone or something on all sides.

surroundings *noun* The surrounding things and places.

survey[1] *noun* (surveys) **1** A general look

at something. **2** An examination of something, an investigation. *a traffic survey*.

survey[2] *verb* (surveys, surveying, surveyed) To make a survey. **surveyor** *noun*.

survive *verb* (survives, surviving, survived) To continue to live after the death of another person or after some serious danger. **survivor, survival** *nouns*.

suspect[1] *verb* (suspects, suspecting, suspected) **1** To have a suspicion about something. **2** To have a feeling that someone is guilty of something.

suspect[2] *noun* (suspects) A person who is suspected of a crime.

suspend *verb* (suspends, suspending, suspended) **1** To hang something up. **2** To put a stop to something for a time. **3** To deprive somebody for a time of a job or a place in a team. **suspension** *noun*.

suspense *noun* Uncertainty, strain.

suspension bridge A bridge supported by steel cables hanging from a framework.

suspicion *noun* (suspicions) **1** A feeling that something is wrong. **2** A feeling that someone is not to be trusted or is guilty of something. **suspicious** *adjective*, **suspiciously** *adverb*.

swag *noun* (informal) Stolen goods.

swagger *verb* (swaggers, swaggering, swaggered) To walk or behave in a conceited way.

swallow[1] *verb* (swallows, swallowing, swallowed) **1** To allow food to pass down the throat. **2** To take something in, to enclose it. *The ship was swallowed up in the fog.*

swallow[2] *noun* (swallows) A kind of small bird with a forked tail.

swam *See* swim[1]

swami *noun* (swamis) A Hindu religious teacher.

swamp[1] *noun* (swamps) A marsh, a bog. **swampy** *adjective*.

swamp[2] *verb* (swamps, swamping, swamped) **1** To flood something with water. **2** To overwhelm, to overload.

swan *noun* (swans) A large white water bird with a long neck.

swank *verb* (swanks, swanking, swanked) (informal) To boast.

swarm[1] *noun* (swarms) **1** A large number of bees clustering together. **2** A crowd.

swarm[2] *verb* (swarms, swarming, swarmed) **1** To move in a swarm. **2** To climb something by clinging with the arms and legs.

swarthy *adjective* (swarthier, swarthiest) With a dark complexion.

swat *verb* (swats, swatting, swatted) To slap and crush something. *to swat a fly.* **swatter** *noun*.

sway *verb* (sways, swaying, swayed) To move from side to side.

swear *verb* (swears, swearing, swore, sworn) **1** To make a solemn promise, to take an oath. *He swore to tell the truth.* **2** To use swear-words.

swear-word *noun* (swear-words) A rude or offensive word sometimes used when people are angry or hurt or excited.

sweat *verb* (sweats, sweating, sweated) To give off liquid through the pores of the skin.

sweater *noun* (sweaters) A knitted pullover or jumper.

sweat-shirt *noun* (sweat-shirts) A light cotton sweater with sleeves.

swede[1] *noun* (swedes) A root vegetable.

Swede[2] *noun* (Swedes) A Swedish person.

Swedish *adjective* Of or from Sweden.

sweep[1] *verb* (sweeps, sweeping, swept) **1** To clean with a brush or broom. **sweeper** *noun*. **2** To move something quickly. *The wind swept Ann's hat away.* **3** To move along quickly or importantly. *A large car swept past.*

sweep[2] *noun* (sweeps) **1** A sweeping movement. **2** A person who cleans chimneys.

sweet[1] *adjective* (sweeter, sweetest) **1** Having a taste like that of sugar. **2** Pleasant, attractive. **sweetly** *adverb*, **sweetness** *noun*.

sweet[2] *noun* (sweets) **1** A small piece of something to eat made mainly from sugar or chocolate. **2** A sweet food eaten after a meat course, such as jelly, tart, or trifle.

sweet corn *noun* Maize.

sweeten *verb* (sweetens, sweetening, sweetened) To make sweeter. **sweetener** *noun*.

sweetheart *noun* (sweethearts) A lover.

swell[1] *verb* (swells, swelling, swelled, swollen) To get bigger or louder.

swell[2] *noun* The slow rise and fall of the open sea.

swelling *noun* (swellings) A swollen place.

sweltering *adjective* Very hot.

swept *See* **sweep**[1]

swerve *verb* (swerves, swerving, swerved) To change direction suddenly in the course of a movement.

swift[1] *adjective* (swifter, swiftest) Fast, moving at speed. **swiftly** *adverb*, **swiftness** *noun*.

swift[2] *noun* (swifts) A bird like a swallow.

swig *verb* (swigs, swigging, swigged) (informal) To take a drink of something.

swill[1] *verb* (swills, swilling, swilled) To clean with water.

swill[2] *noun* Waste food given to pigs.

swim[1] *verb* (swims, swimming, swam, swum) **1** To move yourself through the water. **swimmer** *noun*. **2** To cross something by swimming. *Ruth swam the river easily.* **3** To feel dizzy. *My head's swimming.*

swim[2] *noun* (swims) A time spent swimming.

swimming-bath, swimming-pool *nouns* (swimming-baths, swimming-pools) A pool specially made for people to swim in.

swindle *verb* (swindles, swindling, swindled) To cheat someone.

swine *noun* (swine) A pig.

swing[1] *verb* (swings, swinging, swung) **1** To move to and fro like a pendulum or a door blown by the wind. **2** To turn suddenly. *He swung round to see what the noise was.*

swing[2] *noun* (swings) **1** A swinging movement. **2** A seat hung from a tree or frame for a child to swing on. **in full swing** full of activity.

swipe *verb* (swipes, swiping, swiped) **1** To hit hard. **2** (informal) To steal.

swirl *verb* (swirls, swirling, swirled) To move with twists and turns. *The water swirled round.*

swish *verb* (swishes, swishing, swished) To make a rustling or hissing sound.

Swiss *adjective* Of or from Switzerland.

switch[1] *noun* (switches) A device for turning electricity on or off.

switch[2] *verb* (switches, switching, switched) **1** To turn an electric current on or off. **2** To turn suddenly from one thing to another.

switchboard *noun* (switchboards) An apparatus for connecting telephone wires when calls are being made.

swivel *verb* (swivels, swivelling, swivelled) To turn, to swing right round.

swollen *See* **swell**[1]

swoop *verb* (swoops, swooping, swooped) **1** To dive through the air. **2** To make a sudden attack.

swop *verb* (swops, swopping, swopped) (informal) To exchange one thing for another.

sword *noun* (swords) A weapon with a long steel blade.

swore, sworn *See* **swear**

swot *verb* (swots, swotting, swotted) (informal) To study hard.

swum *See* **swim**[1]

swung *See* **swing**[1]

sycamore *noun* (sycamores) A kind of maple tree.

syllable *noun* (syllables) A word or a part of a word containing one vowel sound.

syllabus *noun* (syllabuses) An outline or summary of things to be studied.

symbol *noun* (symbols) A sign which has come to represent something. **symbolic** *adjective*, **symbolically** *adverb*.

symbolize *verb* (symbolizes, symbolizing, symbolized) To be a symbol of something.

symmetrical *adjective* Having exactly corresponding shapes on each side of an imaginary dividing line. **symmetrically** *adverb*, **symmetry** *noun*.

sympathize *verb* (sympathizes, sympathizing, sympathized) To have sympathy for others. **sympathizer** *noun*.

sympathy *noun* (sympathies) The ability to understand and share other people's feelings. **sympathetic** *adjective*, **sympathetically** *adverb*.

symphony *noun* (symphonies) A kind of composition for an orchestra.

symptom *noun* (symptoms) One of the things that you notice is wrong with you when you are ill.

synagogue *noun* (synagogues) A place where Jews meet to worship.

synchronize *verb* (synchronizes, synchronizing, synchronized) **1** To make things happen at the same time. **2** To make two or more clocks or watches show the same time. **synchronization** *noun*.

synonym *noun* (synonyms) A word with the same meaning as another word. **synonymous** *adjective*.

synthetic *adjective* Artificial. **synthetically** *adverb*.

synthesizer *noun* (synthesizers) A keyboard instrument that can imitate most other instruments.

syringe *noun* (syringes) An instrument for giving injections.

syrup *noun* A thick sweet liquid.

system *noun* (systems) **1** A set of things which together make up one complex unit. *a computer system.* **2** An organized set of ideas, a planned way of doing something.

systematic *adjective* Organized, planned. **systematically** *adverb*.

Tt
•••••

tabby *noun* (tabbies) A cat with striped fur.

table *noun* (tables) **1** A piece of furniture with legs and a wide, flat top. **2** A list, information arranged in an orderly way. *multiplication tables.*

table-cloth *noun* (table-cloths) A cloth to cover a table.

tablespoon *noun* (tablespoons) A large spoon used for serving food.

tablet *noun* (tablets) **1** A pill. **2** A piece of soap. **3** A flat slab of stone with carved writing.

table-tennis *noun* A game played with bats and a ball on a table with a net.

tachograph *noun* (tachographs) An instrument that records the details of a vehicle's journeys.

tack[1] *noun* (tacks) A small nail with a broad head.

tack[2] *verb* (tacks, tacking, tacked) **1** To fix something with tacks. **2** To sew something quickly with long stitches. **3** To sail a zig-zag course against the wind.

tackle[1] *noun* Equipment.

tackle[2] *verb* (tackles, tackling, tackled) **1** In football and other games, to go to the player with the ball and try to get it from him. **2** To deal with a job.

tacky *adjective* (tackier, tackiest) Sticky. **tackiness** *noun*.

tact *noun* Skill in not hurting somebody's feelings. **tactful, tactless** *adjectives*, **tactfully, tactlessly** *adverbs*.

tactics *noun* The art of organizing battles. **tactical** *adjective*, **tactically** *adverb*.

tadpole *noun* (tadpoles) A creature that grows up to become a frog or a toad.

taffeta *noun* A kind of silky fabric.

tag[1] *noun* (tags) **1** A label. **2** A chasing game.

tag[2] *verb* (tags, tagging, tagged) **1** To fix a label on something. **2** To follow somebody closely.

tail[1] *noun* (tails) **1** A projecting part at the end of the back of animals, birds, and fish. **tailless** *adjective*. **2** The end part of something. **3** The side of a coin opposite the side with the head on it. **tail light** a light at the rear of a vehicle.

tail[2] *verb* (tails, tailing, tailed) To follow somebody or something. **tail off** to become smaller, to become less successful.

tailback *noun* (tailbacks) A queue of traffic not able to move freely.

tailor *noun* (tailors) A person whose job is making clothes.

take *verb* (takes, taking, took, taken) **1** To get hold of something. *Take my hand.* **2** To capture. *They took many prisoners.* **3** To carry, to remove. *You can take your work home.* **4** To guide, to accompany. *I will take Tim home.* **5** To have, to use. *Do you take sugar?* **6** To get, to accept. *Take my advice!* **7** To need. *How long will the job take?* **8** To suppose, to understand. *Judging by your expression, I take it that you disapprove.* **9** To organize something, to be in charge of it. *Who is taking us for games tomorrow?* **take notes** to write notes of what you hear or read. **take a photograph** to use a camera to make a photograph. **take in** to deceive someone. **take off** to begin a flight. **take place** to happen.

takings *noun* Money received.

talc or **talcum powder** *noun* A soft powder used on the skin.

tale *noun* (tales) A story. **tell tales** to tell about someone's wrongdoing.

talent *noun* (talents) A special ability to do something.

talented *adjective* Skilful at something, having talent. *Celia is a talented musician.*

talk[1] *verb* (talks, talking, talked) To speak, to say things. **talker** *noun*.

talk[2] *noun* (talks) **1** Conversation, discussion. **2** A lecture.

talkative *adjective* Fond of talking.

tall *adjective* (taller, tallest) **1** Of more than average height. *James is tall for his age.* **2** In height. *John is almost two metres tall.*

tallish *adjective* Rather tall.

Talmud *noun* A collection of ancient Jewish religious books.

talon *noun* (talons) A claw.

tambourine *noun* (tambourines) A small shallow drum with jingling discs round the edge.

tame[1] *adjective* (tamer, tamest) **1** Not wild or fierce, not dangerous to humans. *tame animals.* **2** Dull, uninteresting. **tamely** *adverb*, **tameness** *noun*.

tame[2] *verb* (tames, taming, tamed) To make an animal tame. **tamer** *noun*.

tamper *verb* (tampers, tampering, tampered) To meddle with something.

tan[1] *verb* (tans, tanning, tanned) **1** to develop a brown colour in the skin by being in the sun. **2** To make an animal's skin into leather. **tanner** *noun*.

tan[2] *noun* A colour, yellowish-brown.

tan[3] *noun* A suntan.

tandem *noun* (tandems) A bicycle for two people.

tandoori *noun* A kind of Indian cookery.

tang *noun* A sharp taste.

tangerine *noun* (tangerines) A kind of small orange.

tangible *adjective* Able to be touched, real.

tangle *verb* (tangles, tangling, tangled) **1** To become confused and muddled. *tangled string.* **2** To make something into a confused muddle.

tank *noun* (tanks) **1** A container for a liquid or a gas. *a petrol tank.* **2** An armoured fighting vehicle.

tankard *noun* (tankards) A kind of mug.

tanker *noun* (tankers) **1** A ship designed to carry oil. **2** A lorry with a large tank for carrying liquid. *a milk tanker.*

tantalize *verb* (tantalizes, tantalizing, tantalized) To torment somebody with the offer of something which he or she can never have. **tantalizingly** *adverb*.

tantrum *noun* (tantrums) A fit of bad temper.

tap¹ *noun* (taps) **1** A device for controlling the flow of a liquid or a gas. *a water tap, a gas tap.* **2** A quick light hit.

tap² *verb* (taps, tapping, tapped) To hit something quickly and lightly.

tap-dancing *noun* A kind of dancing in which you make tapping steps on the floor.

tape¹ *noun* (tapes) **1** A narrow strip of cloth, paper, or plastic. *sticky tape, insulating tape.* **2** A plastic tape coated with a magnetic substance used to make sound or video recordings.

tape² *verb* (tapes, taping, taped) **1** To fasten or surround something with tape. **2** To record sound on tape.

tape-measure *noun* (tape-measures) A tape marked in centimetres or inches.

taper *verb* (tapers, tapering, tapered) To become gradually narrower towards one end.

tape-recorder *noun* (tape-recorders) An apparatus for recording and playing back sound using magnetic tape. **tape-recording** *noun*.

tapestry *noun* (tapestries) A piece of cloth with pictures or patterns woven into the material.

tar¹ *noun* A black sticky substance used in road-making. **tarry** *adjective*.

tar² *verb* (tars, tarring, tarred) To put tar on something.

tarantula *noun* (tarantulas) A kind of large spider.

target *noun* (targets) Something to be aimed at.

tarmac *noun* An area made of crushed stones and tar such as a school playground.

tarnish *verb* (tarnishes, tarnishing, tarnished) To become dull or discoloured instead of shiny.

tarpaulin *noun* (tarpaulins) A large thick waterproof sheet.

tart¹ *adjective* Sour, sharp-tasting. **tartly** *adjective*, **tartness** *noun*.

tart² *noun* (tarts) **1** Pastry with jam or fruit on it. **2** A shallow fruit pie.

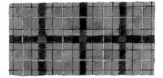

tartan *noun* A kind of cloth from the Scottish Highlands with a criss-cross pattern.

task *noun* (tasks) A piece of work to be done.

task-force *noun* (task-forces) A group of people with orders to carry out a particular operation.

tassel *noun* (tassels) A bunch of loose threads decorating the end of a cord.

taste¹ *verb* (tastes, tasting, tasted) **1** To use the tongue to recognize or get to know things. **2** To have a taste or flavour. *This tastes of onion.*

taste² *noun* (tastes) **1** The ability to taste. *the sense of taste.* **2** Flavour, the quality of a thing which a person can taste. **3** The ability to appreciate beautiful things. *good taste in clothes.* **tasteful, tasteless** *adjectives*, **tastefully, tastelessly** *adverbs*.

tasty *adjective* (tastier, tastiest) Pleasant to the taste.

tattered *adjective* Torn, in rags.

tatters *noun* Rags.

tattoo¹ *noun* (tattoos) **1** Something tattooed on a person's skin. **2** A drumbeat. **3** A display given by troops for entertainment.

tattoo² *verb* (tattoos, tattooing, tattooed) To make a design on a person's skin by pricking it and putting in colouring.

tatty *adjective* (tattier, tattiest) (informal) Shabby, ragged.

taught See **teach**

taunt verb (taunts, taunting, taunted) To mock someone with insults.

taut adjective Tightly stretched.

tavern noun (taverns) An inn, a public house.

tawdry adjective Showy but of no value.

tawny adjective Yellowish-brown.

tax[1] noun (taxes) Money which people have to pay to the government in order to run the affairs of the country.

tax[2] verb (taxes, taxing, taxed) To put a tax on somebody or something. **taxable** adjective.

taxi[1] noun (taxis) A car with a driver which may be hired for short journeys.

taxi[2] verb (taxies, taxiing, taxied) To move along the ground before or after flying. The plane taxied across the aerodrome.

tea[1] noun 1 The dried leaves of an Asian shrub, used to make a hot drink. 2 This drink. 3 (teas) An afternoon meal at which you usually drink tea.

tea-bag noun (tea-bags) A small bag containing enough tea for one drink.

teach verb (teaches, teaching, taught) 1 To pass on knowledge or skill to somebody. Ethel taught me how to stand on my head. 2 To give instruction in a particular subject. Mrs Harding teaches the piano. **teacher** noun.

teachable adjective Able to be taught.

tea-cloth noun (tea-cloths) A cloth used to dry dishes.

teak noun A hard wood from the Far East.

team noun (teams) 1 A set of people playing on the same side in a game. 2 A group working together.

team-work noun Co-operation.

teapot noun (teapots) A pot with a spout, in which tea is made.

tear[1] verb (tears, tearing, tore, torn) 1 To pull apart, to pull into pieces, to pull away from the proper place. 2 To rush. He tore down the road with the police after him.

tear[2] noun (tears) A drop of salty water coming from somebody's eye. **tearful** adjective, **tearfully** adverb. **tear gas** a gas that makes people's eyes water painfully.

tear-drop noun (tear-drops) A tear.

tease verb (teases, teasing, teased) To make fun by bothering somebody or by making joking remarks.

teaspoon noun (teaspoons) A small spoon used for stirring tea.

teat noun (teats) 1 A nipple through which a mother gives her baby milk. 2 The rubber cap on a baby's feeding bottle.

technical adjective Concerned with machinery or with the way things work.

technician noun (technicians) A mechanic, a technical assistant.

technique noun (techniques) A skilled way of doing something.

technology noun The science of machines and their uses. **technologist** noun.

teddy-bear noun (teddy-bears) A stuffed toy bear.

tedious adjective Long and boring. **tediously** adverb.

teem verb (teems, teeming, teemed) 1 To swarm, to be present in large numbers. 2 To rain hard.

teenage adjective Connected with teenagers.

teenager noun (teenagers) A person aged from 13 to 19.

teens noun The period of your life from 13 to 19 years of age.

teeny adjective (teenier, teeniest) Tiny.

teeth See **tooth**

teething adjective Beginning to grow teeth.

teetotaller noun (teetotallers) A person who never drinks alcoholic drink.

telecommunications *noun* Communications over considerable distance by such means as radio, TV, and the telephone.

telegram *noun* (telegrams) A short message delivered quickly by the post office.

telegraph pole A pole carrying telephone wires.

telepathy *noun* The ability to understand what is in the mind of someone else without the help of speaking, writing, or other signs. **telepathic** *adjective*.

telephone¹ *noun* (telephones) An instrument connected by wires to other apparatus which enables one person to speak to another a long distance away.

telephone² *verb* (telephones, telephoning, telephoned) To speak by telephone.

telephoto lens A camera lens which makes distant objects appear nearer.

telescope¹ *noun* (telescopes) An instrument for seeing distant objects more clearly.

telescope² *verb* (telescopes, telescoping, telescoped) To make something shorter by sliding one section inside another like the tubes of a portable telescope. **telescopic** *adjective*.

televise *verb* (televises, televising, televised) To broadcast on television.

television *noun* **1** Broadcasting and receiving pictures through the air by means of radio waves. **2** An apparatus for receiving such pictures. **3** Televised programmes.

tell *verb* (tells, telling, told) **1** To pass on a story or information or instructions by speaking. **teller** *noun*. **2** To distinguish, to decide. *Can you tell the difference between the twins?* **tell off** to tell someone that you are cross with him or her.

telly *noun* (tellies) (informal) Television.

temper *noun* **1** A tendency to become angry. *Take care: that dog's got a temper.* **2** A mood, a condition of the mind. *Dad's in a good temper today.* **lose your temper** to become very angry.

temperament *noun* A person's nature or character.

temperamental *adjective* Liable to quick changes of mood.

temperature *noun* (temperatures) The measurement in degrees of how hot or cold something is. **have a temperature** to have the temperature of your body higher than normal.

tempest *noun* (tempests) A violent storm.

temple *noun* (temples) **1** A building used for worship. **2** The part of the head between the forehead and the ear.

tempo *noun* (tempos) The speed or rhythm of something, especially of a piece of music.

temporary *adjective* For a short time only. **temporarily** *adverb*.

tempt *verb* (tempts, tempting, tempted) To try to persuade somebody to do something which he or she ought not to do. **tempter**, **temptation**. *nouns*.

ten (tens) The number 10. **tenth**.

tenant *noun* (tenants) A person who rents somewhere to live or work.

tend *verb* (tends, tending, tended) **1** To take care of something. **2** To have a tendency.

tendency *noun* (tendencies) An inclination.

tender[1] *adjective* (tenderer, tenderest) **1** Soft, delicate, easily damaged. *tender plants*. **2** Easily cut, easily chewed. *tender meat*. **3** Loving. *a tender kiss*. **tenderly** *adverb*, **tenderness** *noun*.

tender[2] *noun* (tenders) A truck attached to a steam locomotive to carry coal and water.

tennis *noun* A game played with rackets and a ball.

tenor *noun* (tenors) A male singer with a high voice.

tense *adjective* Stretched tight, strained, excited. **tensely** *adverb*, **tension** *noun*.

tent *noun* (tents) A kind of shelter made of canvas or nylon.

tentacle *noun* (tentacles) A thin snake-like part of certain animals. *the tentacles of an octopus*.

tepee *noun* (tepees) A wigwam.

tepid *adjective* Slightly warm.

term *noun* (terms) **1** A period of time when a school or college is open. **2** A word or expression. *We learned some technical terms to do with computers*. **terms 1** Conditions. *If you join our club you must agree to our terms*. **2** Charges. *The hotel's terms are reasonable*. **easy terms** paying by instalments. **on good terms** friendly with one another.

terminal[1] *noun* (terminals) **1** One of the two places on a battery for wires to be attached. **2** A terminus, the end of a transport route. **3** Part of a large computer system, usually consisting of a keyboard and a VDU.

terminal[2] *adjective* Final, ending something.

terminate *verb* (terminates, terminating, terminated) To stop, to end.

terminus *noun* (termini) The end of a railway line or bus route.

terrace *noun* (terraces) **1** A level area in front of a building. **2** A levelled area on a hillside. **3** A row of houses all joined together.

terrestrial *adjective* Belonging to the planet Earth.

terrible *adjective* Frightening, dreadful. **terribly** *adverb*.

terrier *noun* (terriers) A kind of small dog.

terrific *adjective* (informal) **1** Very great. **2** Excellent. **terrifically** *adverb*.

terrify *verb* (terrifies, terrifying, terrified) To fill somebody with fear.

territory *noun* (territories) **1** An area of land. **2** An area of land belonging to an individual or nation. **territorial** *adjective*.

terror *noun* (terrors) Great fear.

terrorist *noun* (terrorists) A person who commits acts of violence for political reasons. **terrorism** *noun*.

terrorize *verb* (terrorizes, terrorizing, terrorized) To fill people with terror.

terse *adjective* Brief. **tersely** *adverb*.

tessellation *noun* A pattern consisting of shapes joined together without spaces between them.

test[1] *noun* (tests) **1** An examination or trial to find out what a person knows or can do, or what the qualities of something are. **2** A test match. **test match** an international match in cricket or Rugby. **test pilot** a pilot who flies aircraft to test them.

test[2] *verb* (tests, testing, tested) To make a test.

testament *noun* (testaments) **Old Testament, New Testament** the two main parts of the Bible.

testicles *noun* The pair of roundish

organs beneath the penis which produce sperm.

testify *verb* (testifies, testifying, testified) To give evidence.

testimony *noun* (testimonies) Evidence.

test-tube *noun* (test-tubes) A glass tube used for experiments in chemistry.

testy *adjective* (testier, testiest) Cross, irritable. **testily** *adverb*.

tether¹ *noun* (tethers) A rope for tying up an animal. **at the end of your tether** unable to put up with something any longer.

tether² *verb* (tethers, tethering, tethered) To tie up with a tether.

text *noun* (texts) **1** The words in a book. **2** A sentence from the Bible.

textbook *noun* (textbooks) A book intended to teach the basic facts about a subject.

textiles *noun* Kinds of cloth.

texture *noun* (textures) The way the surface of a thing feels. *Silk has a smooth texture.*

than *conjunction* A word used when making comparisons. *Cindy is older than Sophie.*

thank *verb* (thanks, thanking, thanked) To tell people that you appreciate something they have done or something they have given. **thankful** *adjective*, **thankfully** *adverb*, **thankfulness** *noun*. **thank you, thanks** polite ways of thanking someone. **thanks to** because of.

that¹ *pronoun* (those) The one there, the one indicated. *Will you have that over there, or this over here?*

that² This word is used in several kinds of sentence including the following: **1** *Have you opened the letter that came this morning?* **2** *I hope that you are well.* **3** *I slept so soundly that I didn't hear the alarm.* **4** *Speak louder so that we can hear.*

thatch¹ *verb* (thatches, thatching, thatched) To make a roof out of straw or reeds. **thatcher** *noun*.

thatch² *noun* Straw or reeds used to make a roof.

thaw¹ *verb* (thaws, thawing, thawed) **1** To become unfrozen. **2** To unfreeze something.

thaw² *noun* (thaws) The melting of snow or ice.

the A particular one, this or that, these or those. *Shut the window and draw the curtains. The rich, the poor*, all rich people, all poor people.

theatre *noun* (theatres) A building designed for the performance of plays to an audience. **operating theatre** a room where a surgeon performs operations.

theatrical *adjective* Of acting or plays.

theft *noun* (thefts) Stealing.

their or **theirs** Belonging to them.

them *See* they

theme *noun* (themes) **1** A subject or topic. **2** One of the main tunes in a musical composition. **theme park** a park with various amusements and rides organized round a particular idea or theme.

themselves *See* they. This word is used in the same ways as **herself.**

then *adverb* **1** At that time. *There were dinosaurs then.* **2** Next, after that time. *The rain stopped and then the sun came out.* **3** In that case. *If you are tired, then have a rest.*

theology *noun* The study of religion.

theory *noun* (theories) **1** An idea suggested to explain something. **2** The general principles of a subject. *the theory of music.* **theoretical** *adjective*.

therapy *noun* (therapies) Treatment.

there *adverb* 1 In that place, at that place, to that place. *Cheer up, we'll soon be there.* 2 This word is also used to call attention to something, or for emphasis. *There she goes! There, what did I tell you?*

therefore *adverb* For that reason.

thermometer *noun* (thermometers) An instrument for measuring temperature.

Thermos *noun* (Thermoses) The trade name for a container which keeps hot drinks hot.

thermostat *noun* (thermostats) An automatic device for keeping a steady temperature. **thermostatic** *adjective*.

thesaurus *noun* (thesauruses) A book which gives you lists of words of similar or related meaning.

these *See* **this**

they *pronoun* (them, themselves) The people or things being talked about.

thick *adjective* (thicker, thickest) 1 Not thin, measuring a comparatively long distance through from one surface to the opposite one. *a thick slice of toast.* 2 Measuring through from one surface to the opposite one. *a beam of wood 10 cm thick.* 3 Dense, hard to see through or to get through. *thick mist, a thick crowd.* 4 Not flowing as quickly as water. *thick gravy.* 5 (informal) Stupid. **thickly** *adverb*, **thickness** *noun*.

thicken *verb* (thickens, thickening, thickened) 1 To make thicker. 2 To become thicker.

thicket *noun* (thickets) A group of trees or shrubs growing closely together.

thief *noun* (thieves) A person who steals.

thigh *noun* (thighs) The part of the leg above the knee.

thimble *noun* (thimbles) A small cap to protect the end of your finger when sewing.

thin¹ *adjective* (thinner, thinnest) 1 Not fat. *a thin person.* 2 Not thick. *a thin slice of bread, thin hair, thin gravy.* **thinly** *adverb*, **thinness** *noun*.

thin² *verb* (thins, thinning, thinned) 1 To make thin. 2 To become thin.

thing *noun* (things) 1 Anything which can be touched or seen, any object, any person, any animal. *What's that thing floating in the water?* 2 An action, a happening. *An odd thing happened to me today.* 3 An idea, a thought. *I have several things on my mind.* **things** circumstances. *Things are getting worse and worse.*

think *verb* (thinks, thinking, thought) To use the mind, to have an idea, to have an opinion. **thinker** *noun*.

third¹ *adjective* Next after the second. **the Third World** the poorer countries of Asia, Africa, and South America.

third² *noun* (thirds) One of the three equal parts into which something is or can be divided.

thirst *noun* (thirsts) A strong desire for something to drink. **thirsty** *adjective*, **thirstily** *adverb*, **thirstiness** *noun*.

thirteen The number 13. **thirteenth.**

thirty (thirties) The number 30. **thirtieth.**

this *pronoun* (these) The one near here, the one being considered.

thistle *noun* (thistles) A wild plant with prickly leaves.

thorn *noun* (thorns) A sharp pointed growth on the stem of a plant. **thorny** *adjective*.

thorough *adjective* Complete, without leaving anything out.

thoroughfare *noun* (thoroughfares) A road, a busy road.

those See **that**[1]

though[1] adverb However. *He never did come back, though, in spite of his promise.*

though[2] conjunction In spite of the fact that. *I did go out, though it was raining.*

thought[1] See **think**

thought[2] noun (thoughts) **1** Thinking. **2** An idea, an opinion. **3** Caring, consideration. *He has no thought for others.* **thoughtful** adjective, **thoughtfully** adverb, **thoughtfulness** noun.

thoughtless adjective Showing no thought for others. **thoughtlessly** adverb, **thoughtlessness** noun.

thousand (thousands) The number 1000. **thousandth.**

thrash verb (thrashes, thrashing, thrashed) **1** To hit repeatedly, to beat someone with a stick or whip. **2** To move the limbs about violently. **3** To defeat someone.

thread[1] noun (threads) **1** A length of cotton, wool, nylon, or other substance which can be used for sewing or for making cloth. **2** A long thin length of any other substance. **3** The raised line and groove which goes round and round a screw.

thread[2] verb (threads, threading, threaded) **1** To pass thread through the eye of a needle. **2** To put things on a thread. *to thread beads.*

threadbare adjective Shabby, badly worn.

threat noun (threats) **1** A warning, a sign of coming trouble or danger. **2** Something or someone likely to cause trouble or danger.

threaten verb (threatens, threatening, threatened) **1** To make threats. **2** To be a threat. **threateningly** adverb.

three (threes) The number 3.

three-dimensional adjective Having depth as well as breadth and height.

thresh verb (threshes, threshing, threshed) To separate the grain from the husks of corn.

threw See **throw**[1]

thrift noun Being thrifty.

thrifty adjective (thriftier, thriftiest) Careful with money. **thriftily** adverb.

thrill[1] noun (thrills) **1** A feeling of great excitement. **2** Something which causes great excitement.

thrill[2] verb (thrills, thrilling, thrilled) To cause a feeling of great excitement. **thrillingly** adverb.

thriller noun (thrillers) An exciting story about crime or spying.

thrive verb (thrives, thriving, thrived or throve) To grow strongly, to develop successfully.

throat noun (throats) **1** The front of the neck. **2** The tube in the neck through which food and air pass into the body.

throb verb (throbs, throbbing, throbbed) To beat with a steady rhythm, to vibrate.

throne noun (thrones) A chair used by a king or queen in official ceremonies.

throng[1] verb (throngs, thronging, thronged) To crowd.

throng[2] noun (throngs) A crowd.

throttle[1] verb (throttles, throttling, throttled) To strangle.

throttle[2] noun (throttles) A device to control the flow of petrol to an engine, an accelerator.

through[1] preposition **1** Into something and out at the other end or side. *We went through a tunnel.* **2** From the beginning to the end of something. *Dad slept through the film.* **3** By means of. *I heard the news through a friend.* **4** Because of. *Accidents happen through carelessness.*

through[2] adverb **1** Through something. *I squeezed through.* **2** Finished. *Wait until I'm through with my homework.* **get through an exam** to pass it. **get through to someone** to communicate or make contact with someone. **see something through** to finish it.

throughout *preposition and adverb* All through, right through.

throw *verb* (throws, throwing, threw, thrown) **1** To make something move through the air by a jerk of the arm. **2** To make somebody or something move suddenly through the air. **3** To move the arms or other parts of the body violently about. **4** To form clay into a pot on a wheel. **thrower** *noun*.

thrush *noun* (thrushes) A song-bird with a light speckled breast.

thrust *verb* (thrusts, thrusting, thrust) To push suddenly or violently.

thud *noun* (thuds) The sound of a hard object hitting something softer.

thug *noun* (thugs) A violent criminal.

thumb *noun* (thumbs) The short thick finger growing separately from the others.

thump *verb* (thumps, thumping, thumped) **1** To hit something heavily. **2** To make a thud.

thunder[1] *noun* **1** The loud sound that follows lightning. **thundery** *adjective*. **2** A loud rumbling sound. **thunderous** *adjective*.

thunder[2] *verb* (thunders, thundering, thundered) To make the sound of thunder.

thunderstruck *adjective* Amazed.

Thursday *noun* (Thursdays) The fifth day of the week.

thus *adverb* In this way.

Tibetan *adjective* Of Tibet.

tick[1] *noun* (ticks) **1** A light regular sound like the sound of a clock. **2** The mark ✔.

tick[2] *verb* (ticks, ticking, ticked) To make a tick. **tick off** (informal) to tell

somebody that you are angry with him or her.

ticket *noun* (tickets) A small piece of paper or card such as you buy to travel on a bus or train.

tickle *verb* (tickles, tickling, tickled) **1** To touch your skin lightly so as to make you laugh or feel irritated. **2** To itch.

ticklish *adjective* **1** Liable to laugh when tickled. **2** Needing care and skill. *a ticklish problem*.

tidal *adjective* To do with or affected by the sea's tides. **tidal wave** an unusually large wave.

tiddler *noun* (tiddlers) (informal) Any tiny fish.

tiddlywinks *noun* A game played with small coloured counters.

tide *noun* (tides) The rising and falling of the sea which happens twice a day.

tidings *noun* (old-fashioned) News.

tidy[1] *adjective* (tidier, tidiest) Neat, carefully arranged. **tidily** *adverb*, **tidiness** *noun*.

tidy[2] *verb* (tidies, tidying, tidied) To make tidy.

tie[1] *verb* (ties, tying, tied) **1** To make a knot. **2** To fasten with string or cord. **3** To finish a game or competition with an equal score or in an equal position.

tie[2] *noun* (ties) **1** A strip of material worn under the collar of a shirt and tied in a knot in front. **2** An equal result in a game or competition.

tiger *noun* (tigers) A large fierce animal of the cat family. **tigress** *noun*.

tight *adjective* (tighter, tightest)
1 Firmly fastened. **2** Closely fitting.
3 Fully stretched. **4** Crowded close
together. *tight as sardines.* **5** (informal) Drunk. **tightly** *adverb*, **tightness** *noun*.

tighten *verb* (tightens, tightening,
tightened) **1** To make tighter. **2** To
become tighter.

tight-rope *noun* (tight-ropes) A tightly
stretched rope for acrobats to
perform on.

tights *noun* A garment which fits
tightly over the legs and lower part
of the body.

tile *noun* (tiles) A thin piece of baked
clay or other material for covering
roofs, walls, or floors.

tiled *adjective* Covered with tiles.

till¹ *conjunction* Until.

till² *noun* (tills) A box or drawer for
money on the counter of a shop.

till³ *verb* (tills, tilling, tilled) To dig
ground to grow crops.

tiller *noun* (tillers) A lever used to turn
a rudder in a boat.

tilt *verb* (tilts, tilting, tilted) To lean.

timber *noun* (timbers) Wood for building or carpentry.

time¹ *noun* (times) **1** The passing by of
minutes, hours, days, or years. *You
don't notice time when you are busy.*
2 A particular moment in time. *The
time is just one o'clock.* **3** A length of
time. *Is there time for another cup of
tea?* **4** A period of history. *Shakespeare
was born in the time of Elizabeth I.*
5 The speed and rhythm of a piece of
music. *If you play in a group you must
keep time with the others.* **times** multiplied by. *4 times 2 is 8 (4 × 2 = 8).* **in
time** not late, eventually. **on time**
punctual.

time² *verb* (times, timing, timed) **1** To
measure the time taken to do something. **2** To note the time at which
something is done. **timer** *noun*.

timely *adjective* Happening at the right
time.

timetable *noun* (timetables) **1** A table
showing when buses, trains, or other
forms of transport come and go. **2** A
table showing when various lessons
take place in school.

timid *adjective* Not very brave. **timidly**
adverb, **timidity** *noun*.

timorous *adjective* Timid. **timorously**
adverb.

timpani *noun* Kettledrums.

tin¹ *noun* A soft silvery metal.

tin² *noun* (tins) A container made of
thin sheet iron coated with tin.

tin³ *verb* (tins, tinning, tinned) To pack
something into tins. *tinned fruit.*

tin-foil *noun* A thin silvery sheet used
in packing food and other products.

tinged *adjective* Coloured slightly.

tingle *verb* (tingles, tingling, tingled)
To have a slight stinging feeling
under the skin.

tinker¹ *noun* (tinkers) A travelling
repairer of pots and pans.

tinker² *verb* (tinkers, tinkering, tinkered) To try to adjust or repair something without the proper knowledge
and skill.

tinkle *verb* (tinkles, tinkling, tinkled)
To make a number of light ringing
sounds.

tinny *adjective* (tinnier, tinniest) **1** Like
tin. **2** Thin and of poor quality.

tin-opener *noun* (tin-openers) A tool
for opening tinned foods.

tinsel *noun* A shiny material used in
decoration.

tint *noun* (tints) A pale shade, a kind of colour. *a light yellow tint.*

tinted *adjective* Slightly coloured.

tiny *adjective* (tinier, tiniest) Very small.

tip[1] *noun* (tips) **1** The thin end of something. **2** A piece fitted to the end of something. **3** A small present of money given to somebody who has done you a service. *Don't forget to give the waiter a tip.* **4** A piece of advice. **5** A place where rubbish is tipped.

tip[2] *verb* (tips, tipping, tipped) **1** To move on to one edge, to overturn. **2** To empty a container thus. **3** To fit a tip or point on something. **4** To give someone money as a tip.

tiptoe *noun* **on tiptoe** on your toes.

tire *verb* (tires, tiring, tired) **1** To become tired. **2** To make a person tired.

tired *adjective* Feeling that you need to rest or sleep. **tiredness** *noun*.

tiresome *adjective* Annoying. **tiresomely** *adverb*.

tissue *noun* (tissues) A piece of soft paper used for cleaning or for blowing your nose.

tissue-paper *noun* Very thin paper.

tit *noun* (tits) A small bird.

titbit *noun* (titbits) A small piece of something good to eat.

title *noun* (titles) **1** The name of a story, or a picture, or a piece of music. **2** A word which shows a person's profession or position, such as *Dr, Lord, Sir, Mrs.*

titter *verb* (titters, tittering, tittered) To give a silly laugh.

TNT A powerful explosive.

to *preposition* **1** In the direction of, towards. *travelling to the moon.* **2** As far as. *They got to their destination.* **3** Rather than, compared with. *Susan prefers dogs to cats.*

to and fro Backwards and forwards.

toad *noun* (toads) A creature like a large frog.

toadstool *noun* (toadstools) A kind of fungus.

toast[1] *verb* (toasts, toasting, toasted) To make something crisp and brown by heating it. **toaster** *noun*.

toast[2] *noun* Toasted bread. **drink a toast** to wish someone happiness or success while drinking a glass of wine.

tobacco *noun* The dried leaves of certain plants prepared for smoking in pipes, cigarettes, or cigars.

tobacconist *noun* (tobacconists) A shopkeeper who sells tobacco.

toboggan *noun* (toboggans) A long narrow sledge. **tobogganing** *noun*.

today *noun* This present day.

toddler *noun* (toddlers) A young child just learning to walk.

to-do *noun* A fuss, much excitement.

toe *noun* (toes) **1** A part of the body at the end of the foot. **2** Part of a shoe or sock covering the toes.

toffee *noun* (toffees) A brown sticky sweet.

together *adverb* **1** In company, side by side. **2** Brought into contact, joined one to the other.

toil[1] *verb* (toils, toiling, toiled) **1** To work hard. **2** To make slow and difficult progress.

toil[2] *noun* Hard work.

toilet *noun* (toilets) A lavatory.

toilet-paper *noun* Paper used in a lavatory.

toilet-roll *noun* (toilet-rolls) A roll of toilet-paper.

token *noun* (tokens) **1** A sign of something. **2** A counter, a voucher. *a bus token, a book token.*

told *See* tell

tolerate *verb* (tolerates, tolerating, tolerated) To put up with something, to endure it, not to protest about it. **tolerable** *adjective*, **tolerance**, **toleration** *nouns*.

toll[1] *verb* (tolls, tolling, tolled) To ring a bell slowly.

toll[2] *noun* A payment, a charge made for using some bridges or roads.

toll-bridge *noun* (toll-bridges) A bridge where a toll is charged.

tomahawk *noun* (tomahawks) A North American Indian axe.

tomato *noun* (tomatoes) A soft juicy fruit.

tomb *noun* (tombs) A place where dead bodies are buried or placed.

tombstone *noun* (tombstones) A stone to mark a tomb.

tomcat *noun* (tomcats) A male cat.

tomorrow *noun* The day after today.

tom-tom *noun* (tom-toms) A kind of drum.

ton (tons) *noun* **1** A unit of weight, 2,240 pounds or about 1,020 kilograms. **2** (informal) 100 miles per hour. **tons** a great amount.

tone[1] *noun* (tones) **1** A musical sound. **2** A quality which indicates the character of something. *There was an angry tone in his voice.* **3** A shade of a colour.

tone[2] *verb* (tones, toning, toned) **tone down** to make something quieter or less violent.

tongs *noun* A tool for picking things up. *coal tongs.*

tongue *noun* (tongues) **1** The long soft movable part of the mouth used in talking, tasting, and licking. **2** Something shaped like a tongue. **3** A language.

tongue-tied *adjective* Unable to speak because of shyness.

tongue-twister *noun* (tongue-twisters) Something which is difficult to say.

tonic *noun* (tonics) Something which makes you stronger and healthier.

tonight *noun* This night, the night which follows today.

tonne *noun* (tonnes) A metric unit of weight, 1,000 kilograms.

tonsillitis *noun* A disease of the tonsils.

tonsils *noun* One of the two soft small organs in the throat.

too *adverb* **1** Also, in addition. *Jamie can come too.* **2** More than is wanted. *The tea is too hot.*

took *See* **take**

tool *noun* (tools) An instrument or device which a person uses to do a certain job.

tooth *noun* (teeth) **1** One of the hard white parts growing in rows in the mouth which are used for biting and chewing. **2** One of a row of pointed parts of something. *the teeth of a saw.*

toothache *noun* Pain in a tooth.

toothbrush *noun* (toothbrushes) A brush for the teeth.

toothless *adjective* Without teeth.

toothpaste *noun* A cleaning paste used on a toothbrush.

top[1] *noun* (tops) **1** The highest part or point of a thing. **2** The upper surface of a thing. **3** The person or thing or team in the highest position. **4** A toy which spins on its point.

top[2] *adjective* Highest. *the top floor.*

top[3] *verb* (tops, topping, topped) **1** To put a top on something. **2** To be the top of something.

top-heavy *adjective* Too heavy at the top.

topic *noun* (topics) A subject for discussion or study.

topical *adjective* In the news.

topple *verb* (topples, toppling, toppled) **1** To throw off. **2** To fall off.

topsy-turvy *adverb and adjective* Upside down, muddled.

Torah *noun* The first five books of the Jewish scriptures.

torch *noun* (torches) A portable electric light.

tore *See* **tear**[1]

toreador *noun* (toreadors) A bull-fighter.

torment *verb* (torments, tormenting, tormented) To cause suffering, to torture. **tormentor** *noun*.

torn *See* **tear**[1]

tornado *noun* (tornadoes) A violent storm.

torpedo[1] *noun* (torpedoes) A weapon which travels under its own power just below the surface of the water to its target.

torpedo[2] *verb* (torpedoes, torpedoing, torpedoed) To attack with torpedoes.

torrent *noun* (torrents) A violent rushing stream.

torrential *adjective* Rushing like a torrent.

tortoise *noun* (tortoises) A kind of slow animal with a hard shell.

torture[1] *verb* (tortures, torturing, tortured) To cause somebody great pain. **torturer** *noun*.

torture[2] *noun* (tortures) Cruel treatment that causes great pain.

Tory *noun* (Tories) A supporter of the Conservative Party.

toss *verb* (tosses, tossing, tossed) **1** To throw. **2** To move about restlessly in bed.

total[1] *adjective* Complete. *a total eclipse.* **totally** *adverb*.

total[2] *noun* (totals) The amount to which something adds up.

total[3] *verb* (totals, totalling, totalled) To add up to something. *The bills totalled over £50.*

totem pole A large post with religious significance, carved by North American Indians.

totter *verb* (totters, tottering, tottered) To walk unsteadily, to wobble. **tottery** *adjective*.

touch[1] *verb* (touches, touching, touched) **1** To put the hand or fingers on something, to feel it. **2** To come into contact with something, to hit it lightly. *The car touched the kerb.* **3** To be in contact, not to be separated. **4** To affect a person's feelings. *Mother was touched by the gift of flowers.* **5** To come up to a certain level briefly. *The temperature touched 23 ° C.* **touch down** to land. **touch up** to improve something by small changes.

touch[2] *noun* (touches) **1** The act of touching something. **2** The sense which enables a person to feel things. *the sense of touch.* **3** A very small amount of something. *There is a touch of frost this morning.* **4** A special skill. *I seem to have lost my touch.* **into touch** across the touch-line.

touch-down *noun* (touch-downs) **1** The landing of an aircraft. **2** In rugby football, the pressing of the ball on the ground behind the goal-line.

touch-line *noun* (touch-lines) A line along the side of a football pitch.

touchy *adjective* (touchier, touchiest) Easily offended. **touchily** *adverb*, **touchiness** *noun*.

tough *adjective* (tougher, toughest) **1** Strong, not easily broken. **2** Hard to cut, hard to chew. *tough meat.* **3** Rough, violent. *a tough criminal.* **4** Difficult. *a tough problem.* **toughly** *adverb*, **toughness** *noun*.

toughen *verb* (toughens, toughening, toughened) **1** To make tougher. **2** To become tougher.

tour[1] *noun* (tours) A journey which passes through various places and ends where it began.

tour[2] *verb* (tours, touring, toured) To make a tour, to travel about on holiday. **tourist** *noun*.

tournament *noun* (tournaments) A series of games or contests.

tow *verb* (tows, towing, towed) To pull a vehicle or boat along.

toward, towards *prepositions* **1** In the direction of. *We set off towards the beach.* **2** As a contribution to. *Colin put his money towards his holiday.* **3** In relation to. *He was very friendly towards us.*

towel *noun* (towels) A cloth for drying things.

tower[1] *noun* (towers) A tall building, a tall part of a building.

tower[2] *verb* (towers, towering, towered) To rise to a great height.

town *noun* (towns) A place where there are many houses with shops, schools, places to work, and so on.

towpath *noun* (towpaths) A path beside a canal or river.

toxic *adjective* Poisonous.

toy *noun* (toys) Something to play with.

trace[1] *verb* (traces, tracing, traced) **1** To copy something by drawing over it on transparent paper. **2** To follow up traces of something or somebody.

trace[2] *noun* (traces) A mark, a sign, a piece of evidence. *The criminals left no traces.*

tracer *noun* (tracers) A bullet or shell which leaves a visible trail.

track[1] *noun* (tracks) **1** A path made by regular use. **2** A trace left by a moving person, animal, or vehicle. **3** A set of rails for trains or other vehicles. **4** A road or path for racing. **5** A metal belt used instead of wheels to drive tanks and some types of tractor. **keep track of** to know where somebody or something is. **track suit** a warm loose suit that athletes wear between events or in training.

track[2] *verb* (tracks, tracking, tracked) To follow the tracks left by something or somebody. **tracker** *noun*.

traction engine A steam engine once used on the roads.

tractor *noun* (tractors) A motor vehicle designed for farm use.

trade[1] *noun* (trades) **1** The buying or selling or exchanging of goods. **2** An occupation, a job. *I worked at the weaver's trade.* **trade union** an organized group of workers.

trade[2] *verb* (trades, trading, traded) To take part in trade, to buy and sell. **trader** *noun*. **trade in** to hand in an old thing as part of the payment for a new one.

trade-mark *noun* (trade-marks) A special sign used by one manufacturer.

tradesman *noun* (tradesmen) **1** A trader, a shopkeeper. **2** A trained worker.

tradition *noun* (traditions) **1** The passing on of ideas, or customs, or stories, or tunes from one generation to another. **2** Something passed on in this way. **traditional** *adjective*, **traditionally** *adverb*.

traffic *noun* **1** Moving vehicles. **2** Trading. *an illegal traffic in drugs.* **traffic lights** signals for controlling traffic. **traffic warden** a person who controls the movement and parking of vehicles in a town.

tragedy *noun* (tragedies) **1** A very sad event. **2** A serious story which tells of terrible events and ends sadly. **tragic** *adjective*, **tragically** *adverb*.

trail[1] *noun* (trails) A track, a trace.

trail[2] *verb* (trails, trailing, trailed) **1** To pull something along behind. **2** To go along behind someone or something. **3** To hang loosely downwards.

trailer *noun* (trailers) **1** A vehicle

designed to be towed by another vehicle. **2** A series of short extracts from a film shown in advance to advertise it.

train[1] *noun* (trains) **1** A number of railway coaches or wagons joined together. **2** A number of people or animals making a journey together. *a camel train.* **3** Part of a dress or robe that trails along the ground. **4** A series of events or ideas. *a train of thought.*

train[2] *verb* (trains, training, trained) **1** To give instruction and practice in doing something. **2** To prepare yourself by practising.

trainer *noun* (trainers) **1** A person who trains people or animals. **2** A kind of soft light shoe.

traitor *noun* (traitors) A person who betrays his or her country or friends.

tram *noun* (trams) A passenger vehicle which runs along lines set in the road.

tramp[1] *noun* (tramps) **1** A homeless person who walks from place to place. **2** The sound of tramping. **3** A long walk.

tramp[2] *verb* (tramps, tramping, tramped) **1** To walk with heavy footsteps. **2** To walk for a long distance.

trample *verb* (tramples, trampling, trampled) To tread heavily on something.

trampoline *noun* (trampolines) A large piece of canvas attached by springs to a rectangular metal frame for use in gymnastics.

trance *noun* (trances) A sleep-like condition.

tranquil *adjective* Calm, peaceful. **tranquilly** *adverb*, **tranquillity** *noun*.

tranquillizer *noun* (tranquillizers) A drug used to make a person calmer.

transatlantic *adjective* Across the Atlantic Ocean.

transfer[1] *verb* (transfers, transferring, transferred) To move something or somebody from one place to another.

transfer[2] *noun* (transfers) **1** A picture or design that can be transferred from one surface to another. **2** The act of transferring something or somebody.

transform *verb* (transforms, transforming, transformed) To change the appearance or character of something. **transformation** *noun*.

transformer *noun* (transformers) A device which changes electrical voltage.

transfusion *noun* (transfusions) Putting blood from one person into another person's body.

transient *adjective* Brief, soon past. **transience** *noun*.

transistor *noun* (transistors) **1** An electronic device used in radios and other equipment. **2** A portable radio made with transistors. **transistorized** *adjective*.

translate *verb* (translates, translating, translated) To give the meaning of something said or written in another language. **translator**, **translation** *nouns*.

translucent *adjective* Allowing light through.

transmit *verb* (transmits, transmitting, transmitted) **1** To pass something on. **2** To send out radio communications or television programmes. **transmitter**, **transmission** *nouns*.

transparency *noun* (transparencies) A transparent photograph for projecting on a screen.

transparent *adjective* Clear enough to see through.

transplant¹ *verb* (transplants, transplanting, transplanted) To take a living thing from one place and put it to grow somewhere else.

transplant² *noun* (transplants) An operation to move an organ from one person's body to another's.

transport¹ *verb* (transports, transporting, transported) To take people or goods from one place to another in a vehicle, ship, or plane.

transport² *noun* **1** Transporting people or goods. **2** Vehicles, ships, or planes used for transport.

trap¹ *noun* (traps) **1** A device for catching animals or people. **2** A small vehicle pulled by a pony.

trap² *verb* (traps, trapping, trapped) To catch in a trap. **trapper** *noun*.

trapdoor *noun* (trapdoors) A kind of door in a floor or ceiling.

trapeze *noun* A pair of long hanging ropes with a cross-bar for an acrobat to perform on.

trash *noun* Rubbish.

travel *verb* (travels, travelling, travelled) To make a journey, to move from place to place. **traveller** *noun*.

trawler *noun* (trawlers) A kind of fishing-boat.

tray *noun* (trays) A flat board with raised edges, used for carrying things.

treacherous *adjective* Not to be trusted. **treacherously** *adverb*, **treachery** *noun*.

treacle *noun* A thick sticky liquid made from sugar. **treacly** *adverb*.

tread¹ *noun* (treads) **1** A sound of walking. **2** The part of a tyre with the pattern cut into it that touches the road.

tread² *verb* (treads, treading, trod, trodden) To walk, to put your foot on something. *Who has trodden on my geraniums?*

treason *noun* Betraying your own country. **treasonable** *adjective*.

treasure¹ *noun* (treasures) **1** A store of money or valuable things. **2** Something or somebody that is highly valued.

treasure² *verb* (treasures, treasuring, treasured) **1** To value highly. **2** To store.

treasury *noun* (treasuries) A place where valuable things are stored.

treat¹ *verb* (treats, treating, treated) **1** To behave in a certain way towards somebody or something. *He treats his dog cruelly.* **2** To give medical attention to somebody. **3** To deal with something to improve or preserve it. *I treated my bike for rust.* **4** To pay for food and drink for somebody. *I'll treat you all to ices.* **treatment** *noun*.

treat² *noun* (treats) **1** Something that gives unusual pleasure. **2** An entertainment or outing that gives someone pleasure.

treaty *noun* (treaties) An agreement between nations. *a peace treaty*.

treble¹ *adjective* Three times as much, three times as many.

treble² *noun* (trebles) A boy with a high singing voice. **treble recorder** a recorder the next size larger than a descant recorder.

tree *noun* (trees) A large plant with a single wooden trunk. **treeless** *adjective*.

trek¹ *noun* (treks) A long and exhausting journey.

trek² *verb* (treks, trekking, trekked) To make a trek.

trellis *noun* (trellises) A criss-cross structure used to support climbing plants.

tremble *verb* (trembles, trembling, trembled) To shake, to shudder.

tremendous *adjective* Enormous, great. **tremendously** *adverb*.

tremor *noun* (tremors) A shaking, a vibrating.

trench *noun* (trenches) A long narrow hole in the ground, a ditch.

trend *noun* (trends) The general direction in which something is going.

trendy *adjective* (trendier, trendiest) (informal) Following the trend of fashion, fashionable. **trendily** *adverb*.

trespass *verb* (trespasses, trespassing, trespassed) To go into another person's property without permission. **trespasser** *noun*.

trestle table A table consisting of boards laid on movable supports called trestles.

trial *noun* (trials) **1** The trying of somebody in a court of law. **2** The trying or testing of someone or something.

triangle *noun* (triangles) **1** A shape with three straight sides and three angles. **2** A percussion instrument consisting of a metal rod bent into a triangle. **triangular** *adjective*.

tribe *noun* (tribes) A society of people living together ruled by a chief. **tribal** *adjective*, **tribesman** *noun*.

tributary *noun* (tributaries) A river which flows into another river.

tribute *noun* (tributes) Something which is said or done or given to show respect or admiration.

trick¹ *noun* (tricks) **1** Something done in order to deceive someone or make someone look foolish. **2** A clever way of doing something. **3** The cards played in a round of whist or other games. **trickery** *noun*.

trick² *verb* (tricks, tricking, tricked) To deceive someone with a trick.

trickle *verb* (trickles, trickling, trickled) To flow slowly or thinly.

tricky *adjective* (trickier, trickiest) **1** Cunning. **2** Skilful. **3** Difficult. **trickily** *adverb*.

tricycle *noun* (tricycles) A three-wheeled vehicle worked by pedals.

tried, trier, tries See **try¹**

trifle *noun* (trifles) **1** A pudding made of custard, cream, pieces of cake, jam, and other ingredients. **2** Something of almost no importance. **3** A small amount.

trifling *adjective* Unimportant.

trigger *noun* (triggers) The lever which fires a gun.

trim¹ *adjective* Neat and tidy. **trimly** *adverb*.

trim² *verb* (trims, trimming, trimmed) **1** To make something trim by cutting away what is not wanted. **2** To decorate. *a hat trimmed with feathers*. **3** To balance the weight of the contents of a boat or aircraft.

Trinity *noun* In Christianity, God known as Father, Son, and Holy Spirit.

trio *noun* (trios) A group of three.

trip¹ *verb* (trips, tripping, tripped) **1** To stumble. **2** To move with light steps.

trip² *noun* (trips) **1** A fall. **2** A journey, an excursion. **tripper** *noun*.

tripe *noun* **1** Part of the stomach of a pig, cow, or ox used as food. **2** (informal) Nonsense.

triple *adjective* Having three parts.

triplet *noun* (triplets) One of three children born to the same mother at one time.

tripod *noun* (tripods) A stand or support with three legs.

triumph¹ *noun* (triumphs) **1** A victory, a great success. **2** A celebration of a triumph. **triumphal, triumphant** *adjectives*, **triumphantly** *adverb*.

triumph² *verb* (triumphs, triumphing, triumphed) To win, to be successful.

trivial *adjective* Not important. **trivially** *adverb*, **triviality** *noun*.

trod, trodden *See* **tread**²

troll *noun* (trolls) An unpleasant supernatural creature in folk tales.

trolley *noun* (trolleys) **1** A small vehicle to be pushed or pulled by hand. **2** A small table on wheels.

trolley-bus *noun* (trolley-buses) An electric bus which gets its power from overhead wires.

trombone *noun* (trombones) A large brass instrument with a sliding tube. **trombonist** *noun*.

troop¹ *noun* (troops) **1** A group of people. **2** A company of scouts. **troops** soldiers.

troop² *verb* (troops, trooping, trooped) To move along in large numbers.

trophy *noun* (trophies) **1** A prize. **2** A souvenir of a victory or success.

tropics *noun* The hot regions of the world on either side of the equator. **tropical** *adjective*.

trot *verb* (trots, trotting, trotted) To move along at a pace between a walk and gallop.

trouble¹ *noun* (troubles) **1** Difficulty, grief, worry. **2** Disturbance, discontent. **3** Illness. *heart trouble*. **take trouble** to take great care over something.

trouble² *verb* (troubles, troubling, troubled) **1** To cause trouble. **2** To take trouble.

trouble-maker *noun* (trouble-makers) A person who causes trouble.

troublesome *adjective* Causing trouble.

trough *noun* (troughs) A long narrow box for animals to feed or drink from.

trousers *noun* A garment with two legs, worn over the lower part of the body.

trout *noun* (trout) A freshwater fish.

trowel *noun* (trowels) **1** A tool for digging small holes. **2** A tool for laying mortar in building.

truant *noun* (truants) A child who stays away from school without a proper excuse. **play truant** to be a truant. **truancy** *noun*.

truce *noun* (truces) An agreement to stop fighting for a time.

truck *noun* (trucks) **1** A lorry, a goods vehicle. **2** A railway wagon. **3** A barrow, a trolley.

trudge *verb* (trudges, trudging, trudged) To walk with tired heavy steps.

true *adjective* (truer, truest) **1** Correct, in agreement with the facts. *a true story*. **2** Loyal, honourable, faithful. *a true friend*. **3** Real, proper, normal, genuine. **4** Exact, accurate, perfectly adjusted. **truly** *adverb*.

trump *noun* (trumps) One of the suits of cards that can beat other suits in whist and some other card-games.

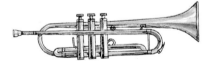

trumpet¹ *noun* (trumpets) A brass instrument which can play high notes. **trumpeter** *noun*.

trumpet² *verb* (trumpets, trumpeting, trumpeted) To make a loud sound like a trumpet.

truncheon *noun* (truncheons) A short club carried by policemen.

trundle *verb* (trundles, trundling, trundled) To roll along noisily or awkwardly.

trunk *noun* (trunks) **1** The main stem of a tree. **2** The main part of a human body. **3** A large case for use when travelling. **4** An elephant's long nose. **trunks** shorts. **trunk road** a main road.

trust¹ *verb* (trusts, trusting, trusted) **1** To believe in the goodness or strength or truth of someone or something. *to trust someone with something*, to allow him or her to look after it. **2** To hope. *I trust you are well?* **trustingly** *adverb*.

trust² *noun* **1** The feeling that someone or something can be trusted. **2** Responsibility. *to be in a position of trust*. **take something on trust** to believe it without having proof. **trustful** *adjective*, **trustfully** *adverb*, **trustfulness** *noun*.

trustworthy *adjective* Reliable, deserving to be trusted.

truth *noun* (truths) Whatever is true, something that is true. **truthful** *adjective*, **truthfully** *adverb*, **truthfulness** *noun*.

try¹ *verb* (tries, trying, tried) **1** To use energy because you want to do something, to make an effort. **trier** *noun*. **2** To test something, to use something in order to find out what it is like. **3** To examine the case against an accused person in a lawcourt. **4** To annoy.

try² *noun* (tries) **1** An attempt. **2** In rugby football, a touch-down which scores points.

T-shirt *noun* (T-shirts) A garment like a vest with short sleeves.

tub *noun* (tubs) A round container.

tuba *noun* (tubas) A large brass instrument which can play very low notes.

tubby *adjective* (tubbier, tubbiest) Short and fat.

tube *noun* (tubes) **1** A hollow length of metal, rubber, plastic, or other material, such as is used to carry water or gas. **2** A container for such things as toothpaste. **3** An underground railway in London.

tuberculosis *noun* A serious disease of the lungs or other parts of the body.

tubular bells *noun* A musical instrument with tube-shaped bells.

tuck *verb* (tucks, tucking, tucked) To push something behind, into, or under something else so that it is hidden or held in place. *I tucked my shirt inside my jeans*. **tuck in** to eat with a good appetite. **tuck up** to tuck the bedclothes round someone comfortably.

Tuesday *noun* (Tuesdays) The third day of the week.

tuft *noun* (tufts) A bunch of things growing together.

tug¹ *noun* (tugs) **1** A sudden pull. **2** A vessel designed for towing ships.

tug² *verb* (tugs, tugging, tugged) To pull hard.

tuition *noun* Teaching.

tulip *noun* (tulips) A cup-shaped flower which grows from a bulb.

tumble *verb* (tumbles, tumbling, tumbled) To fall.

tumble-down *adjective* Almost in ruins.

tumble-drier *noun* (tumble-driers) A machine that tosses washing in warm air to dry it.

tumbler *noun* (tumblers) A flat-bottomed drinking glass.

a b c d e f g h i j k l m

tummy *noun* (tummies) (informal) The stomach.

tumult *noun* (tumults) An uproar, a confused disturbance. **tumultuous** *adjective*.

tuna *noun* (tuna) A large sea-fish.

tune[1] *noun* (tunes) A series of musical notes which make a pleasant pattern of sound. **in tune** at the right pitch. **out of tune** at the wrong pitch. **tuneful** *adjective*, **tunefully** *adverb*.

tune[2] *verb* (tunes, tuning, tuned) **1** To put an instrument in tune. **2** To adjust a radio or television for the best reception of a particular programme. **tuner** *noun*.

tuning-fork *noun* (tuning-forks) A forked piece of metal which when struck sounds a particular musical note.

tunic *noun* (tunics) **1** A kind of jacket like those worn by police officers and members of the armed services. **2** A loose garment hanging from the shoulders to below the waist.

tunnel[1] *noun* (tunnels) An underground passage.

tunnel[2] *verb* (tunnels, tunnelling, tunnelled) To make a tunnel.

turban *noun* (turbans) A covering for the head made by wrapping a length of cloth round it.

turbine *noun* (turbines) A kind of engine which is operated by a jet of gas, steam, or water.

turbot *noun* (turbot *or* turbots) A sea-fish.

turbulent *adjective* Violent, disorderly. **turbulently** *adverb*, **turbulence** *noun*.

turf *noun* (turves) A layer of earth with grass growing on it.

Turk *noun* (Turks) A Turkish person.

turkey *noun* (turkeys) A large bird kept for eating.

Turkish *adjective* Of or from Turkey.

turmoil *noun* Confusion, commotion.

turn[1] *verb* (turns, turning, turned) **1** To move round as a wheel does. **2** To go round a corner, to face a new direction. *Turn left at the lights.* **3** To cause something to turn. *I can't turn the wheel.* **4** To become. *He turned pale.* **5** To control with a switch, knob, or tap. *Turn the light on.* **turn down 1** To reduce the noise from a radio or TV set. **2** To refuse. *He turned down my invitation.* **turn into** to become, change into. *Tadpoles turn into frogs.* **turn out 1** To expel, to send out. *I turned the cat out.* **2** To empty. *Turn out your pockets.* **3** To happen. *It turned out well in the end.* **turn up** to arrive. *Auntie turned up unexpectedly.*

turn[2] *noun* (turns) **1** Turning, the act of turning. **2** The proper time for one person in a group to do something. *It's Robert's turn to bowl next.* **3** (informal) An unpleasant surprise. **4** An attack of an illness. **good turn** a helpful action.

turning *noun* (turnings) A road which joins another road roughly at right angles. *Take the second turning on the left.*

turnip *noun* (turnips) A vegetable with a round white root.

turnstile *noun* (turnstiles) A kind of gate which turns and allows one person through at a time.

turntable *noun* (turntables) The part of a record-player on which the record turns.

turpentine, turps *nouns* A liquid used for thinning paint.

turquoise *adjective* Greenish-blue.

turret *noun* (turrets) **1** A small tower. **2** A revolving shelter for guns.

turtle *noun* (turtles) A sea animal with a hard shell. **turn turtle** to capsize.

tusk *noun* (tusks) A long pointed tooth such as those of the elephant or walrus.

tussle *noun* (tussles) A fight.

tutor *noun* (tutors) A teacher.

TV (informal) Television.

twaddle *noun* (informal) Nonsense.

twang *verb* (twangs, twanging, twanged) To make the sound as of a tight string being plucked.

tweed *noun* (tweeds) A woven woollen cloth.

tweezers *noun* A tool for picking up or gripping small objects.

twelve (twelves) The number 12. **twelfth**.

twenty (twenties) The number 20. **twentieth**.

twice *adverb* Two times.

twiddle *verb* (twiddles, twiddling, twiddled) To turn something aimlessly in the hand.

twig *noun* (twigs) A small piece of a branch of a tree.

twilight *noun* The dim light between day and night.

twin *noun* (twins) **1** One of two children born to the same mother at one time. **2** One of two things exactly alike. *twin beds*.

twine *noun* Thin strong string.

twinge *noun* (twinges) A sudden sharp pain.

twinkle *verb* (twinkles, twinkling, twinkled) To sparkle.

twirl *verb* (twirls, twirling, twirled) To turn round and round.

twist[1] *verb* (twists, twisting, twisted) **1** To turn something round. **2** To turn things round each other. *to twist wires together*. **3** To turn and curve. *The road twisted up the mountain.* **4** To change something into an unnatural or abnormal shape. *The accident twisted my wheel out of shape.*

twist[2] *noun* (twists) A twisting, a turning round. **twisty** *adjective*.

twitch[1] *verb* (twitches, twitching, twitched) To jerk.

twitch[2] *noun* (twitches) A jerk.

twitter *verb* (twitters, twittering, twittered) To chirp continuously.

two (twos) The number 2. **second**

tying *See* tie[1]

type[1] *noun* (types) **1** An example of something, one of a group of people or things with certain characteristics in common. *A peppermint is a type of sweet.* **2** A set or class of people or things with certain characteristics in common.

type[2] *verb* (types, typing, typed) To write with a typewriter. **typist** *noun*.

typewriter *noun* (typewriters) A machine with a keyboard for printing letters on paper.

typhoid *noun* A fever which affects your intestines.

typhoon *noun* (typhoons) A violent windy storm.

typhus *noun* A serious kind of fever.

typical *adjective* Belonging to a certain type, normal, usual. **typically** *adverb*.

tyrannical *adjective* Cruel, like a tyrant.

tyrant *noun* (tyrants) A harsh or cruel ruler who has absolute power.

tyre *noun* (tyres) **1** An air-filled rubber tube round a wheel. **2** A rim of steel or rubber round a wheel.

Uu

udder *noun* (udders) The part of a cow or goat from which milk is drawn.

UFO (UFOs) An unidentified flying object.

ugly *adjective* (uglier, ugliest) **1** Unpleasant to look at. **2** Threatening. **ugliness** *noun*.

ulcer *noun* (ulcers) An open sore.

ultimate *adjective* Last, final. **ultimately** *adverb*.

ultimatum *noun* (ultimatums) A final demand.

ultrasonic *adjective* Sounding so high that you cannot hear it.

umbrage *noun* **take umbrage** to be offended.

umbrella *noun* (umbrellas) A folding framework covered with fabric, held up to keep the rain off.

umpire *noun* (umpires) A referee in games such as cricket and tennis.

unable *adjective* Not able.

unaccountable *adjective* Not able to be explained.

unaccustomed *adjective* Not accustomed, unusual.

unanimous *adjective* With everyone agreeing. **unanimously** *adverb*, **unanimity** *noun*.

unannounced *adjective* Without warning.

unanswerable *adjective* Not able to be answered.

unarmed *adjective* Without weapons.

unassuming *adjective* Modest.

unauthorized *adjective* Not authorized.

unavoidable *adjective* Not able to be avoided.

unaware *adjective* Not aware.

unawares *adverb* Unexpectedly.

unbalanced *adjective* **1** Not balanced. **2** Not sane.

unbearable *adjective* Not endurable. **unbearably** *adverb*.

unbeaten *adjective* Not defeated.

unbecoming *adjective* Not attractive.

unbend *verb* (unbends, unbending, unbent) **1** To straighten. **2** To relax.

unbending *adjective* Firm, not yielding.

unbiased *adjective* Not biased.

uncalled-for *adjective* Not needed, not deserved. *an uncalled-for insult.*

uncanny *adjective* Unnatural, mysterious. **uncannily** *adverb*.

unceasing *adjective* Continuous. **unceasingly** *adverb*.

uncertain *adjective* **1** Changeable, not reliable. **2** Not certain. **uncertainly** *adverb*, **uncertainty** *noun*.

unchangeable *adjective* Not able to be changed.

uncharitable *adjective* Unkind. **uncharitably** *adverb*.

uncharted *adjective* Not explored, not mapped.

uncivilized *adjective* Not civilized, primitive.

uncle *noun* (uncles) **1** A brother of your father or mother. **2** The husband of your aunt.

unclean *adjective* Not clean, dirty.

unclothed *adjective* Naked.

uncomfortable *adjective* Not comfortable.

uncommon *adjective* Rare, unusual, remarkable. **uncommonly** *adverb*.

uncomplimentary *adjective* Not at all flattering, not polite.

unconcerned *adjective* Not concerned, not caring.

unconditional *adjective* Without conditions. **unconditionally** *adverb*.

unconfirmed *adjective* Not confirmed, not proved.

unconscious *adjective* **1** Not conscious. **2** Not aware. **unconsciously** *adverb*, **unconsciousness** *noun*.

uncouth *adjective* Rough, bad-mannered.

uncover *verb* (uncovers, uncovering, uncovered) To take the cover off something, to reveal it.

undamaged *adjective* Not damaged.

undaunted *adjective* Not discouraged.

undecided *adjective* Not decided, not certain.

undeniable *adjective* Not to be denied. **undeniably** *adverb*.

under [1] *preposition* This word has many meanings including the following: **1** Beneath, lower than. *under the table.* **2** Covered by. *under water.* **3** Less than. *under 5 years old.* **4** In the process of, during. *road under construction.* **5** Possessing, using. *He went* *under the name of Sanders.* **6** Subject to, obeying. *The troops were under the command of Wellington.* **under way** moving along in the water.

under ² *adverb* To a lower place. *The ship went under*, it sank.

underarm *adjective and adverb* **bowl underarm** to bowl without raising the arm above the shoulder

undercarriage *noun* (undercarriages) The wheels and landing gear of an aeroplane.

underclothes, underclothing *nouns*, Clothing worn under dresses, skirts, trousers, or other outer garments.

undercover *adjective* Secret.

underdeveloped *adjective* Not fully developed.

underdog *noun* (underdogs) A poor, helpless, or oppressed person.

underdone *adjective* Not cooked thoroughly.

underestimate *verb* (underestimates, underestimating, underestimated) To form too low an estimate of somebody or something.

underfed *adjective* Having had too little food.

underfoot *adverb* On the ground, where you walk.

undergarment *noun* (undergarments) An article of underclothing.

undergo *verb* (undergoes, undergoing, underwent, undergone) To experience something, to suffer it.

undergraduate *noun* (undergraduates) A student at a university who has not yet taken a degree.

underground ¹ *adjective and adverb* **1** Below the ground. **2** Secret.

underground ² *noun* An underground railway.

undergrowth *noun* Shrubs and bushes growing beneath tall trees.

underhand *adjective* Secret, deceitful.

underline *verb* (underlines, underlining, underlined) **1** To draw a line under a word. **2** To emphasize.

undermine *verb* (undermines, undermining, undermined) To dig away at the bottom of something, to weaken it gradually.

underneath *preposition and adverb* Under.

underpaid *adjective* Not paid enough.

underpants *noun* Underclothing for men or boys, worn on the lower half of the body.

underpass *noun* (underpasses) A place where one road passes under another.

underside *noun* (undersides) The lower side of something.

undersized *adjective* Of less than normal size.

understaffed *adjective* Not having enough staff to do the work.

understand *verb* (understands, understanding, understood) **1** To know the meaning of something, to know what it is or how it works. **2** To learn something, to get an impression from what is said or done. *I understand the field is too wet for games today.* **understandable** *adjective*, **understandably** *adverb*.

understanding ¹ *noun* **1** The power to think clearly, intelligence. **2** An agreement. **3** Consideration, sympathy.

understanding ² *adjective* Sympathetic.

understudy *noun* (understudies) An actor who learns another actor's part to be able to take his or her place if necessary.

undertake *verb* (undertakes, undertaking, undertook, undertaken) **1** To agree to do something. **2** To start to do something.

undertaker *noun* (undertakers) A person whose business it is to arrange funerals.

undertone *noun* (undertones) A quiet tone of voice.

undertow *noun* An underwater current.

underwater *adjective and adverb* Below the surface of the water.

underwear *noun* Underclothes.

underwent *See* **undergo**

underworld *noun* **1** The place of the dead in legends. **2** The world of criminals.

undesirable *adjective* Unwelcome, not wanted.

undeveloped *adjective* Not developed.

undid *See* **undo**

undistinguished *adjective* Not special.

undo *adjective* (undoes, undoing, undid, undone) **1** To untie or unfasten something. **2** To destroy the effect of something.

undone *adjective* **1** Not done. **2** Unfastened.

undoubted *adjective* Certain. **undoubtedly** *adverb*.

undress *verb* (undresses, undressing, undressed) To take off your clothes.

undue *adjective* More than is right. **unduly** *adverb*.

unearned *adjective* **1** Not earned. **2** Not deserved.

unearth *verb* (unearths, unearthing, unearthed) **1** To dig up something buried. **2** To discover something.

unearthly *adjective* **1** Supernatural. **2** Very strange.

uneasy *adjective* Anxious, uncomfort-

able. **uneasily** *adverb*, **uneasiness** *noun*.

unemployed *adjective* Without a job, not working. **unemployment** *noun*.

unequal *adjective* Not equal. **unequally** *adverb*.

unerring *adjective* Absolutely accurate. **unerringly** *adverb*.

uneven *adjective* Not even. **unevenly** *adverb*.

unexpected *adjective* Not expected, surprising. **unexpectedly** *adverb*.

unfailing *adjective* Never giving up, reliable. **unfailingly** *adverb*.

unfair *adjective* Not fair. **unfairly** *adverb*, **unfairness** *noun*.

unfaithful *adjective* Not faithful. **unfaithfully** *adverb*, **unfaithfulness** *noun*.

unfamiliar *adjective* **1** Not well known. *unfamiliar surroundings.* **2** Not having knowledge about something. *I am unfamiliar with this district.*

unfasten *verb* (unfastens, unfastening, unfastened) To open fastenings, to unlock.

unfeeling *adjective* Hard-hearted. **unfeelingly** *adverb*.

unfinished *adjective* Not finished.

unfit *adjective* Not fit, not suitable.

unfold *verb* (unfolds, unfolding, unfolded) To open out.

unforeseen *adjective* Unexpected.

unforgettable *adjective* Not able to be forgotten.

unforgiveable *adjective* Not to be forgiven.

unfortunate *adjective* Not fortunate, unhappy, unlucky. **unfortunately** *adverb*.

unfreeze *verb* (unfreezes, unfreezing, unfroze, unfrozen) To change back to a normal condition after being frozen.

unfurl *verb* (unfurls, unfurling, unfurled) To unroll, to spread out.

ungainly *adjective* Clumsy, not graceful.

ungrateful *adjective* Not grateful. **ungratefully** *adverb*.

unguarded *adjective* Not guarded.

unhappy *adjective* (unhappier, unhappiest) Not happy, sad. **unhappily** *adverb*, **unhappiness** *noun*.

unharmed *adjective* Not harmed, safe.

unhealthy *adjective* (unhealthier, unhealthiest) Not healthy. **unhealthily** *adverb*, **unhealthiness** *noun*.

unheard-of *adjective* Not known before.

unhinged *adjective* (informal) Mad.

unicorn *noun* (unicorns) A mythical creature like a horse with a long straight horn.

unidentified *adjective* Not recognized.

uniform [1] *adjective* The same. **uniformly** *adverb*, **uniformity** *noun*.

uniform [2] *noun* (uniforms) An official style of clothes worn by members of an organization or pupils of a school.

unify *verb* (unifies, unifying, unified) To make into one. **unification** *noun*.

unimportant *adjective* Not important.

unintelligible *adjective* Not able to be understood.

uninterested *adjective* Not interested.

uninterrupted *adjective* Without interruptions.

uninvited *adjective* Without being invited.

union *noun* (unions) **1** Uniting or being united. **2** An association of workers. *a trade union.* **Union Jack** the British flag.

unique *adjective* Being the only one of its kind.

unisex *adjective* For use by either sex.

unison *noun* **in unison** exactly together, sounding the same note.

unit *noun* (units) **1** A single thing. **2** A thing that is one of a group of things that belong together. *a kitchen unit.* **3** A quantity or amount used as a basis for measuring or counting. A metre is a unit of length, a dollar a unit of money. **4** An organized group of people and their equipment. *an army unit.*

unite *verb* (unites, uniting, united) To join together, to make or become one.

unity *noun* **1** Being united, being one. **2** Harmony, agreement.

universal *adjective* Concerning everything and everybody, general. **universally** *adverb*.

universe *noun* Everything that exists, the whole of space and everything in it.

university *noun* (universities) A college or group of colleges where people study for degrees or other qualifications.

unjust *adjective* Not fair, not just. **unjustly** *adverb*.

unkempt *adjective* Untidy.

unkind *adjective* Not kind, rather cruel. **unkindly** *adverb*.

unlawful *adjective* Illegal, not lawful.

unleaded *adjective* Containing no lead.

unless *conjunction* **1** If not. **2** Except when.

unlike [1] *preposition* Not like. *Unlike me, she sings well.*

unlike [2] *adjective* Not like, different. *The twins are really quite unlike.*

unlikely *adjective* (unlikelier, unlikeliest) Not likely to happen or to be true.

unload *verb* (unloads, unloading, unloaded) To remove a load from something.

unlock *verb* (unlocks, unlocking, unlocked) To open a lock.

unlucky *verb* (unluckier, unluckiest) Not lucky, unfortunate. **unluckily** *adverb*.

unmanned *adjective* Without a crew.

unmask *verb* (unmasks, unmasking, unmasked) To reveal who someone really is.

unmistakable *adjective* Clear, free from doubt. **unmistakably** *adverb*.

unnatural *adjective* Not natural. **unnaturally** *adverb*.

unnecessary *adjective* Not necessary. **unnecessarily** *adverb*.

unoccupied *adjective* Not occupied.

unofficial *adjective* Not official. **unofficially** *adverb*.

unpack *verb* (unpacks, unpacking, unpacked) To take out things which have been packed.

unpleasant *adjective* Not pleasant, disagreeable. **unpleasantly** *adverb*, **unpleasantness** *noun*.

unpopular *adjective* Disliked. **unpopularity** *noun*.

unpromising *adjective* Not showing promise. **unpromisingly** *adverb*.

unprovoked *adjective* Without having been provoked. *an unprovoked attack.*

unqualified *adjective* Not qualified.

unquestionable *adjective* Beyond doubt. **unquestionably** *adverb*.

unreadable *adjective* Not able to be read.

unreal *adjective* Imaginary, not like real life.

unreasonable *adjective* Not reasonable. **unreasonably** *adverb*.

unreliable *adjective* Not reliable.

unrest *noun* Restlessness, dissatisfaction.

unrestricted *adjective* Not restricted.

unripe *adjective* Not ripe.

unrivalled *adjective* Without close rivals.

unroll *verb* (unrolls, unrolling, unrolled) To undo something that has been rolled up.

unruly *adjective* Not easily controlled, badly behaved.

unsafe *adjective* Not to be relied on, not safe.

unsaid *adjective* Not spoken, not expressed.

unscathed *adjective* Not injured, not harmed.

unscientific *adjective* Not according to the principles of science.

unscrew *verb* (unscrews, unscrewing, unscrewed) To undo something that has been screwed up.

unscrupulous *adjective* Not having a conscience, wicked. **unscrupulously** *adverb*.

unseen *adjective* Not seen, invisible.

unselfish *adjective* Not selfish. **unselfishly** *adverb*, **unselfishness** *noun*.

unsettle *verb* (unsettles, unsettling, unsettled) To make somebody troubled or uncertain.

unsightly *adjective* Ugly.

unsteady *adjective* Not steady. **unsteadily** *adverb*.

unstuck *adjective* Not stuck, not fastened.

unsuitable *adjective* Not suitable.

unsuspected *adjective* Not suspected.

unthinkable *adjective* Not to be considered.

untidy *adjective* Not tidy. **untidily** *adverb*.

untie *verb* (unties, untying, untied) To undo something which has been tied.

until *preposition and conjunction* Up to the time when.

untold *adjective* Not able to be counted.

untouched *adjective* Not touched.

untrue *adjective* Not true.

untruth *noun* (untruths) A lie. **untruthful** *adjective*.

untwist *verb* (untwists, untwisting, untwisted) To straighten something which was twisted.

unused *adjective* Not used.

unusual *adjective* Not usual, rare. **unusually** *adverb*.

unwanted *adjective* Not wanted.

unwary *adjective* Not cautious. **unwarily** *adverb*.

unwelcome *adjective* Not welcome. **unwelcoming** *adjective*.

unwell *adjective* Ill.

unwieldy *adjective* Awkward to handle.

unwilling *adjective* Not willing. **unwillingly** *adverb*, **unwillingness** *noun*.

unwind *verb* (unwinds, unwinding, unwound) 1 To unroll. 2 To relax.

unwise *adjective* Not wise, foolish. **unwisely** *adverb*.

unworthy *adjective* Not worthy. **unworthiness** *noun*.

unwrap *verb* (unwraps, unwrapping, unwrapped) To take something out of its wrapping.

unwritten *adjective* Not written.

unzip *verb* (unzips, unzipping, unzipped) To undo a zip-fastener.

up *adverb and preposition* This word is used in many ways including: 1 To a vertical or standing position, in a vertical or standing position. *to stand up*. 2 To a higher place or condition. *to climb up*. 3 In a high place. *We live up in the hills*. 4 Thoroughly, completely. *Eat your potatoes up*. 5 Out of bed, dressed and ready. *He isn't up yet*. 6 *Your time is up!* your time is finished. **up to 1** Until. *We have up to the end of July to get finished*. 2 Doing.

What are you up to? 3 Capable of. *Is that boy up to the job?* 4 *It's up to us*, we are the people who must do it. 5 *It's not up to much*, it is not very good. **up to date** with all the latest news or improvements.

Upanishad *noun* An important part of the Hindu scriptures.

upbringing *noun* The way you have been brought up.

update [1] *verb* (updates, updating, updated) To make a thing up to date.

update [2] *noun* (updates) The very latest news about something.

upgrade *verb* (upgrades, upgrading, upgraded) To improve something.

upheaval *noun* (upheavals) A violent change.

uphill [1] *adjective* 1 Going up a slope. *an uphill walk*. 2 Difficult. *an uphill task*.

uphill [2] *adverb* Up a slope.

uphold *verb* (upholds, upholding, upheld) To support, to confirm.

upholstery *noun* The padding and covers of chairs and other furniture.

upkeep *noun* The cost of keeping something in good repair.

upland *noun* (uplands) An area of high land.

upmarket *adjective* More expensive, elegant.

upon *preposition* On.

upper *adjective* Higher.

uppermost *adjective* Highest.

upright *adjective* 1 Vertical, erect. 2 Honest.

uprising *noun* (uprisings) A rebellion.

uproar *noun* (uproars) A noisy disturbance. **uproarious** *adjective*, **uproariously** *adverb*.

uproot *verb* (uproots, uprooting, uprooted) To pull something up by the roots.

upset *verb* (upsets, upsetting, upset)

1 To overturn, to tip over.
2 To trouble, to disturb, to offend.

upside-down *adverb and adjective*
1 With the bottom at the top.
2 Untidy, in disorder.

upstairs *adverb and adjective*
1 To a higher floor in a building.
2 On a higher floor.

uptight *adjective* (informal) Tense, annoyed.

up-to-date *adjective* Modern.

upward *adjective* Going towards a higher position. **upwards** *adverb*.

uranium *noun* A valuable metal used as a source of atomic energy.

urban *adjective* Of a city or large town.

urchin *noun* (urchins) A rough boy.

Urdu *noun* One of the languages of India and Pakistan.

urge¹ *verb* (urges, urging, urged)
1 To drive someone or something onwards. 2 To persuade or ask vigorously.

urge² *noun* (urges) A strong desire.

urgent *adjective* To be done at once, needing immediate attention. **urgently** *adverb*, **urgency** *noun*.

urine *noun* The waste liquid passed from the body.

urn *noun* (urns) 1 A metal container with a tap, used for hot drinks.
2 A kind of vase.

us *See* **we**

usable *adjective* Able to be used.

use¹ *verb* (uses, using, used) 1 To employ something for some purpose, to do something with it. *I used my new pen to write the letter.* **user** *noun*. **use up** to consume. *We may soon use up our stock of fuel.* **be used to something** to know it well, to experience it regularly. **used to** did in the past. *People used to travel on horseback.* **used** second-hand.

use² *noun* (uses) 1 Using, being used. 2 The purpose or value of something. *What use is that strange tool?* **in**

use being used. **out of use** not to be used.

useful *adjective* Helpful, capable, producing good results. **usefully** *adverb*, **usefulness** *noun*.

useless *adjective* Not useful. **uselessly** *adverb*, **uselessness** *noun*.

user-friendly *adjective* Helpful, easy to use.

usher *noun* (ushers) A person who shows people to their seats in a theatre or other public place.

usherette *noun* (usherettes) A woman who shows people to their seats in a cinema.

usual *adjective* Normal, customary, such as happens repeatedly. **usually** *adverb*.

utensil *noun* (utensils) A tool, an instrument, a dish or pan.

utilize *verb* (utilizes, utilizing, utilized) To use.

utmost *adjective* Farthest, greatest.

utter¹ *adjective* Complete, total.

utter² *verb* (utters, uttering, uttered) To speak. **utterance** *noun*.

U-turn *noun* (U-turns) A single turn to face in the opposite direction.

Vv
••••••

V 5 in Roman numerals.

v. Versus.

vacant *adjective* Empty, unoccupied. **vacantly** *adverb*, **vacancy** *noun*.

vacation *noun* (vacations) 1 A holiday.
2 A period between terms at a university or college.

vaccinate *verb* (vaccinates, vaccinating, vaccinated) To inoculate someone against smallpox. **vaccination** *noun*.

vaccine *noun* (vaccines) A substance used for inoculations.

vacuum *noun* **1** A space without any air in it. **2** A vacuum cleaner. **vacuum cleaner** an apparatus which sucks up dirt and dust. **vacuum flask** a container used to keep hot liquids hot and cold ones cold.

vagabond *noun* (vagabonds) A tramp.

vagina *noun* (vaginas) In females, the short passage between the womb and the outside of the body.

vagrant *noun* (vagrants) A tramp, a wanderer.

vague *adjective* (vaguer, vaguest) Not clear, not certain. **vaguely** *adverb*, **vagueness** *noun*.

vain *adjective* (vainer, vainest) **1** Proud and conceited. **2** Unsuccessful, useless. **in vain** without useful result. **vainly** *adverb*.

valentine *noun* (valentines) A card you send to someone you love on St Valentine's day, 14th February.

valiant *adjective* Brave. **valiantly** *adverb*.

valid *adjective* Legally acceptable, usable. *This ticket is valid for three months.* **validity** *noun*.

valley *noun* (valleys) A stretch of lower land between hills.

valour *noun* Bravery.

valuable *adjective* Of great value.

valuables *noun* Valuable things.

value¹ *noun* **1** The amount of money that would or should be given for something. **2** The importance or usefulness or worth of something. **valueless** *adjective*.

value² *verb* (values, valuing, valued) **1** To think that something is very good, to regard it highly. **2** To say what you think the value of something is.

valve *noun* (valves) **1** A device for controlling the flow of liquid or gas. **2** An electronic device once common in radios and other equipment.

vampire *noun* (vampires) In legends, a spirit or creature that sucks blood.

van *noun* (vans) A roofed vehicle for carrying goods.

vandal *noun* (vandals) A person who deliberately damages things.

vandalize *verb* (vandalizes, vandalizing, vandalized) To damage someone else's property deliberately. **vandalism** *noun*.

vanguard *noun* (vanguards) The troops at the front of an advancing army.

vanilla *noun* A flavouring used for ice-cream and other foods.

vanish *verb* (vanishes, vanishing, vanished) To disappear.

vanity *noun* Conceit, pride in yourself.

vanquish *verb* (vanquishes, vanquishing, vanquished) To defeat, to conquer.

vaporize *verb* (vaporizes, vaporizing, vaporized) To turn into vapour.

vapour *noun* (vapours) Steam, mist, or some other gas-like substance into which a liquid is changed by heat.

variable *adjective* Varying, changeable. **variably** *adverb*, **variability** *noun*.

variation *noun* (variations) **1** Varying. **2** Something that has been altered.

varied *adjective* Of various sorts.

variety *noun* (varieties) **1** Change, absence of sameness. *I get bored without a bit of variety.* **2** A number of different things. *We made a variety of sandwiches.* **3** A particular kind of something. *This is a tasty variety of* *apple.* **variety show** an entertainment including short musical and comic items.

various *adjective* **1** Different. **2** Several.

varnish *noun* (varnishes) A clear liquid used like paint to give a hard, shiny surface.

vary *verb* (varies, varying, varied) To be different, to alter, to change.

vase *noun* (vases) A container used as an ornament or to hold cut flowers.

vast *adjective* Very large. **vastly** *adverb*, **vastness** *noun*.

vat *noun* (vats) A very large container for liquids.

vault¹ *noun* (vaults) **1** An arched roof. **2** An underground room. **3** A jump made by vaulting.

vault² *verb* (vaults, vaulting, vaulted) To jump over something with the help of the hands or a pole.

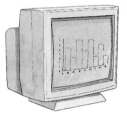

VDU Visual display unit, a screen used in a computer system.

veal *noun* Meat from a calf.

Vedas *noun* Ancient sacred writings of the Hindus.

veer *verb* (veers, veering, veered) To turn, to change direction.

vegetable *noun* (vegetables) A plant, especially a plant used as a food.

vegetarian *noun* (vegetarians) A person who does not eat meat.

vegetation *noun* Plants of all kinds.

vehement *adjective* Strong, eager, violent. **vehemently** *adverb*, **vehemence** *noun*.

vehicle *noun* (vehicles) A device for carrying people or things. Cars, lorries, carts, and sledges are vehicles.

veil *noun* (veils) A thin cloth used to cover something.

vein *noun* (veins) **1** One of the tubes in the body through which blood flows back to the heart. **2** A line like the lines in a leaf or in the wing of an insect.

velocity *noun* Speed.

velvet *noun* A kind of material with a soft texture on one side. **velvety** *adjective*.

vendetta *noun* (vendettas) A quarrel between families in which murders are committed in revenge for other murders.

vending-machine *noun* (vending-machines) A slot-machine where you can get drinks, sweets, or other things.

veneer *noun* (veneers) A thin layer of valuable wood used to cover cheaper wood.

venerable *adjective* Old, worthy of respect.

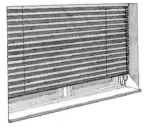

venetian blind A window blind with adjustable horizontal slats.

vengeance *noun* Revenge. **with a vengeance** strongly, thoroughly.

venison *noun* Meat from deer.

venom *noun* The poison from snakes and other poisonous animals.

venomous *adjective* poisonous. **venomously** *adverb*.

vent *noun* (vents) A hole or slit in something.

ventilate *verb* (ventilates, ventilating, ventilated) To allow air freely in and out. **ventilator, ventilation** *nouns*.

ventriloquist *noun* (ventriloquists) An entertainer who seems to make a dummy speak.

venture[1] *noun* (ventures) An adventurous undertaking. **Venture Scout** a senior Scout.

venture[2] *verb* (ventures, venturing, ventured) To risk, to dare.

veranda *noun* (verandas) An open space with a floor and a roof along one side of a house.

verb *noun* (verbs) A word which indicates what someone or something is or does or experiences. In the following sentences, *plays, understands* and *is* are verbs. Helen *plays* the double-bass. Andrew *understands* about computers. Peter *is* old enough for school.

verbal *adjective* In words, spoken rather than written. **verbally** *adverb*.

verdict *noun* (verdicts) The decision reached by a jury at the end of a trial.

verge *noun* (verges) An edge, a border.

verger *noun* (vergers) A caretaker of a church.

verify *verb* (verifies, verifying, verified) To show the truth of something.

vermilion *adjective* Bright red.

vermin *noun* 1 Harmful wild creatures such as rats and mice. 2 Creatures such as fleas and lice which live on people or animals.

verruca *noun* (verrucas) A kind of wart, usually on the foot.

versatile *adjective* Skilful in many ways. **versatility** *noun*.

verse *noun* (verses) 1 A piece of writing consisting of rhymed lines, poetry. 2 A group of rhymed lines in a song or poem. 3 One of the numbered parts of a chapter of the Bible.

version *noun* (versions) 1 A particular account of something. *Ann's version of the quarrel is different from Peter's.* 2 A translation of something. *a new version of the Bible.* 3 A particular way in which something is made or done. *a vegetarian version of shepherd's pie.*

versus *preposition* Against.

vertebra *noun* (vertebrae) One of the bones which make up the backbone.

vertical *adjective* Straight up and down, upright. **vertically** *adverb*.

very[1] *adverb* Extremely, to a great amount or extent.

very[2] *adjective* 1 Exact. *That's the very place.* 2 Extreme. *Go to the very end of the road.*

vessel *noun* (vessels) 1 A container. Cups, bottles, and basins are vessels. 2 A ship, a boat, anything designed to carry people or goods on water.

vest *noun* (vests) An undergarment worn on the upper part of the body.

vestry *noun* (vestries) The room in a church where the minister or choir prepare for services.

vet *noun* (vets) A person trained to look after the health of animals.

veteran *noun* (veterans) A person who has had long experience in something.

veto[1] *noun* (vetoes) A statement forbidding something.

veto[2] *verb* (vetoes, vetoing, vetoed) To forbid. *Dad vetoed our plan.*

vex *verb* (vexes, vexing, vexed) To annoy, to trouble. **vexation** *noun*.

via *preposition* By way of. *We went to France via Dover.*

viable *adjective* Likely to prove possible, likely to be successful.

viaduct *noun* (viaducts) A long bridge with many arches carrying a road or railway.

vibrate *verb* (vibrates, vibrating, vibrated) To move rapidly to and fro, to throb, to quiver. **vibration** *noun*.

vicar *noun* (vicars) A minister in charge of a parish.

vicarage *noun* (vicarages) A vicar's house.

vice[1] *noun* (vices) **1** Evil, wickedness. **2** A fault, a wicked habit.

vice[2] *noun* (vices) An apparatus attached to a workbench for holding things steady.

vice-captain *noun* (vice-captains) A person who may do the job of the captain when necessary.

vice-president *noun* (vice-presidents) The person next in authority under the president.

vice versa The other way round. *We hate them and vice versa*, we hate them and they hate us.

vicinity *noun* The surrounding area, the neighbourhood.

vicious *adjective* Spiteful, evil, wicked. **viciously** *adverb*, **viciousness** *noun*.

victim *noun* (victims) A person who suffers death, injury, hardship, or loss.

victimize *verb* (victimizes, victimizing, victimized) To treat someone unjustly. **victimization** *noun*.

victor *noun* (victors) The winner.

Victorian *adjective* Belonging to the reign of Queen Victoria.

victory *noun* (victories) Success in a battle or competition. **victorious** *adjective*, **victoriously** *adverb*.

video *noun* (videos) **1** A video recorder. **2** A tape you can play on a video recorder. **video recorder** a machine which will record and play back TV programmes on magnetic tape.

view[1] *noun* (views) **1** Beautiful scenery, something you look at from a distance. *There's a fine view from the top of the hill.* **2** The ability to see something because nothing is in the way. *I had a good view of the stage.* **3** An opinion. *What's your view of the problem?* **in view** able to be seen. **on view** displayed for people to see. **with a view to** in order to.

view[2] *verb* (views, viewing, viewed) To look at something, to consider it. **viewer** *noun*.

vigilant *adjective* Watchful. **vigilantly** *adverb*, **vigilance** *noun*.

vigilante *noun* (vigilantes) A member of an unofficial group which tries to deal with crime in a particular area.

vigour *noun* Strength, energy. **vigorous** *adjective*, **vigorously** *adverb*.

Viking *noun* (Vikings) A Scandinavian trader or pirate of the early Middle Ages.

vile *adjective* Shameful, disgusting.

villa *noun* (villas) **1** A kind of house. **2** A country house in Roman times.

village *noun* (villages) A group of houses and other buildings in a country area, smaller than a town. **villager** *noun*.

villain *noun* (villains) A wicked person. **villainous** *adjective*, **villainously** *adverb*, **villainy** *noun*.

vindictive *adjective* Spiteful, determined on revenge. **vindictively** *adverb*.

vine *noun* (vines) A climbing plant that bears grapes.

vinegar *noun* A sour liquid used to flavour food.

vineyard *noun* (vineyards) An area of land planted with vines.

vinyl *noun* A kind of plastic.

viola *noun* (violas) A stringed instrument slightly larger than a violin.

violate *verb* (violates, violating, violated) **1** To break a law or a promise. **2** To treat a person or place without respect. **violation** *noun*.

violent *adjective* Having great force, intense, causing harm. **violently** *adverb*, **violence** *noun*.

violet[1] *adjective* Purple.

violet[2] *noun* (violets) A small purple or white flower.

violin *noun* (violins) A musical instrument with strings, played with a bow. **violinist** *noun*.

viper *noun* (vipers) A small poisonous snake, an adder.

virgin *noun* (virgins) A person who has not had sexual intercourse.

virile *adjective* Manly.

virtually *adverb* As good as, almost. *This coat is virtually new.*

virtue *noun* (virtues) **1** Goodness. **2** Any particular kind of goodness such as honesty, kindness, or justice. **virtuous** *adjective*, **virtuously** *adverb*.

virtuoso *noun* (virtuosi) A highly skilled musician. **virtuosity** *noun*.

virus *noun* (viruses) **1** A microscopic living thing which can cause diseases. **2** A computer program which can spread itself through a computer system causing breakdowns and loss of data.

visa *noun* (visas) An official mark on a passport giving you permission to enter or leave a certain country.

visible *adjective* Able to be seen. **visibly** *adverb*, **visibility** *noun*.

vision *noun* **1** Sight. **2** Imagination, understanding. **3** (visions) A dream or hallucination.

visit [1] *verb* (visits, visiting, visited) **1** To go to see a person or place. **2** To stay somewhere for a while. **visitor** *noun*.

visit [2] *noun* (visits) **1** The act of visiting. **2** Time spent visiting.

visor *noun* (visors) The part of a helmet that closes over the face.

visual *adjective* To do with seeing. **visual aids** pictures and diagrams used by teachers.

visualize *verb* (visualizes, visualizing, visualized) To imagine.

vital *adjective* Essential to life, extremely important. **vitally** *adverb*.

vitality *noun* Energy.

vitamin *noun* (vitamins) Any of a number of substances that are present in various foods and are needed to keep you healthy.

vivacious *adjective* Happy and lively. **vivaciously** *adverb*, **vivacity** *noun*.

vivid *adjective* Bright, lively, clear. **vividly** *adverb*.

vivisection *noun* The performing of scientific experiments on living animals.

vixen *noun* (vixens) A female fox.

vocabulary *noun* (vocabularies) **1** A list of words. **2** All the words a person knows.

vocal *adjective* To do with the voice.

vocalist *noun* (vocalists) A singer.

vodka *noun* A strong alcoholic drink.

vogue *noun* Fashion, popularity.

voice *noun* (voices) **1** The sound of speaking or singing. *I heard her voice in the next room.* **2** The power to speak or sing. *John lost his voice when he was ill.* **voiceless** *adjective*.

void [1] *adjective* Empty. **void of** without.

void [2] *noun* (voids) An empty space, a vacuum.

volcano *noun* (volcanoes) A mountain with an open top out of which molten lava, gases, and ash some-times flow. **volcanic** *adjective*.

vole *noun* (voles) An animal like a small rat.

volley *noun* (volleys) **1** A shower of missiles. **2** In tennis, the hitting back of a ball before it bounces.

volley-ball *noun* A game in which a large ball is thrown over a net.

volt *noun* (volts) A unit for measuring electricity. **voltage** *noun*.

volume *noun* (volumes) **1** The amount of space occupied by a substance, a liquid, or a gas. **2** A quantity or amount of something. *Volumes of smoke poured from the chimney.* **3** The amount of sound produced by a radio set or other apparatus. *Turn up the volume.* **4** A book.

voluntary *adjective* Done willingly, without being paid or compelled. **voluntarily** *adverb*.

volunteer[1] *noun* (volunteers) A person who offers to do something of his or her own free will.

volunteer[2] *verb* (volunteers, volunteering, volunteered) **1** To offer yourself as a volunteer. **2** To offer something voluntarily.

vomit *verb* (vomits, vomiting, vomited) To be sick.

vote[1] *verb* (votes, voting, voted) To show your preference for someone or something by putting a mark on paper, by raising your hand, or by making some other sign. **voter** *noun*.

vote[2] *noun* (votes) The act of voting.

voucher *noun* (vouchers) A kind of ticket or receipt.

vow[1] *noun* (vows) A solemn promise.

vow[2] *verb* (vows, vowing, vowed) To make a vow.

vowel *noun* (vowels) Any of the letters a, e, i, o, u.

voyage *noun* (voyages) A journey in a ship.

vulgar *adjective* Rude, ill-mannered. **vulgarly** *adverb*, **vulgarity** *noun*.

vulnerable *adjective* Easily attacked, easily wounded, easily damaged.

vulture *noun* (vultures) A large bird that feeds on dead animals.

wad *noun* (wads) A pad of soft material.

waddle *verb* (waddles, waddling, waddled) To walk like a duck.

wade *verb* (wades, wading, waded) To walk through water. **wader** *noun*.

wafer *noun* (wafers) A kind of light biscuit sometimes eaten with ice-cream.

wag *verb* (wags, wagging, wagged) To move briskly to and fro.

wage[1] *noun* (wages) Money received regularly for doing work.

wage[2] *verb* (wages, waging, waged) **wage war** to fight a war.

wager *noun* (wagers) A bet.

waggle *verb* (waggles, waggling, waggled) To wag.

wagon *noun* (wagons) **1** An open railway truck. **2** A four-wheeled vehicle pulled by horses or oxen.

wagtail *noun* (wagtails) A kind of bird with a long tail.

wail[1] *verb* (wails, wailing, wailed) To cry, to howl, to complain loudly.

wail[2] *noun* (wails) A wailing sound.

waist *noun* (waists) The part of the body between the hips and the ribs.

waistcoat *noun* (waistcoats) A coat without sleeves, worn under a jacket.

wait[1] *verb* (waits, waiting, waited) **1** To stay in a place or delay doing something until an expected event happens. **2** To act as a waiter.

wait[2] *noun* (waits) A time spent waiting. **lie in wait** to hide ready to attack.

waiter, waitress *nouns* (waiters, waitresses) A person who brings food to the tables in a restaurant.

waiting-list *noun* (waiting-lists) A list of people waiting for something to become available.

waiting-room *noun* (waiting-rooms) A room for people to wait in.

wake[1] *verb* (wakes, waking, woke, waked, woken) **1** To cease sleeping. **2** To arouse somebody from sleep.

wake[2] *noun* (wakes) The track left by a ship in the water.

wakeful *adjective* Unable to sleep.

walk[1] *verb* (walks, walking, walked) To move on foot at an ordinary speed. **walker** *noun*.

walk[2] *noun* (walks) **1** A journey on foot. **2** A way of walking. **3** A path, a route for walking. **walk of life** a job, a profession.

walkie-talkie *noun* (walkie-talkies) (informal) A portable radio telephone.

walking-stick *noun* (walking-sticks) A stick used by a person as a support when walking.

Walkman *noun* The trade name of a small cassette player with headphones.

walk-over *noun* (informal) An easy victory.

wall[1] *noun* (walls) An upright structure of brick, stone, or other material such as that which forms the side of a house.

wall[2] *verb* (walls, walling, walled) To surround something with a wall. *a walled garden.*

wallaby *noun* (wallabies) A kind of small kangaroo.

wallet *noun* (wallets) A pocket case for money and papers.

wallflower *noun* (wallflowers) A garden plant with sweet-smelling flowers.

wallop *verb* (wallops, walloping, walloped) To hit.

wallow *verb* (wallows, wallowing, wallowed) To roll about in mud or water.

wallpaper *noun* (wallpapers) Paper used to cover the walls of rooms.

walnut *noun* (walnuts) A kind of nut.

walrus *noun* (walruses) A large sea animal with two long tusks.

waltz *noun* (waltzes) A kind of dance.

wan *adjective* Sad, pale, looking ill. **wanly** *adverb*.

wand *noun* (wands) A thin rod. *a magic wand.*

wander *verb* (wanders, wandering, wandered) **1** To go about with no particular purpose in mind. **2** To stray from the proper route. **wanderer** *noun*.

wane *verb* (wanes, waning, waned) To become less.

wangle *verb* (wangles, wangling, wangled) (informal) To get something by tricks or persuasion.

want[1] *verb* (wants, wanting, wanted) **1** To feel it would make you happy to have something, to wish for something. **2** To need something, to require it. **3** To be without, to lack.

want[2] *noun* (wants) **1** A lack, a shortage. **2** A need. *in want of money.*

wanton *adjective* Done without reason. *wanton damage*.

war *noun* (wars) **1** Fighting between armies or nations. **2** Any serious struggle.

warble *verb* (warbles, warbling, warbled) To sing.

war-cry *noun* (war-cries) A shout made before and during battle.

ward[1] *noun* (wards) **1** A room for patients in a hospital. **2** A child under the protection of a guardian.

ward[2] *verb* (wards, warding, warded) **ward off** to keep something away.

warden *noun* (wardens) **1** A person in charge of a hostel or other institution. **2** A person with certain official duties. *a traffic warden*.

warder *noun* (warders) A prison guard.

wardrobe *noun* (wardrobes) A cupboard to hang clothes in.

warehouse *noun* (warehouses) A large building used for storing goods.

wares *noun* Goods for sale.

warfare *noun* Making war, fighting.

warhead *noun* (warheads) The explosive end of a torpedo or missile.

warily, wariness *See* **wary**

warlike *adjective* Ready for war, fond of war.

warm[1] *adjective* (warmer, warmest) **1** Fairly hot. **2** Enthusiastic, affectionate. **warmly** *adverb*, **warmth** *noun*.

warm[2] *verb* (warms, warming, warmed) To make or become warmer.

warm-hearted *adjective* Loving, kind.

warn *verb* (warns, warning, warned) To tell somebody in advance about a danger or difficulty.

warning *noun* (warnings) Something that warns.

warp *verb* (warps, warping, warped) To twist out of the proper shape.

war-path *noun* **on the war-path** ready and eager to fight.

warrant *noun* (warrants) An official document giving someone the right to do something.

warren *noun* (warrens) A place where there are many rabbit burrows.

warring *adjective* At war, fighting.

warrior *noun* (warriors) A fighting man.

warship *noun* (warships) A ship for use in war.

wart *noun* (warts) A small hard growth on the skin.

wary *adjective* (warier, wariest) Cautious, watchful. **warily** *adverb*, **wariness** *noun*.

was *See* **be**

wash[1] *verb* (washes, washing, washed) **1** To make a thing clean in water. **2** To be carried along by moving water. *The sailor was washed overboard.* **3** To flow against or over something. *The waves washed against the pier.* **wash up** to wash the dishes after a meal.

wash[2] *noun* **1** The act of washing. **2** Things to be washed, washing. **3** The waves which spread out behind a moving ship.

washable *adjective* Able to be washed safely.

washer *noun* (washers) **1** A ring of rubber, fibre, or metal. **2** A washing-machine.

washing *noun* Clothes to be washed or being washed or which have just been washed.

washing-machine *noun* (washing-machines) A machine for washing clothes.

washing-up *noun* The cleaning of dishes and cutlery after a meal.

wasn't (informal) Was not.

wasp *noun* (wasps) A kind of flying insect with a sting.

wastage *noun* (wastages) An amount wasted or lost.

waste[1] *adjective* **1** Thrown away, no longer needed. *waste paper*. **2** Not cultivated, not in use. *waste land*. **lay waste** to destroy buildings or crops.

waste² *verb* (wastes, wasting, wasted) **1** To use something up with no result, to use too much of something, to let something become valueless by not using it. **2** To lose strength. **waste away** to become weaker.

waste³ *noun* **1** The wasting of something. *a waste of time*. **2** Rubbish, anything that can be thrown away.

watch¹ *verb* (watches, watching, watched) **1** To look at something carefully for some time. **2** To look out for something, to be on guard. **watcher** *noun*.

watch² *noun* (watches) **1** The act of watching. **2** A period of duty on a ship. **watchful** *adjective*, **watchfully** *adverb*, **watchfulness** *noun*.

watch³ *noun* (watches) An instrument worn on the wrist or carried in the pocket for telling the time.

watchman *noun* (watchmen) A person employed as a guard at night.

water¹ *noun* The transparent, colourless liquid which falls as rain or is found in rivers and seas.

water² *verb* (waters, watering, watered) **1** To sprinkle water on seeds or growing plants. **2** To give water to an animal to drink. **3** To fill with water. *My eyes are watering*.

water-closet *noun* (water-closets) A lavatory flushed by water.

water-colour *noun* (water-colours) A kind of paint for mixing with water.

watercress *noun* A plant used in salads.

waterfall *noun* (waterfalls) A fall of water where a stream or river flows over a cliff or big rock.

watering-can *noun* (watering-cans) A container for watering plants.

water-lily *noun* (water-lilies) A kind of flowering plant with broad leaves floating on water.

waterlogged *adjective* Thoroughly soaked or filled with water.

water-main *noun* (water-mains) A thick pipe supplying water.

water-pistol *noun* (water-pistols) A pistol which squirts water.

water-polo *noun* A ball game played by swimmers.

waterproof *adjective* Not allowing water to pass through.

water-skiing *noun* The sport of being towed on skis over water. **water-skier** *noun*.

watertight *adjective* Waterproof.

waterway *noun* (waterways) A channel along which ships or boats may pass.

waterworks *noun* The machinery and buildings from which water is supplied to a district.

watery *adjective* Wet, like water, full of water, containing too much water.

watt *noun* (watts) A unit of electrical power.

wave¹ *verb* (waves, waving, waved) **1** To move your hand to and fro. **2** To move to and fro. *trees waving in the breeze*. **3** To put waves or curls into hair.

wave² *noun* (waves) **1** A ridge of water, especially one in the sea that curls and breaks on the shore. **2** A curve or curl. **3** The act of waving. **4** A vibration or pulse which conveys such things as sound through the air, or light through space, or electrical signals along wires. *radio waves*.

waveband *noun* (wavebands) A group of wavelengths for broadcasting.

wavelength *noun* (wavelengths) **1** A measurement of radio waves or other waves. **2** A particular wavelength used in broadcasting.

waver *verb* (wavers, wavering, wavered) **1** To move unsteadily. **2** To be undecided. **waverer** *noun*.

wavy *adjective* (wavier, waviest) Having waves or curves.

wax *noun* A substance which melts easily into an oily liquid, used for making candles and polish.

waxworks *noun* An exhibition of life-like models of people in wax.

way *noun* (ways) **1** A road, street, lane, path, or passage. **2** A route, a direction, a journey. **3** A series of actions leading to a particular result, a method. *That's not the way to tie a reef-knot.* **4** Normal behaviour or attitude. *It's Susan's way to be generous.* **5** A state, a condition. *Things are in a bad way.*

wayfarer *noun* (wayfarers) A traveller.

wayside *noun* (waysides) The side of a road.

WC A water-closet.

we *pronoun* (us, ourselves) A word you use when referring to yourself and the others with you.

weak *adjective* (weaker, weakest) Feeble, fragile, not strong. **weakly** *adverb*, **weakness** *noun*.

weaken *verb* (weakens, weakening, weakened) To become or make weaker.

weakling *noun* (weaklings) A feeble person.

wealth *noun* Riches.

wealthy *adjective* (wealthier, wealthiest) Rich.

weapon *noun* (weapons) An instrument used to fight with.

wear[1] *verb* (wears, wearing, wore, worn) **1** To have something on your body, to be dressed in it. **2** To have something attached to your clothes. *Naomi wore a badge on her dress.* **3** To cause damage by constant use or rubbing. *My penknife has worn a hole in my pocket.* **4** To last. *Good clothes wear well.* **wear out** to become useless after use. **wear someone out** to make him or her exhausted. **wear off** to become less. *The pain will soon wear off.*

wear[2] *noun* Damage from continued use. **fair wear and tear** normal damage from use.

weary *adjective* (wearier, weariest) Tired. **wearily** *adverb*, **weariness** *noun*.

weasel *noun* (weasels) A small fierce animal with a long, slender body.

weather[1] *noun* The conditions of sunshine, temperature, wind, and rain at a particular time. *stormy weather, fine weather.*

weather[2] *verb* (weathers, weathering, weathered) **1** To come through some difficulty successfully. *to weather the storm.* **2** To become worn by exposure to the weather.

weather-beaten *adjective* Worn or tanned by exposure to the weather.

weave *verb* (weaves, weaving, wove, woven) **1** To make threads into cloth on a loom. **weaver** *noun* **2** To move with many twists and turns.

web *noun* (webs) A net of fine threads spun by a spider.

webbed, web-footed *adjectives* Having the toes joined by pieces of skin.

wed *verb* (weds, wedding, wed, wedded) To marry.

we'd (informal) **1** We would. **2** We had.

wedding *noun* (weddings) A marriage ceremony.

wedding-ring *noun* (wedding-rings) A gold ring worn as a sign of marriage.

wedge[1] *noun* (wedges) A V-shaped object.

wedge[2] *verb* (wedges, wedging, wedged) **1** To fix something with a wedge. **2** To push something into position so that it remains firm.

Wednesday *noun* (Wednesdays) The fourth day of the week.

wee *adjective* (Scottish) Small.

weed[1] *noun* (weeds) A wild plant growing where it is not wanted.

weed[2] *verb* (weeds, weeding, weeded) To remove weeds.

weedy *adjective* (weedier, weediest) **1** Full of weeds. **2** Thin, feeble, weak.

week *noun* (weeks) **1** Seven days from Sunday to Saturday. **2** Any period of seven days.

week-day *noun* (week-days) Any day except Sunday.

week-end *noun* (week-ends) Saturday and Sunday.

weekly *adjective* Once a week.

weep *verb* (weeps, weeping, wept) To cry, to shed tears.

weigh *verb* (weighs, weighing, weighed) **1** To measure the weight of something by the use of scales or some other means. **2** To have a certain weight. *Your parcel weighed three kilograms.* **weigh anchor** to lift the anchor and sail away. **weigh something down** to keep it down with heavy objects. **weigh something up** to consider it.

weight *noun* (weights) **1** The heaviness of something, the amount it is pulled downwards by gravity. **2** A piece of metal of exactly measured heaviness used on scales. **3** A heavy object.

weightless *adjective* Having no weight because of being beyond the pull of gravity. **weightlessness** *noun*.

weighty *adjective* (weightier, weightiest) **1** Heavy. **2** Important.

weir *noun* (weirs) A dam across a river to control the flow of water.

weird *adjective* (weirder, weirdest) Unnatural, strange. **weirdly** *adverb*.

welcome[1] *adjective* Received with pleasure, giving pleasure. *a welcome visit.* **welcome to** allowed to, free to. *You are welcome to borrow my bicycle.*

welcome[2] *noun* (welcomes) A greeting.

welcome[3] *verb* (welcomes, welcoming, welcomed) To show pleasure at the arrival of somebody or something.

weld *verb* (welds, welding, welded) To join two pieces of metal together by heat and pressure.

welfare *noun* Health and happiness.

well[1] *noun* (wells) A deep hole dug or drilled to obtain water or oil from under ground.

well[2] *adverb* (better, best) **1** In a good, right, or satisfactory manner. *Be sure to clean it well.* **2** Indeed, probably. *This may well be our best plan.*

well[3] *adjective* **1** In good health. *You look well.* **2** Successful. *We wish you well.* **well off** rich, fortunate.

we'll (informal) **1** We shall. **2** We will.

well-being *noun* Health, comfort, and happiness.

wellingtons *noun* Knee-length rubber boots.

Welsh *adjective* Of Wales, from Wales.

went *See* **go**

wept *See* **weep**

were *See* **be**

we're (informal) We are.

weren't (informal) Were not.

west[1] *noun* One of the points of the compass, the direction in which the sun sets.

west[2] *adjective and adverb* In or to the west. **west wind** wind blowing from the west.

westerly *adjective* To or from the west.

western[1] *adjective* Of or in the west.

western[2] *noun* (westerns) A film or story about cowboys or American Indians in western North America.

westward *adjective and adverb* Towards the west. **westwards** *adverb*.

wet[1] *adjective* (wetter, wettest) Covered with or soaked in or affected by water or other liquid. *wet weather*, rainy

weather. *wet paint*, paint not yet dry.
wetness *noun*.

wet² *verb* (wets, wetting, wet, wetted)
To make something become wet.

wet-suit *noun* (wet-suits) A rubber
garment worn by skin-divers.

we've (informal) We have.

whack *verb* (whacks, whacking,
whacked) To hit something with
a stick.

whale *noun* (whales) A kind of large
sea animal.

wheel-clamp *noun* (wheel-clamps)
A clamp which can be locked to
a wheel of an illegally parked vehicle
so that you cannot drive it away until
you have paid a fine.

whaler *noun* (whalers) A ship or person
that hunts whales.

wharf *noun* (wharves) A platform at the
edge of the water where ships are
loaded or unloaded.

what *pronoun and adjective* This word is
used in several kinds of sentence
including the following: **1** In questions. *What is the time, please?* **2** In
exclamations. *What a lovely day!* **3** In
pointing something out. *Show me
what you have done.*

whatever *pronoun and adjective* **1** No
matter what. *Whatever happens, don't
panic.* **2** Anything that. *Do whatever
you like.*

wheat *noun* **1** A cereal plant. **2** Its seed,
used for making flour.

wheel¹ *noun* (wheels) A circular framework or disc which turns on an axle.

wheel² *verb* (wheels, wheeling,
wheeled) **1** To move something on
wheels. **2** To move in a curve.

wheelbarrow *noun* (wheelbarrows)
A small cart with one wheel and two
long handles.

wheel-chair *noun* (wheel-chairs)
A chair on wheels for a disabled
person.

wheely *noun* (wheelies) The act of
riding a bicycle with the front wheel
off the ground.

wheeze *verb* (wheezes, wheezing,
wheezed) To make a gasping,
whistling noise as you breathe.

whelk *noun* (whelks) A kind of
shellfish.

when *adverb and conjunction* This word
is used in several kinds of sentence
including the following: **1** At what
time or times. *When can you come?*
2 What time. *Since when have you
worn earrings?* **3** Since, considering
that. *How can you win when you don't
try?*

whenever *conjunction* At whatever
time, every time. *Come and see us
whenever you are passing. Whenever it
rains, water comes in.*

where *adverb and conjunction* This word
is used in several kinds of sentence
including the following: **1** What
place, in what place, to what place.
Where are they? Tell me where they are.
2 In the place in which. *My glasses
were just where I left them.*

whereabouts¹ *adverb* In or near what
place. *Whereabouts did you see him?*

whereabouts² *noun* The place where someone or something is. *Do you know his present whereabouts?*

whereupon *conjunction* After which.

wherever *adverb* In or to whatever place.

whether *conjunction* If.

whey *noun* The watery part of sour milk.

which This word is used in several kinds of sentence including the following: **1** In questions. *Which way did he go?* **2** In pointing something out. *I don't know which to choose. This is the one which I like best.*

whichever *pronoun and adjective* **1** The one which. *Take whichever you like.* **2** No matter which. *Whichever you choose, it will cost the same.*

whiff *noun* (whiffs) A slight smell.

while¹, whilst *conjunctions* **1** During the time that. *I finished my work while you were chatting.* **2** Although, but. *Sue likes tea, while I prefer coffee.*

while² *noun* A period of time. *a long while ago.*

whim *noun* (whims) A sudden impulse.

whimper *verb* (whimpers, whimpering, whimpered) To make weak crying sounds.

whine¹ *noun* (whines) A long complaining cry, a continuous high sound.

whine² *verb* (whines, whining, whined) To make a whine.

whinny *verb* (whinnies, whinnying, whinnied) To make a noise like a horse.

whip¹ *noun* (whips) A cord or strip of leather attached to a handle.

whip² *verb* (whips, whipping, whipped) **1** To beat with a whip. **2** To beat cream until it is stiff. **3** To move or do something suddenly. *She whipped round in a flash. He whipped out a gun.*

whippet *noun* (whippets) A kind of small greyhound.

whirl *verb* (whirls, whirling, whirled) To move rapidly round and round.

whirlpool *noun* (whirlpools) A place in a sea or river where the water whirls round.

whirlwind *noun* (whirlwinds) A violent wind that blows in a spiral.

whisk¹ *noun* (whisks) A device for beating eggs or other foods.

whisk² *verb* (whisks, whisking, whisked) **1** To beat eggs or other foods. **2** To move briskly.

whiskers *noun* Hair or bristles growing on the face.

whisky *noun* A strong alcoholic drink.

whisper *verb* (whispers, whispering, whispered) To speak very softly, to talk secretly.

whist *noun* A card game.

whistle¹ *verb* (whistles, whistling, whistled) **1** To make a shrill sound by blowing air through the lips. **2** To make a similar sound by some other means.

whistle² *noun* (whistles) **1** The sound of whistling. **2** An instrument which makes the sound of whistling.

white¹ *noun* A colour, the colour of fresh snow.

white² *adjective* (whiter, whitest) White or pale in colour. **whiteness** *noun*.

whiten *verb* (whitens, whitening, whitened) To make or become whiter.

whitewash *noun* **1** A liquid used to whiten walls and ceilings. **2** The situation at the end of a series of games when an opponent has been beaten without winning a single game.

whitish *adjective* Rather white.

Whit Sunday, Whitsun The seventh Sunday after Easter.

whiz *verb* (whizzes, whizzing, whizzed) **1** To make a noise like something rushing through the air. **2** To move quickly.

who *pronoun* (whom) Which person.

Who did that? It was the man from whom we bought our car.

whoever *pronoun* Whatever person.

whole[1] *adjective* **1** Complete, entire. *It rained the whole day.* **2** In one piece, unbroken. *The snake swallowed the rabbit whole.*

whole[2] *noun* (wholes) A complete thing. *Two halves make a whole.* **On the whole** considering everything, in general. **wholly** *adverb*.

wholemeal *adjective* Made from flour from which no part of the grain has been removed.

wholesale *adjective* **1** Selling goods in large quantities to shopkeepers. *a wholesale warehouse.* **2** On a large scale, including everyone and everything. *wholesale destruction.*

wholesome *adjective* Favourable to health.

who'll (informal) Who will.

whom *See* **who**

whoop *noun* (whoops) A loud cry.

whooping-cough *noun* A disease accompanied by a gasping cough.

who's (informal) Who is. *Who's coming out?*

whose Of whom, of which. *Whose coat is this?*

why *adverb* For what reason. *Why did you do that? Tell me why you did that.*

wick *noun* (wicks) The thread or strip of material which you light in a candle or oil-lamp.

wicked *adjective* **1** Bad, evil, naughty. **wickedly** *adverb*, **wickedness** *noun*. **2** (slang) Excellent.

wickerwork *noun* Things made from woven reeds or canes.

wicket *noun* (wickets) **1** The three stumps at which you bowl the ball in cricket. **2** The strip of grass between the two wickets.

wicket-keeper *noun* (wicket-keepers) The fielder in cricket who stands behind the wicket.

wide[1] *adjective* (wider, widest) **1** Broad, measuring a long distance from side to side. **2** Measured from side to side. *3 metres wide.* **3** Fully open. *wide eyes.*

wide[2] *adverb* **1** Completely, fully. *I was wide awake.* **2** Away from the target. *My shot went wide.*

widely *adverb* In many places, over a wide area. *This dictionary is widely available in book shops.*

widen *verb* (widens, widening, widened) To make or become wider.

widespread *adjective* Found in many places, common.

widow *noun* (widows) A woman whose husband has died.

widower *noun* (widowers) A man whose wife has died.

width *noun* (widths) Breadth, the distance from one side of something to the opposite side.

wield *verb* (wields, wielding, wielded) To hold and use something.

wife *noun* (wives) A married woman.

wig *noun* (wigs) A covering of false hair.

wiggle *verb* (wiggles, wiggling, wiggled) To wag from side to side.

wigwam *noun* (wigwams) A North American Indian hut or tent.

wild *adjective* (wilder, wildest) **1** Living in the free and natural way, not tamed. *wild animals.* **2** Not cultivated, not inhabited. *wild country.* **3** Violent. *a wild storm.* **4** Reckless, excited. *wild behaviour.* **wildly** *adverb*, **wildness** *noun*.

wilderness *noun* (wildernesses) A desert, a stretch of wild country.

wile *noun* (wiles) A cunning trick. **wily** *adjective*, **wiliness** *noun*.

wilful *adjective* **1** Obstinate. **2** Intentional, deliberate. **wilfully** *adverb*.

will[1] *verb* (would) A word used in sentences which refer to the future. *They will arrive at teatime. They said they would come.*

will[2] *noun* **1** Will-power. **2** A desire or

determination. **3** (wills) A document stating what you wish to be done with your property after you die.

will³ *verb* (wills, willing, willed) To try to control something by will-power.

willing *adjective* Ready to help, ready to do what is needed. **willingly** *adverb*, **willingness** *noun*.

willow *noun* (willows) A kind of tree with thin flexible branches.

will-power *noun* The power of your mind, the strength of your determination.

wilt *verb* (wilts, wilting, wilted) To droop, to become limp.

wily *adjective* (wilier, wiliest) Crafty, cunning.

wimp *noun* (wimps) (informal) An insulting word for a person who is supposed to be feeble or cowardly. **wimpish** *adjective*.

win¹ *verb* (wins, winning, won) **1** To come first in a race, game, or competition. **2** To be victorious in a war or battle. **3** To be successful in gaining something. **winner** *noun*.

win² *noun* (wins) A victory.

wince *verb* (winces, wincing, winced) To make a slight movement because of pain.

winch *noun* (winches) A device for pulling or lifting things by means of a rope wound on a cylinder.

wind¹ *noun* (winds) **1** A steady movement of air, a current of air. **windless** *adjective*. **2** Gas in your stomach or intestines. *Baby has got wind.* **wind instrument** a musical instrument which you play by blowing.

wind² *verb* (winds, winding, wound) **1** To move or go in twists or curves.

The road wound up the mountain. **2** To twist something round and round to make a ball or a coil. *The cotton is wound on a reel.* **3** To turn a handle or key round and round. *Don't forget to wind your watch.*

wind-cheater *noun* (wind-cheaters) A jacket which keeps the wind out.

winded *adjective* Out of breath.

windfall *noun* (windfalls) **1** A fruit blown down from a tree. **2** A piece of unexpected good fortune.

windmill *noun* (windmills) A mill whose power comes from the wind.

window *noun* (windows) An opening in a wall filled with a pane of glass.

window-sill *noun* (window-sills) The shelf at the bottom of a window.

windpipe *noun* (windpipes) A tube in the body from the mouth to the lungs.

windscreen *noun* (windscreens) The window in front of the driver of a car or other vehicle.

windsurfing *noun* The sport of riding on a board like a surf-board with a sail. **windsurfer** *noun*.

windswept *adjective* Exposed to the wind.

windward *adjective* Facing the wind. *the windward side of a ship.*

windy *adjective* (windier, windiest) **1** With a lot of wind. *windy weather, a windy place.* **2** (informal) Scared.

wine *noun* (wines) An alcoholic drink made from grapes or other fruits.

wing *noun* (wings) **1** One of the parts of the body by which a bird or insect flies. **2** One of the flat surfaces which support an aircraft in the air. **3** A part of a building, not the main part. *the north wing.* **4** One of the parts of a motor car which covers the wheels. **5** A player in football or other games whose position is at one side of the pitch.

wink *verb* (winks, winking, winked) **1** To close and open an eye. **2** To shine unsteadily, to flash on and off. **winker** *noun*.

winkle *noun* (winkles) A kind of shellfish.

winnings *noun* Money won by gambling.

winter *noun* (winters) The cold season between autumn and spring. **wintry** *adjective*.

wipe *verb* (wipes, wiping, wiped) To clean or dry something by rubbing it. **wiper** *noun*. **wipe out** to destroy completely.

wire¹ *noun* (wires) **1** Metal drawn out into a long thin rod or thread. **2** A telegram.

wire² *verb* (wires, wiring, wired) **1** To fasten with wire. **2** To fit electrical wiring to something.

wireless *noun* (wirelesses) Radio.

wiring *noun* A system of wires carrying electricity.

wiry *adjective* (wirier, wiriest) **1** Like wire. **2** Lean and strong.

wisdom *noun* The quality of being wise.

wise *adjective* (wiser, wisest) Having understanding, good judgement, and much knowledge. **wisely** *adverb*.

wish¹ *verb* (wishes, wishing, wished) **1** To desire, to want, to long for something. **2** To say that you hope something for somebody. *We wish you a merry Christmas.* **3** To say or think what you would like to happen.

wish² *noun* (wishes) **1** A desire, a longing. **2** The act of wishing.

wishbone *noun* (wishbones) A V-shaped bone from a chicken.

wishful thinking Thinking based on what you wish would happen, not on facts.

wisp *noun* (wisps) A thin, untidy bundle or piece. *a wisp of hair.* **wispy** *adjective*.

wistful *adjective* Rather sad, as if longing for something. **wistfully** *adverb*.

wit *noun* (wits) **1** Intelligence, quickness, cleverness. **2** Witty talk. **3** A witty person.

witch *noun* (witches) A woman who is supposed to have supernatural powers, a woman who can do things by magic. **witchcraft** *noun*.

witch-doctor *noun* (witch-doctors) A male witch among primitive peoples.

with *preposition* **1** Having. *She wore a coat with a red hood.* **2** Accompanied by. *I went out with a friend.* **3** In the same direction as. *We swam with the tide.* **4** Against. *He fought with a lion.* **5** By means of. *She stuck it with glue.* **6** Because of. *I'm stiff with cold.* **7** Concerning. *Be patient with us.*

withdraw *verb* (withdraws, withdrawing, withdrew, withdrawn). **1** To take away something or somebody. **2** To move back from somewhere, to retreat. **withdrawal** *noun*.

wither *verb* (withers, withering, withered) To become dry and shrivelled.

withhold *verb* (withholds, withholding, withheld) To keep something back.

within *preposition and adverb* Inside.

without *preposition* Free from, not having. *I like chips without vinegar.*

withstand *verb* (withstands, withstanding, withstood) To resist.

witness¹ *noun* (witnesses) **1** A person

who sees something happen. **2** A person who gives evidence in a court of law.

witness[2] *verb* (witnesses, witnessing, witnessed) To see something happen.

witty *adjective* (wittier, wittiest) Clever and amusing. **wittily** *adverb*.

wizard *noun* (wizards) A magician, a male witch. **wizardry** *noun*.

wizened *adjective* Dried up, shrivelled.

woad *noun* A kind of blue dye.

wobble *verb* (wobbles, wobbling, wobbled) To move unsteadily from side to side.

woe *noun* (woes) Sorrow, grief, distress. **woeful** *adjective*, **woefully** *adverb*.

wok *noun* (woks) A bowl-shaped pan used in Chinese cookery.

woke, woken *See* **wake**[1]

wolf *noun* (wolves) A fierce wild animal of the dog family.

woman *noun* (women) A grown-up female human being.

womb *noun* The part of a female's body in which the foetus grows until the baby is born.

won *See* **win**[1]

wonder[1] *noun* **1** A feeling of surprise and admiration. **2** (wonders) Something that causes a feeling of surprise and admiration. **wonderful** *adjective*, **wonderfully** *adverb*.

wonder[2] *verb* (wonders, wondering, wondered) **1** To be filled with wonder. **2** To be curious, to ask yourself. *I wonder what that means.*

won't (informal) Will not.

woo *verb* (woos, wooing, wooed) To try to win the love of somebody. **wooer** *noun*.

wood *noun* **1** The hard substance of a tree under the bark. **2** (woods) An area of land where trees grow.

wooded *adjective* Covered with trees.

wooden *adjective* **1** Made of wood. **2** Stiff, without any expression.

woodland *noun* (woodlands) An area of wooded country.

woodlouse *noun* (woodlice) A small insect-like creature with seven pairs of legs.

woodman *noun* (woodmen) A man who works in a forest.

woodpecker *noun* (woodpeckers) A bird that taps trees with its beak to find food.

woodwind *noun* Those wind instruments which can be made of wood, such as flutes, oboes, and clarinets.

woodwork *noun* **1** Carpentry, making things with wood. **2** Things made of wood.

woodworm *noun* (woodworms) A kind of beetle that bores into wood.

woody *adjective* (woodier, woodiest) **1** Covered with trees. **2** Like wood.

wool *noun* **1** The soft hair of sheep and some other animals. **2** Thread or cloth made from this hair.

woollen *adjective* Made of wool.

woollens *noun* Clothes made of wool.

woolly *adjective* (woollier, woolliest) **1** Covered in wool. **2** Made of wool. **3** Like wool. **4** Vague, confused. **woolliness** *noun*.

word[1] *noun* (words) **1** One of the units that make up language. *This sentence contains five words.* **2** Something that is said. *Don't say a word to your mother about this.* **3** A promise. *I give you my word it won't happen again.* **4** An order. *Begin when I give the word.*

word[2] *verb* (words, wording, worded) To put something into words.

word-processor *noun* (word-processors) A computer used to organize words and ideas for printing.

wordy *adjective* (wordier, wordiest) Using too many words.

wore See **wear**[1]

work[1] *noun* **1** An action which needs effort or energy. *Digging the garden is hard work.* **2** Something that has to be done, a person's employment. *Has Mum gone to work yet?* **3** Something produced by work. *Teacher wants to see our work when we have finished.* **works** **1** A factory. **2** The moving parts of a machine.

work[2] *verb* (works, working, worked) **1** To do work. **worker** *noun*. **2** To act or operate in the intended way. *Is the lift working?* **3** To succeed. *Will the idea work?* **4** To make somebody or something work. *Do you know how to work the lift?* **work loose** to become loose gradually. **work out** **1** To happen. *It worked out as we planned.* **2** To calculate. *Can you work out what it will cost?*

workable *adjective* Practicable.

workbench *noun* (workbenches) A bench where people do carpentry or other jobs.

workcard, workcards, worksheet *nouns* (workcards, worksheets) A list of things to be done by pupils.

working *noun* (workings) **1** The way something works. **2** A mine or quarry.

workman *noun* (workmen) A working man.

workmanship *noun* A person's skill in doing work.

work-room *noun* (work-rooms) A room where you work.

workshop *noun* (workshops) A place where things are made or repaired.

world *noun* (worlds) **1** The Earth, its countries and peoples. **2** A particular part of the world, a particular time in its history. *the modern world.* **3** A particular activity. *the world of entertainment.*

worldly *adjective* Concerned with money or status.

worm[1] *noun* (worms) A kind of long thin wriggling creature.

worm[2] *verb* (worms, worming, wormed) To move by crawling or wriggling.

worn See **wear**[1]

worry[1] *verb* (worries, worrying, worried) **1** To trouble someone, to cause anxiety. **2** To be uneasy, to be anxious.

worry[2] *noun* (worries) **1** Being worried. **2** Something that worries you.

worse See **bad**

worsen *verb* (worsens, worsening, worsened) To become or make worse.

worship[1] *noun* **1** Reverence, honour and respect to God. **2** Great respect and admiration paid to someone or something.

worship[2] *verb* (worships, worshipping, worshipped) To give worship. **worshipper** *noun*.

worst See **bad**

worsted *noun* A kind of woollen cloth.

worth[1] *adjective* **1** Having a certain value. *a diamond worth £2,000.* **2** Worthy of. *a castle worth visiting.*

worth[2] *noun* Value or usefulness. *two pounds' worth of flowers,* the quantity that can be bought for £2.

worthless *adjective* Valueless.

worthwhile *adjective* Important enough to do.

worthy *adjective* Deserving respect. **worthiness** *noun*, **worthily** *adverb*. **worthy of** deserving.

would See **will**[1]

wound[1] See **wind**[2]

wound[2] *noun* (wounds) An injury to the body.

wound[3] *verb* (wounds, wounding, wounded) To give a wound to somebody.

wove, woven See **weave**

wrap *verb* (wraps, wrapping, wrapped) To put a covering round something.

wrapper, wrapping *nouns* (wrappers, wrappings) Something used for wrapping.

wrath *noun* Anger. **wrathful** *adjective*, **wrathfully** *adverb*.

wreath *noun* (wreaths) Flowers or leaves woven into a ring.

wreck¹ *noun* (wrecks) A wrecked ship or anything else that has been destroyed or ruined.

wreck² *verb* (wrecks, wrecking, wrecked) To cause the ruin or destruction of something. **wrecker** *noun*.

wreckage *noun* Pieces of a wreck.

wren *noun* (wrens) A tiny brown bird.

wrench¹ *noun* (wrenches) **1** A sudden or painful pull. **2** A tool for twisting nuts and pipes.

wrench² *verb* (wrenches, wrenching, wrenched) To pull or twist violently.

wrestle *verb* (wrestles, wrestling, wrestled) To fight by struggling and trying to throw an opponent down without hitting him or her. **wrestler** *noun*.

wretch *noun* (wretches) **1** An unfortunate or miserable person. **2** A rogue.

wretched *adjective* **1** Feeling very uncomfortable or ill. **2** Poor in quality. **wretchedly** *adverb*, **wretchedness** *noun*.

wriggle *verb* (wriggles, wriggling, wriggled) To move the body about with quick twists.

wring *verb* (wrings, wringing, wrung) **1** To twist something and squeeze it tightly. **2** To get the water out of something by wringing it. **wringer** *noun*. **wringing wet** so wet that water may be wrung out.

wrinkle¹ *noun* (wrinkles) A small crease or line in the skin or on a surface.

wrinkle² *verb* (wrinkles, wrinkling, wrinkled) To form wrinkles.

wrist *noun* (wrists) The joint between the arm and the hand.

write *verb* (writes, writing, wrote, written) **1** To make letters and words on paper or some other surface. **2** To be the author or composer of something. **3** To send a letter. *Don't forget to write.* **writer** *noun*.

writhe *verb* (writhes, writhing, writhed) To twist or roll about.

writing *noun* **1** The act of writing. **2** Handwriting. **3** (writings) Something written.

wrong¹ *adjective* **1** Not right, not just, not fair. *It is wrong to hurt animals.* **2** Not correct. *That answer is wrong.* **3** Not working properly. *My watch is wrong.* **wrongly** *adverb*.

wrong² *adverb* Badly, incorrectly. *I've done it wrong again!*

wrong³ *noun* (wrongs) Something that is wrong. **in the wrong** guilty of some fault.

wrong⁴ *verb* (wrongs, wronging, wronged) To be unfair or unjust to somebody.

wrongdoing *noun* Doing wrong. **wrongdoer** *noun*.

wrongful *adjective* Illegal, not fair. **wrongfully** *adverb*.

wrote *See* **write**

wrung *See* **wring**

wry *adjective* Twisted. *a wry smile.* **wryly** *adverb*.

wudu *noun* For Muslims, washing before prayer.

Xx

X 10 in Roman numerals.

Xerox *noun* The trade name of a type of photocopier.

Xmas *noun* (informal) Christmas.

X-ray[1] *noun* (X-rays) A ray which can penetrate solid things.

X-ray[2] *verb* (X-rays, X-raying, X-rayed) To photograph the inside of someone or something by means of X-rays.

xylophone *noun* (xylophones) A percussion instrument.

Yy
·····

yacht *noun* (yachts) **1** A sailing boat built for racing or cruising. **2** A private ship. **yachtsman** *noun*.

yachting *noun* Sailing in a yacht.

yam *noun* (yams) a kind of tropical vegetable.

yap *verb* (yaps, yapping, yapped) To make short sharp barking sounds.

yard *noun* (yards) **1** A measure of length, 36 inches or about 91 centimetres. **2** An open space with a hard surface, surrounded by buildings and walls.

yarn *noun* (yarns) **1** Thread. **2** (informal) A story.

yashmak *noun* (yashmaks) A veil worn by some Muslim women.

yawn[1] *verb* (yawns, yawning, yawned) **1** To open the mouth widely and breathe in deeply when tired or bored. **2** To be wide open.

yawn[2] *noun* (yawns) The act of yawning.

year *noun* (years) A unit of time, twelve months. It takes one year for the earth to travel round the sun.

yearly *adjective and adverb* Every year, once a year.

yearn *verb* (yearns, yearning, yearned) To long for something.

yeast *noun* A substance used in making bread, beer, and wine.

yell[1] *noun* (yells) A loud cry.

yell[2] *verb* (yells, yelling, yelled) To give a yell, to shout.

yellow[1] *noun* A colour, the colour of buttercups or lemons.

yellow[2] *adjective* (yellower, yellowest) **1** Yellow in colour. **2** Cowardly.

yellowhammer *noun* (yellowhammers) A small bird with a yellow head and throat.

yellowish *adjective* Rather yellow.

yelp *verb* (yelps, yelping, yelped) To make a shrill bark or cry.

Yeoman *noun* (Yeomen) **Yeoman of the Guard** a guard at the Tower of London.

yen *noun* **1** The unit of money in Japan. **2** A yearning.

yes *adverb* A word used to show agreement or consent.

yesterday *noun* The day before today.

yet[1] *adverb* This word has many meanings including the following: **1** Up to this time. *Has the ice-cream man come yet?* **2** At some time in the future. *The gypsy said there were more dangers yet to come.* **3** Ever, still, again. *Jack found that the beanstalk had grown yet taller.*

yet[2] *conjunction* Nevertheless. *He was in great pain, yet he played on.*

yew *noun* (yews) A kind of evergreen tree.

Yiddish *noun* A Jewish language.

yield *verb* (yields, yielding, yielded) **1** To give in, to surrender. **2** To produce a crop. *These trees yield excellent pears.*

yodel *verb* (yodels, yodelling, yodelled) To produce a musical high-pitched call.

yoga *noun* A Hindu method of meditation and self control.

yogi *noun* (yogis) An expert in yoga.

yogurt *noun* A type of food made from milk.

yoke *noun* (yokes) A curved bar put across the shoulders of oxen pulling a cart.

yolk *noun* (yolks) The yellow part of an egg.

Yom Kippur An annual day of fasting for Jews.

you *pronoun* **1** (yourself, yourselves) The person or people being spoken to or written to. **2** Any person. *People say that you should not walk under ladders.*

you'd (informal) You would.

you'll (informal) You will.

young[1] *adjective* (younger, youngest) Having lived or been in existence for a comparatively short time, not old.

young[2] *noun* Young people or young animals.

youngster *noun* (youngsters) A young person.

your, yours Belonging to you.

you're (informal) You are.

yourself, yourselves *See* you. These words are used in the same ways as **herself.**

youth[1] *noun* **1** Being young. **2** The early part of your life. **youthful** *adjective*.

youth[2] *noun* (youths) A young person. **youth club** a club for young people.

you've (informal) You have.

yule, yuletide *nouns* Christmas.

Zz

zany *adjective* Amusingly mad.

zeal *noun* Enthusiasm, eagerness. **zealous** *adjective*, **zealously** *adverb*.

zebra *noun* (zebras) An animal like a horse with black and white stripes. **zebra crossing** *noun* a place marked with black and white stripes for pedestrians to cross the road.

Zen *noun* A form of Buddhism.

zero[1] *noun* (zeros) Nought, the figure 0. **zero hour** the exact time at which an important happening is to begin.

zero[2] *verb* (zeros, zeroing, zeroed) To set figures to zero. **zero in** to aim directly at something.

zest *noun* Great enthusiasm.

zigzag[1] *noun* (zigzags) A line with many sharp turns like this ∿.

zigzag[2] *verb* (zigzags, zigzagging, zigzagged) To move in a zigzag.

zinc *noun* A white metal.

zip[1] *verb* (zips, zipping, zipped) To close something with a zip-fastener.

zip[2], **zip-fastener** *nouns* (zips, zip-fasteners) A device with rows of small teeth for fastening two edges together.

zither *noun* (zithers) A stringed instrument played by plucking.

zodiac *noun* **signs of the zodiac** twelve areas of the sky frequently referred to in astrology.

zone *noun* (zones) An area.

zoo *noun* (zoos) A place where wild animals are kept for people to look at.

zoology *noun* The scientific study of animals. **zoological** *adjective*, **zoologist** *noun*.

zoom *verb* (zooms, zooming, zoomed) **1** To fly suddenly upwards. **2** (informal) To move quickly. **zoom lens** a camera lens that can be adjusted to give close and distant shots from the same position.